# Opel Ascona & Manta Owners Workshop Manual

## J H Haynes Member of the Guild of Motoring Writers
## and Marcus Daniels

**Models covered**
All Opel Ascona and Manta (B Series) models; Saloon, Coupe & Hatchback
1584 cc, 1796 cc, 1897 cc & 1979 cc

*Covers most features of Manta Exclusive models*
*Does not fully cover Ascona i2000*
*Does not cover front-wheel-drive Ascona models*

**ISBN 1 85010 578 2**

Printed in England *(316–2R11)*

ABCDE
FGHIJ
KLMNO
PQ

THE BOOK ®

**Haynes Publishing Group**
Sparkford Nr Yeovil
Somerset BA22 7JJ England

**Haynes Publications, Inc**
861 Lawrence Drive
Newbury Park
California 91320 USA

**British Library Cataloguing in Publication Data**

Daniels, Marcus
Opel Ascona & Manta B-Series owners workshop manual.
1. Cars. Maintenance & repair. Amateur's manual
I. Title     II. Series
629.28'722
ISBN 1-85010-578-2

# Acknowledgements

Our thanks are due to General Motors Limited for the supply of technical information and certain illustrations. Duckhams Oils provided lubrication data and the Champion Sparking Plug Company supplied the illustrations showing the various spark plug conditions.

We are indebted to A.T.Kimpton (Marston Garage) Limited, Marston Magna, Yeovil, who supplied the project Opel Ascona used in our workshops.

Lastly, thanks are due to all of those people at Sparkford who helped in the production of this manual.

# About this manual

## Its aim

The aim of this manual is to help you get the best value from your vehicle. It can do so in several ways. It can help you decide what work must be done (even should you choose to get it done by a garage), provide information on routine maintenance and servicing, and give a logical course of action and diagnosis when random faults occur. However, it is hoped that you will use the manual by tackling the work yourself. On simpler jobs it may even be quicker than booking the car into a garage and going there twice, to leave and collect it. Perhaps most important, a lot of money can be saved by avoiding the costs a garage must charge to cover its labour and overheads.

The manual has drawings and descriptions to show the function of the various components so that their layout can be understood. Then the tasks are described and photographed in a step-by-step sequence so that even a novice can do the work.

## Its arrangement

The manual is divided into thirteen Chapters, each covering a logical sub-division of the vehicle. The Chapters are each divided into Sections, numbered with single figures, eg 5; and the Sections into paragraphs (or sub-sections), with decimal numbers following on from the Section they are in, eg 5.1, 5.2, 5.3 etc.

It is freely illustrated, especially in those parts where there is a detailed sequence of operations to be carried out. There are two forms of illustration: figures and photographs. The figures are numbered in sequence with decimal numbers, according to their position in the Chapter – eg Fig. 6.4 is the fourth drawing/illustration in Chapter 6. Photographs carry the same number (either individually or in related groups) as the Section or sub-section to which they relate.

There is an alphabetical index at the back of the manual as well as a contents list at the front. Each Chapter is also preceded by its own individual contents list.

References to the 'left' or 'right' of the vehicle are in the sense of a person in the driver's seat facing forwards.

Unless otherwise stated, nuts and bolts are removed by turning anti-clockwise, and tightened by turning clockwise.

Vehicle manufacturers continually make changes to specifications and recommendations, and these, when notified, are incorporated into our manuals at the earliest opportunity.

**Whilst every care is taken to ensure that the information in this manual is correct, no liability can be accepted by the authors or publishers for loss, damage or injury caused by any errors in, or omissions from, the information given.**

# Introduction to the Opel Ascona and Manta

The new 'B' series Opel Ascona and Manta models introduced in 1975 have a completely new bodystyle, providing improved passenger accommodation with increased glass area and a lower 'waistline'.

Mechanically the new Ascona and Manta are similar to the previous 'A' series models, which were extremely reliable, therefore only minor modifications have been necessary.

The models covered by this manual comprise the two and four-door saloons, two-door Coupe and Hatchback fitted with a 1.6, 1.8, 1.9 and 2.0 litre engine. The 1.6 litre engine was initially available in a low compression form, with a smaller carburettor and could thus run on two-star fuel. This option has now been discontinued for the UK market.

All models are fitted with servo-assisted disc brakes on the front wheels and drum brakes at the rear. For safety, the system is dual-line with a special anti-locking valve fitted in the hydraulic line to the rear brakes.

Front suspension is of independent coil and wishbones type, while the live rear axle is located by radius arms and a panhard rod and is supported on coil springs and telescopic shock-absorbers. Anti-roll bars are fitted at the front and rear.

Steering is by a forward mounted rack and pinion gear and the steering column is the collapsible mesh, energy absorbing type.

All models are available with four or five-speed all-synchromesh manual gearbox or a three-speed automatic transmission with manual override and kick-down facility.

The Rallye E and 2.0 GTE models are fitted with Bosch fuel injection.

# Contents

Opel Ascona Saloon

Opel Manta Coupe

Opel Manta Berlinetta Hatchback

# General dimensions, weights and capacities

## Dimensions (typical)
Overall length:
| | |
|---|---|
| Ascona | 4321 mm (170.2 in) |
| Manta Coupe | 4445 mm (175.1 in) |
| Manta Hatchback | 4384 mm (172.7 in) |

Overall width:
| | |
|---|---|
| Ascona/Manta (early) | 1670 mm (65.8 in) |
| Manta (later) | 1686 mm (66.4 in) |

Overall height:
| | |
|---|---|
| Ascona | 1380 mm (54.4 in) |
| Manta | 1330 mm (52.4 in) |
| Manta GT/E | 1310 mm (51.6 in) |

## Weights
Nominal kerb weights (typical)*:
| | |
|---|---|
| Ascona/Manta 1.6/1.9 | 1000 kg (2205 lbs) |
| Manta 1.8 Coupe/Hatchback | 1000 kg (2205 lbs)/1025 kg (2260 lbs) |
| Manta 2.0 Coupe/Hatchback | 1040 kg (2293 lbs)/1065 kg (2348 lbs) |
| Manta 2.0 GT/E Coupe/Hatchback | 1065 kg (2348 lbs)/1090 kg (2403 lbs) |

Maximum trailer weight (braked):
| | |
|---|---|
| All engines except 18S | 1300 kg (2867 lbs) |
| 18S | 1200 kg (2646 lbs) |

Maximum roof rack load:
| | |
|---|---|
| All models | 60 kg (132 lbs) |

*Nominal kerb weights quoted are for manual gearbox models only. For automatic transmission, add 35 kg (77 lbs) for 1.6 models, and 20 kg (44 lbs) for all other models.

## Capacities
Engine oil (with filter):
| | |
|---|---|
| 1.6/1.9/2.0 | 3.8 litres (6.7 pints) |
| 1.8 | 3.75 litres (6.6 pints) |

Cooling system (manual gearbox models):
| | |
|---|---|
| 16S | 6.5 litres (11.4 pints) |
| 18S/19E/20E | 6.8 litres (12.0 pints) |
| 19S | 6.1 litres (10.7 pints) |
| 20S | 6.2 litres (10.9 pints) |

Cooling system (automatic transmission models):
| | |
|---|---|
| 16S | 7.2 litres (12.7 pints) |
| 18S/19E/20E | 6.7 litres (11.8 pints) |
| 19S | 7.0 litres (12.3 pints) |
| 20S | 6.1 litres (10.7 pints) |

Manual gearbox:
| | |
|---|---|
| 4-speed | 1.1 litres (1.9 pints) |
| 5-speed | 1.4 litres (2.5 pints) |

Automatic transmission:
| | |
|---|---|
| 1.6/1.9 models | 2.5 to 2.7 litres (4.4 to 4.8 pints) |
| 1.8 models | 2.0 litres (3.5 pints) |
| 2.0 models | 2.1 litres (3.7 pints) |

Rear axle:
| | |
|---|---|
| 1.6/1.9 models | 1.1 litres (1.9 pints) |
| 1.8/2.0 models | 1.2 litres (2.1 pints) |

Fuel tank:
| | |
|---|---|
| All models | 50 litres (11.0 gals) |

# Buying spare parts
# and vehicle identification numbers

### Buying spare parts

Spare parts are available from many sources, for example: G.M garages, other garages and accessory shops, and motor factors. Our advice regarding spare part sources is as follows:

*Officially appointed G.M garages* - This is the best source of parts which are peculiar to your car and are otherwise not generally available (eg. complete cylinder heads, internal gearbox components, badges, interior trim etc). It is also the only place at which you should buy parts if your car is still under warranty - non-G.M components may invalidate the warranty. To be sure of obtaining the correct parts it will always be necessary to give the storeman your car's engine and chassis number, and if possible, to take the 'old' part along for positive identification. Remember that many parts are available on a factory exchange scheme - any parts returned should always be clean! It obviously makes good sense to go straight to the specialists on your car for this type of part for they are best equipped to supply you.

*Other garages and accessory shops* - These are often very good places to buy materials and components needed for the maintenance of your car (eg. oil filters, spark plugs, bulbs, fan belts, oils and greases, touch-up paint, filler paste etc). They also sell general accessories, usually have convenient opening hours, charge lower prices and can often be found not far from home.

*Motor factors* - Good factors will stock all of the more important components which wear out relatively quickly (eg; clutch components, pistons, valves, exhaust systems, brake cylinders/pipes/hoses/seals/shoes and pads etc). Motor factors will often provide new or reconditioned components on a part exchange basis - this can save a considerable amount of money.

### Vehicle identification numbers

The *vehicle identification number plate* is located inside the engine compartment on top of the front end panel. The plate is marked with the vehicle chassis and designation number and the colour code. Also shown is the maximum gross weight for the car.

The *engine number* is stamped on a machined flat located on left-hand side of the cylinder block. The number is prefixed with either '16', '18', '19' or '20', depending on whether the engine is the 1.6 litre, 1.8 litre, 1.9 litre or 2.0 litre type.

Vehicle identification plate

Location of engine number

# Tools and working facilities

## Introduction

A selection of good tools is a fundamental requirement for anyone contemplating the maintenance and repair of a motor vehicle. For the owner who does not possess any, their purchase will prove a considerable expense, offsetting some of the savings made by doing-it-yourself. However, provided that the tools purchased are of good quality, they will last for many years and prove an extremely worthwhile investment.

To help the average owner to decide which tools are needed to carry out the various tasks detailed in this manual, we have compiled three lists of tools under the following headings: Maintenance and minor repair, Repair and overhaul, and Special. The newcomer to practical mechanics should start off with the 'Maintenance and minor repair' tool kit and confine himself to the simpler jobs around the vehicle. Then, as his confidence and experience grows, he can undertake more difficult tasks, buying extra tools as, and when, they are needed. In this way, a 'Maintenance and minor repair' tool kit can be built-up into a 'Repair and overhaul' tool kit over a considerable period of time without any major cash outlays. The experienced do-it-yourselfer will have a tool kit good enough for most repair and overhaul procedures and will add tools from the 'Special' category when he feels the expense is justified by the amount of use these tools will be put to.

It is obviously not possible to cover the subject of tools fully here. For those who wish to learn more about tools and their use there is a book entitled 'How to Choose and Use Car Tools' available from the publishers of this manual.

## Maintenance and minor repair tool kit

The tools given in this list should be considered as a minimum requirement if routine maintenance, servicing and minor repair operations are to be undertaken. We recommend the purchase of combination spanners (ring one end, open-ended the other); although more expensive than open-ended ones, they do give the advantages of both types of spanner.

Combination spanners - 10, 11, 13, 14, 17 mm
Adjustable spanner - 9 inch
Engine sump/gearbox/rear axle drain plug key (where applicable)
Spark plug spanner (with rubber insert)
Spark plug gap adjustment tool
Set of feeler gauges
Brake adjuster spanner (where applicable)
Brake bleed nipple spanner
Screwdriver - 4 in. long x ¼ in. dia. (plain)
Screwdriver - 4 in. long x ¼ in. dia. (crosshead)
Combination pliers - 6 inch
Hacksaw, junior
Tyre pump
Tyre pressure gauge
Grease gun (where applicable)
Oil can
Fine emery cloth (1 sheet)
Wire brush (small)
Funnel (medium size)

## Repair and overhaul tool kit

These tools are virtually essential for anyone undertaking any major repairs to a motor vehicle, and are additional to those given in the basic list. Included in this list is a comprehensive set of sockets. Although these are expensive they will be found invaluable as they are so versatile - particularly if various drives ae included in the set. We recommend the ½ square-drive type, as this can be used with most proprietary torque wrenches. If you cannot afford a socket set, even

bought piecemeal, then inexpensive tubular box spanners are a useful alternative.

The tools in this list will occasionally need to be supplemented by tools from the Special list.

Sockets (or box spanners) to cover range 6 to 27 mm
Reversible ratchet drive (for use with sockets)
Extension piece, 10 inch (for use with sockets)
Universal joint (for use with sockets)
Torque wrench (for use with sockets)
'Mole' wrench - 8 inch
Ball pein hammer
Soft-faced hammer, plastic or rubber
Screwdriver - 6 in. long x 5/16 in. dia. (plain)
Screwdriver - 2 in. long x 5/16 in. square (plain)
Screwdriver - 1½ in. long x ¼ in. dia. (crosshead)
Screwdriver - 3 in. long x 1/8 in. dia. (electricians)
Pliers - electricians
Pliers - needle nosed
Pliers - circlip (internal and external)
Cold chisel - ½ inch
Scriber (this can be made by grinding the end of a broken hacksaw blade)
Scraper (this can be made by flattening and sharpening one end of a piece of copper pipe)
Centre punch
Pin punch
Hacksaw
Valve grinding tool
Steel rule/straight edge
Allen keys
Selection of files
Wire brush (large)
Axle stand
Jack (strong scissor or hydraulic type)

## Special tools

The tools in this list are those which are not used regularly, are expensive to buy, or which need to be used in accordance with their manufacturers instructions. Unless relatively difficult mechanical jobs are undertaken frequently, it will not be economic to buy many of these tools. Where this is the case, you could consider clubbing together with friends (or motorists club) to make a joint purchase, or borrowing the tools against a deposit from a local garage or tool hire specialist.

The following list contains only those tools and instruments freely available to the public, and not those special tools produced by the vehicle manufacturer specifically for its dealer network. You will find occasional references to these manufacturers special tools in the text of this manual. Generally, an alternative method of doing the job without the vehicle manufacturers special tool is given. However, sometimes, there is no alternative to using it. Where this is the case and the relevant tool cannot be bought or borrowed you will have to entrust the work to a franchised garage.

Valve spring compressor
Piston ring compressor
Ball joint separator
Universal hub/bearing puller
Impact screwdriver
Micrometer and /or vernier gauge
Carburettor flow balancing device (where applicable)

*Dial gauge*
*Stroboscopic timing light*
*Dwell angle meter/tachometer*
*Universal electrical multi-meter*
*Cylinder compression gauge*
*Lifting tackle*
*Trolley jack*
*Light with extension lead*

### Buying tools

For practically all tools, a tool factor is the best source since he will have a very comprehensive range compared with the average garage or accessory shop. Having said that, accessory shops often offer excellent quality tools at discount prices, so it pays to shop around.

Remember, you don't have to buy the most expensive items on the shelf, but it is always advisable to steer clear of the very cheap tools. There are plenty of good tools around, at reasonable prices, so ask the proprietor or manager of the shop for advice before making a purchase.

### Care and maintenance of tools

Having purchased a reasonable tool kit, it is necessary to keep the tools in a clean and serviceable condition. After use, always wipe off any dirt, grease and metal particles using a clean, dry cloth, before putting the tools away. Never leave them lying around after they have been used. A simple tool rack on the garage or workshop wall, for items such as screwdrivers and pliers is a good idea. Store all normal spanners and sockets in a metal box. Any measuring instruments, gauges, meters, etc., must be carefully stored where they cannot be damaged or become rusty.

Take a little care when the tools are used. Hammer heads inevitably become marked and screwdrivers lose the keen edge on their blades from time-to-time. A little timely attention with emery cloth or a file will soon restore items like this to a good serviceable finish.

### Working facilities

Not to be forgotten when discussing tools, is the workshop itself. If anything more than routine maintenance is to be carried out, some form of suitable working area becomes essential.

It is appreciated that many an owner mechanic is forced by circumstance to remove an engine or similar item, without the benefit of a garage or workshop. Having done this, any repairs should always be done under the cover of a roof.

Wherever possible, any dismantling should be done on a clean flat workbench or table at a suitable working height.

Any workbench needs a vice: one with a jaw opening of 4 in (100 mm) is suitable for most jobs. As mentioned previously, some clean dry storage space is also required for tools, as well as the lubricants, cleaning fluids, touch-up paints and so on which soon become necessary.

Another item which may be required, and which has a much more general usage, is an electric drill with a chuck capacity of at least 5/16 in (8 mm). This together with a good range of twist drills, is virtually essential for fitting accessories such as wing mirrors and reversing lights.

Last, but not least, always keep a supply of old newspapers and clean, lint-free rags available, and try to keep any working area as clean as possible.

### Spanner jaw gap comparison table

| Jaw gap (in) | Spanner size |
|---|---|
| 0.250 | 1/4 in AF |
| 0.276 | 7 mm |
| 0.313 | 5/16 in AF |
| 0.315 | 8 mm |
| 0.344 | 11/32 in AF; 1/8 in Whitworth |
| 0.354 | 9 mm |
| 0.375 | 3/8 in AF |
| 0.394 | 10 mm |
| 0.433 | 11 mm |
| 0.438 | 7/16 in AF |
| 0.445 | 3/16 in Whitworth; 1/4 in BSF |
| 0.472 | 12 mm |
| 0.500 | 1/2 in AF |
| 0.512 | 13 mm |
| 0.525 | 1/4 in Whitworth; 5/16 in BSF |
| 0.551 | 14 mm |
| 0.563 | 9/16 in AF |
| 0.591 | 15 mm |
| 0.600 | 5/16 in Whitworth; 3/8 in BSF |
| 0.625 | 5/8 in AF |
| 0.630 | 16 mm |
| 0.669 | 17 mm |
| 0.686 | 11/16 in AF |
| 0.709 | 18 mm |
| 0.710 | 3/8 in Whitworth; 7/16 in BSF |
| 0.748 | 19 mm |
| 0.750 | 3/4 in AF |
| 0.813 | 13/16 in AF |
| 0.820 | 7/16 in Whitworth; 1/2 in BSF |
| 0.866 | 22 mm |
| 0.875 | 7/8 in AF |
| 0.920 | 1/2 in Whitworth; 9/16 in BSF |
| 0.938 | 15/16 in AF |
| 0.945 | 24 mm |
| 1.000 | 1 in AF |
| 1.010 | 9/16 in Whitworth; 5/8 in BSF |
| 1.024 | 26 mm |
| 1.063 | 11/16 in AF; 27 mm |
| 1.100 | 5/8 in Whitworth; 11/16 in BSF |
| 1.125 | 11/8 in AF |
| 1.181 | 30 mm |
| 1.200 | 11/16 in Whitworth; 3/4 in BSF |
| 1.250 | 11/4 in AF |
| 1.260 | 32 mm |
| 1.300 | 3/4 in Whitworth; 7/8 in BSF |
| 1.313 | 15/16 in AF |
| 1.390 | 13/16 in Whitworth; 15/16 in BSF |
| 1.417 | 36 mm |
| 1.438 | 17/16 in AF |
| 1.480 | 7/8 in Whitworth; 1 in BSF |
| 1.500 | 11/2 in AF |
| 1.575 | 40 mm; 15/16 in Whitworth |
| 1.614 | 41 mm |
| 1.625 | 15/8 in AF |
| 1.670 | 1 in Whitworth; 11/8 in BSF |
| 1.688 | 111/16 in AF |
| 1.811 | 46 mm |
| 1.813 | 113/16 in AF |
| 1.860 | 11/8 in Whitworth; 11/4 in BSF |
| 1.875 | 17/8 in AF |
| 1.969 | 50 mm |
| 2.000 | 2 in AF |
| 2.050 | 11/4 in Whitworth; 13/8 in BSF |
| 2.165 | 55 mm |
| 2.362 | 60 mm |

# Safety first!

Professional motor mechanics are trained in safe working procedures. However enthusiastic you may be about getting on with the job in hand, do take the time to ensure that your safety is not put at risk. A moment's lack of attention can result in an accident, as can failure to observe certain elementary precautions.

There will always be new ways of having accidents, and the following points do not pretend to be a comprehensive list of all dangers; they are intended rather to make you aware of the risks and to encourage a safety-conscious approach to all work you carry out on your vehicle.

## Essential DOs and DON'Ts

**DON'T** rely on a single jack when working underneath the vehicle. Always use reliable additional means of support, such as axle stands, securely placed under a part of the vehicle that you know will not give way.

**DON'T** attempt to loosen or tighten high-torque nuts (e.g. wheel hub nuts) while the vehicle is on a jack; it may be pulled off.

**DON'T** start the engine without first ascertaining that the transmission is in neutral (or 'Park' where applicable) and the parking brake applied.

**DON'T** suddenly remove the filler cap from a hot cooling system — cover it with a cloth and release the pressure gradually first, or you may get scalded by escaping coolant.

**DON'T** attempt to drain oil until you are sure it has cooled sufficiently to avoid scalding you.

**DON'T** grasp any part of the engine, exhaust or catalytic converter without first ascertaining that it is sufficiently cool to avoid burning you.

**DON'T** allow brake fluid or antifreeze to contact vehicle paintwork.

**DON'T** syphon toxic liquids such as fuel, brake fluid or antifreeze by mouth, or allow them to remain on your skin.

**DON'T** inhale dust — it may be injurious to health (see *Asbestos* below).

**DON'T** allow any spilt oil or grease to remain on the floor — wipe it up straight away, before someone slips on it.

**DON'T** use ill-fitting spanners or other tools which may slip and cause injury.

**DON'T** attempt to lift a heavy component which may be beyond your capability — get assistance.

**DON'T** rush to finish a job, or take unverified short cuts.

**DON'T** allow children or animals in or around an unattended vehicle.

**DO** wear eye protection when using power tools such as drill, sander, bench grinder etc, and when working under the vehicle.

**DO** use a barrier cream on your hands prior to undertaking dirty jobs — it will protect your skin from infection as well as making the dirt easier to remove afterwards; but make sure your hands aren't left slippery. Note that long-term contact with used engine oil can be a health hazard.

**DO** keep loose clothing (cuffs, tie etc) and long hair well out of the way of moving mechanical parts.

**DO** remove rings, wristwatch etc, before working on the vehicle — especially the electrical system.

**DO** ensure that any lifting tackle used has a safe working load rating adequate for the job.

**DO** keep your work area tidy — it is only too easy to fall over articles left lying around.

**DO** get someone to check periodically that all is well, when working alone on the vehicle.

**DO** carry out work in a logical sequence and check that everything is correctly assembled and tightened afterwards.

**DO** remember that your vehicle's safety affects that of yourself and others. If in doubt on any point, get specialist advice.

**IF,** in spite of following these precautions, you are unfortunate enough to injure yourself, seek medical attention as soon as possible.

## Asbestos

Certain friction, insulating, sealing, and other products — such as brake linings, brake bands, clutch linings, torque converters, gaskets, etc — contain asbestos. *Extreme care must be taken to avoid inhalation of dust from such products since it is hazardous to health.* If in doubt, assume that they *do* contain asbestos.

## Fire

Remember at all times that petrol (gasoline) is highly flammable. Never smoke, or have any kind of naked flame around, when working on the vehicle. But the risk does not end there — a spark caused by an electrical short-circuit, by two metal surfaces contacting each other, by careless use of tools, or even by static electricity built up in your body under certain conditions, can ignite petrol vapour, which in a confined space is highly explosive.

Always disconnect the battery earth (ground) terminal before working on any part of the fuel or electrical system, and never risk spilling fuel on to a hot engine or exhaust.

It is recommended that a fire extinguisher of a type suitable for fuel and electrical fires is kept handy in the garage or workplace at all times. Never try to extinguish a fuel or electrical fire with water.

## Fumes

Certain fumes are highly toxic and can quickly cause unconsciousness and even death if inhaled to any extent. Petrol (gasoline) vapour comes into this category, as do the vapours from certain solvents such as trichloroethylene. Any draining or pouring of such volatile fluids should be done in a well ventilated area.

When using cleaning fluids and solvents, read the instructions carefully. Never use materials from unmarked containers — they may give off poisonous vapours.

Never run the engine of a motor vehicle in an enclosed space such as a garage. Exhaust fumes contain carbon monoxide which is extremely poisonous; if you need to run the engine, always do so in the open air or at least have the rear of the vehicle outside the workplace.

If you are fortunate enough to have the use of an inspection pit, never drain or pour petrol, and never run the engine, while the vehicle is standing over it; the fumes, being heavier than air, will concentrate in the pit with possibly lethal results.

## The battery

Never cause a spark, or allow a naked light, near the vehicle's battery. It will normally be giving off a certain amount of hydrogen gas, which is highly explosive.

Always disconnect the battery earth (ground) terminal before working on the fuel or electrical systems.

If possible, loosen the filler plugs or cover when charging the battery from an external source. Do not charge at an excessive rate or the battery may burst.

Take care when topping up and when carrying the battery. The acid electrolyte, even when diluted, is very corrosive and should not be allowed to contact the eyes or skin.

If you ever need to prepare electrolyte yourself, always add the acid slowly to the water, and never the other way round. Protect against splashes by wearing rubber gloves and goggles.

When jump starting a car using a booster battery, for negative earth (ground) vehicles, connect the jump leads in the following sequence: First connect one jump lead between the positive (+) terminals of the two batteries. Then connect the other jump lead first to the negative (–) terminal of the booster battery, and then to a good earthing (ground) point on the vehicle to be started, at least 18 in (45 cm) from the battery if possible. Ensure that hands and jump leads are clear of any moving parts, and that the two vehicles do not touch. Disconnect the leads in the reverse order.

## Mains electricity

When using an electric power tool, inspection light etc, which works from the mains, always ensure that the appliance is correctly connected to its plug and that, where necessary, it is properly earthed (grounded). Do not use such appliances in damp conditions and, again, beware of creating a spark or applying excessive heat in the vicinity of fuel or fuel vapour.

## Ignition HT voltage

A severe electric shock can result from touching certain parts of the ignition system, such as the HT leads, when the engine is running or being cranked, particularly if components are damp or the insulation is defective. Where an electronic ignition system is fitted, the HT voltage is much higher and could prove fatal.

# Routine maintenance

*For modifications, and information applicable to later models, see Supplement at end of manual*

## Introduction

The Routine Maintenance instructions listed are basically those recommended by the vehicle manufacturer. They are sometimes supplemented by additional maintenance tasks proven to be necessary.

The following maintenance instructions should always be used in conjunction with the servicing schedule detailed in the owner's handbook or Protection Plan booklet supplied with each new car, as the servicing requirement may be altered by the manufacturer in the course of time.

In the case of a new car the first free service must be carried out within one month or 500 miles (800 km) from date of delivery followed by the three month or 3,000 miles (5,000 km)' service check-up. Details of these services will be found in the owner's handbook and should be carried out by the authorised dealer.

## Weekly, before a long journey, or every 250 miles (400 km)

**Engine:** Check the level of the engine oil and add oil if necessary.
**Battery:** Check the level of the electrolyte in the battery and top-up with distilled water as necessary. Make sure that the top of the battery is always kept clean and free from moisture.
**Radiator:** Check the level of coolant in the radiator. The coolant should be around ¾ inch above the radiator core top. Add antifreeze solution or plain water as necessary. Remember, if the engine is hot, only turn the filler cap one-quarter of a turn at first, to allow the system to lose pressure; then press the cap down and turn past the safety notch to remove.
**Tyres:** Check the tyre pressures with an accurate gauge and adjust as necessary. *Carefully* inspect the tyre walls (both sides of the tyre) and the treads for damage. The law (UK) requires at least 1 mm deep tread across three quarters of the width of the tyre around the whole periphery of the tyre.
**Hydraulic system:** Check the level of fluid in the brake fluid reservoir and replenish as necessary to the correct level marked on the reservoir. Should the brake system need replenishing weekly, the brake system should be thoroughly checked for leaks. As a matter of routine it is also wise to carefully inspect the flexible brake pipe, use a mirror and torch to view those hidden areas.
**Wheel nuts:** Check the tightness of the wheel nuts.
**Windscreen washer:** Refill the windscreen washer bottle with soft water. Add the special antifreeze sachets in cold weather. *Do not use engine type antifreeze,* it corrodes paintwork. Finally check that the jets operate clearly and accurately.
**Lights, wipers and horns:** Check each electrical system on the vehicle in turn; ensure that all lights work properly and the response of each system is immediate.

Topping-up engine oil

Topping-up coolant

Checking brake fluid level

Windscreen washer reservoir

Location of oil filter

Rear axle oil level plug

## Every 3 months or 3,000 miles (5,000 km)

Under extreme operating conditions such as trailer pulling, frequent short trip operations that prevent the engine really warming up, or operating in dusty terrain, the engine oil should be changed at 3,000 miles (5,000 km) intervals. The weekly checks detailed previously should also be carried out.

## 6,000 miles (10,000 km) or 6 months

**Carry out the 250 miles/weekly checks plus the following:**
**Oil filter:** Renew the oil filter as well as the engine oil every 6,000 miles (10,000 km). The filter is of the full flow cartridge type. It is recommended that the sealing gasket on the new filter be smeared with engine oil before fitting. Once the new filter has been screwed on, tighten the cartridge with hand effort only.
**Battery:** Remove the battery and clean the terminals and connectors.
**Clutch:** The free-travel at the pedal, should be between ¾ inch and 1¼ inch. The procedure for adjusting the clutch is given in Chapter 5.
**Gearbox and rear axle:** Check the level of oil in the gearbox by removing the level/filler plug and topping-up with gear oil until it begins to flow from the plug hole. Replace the plug, the oil does not need to be changed within the life of the gearbox between overhauls. *Automatic:* With the vehicle parked on a level surface and the engine running, select the 'Park' position with the shift lever. Remove and wipe clean the oil reservoir dipstick. Re-insert until the cap is seated, remove and observe level on the stick. Top-up the reservoir to the 'FULL' mark on the stick. Do not overfill the reservoir. The rear axle oil level should be similarly checked and topped-up as necessary.
**Brake pads and linings**
*Front disc brakes:* The minimum allowable thickness of the pad and friction plate is 0.28 inches (7 mm); if any of the four pads has worn below the dimension, all four pads must be renewed. Partial renewal of brake pads will result in unequal braking. Note that the disc brakes are self adjusting and the only running check is to ensure that the brake pistons are functioning properly. The pistons should retract a little into the caliper block to allow a small running clearance between the pad and disc.
*Rear drum brakes:* Remove the brake drums and inspect the drum friction surface for scores. If scores are found refer to Chapter 9. Inspect the brake shoes and linings - if the friction material has been worn down to the rivets, it is time to reline the shoes. If bonded linings are used, then renewal is necessary when the friction material has worn to within 1/16 inch (1.6 mm) of the shoe. Check the adjustment of the brake shoe position after referring to Chapter 9. Turn the individual shoe adjusters until both shoes bind on the drum, then relax the adjusters until the drum can just be rotated freely.
**Handbrake (adjustment):** The handbrake needs adjustment if the brakes are not applied between the fifth and eighth notches of the lever movement. To adjust, tighten the self-locking nut at the handbrake equalizer bracket until the correct lever movement is obtained.
**Suspension and steering:** Carefully check the suspension for slackness or damage. It will be useful to jack-up the wheels so that they may be gripped to force them up-and-down, forward-and-back, and in-and-out. If any slackness is detected, investigate, refer to Chapter 11 and repair immediately. Whilst the front wheels are jacked-up, grip the wheels and force around the steering linkage. As with suspension, if any sloppiness or uneven movement is detected, investigate, refer to Chapter 11 of this manual and repair immediately.
**Exhaust system:** The exhaust system should be closely inspected for cracks, holes, broken shackle parts and gross deterioration. Renovate the system appropriately. Remember that faults such as holes or broken shackles should not be tolerated at all; exhaust fumes can leak into the passenger compartment.
**Ignition system:** Remove the spark plugs and inspect them for colour and electrode gap. The static timing may also be checked using the technique described in Chapter 4.
**Cooling system:** Check fanbelt tension and adjust if necessary. Examine hoses and clips and tighten/renew where necessary.

**General safety checks:**
*Lap and shoulder safety belts:* Inspect the belts and renew them if any fabric and material deterioration is found. Check that the anchorage points are in good order, free from corrosion and the various nuts and bolts tight.
*Heater:* It is always well to check that the defroster system is effective by operating occasionally and sensing that sufficient warm air is being blown onto the windscreen.
*Horn:* Operate the horn occasionally to ensure that it is in working order.
*Seats:* Inspect the front seat adjustment mechanisms. Ensure that all latch pawls are properly engaged and that no components are worn excessively. Remember to inspect the headrest mountings if fitted, checking that they are complete and in proper order.

## 12,000 miles (20,000 km) or 12 months

**Carry out the tasks listed under the weekly and 6 monthly service intervals plus the following:**
**Oil can lubrication:** Apply a spot of oil to the door, bonnet and boot hinges. Also lightly oil the door strikers, check links and lock barrels.
**Cooling system:** Check the strength of the antifreeze in the coolant and top-up if necessary. Inspect the fanbelt for wear and replace if necessary. Adjust the tension of the fanbelt whether it is renewed or not.
**Ignition system:** Clean and reset the spark plug gaps. If the plug points are badly burnt, renew all plugs. Fit a new set of contact breaker points, set the points to the correct gap and apply a spot of oil to the cam lubrication pad. Check the operation of the distributor advance mechanism and ignition timing (see Chapter 4).
**Engine adjustments:** Check the valve, (tappet) clearances and adjust if necessary. Adjust the engine idling speed if it is incorrect.
**Mechanical linkages:** Check the throttle, handbrake and gearchange linkage for wear and adjust/renew where necessary and lubricate.
**Wheel bearings:** Jack the front wheels off the ground and check for wear in the wheel bearings. Adjust the wheel bearings as necessary. Clean and repack with recommended grease. Chapter 11 details the technique for adjusting and cleaning the bearings.
**Carburettor fuel inlet filter:** The in line fuel filter element should be cleaned yearly. A new set of gaskets for this special filter should be used when the filter unit is reassembled. Chapter 3 gives full details of the filter cleaning procedure.
**Carburettor air filter:** The air filter element should be renewed yearly, or more frequently if the vehicle is being used in a dusty environment.
**Positive crankcase ventilation system (PCV):** The PCV metering orifice should be cleaned yearly, or more frequently if the vehicle has been used for: towing trailers, in dusty conditions, for short trips in cold weather, or for trips when the engine idles for protracted periods. Check PCV hoses for blockages or deterioration and renew where necessary. (Refer to Chapter 13).

## 24,000 miles (40,000 km) or 2 years

**Carry out the checks detailed in the weekly, 6 month and yearly service schedules plus the following:**
**Automatic transmission:** Drain, and refill the transmission casing with the recommended lubricant. Inspect the oil pump suction screen and adjust the brake band (see Chapter 6).
**Steering and suspension:** Check the steering gear balljoints for wear using the method described in the 6 monthly checklist. Examine all the steering gear rubber boots for splits or perishing, and renew where necessary. Check all shock absorbers for leaks, and the suspension rubber bushes for deterioration: renew if faults are evident.
**Engine tune:** After two years use, it is a good policy to take the car to a dealer equipped with a Crypton engine tuner, or similar and have the engine completely checked over for faults that would not normally be detected (ie. low compression, incorrect fuel combustion, high speed engine timing, etc).
**Fuel filter (Rallye E).** Fit a new filter and pre-filter to the fuel supply system (Chapter 13).

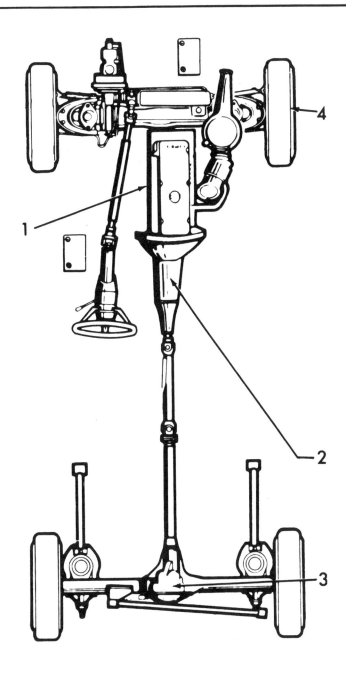

# Recommended lubricants and fluids

| Component or system | Lubricant type/specification | Duckhams recommendation |
|---|---|---|
| 1 Engine | Multigrade engine oil, viscosity range SAE 10W/40 to 20W/50, to API SF/CC | Duckhams QXR, Hypergrade, or 10W/40 Motor Oil |
| 2 Gearbox (manual) 4-speed 5-speed | Hypoid gear oil, viscosity SAE 80EP GM gear oil 90 006 326 | Duckhams Hypoid 80 Duckhams Hypoid 75W/90S |
| 2 Gearbox (automatic) | Dexron type ATF | Duckhams D-Matic |
| 3 Rear axle* Standard differential Limited slip differential | Hypoid gear oil, viscosity SAE 90EP GM special oil 19 42 362 (9 293 688) | Duckhams Hypoid 90S Duckhams Hypoid 90DL |
| 4 Wheel bearings | Multi-purpose lithium based grease | Duckhams LB 10 |

# Chapter 1 Engine

*For modifications, and information applicable to later models, see Supplement at end of manual*

## Contents

## Specifications

### Engine - general

| | |
|---|---|
| Type ... ... ... ... ... ... ... ... ... ... | Four cylinder in-line, camshaft in cylinder head |
| Manufacturer's code: | |
|   1.6 litre ... ... ... ... ... ... ... ... ... | 16S |
|   1.9 litre ... ... ... ... ... ... ... ... ... | 19S |
| Bore: | |
|   1.6 litre ... ... ... ... ... ... ... ... ... | 3.35 in (85 mm) |
|   1.9 litre ... ... ... ... ... ... ... ... ... | 3.66 in (93 mm) |
| Stroke ... ... ... ... ... ... ... ... ... ... | 2.75 in (69.8 mm) |
| Piston displacement: | |
|   1.6 litre ... ... ... ... ... ... ... ... ... | 1584 cc (92 cu in) |
|   1.9 litre ... ... ... ... ... ... ... ... ... | 1897 cc (115.8 cu in) |
| Power output (DIN): | |
|   1.6 litre ... ... ... ... ... ... ... ... ... | 75 bhp at 5000 rpm |
|   1.9 litre ... ... ... ... ... ... ... ... ... | 90 bhp at 4800 rpm |
| Compression ratio ... ... ... ... ... ... ... ... | 8.8 : 1 |
| Valve clearance (with engine at normal operating temperature): | |
|   Inlet ... ... ... ... ... ... ... ... ... ... | 0.012 in (0.30 mm) |
|   Exhaust ... ... ... ... ... ... ... ... ... | 0.012 in (0.30 mm) |
| Lubrication system ... ... ... ... ... ... ... ... | Pressure fed by gear type pump, full-flow filter element |
| Engine oil capacity: | |
|   Dry engine ... ... ... ... ... ... ... ... | 7.2 Imp. pints (4.1 litres) |
|   Refill with filter element change ... ... ... ... | 6.7 Imp. pints (3.8 litres) |
|   Refill without filter element change ... ... ... | 6.2 Imp. pints (3.5 litres) |
| Oil pressure (hot) ... ... ... ... ... ... ... ... | 29 lbf/in$^2$ at 500 rpm |
| Firing order ... ... ... ... ... ... ... ... ... | 1 – 3 – 4 – 2 (No. 1 nearest radiator) |

## Valves and springs

Valve dimensions (intake):

Stem diameter:

| | |
|---|---|
| Standard size     ...     ...     ...     ...     ...     ...     ...     ... | 0.3538 - 0.3543 in (8.987 - 9 mm) |
| 0.003 in (0.075 mm) oversize ...     ...     ...     ...     ...     ... | 0.3567 - 0.3572 in (9.062 - 9.075 mm) |
| 0.0059 in (0.15 mm) oversize ...     ...     ...     ...     ...     ... | 0.3597 - 0.3602 in (9.137 - 9.15 mm) |
| 0.0118 in (0.30 mm) oversize ...     ...     ...     ...     ...     ... | 0.3656 - 0.3661 in (9.287 - 9.3 mm) |
| Total length     ...     ...     ...     ...     ...     ...     ...     ... | 4.843 in (123 mm) |

Valve head diameter:

| | |
|---|---|
| 1.6 litre     ...     ...     ...     ...     ...     ...     ...     ... | 1.574 in (40 mm) |
| 1.9 litre     ...     ...     ...     ...     ...     ...     ...     ... | 1.654 in (42 mm) |

Valve dimensions (exhaust):

Stem diameter:

| | |
|---|---|
| Standard size     ...     ...     ...     ...     ...     ...     ...     ... | 0.3524 - 0.3528 in (8.952 - 8.965 mm) |
| 0.003 in (0.075 mm) oversize ...     ...     ...     ...     ...     ... | 0.3553 - 0.3559 in (9.027 - 9.040 mm) |
| 0.0059 in (0.15 mm) oversize ...     ...     ...     ...     ...     ... | 0.3583 - 0.3588 in (9.102 - 9.115 mm) |
| 0.0118 in (0.30 mm) oversize ...     ...     ...     ...     ...     ... | 0.3642 - 0.3647 in (9.252 - 9.265 mm) |

Total length:

| | |
|---|---|
| 1.6 litre     ...     ...     ...     ...     ...     ...     ...     ... | 4.921 in (125 mm) |
| 1.9 litre     ...     ...     ...     ...     ...     ...     ...     ... | 4.870 in (123.7 mm) |

Valve head diameter:

| | |
|---|---|
| 1.6 litre     ...     ...     ...     ...     ...     ...     ...     ... | 1.339 in (34 mm) |
| 1.9 litre     ...     ...     ...     ...     ...     ...     ...     ... | 1.457 in (37 mm) |

Valve stem clearance:

| | |
|---|---|
| Intake     ...     ...     ...     ...     ...     ...     ...     ... | 0.001 - 0.0025 in (0.025 - 0.063 mm) |
| Exhaust     ...     ...     ...     ...     ...     ...     ...     ... | 0.0024 - 0.0039 in (0.060 - 0.098 mm) |

Max. permissible head to stem runout:

| | |
|---|---|
| Intake     ...     ...     ...     ...     ...     ...     ...     ... | 0.0016 in (0.04 mm) |
| Exhaust     ...     ...     ...     ...     ...     ...     ...     ... | 0.0019 in (0.05 mm) |

Valve seat and correction angle in cylinder head (intake and exhaust):

| | |
|---|---|
| Valve seat angle     ...     ...     ...     ...     ...     ...     ... | 45° |
| Outer correction angle     ...     ...     ...     ...     ...     ... | 30° |
| Valve face angle ...     ...     ...     ...     ...     ...     ...     ... | 44° |

Valve seat width in cylinder head:

| | |
|---|---|
| Intake     ...     ...     ...     ...     ...     ...     ...     ... | 0.049 - 0.059 in (1.25 - 1.50 mm) |
| Exhaust     ...     ...     ...     ...     ...     ...     ...     ... | 0.063 - 0.073 in (1.60 - 1.85 mm) |

Valve stem bores in cylinder head (intake and exhaust):

| | |
|---|---|
| Standard size     ...     ...     ...     ...     ...     ...     ...     ... | 0.3553 - 0.3562 in (9.025 - 9.05 mm) |
| 0.003 in (0.075 mm) oversize     ...     ...     ...     ...     ... | 0.3582 - 0.3592 in (9.1 - 9.125 mm) |
| 0.006 in (0.15 mm) oversize     ...     ...     ...     ...     ... | 0.3615 - 0.3622 in (9.175 - 9.2 mm) |
| 0.0118 in (0.3 mm) oversize     ...     ...     ...     ...     ... | 0.3671 - 0.3681 in (9.325 - 9.35 mm) |

Valve springs - free length:

| | |
|---|---|
| Intake     ...     ...     ...     ...     ...     ...     ...     ... | 2.24 in (56.8 mm) |
| Exhaust (1.6 litre)     ...     ...     ...     ...     ...     ... | 1.93 in (49 mm) |
| Exhaust (1.9 litre)     ...     ...     ...     ...     ...     ... | 2.05 in (52 mm) |

## Cylinder block and pistons

Maximum cylinder bore oversize (reboring):

| | |
|---|---|
| 1.6 litre     ...     ...     ...     ...     ...     ...     ...     ... | + 0.04 in (1 mm) |
| 1.9 litre     ...     ...     ...     ...     ...     ...     ...     ... | + 0.02 in (0.5 mm) |
| Permissible cylinder bore ovality (after rebore)     ...     ...     ... | 0.0005 in (0.013 mm) |
| Permissible cylinder bore taper (after rebore)...     ...     ...     ... | 0.0005 in (0.013 mm) |
| Piston to bore clearance (nominal)     ...     ...     ...     ... | 0.0012 in (0.03 mm) |

Piston ring gaps:

Upper and centre rings:

| | |
|---|---|
| 1.6 litre     ...     ...     ...     ...     ...     ...     ...     ... | 0.0118 - 0.0177 in (0.30 - 0.45 mm) |
| 1.9 litre     ...     ...     ...     ...     ...     ...     ...     ... | 0.0138 - 0.0217 in (0.35 - 0.55 mm) |
| Lower ring     ...     ...     ...     ...     ...     ...     ...     ... | 0.0150 - 0.0551 in (0.38 - 1.40 mm) |

## Crankshaft

| | |
|---|---|
| Main bearing journal diameter ...     ...     ...     ...     ...     ... | 2.282 - 2.283 in (57.99 - 58.003 mm) |
| Connecting rod bearing journal diameter     ...     ...     ...     ... | 2.046 - 2.047 in (51.97 - 51.99 mm) |
| Main bearing journal clearance in bearing     ...     ...     ...     ... | 0.0009 - 0.0025 in (0.02 - 0.06 mm) |
| Connecting rod journal clearance in bearing ...     ...     ...     ... | 0.0006 - 0.0024 in (0.01 - 0.06 mm) |
| Permissible ovality of main and connecting rod journals     ...     ... | 0.0002 in (0.006 mm) |
| Permissible taper of main and connecting rod journals     ...     ... | 0.0004 in (0.01 mm) |
| Crankshaft endfloat     ...     ...     ...     ...     ...     ...     ... | 0.0016 - 0.0063 in (0.04 - 0.016 mm) |

## Camshaft and bearings

Journal diameter:

3 and 4 journal camshaft:

| | |
|---|---|
| First (front)     ...     ...     ...     ...     ...     ...     ... | 1.9266 – 1.9272 in (48.935 – 48.950 mm) |
| Second     ...     ...     ...     ...     ...     ...     ...     ... | 1.9167 – 1.9173 in (48.695 – 48.700 mm) |
| Last     ...     ...     ...     ...     ...     ...     ...     ... | 1.9069 – 1.9075 in (48.435 – 48.450 mm) |

4 journal camshaft:

| | |
|---|---|
| Third     ...     ...     ...     ...     ...     ...     ...     ... | 1.9118 – 1.9124 in (48.560 – 48.575 mm) |

| | | lbf ft | kgf m |
|---|---|---|---|
| Journal clearance in bearing ... ... ... ... ... ... ... | 0.0028 - 0.0043 in (0.070 - 0.110 mm) | | |
| Camshaft endfloat ... ... ... ... ... ... ... ... | 0.004 - 0.008 in (0.10 - 0.20 mm) | | |
| Permissible dimension - cam peak to base ... ... ... ... ... | 1.586 in (40.28 mm) | | |

## Engine lubrication

Oil type/specification ... ... ... ... ... ... ...     Multigrade engine oil, viscosity range SAE 10W/40 to 20W/50, to API SF/CC (Duckhams QXR, Hypergrade, or 10W/40 Motor Oil)

Oil pump gear backlash ... ... ... ... ... ... ...     0.004 - 0.008 in (0.10 - 0.20 mm)
Oil pump gear endfloat in housing ... ... ... ... ... ...     0 - 0.004 in (0 - 0.10 mm)

## Torque wrench settings

| | lbf ft | kgf m |
|---|---|---|
| Connecting rod bolts ... ... ... ... ... ... ... ... | 33 | 4.6 |
| Main bearing cap bolts ... ... ... ... ... ... ... | 81 | 11.1 |
| Flywheel-to-crankshaft bolts ... ... ... ... ... ... | 44 | 6.1 |
| Front pulley to crankshaft ... ... ... ... ... ... | 74 | 10.2 |
| Resonance damper to crankshaft ... ... ... ... ... | 114 | 15.7 |
| Timing chain sprocket to camshaft ... ... ... ... ... | 18 | 2.5 |
| Cylinder head to block ... ... ... ... ... ... ... | 74 | 10.2 |
| Cylinder head to timing cover ... ... ... ... ... ... | 18 | 2.5 |
| Intake manifold to cylinder head ... ... ... ... ... | 26 | 3.6 |
| Exhaust manifold to cylinder head ... ... ... ... ... | 26 | 3.6 |
| Rocker arm stud in cylinder head ... ... ... ... ... | 26 | 3.6 |
| Timing cover to cylinder block ... ... ... ... ... ... | 11 | 1.5 |
| Water pump to cylinder block ... ... ... ... ... ... | 14 | 2.0 |
| Clutch housing to cylinder block ... ... ... ... ... | 36 | 5.0 |
| Spark plugs ... ... ... ... ... ... ... ... | 30 | 4.1 |
| Front engine support to cylinder block ... ... ... ... | 26 | 3.6 |
| Rear engine support to transmission casing ... ... ... ... | 22 | 3.0 |
| Front engine mounting to support bracket ... ... ... ... | 30 | 4.1 |
| Front engine mounting to crossmember ... ... ... ... | 30 | 4.1 |

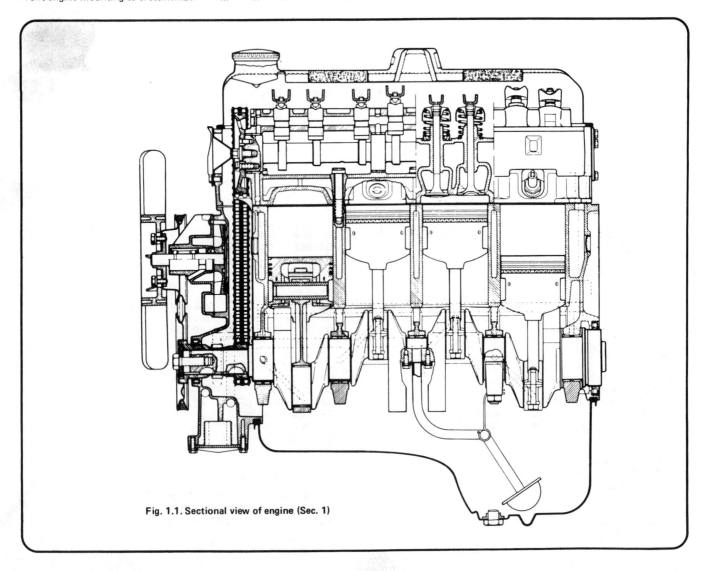

Fig. 1.1. Sectional view of engine (Sec. 1)

## 1 General description

The engines covered in this Chapter comprise the 1.6 and 1.9 litre four cylinder types.

Mechanically the engines are almost identical, the main difference being the bore diameter and the use of three camshaft bearings on the 1.6 engine and four on the 1.9 litre unit. Later engines of both capacities use the same camshaft (with 4 journals), but on the 1.6 litre only 3 journals run in bearings.

On both engines the crankshaft rotates in five main bearings of the replaceable shell type. The connecting-rod (big-end) bearings utilize the same type of bearing. The forward end of the crankshaft protrudes through the front timing cover and drives the camshaft via a sprocket and chain and the oil pump, fuel pump and distributor via a helical gear and shaft (see Fig. 1.2).

The camshaft runs in the cylinder head and operates the valves via solid tappets and stud mounted rocker arms. This gives the advantages of an ohc design but enables the valve clearances to be adjusted without having to remove the camshaft. The double chain that drives the camshaft is fitted with a self-adjusting tensioner.

The valve gear layout coupled with a rigidly supported crankshaft and 'oversquare' bore/stroke configuration, has resulted in an extremely reliable engine with a very respectable power output for the cubic capacity.

The ancillary components (distributor, carburettors, fuel pump, inlet and exhaust manifolds) are all conventional; and detailed descriptions of these items and the systems in which they serve may be found in the relevant Chapters of this manual. Section 19 of this Chapter describes the lubrication system and the overhaul of the major components of that system.

## 2 Major operations possible with engine in place

1 The following major operations may be carried out with the engine in the car:
- i) *Removal and replacement of the cylinder head assembly.*
- ii) *Removal and replacement of the sump (see paragraph 2).*
- iii) *Removal and replacement of the timing chain (see paragraph 2).*
- iv) *Removal and replacement of big-end shells (see paragraph 2).*
- v) *Removal and replacement of camshaft.*
- vi) *Removal and replacement of the water pump.*
- vii) *Removal and replacement of the fuel pump and distributor.*
- viii) *Removal and replacement of the oil pump.*
- ix) *Removal and replacement of the pistons and connecting rods (see paragraph 2).*
- x) *Removal and replacement of the flywheel after removal of the clutch.*

2 It must be stated that whilst the removal of the sump is technically possible with the engine in the car, it involves the detachment of the front suspension frame. The task is therefore probably more complex than the removal of the engine and does not give the benefits of easy access and working which are highly desirable where work on the engine is concerned.

## 3 Major operations requiring engine removal

The following operations can only be carried out with the engine out of the car and on a clean bench or the floor:

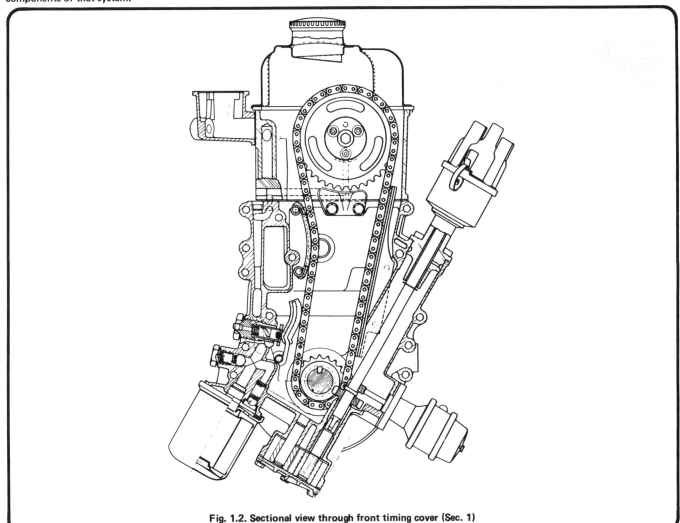

**Fig. 1.2. Sectional view through front timing cover (Sec. 1)**

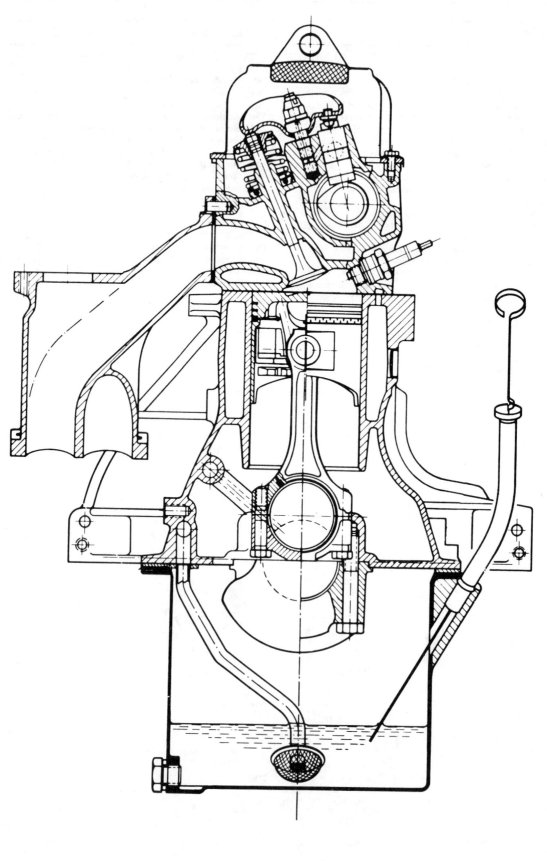

Fig. 1.3. Front sectional view of engine

*i)* Removal and replacement of main bearings.
*ii)* Removal and replacement of the crankshaft.
*iii)* Removal and replacement of the flywheel.

## 4 Methods of engine removal - general

The engine may be lifted out either on its own or in unit with the gearbox. On models fitted with automatic transmission it is recommended that the engine be lifted out on its own, unless a substantial crane or overhead hoist is available, because of the weight factor. If the engine and gearbox are removed as a unit they have to be lifted out at a very steep angle, so make sure that there is sufficient lifting height available.

## 5 Engine - removal (with gearbox)

1   The technique is to detach the engine and its accessories from the car and then lift the assembly out of the engine compartment. Considerable tilt is required to manoeuvre the gearbox underneath the rear engine bulkhead and out of the engine compartment (photos).
2   Before the engine can be removed, it will be necessary to either drive the front of the car onto ramps, or position the vehicle over a pit. Access to the exhaust system and other components is required during engine removal.
3   Open the bonnet and mark the position of the hinges on the bonnet using a pencil or piece of chalk (photo).
4   Get someone to support the weight of the bonnet, remove the hinge bolts and lift away the bonnet.
5   For safety reasons, disconnect the negative battery terminal.
6   Disconnect the radiator bottom hose and drain the coolant into a suitable container.
7   Remove the top hose and, if a radiator cowl is fitted, remove the four retaining screws and lift the cowl away.
8   On cars fitted with automatic transmission it will be necessary to remove the two hoses from the oil cooler at the bottom of the radiator.
9   Remove the centre stud nut retaining the radiator to the bottom strut, and lift the radiator up until it clears the mounting rubbers located on the side panels. Remove the radiator assembly.
10  Make a note of the electrical leads on the alternator and remove them.
11  Disconnect the engine temperature and oil pressure sensor connectors.
12  Remove the distributor boot, disconnect the HT wires from the coil and plugs and remove the distributor cap and rotor.
13  Disconnect the LT wire from the side of the distributor body.
14  Disconnect the brake servo hose from the inlet manifold. Disconnect the heater hoses.
15  Remove the air cleaner and detach the accelerator cable from the linkage on the inlet manifold. On cars fitted with a manual choke, remove the choke cable from the carburettor.
16  Now detach the fuel line to the pump: remember that the tank is above the level of the pump when the vehicle is level. Plug the fuel line with a clean metal bar to prevent spillage.
17  Disconnect the accelerator linkage from the valve spindle on the carburettor. The linkage is retained by a wire clip which passes through the ball joint on the spindle and fastens around the joint socket.
18  Disconnect the fuel lines and the vacuum hoses from the carburettor. Again identification tags on hoses may help during reassembly.
19  Make a note of the electrical connections at the starter motor solenoid and disconnect them.
20  From inside the car: Undo and remove the screws securing the centre console to the transmission tunnel. Lift away the console and then undo the screws which retain the rubber boot that is screwed around the gearlever. Pull the rubber boot up the lever to reveal the joint of the lever to the mechanism on the gearbox. Withdraw the split pin and then the clevis pin which retain the lever in the mechanism. Remove the gearlever and then the boot which protects the whole mechanism.
21  From underneath the car: Disconnect the speedometer cable, the reversing light switch connectors from the gearbox and then the clutch cable from the clutch unit (see Chapter 5).
22  Drain the gearbox oil into a suitable container.
23  Scribe a mark on the propeller shaft rear spider joint and flange, remove the bolts and disconnect the joint (refer to Chapter 7, if necessary). Pull the front end of the shaft out of the gearbox.
24  Remove the exhaust pipe shield which is situated on the first bend of the pipes below the exhaust manifold. Then with a socket spanner and a long extension piece, undo the nuts which retain the pipe to the manifold. Once the pipe is detached from the manifold, remove the pipe support which is attached to the clutch bellhousing.
25  Drain the engine oil and remove the front stone shield.
26  Place a jack beneath the gearbox and undo the bolts which secure the gearbox support member to the bodyshell. Then undo the nuts which secure the member to the mounting on the gearbox and remove the support member completely.
27  Attach a sling to the engine support brackets. The sling should pull in line with the front edge of the bracket. A considerable amount of tilt is required to allow the gearbox to be manoeuvred out of the transmission tunnel and out of the engine compartment.
28  Make sure that, whatever sling arrangement is used, the engine is secured and that rope or chain does not bind on components such as spark plugs.
29  Bring a hoist over the car and connect the sling; take the weight of the engine on the hoist and then undo and remove the nuts securing the engine support brackets to the rubber mounts (photo). Also unbolt one bracket from the cylinder block.
30  Finally check that all electrical connections and pipe connections to the engine have been detached.
31  Once you are satisfied that all is clear and that all the free leads, cables and hoses have been stowed safely, the engine/gearbox assembly may be raised from the car.
32  Lower the jack beneath the gearbox, to allow the assembly to be extracted from the transmission tunnel. Continue to raise the engine until it is hanging freely in the engine compartment. Continue to raise until it can be safely passed over and away from the car.
33  Now that the engine and gearbox assembly is out of the car the two units may be separated. Undo the bolts securing the clutch bellhousing to the cylinder block/crankcase. Remove the starter motor.
34  Lift the gearbox and clutch bellhousing carefully away from the engine, taking particular care to prevent the gearbox input shaft from becoming misaligned in the clutch and flywheel during removal.

5.1a Engine ready for removal

5.1b Lifting out the engine and gearbox (note the angle)

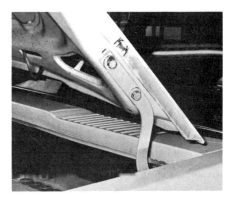

5.3 Bonnet hinge retaining bolts

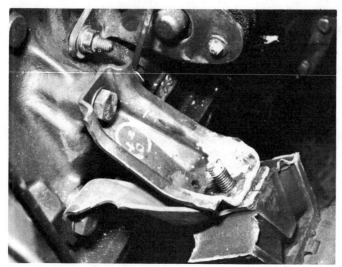

5.29 Engine mounting - L/H side

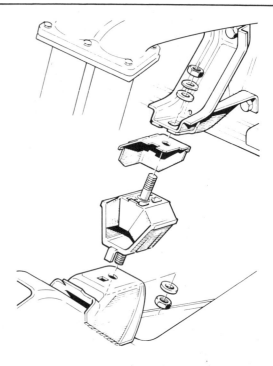

Fig. 1.5. Engine mounting assembly - R/H side (Sec. 5)

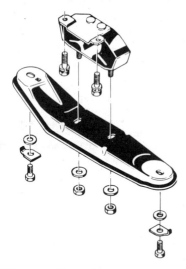

Fig. 1.4. Gearbox mounting and crossmember assembly (Sec. 5)

## 6  Engine - removal (without gearbox)

1  Follow the instructions given in Section 5, paragraphs 2 to 31, with the exception of paragraphs 20, 21, 22, 23 and 26.
2  Support the weight of the gearbox using a jack or blocks.
3  Remove the starter motor retaining bolts and lift away the motor.
4  Remove all the bolts retaining the clutch housing to the rear of the engine (refer to Chapter 6, if necessary).
5  When lifting out the engine, it is necessary to first move it towards the front of the car to clear the gearbox input shaft from the engine flywheel.

## 7  Engine - removal (without automatic transmission)

Because of the weight considerations it is advisable to detach and remove the automatic transmission first, as described in Chapter 6, and then remove the engine, as described in Section 6 of this Chapter.

## 8  Engine - dismantling (general)

1  It is best to mount the engine on a dismantling stand, but if this is not available, stand the engine on a strong bench at a comfortable working height. Failing this, it will have to be stripped down on the floor.
2  During the dismantling process, the greatest care should be taken to keep the exposed parts free from dirt. As an aid to achieving this thoroughly clean down the outside of the engine, first removing all traces of oil and congealed dirt.
3  A good grease solvent will make the job much easier, for, after the solvent has been applied and allowed to stand for a time, a vigorous jet of water will wash off the solvent and grease with it. If the dirt is thick and deeply embedded, work the solvent into it with a strong stiff brush.
4  Finally, wipe down the exterior of the engine with a rag and only then, when it is quite clean, should the dismantling process begin. As the engine is stripped, clean each part in a bath of paraffin or petrol.
5  Never immerse parts with oilways in paraffin (eg. crankshaft and camshaft). To clean these parts, wipe down carefully with a petrol dampened rag. Oilways can be cleaned out with wire. If an air-line is available, all parts can be blown dry and the oilways blown through as an added precaution.
6  Re-use of old gaskets is false economy. To avoid the possibility of trouble after the engine has been reassembled **always** use new gaskets throughout.
7  Do not throw away the old gaskets, for sometimes it happens that an immediate replacement cannot be found and the old gasket is then very useful as a template. Hang up the gaskets as they are removed.
8  To strip the engine, it is best to work from the top down. When the stage is reached where the crankshaft must be removed, the engine can be turned on its side and all other work carried out with it in this position.
9  Wherever possible, refit nuts, bolts and washers finger tight from wherever they were removed. This helps to avoid loss and muddle. If they cannot be refitted then arrange them in a sequence that ensures correct reassembly.
10  Before dismantling begins it is important that special tools are obtained otherwise certain work cannot be carried out. The special tools are shown in Fig. 1.7.

## 9  Engine ancillary components - removal

Before basic engine dismantling begins it is necessary to remove ancillary components as follows:

  1  Alternator                5  Inlet manifold and carburettor
  2  Fuel pump                 6  Exhaust manifold
  3  Thermostat                7  Distributor
  4  Oil filter cartridge      8  Water pump

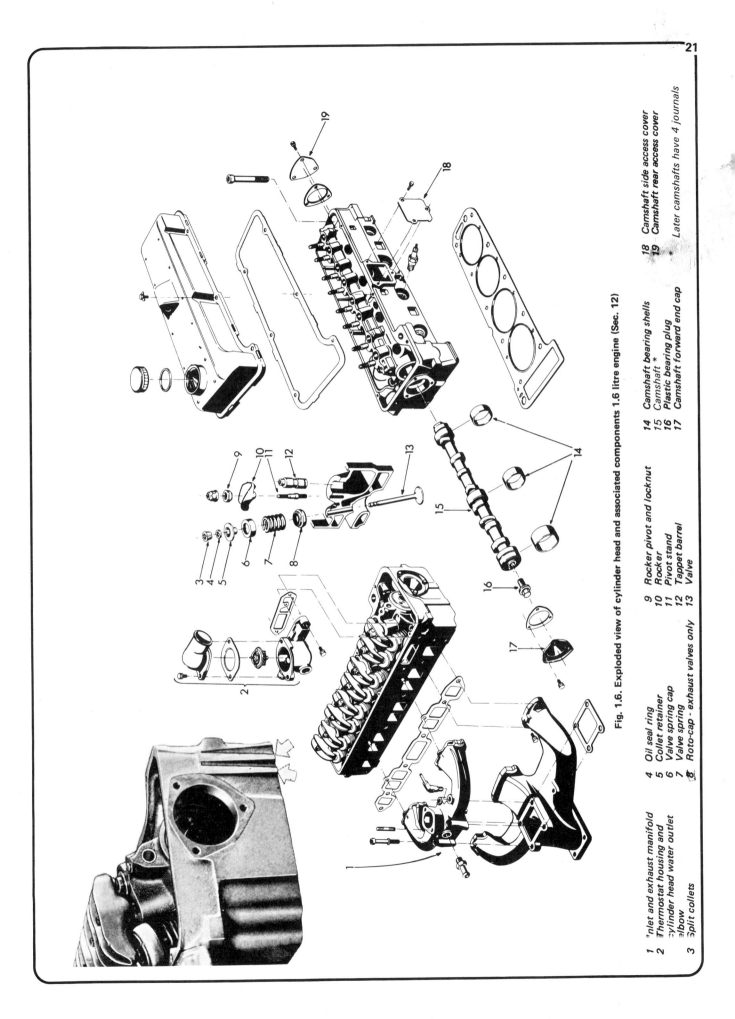

Fig. 1.6. Exploded view of cylinder head and associated components 1.6 litre engine (Sec. 12)

1  Inlet and exhaust manifold
2  Thermostat housing and cylinder head water outlet elbow
3  Split collets
4  Oil seal ring
5  Collet retainer
6  Valve spring cap
7  Valve spring
8  Roto-cap - exhaust valves only
9  Rocker pivot and locknut
10 Rocker
11 Pivot stand
12 Tappet barrel
13 Valve
14 Camshaft bearing shells
15 Camshaft *
16 Plastic bearing plug
17 Camshaft forward end cap
18 Camshaft side access cover
19 Camshaft rear access cover
*  Later camshafts have 4 journals

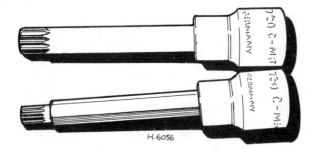

**Fig. 1.7. Special tools required to remove cylinder head and camshaft sprocket bolts. (Sec. 10)**

It is possible to remove any of these components with the engine in place in the car, if it is merely the individual items which require attention.

Presuming the engine to be out of the car and on a bench, and that the items mentioned are still on the engine, follow the procedures described below.

1 Slacken the alternator retaining nuts and bolts; move the unit towards the cylinder block and then remove the fan belt. Continue to remove the nuts and bolts retaining the alternator on the rubber mounting bracket and then lift the unit away. Remove the rubber mounting bracket and store with the alternator and its earthing strap.

2 Fuel pump: Two bolts secure the fuel pump to the engine block. Once the two have been removed, the pump together with the gasket and asbestos spacer can be removed.

3 Thermostat: This item is retained underneath the cylinder head water outlet elbow cap. Again once two bolts have been removed the cap can be lifted up to reveal the thermostat, which can then be simply lifted out of the housing.

4 Oil filter cartridge: This is of the disposable type, and is simply removed by gripping tightly and unscrewing from the engine block.

If the unit is tight, use a strap wrench to release it.

5 Inlet/exhaust manifold and carburettor: Disconnect the carburettor throttle valve spindle from the extension linkage mounted on the inlet manifold. The joint is held together by a wire clip, one part of which passes through the joint ball and socket, the remainder wraps around the clip. Undo and remove the four nuts that secure the carburettor to the manifold and then remove the carburettor. Finally, undo and remove the bolts securing the manifolds to the cylinder head, and remove the manifold.

6 The inlet and exhaust manifolds may be separated by undoing and removing the long bolts which secure them at the centre of the inlet manifold.

7 Distributor: It is necessary to have removed the fuel pump before the distributor can be extracted from the engine block. Once the pump has been removed, remove the distributor as described in Chapter 4.

8 Water pump: Begin by removing the four bolts which secure the fan, and pulley on the water pump shaft flange. Lift the fan and pulley clear, and then undo and remove the six bolts which retain the pump casing to the timing block. Remove the pump.

## 10 Cylinder head - removal (engine in car)

1 It should be noted that the cylinder head bolts and the camshaft sprocket bolts have splined heads that require the use of special tools to remove them (see Fig. 1.7).

2 These tools can be obtained from your G.M. dealer or a good motor accessory or tool factor shop. The part numbers are J-22915 for the cylinder head bolts, and J-23016 for the camshaft bolts. As no other tool will fit these bolts it is essential to obtain the right ones before attempting to dismantle the cylinder head.

3 After removing the bonnet, begin by removing the negative (—) earthing lead from the battery and then drain the cooling system. Remember to set the interior heater at 'hot' and to use the cylinder block drain plug to drain the block fully.

4 Remove the upper radiator hose and interior heater hoses.

5 Disconnect the accelerator cable from the throttle linkage on the carburettor and on cars with a manual choke, the choke cable as well.

Detach the throttle valve spindle from the extension linkage mounted on the inlet manifold. The two are joined at a ball and socket joint by a wire clip which passes through the joint and wraps around the joint cup. Loosen and then remove the four nuts which hold the carburettor on the inlet manifold. Remove the air cleaner, then the fuel and vacuum lines from the carburettor and then the carburettor itself.

6 Next undo and remove the bolts securing the manifolds to the cylinder head. Pull the manifolds clear of the joint face and hold in that position with a length of string.

7 Disconnect the engine temperature sensor and then remove the rocker cover. Remove the camshaft forward end cover. It is secured by three bolts and also governs the end-play on the camshaft.

8 Turn the engine so that No. 4 piston is at its firing position. The procedure to be adopted for turning the engine is to remove all the spark plugs, put the vehicle in top gear and nudge the car forwards. Then leave in gear and apply the handbrake.

9 Unscrew the plug retaining the timing chain tensioner spring and plungers.

10 The indexing hole in the camshaft chainwheel should now be directly above the centre of the wheel. Undo and remove the plastic bolt in the middle of the wheel. Then using the special tool undo and remove the three bolts securing the wheel to the camshaft. Lift the wheel from the camshaft and allow it to rest on the curved bracket immediately beneath the wheel.

11 Now undo and remove the cylinder head bolts with the special tool in the reverse order to tightening (Fig. 1.12.). Note that there are two additional bolts at the front of the cylinder head that thread directly into the timing cover. These should be removed first, using an Allen key, to avoid damaging the aluminium threads in the timing cover as the gasket clamping load is released.

12 The cylinder head should now be free of attachments to the engine and car. It should be appreciated that the cylinder head is very heavy - heavier than its counterparts on other engines - and therefore it is advisable to either use a hoist, or at the very least, an assistant.

13 If the cylinder head appears to be stuck on the engine block, do not try to free it by prising it off with a screwdriver or cold chisel, but tap the cylinder head firmly with a plastic or wooden headed hammer, the mild shocks should break the bond between the gasket, the head and the engine block, allowing the cylinder head to be lifted clear.

## 11 Cylinder head - removal (engine out of car)

Remove the ancillary components listed in Section 9 and then proceed as directed in paragraphs 8 to 12 in the previous Section.

## 12 Cylinder head dismantling - camshaft and tappet removal

The cylinder head is high grade chromium grey cast iron. The camshaft runs on bearings in the cylinder head. The tappet barrels move in bores machined in the cylinder head and the rockers which transmit the tappet movement to the valves, pivot on special fittings screwed into the cylinder head. These valves move in bores machined directly in the cylinder head and the exhaust valves are seated on special inserts of temperature resistant material.

The combustion chamber surface in the cylinder head has been 'alumetised' as well as the seats of the inlet valves. This finish makes for long surface life and inhibits the formation of carbon deposits.

1 Once the cylinder head has been removed, place it on a clean bench and commence the removal of:

    i)         *the rockers and pivots*
    ii)        *the camshaft and tappets*
    iii)       *the valve assemblies (Section 13)*

2 The rockers are removed by simply undoing and removing the locking nuts which retain the rocker pivot pieces on the mounting stud. Store the rockers and pivots in such a manner as to facilitate the refitting of those items into the exact positions from which they were removed.

3 Having already taken off the front camshaft end-cover plate during the cylinder head removal, undo and remove the bolts securing the side and rear camshaft access plates.

4 Turn the cylinder head on its side and extract the tappet barrels and, as with the rockers, store them so that they can be refitted to the bores from which they were taken.

5   The camshaft can now be extracted through the forward end of the cylinder head. Use the access apertures in the cylinder head to support the camshaft and prevent the soft bearing surfaces in the cylinder head being scratched and damaged by the sharp edges of the cam lobes.

6   If the water outlet elbow has not yet been removed, it should be now. It is secured to the cylinder head by three bolts.

### 13 Valves - removal

1   The valves may be removed from the cylinder head by the following method: With a valve spring compressor, compress each spring in turn until the two halves of the collets can be removed. Release the compressor and remove the valve spring cap, spring upper and lower spring seating and finally the valve itself.

2   As usual store all the parts so that they may be refitted into the exact position from which they were taken.

3   If when the valve spring compressor is screwed down, the valve spring cap refuses to free and expose the split collets, do not screw the compressor further in, in an effort to force the cap free. Gently tap the top of the tool directly over the cap with a light hammer. This will free the cap. Whilst you are tapping the tool, hold the compressor firmly with your other hand to prevent the tool jumping off the cap when it is released.

4   As mentioned earlier, there are no valve guide inserts as such in this engine. If on inspection the valve stem bores in the cylinder head are found to be excessively worn, then they will have to be reamed out to the next oversize. Valves with the appropriate oversize stem will need to be fitted when the engine is reassembled.

### 14 Timing chain - removal and refitting

1   The engine has an overhead camshaft driving the inlet and exhaust valves. The distributor, oil pump and fuel pump are all driven from a gear on the forward end of the crankshaft (Fig. 1.10). Such is the design of the engine, that it will be necessary to remove the cylinder head, sump, fuel pump, distributor, timing chain tensioner and water pump before the timing cover (in, and on, which all those items are incorporated), can be removed.

*Adjustment*

2   There is no need to adjust the timing chain tension; a spring loaded plunger acting on a shoe in contact with the chain, holds the chain at the correct tension at all times. The alignment of the drive sprocket and the camshaft chain wheel is dealt with in the next few paragraphs as part of the removal and installation procedure (Fig. 1.9).

*Removal and refitting*

3   Remove the following items:
   i)     *Cylinder head*
   ii)    *Fuel pump*
   iii)   *Distributor*
   iv)    *Sump*
   v)     *Timing chain tensioning plunger*
   vi)    *Water pump*
   vii)   *Crankshaft pulley*

4   The removal of items (i), (ii), (iii) and (vi) has been covered in the previous Sections and in the respective Chapters in this manual.

5   Timing chain tensioner plunger: this has a large hexagon head, which is screwed into the timing case above the oil pressure relief valve - a hexagon headed item just above the oil filter.

6   Sump: Fourteen short bolts secure the sump pan to the crankcase. The sump gasket consists of four parts, and all remnants of the gasket should be removed before reassembly.

7   Crankshaft pulley: a single bolt holds this member in place on the crankshaft. It will be necessary to prevent the crankshaft from turning whilst the bolt is being slackened. Place a chunk of wood between one of the throws on the crankshaft and the crankcase to hold the crankshaft in position. The pulley may need encouragement to slide off the crankshaft - a sprocket puller or similar device is ideal. Do not hit the pulley with a hammer or use excessive force or the pulley will become distorted.

8   Having removed all those items listed in paragraph 3, of this Section,

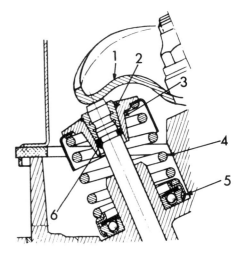

**Fig. 1.8. Section of exhaust valve Components (Sec. 13)**

*1   Rocker*              *4   Spring*
*2   Collets*             *5   Roto-cap*
*3   Collet retainer*     *6   Oil seal ring*

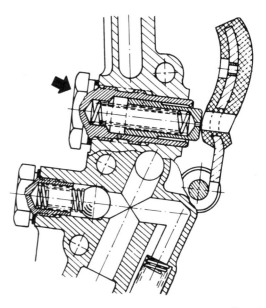

**Fig. 1.9. Timing chain tensioner components (Sec. 14)**

you will have seen why the cylinder head needed to be removed, a small tubular insert in an oil way to the cylinder head registers in both the timing case and cylinder head (Fig. 1.10).

9   The bolts which secure the timing casing to the cylinder block may now be removed and the casing lifted from the engine.

10  The bracket holding the camshaft wheel in its elevated position should be unbolted from the cylinder block to release the camshaft chainwheel and the timing chain itself.

11  The distributor/oil pump/fuel pump drive pinion needs to be pulled off the crankshaft, before the timing sprocket can be removed. Recover the Woodruff keys which locate the sprocket gear and the pulley onto the crankshaft.

12  Reassembly: Because of the detail design of the engine there cannot be any variations on the assembly procedure, which is as follows:

13  Begin by refitting the drive sprocket, ancillary drivegear on the crankshaft. Use the Woodruff keys to locate the two components on the shaft.

14  Refit the straight chain guide and the curved chain guide to the cylinder block.

15  Bring the crankshaft round so that Nos 1 and 4 pistons are at TDC. Hold the camshaft wheel so that its index hole is adjacent to the mark

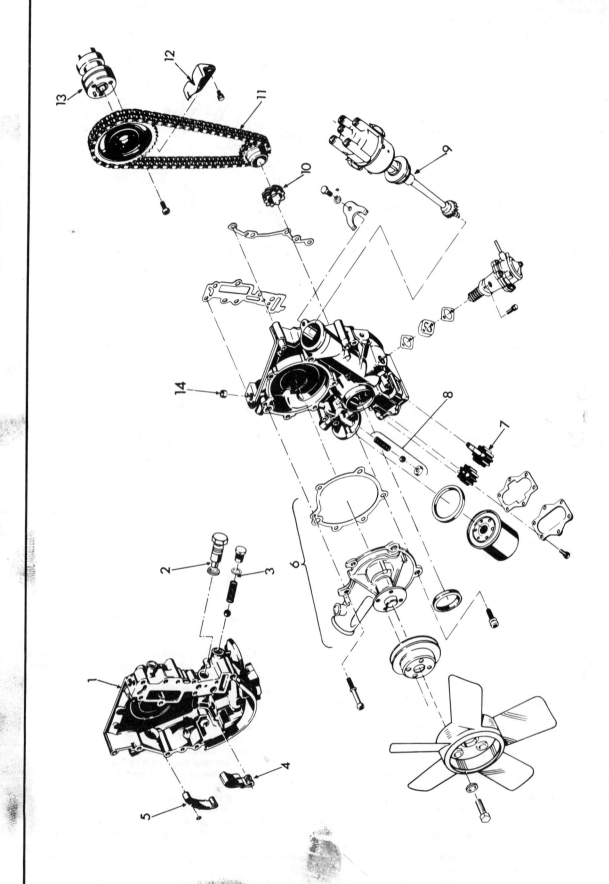

**Fig. 1.10. Exploded view of timing cover and components. (Sec. 14)**

1 Timing casing
2 Chain tensioner plunger
3 Oil pressure relief valve
4 Chain tensioner shoe

5 Chain guide shoe
6 Water pump
7 Oil pump
8 Oil filter by-pass valve

9 Distributor
10 Distributor, oil pump, fuel pump
   drive pinion
11 Timing chain

12 Timing chain wheel support bracket
13 Forward end of camshaft
14 Oil way gasket insert

on the timing plate (see Fig. 1.11). Loop the chain around both wheels, ensuring that their relative alignment is maintained. Again the refitting of those items follows the reversal of their removal procedures, use new gaskets and ensure that all joint surfaces are clean. No fragments of old gaskets must remain.

16 Reset the rockers and tappets - and then proceed to refit the cylinder head back into the car.

## 15 Cylinder block dismantling - flywheel removal

1 Having removed all the ancillary items described in Section 9, the cylinder head as described in Section 10, and then removed the timing case and chain as described in Section 14, the cylinder block should now be ready for further dismantling.

2 Refer to Chapter 5, and remove the clutch from the flywheel. Mark the position of the clutch assembly on the flywheel so that it may be refitted into the exact position from which it was removed. Undo the fixing bolts and remove the clutch mechanism together with the friction disc.

3 It should now be possible to undo and remove the six bolts securing the flywheel to the crankshaft, but note the location of the bolt marked with the letter 'P'. The flywheel can then be lifted from the crankshaft.

4 The final item which is to be removed from the block before the major moving parts are dismantled is the oil collection pipe and strainer. A clip secures the pipe to the main bearing cap No. 4 (second from rear of engine). Remove the clip and remove the two bolts which secure the pipe to the suction port in the crankcase.

5 The engine block is now ready for the major moving parts to be removed.

## 16 Big-end bearings - removal

1 The big-end bearings are the usual shell bearings running on a hardened steel crankpin and the shell surface is very soft. If the shells are scored and worn, it will mean the crankshaft is also worn and it may have to be removed for regrinding (see Section 24).

2 It is only possible to gain access to the big-end bearings (if the engine is to remain in the car), if the front suspension and subframe is lowered. It is felt that such an approach is not satisfactory since it involves a lot of work and in the end does not give you a great deal of freedom of access which the job really demands.

3 If the task is merely to attend to the big-ends and nothing else, the following procedure should be adopted:

4 Remove the engine as directed in Section 5.

5 Work on a strong clean bench and when the engine has been thoroughly cleaned - turn it on its manifold side to give access to the sump.

6 Remove the sump and the oil suction pipe.

7 Wipe the bearing caps clean and check that they have the correct identification markings. Normally the numbers 1 to 4 are stamped on the adjacent sides of the big-end caps and connecting rods, indicating which cap fits which rod and which way round the cap fits the rod; the number '1' should be found on the connecting rod operated by the No. 1 piston at the front of the engine, '2' for the second piston/cylinder, and so on.

8 If for some reason no identification marks can be found, then centre-punch mating marks on the rods and caps. One dot for the rod and cap for the No.'1' piston/cylinder, two for the No. '2' and so on.

9 Undo and remove the big-end cap retaining bolts and keep them in their respective order for correct refitting.

10 Lift off the big-end bearing caps; if they are difficult to remove they may be gently tapped with a soft faced mallet to break the 'stiction' between cap and rod.

11 To remove the shell bearings press the bearing end opposite the groove in both the connecting rod and bearing cap and the shells will slide out easily.

12 If the bearings are being attended to only, and it is not intended to remove the crankshaft, make sure that the pistons do not slide too far down the cylinder bores. The piston could reach a position where the lower piston ring passes out from the bottom of the cylinder bores.

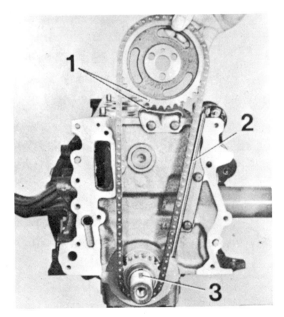

**Fig. 1.11. Correct location of timing chain (Sec. 14 and 47)**

1  Timing marks        2  Chain guide        3  Woodruff key

*Note: No 4 piston will be on its firing stroke with the timing chain in this position*

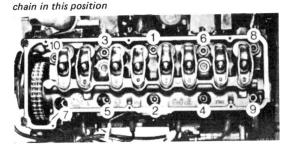

**Fig. 1.12. Correct sequence for tightening the cylinder head bolts (Secs. 10, 14 and 47)**

## 17 Crankshaft and main bearings - removal (including rear crankshaft oil seal)

1 The crankshaft is forged steel and is supported in five main bearings. The endfloat of the shaft is governed by the rear main bearing shell. The rear crankshaft oil seal is mounted in the rear main bearing cap (Fig. 1.13).

2 In order to be able to remove the crankshaft it will be necessary to have completed the following tasks:

   *i)*    *Removal of engine*
   *ii)*   *Separation of engine and gearbox*
   *iii)*  *Removal of the cylinder head*
   *iv)*  *Removal of the sump*
   *v)*   *Removal of the timing case, timing chain*
   *vi)*  *Oil collecting tube and strainer*
   *vii)* *The big-end bearings*

It is not essential to have extracted the pistons and connecting rods, but it makes for a less cluttered engine block during the crankshaft removal.

3 Check that the main bearing caps have identification numbers marked on them, No. 1 should be at the front and No. 5 should be the rear main cap. If for some reason identification cannot be found, use a centre-punch to identify the caps.

4 Before removing the crankshaft it is wise to check the existing endfloat. Use feeler gauges or a dial gauge to measure the gap between the rearmost main bearing journal wall on the crankshaft and the shoulder of the bearing shell in the bearing cap.

5 Move the crankshaft forwards as far as it will go with two tyre levers to obtain a maximum reading. The endfloat should be within the

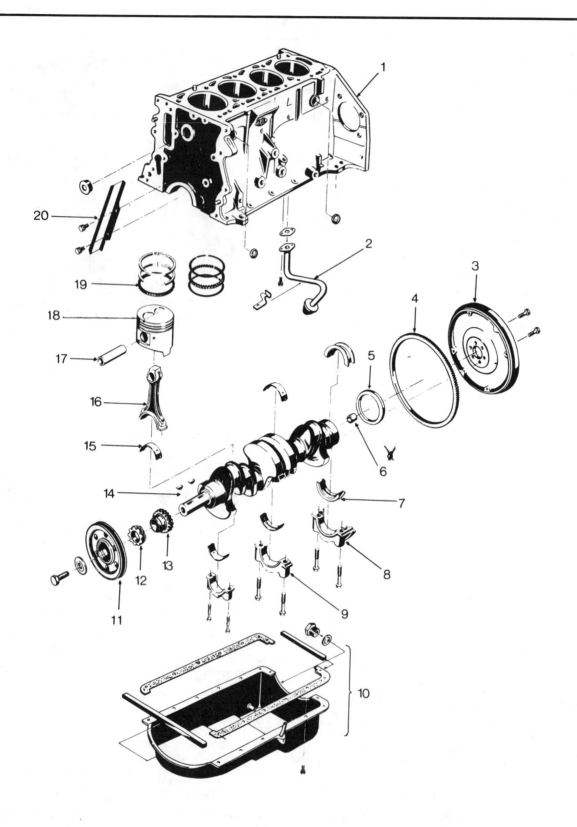

**Fig. 1.13. Exploded view of cylinder block components. (Sec. 17)**

1　Cylinder block
2　Oil collection tube and
　　strainer
3　Flywheel
4　Starter ring gear
5　Rear crankshaft oil seal

6　Centre bearing for gearbox
　　drive shaft location
7　Rear main bearing shell
8　Rear main bearing cap No 5
9　Main bearing cap

10　Sump
11　Crankshaft pulley
12　Auxiliary drive pinion
13　Timing chain sprocket
14　Woodruff keys

15　Big-end bearing shell
16　Connecting rod
17　Gudgeon pin
18　Piston
19　Piston rings
20　Timing chain guide

dimensions given in the Specifications. If the endfloat exceeds those figures, then rear bearing shells with oversize side bearing shoulders should be fitted. See the 'Specifications Section' at the beginning of this Chapter for thrust and main bearing data.

6   Having ensured that the bearing caps have been marked in a manner which facilitates correct refitting, undo the bolts retaining the caps by one turn only to begin with. Once all have been loosened proceed to unscrew and remove them.

7   The bearing caps can now be lifted away together with the shells inside them. Finally the crankshaft can be removed and then the shells seated in the crankcase.

### 18 Connecting rods/pistons and piston rings - removal and dismantling

1   In order to remove the pistons and connecting rods it will have been necessary to have removed the engine from the car, removed the cylinder head, the sump and the big-end bearing caps.

2   With the engine stripped down as indicated - proceed as follows:

3   Extract the pistons and connecting rods out of the top of the cylinder bores; be careful not to allow the rough edges of the connecting rods to scratch and score the smooth surface of the cylinder bore.

4   If it is necessary to separate the pistons from the connecting rods, this is best left to a GM dealer. However, the procedure is described for those having the required equipment and expertise.

5   Do not attempt to separate the pistons and connecting rods unless absolutely essential (eg. in the case where the piston is no longer useable); the interference fit between the gudgeon pin and connecting rod is such that the piston will most certainly be damaged during the removal task.

6   If the pistons are to be scrapped, the gudgeon pins may be removed from the combination in the following manner:

7   It will be necessary to obtain the special mandrel (see Fig. 1.14), or improvise a tool.

8   In a cold condition, press or drift the gudgeon pin out of the piston and connecting rod. Support the reverse side of the piston. **Do not** hold the connecting rod in a vice when the gudgeon pin is being forced out.

9   If you are going to use the improvised tool then certain measurements and checks must be carried out **before** the gudgeon pins are removed (Fig. 1.15).

10 With the design of tool featured in Fig. 1.14 it will be necessary to establish the thickness of the spacing washer on the tool before it is used to refit gudgeon pins.

11 Insert the improvised tool into a connecting rod/piston assembly. Fasten in position. Move the piston along the gudgeon pin away from the tool handle up against the connecting rod. Measure the exposed length of gudgeon pin and fit spacing washers onto the tool, so that the exposed length is achieved when the tool is used to insert gudgeon pins.

12 Piston ring removal: It may be desired to remove the piston rings for ring replacement or ring groove inspection. Gently expand the rings and slide each carefully off the piston taking care not to scratch the aluminium alloy from which the piston is made.

13 It is all too easy to break the cast iron rings if they are pulled off roughly, so this operation must be done with extreme care. It is helpful to use old feeler gauges to bridge empty ring grooves.

14 Lift one end of the ring to be removed out of its groove and insert the end of the feeler gauge under it.

15 Move the feeler gauge around the piston and apply slight upward effort to the ring as it comes out of the groove. The ring should then rest on the land above the slot. The ring can be eased off the piston, using the feeler gauges to prevent it from slipping into other grooves.

### 19 The engine lubrication system - general description

The engine lubrication system is quite conventional (Fig. 1.16). A gear type oil pump draws oil up from the sump, via the suction pipe and strainer, and pumps the oil under pressure into the cartridge oil filter. From the oil filter the oil flows into galleries drilled in the engine block to feed the main bearing on the crankshaft and the moving components of the cylinder head. Oil is bled from the main bearing journals in the crankshaft to supply the big-end bearings.

Therefore, the bearings which receive pressure lubrication are the main crankshaft bearings, the big-end bearings, the camshaft bearings and the tappets.

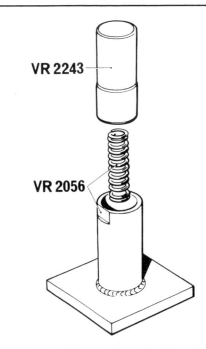

Fig. 1.14. Special tool for removing and refitting the gudgeon pins (Sec. 18)

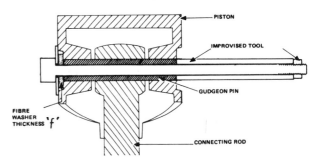

Fig. 1.15. Determining the thickness 'F' of fibre washer prior to removing the gudgeon pin using an improvised tool. (Sec. 18).

The remaining moving parts receive oil by splash or drip feed and these include the timing chain and associated items, the distributor and fuel pump drive, the rockers, the valve stems and to a certain extent the pistons.

The lubrication system incorporates two safeguards. The first is common to all engines and that is a pressure operated ball valve situated in the gallery between the oil pump and oil filter. This is in effect a filter bypass valve and allows oil to pass directly into the engine block gallery - down stream of the filter - when the filter is clogged up and resists the flow of oil (Fig. 1.17).

The second system is an oil pressure relief system, located in the timing casing between the oil filter and timing chain tensioner. It takes oil out of the engine block gallery, downstream of the filter, and passes it back into the sump, when the pressure of oil in that gallery is excessive. On later models the relief valve is located in the oil pump cover.

### 20 Oil pump - removal, dismantling and inspection

1   Access to the oil pump may be gained with the engine in place in the car if so desired - remove the sump stone guard and remove the oil filter cartridge.

2   It is more probable that the pump will not be the only item to require attention for in all probability the engine bearings will have suffered with a pump below par.

3   The pump components are retained in the timing case by a cover; undo and remove the six bolts retaining the cover on the timing case and remove the pump cover.

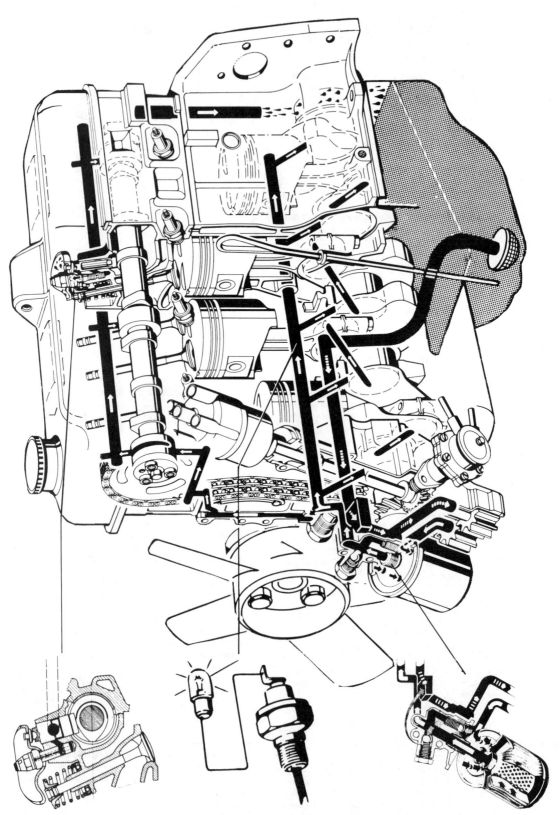

Fig. 1.16. Engine lubrication system. (Sec. 19)

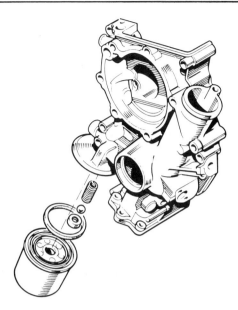

Fig. 1.17. Oil filter and by-pass valve (Sec. 19)

4   Extract the two gears and clean the gears and the inside of the pump with a non-fluffy petrol dampened cloth.

5   Refit the gears and using a straight edge and feeler gauges measure the protrusion of the gear faces above the level of the housing face. **Do not** lubricate the gears before carrying out this check. The permissible protrusion is between 0 and 4 thousandths of an inch (0 - 0.1016 mm) (Fig. 1.18).

6   It is also required to check the backlash between the gears; this may be accomplished using feeler gauges and should be between 0.004 and 0.008 inches (0.1016 and 0.2032 mm) (Fig. 1.19).

7   If the gears prove unsatisfactory on either of those two checks then they must be replaced.

8   It should be noted that when originally produced, it was possible for the bores and the shafts for either or both gears to be 0.008 inch (0.2032 mm) oversize. If an oversize gear had been fitted this will be identified by an '02' being stamped on the edge of the pump housing on the appropriate side. If both gears are oversize then '02' will be found on both sides of the pump (Fig. 1.20).

9   Inspect the interior surface of the pump cover. If it has worn — detectable by passing your finger nail over its surface — it should be renewed.

10 When reassembling the pump, coat the gears liberally with oil and use a new gasket between the cover and housing.

11 Lastly before starting the engine, remove the small plug to be found above the oil pump and fill the pump with engine oil (Fig. 1.21).

---

### 21 Oil pressure relief and bypass valves - removal and overhaul

1   The oil pressure relief valve should be inspected whenever symptoms of low oil pressure occur - that is when the oil pressure warning lamp lights up when the engine is running. The task can be completed with the engine in place.

2   On early models the relief valve is situated above the filter and is seen as a large hexagon headed plug. Unscrew the valve plug and

Fig. 1.18. Checking the oil pump gear-to-cover clearance (Sec. 20)

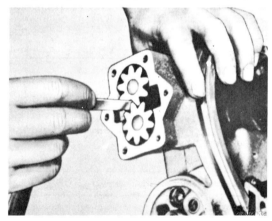

Fig. 1.19. Checking oil pump gear backlash (Sec. 20)

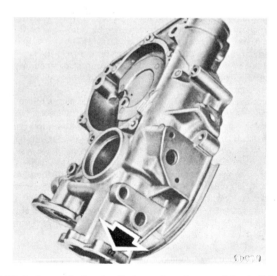

Fig. 1.20. Index mark showing that oversize oil pump driveshaft bushes have been fitted (Sec. 20)

Fig. 1.21. Location of oil pump priming plug (Sec. 20)

extract the sealing washer, spring and steel ball. Use a non-fluffy, petrol dampened rag to clean the valve components and the valve seat in the bore in the timing casing (Fig. 1.22).

3   Inspect the surface of the ball and its seat in the bore. Both surfaces should be smooth and regular.

4   Reinsert the ball and using a small brass drift tap the ball lightly against its seating to ensure the two surfaces conform.

5   If possible use a new valve spring, refit the spring and screw in the valve plug. There is no adjustment to the valve: therefore, start the engine to see whether the oil pressure has been returned to its correct level.

6   On later models undo the six bolts which hold the pump cover in position and take the cover to a clean bench for inspection. Unscrew the valve plug and extract the valve spring and ball. Clean all parts and the valve bore in the cover with a petrol dampened non-fluffy rag. Reassemble the valve and refit the cover to the pump. Remember to prime the pump before starting the engine as directed at the end of Section 20 of this Chapter.

7   The presence of foreign matter between the valve ball and the seat can allow sufficient oil to pass to reduce the pressure in the distribution galleries.

8   If you have not met with success, the oil bypass valve should be inspected. Again this task can be completed with the engine in place in the car.

9   Begin by removing the oil filter cartridge. The relief valve is then exposed in the timing casing inside the contact area of the filter.

10   It is worth noting at this point that you had better check with your spares dealer whether the bypass valve retaining sleeve, and the valve ball and spring are available as spares. It is unlikely that the retaining sleeve can be removed without damaging it beyond re-use. If spares are not available then renew the oil filter, if then the oil pressure returns to normal again, you know that the old filter was clogged and that the bypass valve was not working. Replacement parts for the bypass valve can then be ordered and fitted before the filter clogs up again.

11   The valve sleeve can be hooked or drifted out and then both ball and spring can be extracted. When fitting the new valve components in place take care not to distort the new sleeve as it is being driven into place.

## 22 Oil filter cartridge - renewal

1   When work is of a routine maintenance nature and the filter is due for renewal, a useful tool to loosen a disobliging filter cartridge is a small chain strap wrench. This type of wrench will grip the old filter firmly and enable the most obstinate of cartridges to be freed. Do not use a wrench to tighten the new filter.

## 23 Engine examination and renovation - general

1   With the engine stripped and all parts thoroughly cleaned, every component should be examined for wear. The items listed in the Sections following should receive particular attention and where necessary be renewed or renovated.

2   So many measurements of engine components require accuracies down to tenths of a thousandth of an inch. It is advisable therefore to either check your micrometer against a standard gauge occasionally to ensure that the instrument zero is set correctly, or use the micrometer as a comparative instrument. This last method however necessitates that a comprehensive set of slip and bore gauges is available.

## 24 Crankshaft - examination and renovation

1   Examine the crankpin and main journal surfaces for signs of scoring or scratches and check the ovality and taper of the crankpins and main journals. If the bearing surface dimensions do not fall within the tolerance ranges given in the Specifications at the beginning of this Chapter, the crankpins and/or main journals will have to be reground.

2   Big-end and crankpin wear is accompanied by distinct metallic knocking, particularly noticeable when the engine is pulling from low revs.

3   Main bearing and main journal wear is accompanied by severe engine vibration rumble - getting progressively worse as engine revs increase.

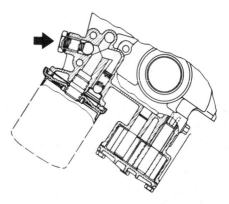

Fig. 1.22. Location of oil pressure relief valve (Sec. 21)

4   If the crankshaft requires regrinding, take it to an engine reconditioning specialist, who will machine it for you and supply the correct undersize bearing shells.

## 25 Big-end and main bearing shells - examination and renovation

1   Big-end bearing failure is accompanied by a noisy knocking from the crankcase and a slight drop in oil pressure. Main bearing failure is accompanied by vibration which can be quite severe as the engine speed rises and falls, and a drop in oil pressure.

2   Bearings which have not broken up, but are badly worn will give rise to low oil pressure and some vibration. Inspect the big-ends, main bearings and thrust washers for signs of general wear, scoring, pitting and scratches. The bearings should be matt grey in colour. With lead-indium bearings, should a trace of copper colour be noticed, the bearings are badly worn as the lead bearing material has worn away to expose the indium underlay. Renew the bearings if they are in this condition or if there is any sign of scoring or pitting. **You are strongly advised to renew the bearings - regardless of their condition. Refitting used bearings is a false economy.**

3   The undersizes available are designed to correspond with crankshaft regrind sizes, ie. 0.020 inch (0.508 mm) bearings are correct for a crankshaft reground - 0.020 inch (0.508 mm) undersize. The bearings are in fact, slightly more than the stated undersize as running clearances have been allowed for during their manufacture.

## 26 Cylinder bores - examination and renovation

1   The cylinder bores must be examined for taper, ovality, scoring and scratches. Start by carefully examining the top of the cylinder bores. If they are at all worn a very slight ridge will be found on the thrust side. This marks the top of the piston ring travel. The owner will have a good indication of the bore wear prior to dismantling the engine, or removing the cylinder head. Excessive oil consumption accompanied by blue smoke from the exhaust is a sure sign of worn cylinder bores and piston rings.

2   Measure the bore diameter just under the ridge with a micrometer and compare it with the diameter at the bottom of the bore, which is not subject to wear (Fig. 1.23). If the difference between the two measurements is more than 0.006 inch (0.15 mm) then it will be necessary to fit oversize pistons and rings. If no micrometer is available, remove the rings from a piston and place the piston in each bore in turn about three quarters of an inch below the top of the bore. If an 0.010 inch (0.25 mm) feeler gauge can be slid between the piston and the cylinder wall on the thrust side of the bore then remedial action must be taken. Oversize pistons are available in the following sizes:

*1.6 litre engine   — 0.020 in (0.5 mm) and 0.040 in (1.0 mm)*
*1.9 litre engine   — 0.020 in (0.5 mm) only*

3   If the bores are slightly worn but not so badly worn as to justify reboring them special oil control rings can be fitted to the existing pistons which will restore compression and stop the engine burning oil. Several different types are available and the manufacturer's instructions concerning their fitting must be followed closely.

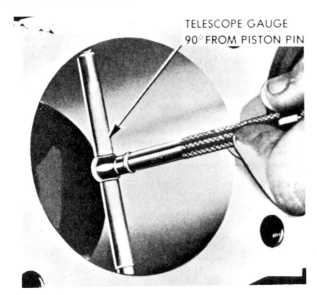

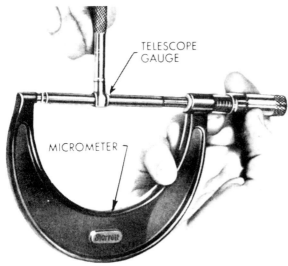

**Fig. 1.23. Measuring the cylinder bores (Sec. 26)**

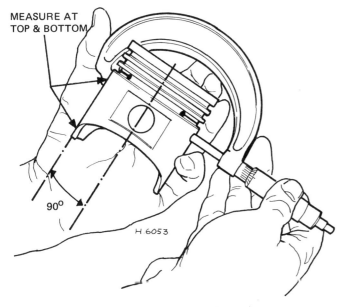

MEASURE AT TOP & BOTTOM

90°

H.6053

**Fig. 1.25. Measuring the piston diameter (Sec. 27)**

## 27 Pistons and piston rings - examination and renovation

1 If the old pistons are to be refitted carefully remove the piston rings and thoroughly clean them. Take particular care to clean out the piston ring grooves. At the same time do not scratch the aluminium. If new rings are to be fitted to the old pistons, then the top ring should be stepped to clear the ridge left above the previous top ring. If a normal but oversize new ring is fitted, it will hit the ridge and break, because the new ring will not have worn in the same way as the old, which will have worn in unison with the ridge.

2 Before fitting the rings on the pistons each should be inserted approximately 3 inches (75 mm) down the cylinder bore and the gap

**Fig. 1.24. Checking piston ring gap (Sec. 27)**

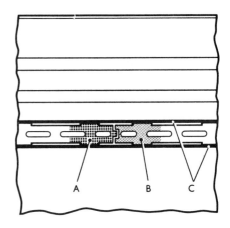

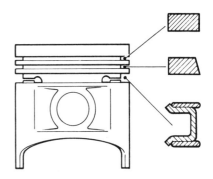

**Fig. 1.26. Correct location of piston rings (Secs. 27 and 39)**
*A and B centre scraper ring ends must not overlap*
*C Location of spacer rings*

measured with a feeler gauge as shown in Fig. 1.24. This should be as detailed in the Specifications at the beginning of this Chapter. It is essential that the gap is measured at the bottom of the ring travel. If it is measured at the top of a worn bore and gives a perfect fit it could easily seize at the bottom. If the ring gap is too small rub down the ends of the ring with a fine file, until the gap, when fitted, is correct. To keep the rings square in the bore for measurement, line each up in turn with an old piston down about three inches. Remove the piston and measure the piston ring gap.

3   When fitting new pistons and rings to a rebored engine the ring gap can be measured at the top of the bore as the bore will now not taper. It is not necessary to measure the side clearance in the piston ring groove with rings fitted, as the groove dimensions are accurately machined during manufacture.

4   The centre piston ring has a tapered sliding edge, and when refitting ensure that the top narrow side of the ring - marked with a 'T' is uppermost.

5   The lower ring which is a combination of three items must be assembled onto the piston, in the following manner: Install the intermediate ring first, making sure that the gap is not aligned with those in the top rings (Fig. 1.26).

6   Then fit the two steel rings onto the upper and lower side of the intermediate ring. Once all are in place check that the ring assembly is not jammed.

## 28 Connecting rods - examination and renovation

1   The connecting rods are not subject to wear but can, in the case of engine seizure, become bent or twisted. If any distortion is visible or even suspected the rod must be renewed.

2   The rods should also be checked for hairline cracks or deep nicks and if in evidence the rod discarded and a new one fitted.

## 29 Camshaft and camshaft bearings - examination and renovation

1   Carefully examine camshaft bearings for wear. If the bearings are obviously worn or pitted or the metal underlay just showing through, then they must be renewed. This is an operation for your local G.M. agent or automobile engineering works, as it demands the use of specialised equipment. The bearings are removed using a special drift after which the new bearings are pressed in, care being taken that the oil holes in the bearings line up with those in the block. With another special tool the bearings are then reamed in position.

2   The camshaft itself should show no signs of wear, but, if very slight scoring marks on the cams are noticed, the score marks can be removed by very gentle rubbing down with a very fine emery cloth or an oil stone. The greatest care should be taken to keep the cam profiles smooth.

3   All new camshafts have 4 journals, and these may be used in engines with 3 or 4 bearings.

## 30 Tappets - examination and renovation

1   Examine the bearing surface of the tappets which lie on the camshaft. Any indentation in this surface or any cracks indicate serious wear, and the tappets should be renewed. Thoroughly clean them out removing all traces of sludge. It is most unlikely that the sides of the tappets will be worn but if they are a very loose fit in their bores and can be readily rocked, they should be discarded and new tappets fitted. The tappets should be renewed whenever a new camshaft is fitted.

## 31 Valves and valve seats - examination and renovation

1   Examine the heads of the valves for pitting and burning especially the heads of the exhaust valves. The valve seatings should be examined at the same time. If the pitting on the valve and seats is very slight the marks can be removed by grinding the seats and valves together with coarse, and then fine, valve grinding paste. Where bad pitting has occurred to the valve seats it will be necessary to recut them to fit new

valves. If the valve seats are so worn that they cannot be recut, then it will be necessary to fit valve seat inserts. These latter two jobs should be entrusted to the local G.M. dealer or automobile engineering works. In practice it is very seldom that the seats are so badly worn that they require renewal. Normally, it is the valve that is too badly worn for replacement, and the owner can easily purchase a new set of valves and match them to the seats by valve grinding.

2   Valve grinding is carried out as follows: Place the cylinder head upside down on a bench with a block of wood at each end to give clearance for the valve stems. Alternatively, place the head at 45° to a wall with the combustion chambers away from the wall.

3   Smear a trace of coarse carborundum paste on the seat face and apply a suction grinder tool to the valve heads. With a semi-rotary action, grind the valve head to its seat, lifting the valve occasionally to

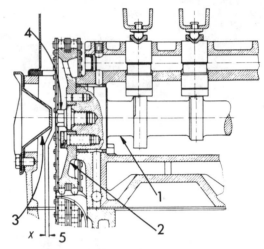

**Fig. 1.27. Forward end of camshaft installation (Sec. 29)**

| | |
|---|---|
| 1   Camshaft | 4   Plastic bearing plug |
| 2   Chain wheel | 5   Camshaft end play gap |
| 3   End cap | |

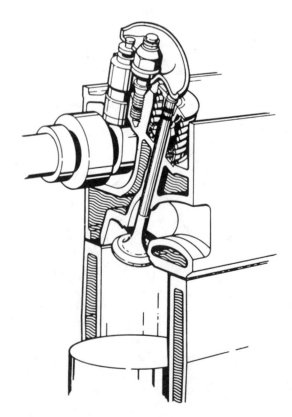

**Fig. 1.28. Sectional view of valve installation (Sec. 31)**

redistribute the grinding paste. When a dull matt even surface finish is produced on both the valve seat and the valve, then wipe off the paste and repeat the process with the carborundum paste, lifting and turning the valve to redistribute the paste as before. A light spring placed under the valve head will greatly ease this operation. When a smooth unbroken ring of light grey matt finish is produced, on both valve and the valve seat faces, the grinding operation is complete.

4   Scrape away all carbon from the valve head and the valve stem. Carefully clean away every trace of grinding compound, taking great care to leave none in the ports or in the valve guides. Clean the valves and valve seats with a paraffin soaked rag, then with a clean rag, and finally if an airline is available, blow the valve, valve guides and valve ports clean.

## 32 Valve guides - examination and renovation

1   There are no valve guide inserts fitted, the valves slide in bores machined directly in the cylinder head material.
2   If the valve guide bores are found to be worn and even proper size valve stems move sloppily in the bores, then the bores must be reamed oversize.
3   Having cut the bores to a new oversize, the appropriate valve with the correct oversize stem must be fitted.
4   When the bores have been recut it will also be necessary to recut the valve seats to ensure that the new valves will seal properly.
5   The task of reaming the valve guide bores and recutting the valve seats is really a job for the professional or for someone with a lot of workshop experience.

## 33 Cylinder head - decarbonisation

1   It is very unlikely that with modern fuels and oils, decarbonisation will be necessary at anything shorter than 60,000 mile intervals.
2   This operation can be carried out with the engine either in or out of the car. With the cylinder head off, carefully remove with a wire brush and blunt scraper, all traces of carbon deposits from the combustion spaces and ports. The valve stems and valve guides should be also freed from any carbon deposits. Wash the combustion spaces and ports down with petrol and scrape the cylinder head surface of any foreign matter with the side of a steel rule or a similar article. Take care not to scratch the surface.
3   Clean the pistons and top of the cylinder bores. If the pistons are still in the cylinder bores then it is essential that great care is taken to ensure that no carbon gets into the cylinder bores as this could scratch the cylinder walls or cause damage to the piston and rings. To ensure that this does not happen, first turn the crankshaft so that two of the pistons are on top of the bores. Place clean non-fluffy rag into the other two bores or seal them off with paper and masking tape. The waterways and pushrod holes should also be covered with a small piece of masking tape to prevent particles of carbon entering the cooling system and damaging the water pump, or entering the lubrication system and damaging the oil pump or bearing surfaces.
4   Press a little grease into the gap between the cylinder walls and the two pistons which are to be worked on. With a blunt scraper carefully scrape away the carbon from the piston crown, taking care not to scratch the aluminium. Also scrape away the carbon from the surround-ing lip of the cylinder wall. When all carbon has been removed, scrape away the grease which will now be contaminated with carbon particles, taking care not to press any into the bores. To assist prevention of carbon build up the piston crown can be polished with a metal polish. Remove the rags or masking tape from the other two cylinders and turn the crankshaft so that the two pistons which were at the bottom are now at the top. Place non-fluffy rag into the other two bores or seal them off with paper and masking tape. Do not forget the waterways and oilways as well. Proceed as previously described.

## 34 Distributor, oil pump and fuel pump drive - examination and renovation

1   The drive for the distributor, oil pump and fuel pump is taken from a helical gear on the forward end of the crankshaft. The driven gear is mounted on the distributor driveshaft. The base of this shaft runs on a bushing in the timing case and is keyed into the oil pump. The fuel pump is actuated by a cam adjacent to the driven gear.

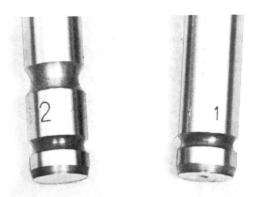

**Fig. 1.29. Markings identifying oversize valves (Sec. 32)**

**Fig. 1.30. Splitting off the ring gear to remove it from the flywheel (Sec. 35)**

2   Though the distributor driveshaft and oil pump shafts run in bushing in the timing case, it is not possible to replace the bushing itself.
3   If the bushing is found to have worn and proper sized distributor and oil pump shafts move sloppily in the bush bore, then the whole timing case will have to be renewed. Exchange pump parts to fit the replacement timing case will also have to be obtained. See Section 20 of this Chapter, regarding renovation of the oil pump.

## 35 Flywheel and starter ring gear - examination and renovation

1   The flywheel assembly is a finely balanced item and really there are few jobs which can be undertaken by the home mechanic.
2   Having removed the flywheel from the engine examine the driving face of the flywheel for scores and roughness that will give excessive wear on the clutch disc and a rough 'pick-up' of drive. If the surface is rough and needs re-machining then this task should be entrusted to reputable motor repairers.
3   It will not be a matter of just skimming the surface of the flywheel but also rebalancing it.
4   Starter ring gear: The ring gear is an interference fit on the periphery of the flywheel. If on inspection several teeth are found to be missing and the state of the other teeth is also shabby, the gear should be replaced. As usual check that a spare gear is available before removing the old one.
5   The ring gear may be removed by drilling a 0.24 inch (6 mm) diameter hole, some 0.32 inches (8 mm) deep into the ring gear. This hole should weaken the gear sufficiently for a sharp blow with a cold chisel, right by the drilled hole, to break the gear. Once the gear is broken it can be lifted from the flywheel (Fig. 1.30).
6   The new ring gear should be put into an oven (domestic electric) and heated to between 190° and 220°C (366 to 416°F). Maintain that temperature for five minutes, to ensure that the ring is fully expanded.
7   Quickly remove the ring from the oven, and place onto the flywheel, with the inner chamfer towards the flywheel. Using a soft metal drift

(eg. brass) tap the still hot ring gear evenly into position on the flywheel (Fig. 1.31). Do not quench, but allow to cool naturally.

8  The lateral run-out of the installed gear must not exceed 0.020 inches (0.5080 mm) measured with a dial gauge.

## 36  Engine - reassembly (general)

1  To ensure maximum life with minimum trouble from a rebuilt engine, not only must every part be correctly assembled, but everything must be spotlessly clean, all the oilways must be clear, locking washers and spring washers must always be fitted where indicated and all bearings and other working surfaces must be thoroughly lubricated during assembly. Before assembly begins renew any bolts or studs whose threads are in any way damaged; whenever possible use new spring washers.

2  Apart from your normal tools, a supply of non-fluffy rags, an oil can filled with engine oil (an empty washing-up fluid plastic bottle thoroughly clean and washed out will invariably do just as well), a supply of new spring washers, a set of new gaskets and a torque wrench should be collected together.

3  The order of assembly for the engine is as follows:

   *i)*   *Assemble crankshaft into engine block*
   *ii)*  *Assemble piston and conrods*
   *iii)* *Assemble piston/conrods into engine*
   *iv)* *Fit big-end bearings*
   *v)*  *Fit the flywheel onto the engine*
   *vi)* *Assemble timing chain and associated components onto engine*
   *vii)* *Assemble the timing case onto the engine*
   *viii)* *Fit the sump*
   *ix)* *Assemble the cylinder head*
   *x)*  *Fit the cylinder head to the engine*
   *xi)* *Fit oil pump, fuel pump, distributor, water pump and clutch*
   *xii)* *Join engine to the gearbox*

4  The engine should then be ready for refitment to the car.

5  Details of the engine assembly tasks are given in the following Sections.

## 37  Crankshaft - refitting

1  Ensure that the crankcase is thoroughly clean and that all oilways are clear. A thin twist drill is useful for clearing the oilways, or if possible they may be blown out with compressed air. Treat the crankshaft in the same fashion, and then inject engine oil into the oilways.

2  Never re-use old bearing shells; wipe the shell seats in the crankcase clean and then fit the upper halves of the main bearing shells into their seats (photo).

3  Note that there is a tab on the back of each bearing which engages with a groove in the shell seating (in both crankcase and bearing cap). Wipe away all traces of protective grease on the new shells.

4  Now fit the remaining shells into the bearing caps.

5  Four sets of shells are identical and fit onto the main bearings at positions 1 to 4. The rearmost main bearing shells incorporate the thrust

**Fig. 1.31. Fitting a new ring gear (Sec. 35)**

bearing (photo). The rearmost shells are supplied with various thicknesses of flange in order to be able to set the crankshaft endfloat. Having already measured the endfloat and the old bearing flange thickness when the engine was dismantled (Section 17, paragraph 5) use a new bearing with a flange thickness which will create the required endfloat.

6  Ensure that the holes in the shells fitted in the crankcase seats line up and do not diminish the oil supply hole in the crankcase. Inject oil into each supply oilway and coat the shells liberally with new engine oil (photo).

7  Lower the crankshaft into position and fit each cap in turn. The mating surfaces of the cap and crankcase must be spotlessly clean. Screw in the cap bolts and tighten each bolt a little. Check the crankshaft for ease of rotation (photos).

8  Should the crankshaft be stiff to turn or possess high spots, a most careful inspection should be made, preferably by a skilled mechanic, to trace the cause of the trouble; fortunately it is very seldom that any trouble of this nature will be experienced when fitting a crankshaft.

9  Tighten all the main bearing cap bolts, progressively to the specified torque and recheck the crankshaft for freedom of rotation (photo).

10  Use feeler gauges or a clock gauge to check the crankshaft endfloat which should be within the dimensions given in the Specifications. Various thicknesses of rear bearing flange are available.

11  Use sealing compound near and around the step in the rear main bearing cap seating to ensure that the joint is oil tight.

12  Insert the rear crankshaft oil seal into its seating in the rear bearing cap and crankcase (photo).

13  The crankshaft is now ready to receive the piston and connecting rod assemblies.

## 38  Pistons and connecting rods - assembly

1  The pistons and connecting rods are supplied separately and

37.2 Fitting the main bearing shells

37.5 Rear main bearing cap and shell bearing

37.6 Lubricating the crankshaft prior to bearing cap installation

37.7a Installing the crankshaft

37.7b Fitting the rear main bearing cap

37.9 Tightening the main bearing cap bolts

37.12 Fitting the crankshaft rear oil seal

whenever the engine block has been rebored the machine shop will supply the correct pistons and piston rings.

2   As mentioned in Section 18, it is essential that the gudgeon pin be inserted quickly into its correct position using either the special G.M. tool or the tool described in Section 18. Once the pin is in the piston and connecting rod, there is no chance of adjusting its position without damaging the piston.

3   The technique for assembling the piston and connecting rod is to heat the rod up to 280°C (536°F) and then place the rod and piston together and insert the gudgeon pin while the rod is still hot.

4   Place all four connecting rods in an oven (domestic) and heat to a temperature of around 280°C (536°F). Alternatively, use temperature indicator crayons and a hot plate to bring the small end of the connecting rod to the required temperature. A gas torch can be used directly on the connecting rod but only if you have had experience with such methods before. Care must be taken to 'brush' the small end of the rod evenly with the flame, so that hot spots are not created. It requires care to judge when the material has reached the required temperature - any overheating will seriously weaken the rod. One guide as to when the rod reaches the right temperature is when the clean metal surface is just changing colour to a darker shade of grey.

5   The importance of getting the connecting rod to the correct temperature and maintaining it whilst the gudgeon pin is fitted, cannot be overstressed. If the pin is caught by the contracting small end of the rod before the pin has been positioned properly, the piston will most

probably be damaged if any attempt is made to adjust the pin's position.

6   Having heated the rod, place the rod into a vice; hold the piston over the small end. Make sure that you have the connecting rod and piston in the correct relative positions (ie. the notch in the top of the piston should be to the right and the oil squirt hole in the connecting rod should be towards you, the notch in the big-end cap should be to the left) (Fig. 1.32).

7   Push the gudgeon pin into position with the tool chosen. When the connecting rod has cooled down, remove the assembly from the vice and check the gudgeon pin position in the assembly. The pin should be exactly central in the piston when the connecting rod is held centrally in the piston.

8   The assembly is now ready to accept the piston rings.

## 39 Piston rings - refitting

1   Check that the piston ring grooves and oilways are thoroughly clear. Always move the rings into position from the top of the piston.

2   The easiest method of fitting piston rings is to use a 0.015 inch (0.00 mm) feeler gauge (or similar) around the top of the piston and move the rings into position over the feeler gauge. This sequence is the reversal of the removal procedure detailed in Section 18 of this Chapter.

3   Note that as far as the oil control ring (the lowest), is concerned, it

is necessary to fit the central spring ring first and then the two steel bands immediately above and below the spacer ring; then ensure that the steel band rings are free to move (Fig. 1.26).

4  The two compression rings have a 'T' or 'Top' mark on the top side, and these rings must be fitted the correct way round.

5  When all the rings are in position on the pistons move them around to bring each ring gap to be some 120° away from the adjacent ring. This rule also applies to the individual rings that comprise the oil control ring.

### 40  Pistons and connecting rods - refitting

1  Lay the piston/connecting rod assemblies out in their correct order ready for refitting into their respective bores in the cylinder block. Remember that the connecting rods have been numbered to indicate to which cylinder they are to be fitted.

2  Clean the cylinder bores with a clean non-fluffy rag.

3  Apply some engine oil to the piston rings and then wrap the piston ring compressor around the first assembly to be fitted. A large diameter worm drive hose clip will serve as a ring compressor if a proper tool is not available.

4  Insert the connecting rod and piston into the top of the cylinder block and gently tap the piston through the ring compressor into the

cylinder bore with a wooden or soft headed mallet. Guide the big-end of the connecting rod near to its position on the crankshaft (photo).

5  Repeat the sequence described for the remaining three piston-connecting rod assemblies.

6  Check that all the pistons and connecting rods are the correct way around in the cylinder block. The notches in the top of the pistons should be towards the front of the engine; the oil squirt holes near the big-ends on the connecting rods should be on the manifold side of the engine. The notches in the big-end caps should all be to the rearward end of the engine.

### 41  Connecting rods/big-end bearings - refitting to crankshaft

1  Wipe the shell seat in the big-end of the connecting rod clean, and the underside of the new shell bearing. Fit the shell into position in the connecting rod with its locating tongue engaged with the appropriate groove in the big-end. Check that the oil squirt hole in the rod is aligned with the hole in the bearing shell.

2  Generously lubricate the crankpin journals with engine oil and turn the crankshaft so that it is in its most advantageous position for the rod to be drawn onto it.

3  Wipe the bearing shell seat in the bearing cap clean, and then the underside of the new shell. Fit the shell into the cap, engaging the shell tongue with the groove in the cap.

4  Draw the big-end of the connecting rod onto the crankpin and then fit the cap into position. Make sure it is the correct way around, and then insert the two retaining bolts (photo).

5  Tighten the big-end bolts a little at first, and do not tighten fully to the specified torque until all the piston/connecting rod assemblies have

Fig. 1.32. Correct assembly of piston to connecting rod (Sec. 38)

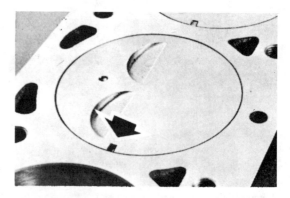

Fig. 1.33. Notch in piston must face towards the front of engine (Sec. 40)

40.4 Installing a piston - note the piston ring compressor

41.4 Fitting a big-end bearing cap

41.5 Tightening the big-end bolts

been fitted and the rotational freedom of the crankshaft checked (photo).

## 42 Flywheel - refitting

1 Offer up the flywheel to the rear end of the crankshaft and align, relative to the shaft, so that the centering bolt marked 'P' fits into the same hole in the flywheel as it did before (photo). The centering hole should have been marked as detailed in Section 15 of this Chapter.

2 Insert the remaining bolts and tighten to the specified torque.

3 Note that if a new flywheel is being fitted, the narrowest hole of the six should be used with the bolt marked 'P'.

4 If the needle roller bearing has been removed from the centre of the rear end of the crankshaft, it should now be refitted. Pack the rollers with grease and insert the bearing into the crankshaft.

5 The clutch disc and clutch mechanism can be refitted at this point if desired. Remember to align the '2' marks on the clutch unit and flywheel and hold the friction disc centrally on the flywheel with a suitable mandrel. Torque the clutch mechanism retaining bolts progressively and evenly to the specified torque (photo).

## 43 Timing chain, timing case and sump - reassembly

1 The engine should now be in a condition to accept the timing components and the auxiliary drive assembly.

2 Begin by placing the Woodruff key in the slots in the forward end of the crankshaft. Gently tap the timing sprocket and auxiliary drive

Fig. 1.34. Identification of flywheel locating bolt (Sec. 42)

pinion onto the shaft - over the keys. Note that the sprocket teeth should be next to the shoulder on the crankshaft (photo).

3 Fit the straight chain guide onto the cylinder block and then fit the curved chain wheel support to the top of the block.

4 The engine needs to be upside down or on its side whilst the crankshaft is turned to bring the number 1 and 4 pistons to TDC.

5 Hold the crankshaft in that position whilst the timing chain and

42.1 The shouldered flywheel bolt is marked with the letter 'P'

42.5 Refitting the clutch assembly

43.2 Correct position of the timing sprocket and auxiliary drive gear

43.5 Fitting the timing chain

43.7 Fitting the timing cover

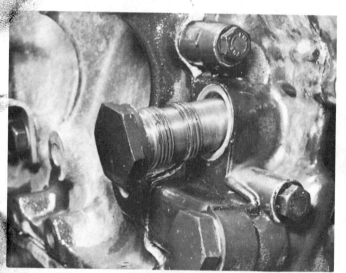

43.10 Insert the timing chain tension plunger

43.11 Oil collector pipe installed

camshaft chain wheel are fitted. The wheel should be positioned with
the index dimple on the periphery of the wheel adjacent to the notch
in the wheel support bracket (photo).

6   Now fit the crankshaft forward oil seal into the timing casing and
the curved chain tensioner. Do not fit the tensioner plunger at this
point.

7   Clean the mating faces of the cylinder block and the timing case,
and fit new gaskets in position. Offer up the casing to the block and
when in position, insert and tighten the retaining bolts. Tighten these
bolts to the specified torque (photo).

8   Check that the chainwheel and crankshaft are still in correct relative
position.

9   Insert the oil pump components as directed in Section 20, of this
Chapter.

10   Insert the chain tensioner plunger but do not tighten the plug at
this stage (photo).

11   Bolt the oil collector pipe and strainer onto the crankcase and No.
4 main bearing cap (photo).

12   Clean the mating surfaces of the sump and crankcase. Remember
the groove in the timing case and rear main bearing cap which accepts
the sump.

13   Smear grease over the mating surfaces of both sump and crankcase
and stick the new pieces of gasket into position, use a sealant at the
corners of the front and rear gasket sections.

14   Fit the sump into position and secure with bolts. Do not squeeze

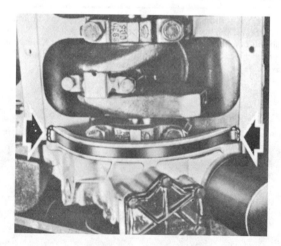

Fig. 1.35. Use of sealant on oil sump end gaskets (Sec. 43)

the soft gasket material from the joint by overtightening the bolts.
15 The engine may now be stood upright on the sump and prepared for the fitting of the cylinder head (Section 47).

## 44 Cylinder head - reassembly

1 The sequence for reassembly of the cylinder head is as follows:
   i) *Refit the inlet and exhaust valve assemblies*
   ii) *Refit the camshaft and tappet barrels*
   iii) *Refit the rockers*
   iv) *Refit the rear and side camshaft access covers and water outlet elbow*

2 It is advisable to refit the cylinder head to the engine with the rockers slack, so there is no chance of the valve interfering with the top of the cylinder block or pistons during refitting.

## 45 Valve assemblies - refitting to cylinder head

1 To refit the valves and valve springs to the cylinder head proceed as follows:
2 Lay the cylinder head on its side with the spark plug apertures facing downward.
3 Fit the valves into the same guides from which they were removed. (photo).
4 Fit the inlet valve stem oil seals in position over the guide protrusion (photo).
5 Place the lower spring seat in position, then the spring and then the oil seal and spring cap (photo).
6 Note that the exhaust valve springs are different from the inlet valve springs. The exhaust springs are shorter than the inlet springs, and the narrow windings should be away from the cylinder head, and the spring should be seated on the special 'roto cap' spring seat (photo).
7 Fit the spring compressor into position and compress the spring sufficiently for the cotters to be slipped into place in the groove machined in the top of the valve stem (photo).
8 Remove the spring compressor and repeat this procedure until all eight valves have been assembled into the cylinder head.

## 46 Camshaft and tappet barrels - refitting

1 Take the camshaft and wipe the lobes and journals clean with a non-fluffy rag, and then liberally coat with new engine oil.
2 Clean and then lubricate the bearing bores in the cylinder head.
3 Carefully insert the camshaft into the cylinder head being careful not to scratch the surfaces of the bearings in the head. Support the shaft through the access aperture, whilst it is being passed down into position (photo).
4 Once the camshaft is in position the tappets may be refitted into their respective bores (photo).
5 The rockers may be refitted onto the pivot studs now, but do not tighten down and set tappet gaps at this point: this should be done once the cylinder head is fitted on the engine and the camshaft bolted to its timing chain wheel (photo).

## 47 Cylinder head - refitting

1 As already mentioned in other Sections, the rockers should all be slack, so that all valves are closed. This will ensure that neither valves nor pistons are damaged during the fitting of the cylinder head.
2 With the engine standing on its sump, check that the crankshaft sprocket keyway is uppermost. The camshaft timing mark will not be visible, but should still be aligned with the mark on the timing plate (see Fig. 1.11).
3 Locate the oilway insert which engages both cylinder head and timing casing into the top of the timing casing (photo).
4 Place a new cylinder head gasket onto the cylinder block. The gasket is marked as to which way up it should be.
5 Lower the cylinder head carefully onto the engine, taking care not to disturb the camshaft chainwheel which needs to pass into the forward space in the cylinder head casting. Insert a few attachment bolts in the manifold side of the block (photo).
6 Turn the camshaft (access through the apertures in the side and rear end of the cylinder head) so that it can engage the chainwheel. Push the chainwheel onto the camshaft and secure with the three special bolts.
7 The camshaft has grooves machined in it which will now permit the cylinder head attachment bolts to be inserted in the camshaft side of the cylinder head. The bolts need to pass by the camshaft (photo).
8 Tighten the cylinder head bolts progressively and evenly in the order shown in Fig. 1.12 to the specified torque (photo). After this has been done, refit and tighten the two Allen headed bolts at the front of the cylinder head which thread into the timing cover.
9 Now tighten the camshaft chainwheel bolts to the specified torque and then insert the plastic plug into the centre of the camshaft wheel assembly (photo).
10 Fit the forward end camshaft cover plate (photo), use new gaskets and tighten the bolts, then measure the endfloat of the camshaft; a dial gauge will be easier to use although a feeler gauge pushed between the plug and the forward access cover should yield the same result. The endplay should be between 0.004 and 0.008 inches (0.10 and 0.20 mm).
11 The endplay is adjusted by mechanical deformation of the forward access cover. Depending on the adjustment required, the bearing tip of the cover will need to be **lightly** tapped inwards, or the cover removed and the tip tapped outwards.
12 The rear and side camshaft covers may now be refitted - as usual use new gaskets and tighten the attachment bolts.
13 Tighten the timing chain tensioner plug, then adjust the valve clearances as described in Section 48.
14 Remembering that the timing chain, camshaft and cylinder head have been fitted with No 4 piston at TDC on its firing stroke, rotate the crankshaft through 360° (thus bringing No 1 piston to TDC on its firing stroke) in preparation for fitting the distributor.

## 48 Valve clearances - adjustment

1 If the engine is in the course of reassembly, and the cylinder head has just been refitted, tighten the nuts on the rocker pivot studs so that as the engine is turned, the rocker transmits progressively more

45.3 Inserting the valve

45.4 Valve stem oil seal correctly fitted

45.5 Installing an exhaust valve spring and cap

45.6 Inlet and exhaust valve springs and caps, (note that exhaust spring is shorter)

45.7 Compressing the valve spring

46.3 Refitting camshaft

46.4 Refitting a tappet

46.5 Installing a rocker arm

47.3 Rubber insert and cylinder head gasket

47.5 Cylinder head refitted

47.7 Cut-out in camshaft

47.8 Tightening the cylinder head bolts

47.9 Tightening the camshaft sprocket bolts

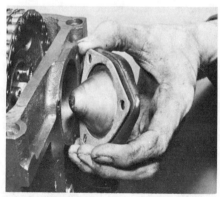

47.10 Refitting the camshaft retaining plate

48.5 Setting the valve clearances

movement to the valve. Do not tighten to the point where the rocker ceases to become slack at some time during the rotation of the engine.

2  As an initial setting to enable the engine to be started-up, the tappets should be set to 0.012 in (0.30 mm). After the engine has been refitted in the car and thoroughly warmed up, the clearances must be rechecked and adjusted with the engine running at idling speed.

3  Make up a temporary chain guard to the dimensions shown in Fig. 13.3 (Chapter 13).

4  With the rocker cover removed and the temporary chain guard fitted, start the engine and allow it to achieve normal operating temperature.

5  With the engine running at idling speed, adjust the rocker nut until a 0.012 in (0.30 mm) feeler gauge can just be inserted between the head of the valve stem and the rocker arm.

6  The importance of correct rocker/valve adjustment cannot be overstressed. If the gap is too large, the valves will not open fully and the engine 'breathing' will be constricted. If the gap is too small, the valves and pistons may damage each other, and the engine 'breathing' will deteriorate because during the engine cycle both inlet and exhaust valves will open for longer periods than intended. Both effects will reduce engine economy and power.

7  Once the valve/rocker gaps have been adjusted the rocker cover may be fitted. Ensure that the mating surfaces of the cover and cylinder head are perfectly clean and clear off any fragments of old gaskets.

8  Smear a new gasket with a little grease and then position on the cylinder head. Lower the cover into place and secure with the six bolts.

49.2 Static timing mark on flywheel

### 49  Distributor - refitting

1  Just as it is necessary to synchronise the camshaft with the crankshaft, to ensure that the valves open and close at the correct moments, so it is important to ensure that the distributor is correctly fitted. The spark which ignites the fuel/air charge in the cylinder must arrive at the correct instant to ensure that the maximum amount of energy is extracted from the combustion.

2  The crankshaft should already have been turned to bring No 1 piston to TDC on its firing stroke (see Section 47); in this position, the ball in the flywheel is aligned with the pointer in the aperture in the rear cylinder block flange (photo).

3  Take the distributor assembly, complete but for the cap, and turn the centre shaft so that the rotor arm is aligned as shown in Chapter 4.

4  Holding the distributor in this position feed the unit down into the timing casing and allow the shaft gear to mesh with the drive pinion on the crankshaft (photo).

5  The gears are cut on a helix and therefore it will be necessary to allow the distributor assembly to turn with the shaft whilst the gears fall into mesh. The reference mark made before dismantling indicates the final position for the distributor (Figs. 1.36 and 1.37).

6  Note the position of the vacuum advance/retard unit on the distributor. If the distributor is turned so that the advance/retard unit is not 'parallel' with the side of the engine, and on the opposite side of the distributor to the engine, then lift the distributor out of the engagement with the crankshaft drive pinion and turn the assembly so that as it is lowered into position again it finishes in the desired orientation relative to the engine.

7  Note that the rotor arm should still be aligned with the notch in the distributor casing and the ball in the flywheel aligned with the point in the cylinder bolt.

8  Fit the distributor clamp plate and bolt and tighten the bolt to a small extent (photo).

9  Check and adjust the 'static timing' of the distributor as directed in Chapter 4, before proceeding to the final assembly of the engine.

Fig. 1.36. Position of distributor shaft when No 1 piston is at top-dead-centre. (Delco-Remy type). (Sec. 49)

### 50  Final assembly - general

1  The following components should be assembled onto the engine, before it is refitted into the car. Refer to the relevant Chapters of this manual if you are in any doubt as to points of procedure of reassembly.

2  Refit the water pump, pulley and fan (photo).

3  Refit the crankshaft pulley (photo). Note that if a new pulley is being fitted and it is not provided with a timing notch, a notch must be cut using the old pulley as a template.

4  Refit the alternator support bracket.

5  Refit the fanbelt.

Fig. 1.37. Position of distributor rotor when No 1 piston is at top-dead-centre. (Bosch type). (Sec. 49)

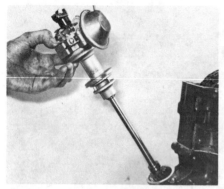

49.4 Refitting the distributor and driveshaft

49.8 Distributor clamping plate and bolt

50.2 Refitting the water pump

50.3 Refitting the crankshaft pulley

50.6 Installing the fuel pump

50.8 Gearbox refitted to engine

50.10 Refitting the thermostat housing

6   Refit the fuel pump (photo).
7   Refit the oil filter cartridge.
8   Reconnect the gearbox to the engine (photo).
9   Refit the starter motor.
10  Refit the cylinder head water outlet elbow and thermostat (photo).
11  Refit the engine main support brackets.

## 51 Engine - refitting

1   Although it is possible for the engine and gearbox assembly to be refitted by one man, providing he has the correct equipment, it is much easier if two are present.
2   Generally the refitting procedure is the reversal of the removal sequence. In addition, however:
3   Ensure that all loose leads, pipes, cables etc., are tucked out of the way of the engine/gearbox as it is refitted. It is easy to trap and damage one of these minor items and necessitate a lot of extra work after the engine is replaced.
4   The engine refitment sequence is as follows:
   a)  Lower engine and gearbox into position (photo).
   b)  Fit the mounting nuts and bolts.
   c)  Fit the gearbox support member and attach flexible mounting.
   d)  Reassemble the propeller shaft onto the gearbox and rear propeller shaft (photo).
   e)  Refit the gearbox gearshift lever mechanism (photo).
   f)  Refit the centre console inside the car (photo).
   g)  Refit the clutch cable and adjust the cable/pedal position.
   h)  Reconnect the speedometer cable and reversing light switch.
   i)  Reconnect the oil pressure and water temperature sensor leads.
   j)  Refit the exhaust and inlet manifolds (photo).
   k)  Refit the exhaust system to the manifold.
   l)  Refit the carburettor and reconnect all the vacuum hoses and air hoses.
   m)  Refit the accelerator linkage (and choke linkage 1.6 litre engines only) (photo).
   n)  Refit the radiator and reconnect the upper and lower water hoses and the heater hoses. (On cars fitted with automatic transmission, refit the oil cooler hoses).
   o)  Reconnect the fuel lines to the pump and carburettor.
   p)  Refit the air cleaner and associated hoses.
   q)  Refit the electrical leads to the starter motor, alternator and distributor.
   r)  Check the static timing of the distributor.
   s)  Refit the spark plugs.
   t)  Refit the distributor cap and reconnect the HT leads to the coil and spark plugs.
   u)  Refit the engine compartment bonnet.

51.4a Lowering the engine into the car

51.4d Inserting the prop shaft into the gearbox

51.4e Refitting the gearstick

51.4f Replacing the centre console

51.4j Refitting the manifolds and carburettor

51.4m Refitting the throttle cable - typical

*v) Reconnect the battery.*
*w) Fill the engine with new oil, check the gearbox oil and refill the cooling system.*

## 52 Engine - initial start-up after overhaul

1 Make sure that the battery is fully charged and that all lubricants, coolant and fuel are replenished.

2 If the fuel system has been dismantled it will require several revolutions of the engine on the starter motor to pump the petrol up to the carburettor.

3 As soon as the engine fires and runs, keep it going at a fast tickover only (no faster), and bring it up to the normal working temperature.

4 As the engine warms up there will be odd smells and some smoke from parts getting hot and burning off oil deposits. The signs to look for are leaks of water or oil which will be obvious if serious. Check also the exhaust pipe and manifold connections, as these do not always 'find' their exact gas tight position until the warmth and vibration have acted on them, and it is almost certain that they will need tightening further. This should be done of course, with the engine stopped.

5 When normal running temperature has been reached adjust the engine idling speed, as described in Chapter 3.

6 Stop the engine and wait a few minutes to see if any lubricant or coolant is dripping out when the engine is stationary.

7 Road test the car to check that the timing is correct and that the engine is giving the necessary smoothness and power. Do not race the engine - if new bearings and/or pistons have been fitted it should be treated as a new engine and run in at a reduced speed for the first 300 miles (500 km).

## 53 Fault diagnosis - engine

| Symptom | Reason/s | Remedy |
|---|---|---|
| **Engine fails to turn over when starter control operated** | | |
| No current at starter motor | Flat or defective battery | Charge or replace battery. Push start car. |
| | Loose battery leads | Tighten both terminals and earth ends of earth leads. |
| | Defective starter solenoid or switch or broken wiring | Run a wire direct from the battery to the starter motor or by-pass the solenoid. |
| | Engine earth strap disconnected | Check and retighten strap. |

| Symptom | Reason/s | Remedy |
|---|---|---|
| Current at starter motor | Jammed starter motor drive pinion | Place car in gear and rock to and fro. |
| | Defective starter motor | Remove and recondition. |
| **Engine turns over but will not start** | | |
| No spark at spark plug | Ignition damp or wet | Wipe dry the distributor cap and ignition leads. |
| | Ignition leads to spark plugs loose | Check and tighten at both spark plug and distributor cap ends. |
| | Shorted or disconnected low tension leads | Check the wiring on the − and + terminals of the coil and to the distributor. |
| | Dirty, incorrectly set, or pitted contact breaker points | Clean and adjust, or renew. |
| | Faulty condenser | Check contact breaker points for arcing, remove and fit new. |
| | Defective ignition switch | By-pass switch with wire. |
| | Ignition leads connected wrong way round | Remove and replace leads to spark plugs in correct order. |
| | Faulty coil | Remove and fit new coil. |
| | Contact breaker point spring earthed or broken | Check spring is not touching metal part of distributor. Check insulator washers are correctly placed. Renew points if the spring is broken. |
| No fuel at carburettor float chamber or at jets | No petrol in petrol tank | Refill tank! |
| | Vapour lock in fuel line (in hot conditions or at high altitude) | Blow into petrol tank, allow engine to cool, or apply a cold wet rag to the fuel line. |
| | Blocked float chamber needle valve | Remove, clean and replace. |
| | Fuel pump filter blocked | Remove, clean and replace. |
| | Choked or blocked carburettor jets | Dismantle and clean. |
| | Faulty fuel pump | Remove, overhaul and replace. |
| **Engine stalls and will not start** | | |
| Excess of petrol in cylinder or carburettor flooding | Too much choke allowing too rich a mixture to wet plugs | Remove and dry spark plugs or with wide open throttle, push start the car. |
| | Float damaged or leaking or needle not seating | Remove, examine, clean and replace float and needle valve as necessary. |
| | Float level incorrectly adjusted | Remove and adjust correctly. |
| No spark at spark plug | Ignition failure - sudden | Check over low and high tension circuits for breaks in wiring. |
| | Ignition failure - misfiring precludes total stoppage | Check contact breaker points, clean and adjust. Renew condenser if faulty. |
| | Ignition failure - in severe rain or after traversing water splash | Dry out ignition leads and distributor cap. |
| No fuel at jets | No petrol in petrol tank | Refill tank! |
| | Petrol tank breather choked | Remove petrol cap and clean out breather hole or pipe. |
| | Sudden obstruction in carburettor(s) | Check jets, filter, and needle valve in float chamber for blockage. |
| | Water in fuel system | Drain tank and blow out fuel lines. |
| **Engine misfires or idles unevenly** | | |
| Intermittent spark at spark plug | Ignition leads loose | Check and tighten as necessary at spark plug and distributor cap ends. |
| | Battery leads loose on terminals | Check and tighten terminal leads. |
| | Battery earth strap loose on body attachment point | Check and tighten earth lead to body attachment point. |
| Intermittent sparking at spark plug | Engine earth lead loose | Tighten lead. |
| | Low tension leads to + and − terminals on coil loose | Check and tighten leads if found loose. |
| | Low tension lead from − terminal side to distributor loose | Check and tighten if found loose. |
| | Dirty, or incorrectly gapped plugs | Remove, clean and regap. |
| | Dirty, incorrectly set, or pitted contact breaker points | Clean and adjust, or renew. |
| | Tracking across inside of distributor cover | Remove and fit new cover. |
| | Ignition too retarded | Check and adjust ignition timing. |
| | Faulty coil | Remove and fit new coil. |

| Symptom | Reason/s | Remedy |
|---|---|---|
| Fuel shortage at engine | Mixture too weak | Check jets, float chamber needle valve, and filters for obstruction. Clean as necessary. Carburettors incorrectly adjusted. |
| | Air leak in carburettor | Remove and overhaul carburettor. |
| | Air leak at inlet manifold to cylinder head, or inlet manifold to carburettor | Test by pouring oil along joints. Bubbles indicate leak. Renew manifold gasket as appropriate. |
| **Lack of power and poor compression** | | |
| Mechanical wear | Incorrect valve clearances | Adjust rocker arms to take up wear. |
| | Burnt out exhaust valves | Remove cylinder head and renew defective valves. |
| | Sticking or leaking valves | Remove cylinder head, clean, check and renew valves as necessary. |
| | Weak or broken valve springs | Check and renew as necessary. |
| | Worn valve guides or stems | Renew valve guides and valves. |
| | Worn pistons and piston rings | Dismantle engine, renew pistons and rings. |
| Fuel/air mixture leaking from cylinder | Burnt out exhaust valves | Remove cylinder head, renew defective valves. |
| | Sticking or leaking valves | Remove cylinder head, clean, check, and renew valves as necessary. |
| | Worn valve guides and stems | Remove cylinder head and renew valves and valve guides. |
| | Weak or broken valve springs | Remove cylinder head, renew defective springs. |
| | Blown cylinder head gasket (accompanied by increase in noise) | Remove cylinder head and fit new gasket. |
| | Worn pistons and piston rings | Dismantle engine, renew pistons and rings. |
| | Worn or scored cylinder bores | Dismantle engine, rebore, renew pistons and rings. |
| Incorrect adjustments | Ignition timing wrongly set. Too advanced or retarded | Check and reset ignition timing. |
| | Contact breaker points incorrectly gapped | Check and reset contact breaker points. |
| | Incorrect valve clearances | Check and reset rocker arm to valve stem gap. |
| | Incorrectly set spark plugs | Remove, clean, and regap. |
| | Carburation too rich or too weak | Tune carburettor for optimum performance. |
| Carburation and ignition faults | Dirty contact breaker points | Remove, clean and replace. |
| | Fuel filters blocked causing poor top end performance through fuel starvation | Dismantle, inspect, clean, and replace all fuel filters. |
| | Distributor automatic balance weights or vacuum advance and retard mechanisms not functioning correctly | Overhaul distributor. |
| | Faulty fuel pump giving top end fuel starvation | Remove, overhaul, or fit exchange reconditioned fuel pump. |
| **Excessive oil consumption** | Excessively worn valve stems and valve guides | Remove cylinder head and fit new valves and valve guides. |
| | Worn piston rings | Fit oil control rings to existing pistons or purchase new pistons. |
| | Worn pistons and cylinder bores | Fit new pistons and rings, rebore cylinders. |
| | Excessive piston ring gap allowing blow-up | Fit new piston rings and set gap correctly. |
| | Piston oil return holes choked | Decarbonise engine and pistons. |
| **Oil being lost due to leaks** | Leaking oil filter gasket | Inspect and fit new gasket as necessary. |
| | Leaking rocker cover gasket | Inspect and fit new gasket as necessary. |
| | Leaking timing gear cover gasket | Inspect and fit new gasket as necessary. |
| | Leaking sump gasket | Inspect and fit new gasket as necessary. |
| | Loose sump plug | Tighten, fit new gasket if necessary. |
| **Unusual noises from engine** | | |
| Excessive clearances due to mechanical wear | Worn valve gear (noisy tapping from rocker box) | Inspect and renew rocker shaft, rocker arms, and ball pins as necessary. |
| | Worn big-end bearing (regular heavy knocking) | Drop sump, if bearings broken up clean out oil pump and oilways, fit new bearings. If bearings not broken but worn fit bearing shells. |
| | Worn timing chain and gears (rattling from front of engine) | Remove timing cover, fit new timing wheels and timing chain. |
| | Worn main bearings (rumbling and vibration) | Drop sump, remove crankshaft, if bearing worn but not broken up, renew. If broken up strip oil pump and clean out oilways. |
| | Worn crankshaft (knocking, rumbling and vibration) | Regrind crankshaft, fit new main and big-end bearings. |

# Chapter 2 Cooling system

*For modifications, and information applicable to later models, see Supplement at end of manual*

## Contents

## Specifications

### Cooling system

| | | |
|---|---|---|
| Type ... ... ... ... ... ... ... ... ... ... | Pressurized system | |
| Cooling system capacity (including heater): | **16S** **19S** | **19E** |
|    Manual gearbox models ... ... ... ... ... ... | 11.4 pt (6.5 litre) 10.7 pt (6.1 litre) | 12.0 pt (6.8 litre) |
|    Automatic transmission models ... ... ... ... ... | 12.7 pt (7.2 litre) 12.3 pt (7.0 litre) | 11.8 pt (6.7 litre) |
| Operating pressure of system ... ... ... ... ... ... | 13.2 to 15.2 psi (0.42 to 1.06 kg/sq cm) | |
| Water temperature control ... ... ... ... ... ... | Thermostat and bypass | |
| Thermostat opens at ... ... ... ... ... ... | 189°F (87°C) | |
| Water circulation ... ... ... ... ... ... ... | Centrifugal pump driven by fanbelt | |

### Torque wrench setting

| | lb f ft | kg f m |
|---|---|---|
| Water pump to cylinder block ... ... ... ... ... ... | 14 | 1.9 |

## 1 General description and maintenance

Engine cooling is achieved by a conventional pump assisted thermo-syphon system. Inlet manifold and carburettor heating as well as car interior heating provisions are included as usual. The coolant is pressurized to prevent premature boiling in adverse conditions and to allow the engine to run at its most efficient running temperature.

The system functions as follows: cold water from the radiator circulates up the lower radiator hose to the water pump where it is impelled into the cylinder block around the water passages. The water then travels up into the cylinder head, around the combustion spaces and valve seats absorbing heat before finally passing out through the thermostat. When the engine is running at its correct temperature the water flow from the cylinder head diverges to flow through the inlet manifold, car interior heater and the radiator. However, when the engine is cool - below its correct operating temperature, the thermostat valve prevents the coolant from flowing into the radiator and therefore the flow is restricted to the engine.

The restriction in the flow of coolant ensures that the engine quickly warms to its correct operating temperature.

The coolant temperature is monitored by a variable resistance transducer screwed into the thermostat housing, just below the thermostat valve. The transducer together with the gauge on the instrument panel gives a continuous indication of coolant temperature.

Normal maintenance consists of checking the level of water in the radiator at regular intervals and inspecting the hoses and joints for signs of leaks or material deterioration.

## 2 Cooling system - draining

With the car on level ground, drain the system as follows:
1 With the cooling system cold, remove the filler cap and move the car interior heater control to 'HOT'. **Do not attempt to drain system when the engine coolant is still hot.**
2 There is no tap or plug fitted to the bottom of the radiator, therefore

it is necessary to loosen the clip retaining the lower radiator hose to the lower radiator union and pull the hose from the radiator.
3 If antifreeze is being used in the cooling system, efforts should be made to collect it. Make sure that any splashes of antifreeze solution on the bodywork are cleaned off with water - the solution will erode paintwork.
4 If the cylinder head is going to be removed, or the water pump, or the engine removed from the car, the cylinder block should be properly drained of water.
5 Remove the cylinder block drain plug, which is set behind the exhaust pipe and manifold - another reason for working on a cold engine.
6 To make certain that all coolant has been drained from the engine block, the plug orifice should be probed to dislodge any fragments of rust or sediment which might be preventing complete drainage of coolant.

## 3 Cooling system - flushing

1 Generally, even with proper use the cooling system will gradually lose efficiency as the radiator becomes choked with rust scale, deposits from the coolant and other sediment. To clean the system out, remove the radiator filler cap, cylinder block plug and bottom hose and leave a pipe from a water tap running into the filler hole for about fifteen minutes.
2 Reconnect the bottom hose, refit the cylinder block plug and refill the cooling system as described in Section 4 adding a proprietary cleaning compound. Run the engine for fifteen minutes, all sediment and sludge should be loosened and may be removed by flushing the cooling system once more.
3 In very bad cases the radiator should be reverse flushed. This can be done with the radiator in position. The cylinder block plug is left in position and the pipe from a mains water tap inserted into the bottom union of the radiator. The mains pressure will force the water up the radiator and out of the filler plug hole and after several minutes the radiator core should have been thoroughly cleared of deposits.

## 4 Cooling system - filling

1 The lower radiator hose should be reconnected and all hoses and connections secured. If the cylinder block drain plug has been removed, it should be refitted and tightened.
2 Set the car interior heater control at 'HOT'.
3 Fill the cooling system slowly to prevent air locks developing. The water used in the cooling system ideally ought to be soft; if the local supply is hard it may be boiled to remove the temporary hardness.
4 The final level of coolant in the radiator should be about ¾ inch above the top of the tubes in the radiator.
5 Start the engine and run for several minutes, enough time for minor air pockets to clear. Once the engine has been run, re-check the level of coolant in the radiator.
6 For information concerning antifreeze and corrosion inhibitors, refer to Section 13.

## 5 Radiator - removal and refitting

1 Drain the cooling system as directed in Section 2 of this Chapter. Remove the top hose (photo).

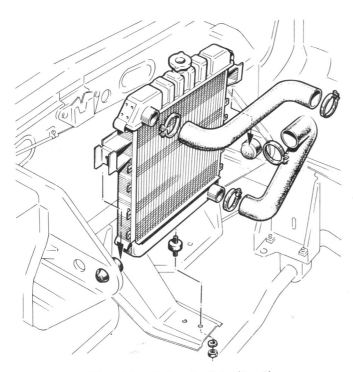

**Fig. 2.1. Installation of radiator (Sec. 5)**

2 On vehicles with automatic transmission unscrew the transmission oil cooler lines from the connectors on the bottom of the radiator. It is essential that no dirt gets into the lines or oil cooler, therefore hold the connectors away from the radiator and plug the lines to the transmission.
3 If a radiator cowl is fitted, remove the securing screw and lift the cowl rearwards over the fan.
4 Remove the lower attaching nut and slide the radiator out of its supports in the engine compartment (photos).
5 Refitting follows the reversal of the removal procedure. On automatic transmission cars the oil lines connecting to the oil cooler must be tightened to a torque of 11 to 15 lb f ft (1.5 to 2.1 kg f m).
6 Make absolutely sure that no dirt has managed to get into the transmission oil lines or oil cooler.
7 Install the top and bottom hoses and refill the cooling system as directed in Section 4 of this Chapter.

## 6 Radiator - inspection and cleaning

1 With the radiator out of the car, leaks may be soldered up or repaired with compounds such as 'Cataloy'. Clean out the radiator by flushing as detailed in Section 3. It should be mentioned that solder repairs are best completed professionally; it is too easy to damage other radiator parts by excessive heating.
2 Clean the exterior of the radiator by hosing down the matrix core with a strong jet of water. There will probably be quite an accumulation of mud and dead insects in the core of the radiator.
3 Inspect the upper and lower hoses for signs of surface deterioration - both inside and outside. Renew the hoses as necessary.
4 Examine the hose clips and renew them also, if they are rusted or distorted.

## 7 Thermostat - removal, testing and replacement

1 Typical symptoms of thermostat malfunction are either a slow warm up of the engine, anything in excess of 7 to 8 minutes, or an overheating engine, betrayed by pinking, 'running on' or excessive evaporation of coolant.
2 The thermostat valve is held underneath an aluminium alloy cover which also acts as the upper hose union.
3 It will only be necessary to partially drain the cooling system if the thermostat is going to be removed; though considering the method of draining the cooling system (Section 2) the system might as well be fully drained.
4 Once the coolant has been drained away, the top radiator hose may be removed and the thermostat cover unbolted from the thermostat elbow/housing on the cylinder head.
5 The thermostat valve is now exposed and may be lifted out for closer inspection and testing (photo).
6 To test the thermostat, suspend it in a container of cold water, then proceed to heat the water and note the temperature at which the valve begins to open. The valve should start to open at 189°F (87°C) and be fully open when the water reaches 212°F (100°C).
7 Discard the thermostat if the valve opens too early, or is not fully open at 212°F (100°C). Again if the valve does not fully close, the

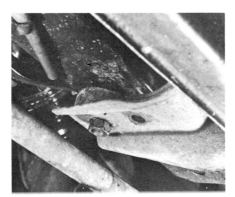

5.1 Radiator filler cap and top hose

5.4a Radiator lower attachment point

5.4b Lifting out the radiator

7.5 Removing the thermostat

thermostat must be discarded.

8   Refitting the thermostat follows the reversal of the removal procedure. Always ensure that the cover and thermostat elbow/housing mating surfaces are perfectly clean and flat. If the cover is badly corroded inside it may be renewed. A new gasket should be used, but do not use sealing compounds because it will make removal very difficult next time.

## 8  Water pump - removal and refitting

1   The water pump has been designed and made in a manner which results in it being unrepairable. Only the complete water pump is available as a spare.
2   Begin the removal of the water pump by draining the cooling system. There is no necessity to drain the cylinder block. Remove the radiator as directed in Section 5 of this Chapter.
3   Slacken the bolts on the alternator mounting to permit the unit to be moved inwards to slacken the fanbelt. Remove the fanbelt.
4   Next unbolt the fan and pulley from the pump shaft flange fitting.
5   Disconnect the lower radiator hose from the pump inlet port and

the interior heat pipe from the pump.
6   The bolts which secure the pump to the timing cover and cylinder block may now be removed and the pump unit lifted away.
7   If any feature of the pump - water seals, bearing play or impeller condition are found suspect, the whole assembly must be replaced.
8   Refitting the pump follows the reversal of the removal procedure. Make sure the mating surfaces of the pump and timing cover are perfectly clean and flat, and always use a new gasket when refitting the pump onto the engine.
9   Once the pump is in position, with the new gasket, the securing bolts must be tightened evenly to the specified torque setting.
10 Refit the radiator, hoses and car interior heater pipe. Refit the fan and pulley and then the fanbelt.
11 Finally when everything is refitted and secure, refill the cooling system.

## 9  Fanbelt - removal and replacement

1   If the fanbelt is worn or has over stretched it should be renewed. Sometimes the reason for replacement is that the belt has broken in service. It is therefore recommended that a spare belt is always carried in the car. Replacement is a reversal of the removal procedure, but if replacement is due to breakage:
2   Loosen the alternator pivot and slotted link bolts and move the alternator towards the engine.
3   Carefully fit the belt over the crankshaft, water pump and alternator pulleys.
4   Adjust the belt, as described in Section 10, and tighten the alternator mounting bolts. **Note:** after fitting a new belt it will probably require further adjustment after about 250 miles (400 km).

## 10  Fanbelt - adjustment

1   It is important to keep the fanbelt correctly adjusted and it should be checked every 6,000 miles (10,000 km) or 6 months. If the belt is slack, it will slip, wear rapidly and cause the alternator and water pump to malfunction. If the belt is too tight, the alternator and water pump bearings will wear rapidly and result in premature failure.
2   The fanbelt tension is correct when there is 0.5 inch (13 mm) of lateral movement at the midpoint position between the alternator pulley and the crankshaft pulley. To adjust the belt tension slacken the alternator bolts just sufficiently for the unit to be gently levered, with a long screwdriver, away from the engine. Once a new position of the alternator has been obtained for the correct belt tension, the unit's bolts can be tightened (photo).

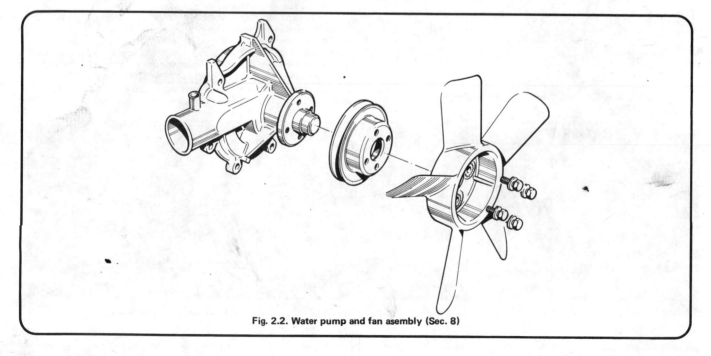

Fig. 2.2. Water pump and fan asembly (Sec. 8)

Fig. 2.3. Alternator mounting bolts (Secs. 9 and 10)

1 Lower mounting bolt
2 Top mounting bolt
3 Adjusting bolt

## 11 Temperature gauge - fault diagnosis

1 If the temperature gauge fails to work, either the gauge, the sender unit, the wiring or the connections are at fault.
2 It is not possible to repair the gauge or the sender unit and they must be replaced by new units if at fault.
3 First check that the wiring connections are sound. Check the wiring for breaks using an ohmmeter. The sender unit and gauge should be tested by substitution.

## 12 Temperature gauge and sender unit - removal and refitting

1 Refer to Chapter 10, for removal of the temperature gauge.
2 To remove the sender unit, disconnect the wire from the terminal and unscrew the unit from the side of the thermostat housing using the correct size spanner (photo).
3 When replacing the sender unit, smear some jointing compound on the threads to ensure a watertight joint.

## 13 Antifreeze and corrosion inhibitors - general

1 In circumstances where it is likely that the temperature will drop below freezing it is essential that some of the water is drained and an adequate amount of ethylene glycol antifreeze is added to the cooling system. If antifreeze is not used, it is essential to use a corrosion inhibitor in the cooling system in the proportion recommended by the inhibitor manufacturer.
2 Any antifreeze which conforms with specifications BS3151, BS3152 or BS6580 can be used (Duckhams Universal Antifreeze and Summer Coolant). Never use an antifreeze with an alcohol base as evaporation is too high.

10.2 Checking the fanbelt tension

12.2 Temperature gauge sender unit

3 Antifreeze with an anti-corrosion additive can be left in the cooling system for up to two years, but after six months it is advisable to have the specific gravity of the coolant checked at your local garage, and thereafter once every three months.
4 The table below gives the proportion of antifreeze and degree of protection:

| Antifreeze | Commences to freeze | | Frozen | |
|---|---|---|---|---|
| % | $^{o}C$ | $^{o}F$ | $^{o}C$ | $^{o}F$ |
| 25 | -13 | 9 | -26 | -15 |
| 33 1/3 | -19 | -2 | -36 | -33 |
| 50 | -36 | -33 | -48 | -53 |

**Note:** Never use antifreeze in the windscreen washer reservoir as it will cause damage to the paintwork.

**Warning:** Ethylene glycol is poisonous, keep out of reach of children.

## 14 Fault diagnosis - Cooling system

| Symptom | Reason/s | Remedy |
|---|---|---|
| Overheating | Insufficient water in cooling system | Top up radiator. |
| | Fanbelt slipping (accompanied by a shrieking noise on rapid engine acceleration) | Tighten fanbelt to recommended tension or replace if worn. |
| | Radiator core blocked or radiator grille restricted. | Reverse flush radiator, remove obstructions. |
| | Bottom water hose collapsed, impeding flow | Remove and fit new hose. |
| | Thermostat not opening properly | Remove and fit new thermostat. |
| | Ignition advance and retard incorrectly set (accompanied by loss of power, and perhaps, misfiring) | Check and reset ignition timing. |
| | Carburettor incorrectly adjusted (mixture too weak) | Tune carburettor. |
| | Exhaust system partially blocked | Check exhaust pipe for constrictive dents and blockages. |
| | Oil level in sump too low | Top up sump to full mark on dipstick. |
| | Blown cylinder head gasket (water/steam being forced down the radiator overflow pipe under pressure) | Remove cylinder head, fit new gasket. |
| | Engine not yet run-in | Run-in slowly and carefully. |
| | Brakes binding | Check and adjust brakes if necessary. |
| Underheating | Thermostat jammed open | Remove and renew thermostat. |
| | Incorrect thermostat fitted allowing premature opening of valve | Remove and replace with new thermostat which opens at a higher temperature. |
| | Thermostat missing | Check and fit correct thermostat. |
| Loss of cooling water | Loose clips on water hoses | Check and tighten clips if necessary. |
| | Top, bottom, or bypass water hoses perished and leaking | Check and replace any faulty hoses. |
| | Radiator core leaking | Remove radiator and repair. |
| | Thermostat gasket leaking | Inspect and renew gasket. |
| | Radiator pressure cap spring worn or seal ineffective | Renew radiator pressure cap. |
| | Blown cylinder head gasket (pressure in system forcing water/steam down overflow pipe) | Remove cylinder head and fit new gasket. |
| | Cylinder wall or head cracked | Dismantle engine, despatch to engineering works for repair. |

# Chapter 3 Carburation; fuel and exhaust systems

*For modifications, and information applicable to later models, see Supplement at end of manual*

## Contents

## Specifications

### Fuel pump
| | |
|---|---|
| Type ... ... ... ... ... ... ... ... ... ... | Mechanical, driven from distributor drive |
| Pressure (1950 rpm) ... ... ... ... ... ... ... ... | 3.1 to 3.7 psi |

### Fuel tank
| | |
|---|---|
| Capacity ... ... ... ... ... ... ... ... ... ... | 11 Imp. gallons (50 litres) |
| Location ... ... ... ... ... ... ... ... ... ... | Behind rear seat |

### Fuel filter
... ... ... ... ... ... ... ... ...    Mesh type in fuel pump

### Air cleaner
... ... ... ... ... ... ... ... ...    Replaceable paper element

### Carburettor specification (Solex type 35 PDSI)
| | |
|---|---|
| Auxiliary system ... ... ... ... ... ... ... ... | Additional idling air |
| Float needle valve ... ... ... ... ... ... ... ... | 1.75 mm |
| Float needle valve washer ... ... ... ... ... ... | 2.0 mm |
| Venturi diameter ... ... ... ... ... ... ... ... | 26.0 mm |
| Mixture outlet ... ... ... ... ... ... ... ... | 2.4 |
| Main jet ... ... ... ... ... ... ... ... ... | X 127.5 |
| Air correction jet ... ... ... ... ... ... ... | 80 |
| Idling jet ... ... ... ... ... ... ... ... | 50 |
| Injector tube ... ... ... ... ... ... ... ... | 50 |
| Enrichment: | |
|     Main jet system ... ... ... ... ... ... ... | 50 |
|     Tube in cover ... ... ... ... ... ... ... | 75 |
| Additional idling fuel jet ... ... ... ... ... ... | 45 |
| Additional idling mixture jet ... ... ... ... ... ... | 60 |
| Idling speed (engine hot) ... ... ... ... ... ... | 800 to 850 rpm |
| Ignition control vacuum: | |
|     mm Hg ... ... ... ... ... ... ... ... | 1 to 15 |
|     in Hg ... ... ... ... ... ... ... ... | 0.1 to 0.6 |
|     mm $H_2O$ ... ... ... ... ... ... ... | 20 to 200 |
|     in $H_2O$ ... ... ... ... ... ... ... | 0.8 to 8.0 |
| Exhaust gas emission at idling speed ... ... ... ... ... | 1.5 to 2.5% CO |

### Carburettor specifications (Solex type 32/32 DIDTA)

| | Primary | Secondary |
|---|---|---|
| Auxiliary system ... ... ... ... ... ... ... ... | Additional idling air | |
| Float needle valve ... ... ... ... ... ... ... ... | 2.0 mm | |
| Float needle valve washer ... ... ... ... ... ... | 1 mm | |
| Venturi diameter ... ... ... ... ... ... ... ... | 26 mm | 26 mm |
| Mixture outlet ... ... ... ... ... ... ... ... | 2.8 | 3.2 |
| Main jet ... ... ... ... ... ... ... ... ... | X 135 | X 145 |
| Air correction jet ... ... ... ... ... ... ... | 140 | 125 |
| Idling jet ... ... ... ... ... ... ... ... | 50 | — |
| Progression jet ... ... ... ... ... ... ... | — | 60 |
| Progression air jet ... ... ... ... ... ... ... | — | 100 |
| Injector tube ... ... ... ... ... ... ... ... | 45 | — |

| | | |
|---|---|---|
| Enrichment: | | |
|    main jet system    ...    ...    ...    ...    ...    ...    ...    ... | 100 | — |
|    tube in cover ...    ...    ...    ...    ...    ...    ...    ... | 80 | — |
| Idling speed (engine hot)    ...    ...    ...    ...    ...    ... | 800 - 850 rev/min | |
| Ignition control vacuum: | | |
|    mm Hg    ...    ...    ...    ...    ...    ...    ...    ...    ... | 1 - 15 | |
|    in Hg    ...    ...    ...    ...    ...    ...    ...    ...    ... | 0.1 - 0.6 | |
|    mm $H_2O$    ...    ...    ...    ...    ...    ...    ...    ...    ... | 20 - 200 | |
|    in $H_2O$    ...    ...    ...    ...    ...    ...    ...    ...    ... | 0.8 - 8 | |
| Exhaust Gas Emission at idling speed: | | |
|    air/fuel ratio ...    ...    ...    ...    ...    ...    ...    ... | 14 : 1 - 13.7 : 1 | |
|    carbon monoxide (CO)    ...    ...    ...    ...    ...    ... | 1.5 - 2.5% | |
| Fast idling speed (engine hot)    ...    ...    ...    ...    ... | 3200 rev/min | |
| Float chamber vent valve setting    ...    ...    ...    ... | 4/4.5 mm | |
| Throttle flap gap (secondary barrel)    ...    ...    ...    ... | 0.5 mm (0.002 in) | |
| Choke flap gap    ...    ...    ...    ...    ...    ...    ...    ... | 2.5 to 3 mm | |

## Carburettor specifications (Zenith type 35/40 INAT)

| | Primary | Secondary |
|---|---|---|
| Auxiliary system    ...    ...    ...    ...    ...    ...    ...    ... | Additional idling mixture | |
| Float needle valve    ...    ...    ...    ...    ...    ...    ... | 2 mm | |
| Float needle valve washer    ...    ...    ...    ...    ...    ... | 1 mm | |
| Venturi diameter    ...    ...    ...    ...    ...    ...    ... | 26 mm | 32 mm |
| Mixture outlet    ...    ...    ...    ...    ...    ...    ...    ... | 3.1 | 3.1 |
| Main jet    ...    ...    ...    ...    ...    ...    ...    ...    ... | X 135 | X 165 |
| Air correction jet    ...    ...    ...    ...    ...    ...    ... | 120 | 140 |
| Emulsion tube    ...    ...    ...    ...    ...    ...    ...    ... | 9S | 4K |
| Idling jet ...    ...    ...    ...    ...    ...    ...    ...    ... | 45 | — |
| Progression jet    ...    ...    ...    ...    ...    ...    ...    ... | — | 120 |
| Progression air jet    ...    ...    ...    ...    ...    ...    ... | — | 1.0 |
| Injector tube    ...    ...    ...    ...    ...    ...    ...    ... | 45 | 50 |
| Enrichment: | | |
|    main jet system    ...    ...    ...    ...    ...    ...    ... | 40 | — |
| Additional idling fuel jet    ...    ...    ...    ...    ...    ... | 55 | — |
| Additional idling mixture jet    ...    ...    ...    ...    ... | 50 | — |
| Idling speed (engine hot)    ...    ...    ...    ...    ...    ... | 800 - 850 rev/min | |
| Ignition control vacuum: | | |
|    mm Hg    ...    ...    ...    ...    ...    ...    ...    ...    ... | 1 - 15 | |
|    in Hg    ...    ...    ...    ...    ...    ...    ...    ...    ... | 0.1 - 0.6 | |
|    mm $H_2O$    ...    ...    ...    ...    ...    ...    ...    ...    ... | 20 - 200 | |
|    in $H_2O$    ...    ...    ...    ...    ...    ...    ...    ...    ... | 0.8 - 8 | |
| Exhaust gas emission at idling speed: | | |
|    air/fuel ratio ...    ...    ...    ...    ...    ...    ...    ... | 14 : 1 - 13.7 : 1 | |
|    carbon monoxide (CO)    ...    ...    ...    ...    ... . | 1.5 - 2.5% | |
| Fast idling speed (engine hot)    ...    ...    ...    ...    ... | 2700 rev/min | |
| Float chamber vent valve setting    ...    ...    ...    ... | 1.5/1.8 mm | |
| Throttle flap gap (secondary barrel)    ...    ...    ...    ... | 0.5 mm (0.002 in) | |
| Choke flap gap    ...    ...    ...    ...    ...    ...    ...    ... | 2.7 to 2.9 mm | |

## Torque wrench setting

| | lb f ft | kg f m |
|---|---|---|
| Exhaust pipe to manifold    ...    ...    ...    ...    ...    ...  ..  ... | 14 | 2 |

## 1  General description

The basic layout of the fuel system on all models comprises a fuel tank mounted behind the rear seat, a fuel pump mechanically operated by a cam on the distributor driveshaft and a carburettor and inlet manifold. The interconnecting fuel lines are small-bore metal pipes with flexible hose connections where necessary.

The Zenith type 35/40 INAT and Solex type 32/32 DIDTA carburettors are the twin-barrel type fitted with an electrically-operated automatic choke. The Solex 35 PDSI type has a single stage barrel with a manually operated choke.

The carburettor on all models is connected to the accelerator pedal by a cable, and on cars fitted with automatic transmission an additional cable is used to control the 'kick-down' facility.

## 2  Air filter element - removal and replacement

1  Under normal driving conditions the filter element will require renewal every 24,000 miles (40,000 km). Using the vehicle in dusty areas will necessitate more frequent renewal.
2  To gain access to the filter element, release the toggle clips located around the top of the filter casing and remove the centre nut if fitted (photo).
3  Lift away the top cover and remove the filter element (photo).
4  When fitting the new element, ensure that it is correctly seated in the bottom of the filter casing before replacing the top cover.
5  A sealing ring is fitted on the outer rim of the top cover and this should be checked periodically for possible deterioration and replaced if necessary.
6  To remove the complete filter assembly, first undo the centre screw or, depending on the type of carburettor, slacken the clamp holding the filter casing to the carburettor air intake.
7  Carefully pull off the crankcase ventilation hose and vacuum control pipe if fitted.
8  Lift away the filter assembly straight upwards, detaching the inlet pipe from the warm air duct if fitted.

## 3  Heated air intake system - description

1  On some cars the air filter system incorporates an inlet manifold vacuum and inlet air temperature governed warm air supply line. This line comprises an air horn attached to the exhaust manifold and a duct to the air cleaner which houses a vacuum operated flap valve situated on the line aperture in the cleaner box (Fig. 3.2).
2  The vacuum line to this valve is itself governed by a thermally

**Fig. 3.1. Air filter cover toggle clips and centre screw (the latter on some models only). (Sec. 2)**

2.2 Air filter toggle catch

2.3 Air filter element

sensitive valve situated in the cleaner. The valve uses bimetal strip to activate the device.

3   The air supply operates as follows:

(i) *In cold conditions, the thermal valve is open to allow the inlet vacuum to activate the valve in the air cleaner supply duct, so as to open the warm air line from the exhaust manifold surface and close the line through the cool air intake.*

(ii) *As the engine warms up, so the air drawn in from the exhaust manifold warms the thermally sensitive valve which closes the vacuum line to the air inlet control valve. Air is then solely drawn through the cool air intake.*

### 4   Carburettor - description and operation

The Zenith and Solex 32/32 twin-barrelled carburettors are almost identical in operation although they differ slightly in construction. Both types provide highly efficient fuel metering throughout all engine demands from the cold start condition through hard acceleration and fast cruising.

The Solex PDSI single barrel type is considerably more simple in construction and although not providing the greater performance capabilities of the twin barrel type, does offer improved fuel economy.

The following description of the basic modes of carburettor operation apply to all types, although any reference to the secondary barrel function obviously does not apply to the Solex PDSI model.

1   The basic function of the carburettor is to mix a measured amount of fuel vapour with air in order to make the most effective fuel/air charge for the engine to 'breathe'. This basic function of the device is clearly illustrated by taking the medium speed cruising mode of operation.

2   *Medium speed mode:* In this mode, the carburettor is receiving fuel from the pump and is holding it in the float chamber. The float regulates the level of fuel in the chamber in the same way as its counterpart in a domestic cold water cistern: if the level of fuel drops the float admits more fuel into the chamber; as the level rises the buoyant force of the float closes the inlet valve to prevent more fuel entering the chamber. The level of the fuel in the float chamber is very critical because it affects the operation of the emulsion tube.

Under steady running conditions air is being drawn through the barrel of the carburettor at sufficient speed to cause a slight depression (vacuum) in the throat region of the venturi. This depression draws

fuel from the float chamber through the main jet in the base of the float chamber, then through the emulsion tube and finally through the mixing orifice in the centre of the minor venturi.

In order to improve the mixing of the fuel and air and to prevent excessive amounts of fuel being drawn into the venturi by the depression, some of the incoming air is allowed to pass through an 'air correction jet' and flow down around the emulsion tube. The emulsion tube has holes machined in it which permit the air to blow into the fuel and create an emulsion of fuel and air. More air is added to this emulsion as it passes the 'vent jet' on its way to the mixing orifice in the minor venturi.

The vent jet and air correction jet effect is to lower the level of fuel in the emulsion tube and to form a first stage mixture - the emulsion. Both these features are necessary since without them the depression tends to draw too much fuel into the air stream and the mixing of the fuel with the air is less efficient.

Having established the steady state of functioning of the carburettor, it is necessary to consider the remaining modes of operation to establish the functions of the other minor jets and devices.

3   *Cold starting:* The engine needs a rich mixture in order to compensate condensation of fuel onto the inlet manifold and to provide sufficient power to drive the car. With the throttle valve only partly open, insufficient depression is created in the primary venturi to draw the fuel required into the air stream.

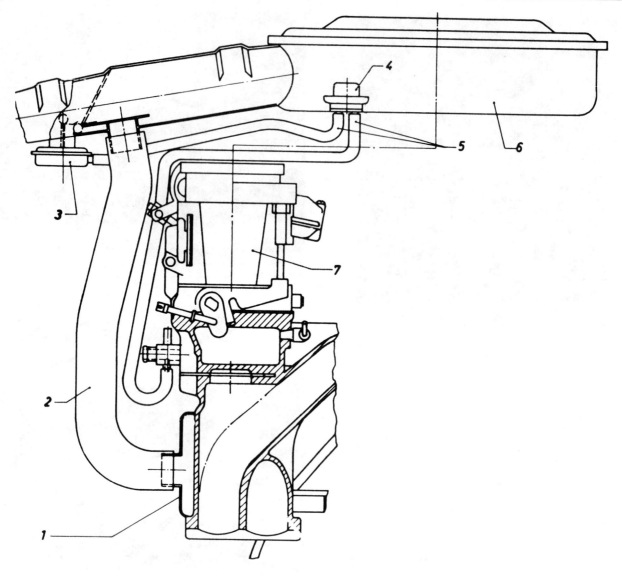

**Fig. 3.2. Warm air filter system**

| | | |
|---|---|---|
| 1   Warm air horn at the<br>     exhaust manifold | 3   Vacuum actuated flap<br>     control device | 5   Vacuum hoses |
| 2   Connecting hose | 4   Thermal valve controlling<br>     the vacuum line | 6   Air cleaner<br>7   Carburettor |

A choke flap or valve is therefore fitted in the top of the primary barrel air inlet which closes when the engine is cold, and opens when the engine reaches normal running temperature. On twin-barrel carburettors the operation of the choke is automatic, being operated by an ignition controlled heater element and bi-metal spring within the choke control housing. The choke valve on the Solex PDSI carburettor is manually operated by a cable and control knob on the instrument panel. When the choke flap valve is closed, a large depression is formed throughout the whole barrel of the carburettor which is sufficient to draw the required amount of fuel into the air stream. The flap pivot spindle is eccentric on the flap, to allow the depression in the barrel to open the flap depending on the magnitude of the depression.

It is possible with this arrangement however that when the engine is accelerated when cold, the choke flap could be impelled to open to an extent which would significantly reduce the depression in the barrel. The reduction could be sufficient to prevent fuel being drawn into the air stream in the required quantities.

On the twin-barrel carburettors a second vacuum diaphragm system has been included to prevent the choke flap from opening excessively during cold acceleration.

The system senses the vacuum in the carburettor primary barrel.

4   *Engine idling and low rpm:* When the engine air demand is low, insufficient depression is created in the venturi to draw the required amount of fuel into the air stream. There is a depression formed however in the vicinity of the edge of the throttle flap. A formation of small jets has therefore been positioned in the lower area of the barrel. near the throttle flap. When the engine is idling or is turning at low revolutions per minute, air passes down the primary barrel and past the throttle flap. As it 'squeezes' by the flap it draws fuel from the idling and low speed jets in the side of the throttle barrel. Once engine speed increases, the depression 'moves' from around the idle jets to the venturi and then continues to draw in fuel from the main emulsion tube.

5   *Engine accelerating:* The engine requires an enriched mixture of fuel and air to develop the extra power. The engine will respond quicker if the carburettor anticipates the need for more air and fuel. This anticipation is accomplished mechanically by coupling the throttle linkage to a diaphragm fuel pump on the carburettor. This pump injects additional fuel through the acceleration jet directly into the air stream in the primary venturi. The linkage is designed to allow the pump to deliver a shot of fuel over a finite time and there is some relative movement between the throttle linkage and the pump actuating lever.

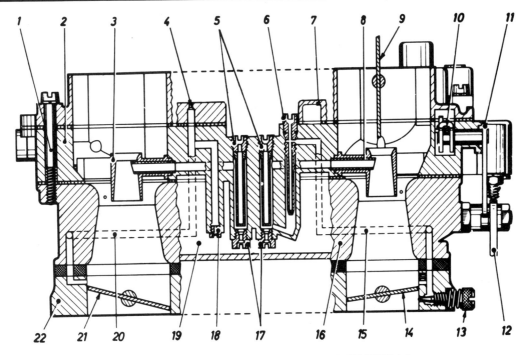

**Fig. 3.3. Side sectional view of the Zenith 35/40 INAT carburettor**

1 Carburettor cover screw
2 Jet housing assembly
3 Secondary barrel venturi
4 Compensating air bore
5 Air correction jets
6 Idling speed air bore
7 Carburettor cover

8 Primary barrel discharge tube
9 Choke flap
10 Internal lever, acceleration pump
11 External lever, acceleration pump
12 Actuating lever, acceleration pump
13 Idling speed mixture control screw
14 Primary barrel throttle flap

15 Idling speed mixture passage
16 Float chamber housing
17 Metering jets
18 Secondary barrel progression jet
19 Float chamber
20 Secondary barrel progression passage
21 Secondary barrel throttle flap
22 Throttle flap body

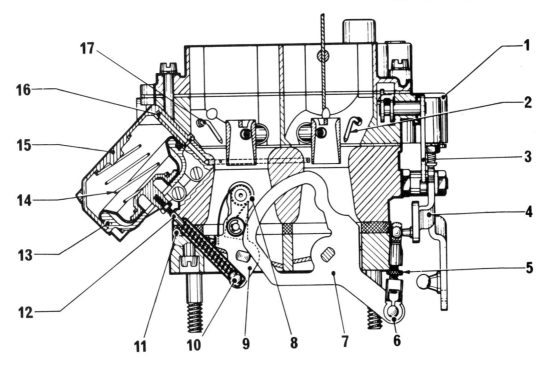

**Fig. 3.4. End sectional view of Zenith INAT carburettor**

1 Float chamber ventilator housing
2 Injection tube, primary barrel
3 Acceleration pump lever
4 Throttle lever
5 Ventilator adjusting screw
6 Throttle connecting rod

7 Throttle flap lever, primary barrel
8 Throttle flap link lever
9 Throttle flap lever, secondary barrel
10 Ball on throttle flap lever
11 Insulator

12 Connecting rod
13 Rubber diaphragm
14 Diaphragm return spring
15 Vacuum housing
16 Vacuum passage for secondary actuation
17 Injection tube, secondary barrel

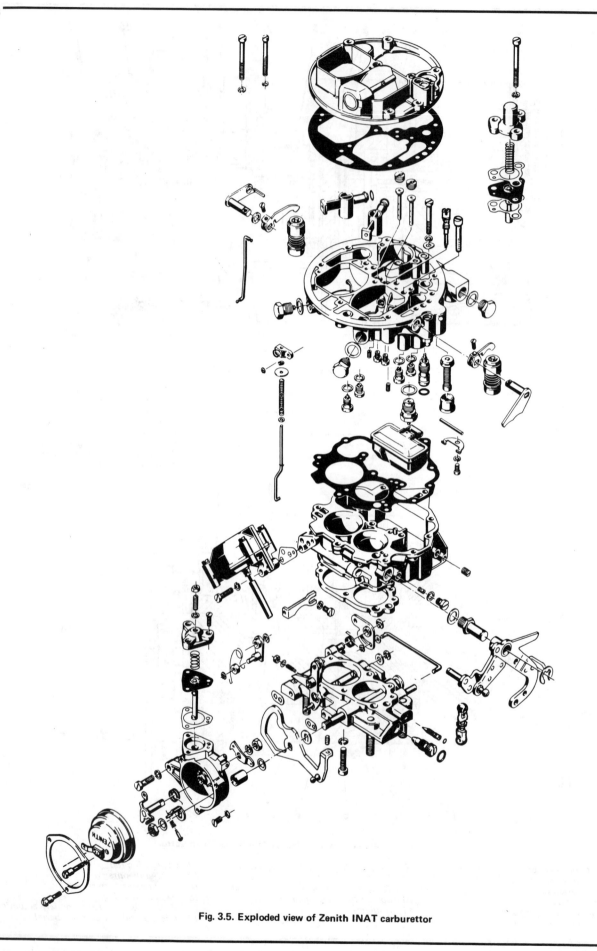

Fig. 3.5. Exploded view of Zenith INAT carburettor

6 *Engine between medium and high speeds:* The engine's consumption of air is more or less proportional to its speed and because the carburettor has a fixed barrel and venturi size, the velocity of the air through the venturi is also proportional to engine speed. It is also a feature of this type of carburettor that the main jet is only effective within a moderate band of air speeds through the carburettor (hence the need for slow running and idle jets). In order to improve the versatility of this carburettor, a second barrel and venturi have been added to augment the primary barrel at high engine speeds. Once the demand on air and fuel reaches a predetermined level - appropriate to the maximum desirable air speed for the primary barrel - the throttle valve in the secondary barrel opens and that barrel supplies the extra air.

The carburettor adjusts to a twin barrel system and the air speeds through the venturis are maintained at levels at which carburation is most effective.

The secondary barrel has the slow running jets incorporated to cater for the case when its throttle valve has not opened sufficiently for the air speed in the secondary barrel to reach its optimum level.

The Solex single-barrel carburettor is fitted with a high speed enrichment jet to compensate for the reduced effectiveness of the main jet at high speeds (high engine speeds), through the barrel.

At high speeds the depression (slight vacuum) in the throat of the barrel is sufficient to open a small valve in a direct line to the float chamber. The air will then draw fuel directly from the float chamber into the stream through the venturi by passing the now relatively ineffective emulsion tube and main jet. In this way the engine may still 'breathe' a proper mixture of fuel and air at high speeds.

7 A similar enrichment capability is built into the twin-barrel carburettors to augment the main jet during medium speed engine demands. The valve is vacuum actuated and is located above the float chamber (Fig. 3.6).

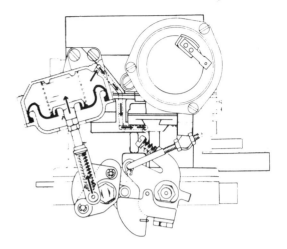

**Fig. 3.6. Operation of vacuum controlled throttle valve on the secondary barrel of the Solex DIDTA carburettor. (Sec. 4)**

5.3 Choke control cable - single barrel carburettor

## 5 Carburettor - removal and refitting

1 The procedure for removing the Solex and Zenith carburettors is virtually the same.

2 First remove the air cleaner, using the procedure described in Section 2.

3 On automatic choke carburettors, disconnect the wire terminal from the choke housing. If a manually operated choke is fitted, slacken the cable securing screw and withdraw the cable (photo).

4 Remove the throttle cable ball joint from the carburettor lever and the outer cable from the bracket (photo).

5 Slacken the clip and pull off the petrol feed pipe from the carburettor.

6 Remove any vacuum pipes that may be attached to the carburettor.

7 Finally undo and remove the four nuts which secure the carburettor to the inlet manifold.

8 Refitting the carburettor follows the exact reversal of the removal procedure. It is recommended that new gaskets be used each time the carburettor is separated from the inlet manifold.

9 Once the carburettor has been refitted, check the idling speeds and mixture as detailed in the next Section of this Chapter.

## 6 Carburettor - setting and adjustment

1 There is very little in the way of mixture adjustment that may be carried out on fixed choke carburettors. All jet sizes are fixed and are determined by the carburettor and engine manufacturers' jointly.

2 The carburettors on all models are expertly set at the factory to achieve optimum fuel metering in conjunction with ignition vacuum advance control. The throttle flap stop screw is then sealed with a plastic cap.

3 Incorrect adjustment of the throttle stop screw by inexperienced hands could seriously affect the ignition advance timing and the progression system of the carburettor primary barrel.

4 Correct adjustment of idle speed and mixture require the use of a CO meter, and it is inadvisable to tamper with either the mixture or the throttle stop screw. Minor adjustments can be made and these are detailed in Chapter 13.

5.4 Throttle control cable - typical

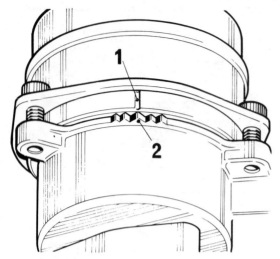

Fig. 3.7. Automatic choke adjustment - Solex (Sec. 7)

1   Mark on outer cover
2   Reference notches on main body

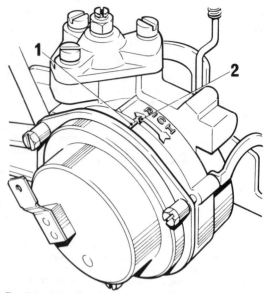

Fig. 3.8. Automatic choke adjustment - Zenith (Sec. 7)

1   Mark on outer cover          2   Inner pointer

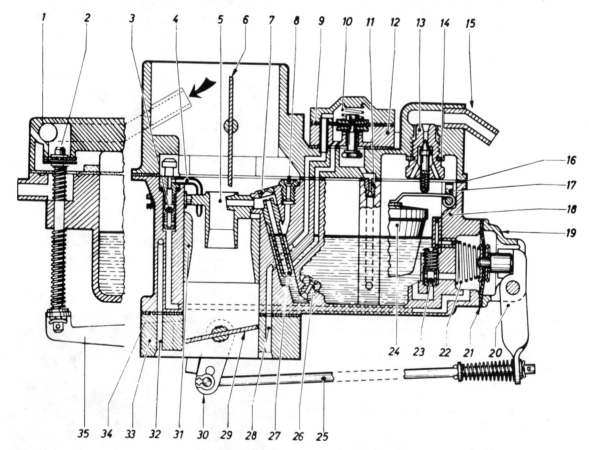

Fig. 3.9. End section of Solex DIDTA carburettor

| | | |
|---|---|---|
| 1 Carburettor | 10 Thrust spring | 19 Accelerator pump cover |
| 2 Float chamber vent valve | 11 Enrichment metering orifice - jet | 20 Pump lever |
| 3 Ball valve (pressure) | 12 Enrichment valve block | 21 Pump diaphragm |
| 4 Accelerator jet injector tube | 13 Float inlet needle valve | 22 Spring |
| 5 Minor venturi | 14 Valve sealing ring | 23 Ball (suction) valve |
| 6 Choke valve | 15 Fuel line inlet tube | 24 Float |
| 7 Air vent jet | 16 Carburettor cover gasket | 25 Pump connecting link |
| 8 Air connect jet | 17 Leaf spring | 26 Metering jet |
| 9 Enrichment valve diaphragm | 18 Float chamber | 27 Emulsion tube |
| | | 28 Vacuum passage for enrichment |

| |
|---|
| 29 Throttle valve |
| 30 Intermediate lever - actuating accelerator pump |
| 31 Main primary venturi |
| 32 Vacuum passage for automatic choke overide |
| 33 Carburettor barrel |
| 34 Gasket |
| 35 Vent valve lever |

## 7  Automatic choke - adjustment

1 Check that the mark on the outer choke cover is aligned  with the pointer on the inner thermostat cover; on Solex carburettors the centre pointer is the correct one. (See Figs.3.7 and 3.8). At this setting ,the choke flap should  open fully  within 3 to 5 minutes of the ignition being switched on.

*2 Solex carburettor.* To adjust the operation of the choke, slacken the three cover screws slightly and rotate the outer cover anticlockwise to weaken the effectiveness of the choke or clockwise to strengthen it.

*3 Zenith carburettor.* To adjust the operation of the choke , slacken the three cover screws slightly and rotate the outer cover clockwise to weaken the effectiveness of the choke or anticlockwise to strengthen it.

*4 All carburettors.* When the required setting has been achieved ,tighten the retaining screws and make a new alignment mark on the cover housing.

## 8  Solex carburettors - dismantling, inspection and reassembly

1   To avoid dropping screws etc, down the inlet manifold the carburettor **must** be removed from the engine before attempting to dismantle it.

2   Remove the carburettor, as described in Section 5.

3   Place some clean paper on the worktop and as each item is dismantled lay it out on the paper in the order of removal.

4   The dismantling procedure described applies to the DIDTA carburettor; the PDSI is of simpler design and the same procedures apply.

5   With the carburettor off the engine and brushed clean, commence dismantling as follows:

Undo and remove the outer nut from the end of the link connecting

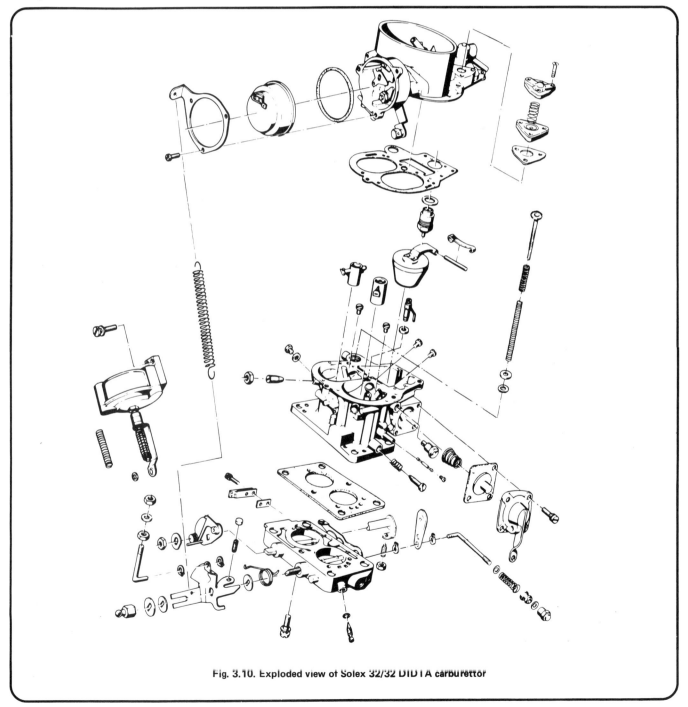

Fig. 3.10. Exploded view of Solex 32/32 DIDTA carburettor

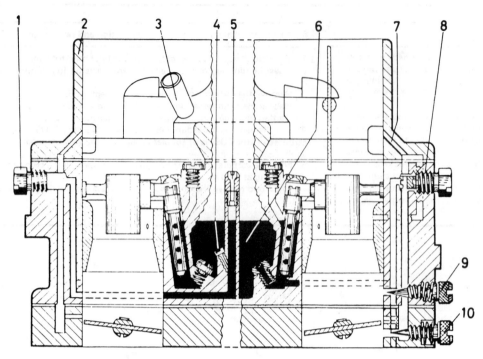

Fig. 3.11. Side section of Solex DIDTA carburettor

1  Plug (secondary barrel pass over mechanism vacuum channels)
2  Carburettor cover
3  Float chamber vent tube
4  Pass-over jet
5  Pass-over air jet
6  Float chamber
7  Idle air passage
8  Idle air jet
9  Idle air adjusting screw
10 Mixture adjusting screw

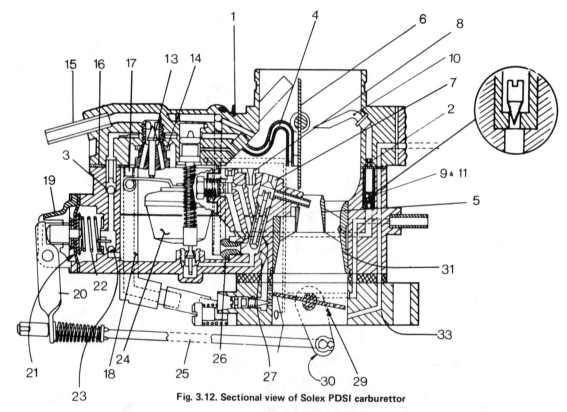

Fig. 3.12. Sectional view of Solex PDSI carburettor

1  Carburettor top cover
2  Calibration jet
3  Ball valve (pressure)
4  Accelerator jet injector tube
5  Minor venutir
6  Choke valve
7  Air vent jet
8  Air connect jet
9  Enrichment valve diaphragm
10 Enrichment tube
11 Enrichment metering orifice-jet
13 Float inlet needle valve
14 Valve sealing ring
15 Fuel line inlet tube
16 Carburettor cover gasket
17 Leaf spring
18 Float chamber
19 Accelerator pump cover
20 Pump lever
21 Pump diaphragm
22 Spring
23 Ball (Section) valve
24 Float
25 Pump connecting link
26 Metering jet
27 Emulsion tube
29 Throttle valve
30 Intermediate lever actuating accelerator pump
31 Main primary venturi
33 Carburettor barrel

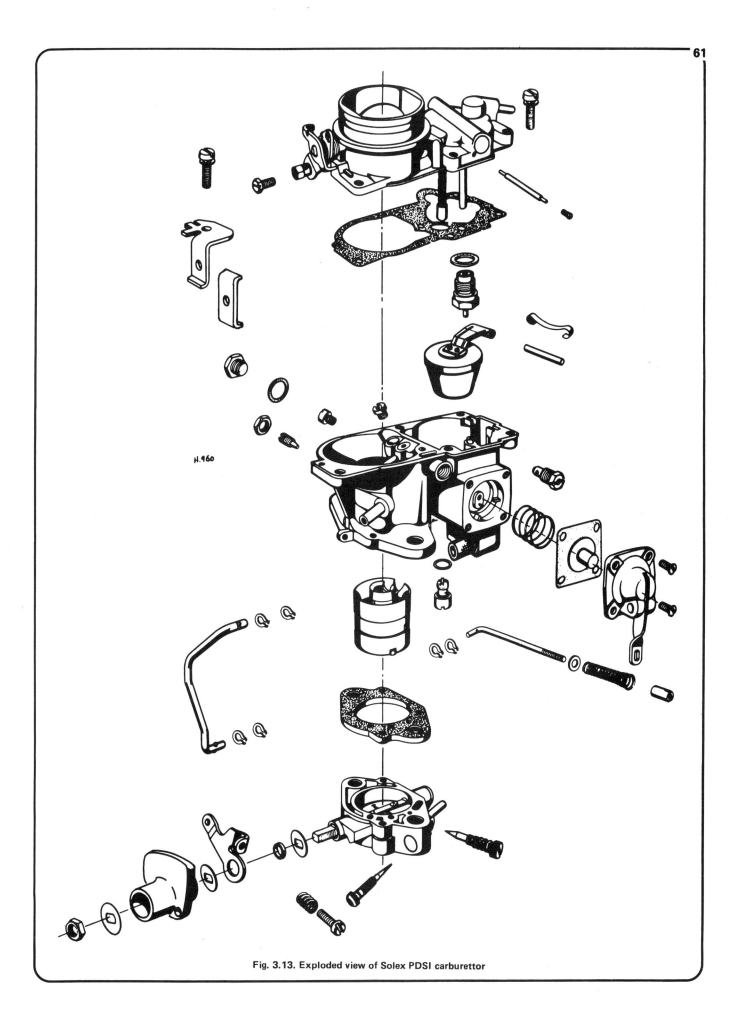

H.960

Fig. 3.13. Exploded view of Solex PDSI carburettor

the throttle lever and choke.

6 *DIDTA carburettor only:* Prise the vacuum unit lever off the secondary barrel throttle lever.

Undo and remove the screws which secure the carburettor cover to the main body (Fig. 3.14).

7 The float chamber inlet needle valve may now be unscrewed from the carburettor cover and the copper sealing ring recovered.

8 Undo and remove the screws securing the cover of the mixture enrichment valve. Remove the cover and inspect the diaphragm and associated parts (Fig. 3.15).

9 Undo and remove the three screws securing the cover of the vacuum actuated choke valve overide mechanism. Remove the cover and inspect the diaphragm (Fig. 3.16).

10 Undo the screws securing the vacuum device, which actuates the secondary barrel throttle, from the carburettor cover.

11 Remove the reduction jet and then thoroughly clean all parts in petrol. Blow dry with a blast of compressed air. Do not use rags or pipe cleaners, the bores and holes in the carburettor components are so fine that any foriegn matter will reduce their effectiveness.

12 Turn your attention now to the carburettor body and commence its overhaul by removing the injection tube and ball valve from the float chamber. If the sealing ring is damaged, a new one must be used when reassembling the unit.

13 Undo and remove the four screws retaining the accelerator pump cover. Lift off the cover and inspect the pump diaphragm and component parts.

14 It is now possible to unscrew all the jet inserts from inside the float chamber and carburettor barrel (Fig. 3.17). Unscrew the threaded plug and ball valve - the accelerator pump suction valve.

15 Clean the parts in petrol and blow dry with compressed air. Blow the carburettor barrel and float chamber fuel/air passages in the direction of fuel flow.

16 Function the float chamber vent valve by hand and inspect the valve and seating. (DIDTA only: Fig. 3.18).

17 Check that all jet inserts are according to the carburettor specification.

18 Replace all gaskets and seal rings.

Fig. 3.14. DIDTA carburettor - screws (arrowed) securing cover to the mainbody (Sec. 8)

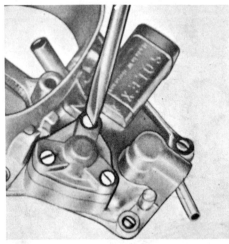

Fig. 3.15. DIDTA carburettor - removing the enrichment valve cover (Sec. 8)

Fig. 3.16. DIDTA carburettor - automatic choke over-ride unit cover screws (Sec. 8)

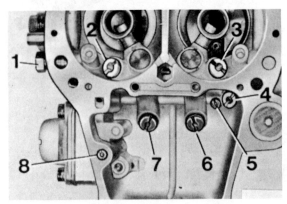

Fig. 3.17. Location of DIDTA carburettor jets (Sec. 8)

1   *Idling speed air jet*
2   *Primary barrel air correction jet*
3   *Secondary barrel air correction jet*
4   *Progression air jet*
5   *Progression jet*
6   *Secondary barrel main jet*
7   *Primary barrel main jet*
8   *Enrichment air jet*

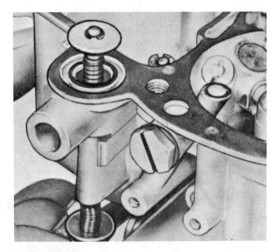

Fig. 3.18. DIDTA carburettor float chamber vent valve (Sec. 8)

Reassembly follows the reversal of the dismantling procedure and the following adjustments and checks should be made before the carburettor is refitted to the engine.

19 Carburettor assembly adjustments and checks:

(i) *Float chamber vent valve mechanism clearance.*
(ii) *Hot idle compensator.*
(iii) *Secondary barrel throttle valve stop.*
(iv) *Accelerator pump linkage.*
(v) *Automatic choke - can be completed with the carburettor fitted to the engine.*
(vi) *Fast idle speed adjustment.*

20 *Float chamber vent valve mechansim:* The vent valve is actuated by a slave lever on the throttle valve spindle. The lever is joined to the valve stem, being retained by a split pin and washer. The clearance that has to be checked is that between the lever and washer, when the lever has fully compressed the spring on the valve stem. This clearance should be 0.24 inches (6 mm) and it is adjusted by bending the tongue on the slave lever (Figs. 3.19 and 3.20).

21 *Hot idler compensator:* The purpose of this device is to prevent the throttle valve from closing completely onto its slow idle stop. During deceleration or idling when the throttle valve is normally closed, the engine is drawing in a richer fuel/air mixture than it needs (Fig. 3.21). This richer mixture when burnt gives a high proportion of Carbon Monoxide. In order to meet the new exhaust emission regulation's requirements, a hot idle device has been incorporated to prevent the throttle from closing fully, thereby maintaining a proper mixture of fuel and air for the engine.

22 The compensator device should open at 90°C (194°F) and is simply checked by immersing it in hot water (nearly boiling). If the device does not open at this temperature - it should be replaced.

23 *Secondary barrel throttle valve stop:* The stop screw should be adjusted so that there is a 0.002 inch (0.05 mm) gap at the edge of the butterfly valve. This adjustment may be accomplished by loosening the screw and locking nut until the valve is fully closed. Then turn in the stop screw ¾ turn to open the valve the requisite amount. Hold the screw in position and lock with the locking nut. The gap around the valve is necessary to prevent the valve from sticking closed (Fig. 3.22).

24 *Accelerator pump linkage:* It is necessary to have the linkage refitted correctly because it affects the amount of fuel which the pump will inject into the carburettor barrel. Pay attention to the positions of the parts of the linkage. Note that the link fits into the hole nearest the throttle spindle. The split pin and washer fit on the link on the endmost position.

25 *Automatic choke - adjustment:* Mount the automatic choke device on the carubrettor so that the mark on the thermal device coincides with the centre mark on the carburettor body.

26 *Fast idle speed:* Adjust the throttle stop screw (primary barrel) so that the gap between the valve and barrel side is between 0.029 and 0.033 inches (0.75 to 0.85 mm).

Then open the throttle valve, close the choke valve and then close the throttle valve back onto its idle stop. The abutment lever in the automatic choke body should now be resting on the outer step of the cam with the throttle valve slightly open.

The adjustment of the choke can be completed when the carburettor has been completely assembled and refitted to the engine.

Run the engine until it has reached its proper operating temperature. Release the throttle pedal to allow the valve to rest on the fast idle linkage.

Check the engine speed - for fast idle - it should be around 3200 rpm. Correct the speed to this figure by altering the effective length of the

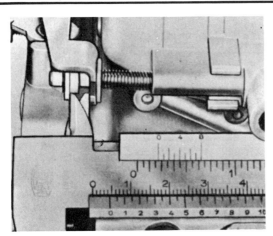

Fig. 3.23. Checking vent valve clearance (Sec. 8)

Fig. 3.20. Adjusting vent valve clearance (Sec. 8)

Fig 3.21 Carburettor temperature compensator (Sec. 8)

1 Tapered plug        2 Bi-metal spring

Fig. 3.22. Adjusting the secondary throttle valve stop screw (Sec. 8)

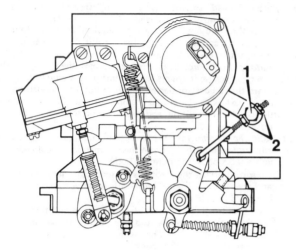

Fig. 3.23. Fast idle adjustment rod (Sec. 8)

1  Swivel link                    2  Adjuster nuts

throttle/choke device connecting link. If the engine speed is too high
loosen the lower nut and 'tighten' the upper nut - and if too low
loosen the high nut and tighten the lower (Fig. 3.23)

## 9  Zenith carburettor - dismantling, inspection and reassembly

1  Remove the carburettor, as described in Section 5, and lay out a
clean sheet of paper on the worktop so that each part of the carburettor
can be laid out in the order of removal.
2  Clean off all exterior dirt from the carburettor body before dismantling it.
3  To remove the top section of the carburettor, remove the plastic
plug from the side and slacken the screw securing the automatic choke
rod (Fig. 3.24). Remove the ten screws securing the top section (one
is inside the air filter securing screw recess) and lift off the cover.
4  Disconnect the accelerator pump linkage and the three retaining
screws, and remove the jet housing assembly from the float body (see
Fig. 3.25).
5  Lift out the primary accelerator pump piston past the operating
lever (Fig. 3.26).
6  To remove the secondary pump piston, first remove the screw
securing the operating lever to the shaft and remove piston and lever.
7  The two air correction jets can be unscrewed from the jet housing,
but keep them in the right order as they are different sizes (see Fig. 3.27).
8  The emulsion tubes can now be lifted out, but make a careful note
of their position to ensure correct installation (Fig. 3.28).
9  The various jets can be removed from the jet housing assembly
as required, (See Fig. 3.29). Clean the jets using clean petrol and an
airline, if available.
10 The float assembly can be removed by undoing the single screw
retaining the bracket.

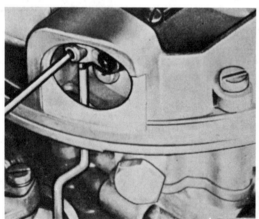

Fig. 3.24. Zenith carburettor - removing choke rod clamping screw
(Sec. 9)

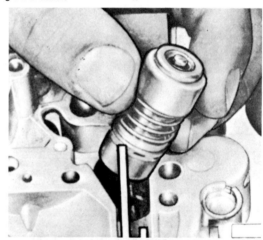

Fig. 3.26. Lifting out primary accelerator pump piston (Sec. 9)

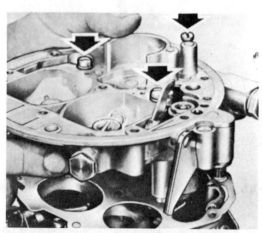

Fig. 3.25. Removing the jet housing assembly - Zenith carburettor
(Sec. 9)

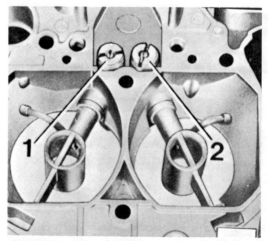

Fig. 3.27. Location of air correction jets - Zenith (Sec. 9)

1  Secondary barrel jet                    2  Primary barrel jet

11 To remove the vacuum control unit, release the control rod from the secondary barrel throttle flap, remove the three securing screws and lift away the vacuum unit (Fig. 3.30).

12 Remove the three screws securing the automatic choke over-ride cover and examine the diaphragm beneath it for damage.

13 The throttle lever can be removed by detaching the spring clip from the end of the shaft and lifting off the lever and two nylon bushes (Fig. 3.31).

14 To gain access to the idling jet inside the float chamber housing, undo the plug from the side of the housing and then unscrew the jet using a suitably-sized screwdriver (Fig. 3.32).

15 Clean the parts in petrol and blow dry with compressed air. Blow the carburettor barrel and float chamber fuel/air passages in the direction of fuel flow.

16 Function the float chamber vent valve by hand and inspect the valve and seating.

17 Check that all jet inserts are according to the carburettor specification.

18 Replace all gaskets and seal rings.

19 Reassemble the carburettor using the reverse procedure to dismantling and carry out the checks and adjustments detailed in Section 6, with the exception of the fast idle adjustment which should be carried out as follows.

Fig. 3.28. Removing the emulsion tubes - Zenith (Sec. 9)

Fig. 3.29. Location of Zenith carburettor jets (Sec. 9)

Carburettor jet and valve details:
1  Primary barrel acceleration pump outlet valve
2  Primary barrel acceleration pump intake valve
3  Enrichment valve
4  Primary barrel metering jet
5  Secondary barrel metering jet
6  Secondary barrel progression jet
7  Secondary barrel acceleration pump intake valve
8  Secondary barrel acceleration pump outlet valve
9  Additional idling mixture air vent
10  Additional idling mixture jet

Fig. 3.30. Removing the vacuum control unit - Zenith (Sec. 9)

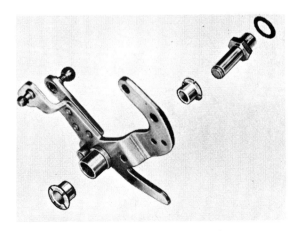

Fig. 3.31. Throttle lever and components (Sec. 9)

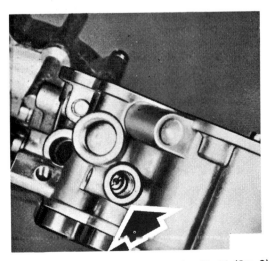

Fig. 3.32. Location of additional idling jet - Zenith (Sec. 9)

20 With the engine stopped, open the throttle fully so that the fast idle screw is visible through the side of the choke housing.
21 Adjust the screw in stages, using a thin-bladed screwdriver until the correct fast idle speed of 2,700 rpm is achieved (Fig. 3.33).

### 10 Fuel pump - removal and refitting

1   It will be advisable to raise the front of the car onto a pair of chassis stands, or car ramps for this task. The fuel tank is slightly above the fuel pump when the car is level and therefore if the pump is removed in that instance, fuel will drain from the tank through the pump inlet pipe.
2   The pump is driven off the distributor driveshaft and in order to gain access to the pump, it is preferable, though not essential, to remove the alternator - (See Chapter 10, Electrical System).
3   Once the alternator has been removed, the two pipes should be plugged with a clean metal rod to prevent both the ingress of dirt and the leakage of fuel.
4   Now that the pipe connections have been removed the bolts securing the pump to the timing casing can be undone and the pump removed. Recover the asbestos spacer and the gaskets.
5   The pump is a sealed unit and cannot be replaced. If a fault is suspected a new unit should be fitted.
6   The fuel pump filter can be removed by removing the single screw retaining the top cover, and lifting out the filter screen (Fig. 3.34).
7   Wash the filter in clean petrol and blow dry with a compressed airline. Clean out any sediment inside the filter bowl.
8   Refitting follows the reversal of the removal procedure; as usual

it is recommended that new gaskets be used at the pump/engine joint (Fig. 3.35).

### 11 Exhaust system - general

1   The exhaust system on all models is in three main sections; the front pipe assembly comprises twin pipes connected to the exhaust manifold on the engine, converging into a single pipe attached to the centre silencer and pipe assembly. This in turn is attached to the rear silencer and tailpipe. Certain models have a third silencer fitted.
2   The front pipes are attached to the engine manifold by means of a flange and gasket, and secured by six bolts. Whenever the joint is dismantled a new gasket should always be used (Fig. 3.36).
3   The centre silencer and rear silencer/tailpipe assembly is secured to the underfloor by means of rubber rings hooked onto brackets (see Fig. 3.37).
4   It is wise to use only properly made exhaust system parts and exhaust pipe shackles. Remember that the exhaust pipes and silencers corrode internally as well as externally and therefore when any one section of pipe or a silencer demands renewal, it often follows that the whole system is best renewed.
5   It is most important when fitting exhaust systems that the twists and contours are carefully followed and that each connecting joint overlaps the correct distance (1.5 inches (32.5 mm) approximately). Any stresses and strains imparted in order to force the system to fit the vehicle will result in premature system failure.
6   When fitting a new part, or a complete system, it is as well to remove the whole system from the car and clean all the joints so that

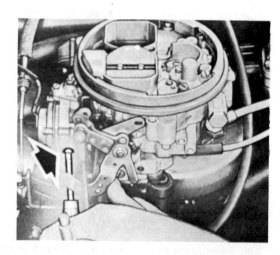

Fig. 3.33. Adjusting the fast idling speed screw through holes in side of the choke housing - Zenith (Sec. 9  )

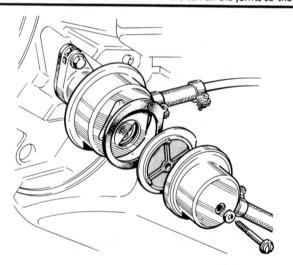

Fig. 3.34. Fuel pump filter bowl removed (Sec. 10)

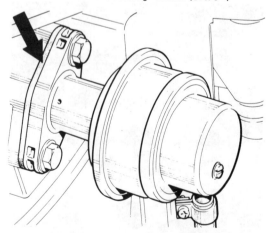

Fig. 3.35. Location of fuel pump insulating gasket (Sec. 10)

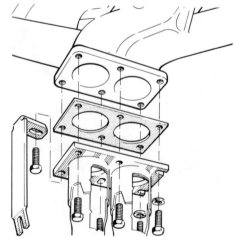

Fig. 3.36. Exhaust manifold attachment flange (Sec. 11)

they will fit together easily.

7   The exhaust manifold and inlet manifold are bolted together at the centre section to provide a hot spot for fuel vapourisation. A gasket is used at the hot spot joint and the manifold/cylinder head face.

8   New gaskets must always be used if the manifold is separated from the head, or the inlet manifold from the exhaust manifold.

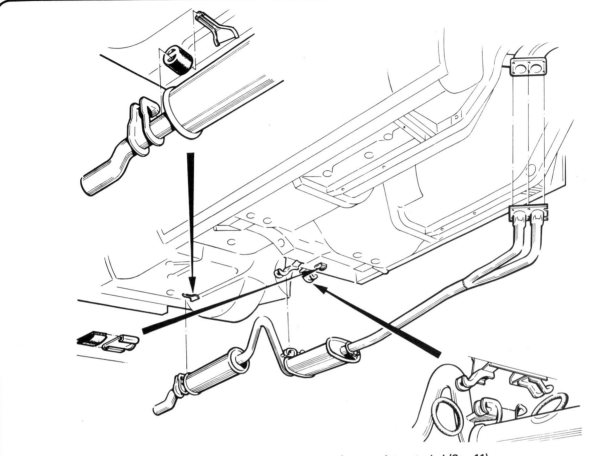

Fig. 3.37. Exhaust system attachment points — typical (Sec. 11)

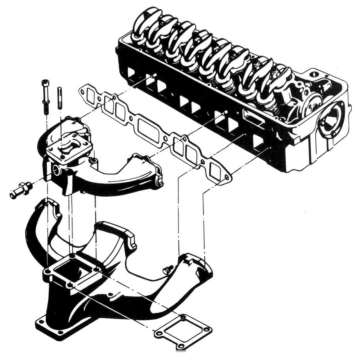

Fig. 3.38. Inlet/exhaust manifolds and gaskets (Sec. 11)

## 12 Fuel tank - removal and refitting

1   The fuel tank is mounted vertically in the luggage compartment immediately behind the rear seat. The tank is secured in position by four bolts. The filler pipe protrudes through the right-hand side rear wing and is retained in place by a rubber grommet. A vent pipe is clipped to the bottom of the tank and leads out through the luggage compartment floor.

2   The fuel gauge sender unit is secured to the top section of the tank by five screws. It is a non-repairable item and if faulty must be replaced with a new unit. When refitting the sender unit, ensure that the wiring terminal is at the 2 o'clock position (see Fig. 3.40).

3   To remove the tank, pick a time when the tank is almost empty and carry out the work in a well ventilated building or, preferably outside.

4   Open the boot lid and release the three retaining buttons and two turn clips securing the tank trim panel, and remove the panel (Fig. 3.41).

5   Using a blunt screwdriver, ease out the large rubber grommet from around the filler neck. Undo the filler pipe clamp and release the filler vent pipe from the top of the tank.

6   Pull the tank vent pipe up through the boot floor and disconnect the sender unit wire.

7   From beneath the car, place a suitable container beneath the tank, slacken the fuel feed pipe clamp and pull off the flexible pipe from the tank.

8   Remove the four bolts from the sides of the tank. Push the filler and vent pipe far enough to the right to clear the tank and carefully lift out the tank assembly.

9   Refit the tank using the reverse procedure to removal.

## 13 Fuel gauge and sender unit - general

1   The fuel gauge and sender unit are integrated into the electrical system of the car and therefore the description and all notes regarding the fuel sensor system are included in Chapter 10.

## 14 Accelerator cable - renewal and adjustment

1   The accelerator cable cannot be lubricated, and if the throttle action is stiff or jerky the complete cable assembly must be renewed.

2   First remove the inner cable ball end from the carburettor lever and detach the outer sleeve from the bracket (Fig. 3.42).

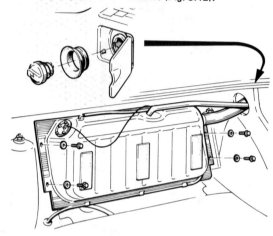

Fig. 3.39. Location of fuel tank and filler neck (Sec. 12)

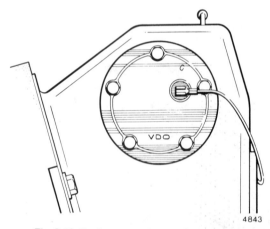

Fig. 3.40. Fuel gauge sender unit (Sec. 12)

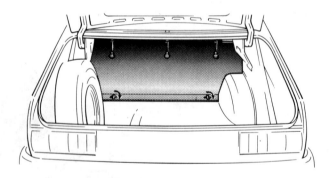

Fig. 3.41. Fuel tank trim panel securing points (Sec. 12)

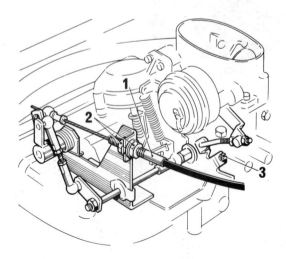

Fig. 3.42. Throttle cable details - typical (Sec. 14)

1   *Outer cable*          2   *Adjusting nuts*          3   *Throttle stop screw*

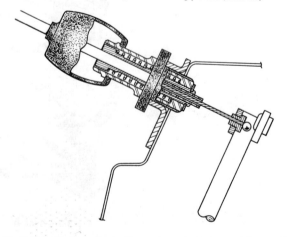

Fig. 3.43. Throttle cable pull-out sleeve in dash panel (Sec. 14)

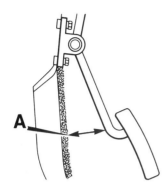

Fig. 3.44. Accelerator pedal height - dimension 'A' should be 2 in (50 mm). (Sec. 14)

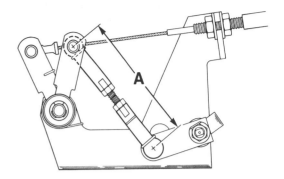

Fig. 3.45. Adjustable rod on carburettor throttle lever, (if fitted). Dimension 'A' should be 3 in (76 mm) . (Sec. 14)

3   On the end of the accelerator lever, unhook the wire and plastic bushing. Then from the engine compartment pull the cable from the bracket on the dash panel (Fig. 3.43).

4   It is important to note that the cable lengths differ with different engines, so pay attention to the part numbers and as a last check compare the old and new cable assemblies.

5   Refitting follows the reversal of the removal procedure - make certain that the ball and plastic bushing on the end of the cable are properly seated in the accelerator pedal lever.

6   To adjust the cable length, first set the accelerator pedal height to the dimension shown in Fig. 3.44 by turning the pedal stop in or out.

7   If the carburettor is fitted with an adjustable control rod set it to the dimension shown in Fig. 3.45.

8   The cable length is adjusted by means of the two locknuts on the outer cable bracket. When correctly adjusted there should be clearance between the throttle stop screw and the fast idle cam with the accelerator pedal stop contacting the dashpanel, throttle closed. With the pedal floored the throttle flap should be fully open.

9   For cars fitted with automatic transmission, refer to Chapter 6 for kick-down cable adjustment.

## 15 Fault diagnosis - fuel system and carburation

*Unsatisfactory engine performance and excessive fuel consumption are not necessarily the fault of the fuel system or carburettor. In fact they more commonly occur as a result of ignition and timing faults. Before acting on the following it is necessary to check the ignition system first. Even though a fault may lie in the fuel system it will be difficult to trace unless the ignition is correct. The faults below therefore, assume that this has been attended to first (where appropriate).*

| Symptom | Reason/s | Remedy |
|---|---|---|
| Smell of petrol when engine is stopped | Leaking fuel lines or unions<br>Leaking fuel line | Repair or renew as necessary.<br>Fill fuel tank to capacity and examine carefully at seams, unions and filler pipe connections.<br>Repair as necessary. |
| Smell of petrol when engine is idling | Leaking fuel line unions between pump and carburettor<br>Overflow of fuel from float chamber due to wrong level setting, ineffective needle valve or punctured float | Check line and unions and tighten or repair.<br><br>Check fuel level setting and condition of float and needle valve, and renew if necessary. |
| Excessive fuel consumption for reasons not covered by leaks or float chamber faults | Worn jets<br>Over-rich jet settings<br>Sticking mechanism | Renew jets or carburettor body if not removable.<br>Adjust jet.<br>Check correct movement of mechanism |
| Difficult starting, uneven running, lack of power, cutting out | One or more jets blocked or restricted<br><br>Float chamber fuel level too low or needle valve sticking<br>Fuel pump not delivering sufficient fuel | Dismantle and clean out float chamber and jets.<br>Dismantle and check fuel level and needle valve.<br>Check pump delivery and clean or repair as required. |

# Chapter 4 Ignition system

## Contents

## Specifications

### Spark plugs

| | |
|---|---|
| AC ... ... ... ... ... ... ... ... ... ... | 42 FS or R42–6 FS |
| Bosch ... ... ... ... ... ... ... ... ... | W200T35 |
| Spark plug gap ... ... ... ... ... ... ... ... | 0.028-0.031 in (0.7-0.8 mm) |

### Ignition coil

| | |
|---|---|
| Type ... ... ... ... ... ... ... ... ... | Bosch or Delco-Remy |
| Primary coil resistance ... ... ... ... ... ... ... | 1.2-1.6 ohms |
| Starting voltage ... ... ... ... ... ... ... ... | 12 volts (approx) |
| Running voltage ... ... ... ... ... ... ... ... | 4.5-6 volts |

### Distributor

| | |
|---|---|
| Type ... ... ... ... ... ... ... ... ... | Bosch or Delco-Remy |
| Contact breaker gap ... ... ... ... ... ... ... | 0.016 in (0.40 mm) |
| Cam dwell angle ... ... ... ... ... ... ... ... | 47° − 53° |
| Ignition timing (static) ... ... ... ... ... ... ... | 5° BTDC |

### Vacuum advance

**1.6 engine**

| Vacuum bar | (in. Hg) | Distributor advance (degrees) |
|---|---|---|
| −0.13 | 3.9 | 0 |
| −0.24 | 7.1 | 1 − 3½ |
| −0.27 | 7.9 | 3½ − 6 |
| −0.33 | 9.8 | 6½ − 9 |
| −0.40 | 11.8 and over | 9 − 11 |

**1.9 engine**

| Vacuum bar | (in. Hg) | Distributor advance (degrees) |
|---|---|---|
| −0.11 | 3.1 | 0 |
| −0.17 | 5.1 | 0 − 5 |
| −0.24 | 7.1 | 4 − 8½ |
| −0.27 | 7.9 and over | 6 − 9 |

### Torque wrench settings

| | lb f ft | kg f m |
|---|---|---|
| Spark plugs ... ... ... ... ... ... ... ... ... | 22 - 29 | 3.1 - 4 |

## 1 General description

In order that the engine can run correctly it is necessary for an electrical spark to ignite the fuel/air mixture in the combustion chamber at exactly the right moment in relation to engine speed and load. The ignition system is based on feeding low tension voltage from the battery to the coil where it is converted to high tension voltage. The high tension voltage is powerful enough to jump the spark plug gap in the cylinders many times a second under high compression, providing that the system is in good condition and that all adjustments are correct.

The ignition system is divided into two circuits, low tension and high tension.

The low tension circuit (sometimes known as the primary) consists of the battery, lead to the control box, lead to the ignition switch, lead from the ignition switch to the low tension or primary coil windings (terminal BAT), and the lead from the low tension coil windings (coil terminal DIST) to the contact breaker points and condenser in the distributor.

The high tension circuit consists of the high tension or secondary coil winding, the heavy ignition lead from the centre of the coil to the windings, the heavy ignition lead from the centre of the coil to the centre of the distributor cap, the rotor arm, and the spark plug leads and spark plugs.

The system functions in the following manner. Low tension voltage is changed in the coil into high tension voltage by the opening and closing of the contact breaker points in the low tension circuit. High tension voltage is then fed via the carbon brush in the centre of the distributor cap to the rotor arm of the distributor cap, and each time it comes in line with one of the four metal segments in the cap, which are connected to the spark plug leads, the opening and closing of the contact breaker points causes the high tension voltage to build up, jump the gap from the rotor arm to the appropriate metal segment and so via the spark plug lead to the spark plug, where it finally jumps the spark plug gap before going to earth.

The ignition is advanced and retarded automatically, to ensure the spark occurs at just the right instant for the particular load at the prevailing engine speed.

The ignition advance is controlled both mechanically and by a vacuum operated system. The mechanical governor comprises two weights, which move out from the distributor shaft as the engine speed rises due to centrifugal force. As they move outwards they rotate the cam relative to the distributor shaft, and so advance the spark. The weights are held in position by two light springs and it is the tension of the springs which is largely responsible for correct spark advancement.

The vacuum control consists of a diaphragm, one side of which is connected via a small bore tube to the carburettor, and the other side to the contact breaker plate. Depression in the inlet manifold and carburettor, which varies with engine speed and throttle opening, causes the diaphragm to move, so moving the contact breaker plate, and advancing or retarding the spark. A fine degree of control is achieved by a spring in the vacuum assembly.

A wiring harness includes a high resistance wire in the ignition coil feed circuit and it is very important that only a 'ballast resistor' type ignition coil is used. The starter solenoid has an extra terminal so that a wire from the solenoid to the coil supplies current direct to the coil when the starter motor is operated. The ballast resistor wire is therefore by-passed and battery voltage is fed to the ignition system so giving easier starting.

## 2  Routine maintenance

1  *Spark plugs:* Remove the plugs and thoroughly clean away all traces of carbon. Examine the porcelain insulator round the central electrode inside the plug. If damaged discard the plug. Reset the gap between the electrodes. Do not use a set of plugs for more than 9,000 miles (15,000 km) - it is false economy.

2  *Distributor:* Every 9,000 miles (15,000km) remove the cap and rotor arm and put one or two drops of engine oil into the centre of the cam recess. Smear the surfaces of the cam itself with petroleum jelly. Do not over-lubricate as any excess could get onto the contact point surfaces and cause ignition difficulties. Every 9,000 miles (15,000km) examine the contact point surfaces. If there is a build-up of deposits on one face and a pit in the other it will be impossible to set the gap correctly and they should be refaced or renewed. Set the gap when the contact surfaces are in order.

3  *General:* Examine all leads and terminals for signs of broken or cracked insulation. Also check all terminal connections for slackness or signs of fracturing of some strands of wire. Partly broken wire should be renewed. The HT leads are particularly important as any insulation faults will cause the high voltage to 'jump' to the nearest earth and this will prevent a spark at the plug. Check that no HT leads are loose or in a position where the insulation could wear due to rubbing against part of the engine.

## 3  Distributor contact breaker points - gap adjustment

1  Release the clips or screws which secure the distributor cap and lift the cap, together with the HT leads cover, from the distributor.

2  Wipe the inside and outside of the cap clean with a dry cloth. Scrape away any small deposits from the four studs and inspect the cover for cracks or surface deterioration. Check the brush in the centre of the

cap, it should protrude about ¼ in (6mm). Renew the cap if cracked or if any of the HT studs are corroded and worn away.

3  Lift the distributor arm from the central shaft and wipe the metal tip clean.

4  Remove the plastic cover which protects the contact breaker mechanism and prevents condensation from settling on the mechanism and reducing its effectiveness.

5  Now that the contact breakers are exposed, gently prise the contacts apart and examine the condition of their faces. If they are rough, pitted or dirty it will be necessary to remove them for resurfacing or for new points to be fitted.

6  Presuming the points are satisfactory, or they have been cleaned or replaced, measure the gap between the points by turning the engine over until the contact breaker arm is on the peak of one of the four cam lobes. A 0.016 in (0.40 mm) thick feeler gauge should now just fit between the points (photo).

7  If the points are too close or too far apart, slacken the contact breaker set mounting screw. Move the 'stationary point' until the correct gap has been achieved and then secure by tightening the set screw in the breaker set mounting plate.

8  Check the gap once again to ensure the adjustment was not disturbed when the set screw was tightened.

9  Replace the plastic cover, then the rotor arm and finally the distributor cap with its plastic cover (Fig. 4.1).

10 Final adjustment of the contact breaker points gap should now be made using a dwell meter, which measures dwell angle. The dwell angle is the number of degrees through which the distributor cam turns between the instants of closure and opening of the contact breaker points.

11 Connect a dwell meter in accordance with the equipment manufacturer's instructions. A meter which can operate with the engine running is to be preferred; otherwise check with the engine cranking.

12 If the dwell angle is too large, increase the points gap, and *vice-versa*. Only very slight adjustments should normally be made before re-checking.

13 If possible, check the dwell angle with the engine running — several adjustments may be required to obtain the correct setting.

14 Always check and adjust the dwell angle before setting the ignition timing, as described in Section 8.

## 4  Distributor contact breaker points - removal and replacement

1  If the contact breaker points are burned, pitted or badly worn, they must be removed and either be renewed or have their faces filed smooth and flat if they are still serviceable.

2  Having removed the distributor cap, rotor arm and contact breaker mechanism cover, proceed to undo and remove the set screw which

3.6 Setting the contact breaker points

Fig. 4.1. Removing the distributor cap cover - arrows indicate the three press studs (Sec. 3)

retains the breaker mechanism to the distributor base plate.

3   *Bosch distributors:* Remove the LT lead spade connector and lift out the complete contact breaker assembly (Fig. 4.2).

4   *Delco-Remy distributors:* Ease the moving contact arm spring from the insulator assembly on the fixed contact plate and remove the condenser and LT spade terminals (Fig. 4.3).

5   Lift off the moving contact arm and spring followed by the fixed contact plate.

6   It is possible to reface the contact points using a fine carborundum stone or emery paper. However, if the points show signs of burning or pitting, it is strongly recommended that they are replaced with a new set.

7   Replacement of the points follows the reverse sequence to removal. When replacing the Delco-Remy type points, ensure that the LT and condenser terminals are fitted in the correct order on the insulator post (see Fig. 4.4).

8   Finally, adjust the points gap, as described in Section 3.

## 5   Condenser - removal, testing and replacement

1   The purpose of the condenser, (sometimes known as a capacitor) is to ensure that when the contact breaker points open there is no sparking across them which would waste voltage and cause wear.

2   The condenser is fitted in parallel with the contact breaker points. If it develops a short circuit, it will cause ignition failure as the points will be prevented from interrupting the low tension circuit.

3   If the engine becomes very difficult to start or begins to miss after several miles running and the breaker points show signs of excessive burning, then the condition of the condenser must be suspect. A further test can be made by separating the points by hand with the ignition switched on. If this is accompanied by a flash it is indicative that the condenser has failed.

4   Without special test equipment the only sure way to diagnose condenser trouble is to replace a suspected unit with a new one and note if there is any improvement.

5   To remove the condenser from the distributor take off the distributor cap, rotor arm and cover.

6   *Bosch distributors:* Firstly pull off the contact points LT lead from the spade terminal located inside the distributor casing.

7   Remove the LT lead connecting the coil to the distributor, from the ignition coil.

8   Undo and remove the screw securing the condenser and LT lead assembly to the distributor case. Note that the condenser is supplied complete with the LT lead to the coil and the LT spade tag and mounting grommet.

9   *Delco-Remy distributors:* Ease out the moving contact arm spring from the insulating post and lift out the condenser spade terminal.

10  Remove the condenser retaining screw and lift out the condenser.

11  Replacement of the condenser follows the reverse procedure to removal.

## 6   Distributor - removal and replacement

1   Begin by removing the battery connections and then go on to remove the distributor cap. Stow the cap aside, so as not to interfere with the task of removing the distributor. If the cap is removed from the car it might be as well to fix identification tags onto the HT leads and coil HT leads to ensure correct reconnection.

2   Remove the spark plugs and put the transmission in neutral.

3   Rotate the engine by means of the fan until the distributor rotor (or shaft), is in the position in Figs. 4.5 and 4.6 (No. 1 piston at TDC).

4   Once the engine has been turned to the position indicated, apply the handbrake and leave in gear. It makes the task of refitting the distributor much easier if the engine remains in that position.

5   Disconnect the LT lead connecting the distributor and ignition coil, from the coil.

6   Remove the petrol pump - refer to Chapter 3. It is necessary to remove the pump because it is actuated by a cam on the distributor shaft. Unless the pump is removed the distributor shaft cannot be extracted from its bore in the timing chain cover (Fig. 4.7.).

7   Undo and remove the distributor clamp bolt and remove the clamp plate. The distributor may now be lifted out of the timing chain cover block.

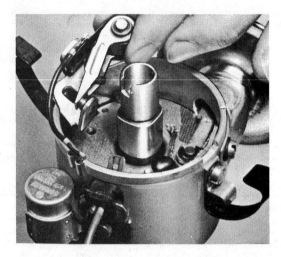

**Fig. 4.2. Lifting out the contact breaker assembly (Bosch distributor) (Sec. 4)**

**Fig. 4.3. Releasing the contact breaker spring from the insulator post (Delco-Remy). Sec. 4)**

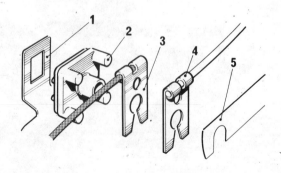

**Fig. 4.4. Correct installation of distributor insulator post (Delco-Remy) (Sec. 4)**

1   *Fixed contact plate*          4   *LT terminal*
2   *Plastic insulator*            5   *Contact breaker spring*
3   *Condenser terminal*

Fig. 4.5. Position of distributor rotor with No 1 piston at TDC (Bosch) (Sec. 6)

Fig. 4.6. Position of distributor shaft with No 1 piston at TDC (Delco-Remy). (Sec. 6)

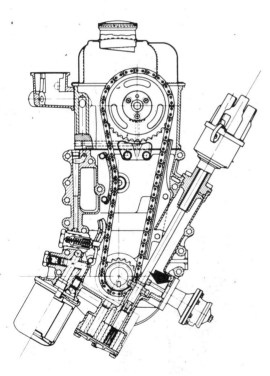

Fig. 4.7. Location of distributor and driveshaft - arrow indicates fuel pump pushrod (Sec. 6)

Fig. 4.8. Position of distributor shaft prior to installing in engine (Delco-Remy). (Sec. 6)

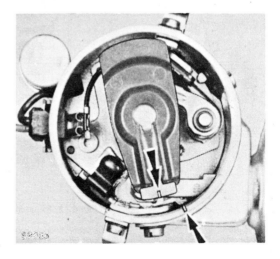

Fig. 4.9. Position of distributor rotor prior to installing in engine (Bosch). (Sec. 6)

8  *Refitting:* Ensure that the engine is in the position when the number 1 cylinder piston is in the firing position. Hopefully the engine will not have been disturbed since the distributor was removed.

9  As the distributor is replaced, the helix on the drive gear will rotate the shaft. To compensate for this, position the rotor (or shaft), as shown in Figs. 4.8 and 4.9 prior to installing the distributor.

10 Holding the distributor and shaft in the correct position, insert the assembly into the timing cover aperture.

11 When the distributor shaft has seated correctly into the oil pump shaft slot check that the distributor driveshaft has rotated to the correct position (Figs. 4.5 and 4.6)

12 Refit the distributor clamp bolt and tighten.

13 Refit the fuel pump and check the static timing as described in Section 8, of this Chapter.

Fig. 4.10. Remove the vacuum advance rod retaining clip (Sec. 7)

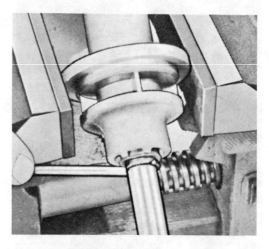

Fig. 4.11. Removal of the snap-ring from the distributor driveshaft (Sec. 7)

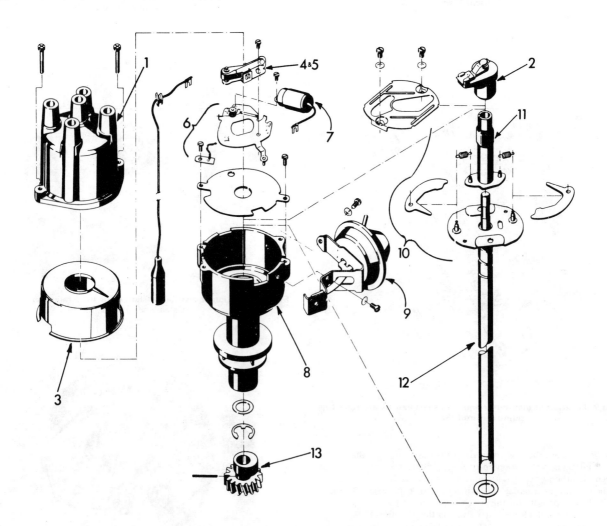

Fig. 4.12. Exploded view of the Delco-Remy distributor (Sec. 7)

| | | | | | | |
|---|---|---|---|---|---|---|
| 1 | Distributor cap | 5 | Contact breaker mounting | 8 | Distributor casing | 11 | Distributor cam |
| 2 | Rotor arm | 6 | Contact breaker base plate | 9 | Vacuum advance, diaphragm | 12 | Drive shaft |
| 3 | Dust shield | | assembly | | unit | 13 | Drive pinion and fuel pump |
| 4 | Contact breaker arm | 7 | Condenser | 10 | Centrifugal advance | | cam |
| | | | | | mechanism | | |

**Measuring plug gap.** A feeler gauge of the correct size (see ignition system specifications) should have a slight 'drag' when slid between the electrodes. Adjust gap if necessary

**Adjusting plug gap.** The plug gap is adjusted by bending the earth electrode inwards, or outwards, as necessary until the correct clearance is obtained. Note the use of the correct tool

**Normal.** Grey-brown deposits, lightly coated core nose. Gap increasing by around 0.001 in (0.025 mm) per 1000 miles (1600 km). Plugs ideally suited to engine, and engine in good condition

**Carbon fouling.** Dry, black, sooty deposits. Will cause weak spark and eventually misfire. Fault: over-rich fuel mixture. Check: carburettor mixture settings, float level and jet sizes; choke operation and cleanliness of air filter. Plugs can be re-used after cleaning

**Oil fouling.** Wet, oily deposits. Will cause weak spark and eventually misfire. Fault: worn bores/piston rings or valve guides; sometimes occurs (temporarily) during running-in period. Plugs can be re-used after thorough cleaning

**Overheating.** Electrodes have glazed appearance, core nose very white – few deposits. Fault: plug overheating. Check: plug value, ignition timing, fuel octane rating (too low) and fuel mixture (too weak). Discard plugs and cure fault immediately

**Electrode damage.** Electrodes burned away; core nose has burned, glazed appearance. Fault: pre-ignition. Check: as for 'Overheating' but may be more severe. Discard plugs and remedy fault before piston or valve damage occurs

**Split core nose (may appear initially as a crack).** Damage is self-evident, but cracks will only show after cleaning. Fault: pre-ignition or wrong gap-setting technique. Check: ignition timing, cooling system, fuel octane rating (too low) and fuel mixture (too weak). Discard plugs, rectify fault immediately

## 7  Distributor - dismantling, inspection and reassembly

1  Before dismantling the distributor, lay a clean sheet of paper on the workbench so that the various items can be laid out in the order of removal.

2  Remove the distributor cap, rotor arm, moisture cover and contact breaker set as described in Section 4 of this Chapter.

3  *On Bosch distributors,* remove the screws securing the cap clips to the sides of the body.

4  *On Delco-Remy distributors,* remove the two screws retaining the baseplate to the distributor body.

5  The spring clip ring which secures the vacuum advance/retard rod to the spigot on the contact breaker mechanism base plate should now be prised off the spigot (Fig. 4.10). Then undo and remove the two screws securing the vacuum diaphragm unit to the distributor casing and remove the diaphragm unit from the distributor assembly.

6  Now prise the spring ring which retains the distributor shaft in the distributor casing out of this slot in the shaft just below the casing (Fig. 4.11).

7  Push the shaft up through the distributor casing and remove the contact breaker base plate assembly.

8  Do not attempt to dismantle the base plate assembly as it can only be renewed as a complete item.

9  The two plates comprising the contact base plate assembly may be separated once the screw securing ball and thrust spring has been

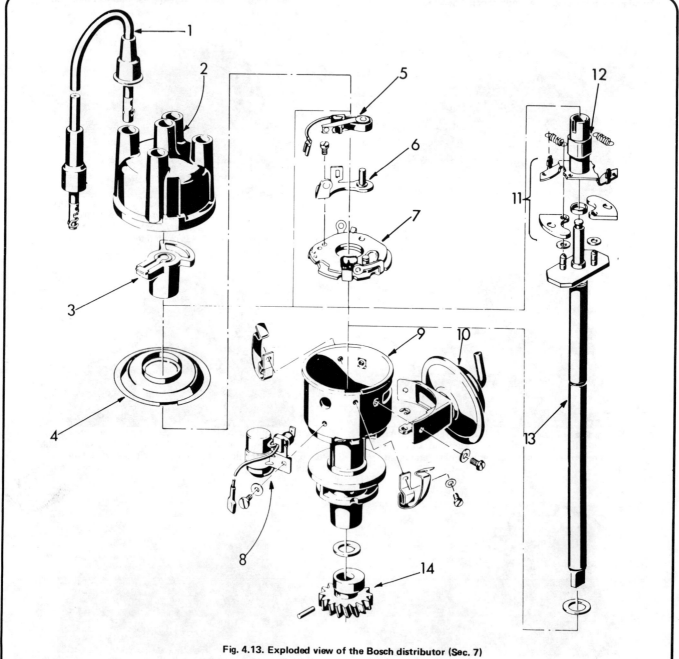

**Fig. 4.13. Exploded view of the Bosch distributor (Sec. 7)**

| | | | |
|---|---|---|---|
| 1  HT leads | 6  Contact breaker mounting | 9  Distributor casing | 12  Distributor cam |
| 2  Distributor cap | and pivot | 10  Vacuum advance, diaphragm | 13  Drive shaft |
| 3  Rotor arm | 7  Contact breaker base plate | unit | 14  Drive pinion and fuel pump |
| 4  Dust shield | assembly | 11  Centrifugal advance | cam |
| 5  Contact breaker mounting | 8  Condenser and LT lead | mechanism | |

removed.

10 It is recommended that the centrifugal advance mechanism should not be dismantled and if it is desired to remove the shaft, complete with centrifugal advance, for cleaning the drive gear and petrol pump the cam is retained to the bottom of the shaft by a single dowel pin.

11 There is no point in dismantling the distributor any further; individual parts other than caps, contact breaker sets and condenser units are difficult to obtain separately.

12 If the distributor shaft bearing is found to be worn, allowing the shaft to move radially, it is to be assumed that the majority of the moving components in the distributor have worn to a similar extent and that a new distributor should be obtained and fitted.

13 Clean all parts in an oil/grease solvent and thoroughly dry, preferably with an air blast to avoid foreign matter re-entering the fine mechanisms.

14 Smear the sliding parts and the springs of the centrifugal advance mechanism with a little medium grease (Fig. 4.14).

15 Check all moving parts for wear at the respective bearings and if replacement parts are not available - replace the whole distributor.

16 *Reassembly:* Fit the contact breaker base plate assembly to the distributor shaft. Inject some oil onto the shaft bearing surface and insert the shaft assembly into the distributor casing.

17 Fit the spacer washer and then the spring ring to the shaft to retain it in the distributor casing.

18 If the drive gear unit was removed, refit now and secure with the dowel pin.

19 Offer the vacuum unit to the distributor, fit the vacuum unit rod over the mating spigot on the breaker base plate assembly and secure the rod in position with the spring 'C' ring clip. Apply a little grease to the spigot/rod bearing.

20 Move the lower breaker base plate around so that the mounting lugs are aligned with the securing screw holes in the distributor housing.

21 Secure the vacuum unit to the casing with two set screws. Then position the cap retaining clips on the casing and secure with set screws.

22 Fit the condenser unit and then the contact breaker set as described earlier in this Chapter.

23 Oil the sliding parts of the breaker base plate assembly and the felt in the centre of the cam fitting. Apply a *little* high melting point grease to the surface of the cam (Fig. 4.15).

24 Adjust the contact breaker gap to 0.020 inches (0.50 mm) as described in Section 3, of this Chapter.

25 The distributor is now in a condition to be refitted to the engine. Proceed as directed in Section 6, of this Chapter.

## 8 Ignition timing - adjustment

1 It is necessary to time the ignition when it has been upset due to overhauling or dismantling which may have altered the relationship between the position of the pistons and the moment at which the distributor delivers the spark. Also, if maladjustments have affected the engine performance it is very desirable, although not always essential, to reset the timing starting from scratch. In the following procedures it is assumed that the intention is to obtain standard performance from the standard engine which is in reasonable condition. It is also assumed that the recommended fuel octane rating is used.

2 Set the transmission to neutral and remove all four spark plugs.

3 Place a thumb over No. 1 cylinder spark plug hole (front cylinder), and rotate the engine clockwise by means of the fan until pressure is felt building up in the No. 1 cylinder. This indicates that the No. 1 piston is approaching top-dead-centre (TDC) on the firing stroke.

4 Continue to rotate the engine until the notch in the crankshaft pulley is directly opposite the mark on the timing cover (Fig. 4.16).

**Note:** *On some early engines there are four timing marks on the timing cover and the longer central mark should be aligned with the notch in the pulley.*

Also on some engines, the timing position must be checked by removing the plug from the aperture in the flange on the rear of the cylinder block and rotating the engine until the ball set in the flywheel is in line with the pointer on the engine flange (photo).

5 Remove the distributor cap and check that the distributor rotor (or shaft) is in the position described in Section 6, of this Chapter.

6 Slacken the distributor clamp bolt and rotate the distributor body

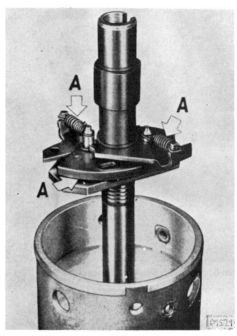

**Fig. 4.14. Lubrication points on the centrifugal advance mechanism (Sec. 7)**

**Fig. 4.15. Lubrication points on the upper distributor assembly (Sec. 7)**

*A  Light smear of medium grease*  *B  Engine oil*
*C  Engine oil*

**Fig. 4.16. Crankshaft pulley and front cover timing marks (Sec. 8)**

8.4 Static timing ball and pointer on flywheel

**Fig. 4.17. Rotating the distributor to correct the timing**

A   Advance ignition
B   Retard ignition

until the contact breaker points are just opening. Tighten the clamp
bolt (Fig. 4.17).

7   Difficulty is sometimes experienced in determining exactly when
the contact breaker points open. This can be ascertained most accurately
by connecting a 12v bulb in parallel with the contact breaker points
(one lead to earth and the other from the distributor low tension
terminal). Switch on the ignition and turn the distributor body anti-
clockwise until the bulb lights up, indicating the points have just
opened.

8   If it was not found possible to align the rotor arm correctly one of
two things is wrong. Either the distributor drive shaft has been incorrectly fitted in which case the distributor must be removed and replaced
as described in Section 6, of this Chapter and in Chapter 1, or the
distributor cam assembly has been incorrectly fitted on the driveshaft.
To rectify this, it will be necessary to partially dismantle the distributor
and check the position of the cam assembly on the centrifugal advance
mechanism; it may be 180⁰ out of position.

9   As a final check on the ignition timing the best method is to use a
strobe lamp.

10  Put a spot of white paint on the notch in the crankshaft pulley and
the pointer on the timing cover and connect the strobe light into the
No. 1 cylinder HT circuit. Disconnect and plug the distributor vacuum
pipe.

11  Run the engine at idling speed and point the strobe lamp at the
timing marks. At idling speed the white paint marks should be immediately opposite each other; open the throttle slightly and check that
as the engine revolutions rise the spot on the crankshaft pulley moves
anticlockwise. This indicates the advance mechanism is operating
correctly. **Note:** On engines with the timing mark on the flywheel, the
paint spot should be applied on the ball in the flywheel and the pointer
on the crankcase flange.

---

## 9   Ignition resistance wire - testing

To promote longer ignition system life the actual running voltage
used in the system is reduced by means of a resistance wire positioned
between the ignition switch and the ignition coil.

This circuit is alive when the ignition switch is on in the normal
running position but is bypassed while the ignition switch is in the
start position thereby applying full battery voltage for easier engine
starting.

If the condition exists where the engine will start but will not run
with the switch in the running position the resistance wire should be
suspect and checked. To carry out this check proceed as follows:

1   Connect up a voltmeter as shown in Fig. 4.18.
2   Fit a jump wire from the distributor terminal of the coil to a good
earth.
3   Make sure that all the accessories and lights are switched off.
4   Turn on the ignition.
5   The voltmeter should read between 4.5 and 6 volts. If the reading
is above or below these limits the resistance wire should be renewed.

---

## 10  Spark plugs and HT leads - general

1   The correct functioning of the spark plugs is vital for the correct
running and efficiency of the engine.

2   At intervals of 6,000 miles (10,000km) the plugs should be removed,
examined, cleaned, and if worn excessively, replaced. The condition of
the spark plug will also tell much about the overall condition of the
engine (Fig. 4.19).

3   If the insulator nose of the spark plug is clean and white, with no
deposits, this is indicative of a weak mixture, or too hot a plug (a hot
plug transfers heat away from the electrode slowly, a cold plug transfers
heat away quickly).

4   The plugs fitted as standard are one of those as specified at the
beginning of this Chapter. If the top and insulator nose is covered with
hard black-looking deposits, then this is indicative that the mixture is
too rich. Should the plug be black and oily, then it is likely that the
engine is fairly worn, as well as the mixture being too rich.

5   If the insulator nose is covered with light tan to greyish brown
deposits, then the mixture is correct and it is likely that the engine is
in good condition.

**Fig. 4.18. Checking the ignition coil resistor wire ('V' is voltmeter)**

6  If there are any traces of long brown tapering stains on the outside of the white portion of the plug, then the plug will have to be renewed, as this shows that there is a faulty joint between the plug body and the insulator, and compression is being allowed to leak away.

7  Plugs should be cleaned by a sand blasting machine, which will free them from carbon more than cleaning by hand. The machine will also test the condition of the plugs under compression. Any plug that fails to spark at the recommended pressure should be renewed.

8  The spark plug gap is of considerable importance, as, if it is too large or too small, the size of the spark and its efficiency will be seriously impaired. For the best results the spark plug gap should be set in accordance with the 'Specifications' at the beginning of this Chapter (Fig. 4.19A).

9  To set it, measure the gap with a feeler gauge, and then bend open, or close, the outer plug electrode until the correct gap is achieved. The centre electrode should never be bent as this may crack the insulation and cause plug failure if nothing worse.

10 When replacing the plugs, remember to use new washers, and replace the leads from the distributor in the correct firing order, which is 1 - 3 - 4 - 2, No. 1 cylinder being the one nearest the distributor.

11 The plug leads require no routine attention other than being kept clean and wiped over regularly. At intervals of 6,000 miles (10,000km), however, pull each lead off the plug in turn and remove it from the distributor. Water can seep down into the joints giving rise to a white corrosive deposit which must be carefully removed from the end of each cable.

## 11 Coil - general

1  The coil is an auto-transformer and has two sets of windings wound around a core of soft iron wires. The resistances of the two windings are given in the 'Specifications' at the beginning of this Chapter.

2  If the coil is suspect then these resistances may be checked and if faulty it may readily be replaced after undoing the mounting bolts (photo).

## 12 Ignition system - fault diagnosis

By far the majority of breakdown and running troubles are caused by faults in the ignition system either in the low tension or high tension circuits.

There are two main symptoms indicating faults. Either the engine

11.2 Delco-Remy type coil

will not start or fire, or the engine is difficult to start and misfires. If it is a regular misfire, (ie. the engine is running on only two or three cylinders), the fault is almost sure to be in the secondary or high tension circuit. If the misfiring is intermittent the fault could be in either the high or low tension circuits. If the car stops suddenly, or will not start at all, it is likely that the fault is in the low tension circuit. Loss of power and overheating, apart from faulty carburation settings, are normally due to faults in the distributor or to incorrect ignition timing.

### Engine fails to start

1  If the engine fails to start and the car was running normally when it was last used, first check there is fuel in the petrol tank. If the engine turns over normally on the starter motor and the battery is evidently well charged, then the fault may be in either the high or low tension circuits. First check the HT circuit. **Note:** If the battery is known to be fully charged, the ignition light comes on, and the starter motor fails to turn the engine **check the tightness of the leads on the battery terminals and also the secureness of the earth lead to its connection to the body.** It is quite common for the leads to have worked loose, even if they look and feel secure. If one of the battery terminal posts gets very hot when trying to work the starter motor this is a sure indication of a faulty connection to that terminal.

2  One of the commonest reasons for bad starting is wet or damp spark plug leads and distributor. Remove the distributor cap. If condensation is visible internally dry the cap with a rag and also wipe over the leads. Refit the cap.

3  If the engine still fails to start, check that voltage is reaching the plugs by disconnecting each plug lead in turn at the spark plug end, and holding the end of the cable about ¼ inch (6 mm) away from the cylinder block. Spin the engine on the starter motor.

4  Sparking between the end of the cable and the block should be fairly strong with a strong regular blue spark. (Hold the lead with rubber to avoid electric shocks). If voltage is reaching the plugs, then remove them and clean and regap them. The engine should now start.

5  If there is no spark at the plug leads, take off the HT lead from the centre of the distributor cap and hold it to the block as before. Spin the engine on the starter once more. A rapid succession of blue sparks between the end of the lead and the block indicate that the coil is in order and that the distributor cap is cracked, the rotor arm is faulty, or the carbon brush in the top of the distributor cap is not making good contact with the spring on the rotor arm. Possibly, the points are in bad condition. Clean and reset them as described in this Chapter, Section 2 or 3.

6  If there are no sparks from the end of the lead from the coil, check the connections at the coil end of the lead. If it is in order start checking the low tension circuit.

7  Use a 12v voltmeter or a 12v bulb and two lengths of wire. With the ignition switched on and the points open, test between the low tension wire to the coil (it is marked 15 or +) and earth. No reading indicates a break in the supply from the ignition switch. Check the connections at the switch to see if any are loose. Refit them and the engine should run. A reading shows a faulty coil or condenser, or broken lead between the coil and the distributor.

8  Take the condenser wire off the points assembly and with the points open test between the moving point and earth. If there now is a reading then the fault is in the condenser. Fit a new one and the fault is cleared.

9  With no reading from the moving point to earth, take a reading between earth and the − or 1 terminal of the coil. A reading here shows a broken wire which will need to be replaced between the coil and distributor. No reading confirms that the coil has failed and must be replaced, after which the engine will run once more. Remember to refit the condenser wire to the points assembly. For these tests it is sufficient to separate the points with a piece of dry paper while testing with the points open.

### Engine misfires

1  If the engine misfires regularly run it at a fast idling speed. Pull off each of the plug caps in turn and listen to the note of the engine. Hold the plug cap in a dry cloth or with a rubber glove as additional protection against a shock from the HT supply.

2  No difference in engine running will be noticed when the lead from the defective circuit is removed. Removing the lead from one of the good cylinders will accentuate the misfire.

3   Remove it about ¼ inch (6mm) away from the block. Re-start the engine. If the sparking is fairly strong and regular, the fault must lie in the spark plug.

4   The plug may be loose, the insulation may be cracked, or the points may have burnt away giving too wide a gap for the spark to jump. Worse still, one of the points may have broken off. Either renew the plug, or clean it, reset the gap, and then test it.

5   If there is no spark at the end of the plug lead, or if it is weak and intermittent, check the ignition lead from the distributor to the plug. If the insulation is cracked or perished, renew the lead. Check the connections at the distributor cap.

6   If there is still no spark, examine the distributor cap carefully for tracking. This can be recognised by a very thin black line running between two or more electrodes, or between an electrode and some other part of the distributor. These lines are paths which now conduct electricity across the cap thus letting it run to earth. The only answer is a new distributor cap.

7   Apart from the ignition timing being incorrect, other causes of misfiring have already been dealt with under the Section dealing with the failure of the engine to start. To recap, these are that

a)   *The coil may be faulty giving an intermittent misfire;*
b)   *There may be a damaged wire or loose connection in the low tension circuit;*
c)   *The condenser may be faulty; or*
d)   *There may be a mechanical fault in the distributor (broken driving spindle or contact breaker spring).*

8   If the ignition timing is too far retarded, it should be noted that the engine will tend to overheat, and there will be a quite noticeable drop in power. If the engine is overheating and the power is down, and the ignition timing is correct, then the carburettor should be checked, as it is likely that this is where the fault lies.

# Chapter 5 Clutch

*For modifications, and information applicable to later models, see Supplement at end of manual*

## Contents

## Specifications

### Clutch

| | |
|---|---|
| Type ... ... ... ... ... ... ... ... ... ... | Single plate, dry disc |
| Pedal free-travel ... ... ... ... ... ... ... ... | Nil |
| Friction plate facings ... ... ... ... ... ... ... | Woven asbestos |
| Facing attachment ... ... ... ... ... ... ... ... | Rivets |
| Vibration damping ... ... ... ... ... ... ... ... | 4 torsional springs |

### Torque wrench settings

| | lb f ft | kg f m |
|---|---|---|
| Flywheel to crankshaft, bolt ... ... ... ... ... ... ... | 43 | 6 |
| Clutch cover to flywheel, bolt ... ... ... ... ... ... | 15 | 2 |
| Gearbox to clutch bellhousing, bolt ... ... ... ... ... | 32 to 36 | 4.4 to 5 |
| Starter to clutch bellhousing, bolt ... ... ... ... ... | 40 | 5.5 |
| Actuating lever pivot bolt, lock nut ... ... ... ... ... | 4 | 0.55 |
| Intake and exhaust manifolds, bolt ... ... ... ... ... | 33 | 4.5 |
| Bellhousing to cylinder block ... ... ... ... ... ... | 36 | 5 |

## 1 General description

All models are fitted with a single plate dry disc clutch. The friction disc is retained by a diaphragm spring acting on a pressure plate. The whole clutch unit is held within a pressed steel cover, which is bolted to the flywheel. The gearbox driveshaft projects through the clutch to run in a roller bearing held in the centre of the engine crankshaft. The clutch friction plate runs on splines on the gearbox driveshaft.

The clutch is actuated mechanically, via a Bowden cable. From its connection on the clutch pedal this cable runs through a sleeve, retained by a damper, in the engine compartment firewall, an eye fitting on the

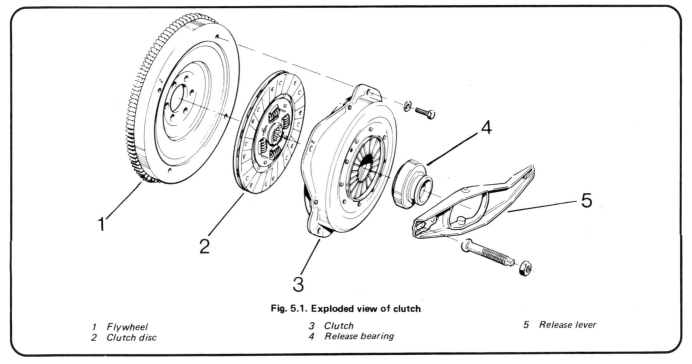

**Fig. 5.1. Exploded view of clutch**

| | | |
|---|---|---|
| *1  Flywheel* | *3  Clutch* | *5  Release lever* |
| *2  Clutch disc* | *4  Release bearing* | |

clutch bellhousing - to emerge and connect to the clutch actuating lever. The lever has the clutch thrust bearing mounted centrally and its furthest end pivots on a ball headed bolt, screwed into the clutch bellhousing.

The clutch operates as follows: When the clutch pedal is depressed, the cable is pulled to move the outside end of the actuating lever forwards. As the lever is moved forwards, it pivots about the ball headed bolt and pushes the thrust bearing into the clutch diaphragm spring. When the centre of the spring is pushed inwards its periphery is moved outwards pulling the clutch pressure plate with it. Now that the pressure plate has been lifted from the friction disc, the disc no longer transmits the engine torque from the flywheel to the gearbox driveshaft. As the clutch pedal is released, the cable returns allowing the actuating lever to move rearwards. As the lever moves back, the thrust bearing is retracted from the centre of the clutch. The diaphragm spring now forces the pressure plate back against the friction disc and flywheel. The friction disc now being held hard against the flywheel is once more capable of transmitting engine power from the flywheel to the gearbox driveshaft.

As the friction linings on the friction disc wear, the pedal 'rest' position moves towards the driver and also towards the 'clutch worn' light warning switch. The switch is mounted on the pedal support bracket. The actuating mechanism is such that there is no pedal lash or free movement. The tension spring acting on the pedal serves to maintain light pressure on the clutch thrust bearing and diaphragm spring.

## 2  Clutch pedal - travel adjustment (early models)

1   As stated in the previous Section, there should be no free movement of the pedal. Generally the pedal travel will only need adjustment when the clutch has worn to the point when the pedal closes the 'clutch worn' warning light switch, or when a new cable has been fitted.
2   Refer to Fig. 5.2 for the measurement position.
3   If the parking brake is fitted with a warning lamp, the brake must be released. The same lamp is used to indicate a brake or clutch fault.
4   From underneath the car loosen the locknut on the clutch lever pivot bolt, which is on the right-hand side of the bellhousing. It was found to be a little difficult to reach this pivot bolt, but with a little perseverance and a slim spanner it is possible.
5   Turn the pivot bolt until the distance between the clutch actuating lever and the bellhousing front face is 4.29 in (109 mm).
6   Once this has been achieved, the pivot bolt should be tightened to 4 lb f ft (0.5 kg f m).
7   See Chapter 13 for cars having a clutch cable with a screwed adjuster.

## 3  Clutch cable - removal and replacement (early models)

1   The clutch cable should be renewed if the action of the clutch pedal is jerky or stiff or, more obviously, if the cable has broken.
2   First jack-up the front of the car and support it on axle stands.
3   From beneath the car, remove the nylon collar from the end of the clutch cable and slide the cable ball end out of the clutch fork (Fig. 5.3).
4   Withdraw the cable and rubber sleeve through the hole in the side of the clutch bellhousing.
5   From the engine compartment, prise out the circlip from the outer cable at the point where the cable passes through the rear engine bulkhead (see Fig. 5.4).
6   Push the cable through the rubber grommet just enough to enable the end to be unhooked from the clutch pedal.
7   Detach the bracket retaining the cable to the body and remove the complete cable assembly.
8   To refit the cable, insert the lower end with the rubber sleeve through the hole in the side of the clutch bellhousing (photo).
9   Fit the ball end through the slot in the clutch lever and push on the nylon retaining collar.
10  Push the cable through the damper assembly in the engine compartment bulkhead and hook the inner cable end onto the clutch pedal lever.
11  To adjust the cable length, pull the cable out of the damper until the clutch pedal arm is just touching the plunger of the clutch warning switch (an assistant will be necessary).
12  Hold the cable in this position and fit the circlip on the cable so that   there are three grooves between the circlip and damper (Fig. 5.5).

**Fig. 5.2. Clutch adjustment points. (Sec. 2)**

    *1   Locknut*
    *2   Pivot bolt*
    *X   This dimension is 4.29 in (109 mm)*

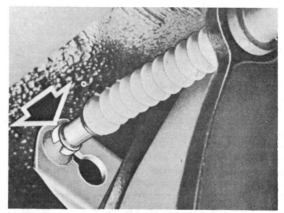

**Fig. 5.3. Nylon retaining ring on clutch fork (Sec. 3)**

13  Push the outer cable through the damper so that the circlip is against the washer and press the clutch pedal several times to seat the cable.
14  Measure the distance between the outer rim of the steering wheel and the clutch pedal pad, first with the pedal fully depressed, then with the pedal released. The difference between the two measurements should be 5.9 in (150 mm), and can be altered, if necessary, by relocating the cable circlip in a different groove from that set at paragraph 12.
15  Bolt the cable bracket back onto the bodywork and check the pedal position, as described in Section 2.
16  See Chapter 13 for cars having a clutch cable with a screwed adjuster.

## 4  Pedal travel warning light circuit - general

1   The pedal height varies according to the state of wear of the clutch friction disc. As the plate lining wears the pedal follows and moves upwards towards the driver. A switch has been fitted to the clutch pedal support bracket to register when the pedal height has moved to a point at which the actuating mechanism requires adjustment.
2   The pedal travel warning light is on the same circuit as the handbrake-on warning switch, and brake hydraulic system warning switch. If any of the switches close, the warning lamp will light up.
3   The switch is arranged on the 'earth' (ground) side of the warning

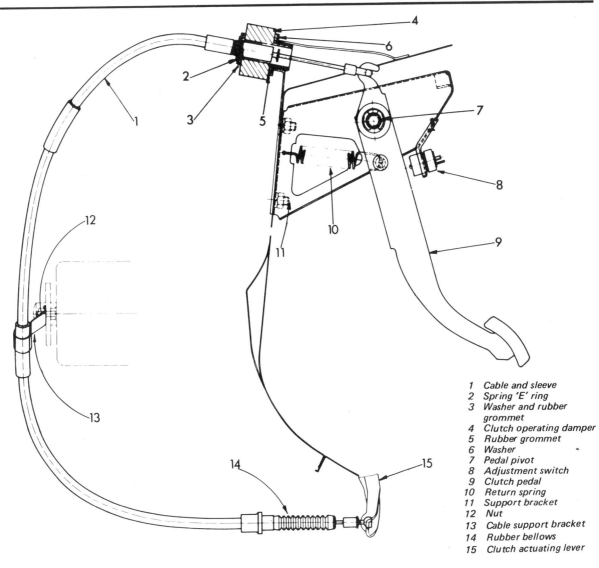

1    Cable and sleeve
2    Spring 'E' ring
3    Washer and rubber
     grommet
4    Clutch operating damper
5    Rubber grommet
6    Washer
7    Pedal pivot
8    Adjustment switch
9    Clutch pedal
10   Return spring
11   Support bracket
12   Nut
13   Cable support bracket
14   Rubber bellows
15   Clutch actuating lever

Fig. 5.4. Clutch cable and pedal assembly

Fig. 5.5. Clutch cable adjustment · dimension 'A' indicates three grooves (Sec. 3)

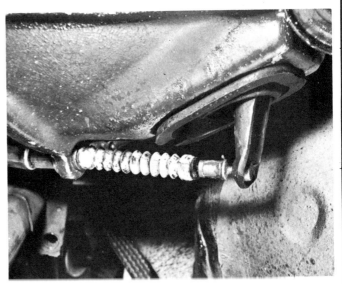

3.8. Lower end of clutch cable and rubber sleeve

lamp, and the circuit and components may be checked as follows:

4   Remove the leads from the clutch switch and touch them onto the bodyshell nearby. The warning lamp should light up. If the lamp does not light, then refer to Chapter 10, and remove.

5   If, however, the warning lamp does light up; reconnect the switch and discard. It is not repairable.

6   Removal of the switch is quite straightforward, being a matter of detaching the leads and unscrewing the switch from the support bracket.

### 5   Clutch release bearing - removal

1   Wear of the clutch release bearing is indicated by a squealing noise when the clutch pedal is depressed with the engine running.

2   To gain access to the release bearing, remove the gearbox and clutch housing, as described in Chapter 6 (photo).

3   Remove the pivot bolt locknut and screw the pivot bolt into the clutch housing (Fig. 5.2).

4   Remove the release lever from the pivot bolt and slide the lever and release bearing off the gearbox shaft.

5   Remove the bearing assembly from the spigots in the release lever.

6   The release mechanism is now dismantled as far as it will go. If any component is found unserviceable, it should be discarded and a new part fitted in its place.

7   The release bearing assembly should feel smooth and be quiet when turned. If any roughness is heard or felt the bearing assembly should be renewed.

8   The refitting procedure is the exact reversal of the removal sequence. Remember to tighten all nuts and bolts to the specified torques (see Specifications at the beginning of this Chapter).

### 6   Clutch assembly - removal and replacement

1   Remove the gearbox and clutch housing, as described in Chapter 6.

2   Once the clutch assembly on the flywheel has been exposed, scribe a mark onto the flywheel and clutch cover to indicate their relative positions. This will ensure correct refitment if the original parts are reused (photo).

3   Remove the clutch assembly by unscrewing the four bolts holding the cover to the rear face of the flywheel. Unscrew the diagonally opposite bolts, half a turn at a time, to prevent distortion of the cover flange.

4   With the bolts and spring washers removed, lift the clutch assembly off the flywheel. The driven plate or clutch disc will fall out at this stage - as it is not attached to the clutch cover assembly, or the flywheel. Carefully make a note of which way round it is fitted (photo).

5   It is important that no oil or grease gets on the clutch disc friction linings, or the pressure plate and flywheel faces. It is advisable to handle the parts with clean hands and to wipe down the pressure plate and flywheel faces with a clean dry rag before inspection or refitting commences.

6   To refit the clutch, place the clutch disc against the flywheel. Early clutch discs should be fitted with the *longer* side of the central boss towards the flywheel. Later clutch discs should be fitted with the *shorter* side of the central boss towards the flywheel. Later type clutch discs can be identified by the circlip (arrowed in Fig. 5.6) which

retains the central boss; early type clutch discs have no circlip. On no account should the clutch disc be replaced the wrong way round as it will be found quite impossible to operate the clutch.

7   Place the clutch cover assembly on the flywheel. Replace the four bolts and spring washers and tighten them finger tight so that the clutch disc is gripped but can still be moved.

8   The clutch disc must now be centralised so that when the engine and gearbox are mated, the gearbox input shaft splines will pass through the splines in the centre of the hub.

9   Centralisation can be carried out quite easily, by inserting a round bar or long screwdriver through the hole in the centre of the clutch, so that the end of the bar rests in the small hole in the end of the crankshaft containing the input shaft bearing bush. Moving the bar sideways or up and down will move the clutch disc in whichever direction is necessary to achieve centralisation.

10  Centralisation is easily judged by removing the bar and viewing the driven plate hub in relation to the hole in the centre of the diaphragm spring. When the hub appears exactly in the centre of the release bearing hole, all is correct. Alternatively, if an old input shaft can be borrowed this will eliminate all the guesswork, obviating the need for visual alignment.

11  Tighten the clutch bolts firmly in a diagonal sequence to ensure that the cover plate is pulled down evenly without distortion of the flange. Tighten the bolts to the torque wrench setting given in the Specifications.

12  Refit the gearbox and clutch housing onto the engine and after refitting the clutch cable check the pedal travel adjustment, as described in Section 2.

### 7   Clutch assembly - inspection

1   In the normal course of events, clutch dismantling and reassembly, is the term used for simply fitting a new clutch pressure plate and friction disc. Under no circumstances should the diaphragm spring clutch unit be dismantled. If a fault develops in the pressure plate assembly, an exchange replacement unit must be fitted.

2   If a new clutch disc is being fitted it is false economy not to renew the release bearing at the same time. This will preclude having to replace it at a later date when wear on the clutch linings is very small.

3   Examine the clutch disc friction linings for wear or loose rivets, the disc for rim distortion, cracks and worn splines. If any of these faults are evident the disc must be replaced with a new one.

4   Check the machined faces of the flywheel and the pressure plate. If either is badly grooved it should be machined until smooth, or replaced with a new item. If the pressure plate is cracked or split it must be renewed.

5   Examine the hub splines for wear and also make sure that the centre hub is not loose.

### 8   Clutch pedal - removal and refitting

The clutch pedal is attached to the same supports as the brake pedal. Refer to Chapter 9 for removal and refitting procedures for both pedals.

5.2 Gearbox and clutch housing prior to removal from engine

6.2 Alignment marks on clutch cover and flywheel

6.4 Clutch friction disc and pressure plate

## 9 Fault diagnosis - clutch

There are four main faults to which the clutch and release mechanism are prone. They may occur by themselves or in conjunction with any of the other faults. They are clutch squeal, slip, spin and judder.

### Clutch squeal - diagnosis and cure

1 If on taking up the drive or when changing gear, the clutch squeals, this is a sure indication of a badly worn clutch release bearing.
2 As well as regular wear due to normal use, wear of the clutch release bearing is much accentuated if the clutch is ridden, or held down for long periods in gear, with the engine running. To minimise wear of this component the car should always be taken out of gear at traffic lights and for similar holdups.

### Clutch slip - diagnosis and cure

1 Clutch slip is a self evident condition which occurs when the clutch friction plate is badly worn, when oil or grease have got onto the flywheel or pressure plate faces, or when the pressure plate itself is faulty.
2 The reason for clutch slip is that, due to one of the faults listed above, there is either insufficient pressure from the pressure plate, or insufficient friction from the friction plate to ensure solid drive.
3 If small amounts of oil get onto the clutch, they will be burnt off under the heat of clutch engagement, and in the process, gradually darken the linings. Excessive oil on the clutch will burn off leaving a carbon deposit which can cause quite bad slip, or fierceness, spin and judder.
4 If clutch slip is suspected, and confirmation of this condition is required, there are several tests which can be made.
5 With the engine in top gear and pulling lightly up a moderate incline sudden depression of the accelerator pedal may cause the engine to increase its speed without any increase in road speed.
6 In extreme cases of clutch slip the engine will race under normal acceleration conditions.
7 If slip is due to oil or grease on the linings a temporary cure can sometimes be effected by squirting carbon tetrachloride into the clutch.

The permanent cure is, of course, to renew the clutch driven plate and trace and rectify the oil leak.

### Clutch spin - diagnosis and cure

1 Clutch spin is a condition which occurs when the release arm travel is excessive, there is an obstruction in the clutch either on the primary gear splines or in the operating lever itself, or the oil may have partially burnt off the clutch linings and have left a resinous deposit which is causing the clutch to stick to the pressure plate or flywheel.
2 The reason for clutch spin is that due to any, or a combination of the faults just listed, the clutch pressure plate is not completely freeing from the centre plate even with the clutch pedal fully depressed.
3 If clutch spin is suspected, the condition can be confirmed by extreme difficulty in engaging first gear from rest, difficulty in changing gear, and very sudden take up of the clutch drive at the fully depressed end of the clutch pedal travel as the clutch is released.
4 Check that the clutch cable is correctly adjusted and, if in order, the fault lies internally in the clutch. It will then be necessary to remove the clutch for examination, and to check the gearbox input shaft.
5 This condition may also be due to the driven plate being rusted to the flywheel or pressure plate. It is possible to free it by applying the handbrake, depressing the clutch pedal, engaging top gear and operating the starter motor. If really badly corroded, then the engine will not turn over, but in the majority of cases the driven plate will free. Once the engine starts, rev it up and slip the clutch several times to clear the rust deposits.

### Clutch judder - diagnosis

1 Clutch judder is a self evident condition which occurs when the gearbox or engine mountings are loose or too flexible, when there is oil on the faces of the clutch friction plate, or when the clutch pressure plate has been incorrectly adjusted during assembly.
2 The reason for clutch judder is that due to one of the faults just listed, the clutch pressure plate is not freeing smoothly from the friction disc, and is snatching.
3 Clutch judder normally occurs when the clutch pedal is released in first or reverse gears, and the whole car shudders as it moves backwards or forwards.

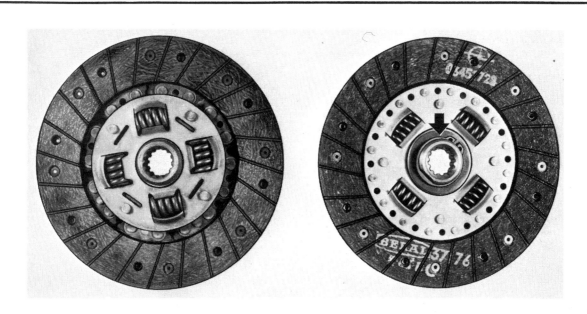

**Fig. 5.6. Early and later type clutch discs (Sec 6)**

*Later type clutch disc (right) has circlip (arrowed) to retain central boss. Early type clutch disc (left) has no circlip*

# Chapter 6 Manual gearbox and automatic transmission

*For modifications, and information applicable to later models, see Supplement at end of manual*

## Contents

## Specifications

## Manual gearbox

| | |
|---|---|
| Type ... ... ... ... ... ... ... ... ... ... | 4 forward speeds, plus reverse. Synchromesh on all forward ratios |

### Ratios
| | |
|---|---|
| 1st gear ... ... ... ... ... ... ... ... ... | 3.428 |
| 2nd gear ... ... ... ... ... ... ... ... ... | 2.156 |
| 3rd gear ... ... ... ... ... ... ... ... ... | 1.366 |
| 4th gear ... ... ... ... ... ... ... ... ... | 1.000 |
| Reverse ... ... ... ... ... ... ... ... ... | 3.317 |

### Oil type/specification
Oil type/specification ... ... ... ... ... ... — Hypoid gear oil, viscosity SAE 80EP (Duckhams Hypoid 80)

### Oil capacity
Oil capacity ... ... ... ... ... ... ... ... — 2 Imp pints (1.1 litres)

### Adjustment and installation specifications

| | |
|---|---|
| Distance of gearshift lever bellows between end of bellows on gearshift lever and gearshift lever knob upper edge ... ... ... ... ... | 8.1 in (205 mm) |
| Free-travel of reverse gearshift blocker pull ring on installed gearshift lever (approx) ... ... ... ... ... ... ... ... ... | 0.04 - 0.8 in (1 - 2 mm) |
| Distance between reverse gearshift blocker pull ring and gearshift lever knob lower edge after installation of knob - knob heated up to 176°F (80°C) in boiling water ... ... ... ... ... ... ... | 0.3 in (7 mm) |
| Axial play of intermediate shift lever pivot pin ... ... ... | 0.004 - 0.012 in (0.1 - 0.3 mm) |
| Adjusting reverse gearshift blocker on selector shaft ... ... ... | Engage second gear. Adjust selector ring screwed onto selector shaft so that the shifter lug of the gearshift lever rests clearance free against the stop of the intermediate shift lever. Turn back selector ring ¼ turn and secure with lock nut. |

### Torque wrench settings (manual gearbox)

| | lb f ft | kg f m |
|---|---|---|
| Rubber support block to the gearbox ... ... ... ... ... | 22 | 3.1 |
| Bellhousing to the engine block ... ... ... ... ... ... | 29 | 4 |
| Gearbox to clutch bellhousing ... ... ... ... ... ... | 32 - 36 | 4.4 - 5 |
| Gearbox rear extension to main casing ... ... ... ... ... | 21 | 3 |
| Baseplate to main casing ... ... ... ... ... ... | 7 - 10 | 0.96 - 1.38 |

## Automatic transmission

### Marking on yellow identification plate
| | |
|---|---|
| 1.6 engine ... ... ... ... ... ... ... ... ... | OH |
| 1.9 engine .. ... ... ... ... ... ... ... ... | OG |

### Ratios (mechanical)
| | |
|---|---|
| 1st gear ... ... ... ... ... ... ... ... ... | 2.40 : 1 |
| 2nd gear ... ... ... ... ... ... ... ... ... | 1.48 : 1 |
| 3rd gear ... ... ... ... ... ... ... ... ... | 1.00 : 1 |
| Reverse ... ... ... ... ... ... ... ... ... | 1.92 : 1 |

| | |
|---|---|
| Selector lever ... ... ... ... ... ... ... ... ... | On tunnel console |

**Selector lever positions**

| | |
|---|---|
| P ... ... ... ... ... ... ... ... ... ... | Rear wheels locked. Starting possible |
| R ... ... ... ... ... ... ... ... ... ... | Back-up lamp switched on, reverse gear selected |
| N ... ... ... ... ... ... ... ... ... ... | Starting possible |
| D ... ... ... ... ... ... ... ... ... ... | Automatic shifts 1 - 2 - 3 - 2 - 1 |
| S ... ... ... ... ... ... ... ... ... ... | Only 1st and 2nd gear 1 - 2 - 1 |
| L ... ... ... ... ... ... ... ... ... ... | Only 1st gear |

| | |
|---|---|
| **Shift points** ... ... ... ... ... ... ... ... | Refer to separate table |
| **Shifting** ... ... ... ... ... ... ... ... ... | Automatic, depending on engine vacuum (throttle valve) and vehicle speed (governor) |
| **Kickdown control** ... ... ... ... ... ... ... | Mechanical, bowden control wire |

**Torque converter**

| | | |
|---|---|---|
| Diameter ... ... ... ... ... ... ... ... ... | 9 in nominal (approx. 247 mm) | |
| Paint marking ... ... ... ... ... ... ... ... | yellow | green |
| Torque ratio ... ... ... ... ... ... ... ... | 2.4 : 1 | 2.1 : 1 |

| | |
|---|---|
| **Oil type/specification** ... ... ... ... ... | Dexron type ATF (Duckhams D-Matic) |

**Oil capacity**

| | |
|---|---|
| Oil change ... ... ... ... ... ... ... ... | 4.5 - 5 Imp pints (2.5 - 2.7 litres) |
| Complete refill (torque converter 'dry') ... ... | 9 - 9.2 Imp pints (5 - 5.2 litres) |
| Topping-up (difference between 'Add' and 'F' marks on dipstick) ... | 0.9 Imp pints (0.5 litre) |

**Torque wrench settings (automatic transmission)**

| | lb f ft | kg f m |
|---|---|---|
| Oil pan to case ... ... ... ... ... ... ... ... | 7 - 10 | 0.96 - 1.38 |
| Transfer plate to valve body ... ... ... ... ... ... | 6 - 8 | 0.82 - 1.1 |
| Reinforcement plate to case ... ... ... ... ... ... | 13 - 15 | 1.79 - 2 |
| Valve body to case ... ... ... ... ... ... ... | 13 - 15 | 1.79 - 2 |
| Servo cover to case ... ... ... ... ... ... ... | 16 - 19 | 2.2 - 2.6 |
| Modulator assembly ... ... ... ... ... ... ... | 12 - 15 | 1.65 - 2 |
| Converter housing to oil pump ... ... ... ... ... | 13 - 17 | 1.79 - 2.3 |
| Converter housing to case ... ... ... ... ... ... | 22 - 26 | 3.1 - 3.59 |
| Selector lever jam nut ... ... ... ... ... ... | 8 - 11 | 1 - 1.4 |
| Governor body to governor ... ... ... ... ... ... | 6 - 8 | 0.82 - 1.1 |
| Extension housing to case ... ... ... ... ... ... | 20 - 30 | 2.76 - 4.14 |
| Servo adjusting bolt lock nut ... ... ... ... ... | 12 - 15 | 1.65 - 2 |
| Planetary carrier lock plate ... ... ... ... ... | 5 - 7 | 0.69 - 0.96 |
| Oil pressure check plug ... ... ... ... ... ... | 5 - 7 | 0.69 - 0.96 |
| Flex plate to crankshaft ... ... ... ... ... ... | 36 - 51 | 5 - 8.3 |
| Converter to flex plate ... ... ... ... ... ... | 38 - 42 | 5.25 - 5.8 |
| Converter housing to cylinder block ... ... ... ... | 38 - 42 | 5.25 - 5.8 |
| Intermediate selector lever to console selector lever shaft ... ... | 18 - 20 | 2.48 - 2.765 |
| Rear engine support to transmission case extension ... ... | 18 - 22 | 2.48 - 3.1 |
| Outer transmission selector lever to transmission selector lever shaft ... | 13 - 16 | 1.79 - 2.2 |
| Oil cooler line connector ... ... ... ... ... ... | 10 - 13 | 1.38 - 1.79 |
| Oil cooler line to connector ... ... ... ... ... | 11 - 15 | 1.4 - 2 |
| Oil cooler line to oil cooler hose ... ... ... ... | 11 - 15 | 1.4 - 2 |
| Oil cooler hose to oil cooler ... ... ... ... ... | 11 - 15 | 1.4 - 2 |
| Brake band adjusting screw ... ... ... ... ... ... | 3.3 | 0.5 |
| Brake band adjusting screw locknut ... ... ... ... | 12 to 15 | 1.7 to 2.1 |
| Brake band servo cover bolts ... ... ... ... ... | 17 to 19 | 2.3 to 2.6 |
| Transmission oil pan bolts ... ... ... ... ... ... | 7 to 9 | 1.0 to 1.3 |

## 1 General description - manual gearbox

1 The same manual gearbox is fitted to all models; it has synchromesh on all four forward speeds. The reverse gear only is non-synchromesh.
The arrangement of the gearbox is similar to other vehicles made by General Motors; access to the box is provided by a detachable base plate and the gear selector mechanism comprises the gear lever, pivot member relay rods, a transverse shaft in the gearbox and finally the selector forks on their shafts. The forks act on the synchronising rings on a hub splined to the mainshaft. The rings are impelled forwards or rearwards against the gear train to be engaged. A female cone is carried with the synchronising ring against a male cone on the gear being engaged. The friction between the two cones as they come together serves to bring the gear train speed to that of the synchronising ring and the mainshaft. Once the speeds are matched, the ring can pass further to fully engage the dogs on the gear train. Keys sprung in the ring hub act to keep the ring in place once it has positively engaged a gear train.
2 The construction of the box is conventional; when being disman-

tled, the mainshaft (output) is removed complete with the rear gearbox extension, all the synchromesh assemblies and the 1st, 2nd and 3rd gear driven gears.
3 The input shaft can be removed once the bellhousing has been unbolted from the gearbox, and comes complete with its bearing and gear which drives the layshaft.
4 The layshaft is in the bottom of the gearbox and runs on two sets of needle roller bearings on a central shaft. Access to the box is via a base plate on the gearbox. There are no repair tasks on the gearbox (except minor jobs on the exterior gearshift mechanism) that can be completed with the gearbox in place. The dismantling of this gearbox is only possible in a particular set sequence detailed in Sections 3, 5, and 6.

## 2 Gearbox (manual) - removal and replacement

1 The gearbox may be removed without significantly disturbing the engine. It will be as well if there were assistance from one person at

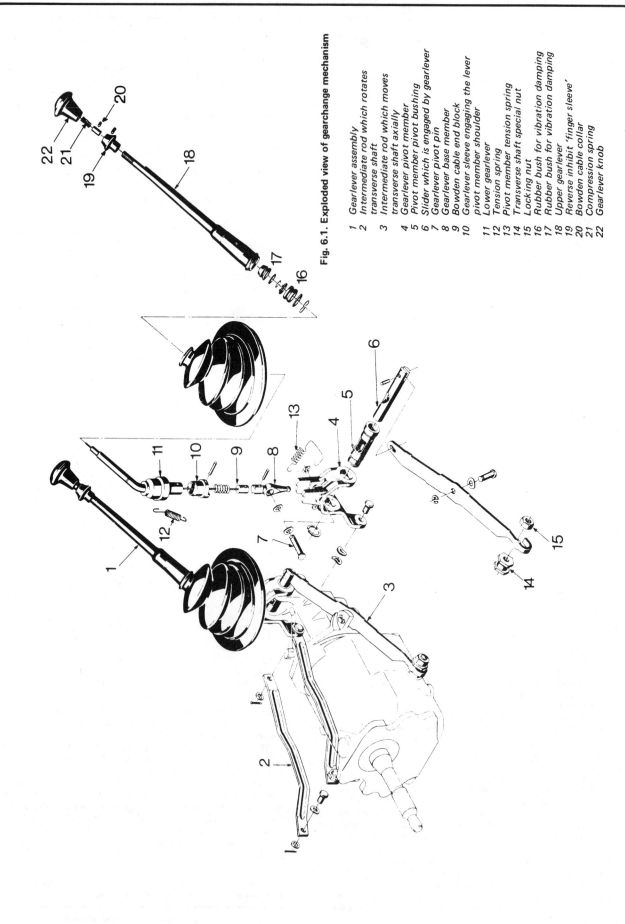

**Fig. 6.1. Exploded view of gearchange mechanism**

1 Gearlever assembly
2 Intermediate rod which rotates transverse shaft
3 Intermediate rod which moves transverse shaft axially
4 Gearlever pivot member
5 Pivot member pivot bushing
6 Slider which is engaged by gearlever
7 Gearlever pivot pin
8 Gearlever base member
9 Bowden cable end block
10 Gearlever sleeve engaging the lever pivot member shoulder
11 Lower gearlever
12 Tension spring
13 Pivot member tension spring
14 Transverse shaft special nut
15 Locking nut
16 Rubber bush for vibration damping
17 Rubber bush for vibration damping
18 Upper gearlever
19 Reverse inhibit 'finger sleeve'
20 Bowden cable collar
21 Compression spring
22 Gearlever knob

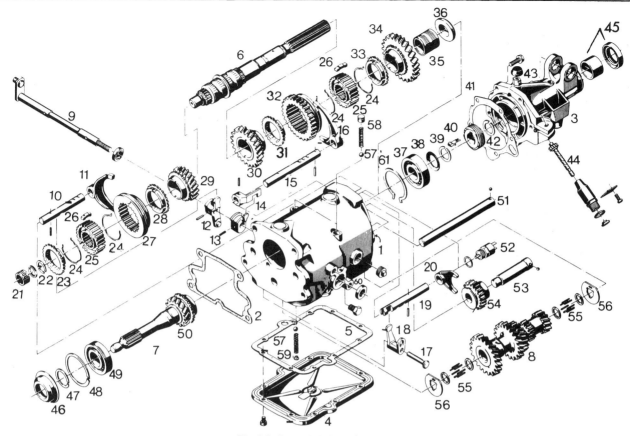

**Fig. 6.2. Exploded view of manual gearbox**

| | | | |
|---|---|---|---|
| 1 | Gearbox main casing | 18 | Reverse gear relay lever |
| 2 | Front gasket | 19 | Reverse gear selector shaft |
| 3 | Gearbox rear extension | 20 | Reverse gear selector fork |
| 4 | Gearbox base plate | 21 | Forward needle roller bearing |

1  Gearbox main casing
2  Front gasket
3  Gearbox rear extension
4  Gearbox base plate
5  Plate gasket
6  Gearbox mainshaft
7  Gearbox input shaft
8  Layshaft
9  Selector transverse shaft
10  4th/3rd gear selector fork shaft
11  4th/3rd gear selector fork
12  Transverse shaft relay lever - 3rd/4th gears
13  Transverse shaft relay lever - 1st/2nd and reverse gears
14  1st/2nd gear selector shaft dog
15  1st/2nd gear selector shaft
16  1st/2nd gear selector fork
17  Reverse gear relay lever pivot

18  Reverse gear relay lever
19  Reverse gear selector shaft
20  Reverse gear selector fork
21  Forward needle roller bearing on mainshaft
22  4th/3rd synchromesh retaining circlip
23  4th gear synchronising loose cone
24  Synchromesh dog retaining spring
25  4th/3rd synchromesh hub
26  Synchronising ring locating key
27  4th/3rd synchromesh ring
28  3rd gear synchromesh loose cone
29  3rd gear on mainshaft
30  2nd gear on mainshaft
31  2nd gear synchromesh loose cone

32  1st/2nd synchromesh selector ring, with reverse gear
33  1st gear synchromesh loose cone
34  1st gear on the mainshaft
35  Mainshaft bearing sleeves
36  Bevelled spacer
37  Mainshaft centre bearing
38  Belvil washer
39  Mainshaft bearing retaining circlip
40  Speedometer drive gear
41  Rear extension gasket
42  Mainshaft circlip
43  Oil breather cap
44  Speedometer drive
45  Rear extension bushing and oil seal
46  Input shaft oil seal

47  Input shaft bearing retaining circlip
48  Bearing outer circlip
49  Input shaft bearing
50  Layshaft drive gear on the input shaft
51  Layshaft centre bearing shaft
52  Reverse light switch
53  Reverse idler gear shaft
54  Reverse idler gear
55  Layshaft needle roller bearing
56  Layshaft end bearing pads
57  Gear selector shaft locking ball and spring
59  Spring end cap
60  Transverse shaft oil seal
61  Mainshaft bearing retaining circlip

least; the gearbox is a heavy assembly and a trifle unwieldy.

2   Raise the car so that there is approximately a 2 ft high space underneath the engine and gearbox region. Put chassis stands underneath the front of the car and chock the rear wheels. It is essential to ensure that the car is safe in its raised position because when working underneath it, the efforts made to loosen bolts and remove the gearbox could easily topple an inadequately supported vehicle. Drain the gearbox oil and disconnect the battery.

3   The sequence to be followed for gearbox removal is as follows:

  *i) Remove the gearshift lever and protective rubber boots.*
  *ii) Remove the forward section of the propeller shaft.*
  *iii) Remove the speedometer cable reversing light switch and clutch actuating cable.*
  *iv) Remove the starter motor, disconnect the exhaust and then undo the nuts/bolts securing the clutch housing to the engine block. Alternatively the gearbox may be unbolted from the rear of the clutch housing, and the clutch housing removed from the engine seperately.*

  *v) Lift gearbox from the engine, lower it to the ground and pull from underneath the car.*

4   *Gearshift lever removal:* It will be necessary to first remove the centre console moulding. This is retained by four screws concealed beneath plastic caps (Fig. 6.3). After removing the caps and screws, lift the console forward over the handbrake lever and withdraw it from the car.

5   Slide the upper gearlever boot up the lever and then pull the lower boot away from the transmission housing to expose the gearlever linkage (photo).

6   Unhook the small spring from the end of the lever and then remove the spring 'C' ring from the end of the cotter pin on which the gearshift lever pivots. Remove the cotter pin and lift out the gearlever.

7   From beneath the car, unbutton the lower rubber boot from around the gearlever pivot mechanism.

8   *Propeller shaft forward section:* Chapter 7 details all aspects of the propeller shaft removal, refitting and maintenance; the removal of the forward shaft involves the undoing of the coupling bolts which retain the rear universal joint on the forward propeller shaft to the yoke on

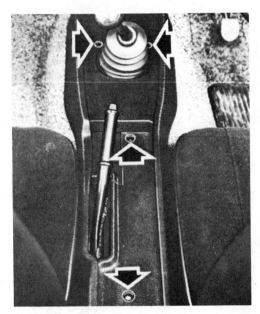

**Fig. 6.3. Location of centre console securing screws (Sec. 2)**

2.5 Removing the gearlever

the forward end of the rear shaft. It is necessary to mark the flanges so that they can be reassembled into exactly the same position.

9   Once the rear spider is detached from the rear propeller shaft yoke the forward shaft can then be moved slightly forwards, the rear end lowered clear of the car and then the whole lifted rearwards out of the gearbox rear extension. The thrust spring in the gearbox rear extension should be extracted and stored with the propeller shaft.

10  *Speedometer cable, stoplight switch and clutch cable:* At this point it is only necessary to detach the cable and sleeve and the electrical leads respectively. Sections 9 and 10 of this Chapter give full details of the complete assemblies and their maintenance.

11  The cable and sleeve is retained by a single knurled nut; once this nut has been undone the cable and sleeve can be detached from the gearbox. The clutch cable removal is detailed in Chapter 5. It involves the unhooking of the cable return spring from the actuating arm projecting out of the bellhousing and then ideally the relaxing of the cable by screwing the clutch actuating arm pivot bolt out of the bellhousing. Unfortunately the pivot bolt is difficult to get at, and therefore it may be necessary to use force to pull the cable from the eye of the actuating lever. The cable and sleeve can then be detached from the bellhousing.

12  *Starter motor, exhaust and clutch bellhousing attachments:* It will be necessary to remove the negative earthing connector on the battery before the starter is removed.

Once the battery has been disconnected, the leads connected to the starter motor assembly may be detached.

13  The nuts and bolts retaining the starter to the cylinder block flange and clutch bellhousing should be undone and the starter lifted clear.

14  Support the weight of the engine/gearbox assembly by placing a jack and flat wooden block beneath the sump.

15  Proceed to undo the nuts and bolts securing the clutch bellhousing to the engine, then disconnect the exhaust pipe at the manifold.

16  Having removed all the nuts and bolts securing the gearbox and clutch bellhousing to the engine, and having supported the engine beneath the sump, the bolts securing the gearbox rear support cross-member to the car bodyshell may now be slowly removed. At the same time it will be as well to place another jack underneath the gearbox to support it before its removal.

17  Once all attachments to the car have been removed the gearbox should be tugged rearwards first so that the gearbox input shaft can disengage the clutch unit, the bellhousing and the positioning spigots on the cylinder block.

18  The gearbox should be tilted or lowered until it has been completely separated from the engine block, and in particular the clutch unit on the flywheel.

19  *Replacement of the gearbox:* As usual, replacement follows the

reversal of the removal procedure. The sequence is as follows:

20  Lift the gearbox up so that it is aligned with the engine, and then move it forward to offer the gearbox input shaft into the clutch and flywheel.

**Do not use** force to engage the input shaft with the clutch, if necessary, turn the input shaft a little so that the splines on the shaft may be in a better position to engage the clutch.

21  The clutch is a delicate mechanism and it can be damaged by an incorrectly aligned gearbox input shaft.

22  Once the engine and gearbox units have been joined, refit the rear gearbox support crossmember and then the starter motor and exhaust.

23  Continue by refitting the clutch cable, speedometer cable and reversing light switch leads.

24  Recouple the propeller shaft and refit the gearshift lever together with the centre console.

## 3   Gearbox (manual) - dismantling

1   As with other units on the car such as the differential and engine it is possible to obtain complete reconditioned gearboxes for 'transplant' into your vehicle. This course of action should be considered, particularly when it is known that the old box has been used for more than 60,000 miles (96,000 km), since it would be uneconomic in time and probably spare parts, to dismantle and repair the gearbox yourself.

2   Assuming that the decision has been made to dismantle the box for general overhaul, or to replace a component known to be broken or worn - proceed as follows:

3   Begin by cleaning the exterior of the gearbox throughly using a solvent such as paraffin or 'Gunk'. After the solvent has been applied and allowed to stand for a time, a vigorous jet of water will wash off the solvent together with the oil and dirt. Finally wipe the unit dry with a non-fluffy rag.

4   The method for dismantling the gearbox is as follows:

i)      Drain the oil from the gearbox.
ii)     Remove the clutch actuating lever and thrust race.
iii)    Remove the clutch bellhousing.
iv)     Remove the gearshift rods and levers.
v)      Remove the base of the box.
vi)     Remove the speedometer drive.
vii)    Remove the layshaft.
viii)   Remove the gear selector forks and shafts.
ix)     Remove reverse idle gear.
x)      Extract the mainshaft.
xi)     Extract the input shaft.

5   The dismantling of the mainshaft and input shaft, is described in detail in Sections 5 and 6, of this Chapter.

6   After draining the oil from the gearbox, remove the clutch actuating

lever, as follows: Unscrew the lever pivot bolt lock nut and then screw the bolt into the bellhousing. It will be necessary to screw the bolt completely out of the housing before the actuating lever and thrust race can be lifted from the sleeve over the gearbox input shaft.

7 Once the clutch actuating lever has been removed, the bellhousing may be separated from the gearbox. Four bolts hold the two units together. Remove the old gasket.

8 *Removal of gearshift levers and rods:* Begin by removing the spring action on the pivot member in the mechanism (photo). Remove the circlip retaining the slider in the bush bore and then remove the clevis pin on which the left-hand lever pivots. Push the slider out of the bush bore (photo). Disengage the lever from the end of the selector shaft which runs transversely through the gearbox.

9 Clevis pins retain the right-hand rod to the selector shaft arm and gearshift mechanism. Once the pins have been removed the rod can be lifted clear.

10 *Removal of base of gearbox:* Undo and remove the ten bolts which secure the base to the gearbox casing. Lift away the base plate and its gasket. Recover the gear selector shaft locking balls and springs that were retained in their bores in the gearbox casing by the base plate (photo).

11 *Removal of the speedometer drive:* The unit is retained in the rear extension of the box by a plate which engages a slot in the exterior of the drive unit. Undo and remove the single bolt securing this plate to the gearbox, then withdraw it from the slot and finally pull the drive unit from the rear extension (photo).

12 *Removal of layshaft:* Undo and remove the bolts securing the gearbox rear extension to the main casing, and then rotate the extension until the end of the layshaft locating shaft is exposed.

13 With a soft metal drift tap the centre shaft rearwards out of the gearbox and layshaft (photo).

14 The layshaft can now be lifted from the gearbox and the end bearings and layshaft needle bearings recovered. The single ball bearing in the centre bearing shaft should also be recovered.

15 *Removal of the gear selector forks and shafts:* Begin by removing the pivot pin for the reverse gear selector relay lever. Use a soft metal

drift to drive the pin out of the casing into the gearbox (photo).

Then remove the pin and lever from the gearbox assembly.

16 Turn the gearbox the right way up and knock out the two plugs which retain another pair of selector shaft locking balls and the thrust springs. Sharp blows onto the side of the plug should release them (photo).

17 Now turn the transverse shaft through nearly 90º so that the inner arm is horizontal. Then drive out the spring pin, which retains this arm onto the transverse shaft, with a square face drift. It is unwise to use a pointed drift because it will tend to pass into the spring pin and hinder its removal.

18 Once the pins have been removed the transverse shaft may be pulled from the gearbox and the two relay levers recovered (photo).

19 Drift out the spring pin which secures the reverse gear selector fork onto the selector shaft, then unscrew the reverse light switch and extract the reverse gear selector shaft, and remove the selector fork from the reverse idle gear.

20 Using a soft metal drift, drive the shaft on which the reverse idle gear runs out of the bores in the gearbox (photo). Recover the reverse idler gear. Remember that it will be necessary to turn the rear gearbox extension into a position where it is possible for the reverse gear shaft to pass out of the gearbox.

21 With the same square ended drift as before, drive the other spring pins which secure the 1st/2nd and 3rd/4th gear selector forks on their respective shafts. Once all levers and forks have been released from the two selector shafts running down each side of the gearbox, they too can be extracted from the forward end of the box (photo).

22 *Extract the mainshaft:* Once the selector forks and shafts have been removed, a sharp tug on the rear extension housing should be all that is required to separate the mainshaft assembly from the gearbox. Be careful to recover all the rollers and parts to the bearing on the forward end of the mainshaft (photo).

23 *Extract the gearbox input shaft:* This shaft assembly should also only require a sharp tug to release it from the gearbox casing.

24 The dismantling of the mainshaft and input shaft assemblies is detailed in Sections 5 and 6, of this Chapter.

3.8a The pivot spring being removed

3.8b Withdrawing the slider shaft

3.10 Lifting off the gearbox baseplate

3.11 Speedometer drive removal

3.13 Removing the layshaft

3.15 Tapping out the reverse gear lever pivot pin

3.16 The plug on the top of the gearbox retains the selector shaft locking ball and spring

Fig. 6.4. Transverse shaft selector fork spring pins (Sec. 3)

3.18 Removal of transverse selector shaft

Fig. 6.5. Longitudinal selector shaft spring pins (Sec. 3)

3.20 Removing the reverse gear idler shaft

3.21 Withdrawing the selector fork shafts

3.22 Removal of mainshaft assembly from gearbox

### 4 Gearbox (manual) - examination and renovation of components

1 The gearbox has been stripped, presumably because of wear or malfunction, possibly excessive noise, ineffective synchromesh or failure to stay in a selected gear. The cause of most gearbox ailments is failure of the ball bearings on the input or mainshaft and wear of the synchronising system (cones and dogs). The nose of the mainshaft which runs in the needle roller bearing in the input shaft is also subject to wear. This can prove very expensive as the mainshaft would need replacement and this represents about 20% of the total cost of a new gearbox.

2 Examine the teeth of all gears for signs of uneven or excessive wear and, of course, chipping. If a gear on the mainshaft requires replacement, check that the corresponding laygear is not equally damaged. If it is the whole laygear may need replacing also.

3 All gears should be a good running fit on the shaft with no signs of rocking. The hubs should not be a sloppy fit on the springs.

4 Selector forks should be examined for signs of wear or ridging on the faces which are in contact with the operating sleeve.

5 Check for wear on the selector rod and interlock spool.

6 The ball bearings may not be obviously worn but if one has gone to the trouble of dismantling the gearbox it would be short sighted not to renew them. The same applies to the four synchronizer rings although for these the mainshaft has to be completely dismantled for the new ones to be fitted.

7 The input shaft bearing retainer is fitted with an oil seal and this should be removed if there are signs that oil has leaked past it into the clutch housing, or, of course, if it is obviously damaged. The rear extension has an oil seal at the rear as well as a ball bearing race. If either has worn or oil has leaked past the seal the parts should be renewed.

8 Before finally deciding to dismantle the mainshaft and replace parts it is advisable to make enquiries regarding the availability of parts and their cost. It may still be worth considering an exchange gearbox even at this stage. You should reassemble it before exchange.

### 5 Input shaft (manual gearbox) - dismantling and reassembly

1 Place the input shaft in a vice, splined end upwards, and with a pair of circlip pliers, remove the circlip which retains the ball bearing in place. Lift away the spacer.

2 With the bearing resting on the top of the open jaws of the vice, and splined end upwards, tap the shaft through the bearing with a soft faced hammer.

3 Note that the offset circlip groove in the outer track of the bearing is towards the front of the input shaft.

4 Lift away the oil slinger.

5 Remove the caged needle roller bearing from the centre of the rear of the input shaft - if it is still in place.

6 Remove the circlip from the old bearing and transfer it to the new bearing.

7 Assembly of the shaft follows the reversal of dismantling as usual. Replace the oil filter and with the aid of a block of wood and vice, tap and slide the bearing onto the shaft, ensuring that it is the correct way

round and tap into place with a soft faced hammer.

8 Finally refit the spacer and bearing retaining circlip.

### 6 Mainshaft (manual gearbox) - dismantling and reassembly

1 Remove the needle roller bearing on the front end of the mainshaft if it is still in place, and then proceed to remove the circlips between the spline and speedometer drive, and at the front end of the shaft (photo).

2 Next to be removed is the nylon speedometer drivegear. It is retained by a spring steel clip which needs to be depressed to release the gear and permit its removal (photo).

3 Once the speedometer gear is clear, the circlip holding the centre mainshaft bearing in place on the shaft should be removed.

4 Hold the first speed gear wheel in and tap the shaft out of the bearing and gear with a soft faced hammer (photo).

5 The third gear wheel and 3rd/4th synchronising mechanism can be removed with the aid of a hub/wheel puller. The puller should act on the gearwheel and the forward end of the mainshaft (photo).

6 All that remains now is to remove the end gear wheel, reverse gear and the 1st/2nd synchroniser assembly from the mainshaft. These must be driven to the rear end of the mainshaft.

7 It takes considerable effort to remove this last gear assembly from the mainshaft using a stout tubular drift acting on the front side of the 2nd gear wheel. Note there is a shoulder preventing the movement of the 2nd gear wheel towards the forward end of the mainshaft (photo).

8 The sleeve on which the 1st gear wheel runs is removed with the 2nd gear wheel, reverse and 1st/2nd gear synchroniser assembly (photo).

9 *Reassembly:* The procedure is as usual the reverse of the dismantling procedure, but there are several points to watch as the mainshaft is reassembled.

10 When the end gear, reverse and 1st/2nd gear synchroniser is being slid into position, the sleeve on which the 1st gear runs must follow. This sleeve is an interference fit on the mainshaft when cold, but it can be slid into position quite easily if heated to only between 120 and 150ºC (248 and 302ºF).

11 *Synchronisers:* If the synchronisers have been dismantled or come apart during the dismantling of the mainshaft, their reassembly should be conducted as follows:

12 Take the synchroniser hub and position the two springs so that the turned ends project into the same key slot (Fig. 6.6). Note that the springs should run in opposite directions.

13 The three keys should be put in their slots in the synchroniser hub, so that the arrows embossed on the key point to the shifter fork groove in the synchroniser ring (Fig. 6.7). The key which has been hollowed out should be located in the hub slot so that the spring turned ends project into the key (Fig. 6.6).).

14 The loose synchroniser cones fit between the fixed cone on the gear wheel and the synchroniser hub.

15 Reassembly sequence for mainshaft:

   *i)   Move the 2nd gear and 1st/2nd synchroniser assembly onto the mainshaft.*

   *ii)   Warm the 1st gear sleeve to between 120 and 150ºC (248 and 302ºF) and slide into position behind the 2nd gear*

6.1 Removal of circlip from front of mainshaft

6.2 Removing speedometer drive circlip

6.4 Removing mainshaft bearing and first gear

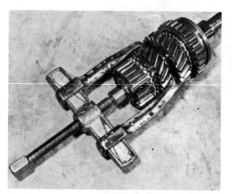

6.5 Using a hub puller to remove the third gear

6.7 Removing the second gear from the mainshaft

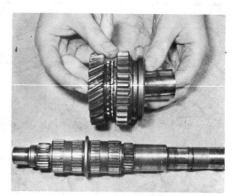

6.8 The second gear, 1st/2nd and reverse gear synchroniser and first gear sleeve.

Fig. 6.6. Location of synchroniser springs (Sec. 6)

Fig. 6.7. Correct location of synchroniser hub keys (Sec. 6)

6.15ii Refitting the mainshaft sleeve

6.15iii Refitting 3rd gear and synchro-cone

6.15iv 3rd/4th gear synchro-hub

and 1st/2nd synchroniser (photo).

iii)   *Move the 3rd gear and synchroniser cone into position onto the front of the mainshaft (photo).*

iv)   *Mount the 3rd/4th synchroniser assembly into position on the front of the mainshaft (photo).*

v)   *Retain the 3rd gear and 3rd/4th synchroniser on the mainshaft with a circlip.*

vi)   *Move the 1st gear and loose cone into position from the rear end of the mainshaft (photo).*

vii)   *Fit the bevelled spacer behind the 1st gear wheel and then move the large circlip which eventually locates the mainshaft in the gearbox rear extension (photo).*

viii)   *Slide the mainshaft centre bearing into position and*

retain with the Belville washer and circlip (photos).

ix)   *Refit the speedometer drive wheel onto the mainshaft. Make sure that the retaining clip is located in the hole in the mainshaft and is the correct way round (photo).*

x)   *Put the last circlip into position between the speed-ometer drive and rear mainshaft splines.*

xi)   *Examine the oil seal in the rear gearbox extension, and if it is not in virtually new condition, renew the seal.*

xii)   *Offer the assembled mainshaft into the rear gearbox extension. The mainshaft is retained in the extension by a large circlip which holds the centre bearing in position in the extension. The mainshaft assembly is now complete (photo).*

6.15vi 1st gear and cones being refitted

6.15vii Refitting bevelled spacer and large circlip

6.15viiia Refitting mainshaft bearing and washer

6.15viiib Securing mainshaft bearing with circlip

6.15ix Refitting speedometer drive

6.15xii Inserting mainshaft into the rear gearbox extension

7.1 Installing the mainshaft into gearbox casing

7.5 Refitting the 1st/2nd gear selector fork and shaft

7.7 Tapping in the spring pins securing the selector forks to their shafts

## 7  Gearbox (manual) - reassembly

1   The reassembly commences with the mounting of the mainshaft assembly into the gearbox main casing. Use a new gasket and stick it onto the rear extension with some medium grease. It will be convenient at this point to screw in a couple of bolts lightly, just to hold the shaft assembly in position whilst the rest of the gearbox is reassembled (photo).

2   Assemble the needle roller bearing onto the forward end of the mainshaft and liberally coat with gearbox oil.

3   Move the input shaft assembly into position in the gearbox.

4   Next mount the 3rd/4th gear selector fork onto the groove in the synchroniser ring, and then slide the shaft on which it is mounted, into position.

5   Mount the 1st/2nd gear selector fork into position in the groove in the synchroniser ring. Slide the shaft onto which it is mounted, into position (photo).

6   Now slide the reverse gear selector fork shaft into position together with the selector fork. Then undo the couple of bolts holding the rear extension in position, and rotate the extension so that the reverse idler gear shaft can be inserted into the gearbox. Mount the idler gear on the shaft having engaged it with the selector fork.

7   The spring pins which retain the selector forks onto their shafts should be driven into position now. Use a square ended drift to drive the pins into position; a pointed drift will work into the pin and prevent its full insertion (photo). Refer to Figs. 6.8 and 6.9 and check the positions of the forks and shafts.

8   Once the selector forks and shafts are in position, the transverse selector shaft should be inserted into the gearbox. The relay levers mounted on the shaft are retained by spiral pins (photo).

9   Turn the transverse shaft into its correct position with the relay lever vertical inside the box. Next mount the reverse gear selection relay lever on its pivot pin which needs to be driven into the side of the box (photo). Return the shaft to its usual position and install the reverse gear relay lever and pivot pin (Fig. 6.10).

7.8 Refitting the selector relay levers to the transverse shaft

7.9 Refitting the reverse selector relay lever

7.10a Inserting the selector shaft locking bolt and spring

7.10b Refitting retaining plug

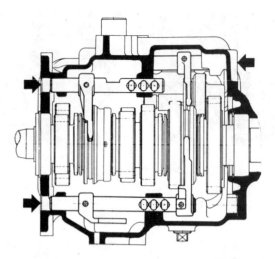

Fig. 6.8. Installation of the selector shafts (Sec. 7)

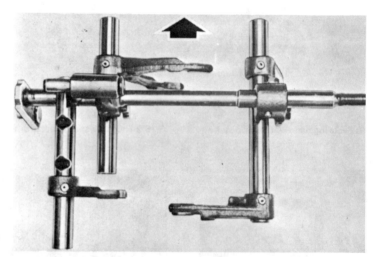

Fig. 6.9. Correct layout of the selector forks and shafts (Sec. 7)

Fig. 6.10. Installing the reverse gear selector lever (dimension 'A' is 0.004 - 0.012 inches/0.10 - 0.30 mm)

10 It is now time for the selector shaft locking balls to be inserted into position. Turn the gearbox the right way up, and drop the balls and their springs into the appropriate bores. The lock balls and springs are retained by plugs which have to be driven into the bores (photos).
11 The layshaft should be mounted into the gearbox next. Begin by gathering the shaft, its end bearings and its needle roller bearings (photo).
12 Put the layshaft bearing shaft into the layshaft, then push the needle bearing washer into position (photo).
13 Pack the needles around the shaft into the counter bore in the layshaft (photo).
14 Put the second bearing washer into position on the outer end of the needle roller bearing.
15 Extract the centre bearing shaft, and then position the two end bearing pads onto the gearbox casing (photo). Insert the layshaft and slide the centre bearing shaft through the gearbox and layshaft. The shaft must be inserted from the rear end of the box and the rear

extension will need to be rotated again to allow the shaft to pass into the gearbox. Ensure that the ball which locks the bearing shaft in position is fitted in the bearing shaft (photo).
16 Now the rear extension can be bolted permanently in position. Tighten the bolts to their correct torque.
17 Turn your attention to the clutch bellhousing; insert the input shaft oil seal into the counter bore in the bellhousing gearbox joint faces with a little medium grease (photo).
18 Bolt the gearbox onto the bellhousing. Take care when inserting the input shaft through the housing; the seal is delicate.
19 Insert the last selector fork shaft locking ball and the springs into the bore in the sides of the gearbox casing (photos).
20 Refit the gearbox base plate. Use a little medium grease to stick the new gasket in position whilst the plate is being refitted (photo).
21 Refit the speedometer drive unit and screw the reversing light switch into position (photos).
22 Next fit the gearshift lever which connects the box transverse shaft

7.11 Layshaft gear cluster and components

7.12 Refitting the needle roller washer into layshaft

7.13 Packing the needle rollers around the shaft

7.15a Positioning the layshaft thrust washers

7.15b Refitting layshaft gearcluster shaft

7.17 Installing the input shaft seal

7.19a Inserting the selector shaft ball and spring

7.19b Refitting the spring end caps

7.20 Refitting the gearbox baseplate

7.21a Installing the speedometer drive

7.21b Refitting the reversing light switch

7.22 Location of lever on the transverse
selector shaft

7.25 Split pin retaining RH lever to transverse
selector shaft

7.26 Clutch actuating lever and bearing
assembled in the clutch bellhousing

to the slider in the gearlever pivot. The forked end of the lever fits
over a special nut which is screwed onto the end of the transverse
shaft (photo).
23 The special nut is locked with another nut. The side lever pivots
on a clevis pin which fits in lugs moulded in the rear gearbox extension.
24 Another clevis pin retains the lever in the slider. All clevis pins are
retained with a washer and split pin.
25 The other side gearshift lever which acts to rotate the transverse
rod in the gearbox, should be fitted now. It too is retained by clevis
pins (photo). Adjust the mechanism as directed in Section 8, of this
Chapter.
26 The final items to be assembled before the gearbox is ready to be
refitted to the car are the clutch actuating lever and thrust bearing.
Mount the thrust bearing and pivot bolt onto the lever and then offer
the group into the bellhousing. The thrust bearing should pass over
the gearbox input shaft sleeve. The pivot bolt should be screwed into
the housing to draw the lever into its operating position (photo).

## 8  Gearshift mechanism and gearlever (manual gearbox) - general

1   This Section describes the gearshift mechanism, outside the gearbox,
and the gearlever itself which incorporates a bowden cable and interlock
device used when selecting reverse gear.
2   Beginning with the shift mechanism exterior to the box: this comprises two members which act on the box transverse shaft to move it
rotationally and axially.
3   The two members are connected to the gearlever pivot fitting. The
pivot fitting rotates about a slider; this slider, attached to the left-hand
lever member transmits the sideways movement of the gearlever to the
transverse shaft in the box.
4   The pivot fitting also extends downwards to join the right-hand rod
to transmit fore-aft movement of the gearlever as rotational movement
of the transverse shaft in the box (photo).
5   Wear in the exterior mechanism is simply detected and repaired.
Clevis pins are easily removed. The only item which will necessitate
the removal of the gearbox if it needs to be renewed is the bush in

which the slider moves and on which the gearlever pivot member
pivots.
6   To remove the pivot bushing, remove the snap-ring and drive the
bush out of the rear extension bores from the snap-ring side (photo).
7   The bushing needs to be removed to free the gearlever pivot
member if that needs renewal for some reason.
8   When reassembling the left-hand side lever onto the gearbox it is
necessary to ensure the correct positioning of the lever on the transverse shaft.
9   Temporarily mount the gearlever in the pivot member. Move to
engage 2nd gear; once engaged, turn the special nut on the end of the
transverse shaft to bring the gearlever shoulder against the stop on the
pivot member (Fig. 6.11).
10  Then turn the special nut back by ¼ turn and lock in position with
the lock nut. Check the operation of the gearshift mechanism again.
11  *Gearlever:* The gearlever incorporates a mechanism which prevents
reverse gear being selected accidentally. A 'finger sleeve' is attached to
a bowden cable which at its lower end is connected to a plunger. The
plunger prevents the lever from passing into the 'reverse position' until
the 'finger sleeve' is raised and the plunger withdrawn.
12  If difficulty is experienced in selecting reverse because the lever
will not pass into the correct position, it is likely that the cable is
either broken completely or partly. Either way the working of this
mechanism should be checked before proceeding to investigate the
main gearbox.
13  To inspect and dismantle the gearlever begin by removing the
lever. Undo the screws (3 or 4 depending on centre console pattern)
which secure the centre console to the transmission tunnel and then
remove the console and gearshift mechanism protective rubber boots.
The lower boot is buttoned around the mechanism, and is reached
from underneath the car.
14  Remove the clevis pin on which the gearlever pivots and remove
the tension spring acting on the lever sleeve.
15  Once the lever is removed, pull the knob off and unscrew the two
grub screws which retain the bowden cable in the 'finger sleeve' and
collar. Note that the knob cannot be refitted and a new one must be
obtained.

8.4 The gearlever pivot assembly

8.6 Snap-ring removed from pivot bushing

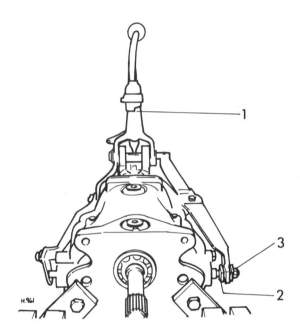

Fig. 6.11. Chearchange mechanism (Sec. 8)

*1 Shoulder stop on the gearlever pivot member*
*2 Special nut which engages the intermediate lever*
*3 Locknut*

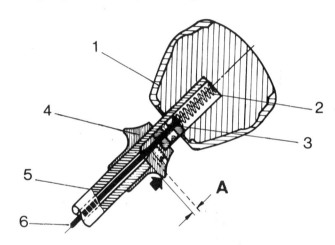

Fig. 6.12. Section through gearchange lever (Sec. 8)

*1 Gear knob*
*2 Compression spring*
*3 Bowden cable collar*
*4 Finger sleeve*
*5 Gearlever*
*6 Bowden cable*
*Dimension 'A' should be 0.040 - 0.080 in (1 - 2 mm)*

16 The lower end of the bowden cable is attached to a cylindrical member which is secured to the outer stop sleeve with a spiral pin. The base of the lever is secured to the gear lever end fitting by another spiral pin.

17 Drive out both spring pins with a square ended drift to release the end fitting and the cable end from the outer 'stop' sleeve.

18 The cable can then be extracted from the base of the lever.

19 Reassembly follows the reversal of removal sequence. The new gearlever knob needs to be heated in boiling water before refitting to the gearlever.

20 *Gearlever rubber damping renovation:* Above the bend of the lever, there is a join which houses rubber bushes that isolate the top of the lever from a lot of gearbox vibration.

21 To renew these bushes, remove the gearlever and then the lever knob. Loosen the screws in the collar and finger sleeve which grip the top of the bowden cable. Note that the old knob cannot be re-used once removed, and a new one must be used on assembly.

22 Remove the wire clip in the bottom end of the upper lever and then pull the top of the lever from the lower part. The two rubber bushes are then exposed and can be renewed.

23 Reassembly follows the reversal of dismantling - remember to heat the new knob in boiling water so that it can be pushed onto the top of the lever.

## 9 Speedometer cable - general

1 The speedometer cable is attached to the drive fitting on the gearbox rear extension by a knurled nut. Undo the nut, then the cable and sleeve can be removed from the drive.

2 The drive unit is secured in the rear extension by a single plate and bolt, which engages in a slot in the side of the drive.

3 The cable is retained in the speedometer casing by a spring clip which should be pressed down to release the cable. It might be necessary to remove the right lower instrument panel to gain access (Chapter 13, Section 16).

## 10 Reversing light switch (manual gearbox) - general

1 The switch screws into the rear of the main box and is actuated by the movement of the reverse gear selector shaft.

2 Pull the electrical lead and simply unscrew the switch. The switch cannot be repaired, therefore renewal is the only action practicable if the existing switch is deemed faulty.

**11 Fault diagnosis - manual gearbox**

| Symptom | Reason/s | Remedy |
| --- | --- | --- |
| Weak or ineffective synchromesh | Synchronising cones worn, split or damaged | Dismantle and overhaul gearbox. Fit new gear wheels and synchronising cones. |
| | Synchromesh dogs worn, or damaged | Dismantle and overhaul gearbox. Fit new synchromesh unit. |
| Jumps out of gear | Broken gearchange fork rod spring | Dismantle and replace spring. |
| | Gearbox coupling dogs badly worn | Dismantle gearbox. Fit new coupling dogs. |
| | Selector fork rod groove badly worn | Fit new selector fork rod. |
| Excessive noise | Incorrect grade of oil in gearbox or oil level too low | Drain, refill, or top up gearbox with correct grade of oil. |
| | Gearteeth excessively worn or damaged | Dismantle and overhaul gearbox. Renew gear wheels. |
| | Laygear thrust washers worn allowing excessive end play | Dismantle and overhaul gearbox. Renew thrust washers. |
| Difficulty in engaging gears | Clutch pedal adjustment incorrect | Adjust clutch pedal correctly. |

**12 Automatic transmission - general**

The automatic transmission fitted is manufactured by General Motors. There are differences in detail between units fitted to 1.6 litre and 1.9 litre cars that accommodate the different amount of power which these engines develop.

The transmission comprises two basic systems: the torque converter and a torque/speed responsive hydraulically operated epicyclic gearbox.

The gearbox provides three forward speeds and one reverse.

Due to the complexity and fine engineering of an automatic transmission, if the performance is not up to standard or an overhaul is necessary, the work should be entrusted to a G.M. main dealer who will have the equipment necessary for accurate fault diagnosis and rectification.

Therefore the following Sections contain solely general and servicing information.

**13 Fluid level and maintenance (automatic transmission)**

1  G.M. recommend the use of DEXRON oil (Duckhams D-Matic) in the automatic transmission for both the torque converter and gearbox.
2  Maintenance of the automatic transmission involves the following

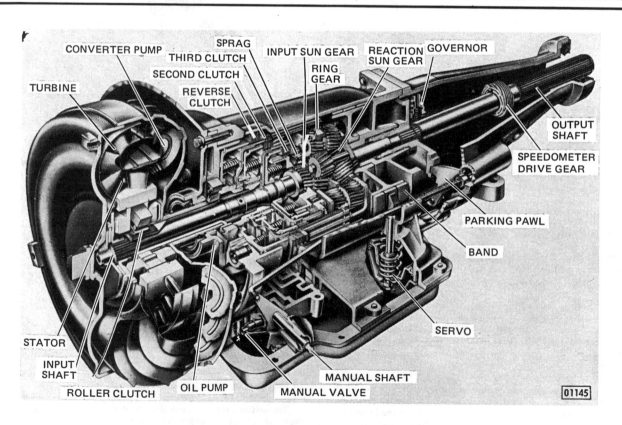

Fig. 6.13. General view of the automatic transmission

tasks:

i)   *Every engine oil change, check the level of oil in the transmission oil reservoir.*

ii)  *Every 24,000 miles (40,000km) or two years the oil pan should be drained and new oil added to the correct level in the reservoir.*

iii) *If the car has been used in heavy city traffic or used commercially, it is recommended that the oil and strainer be renewed every 12,000 miles (20,000km) or yearly.*

3  *Checking the transmission oil level:* The transmission is designed so that the oil should reach the 'full' mark on the reservoir dipstick when the unit has reached its running temperature of 180°F (82.2°C). This normal running temperature is usually attained after 30 minutes motoring.

4  With the transmission at its normal operating temperature, stop on level ground and move the selector to the 'park' position. Check the level of the oil now, with the engine running. The oil should be up to the 'full' mark. The distance between the 'add' mark and 'full' is 1 Imp. pint (0.56 litre) of oil in the reservoir.

5  If it is only possible to check the level of oil when the unit is cold put the control lever into 'park' and start the engine. Let the engine idle and move the control lever steadily through each position and then back to 'park'. When the oil is cold, the correct level with the engine running, and after the functioning described, is ¼ inch (6.3mm) below the 'add' mark. As usual it is essential for the vehicle to be stood on level ground for these checks.

6  It may be realised now that the extent to which the oil expands between 70 and 180°F (21.1 and 82.2°C) is considerable, enough in fact to take the level of oil from ¼ inch (6.3mm) below the 'add' mark to the 'full' mark on the reservoir dipstick. **Do not overfill** the reservoir.

7  *Draining oil and strainer replacement:* Raise the front of the car onto ramps, or chassis stands; there should be sufficient space underneath the vehicle to gain access to the base of the transmission. A bucket or container to collect about 3 Imp. quarts (3.4 litres) of oil is required.

8  Undo the bolts securing the oil pan to the gearbox, remove the oil pan and gasket and collect the oil.

9  Next remove the strainer and its gasket and discard both. Fit a new strainer and gasket. Tighten the strainer screen bolts to 13 - 15 lb f ft (1.8 to 1.9 kg f m).

10  Clear the oil pan and when dry and clean, refit to the gearbox using a new gasket. The bolts securing the pan to the box should be tightened to between 7 and 10 lb f ft (0.9 and 1.3 kg f m).

11  Lower the car back to the ground and fill the transmission, through the filter tube, with approximately 2 to 3 Imp. quarts (2.2 to 3.4 litres) of transmission fluid.

12  Check the level of oil in the transmission, as described in paragraphs 5 and 6 of this Section.

13  Add oil to ¼ inch (6.3mm) below the 'add' mark on the dipstick - **Do not overfill.**

14  *Filling a dry gearbox and torque converter:* If the gearbox only was renewed or rebuilt up to 3.1 Imp. quarts (3.52 litres) of oil will be required.

15  If the torque converter was renewed as well, 5.3 to 5.5 Imp. quarts (6 to 6.2 litres) of oil will be required.

16  The oil level should be checked as described in paragraphs 5 and 6 of this Section.

## 14 Automatic transmission unit - removal and replacement

### Removal

1  Begin by disconnecting the battery, stow the leads and connections away safely.

2  Next remove the air cleaner, and then undo the transmission to engine bolts down to the level of the starter.

3  Remove the dipstick from the transmission oil filler tube.

4  Now jack-up the car so that there is nearly 2 feet (0.6m) of clear space underneath the transmission. The transmission is removed from beneath the vehicle and so space is required to move the assembly under the car.

5  Undo the oil pan drain plug and collect the oil. Once all the oil has been recovered replace the drain plug.

6  Remove the radiator cowl mounting bolts from the radiator and locate the cowl over the fan blades.

7  Support the engine with a jack raised underneath the sump. Then remove the engine/bellhousing brackets, on both sides of the sump. Disconnect the wiring and remove the starter motor.

8  Next unbolt the cover plate on the bottom of the bellhousing. On some models the cover plate clips into position.

9  Unbolt the exhaust pipe from the manifold. This task can be difficult if suitable tools are not available. Remove the pipe shroud and use a socket spanner with a long extension to reach the bolts in the manifold/pipe joint.

10  Unhook the pipe rubber suspension.

11  Remove the front section of the propeller shaft. Check Chapter 7 for details of this procedure.

12  Disconnect the transmission oil cooler lines. Close the pipes, to prevent spillage of oil or ingress of dirt, with plugs or caps.

13  Detach the front anti-roll bar from the bodyshell, and loosen the attachment bolts at the lower arms on the front suspension. It is necessary to lower the bar to permit the transmission to be lowered from the engine.

14  Place another jack underneath the transmission and then remove the support crossmember.

15  Lower the transmission and engine enough to remove the kickdown cable and modulator vacuum line.

16  Next remove the speedometer cable - as per manual transmission, and the gear selector lever.

17  Mark the flex plate and converter casing so that they may be reassembled into the same position; then undo the bolts which secure the torque converter to the flex plate.

18  Finally undo the last nuts and bolts which retain the bellhousing to the engine block.

Prise the transmission off the engine and lower away.

Keep the rear of the transmission below the front to prevent the converter from falling.

19  If possible arrange to support the converter on the bellhousing with an improvised prop.

### Replacement

20  Raise the transmission assembly into position behind the engine. Rotate the torque converter (if original one still being used) so that the marks made prior to disassembly are aligned. Remove any converter support that has been employed during handling of the transmission (Fig. 6.14).

21  Bolt the converter bellhousing to the engine block, tightening those bolts to the specified torque. Refit the transmission filler tube.

22  Secure the converter to the flex plate and torque the bolts to the

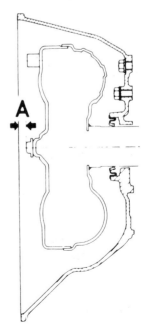

Fig. 6.14. Correct installation of the torque converter in the bellhousing (dimension 'A' is 0.20 to 0.28 inches/0.50 to 0.71 mm). (Sec. 14)

specified torque.

23 Connect the oil cooler lines and the kickdown cable to the transmission. Continue by connecting the gearshift linkage vacuum modulator line and the speedometer cable.

24 Fit the lower starter motor flange bolt and tighten it to the specified torque.

25 Refit the rear transmission support crossmember and then install the forward section of the propeller shaft - check Chapter 7 for details.

26 Refit the brackets which couple the engine block to the bellhousing each side of the sump.

27 Reconnect the exhaust system, and refit the front suspension anti-roll bar. Remember to retighten the bolts securing the bar to the lower arms of the front suspension.

28 Lower the car from the chassis stands and then refit the battery connections, and the bolt to the upper starter motor flange if not already in place.

29 Fill the transmission as directed in the preceding Section.

## 15 Separating the torque converter and gearbox unit (automatic transmission)

1   Remove the automatic transmission from the car as directed in the previous Section; transfer the unit to a clean bench.

2   The converter can be pulled straight off the gearbox input shaft. It contains a large quantity of oil.

3   The two units are joined quite simply by sliding the converter over the gearbox shaft. To ensure the converter has been correctly refitted, ie, the converter hub is meshing with the oil pump gear wheel in the transmission, measure the distance between the converter housing flange and centre spigot as shown in Fig. 6.14. If the measurement taken is not within the specification stated, it is possible that the converter hub is not meshing correctly. Rotate the converter until the gears can be felt to mesh and recheck the clearance.

4   Any further dismantling of the transmission is not recommended.

## 16 Kickdown control cable adjustment (automatic transmission)

1   It is essential, when considering kickdown control cable adjustment, that the accelerator cable is first correctly adjusted (see Section 14, Chapter 3).

2   Fully depress the accelerator pedal and place a 10 mm thick block between the pedal stop on the toe-board and the pedal (Fig. 6.16). Use a heavy object to retain pedal in this position.

3   Referring to Fig. 6.15 release the cable clamp pinch bolt (2) and then pull sleeve (1) through clamp until the cable nipple can be felt against the sleeve in the accelerator shaft bracket.

4   Continue to hold the sleeve in this position and tighten the cable clamp pinch bolt.

5   Remove the object used to hold down the accelerator pedal and retrieve the 10 mm block.

6   Check for correct operation of the carburettor throttle valves by operating the accelerator pedal. Also check that the kickdown operates when the pedal is fully depressed.

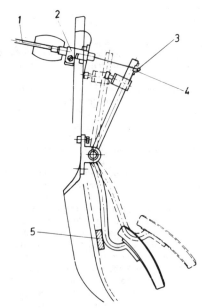

Fig. 6.16 Kickdown cable adjustment components (Sec. 16)

| | |
|---|---|
| 1   Kickdown cable control | 4   Accelerator pedal shaft |
| 2   Cable clamp | sleeve |
| 3   Kickdown cable nipple | 5   10 mm block |

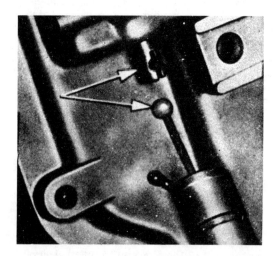

Fig. 6.17. Kickdown inner cable attachment point (Sec. 16)

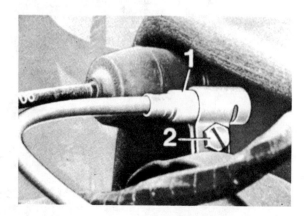

Fig. 6.15 Kickdown cable adjusting sleeve (1) and clamp bolt (2) (Sec. 16)

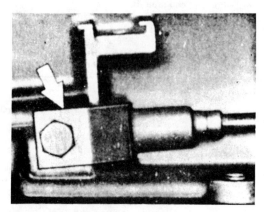

Fig. 6.18. Bracket retaining kickdown cable sleeve to gearbox (Sec. 16)

**17 Gear selector lever assembly (automatic transmission) - removal, replacement and adjustment**

*Gear selector lever assembly — removal and replacement*

1   Begin by prising off, from its rear, the selector lever cover; then, by passing the selector lever through a slot in one of its edges, remove the gear selector sliding plate.

2   To remove the centre console, first release the four retaining screws (Fig. 6.19) and then, by manoeuvring the console to enable the selector lever T-handle to pass through the gear selector slot, lift away the console.

3   Remove the starter inhibitor/reversing light switch by unscrewing it from the lever bracket on the right-hand side of the selector lever, then withdraw the selector indicator lamp socket from the opposite side of the selector lever. It is not considered necessary to disconnect the selector indicator wiring.

4   Raise the front of the car and support on axle stands. From beneath the left-hand side of the gearbox seperate the selector lever extension arm from the intermediate rod by removing the wire clip and clevis pin.

5   Undo and remove the four self-tapping screws that secure the selector lever assembly to the transmission tunnel and withdraw the assembly.

6   The lever pivot bracket is secured to the assembly support by three bolts. There is little point in dismantling the assembly further, but for those interested Fig. 6.21 shows the component parts of the assembly.

7   Refitting is a reversal of the removal procedure noting the following points:

a)   *The working surfaces of the gear selector assembly should be lightly coated with a graphite grease.*

b)   *A bead of plastic sealing compound should be applied to the joint faces of the gear selector assembly case and transmission tunnel before refitting.*

*Gear selector linkage — adjustment*

**Note:** *As this task is carried out beneath the car, observe the safety precautions given earlier in this Section.*

8   Disconnect the forked end of the intermediate rod from the transmission selector lever, noting its fitted position.

9   Move both the gear selector lever and transmission selector lever to position '1'.

10 Adjust the length of the intermediate rod at the forked end to align the two bolt holes of the fork with the single bolt hole of the transmission selector lever.

11 Now lengthen the intermediate rod by a further 4½ turns of the forked end and, without disturbing this adjustment, reconnect the rod to the transmission selector lever and lock the fork in position (Fig. 6.22).

12 By moving the gear selector lever, check for correct engagement of all gear positions and, if necessary, re-adjust the length of the intermediate rod.

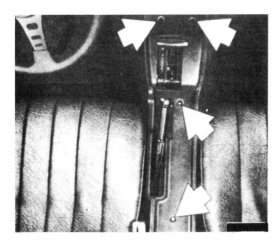

Fig. 6.19. Console retaining screws (automatic transmission). (Sec. 17)

Fig. 6.20. Automatic transmission selector lever retaining screws and inhibit switch 'A' (Sec. 17)

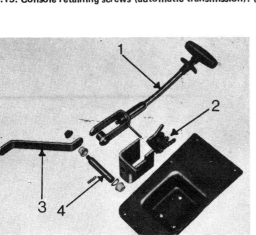

Fig. 6.21. Gear selector lever components (Sec. 17)

1   *Gearlever*
2   *Lever gate*
3   *Lever extension*
4   *Pivot bar*

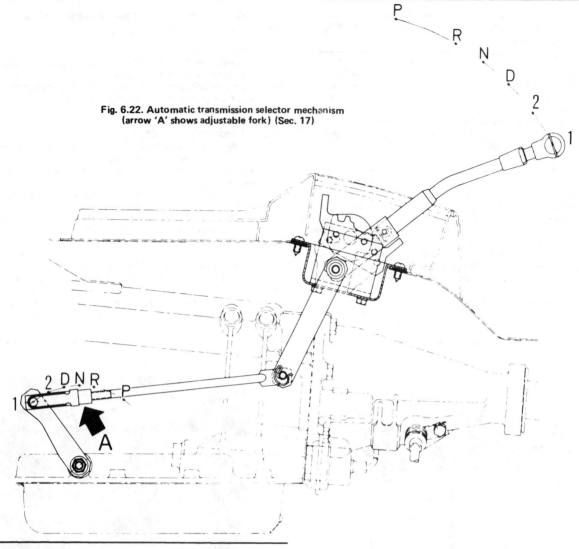

**Fig. 6.22. Automatic transmission selector mechanism (arrow 'A' shows adjustable fork) (Sec. 17)**

## 18 Carburettor throttle linkage (automatic transmission) - dashpot adjustment

1    The adjustment should be carried out with the engine idling - having reached its normal operating temperature, and with the gear selector in the 'N' position.

2    Idle RPM are as follows:

| | | |
|---|---|---|
| 1.6 litre | S Engine | 750 to 800 rpm |
| 1.9 litre | S Engine | 750 to 800 rpm |

3    Loosen the dashpot locknut below the support bracket, and then turn the dashpot so that in the condition described in paragraph 1, the plunger is pushed in by 0.14 inch (3.5mm). Tighten the locknut to maintain the dashpot in the correct position (Fig. 6.23).

## 19 Starter inhibit and reversing light switch (automatic transmission) - general

1    This switch is situated at the pivot of the gear selector lever. It is exposed by removing the central console and is simply bolted onto the lever pivot bracket. The switch is actuated by a spigot near the pivot on the selector lever. The switch is not repairable, and when deemed faulty, it should be replaced.

## 20 Towing - precautions for automatic transmission models

1    There are no particular rules to abide by when using the vehicle for

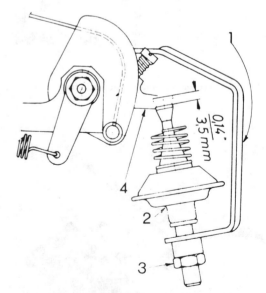

**Fig. 6.23. Accelerator linkage dashpot (Sec. 18)**

| | |
|---|---|
| 1    Dashpot support | 3    Dashpot locknut |
| 2    Dashpot | 4    Throttle lever extension |
| | compression 0.14 inches |
| | (0.35 mm) |

towing - but if the vehicle is **being** towed there are precautions to be taken.

2   If the vehicle is to be towed in any of the three conditions listed below, the forward half of the propeller shaft must be detached from the rear half, and tied securely to one side:

   i)      If towing speeds greater than 35 mph are necessary.
   ii)     The transmission is malfunctioning.
   iii)    If the vehicle is going to be towed for a distance greater than 50 miles (80k m).

## 21  Brake band - adjustment

1   The brake band requires re-adjustment every time the transmission oil is changed.

2   The adjustment is important because, in addition to ensuring the correct amount of play between the brake band and the drum, it also affects the loading of the piston relief spring of the band servo and has a direct influence on the engagement of the third gear clutch.

3   Remove the drain plug from the transmission oil pan and allow the fluid to drain out.

4   Ensure that the surroundings are clean and then remove the oil pan retaining bolts; take off the oil pan and gasket.

5   Remove the bolts from the brake band servo cover and remove the cover.

6   Release the locknut of the brake band adjusting screw.

7   With a 3/16 in hexagon bit, tighten the brake band adjusting screw to the specified torque and then, while holding the adjusting sleeve in a spanner to prevent it from rotating, slacken the adjusting screw five complete revolutions.

8   While still holding the adjusting sleeve with a spanner, tighten the adjusting screw locknut to the specified torque.

9   Clean the mating faces of the brake band servo cover and the transmission casing and, using a new gasket which is absolutely dry, install the cover and tighten the bolts to the specified torque.

10  Clean the mating faces of the oil pan and the transmission casing. Install the oil pan, using a new gasket and tighten the oil pan bolts to the specified torque.

11  Fill the transmission with the correct fluid and check the level as detailed in Section 13.

## 22  Fault diagnosis - automatic transmission

Faults in these units are nearly always the result of low fluid level or incorrect adjustment of the selector linkage or downshift cable. Internal faults should be diagnosed by your G.M. main dealer who has the necessary equipment to carry out the work.

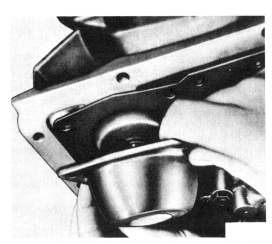

Fig. 6.24. Removing the brake band servo cover (Sec. 21)

Fig. 6.25. Tightening the brake band adjusting screw (Sec. 21)

Fig. 6.26. Tightening the locknut while holding the adjusting sleeve (Sec. 21)

# Chapter 7 Propeller shaft

*For modifications, and information applicable to later models, see Supplement at end of manual*

## Contents

## Specifications

| Description ... ... ... ... ... ... ... ... ... | A two section propeller shaft is used. The forward section comprises a conventional tubular shaft fitted with a universal joint at each end. The rear section is a solid shaft running inside a tubular axle extension. |
|---|---|

### Torque wrench settings

| | lb f ft | kg f m |
|---|---|---|
| Rear shaft flange to centre universal joint - bolt ... ... ... ... | 11 | 1.4 |
| Central joint support beam to bodyshell anchor point - bolt ... ... | 36 | 5 |
| Support block bolt ... ... ... ... ... ... ... | 29 | 4 |
| Central joint support to rubber block ... ... ... ... ... | 15 | 2 |
| Tube rubber block to torque tube ... ... ... ... ... | 15 | 2 |
| Rear shaft - forward end - nut ... ... ... ... ... ... | 87 | 12 |

## 1 General description

The propeller shaft is in two parts: a forward tubular section and a rearward solid section running in a tubular extension of the final drive housing. The forward section is conventional in design, having a universal joint at each end and at the forward end a splined coupling which slides on the gearbox output shaft. The rear solid propeller shaft is connected to the drive pinion shaft by an internal splined sleeve which slides onto the barrel splined fitting on the pinion shaft. The forward end of the shaft runs in a bearing seated in a rubber cushion block. The rear shaft runs in a tubular member which is secured to the final drive casing by four bolts. The forward end of the tubular member rests on two rubber blocks mounted in the propeller shaft central support. The central joint support is in turn supported by a beam which runs transversely across the underside of the car, between anchorages adjacent to those for the rear suspension trailing arms (Fig. 7.2).

## 2 Propeller shaft - removal and refitting

1 Since it is unlikely that both sections of the shaft will need to be removed at the same time, the procedures for the separate removal of those sections follows:

### Forward section propeller shaft (Fig. 7.1)

2 Begin by raising the vehicle onto chassis stands placed underneath the rear jacking points. It is necessary to be able to get comfortably underneath the centre of the car. Remember to chock the front wheels.

3 Then remove the handbrake cable yoke/tension equaliser bracket from the brake rod; then detach the exhaust system from the underside of the car to gain space in the vicinity of the forward propeller shaft.

4 If it is anticipated that the existing shaft will be refitted - mark the rear universal joint spider and rear joint flange (which is attached to the rear propeller shaft) in order to ensure correct alignment when

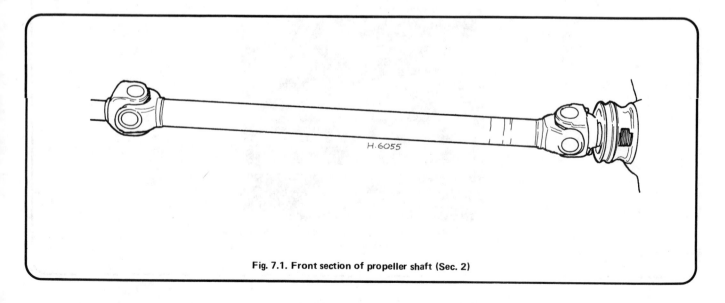

H.6055

Fig. 7.1. Front section of propeller shaft (Sec. 2)

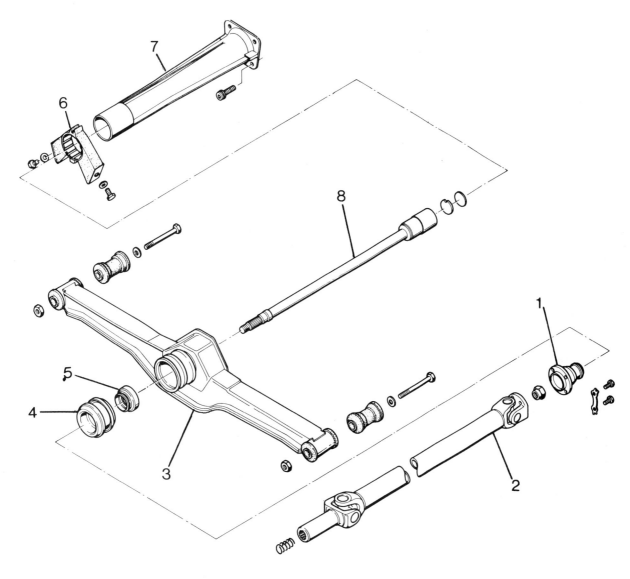

**Fig. 7.2. Exploded view of propeller shaft assembly**

1  Pinion flange
2  Forward propeller shaft (tubular)
3  Crossmember
4  Centre bearing rubber support
5  Centre bearing
6  Extension housing mounting
7  Extension housing
8  Rear propeller shaft (solid)

refitting (photo).
5  Bend back the locking tabs and remove the four bolts.
6  Push the forward propeller shaft slightly forward to permit the rear end to be lowered clear of the central joint support structure.
7  Slide the propeller shaft out of the gearbox rear extension and off its output shaft. Recover the thrust spring from inside the splined coupling on the front of the propeller shaft.
8  It may be necessary to cover or plug the open end of the gearbox rear extension to prevent the ingress of dirt or leakage of gear oil.
9  Refitting the propeller shaft is a reversal of the removal procedure. Make absolutely certain that if any new parts are being used - including nuts and bolts - that they are the correct part with the correct number and are genuine G.M. parts. Coat the forward coupling splines with EP90 gear oil before fitting the propeller shaft.
10  Failure of nuts, bolts and other components on the propeller shaft system could be catastrophic and therefore non-standard parts should not be used.
11  If the existing propeller shaft is being re-used remember to align the rear joint spider and the rear shaft yoke according to the marks made prior to disassembly.

*Rear section propeller shaft*
12  The rear section of the shaft is removed complete with the tubular extension to the final drive housing and the central joint support beam.

13  Begin by raising the vehicle onto chassis stands placed under the rear axle end fittings.
14  Remove the handbrake cable yoke/tension equaliser bracket from the handbrake rod. Detach the return spring from the brake rod.
15  Next detach the exhaust pipes from the underside of the vehicle to give extra access to the forward and rearward sections of the propeller shaft.
16  To ensure correct alignment when reassembling the propeller shaft - mark the rear universal joint spider and the pinion flange splined onto rear shaft.
17  Undo and remove the bolts which secure the spider to the yoke and lift the forward section to one side.
18  Bring a jack underneath the central joint support beam and bring into contact with that beam to apply a little force to the beam. Now the nuts and bolts securing the central beam to the bodyshell anchorages may be undone and removed.
19  Detach the brake hydraulic line support bracket from the tubular extension of the final drive unit (photo).
20  Lower the central joint support beam just a little and then unbolt the tubular extension (torque tube) from the flange on the final drive housing using an M8 size tri-square socket bit (see Fig. 7. 3).
21  The whole rear shaft assembly may now be removed from the underside of the car (Fig. 7.4).

2.4 Rear universal joint

2.19 Location of brake pipe on extension housing

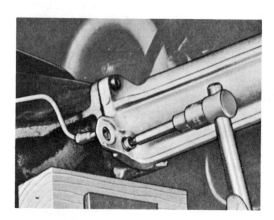

**Fig. 7.3. Removing the extension housing bolts (Sec. 2)**

**Fig. 7.4. Lifting the extension housing away from the car (Sec. 2)**

22 The refitting of the rear section of the propeller shaft is a reversal of the removal sequence described.

23 The comments made in paragraphs 9, 10 and 11 earlier in this Section apply equally to the rear propeller shaft installation.

24 If the brake hydraulic system was disturbed, bleed the rear brakes and in any event check the adjustment of the handbrake. Both tasks are described in Chapter 9 of this manual.

25 Remember to tighten all vital nuts and bolts to the torques specified at the beginning of this Chapter.

## 3 Universal joints - inspection, removal and repair

1 Wear in the needle roller bearings is characterised by vibration in the transmission, 'clonks' on taking up the drive, and in extreme cases of lack of lubrication, metallic squeaking, and ultimately grating and shrieking sounds as the bearings break up.

2 It is easy to check if the needle roller bearings are worn with the propeller shaft in position, by trying to turn the shaft with one hand, and the other hand holding the rear flange when the rear universal joint is being checked, and the front coupling when the front universal joint is being checked. Any movement between the propeller shaft and the front, or rear couplings is indicative of considerable wear. If worn, the old bearings and spider will have to be discarded and a repair kit, comprising new universal joint spiders, bearings, oil seals, and retainers purchased. Make sure this kit is available to you before dismantling. Check also by trying to lift the shaft and noticing any movement in

the splines.

3 Test the propeller shaft for wear, and if worn it will be necessary to purchase a new forward half coupling, or if the yokes are badly worn, an exchange half propeller shaft. It is not possible to fit oversize bearings and journals to the trunnion bearing holes.

### Dismantling

4 Clean away all traces of dirt and grease from the universal joint yoke. Using a very small and sharp chisel remove the metal that has formed a lip over the bearing cup faces by peening. This will take some time and great care.

5 Hold the propeller shaft and using a soft faced hammer tap the universal joint yoke so as to remove the bearing cups by 'shock' action.

6 If the cups cannot be extracted using this method, use two sockets, one slightly smaller than the cups and the other larger.

7 Hold the yoke in a vice with the sockets located on opposite bearing cups and slowly close the vice so that the smaller socket forces one cup inwards and pushes the other cup out of the yoke. Remove the assembly from the vice and pull the cup out of the yoke using a pair of grips.

8 Remove the remaining cups in the same manner and lift out the spider assembly.

### Reassembly

9 Thoroughly clean out the yokes and journals.

10 Fit new seals and retainers on the spider journals, place the spider

on the propeller shaft yoke and assemble the needle rollers into the bearing cups retaining them with some thick grease.
11 Fill each bearing cup about 1/3 full with Duckhams LB 10 grease or similar. Also fill the grease holes in the journal spider with grease taking care that all air bubbles are eliminated.
12 Refit the bearing cups on the spider and tap the bearings home so that they lie squarely in position.
13 Using a centre punch peen over the end of the bearing cup bores to stop the cups from working out.

## 4  Rear propeller shaft assembly - renovation

1  There are two sets of rubber supports in the centre propeller shaft joint area; firstly there is the block which supports the rear shaft forward end support bearing and secondly there are the two blocks which support the forward end of the torque tube in the rear propeller shaft.
2  The shaft support bearing, the shaft and the blocks cannot be removed in situ, therefore begin by removing the rear section of the propeller shaft as described in the previous Section.
3  With the rear propeller assembly on a bench, undo and remove the nut which retains the centre universal joint yoke onto the forward end of the shaft. Restrain the shaft by holding the yoke with a bar suitably bolted to the yoke fitting.
4  Once the nut has been removed, the yoke may be gently tapped off the shaft with a soft mallet. If it is tight a universal puller should enable it to be removed.
5  The propeller shaft may now be driven out of the forward bearing and the torque tube using a soft mallet.

### Centre bearing and rubber support
6  Once the shaft has been removed from the assembly the centre bearing may be pulled from its rubber support complete with its metal casing. The rubber cushion support is retained in the central joint support by tabs which have been bent inwards around the outer lips of the rubber moulding. Once those tabs have been eased back off the rubber, the moulding can be extracted from the joint support fitting (Fig. 7.5).
   Refitting the two items follows the reversal of the removal sequence. The space in front of the centre bearing must be packed with water resistant grease (Fig. 7.6).

### Extension tube rubber mounting
7  To remove the extension tube mounting assembly it is necessary to carefully cut through the mounting with a hacksaw (Fig. 7.7).
8  Drive the mounting off the extension tube using a soft faced hammer.
9  When fitting the new mounting make sure the groove in the mounting assembly is in line with the upper rib on the housing (see Fig. 7.8).
10 Drive the new mounting on squarely, using a block of wood and hammer, until the end of the housing protrudes 0.004 in (0.1mm) beyond the mounting.

### Reassembly of the rear propeller shaft unit
11 The propeller shaft should be inserted into the rear end of the torque tube and driven through the forward support bearing with a soft mallet. Be careful not to strain the rubber support of the forward bearing.

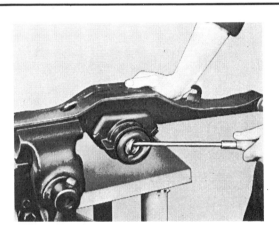
Fig. 7.5. Removing the centre bearing (Sec. 4)

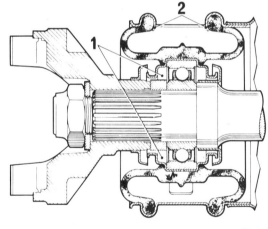
Fig. 7.6. Sectional view of centre bearing assembly (Sec. 4)
1  Grease packing points     2  Retaining tabs

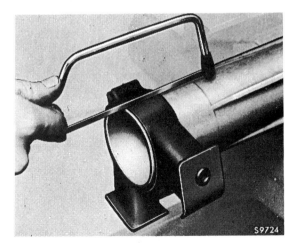
Fig. 7.7. Cutting off the rubber mounting from the extension housing (Sec. 4)

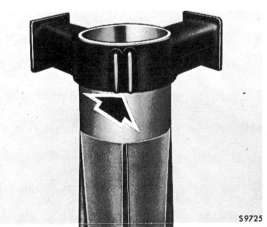
Fig. 7.8. Correct position of new rubber mounting on extension housing (Sec. 4)

12 Refit the universal joint yoke: use a soft mallet again, to drive the yoke fitting home on the splines on the shaft.

13 Restrain the yoke with an improvised tool bolted to the yoke fitting and secure the yoke with a new self-locking nut on the end of the shaft. Tighten the nut to the specified torque.

14 Refit the rear propeller shaft to the vehicle as detailed in Section 2, of this Chapter.

## 5  Fault diagnosis - propeller shaft

1  The main symptom of a faulty propeller shaft is a severe low frequency vibration, the intensity of which is variable with the road speed of the car. The vibration will be unaffected by whether the car is accelerating or decelerating.

2  The faults can be in several places:

  i)    *One or both of the universal joints.*
  ii)   *The forward joint sliding splines on the gearbox output shaft.*
  iii)  *A worn centre support bearing.*
  iv)   *Deterioration of centre bearing support rubbers.*
  v)    *Out of balance forward propeller shaft (eg. a bent shaft or shaft unevenly coated with paint, underseal or even dirt).*

3  The propeller shaft is finely balanced and the smallest noticeable amounts of wear can excite severe vibration.

4  Check for wear of the bearings and joints by gripping each side of the bearing or joint and try to force radial or axial relative movement as appropriate.

# Chapter 8 Rear axle

*For modifications, and information applicable to later models, see Supplement at end of manual*

## Contents

## Specifications

| | |
|---|---|
| **Axle type** ... ... ... ... ... ... ... ... ... | Semi-floating, hypoid |

**Axle ratios**

| | |
|---|---|
| 1.6 engine ... ... ... ... ... ... ... ... ... | 3.70 : 1 |
| 1.6S engine ... ... ... ... ... ... ... ... ... | 3.67 : 1 |
| 1.9 engine ... ... ... ... ... ... ... ... ... | 3.67 : 1 |

**Oil capacity**

| | |
|---|---|
| All models ... ... ... ... ... ... ... ... ... | 1.9 Imp pints (1.1 litres) |

**Oil type**

| | |
|---|---|
| Axle with standard differential: | |
| During the first 10,000 miles or if a new axle is fitted ... ... ... | GM special oil 19 42 362 (9 293 688) (Duckhams Hypoid 90DL) |
| Normal topping up ... ... ... ... ... ... ... ... | Hypoid gear oil, viscosity SAE 90EP (Duckhams Hypoid 90S) |
| Axle with limited slip differential ... ... ... ... ... ... | GM special oil 19 42 362 (9 293 688) (Duckhams Hypoid 90DL) |

**Pinion bearing preload**

| | |
|---|---|
| New bearings ... ... ... ... ... ... ... ... ... | 6.2 - 11.5 lb f inches (0.70 - 1.30 Nm) |
| Used bearings ... ... ... ... ... ... ... ... ... | 5.3 - 8.0 lb f inches (0.60 - 0.90 Nm) |

**Torque wrench settings**

| | lb f ft | kg f m |
|---|---|---|
| Propeller shaft/drive pinion flange (nut and bolt) ... ... ... ... | 11 | 1.5 |
| Flange to drive shaft extension (nut) ... ... ... ... ... ... | 37 | 5.1 |
| Crownwheel gear to differential case (bolt) ... ... ... ... ... | 47 | 6.5 |
| Differential bearing cap (bolt) ... ... ... ... ... ... ... | 33 | 4.5 |
| Differential housing rear cover (bolt) ... ... ... ... ... ... | 22 | 3 |
| Anti-roll bar to rear axle shackle (nut and bolt) ... ... ... ... | 25 | 3.5 |
| Anti-roll bar location to bodyshell (bolt) ... ... ... ... ... | 15 | 2 |
| Track rod to rear axle (nut) ... ... ... ... ... ... ... | 81 | 11 |
| Track rod to bodyshell member ... ... ... ... ... ... | 72 | 9.8 |
| General: | | |
| 10 mm bolts and nuts ... ... ... ... ... ... ... ... | 36 | 5 |
| 8 mm bolts and nuts ... ... ... ... ... ... ... ... | 15 | 2 |
| 6 mm bolts and nuts ... ... ... ... ... ... ... ... | 5 | 0.69 |

## 1 General description

The rear axle assembly comprises a hypoid gear differential assembly housed in a banjo type solid axle casing.

Coil spring suspension is used in conjunction with trailing arms which controls the fore-and-aft movement of the axle. Sideways movement is prevented by means of a Panhard rod (track rod).

An extension housing is bolted to the front of the differential casing and is supported in a rubber mounting attached to a crossmember. The drive from the axle pinion to the propeller shaft is transmitted by a solid shaft located within the extension housing.

The axle shaft (halfshaft), are splined at their inner ends into the differential gears, while the outer ends are supported by ball bearings. Oil is prevented from leaking from the axle casing into the brake assemblies by means of lip-type oil seals.

The axle casing is not fitted with a drain plug and it is necessary to remove the end cover plate to drain the axle oil.

The overhaul and repair of a differential assembly is a highly skilled task requiring special tools and it is not recommended that the DIY mechanic should attempt the job. The best policy in the event of differential failure or excessive noise, is to obtain a factory reconditioned unit which will be guaranteed.

## 2 Rear axle - removal and refitting

1 Complete removal of the rear axle will only be necessary when fitting a factory reconditioned unit, or for overhaul by a garage or specialist workshop.

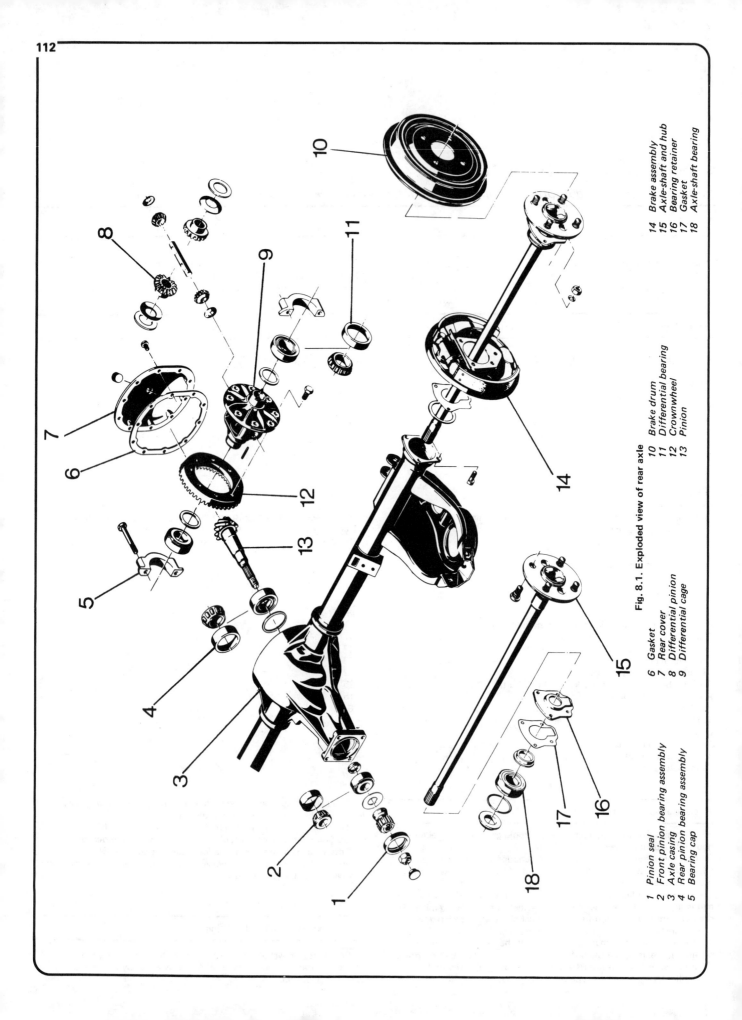

**Fig. 8.1. Exploded view of rear axle**

1   Pinion seal
2   Front pinion bearing assembly
3   Axle casing
4   Rear pinion bearing assembly
5   Bearing cap
6   Gasket
7   Rear cover
8   Differential pinion
9   Differential cage
10   Brake drum
11   Differential bearing
12   Crownwheel
13   Pinion
14   Brake assembly
15   Axle-shaft and hub
16   Bearing retainer
17   Gasket
18   Axle-shaft bearing

**Fig. 8.2. Sectional view of rear axle**

1   Rear axle casing
2   Final drive housing
3   Final drive cover
4   Differential casing
5   Crownwheel gear and drive
     pinion
6   Differential side gears
7   Differential (pinions gears)
8   Side gear thrust washers
9   Side gear shims
10  Differential side bearings
11  Differential side bearing
     retaining caps
12  Axle-shaft
16  Rear axle extension - torque
     tube
17  Propeller shaft - rear portion
18  Centre bearing support beam
19  Centre bearing and rubber
     support
21  Differential pinion gear bearing
     shaft
22  Drive pinion positioning shims
23  Collapsible spacer
24  Barrel spline fitting
25  Drive pinion shaft oil seal
26  Yoke fitting on forward end of
     rear propeller shaft

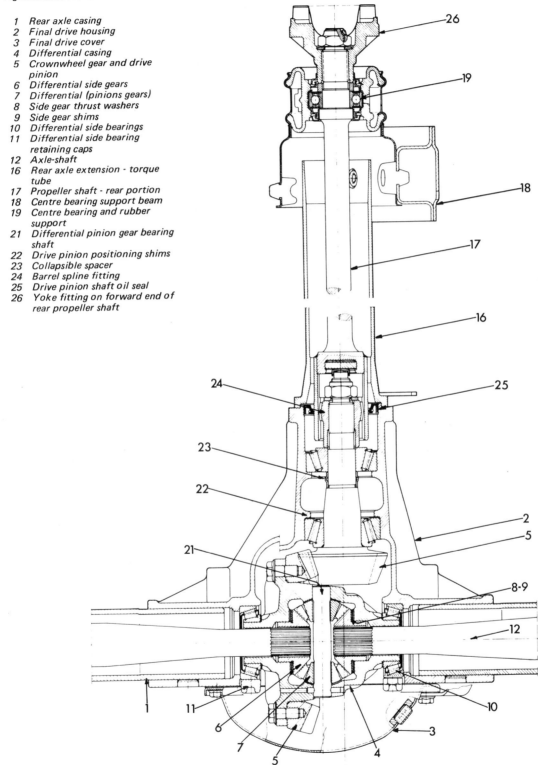

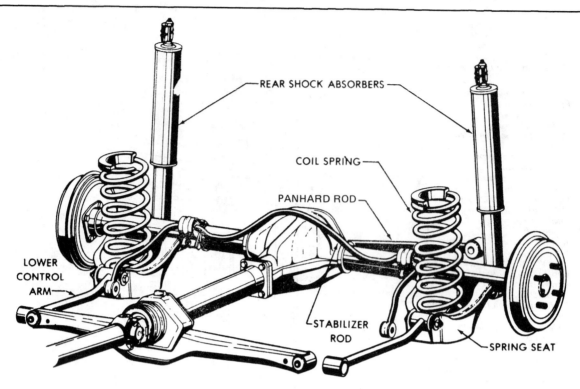

Fig. 8.3. Layout of rear axle assembly

2   Begin by raising the vehicle until both rear wheels are clear of the
ground and place chassis stands under the rear jacking points on each
side of car. Remove the rear wheels and then the brake drums. Make
absolutely certain that the vehicle is properly supported - you will
be working underneath and several tasks will require efforts which will
easily topple a car if inadequately supported. Support the rear axle
with a trolley jack.
3   Working on the handbrake mechanism, remove the handbrake cable
tension equalizer from the brake link rod. Remove the return spring.
4   Undo and remove the nuts and bolts retaining the lower end of the
shock absorbers in the forks on the axle casing.
5   Undo and remove the nut and bush retaining the Panhard rod to the
end of the axle casing (Fig. 8.4).
6   Undo and remove the nuts and bolts securing the anti-roll bar to the
rear axle (Fig. 8.5).
7   Mark the central universal joint mating areas to ensure correct
alignment when the transmission is reassembled. Undo and remove the
bolts retaining the propeller shaft coupling to the rear shaft yoke.
Tie the propeller shaft to one side.
8   Disconnect the rear brake flexible hose from the bracket on the

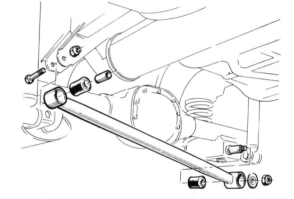

Fig. 8.4. Location of Panhard rod (Sec. 2)

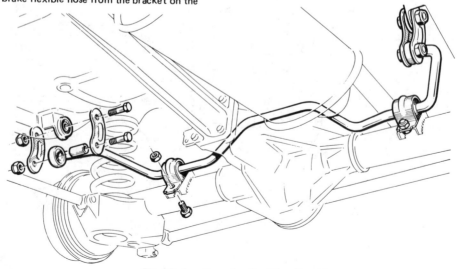

Fig. 8.5. Location of anti-roll bar (Sec. 2)

differential casing. Plug ends to prevent ingress of dirt.

9   Lower the axle far enough to free the two coil springs (Fig. 8.6).

10   Remove the nuts and bolts which secure the ends of the transmission central joint support to the bodyshell.

11   Finally undo and remove the nuts and bolts securing the suspension trailing rods ends in the forks of the rear axle fitting.

12   Slide the rear axle assembly from underneath the vehicle (Fig. 8.7).

13   *Refitting of rear axle to vehicle:* It is essential to use the proper nuts and bolts when reassembling the suspension and axle onto the car and to tighten those parts to the correct torques. The nuts and bolts are vital components and only genuine G.M parts should be used as replacements.

14   Begin refitment by moving the axle assembly underneath the car and offering it up to its installed position.

15   Insert the fixing bolts through the ends of the transmission central joint support beam and anchorages. Secure by attaching the washers and nuts - tightened finger tight.

16   Lower the axle unit to the point when the springs and spring seat rubbers can be inserted. Make certain they are properly aligned before raising the axle again to allow the Panhard rod to be attached.

17   Attach the trailing arms to axle fork brackets, tighten nuts a little but not yet to the torque specified.

18   Attach the track/Panhard rod to the axle, tighten the nut and bolt a little, but not yet to the torque specified.

19   Jack the vehicle up off the chassis stands under the jacking points and place shorter stands underneath the axle unit. Let down the car until the stands under the axle are taking ALL the load of the rear of the car. Remove the jacks.

20   Now, while underneath the car, the nuts and bolts securing the transmission centre joint support beam to the bodyshell, and the suspension arms to the axle nut and anchorages on the bodyshell must be tightened to the torques specified. **Do not attempt to tighten the suspension fastening nuts and bolts to their appropriate torques without the weight of the car being supported on the axle.**

21   Re-attach the shock absorbers to the axle unit and tighten the fixing nuts and bolts to the torque specified at the beginning of this Chapter.

22   Refit the anti-roll bar to the axle unit - remembering to torque the bolts to the specified torques.

23   Untie the propeller shaft from its stowed position and align the marks made before it was detached from the rear part of the shaft in the torque tube unit extension.

24   Fit the bolts to connect the coupling to the rear shaft yoke. Tighten nuts to the specified torque and bend over tabs to secure the nuts in position. It is advisable to use new tab washer plates each time the unit is dismantled.

25   Refit the handbrake cables to their respective rear brake shoes and refit the brake drums.

26   The hydraulic brake circuit may now be reconnected to the rear axle unit and the braking system bled. Refer to Chapter 9 - Braking System.

27   Adjust the handbrake linkage, if the equalizer bracket has been disturbed during the removal - refitting of the axle.

28   Fit the rear wheels and tighten the wheel nuts.

29   A jack may be positioned under the axle and the axle unit (and vehicle) raised off the stands underneath the ends of the axle. Remove the stands and lower the car to the ground. Check and if necessary top-up the oil level.

---

### 3   Axle-shaft (halfshaft), bearings and oil seals - removal, inspection and refitting

---

1   Jack-up the rear of the car and support on axle stands placed either beneath the jacking points or beneath the axle unit.

2   Remove the rear wheels, mark the position of the brake drum in relation to the axleshaft and remove the drums.

3   Using a socket through the access holes in the axleshaft flange, remove the four nuts retaining the bearing plate to the axle casing flange (Fig. 8.8).

4   It should now be possible to pull the axle-shaft and bearings assembly out of the axle casing. If difficulty is experienced, refit the roadwheel onto the axle flange and carefully pull the shaft out using the wheel for leverage.

**Note:** Care should be taken to avoid damaging the shaft inner splines

Fig. 8.6. Removing the coil springs after lowering the axle assembly (Sec. 2)

Fig. 8.7. Lifting out the complete axle assembly (Sec. 2)

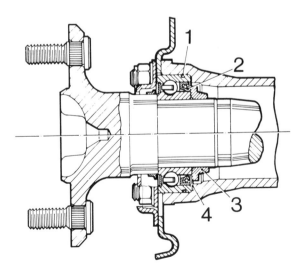

Fig. 8.8. Sectional view of axle-shaft bearing (Sec. 3)

1   *Outer sealing ring*          3   *Bearing retainer ring*
2   *Inner seal*                  4   *Shims*

while withdrawing them through the axle casing.

5    It can now be seen that the bearings, retaining plate and oil seal are held in position by a ring which is an interference fit on the shaft next to the bearing.

6    To renew any of the parts mentioned it is necessary to remove the ring. The method is to be adopted is to break the ring with a cold chisel (Fig. 8.9).

7    The bearing must now be pulled off to free the retaining plate and seal. Pull the seal off the bearing.

8    A forked plate should be placed behind the bearing and the shaft tapped with a soft mallet through the bearing inner race. The bearing retainer plate will need to be moved away from the bearing.

9    Once all the parts have been freed they may be inspected and renewed as necessary.

10   **Note:** All components associated with the axleshaft are **vital** and only genuine G.M parts with the correct part number should be used. This stipulation includes nuts and bolts. It is equally important to tighten all fastenings to the correct torques when reassembling the components.

11   Check the radial run out of the axleshaft at the bearing seating and the lateral (lengthwise) run out of the axleshaft flange at its largest diameter. The maximum radial run out is 0.002 in (0.50 mm) and the maximum lateral is 0.004 in (0.10 mm). A shaft which does not meet these demands in either case must be renewed.

12   With all the components ready for reassembly, locate the bearing retainer plate onto the upper seating on the end of the axleshaft.

13   Next offer the bearing onto the smaller diameter seating on the end

of the shaft. Make sure that the oil seal retaining groove on the bearing is towards the inner splined end of the axle-shaft. (Fig. 8.10).

14   Considerable force (in excess of 2,500 lb f, 1135 kg f) will be required to force the bearing home on its seating. The bearing retaining ring will require a larger force. Both are pressed on in a cold condition and no lubricant is required. It is clearly a case for special workshop equipment.

15   Before the axleshaft is inserted into the casing, the depth of the bearing seat in the end of the axle casing must be measured with a depth gauge. The depth must be measured with the backing plate and gaskets in place (Fig. 8.11).

16   Then measure the width of the bearing outer race and the difference in the two measurements is the required thickness of the shims. The maximum permissible difference in 'shim + bearing width' and bearing seat width is 0.002 in (0.05 mm). Add 0.004 (0.10 mm) thick shims as necessary behind the bearing (Fig. 8.12).

17   If the old bearing is being reused there should be no need to alter the shims that have been fitted.

18   Apply some EP90 gear oil to the splines on the inner end of the axleshaft into the axle casing. The shaft may need turning a little to mate the splines on the shaft with those in the differential. Drive the shaft home with a soft mallet, ensuring that the bearing is fully seated in the axle casing.

19   Fit the retaining plate in position and secure with the nuts. Tighten the nuts to the specified torque.

20   Refit the brake drum and wheel and tighten the wheel nuts.

21   Raise the car off the stands and lower to the ground.

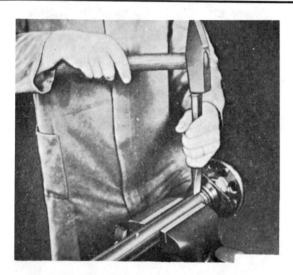

Fig. 8.9. Cutting off the bearing retainer ring (Sec. 4)

Fig. 8.10. Check that the bearing seal groove faces inwards (Sec. 4)

Fig. 8.11. Measuring the depth of the axle-shaft bearing recess (Sec. 4)

Fig. 8.12. Fitting an axle-shaft bearing shim (Sec. 4)

## 4 Pinion shaft oil seal - removal and replacement

1 The pinion shaft oil seal runs on the outside of the splined sleeve

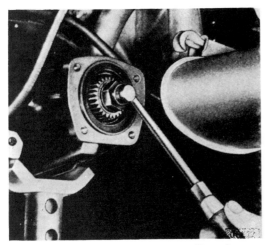

Fig. 8.13. Prising out the pinion seal (Sec. 4)

which couples the rear propeller shaft to the pinion shaft.
2 It will be necessary to remove the whole rear part of the propeller shaft together with the torque tube and central joint support beam - see Chapter 7.
3 Once the torque tube and propeller shaft which runs inside the tube have been removed, the seal is clearly seen at the edge of the bore in the differential case which accepts the pinion shaft.
4 Simply prise the old seal out with a screwdriver and clean the seating in the differential casing ready for the fitment of the new seal.
5 Soak the new seal in gear oil for one hour before fitting. Gently press the seal into the seating - make sure the lip of the seal faces inwards. Press evenly around the seal - it must not be distorted.
6 Reassemble the propeller shaft and torque tube as described in Chapter 7.
7 Check the level of oil in the rear axle before lowering the vehicle back to the ground.

## 5 Limited slip differential - description and checking

1 The 'Limited Slip' differential is available as an optional extra. The object of this type of differential is to reduce the maximum possible difference in rotational speeds of the rear wheels to a reasonable

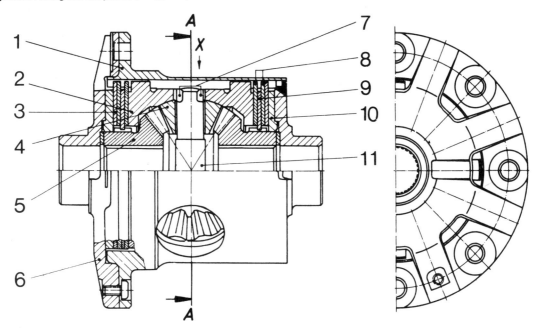

Fig. 8.14. Sectional view of a limited-slip differential (Sec. 5)

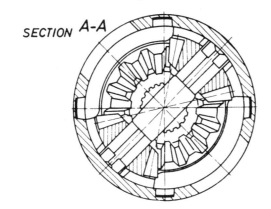

SECTION A-A

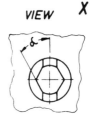

VIEW X

| | | | |
|---|---|---|---|
| 1 Differential case | 4 Differential pinions | 7 Differential shaft chamfer | 10 Radial guide plate |
| 2 Pressure plate | 5 Side gears | 8 Outer friction plates | 11 Differential shaft(s) |
| 3 Thrust spring | 6 Cover | 9 Inner friction plates | |

**Fig. 8.15. Using a wheel rim and suspended weight to test the limited-slip differential (Sec. 5)**

minimum. Such a capability gives the following advantageous features:

i)   *Reduced rear wheelspin, when starting and when one wheel has poor contact.*
ii)  *The likelihood of skidding reduced at high speed when there are different loads on the rear wheels eg. cornering, braking.*
iii) *Reduced wheelspin occasioned by wheel hop on a rough road.*

2   It is considered that the limited slip unit is not suited for DIY repair and therefore if a fault is suspected then either the car should be taken to the nearest G.M dealer - or the unit may be removed from the axle and exchanged or repaired professionally.

### *Checking the limited slip unit (in situ):*
3   The limited slip differential effectiveness may be checked without removing the unit from the car.
4   You will need an old wheel rim - 5½J x 13 or 5J x 13 preferably to fit the rear wheel studs, some strong cable and a weight of 100 lbs (45.3 kg). Finally you will need a torque wrench capable of reading up to 150 lb f ft (21 kg f m), and an adaptor capable of taking the torque wrench load and distributing it to at least two wheel studs.
5   Raise the car onto chassis stands placed beneath the rear jacking points or rear axle casing. Chock the front wheels.

**6   Fault diagnosis - rear axle**

**Fig. 8.16 Applying the test torque to the differential (Sec. 5)**

6   Remove one rear wheel and fit the special wheel rim which has the cable wrapped around its periphery.
7   Move, or assemble, the 100 lb (45.3 kg) mass beneath the free end of the cable on the wheel rim. Attach the cable to the mass securely (Fig. 8.15).
8   Release the handbrake and fit the adaptor and torque wrench to the rear wheel on the other side of the car (Fig. 8.16).
9   Turn the wrench until the weight is raised a little. Note the torque on the wrench when this has been achieved.
10  Repeat the test once or twice to determine a consistent average torque reading; and then calculate the limited slip "Lock Coefficient" using the formula below:

$$LC = \frac{T - TC}{T + TC} \times 100\%$$

$T$  =  *Torque Reading of the wrench*

$TC$  =  *Applied torque of the mass on the other side of the axle. If the 100 lbs was applied on a 13" min wheel, (weight x radius of wheel) TC 53 lbs ft.*

11  The nominal value for LC is 40%. If after the tests the value of LC is found to be less than 25% the limited slip unit should be removed for overhaul or exchange.

| Symptom | Reason/s |
|---|---|
| Vibration | Worn axle-shaft bearings. Loose drive flange bolts. Out of balance propeller shaft. Wheels require balancing. |
| Noise | Insufficient lubrication. Worn gears and differential components generally. |
| 'Clunk' on acceleration or deceleration | Incorrect crownwheel and pinion mesh. Excessive backlash due to wear in crownwheel and pinion teeth. Worn axle-shaft or differential side gear splines. Loose drive flange bolts. Worn drive pinion flange splines. |
| Oil leakage | Faulty pinion or axle-shaft oil seals. May be caused by blocked axle housing breather. |

# Chapter 9 Braking system

*For modifications, and information applicable to later models, see Supplement at end of manual*

## Contents

## Specifications

| | |
|---|---|
| **System type** ... | Discs front, drums rear, dual hydraulic circuit - servo assisted |
| **Brake pedal free-travel** ... | 0.24 - 0.31 in (6 - 8 mm) |

**Master cylinder**

| | |
|---|---|
| Type ... | Tandem |
| Nominal diameter ... | 13/16 in (20.64 mm) |
| Maximum housing diameter ... | 0.817 in (20.75 mm) |
| Smallest piston diameter ... | 0.807 in (20.49 mm) |
| Maximum permissible piston clearance ... | 0.010 in (0.26 mm) |

**Disc brakes**

| | |
|---|---|
| Disc diameter ... | 9.2 in (234 mm) |
| Disc thickness ... | 0.5 in |
| Minimum thickness of disc after refacing ... | 0.46 in (11.7 mm) |
| Permissible runout ... | 0.009 in (0.22 mm) |
| Minimum permissible pad thickness ... | 0.06 in (1.5 mm) |

**Drum brakes**

| | |
|---|---|
| Drum diameter ... | 9.0 in (228 mm) |
| Maximum drum diameter after refacing ... | 9.09 in (231 mm) |
| Maximum permissible runout of drums ... | 0.004 in (0.1 mm) |

**Servo unit**

| | |
|---|---|
| Type ... | 7 in (177.8 mm): Single diaphragm |
| Boost ratio ... | 2.64 : 1 |

**Handbrake**

| | |
|---|---|
| Type ... | Mechanically operated - actuating rear brakes only |

| Torque wrench settings | lb f ft | kg f m |
|---|---|---|
| Brake caliper to steering knuckle ... | 61 | 8.5 |
| Brake disc to wheel hub ... | 36 | 5 |
| Brake disc shield to steering knuckle and steering arm ... | 47 | 6.5 |
| Brake pipe to caliper ... | 22 | 3.1 |
| Brake hose to front wheel brake cylinder ... | 22 | 3.1 |
| Brake backing plate to steering knuckle (upper bolts) ... | 22 | 3.1 |
| Brake backing plate to steering knuckle and steering arm (lower bolts) ... | 47 | 6.5 |
| Backing plate to rear axle housing ... | 43 | 5.95 |
| Master cylinder actuator rod to brake pedal ... | 5 | 0.69 |
| Wheel brake cylinder to brake backing plate ... | 5 | 0.69 |
| Master cylinder to brake booster ... | 12 | 1.65 |
| Brake booster to support ... | 11 | 1.5 |

## 1  General description

All models are fitted with disc brakes on the front wheels and drum brakes on the rear. They are operated hydraulically by a master cylinder when the brake pedal is depressed.

The system uses special hydraulic fluid which is fed to the respective slave cylinders from the master cylinder and reservoir by a system of metal and flexible pipes and hoses.

A servo system is fitted as standard to all models, and this uses the vacuum in the inlet manifold to drive the master cylinder pushrod when the brake pedal is depressed. The effort which is required from the driver to operate the servo unit is thus reduced.

The front disc brakes are the conventional fixed caliper design. Each half of the caliper contains a piston which moves in a bore; they are interconnected so that under hydraulic pressure the pistons move towards each other. With this action they clamp the rotating disc between two special friction pads to slow the rotation of the disc. The seals fitted between the piston and the bore are shaped so that they are stretched slightly when the piston moves to apply the brake and then, when the hydraulic pressure is released, they contract and draw the piston back slightly from the friction pads and disc. This characteristic of the piston/bore seal provides a running clearance between the disc and pads. As the pads wear, the piston is able to move through the seal, allowing wear to be taken up continuously (Fig. 9.1).

The rear drum brakes are of the internally expanding type. The action of both the handbrake mechanism and the single hydraulic cylinder in each drum is to move the brake shoes outwards against the inside surface of the drum. A pair of springs acting between two brake shoes in each drum serve to maintain a running clearance between the shoe linings and drum under normal running.

The master cylinder is a dual piston design, for safety. The primary piston acts to supply fluid to the rear brakes and the secondary piston to the front brakes. The front brake and the rear brake systems are **not** linked hydraulically and either will maintain full operation in the event of failure of the other system.

## 2  Bleeding the hydraulic system

1  Whenever the brake hydraulic system has been dismantled to renew a pipe or hose or other major part, air will have inevitably been introduced into the pipe system. The system will therefore require 'bleeding' in order to remove this air and restore the effectiveness of the system.
2  During the 'bleeding' operation the level of hydraulic fluid in the reservoir must be maintained at least half full, to prevent more air from being taken into the system via the reservoir and master cylinder.
3  Obtain a clean glass jar, some plastic tube (15 inches long and a suitable diameter to fit tightly over the bleed valves). A can of **new** brake fluid will also be required.
4  Clean all the brake pipes and hoses and check that all connections are tight and bleed valves closed.
5  It will be easier to gain access to the bleed valves and the rear of the brake assemblies if the appropriate roadwheel is removed. Chock the other wheels whilst the system is being bled. Release the handbrake.
6  Fill the master cylinder reservoir, and the bottom inch of the jar, with hydraulic fluid. Take extreme care that no fluid is allowed to come into contact with the paintwork, as it acts as a solvent and it will damage the finish.
7  Remove the rubber dust cap (if fitted) from the end of the bleed valve on the front disc brake caliper which is furthest away from the master cylinder. Insert the other end of the bleed tube in the jar containing 1 inch of hydraulic fluid.
8  Use a suitable open-ended spanner and unscrew the bleed valve about half a turn.
9  An assistant should now pump the brake pedal by first depressing it one full stroke, followed by three short but rapid strokes and allowing the pedal to return of its own accord. Check the fluid level in the reservoir. Carefully watch the flow of fluid into the glass jar and, when air bubbles cease to emerge with the fluid, during the next down stroke, tighten the bleed valve. Remove the plastic bleed tube and tighten the bleed valve. Replace the rubber dust cap.
10  Repeat operations in paragraphs 5 to 9 for the second front brake.
11  The rear brakes should be bled in the same manner as the front,

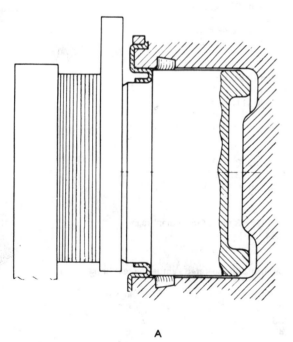

A = BRAKE ON
THE RUBBER FLUID SEAL TIGHTLY GRIPPING PISTON
IS DEFLECTED IN DIRECTION OF PISTON TRAVEL

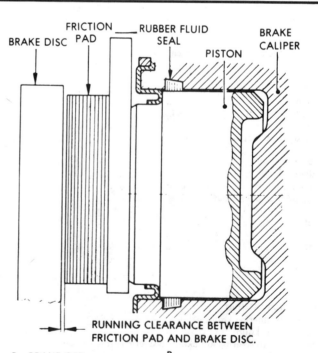

B = BRAKE OFF
THE PISTON IS RETRACTED BY THE AMOUNT OF
RUBBER FLUID SEAL DEFLECTION. THIS AMOUNT
IS EQUAL TO RUNNING CLEARANCE.

**Fig. 9.1. Operation of disc caliper piston (Sec. 1)**

except that each brake pedal stroke should be slow with a pause of three to four seconds between each stroke.

12  Sometimes it may be found that the bleeding operation for one or more cylinders is taking a considerable time. The cause is probably due to air being drawn past the bleed valve threads when the valve is loose. To counteract this condition, it is recommended that, at the end of each downward stroke, the bleed valve be tightened to stop air being drawn past the threads.

13  If, after the bleed operation has been completed, the brake pedal operation still feels spongy, this is an indication that there is still air in the system, or that the master cylinder is faulty.

14  Check and top up the reservoir fluid level with fresh hydraulic fluid. Never re-use the old brake fluid.

---

### 3  Front disc brake caliper pads - removal and refitting

1  Chock the rear wheels, apply the handbrake, jack-up the front of the car and support on firmly based axle stands. Remove the road-wheel.

2  Either 'Girling' or 'Ate' brake calipers are fitted. Both types are similar in construction, the main differences being that the pad retaining pins on the Ate calipers are secured by spring collars. To remove this type of pin, simply drive it in towards the centre of the car, using a thin punch. (See Fig. 9.2 and photo).

3  The pad retaining pins on the Girling calipers are secured by spring clips and the pins are driven outwards to remove them (see Fig. 9.3).

4  Lift away the brake pads and spring clip, and inspect the thickness of the friction material. If the material is less than 1/16 inch (1.6mm) thick the pads must be renewed. If one of the pads is found to be more worn than the other, it is permissible to change these round - as long as the disc is not heavily scored (photo).

5  When refitting new pads, ensure that they have been manufactured to the specifications given at the beginning of this Chapter.

6  **Do not** renew just one or two pads at any one time; the pads on both front brakes must be renewed at the same time, even in the unlikely event that they do not all warrant it from the point of view of wear.

7  Inspect the brake disc surface; concentric scores up to 0.020 inch (0.5 mm) deep can be accepted; however, if deeper scores are found, the brake disc must either be skimmed or renewed (Section 5).

8  To refit the pads, begin by extracting a small amount of brake fluid from the system. This is achieved with the aid of a glass jar and some plastic tubing as used for bleeding the brakes.

9  Fit the plastic tube over the bleed valve and immerse the free end into 1 inch of clean hydraulic fluid in the jar. Slacken off the bleed valve one turn and press the caliper pistons back into their bores. Tighten the bleed valve and remove the bleed tube.

10  Wipe the exposed end of the pistons and the recesses of the caliper, free of dust and road dirt.

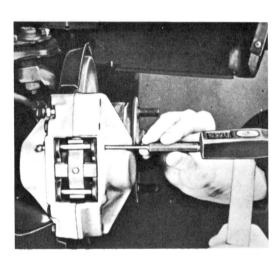

**Fig. 9.2. Extracting the brake pad retaining pins ('Ate' type brakes) (Sec. 3)**

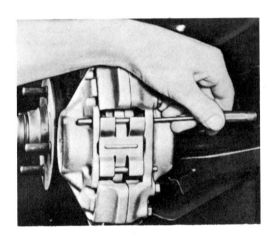

**Fig. 9.3. Extracting the brake pad retaining pins ('Girling' type brakes) (Sec. 3)**

3.2 Removing the disc brake pad retaining pins

3.4 Lifting out the disc brake pads

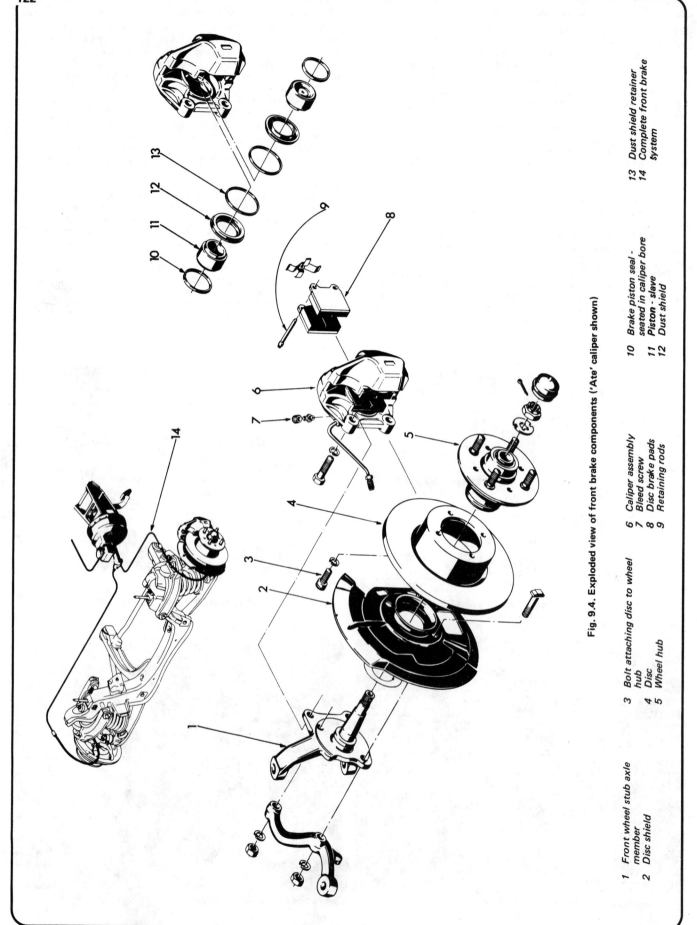

**Fig. 9.4. Exploded view of front brake components ('Ate' caliper shown)**

1  Front wheel stub axle member
2  Disc shield
3  Bolt attaching disc to hub
4  Disc
5  Wheel hub
6  Caliper assembly
7  Bleed screw
8  Disc brake pads
9  Retaining rods
10  Brake piston seal - seated in caliper bore
11  Piston - slave
12  Dust shield
13  Dust shield retainer
14  Complete front brake system

11 Refitting the pads is now the reversal of the removal sequence, but the following points must be observed:

a) *If it is suspected that air has entered the system during the operation described in paragraph 9, the whole system must be bled as described in Section 2.*

b) *The pad retaining pins must be a tight fit in the caliper. Pins which do not fit tightly must be renewed.*

12 Wipe the top of the brake fluid reservoir and remove the cap. Top up the reservoir and then depress the brake pedal several times to settle the pads. Re-check the brake fluid level.

13 If the brakes feel 'spongy' bleed them, as directed in Section 2.

### 4 Front disc brake caliper - removal and refitting

1 Apply the handbrake, chock the rear wheels and jack-up the front of the car. Support the front of the car securely on axle stands and then remove the appropriate roadwheel.

2 Wipe the top of the brake fluid reservoir, unscrew the cap and place a thin sheet of polythene over the top. Refit the cap. This measure will stop the leakage of fluid from the system when subsequently dismantled.

3 Wipe clean the area around the caliper flexible hose to metal pipe connection and the hose to caliper connection. Detach the metal pipe from the hose. Hold the fixed end of the hose with a spanner whilst the union fitting on the pipe is unscrewed from the pipe. Then remove the nut which retains the hose in the support bracket.

4 Once the inside end of the hose is detached, proceed to remove the brake pads and store them safely so that the surfaces will not be contaminated with oil or dirt.

5 Finally, undo the two bolts which secure the caliper to the wheel support (Fig. 9.5).

6 Refitting follows the reversal of the removal procedure. Remember to tighten the caliper to wheel hub support bolts to the specified torque and bleed the brake system once everything has been reassembled.

7 When refitting a brand new caliper assembly, the pistons may stick to the seals in the caliper bores. In that instance refit the new caliper with an old thin pair of brake pads. Reconnect the hydraulics, bleed and then depress the brake pedal to function the new caliper. The seal should now be properly seated in the bore and any stickiness on the piston erased.

8 Remove the old pads and fit new ones, as detailed in the previous Section.

### 5 Front brake disc - removal and refitting

1 Chock the rear wheels, apply the handbrake and jack-up the front of the car. Support the vehicle on firmly based axle stands and then remove the roadwheels.

2 Refer to Section 4 of this Chapter and remove the caliper assembly. Though complete removal of the caliper and its brake hose is not strictly necessary - the caliper may be detached from the wheel hub support and hung on the suspension. The brake system need not then be disconnected - removal of the complete caliper assembly is recommended as it gives greater freedom of access to the suspension assembly.

3 Use a wide bladed screwdriver and lever off the hub grease cap. Now remove the nut retaining the wheel hub and disc and then the hub and disc assembly.

4 The disc can only be separated from the hub with the special serrated socket headed wrench. **Note:** This tool is the same form as those required for the camshaft and cylinder head bolts.

5 On refitting the hub and disc, coat the wheel bearings with medium lithium based grease. Tighten the disc to hub bolts to the specified torque.

6 To ensure that the braking effort by each disc is equal, both discs must have the same surface condition. It follows therefore that they must either be renewed or skimmed as a pair; see the Specifications at the beginning of this Chapter, for minimum disc thickness after skimming.

7 When refitting the disc to the hub ensure that the joint faces are perfectly clean. Secure the two parts together with the four bolts and tighten progressively to the specified torque.

8 Adjust the front wheel bearings as directed in Chapter 11.

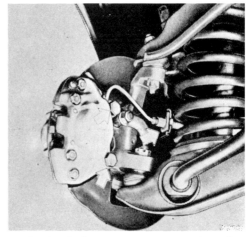

**Fig. 9.5. Brake caliper attaching bolts (Sec. 4)**

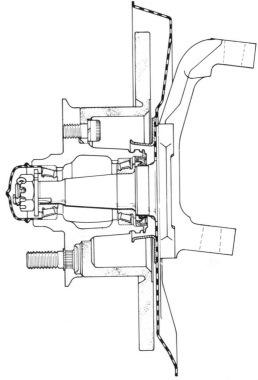

**Fig. 9.6. Sectional view of brake disc and hub (Sec. 5)**

9 Once the bearings have been adjusted, check the runout of the disc periphery against the figure in the 'Specifications' Section.

### 6 Front disc brake caliper - overhaul

1 Remove the caliper from the wheel support as detailed in Section 4, of this Chapter.

2 Remove both brake pads and their retaining pins and clips.

3 Temporarily, reconnect the caliper to the hydraulic system and support its weight. Do not allow the caliper to hang on the flexible hose; support its weight.

4 Use a small 'G' clamp to hold the piston in the mounting half of the caliper, in place, whilst the footbrake is gently depressed to force the other piston out of the caliper.

5 It will be necessary to remove the pistons over a catchment tray to collect the spilled hydraulic fluid. It may also be necessary to partially bleed the system to the front wheel installation being overhauled in order to enable the fluid to force the free piston out.

6 As the piston comes out of the caliper block extract the dust seal and once it is completely out, use a plastic knitting needle or

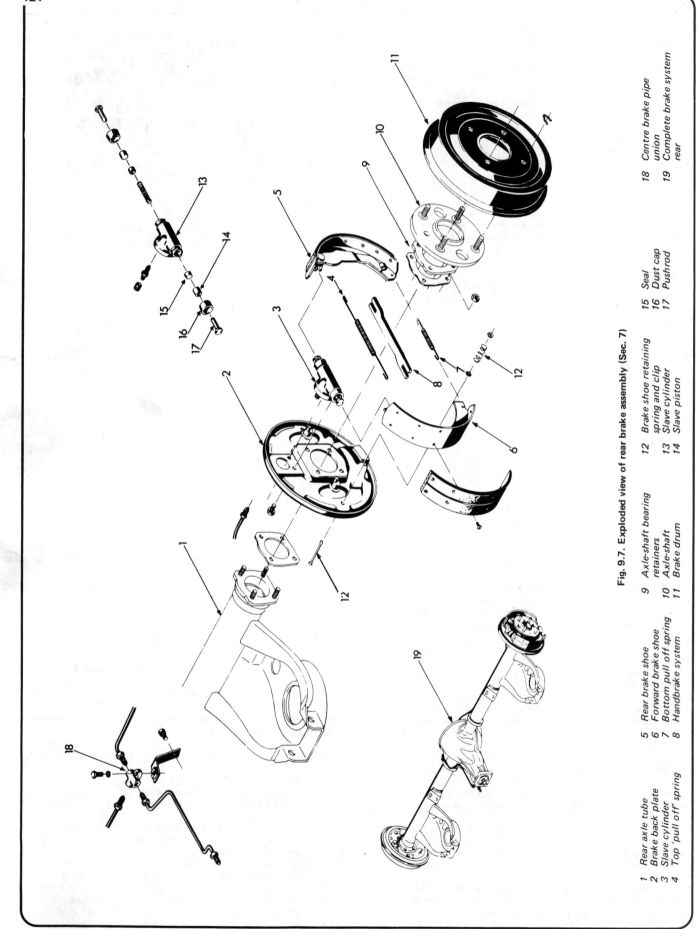

**Fig. 9.7. Exploded view of rear brake assembly (Sec. 7)**

1  Rear axle tube
2  Brake back plate
3  Slave cylinder
4  Top 'pull off spring

5  Rear brake shoe
6  Forward brake shoe
7  Bottom pull off spring
8  Handbrake system

9  Axle-shaft bearing
   retainers
10 Axle-shaft
11 Brake drum

12 Brake shoe retaining
   spring and clip
13 Slave cylinder
14 Slave piston

15 Seal
16 Dust cap
17 Pushrod

18 Centre brake pipe
   union
19 Complete brake system
   rear

thin wooden rod to remove the seal ring in the caliper bore.

7 The piston in the mounting side is removed in the same manner as described in the previous paragraphs. The piston freed first is temporarily re-inserted into its old bore - without seals - and retained by a small 'G' clamp. The 'mounting side' piston is forced out under hydraulic pressure as its partner was.

8 Thoroughly clean the caliper and pistons in Girling Cleaning Fluid or methylated spirits. Any other fluids will damage the internal seals between the two halves of the caliper. **Do not separate the two halves of the caliper.**

9 Inspect the caliper bores and piston surfaces for signs of scoring or corrosion - which, if evident, means a new assembly must be fitted.

10 To reassemble the caliper, first wet the new piston seal ring with new brake fluid and carefully insert it into its groove in the caliper bore.

11 Then refit the dust cover into its special cover in the caliper bore rim. Release the bleed valve in the caliper by one complete turn.

12 Coat the sides of the piston with hydraulic fluid and then position the piston squarely over the top of the caliper bore.

Once in position at the top of the bore, ease the piston gently into the bore until just over ¼ inch (6mm) is left protruding from the caliper. Engage the dust seal onto the groove on the rim of the piston and then push the piston as far as it can go into the caliper. Fit the cover retaining ring.

13 Repeat the operations described in paragraphs 10, 11, and 12 to refit the other piston into the caliper.

14 The pads may be fitted to the caliper assembly before it is refitted to the car. In any event bleed the brakes when the complete caliper has been refitted to the car.

## 7 Rear brake shoes and drums - inspection, removal, refitting and adjustment

1 After high mileages it will be necessary to fit replacement shoes with new linings. Refitting new brake linings to shoes is not considered economic or even possible without the use of specialist equipment.

2 In any event, ensure that the lining shoes and linings have been made to the correct specification.

3 Begin inspection by chocking the front wheels and jacking-up the rear of the car. Support the car on firmly based axle or chassis stands.

4 Then remove the roadwheels, and mark the relative position of the drum to the rear axle-shaft at its centre.

5 Remove the spring clamps from the wheel studs (if fitted) and then turn both shoe adjusters on the inside of the brake back plate to allow the shoes to move inwards off the inside of the drum.

6 Now ease the drum off the brake assembly to expose the brake shoes, the slave cylinder and the handbrake mechanism. If the drum

is sticking to the axle-shaft flange, it should be loosened with light hammer strokes on the inside edge of the drum.

7 When refitting the drum it is wise to smear a little medium grease over the contact area of the drum, and axle flange. This measure will help to provide for an easy removal of the brake drum next time.

8 The brake shoes should be visually inspected. If any have been contaminated with oil or grease - black glazed surface - or if the friction material is less than 1/16 inch at its thinnest point, both must be replaced.

9 If riveted linings are in place, see whether the heads of the rivets are wearing in contact with the drum. The linings must be replaced, preferably before the rivet heads show signs of wear.

10 To remove the brake shoes begin by removing the shoe retaining springs in the centre of the shoes (photo). Use a pair of pliers to release the spring retainers by rotating them through 90 degrees. Lift away the springs, retainers and washers from each shoe web.

11 Use a sturdy screwdriver to ease the bottom of the shoes from the anchor. Remove the spring from the bottom of the shoes.

12 The forked strip, which transmits the handbrake efforts to the forward shoe and rear shoe lever, can now be extracted together with the top retaining spring.

13 Pull the end of the handbrake cable from the bottom of the lever attached to the rearward shoe.

14 If the brake shoes are going to be off for some time, the pistons in the slave cylinder should be retained by a loop of string. There is a small spring between the pistons which will slowly act to eject the piston(s) if left unrestrained.

15 Thoroughly clean all traces of dust from the shoes, backplate, and drum, using a stiff brush. **Do not blow the dust clear as it is asbestos based and should not be inhaled.** Brake dust can cause judder and squeal and therefore it is important to clean away all traces.

16 Check that each piston is free in its cylinder and that the rubber dust covers are undamaged and in position. Check also that there are no hydraulic fluid leaks.

17 Finally, check that the slave cylinder and the shoe anchor at the bottom of the backplate are secure.

18 Prior to refitting the brake shoes, smear a trace of brake grease (Duckhams Keenol for instance) on the ends of the brake shoes, the rear shoe/handbrake lever pivot, the steady platform anchor posts and the adjuster surface. Do not allow any of the grease to come into contact with the brake linings or rubber boots (Fig. 9.9).

19 The refitting procedure is the reversal of removal. The two pull off springs should preferably be renewed every time new shoes are fitted and must be refitted into their original web holes. They should be between the shoe web and the backplate when fitted (photo).

20 Once the drum is refitted the shoe positions can be adjusted (Fig. 9.10) and then the roadwheel refitted. Tighten the roadwheel nuts.

21 Finally, road test the car to check the operation and effectiveness of the brakes.

**Fig. 9.8. View of rear brake components (Sec. 7)**

S9674

7.10 Rear brake shoe retainer

Fig. 9.9. Grease points on rear brake backplate (Sec. 7)

7.19 Correct installation of rear brake shoes on wheel cylinder

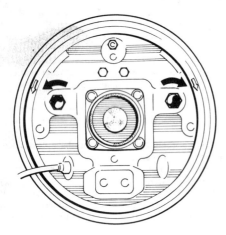

**Fig. 9.10 Adjusting the rear brakes (Sec. 7)**

*Each shoe is adjusted separately by an adjuster which should be turned in the direction of the arrows stamped on the outer edge of the rear flange plate. Turn the adjusters until the shoes are hard against the drum and then turn slightly in the opposite direction until the wheel rotates freely.*

### 8    Rear brake slave cylinder - removal and overhaul

1    The slave cylinder should be removed when the seals need renewal. It is not wise to try to overhaul the cylinder in situ.
2    Remove the brake drums and brake shoes as directed in Section 7 of this Chapter.
3    Next, wipe the top of the brake fluid reservoir and unscrew the cap. Place a thin sheet of polythene over the top and replace the cap. This

measure will prevent loss of fluid from the system when the pipe/hose connections are dismantled on the rear brake backplate.
4    Using an open-ended spanner, unscrew the union fitting retaining the brake pipe in the slave cylinder.
5    Once the brake pipe is detached, the two bolts which retain the cylinder to the backplate can be undone and the cylinder removed.
6    Once the cylinder is removed and on a clean bench, proceed to pull out the pistons, seals, spring and relay plungers which act between the pistons and shoes.
7    Examine the piston and cylinder for signs of wear or scoring, and if there are any the whole assembly must be renewed. If the metal surfaces of the pistons and cylinder are in good condition only the seals need to be replaced (Fig. 9.11).
8    Clean all the parts with hydraulic fluid or methylated spirits. Do not use any other solvent.
9    Immerse the cleaned parts and new seals in new hydraulic fluid, before beginning to reassemble the slave cylinder.
10 Fit the new seal to the piston so that the lip faces away from the centre of the piston. Make sure that the lip enters the cylinder clearly.
11 Once the two pistons are in place and the dust seals in place, the pistons should be retained with a loop of string around the cylinder.
12 Refit the cylinder back to the backplate, reassemble the brake shoes and drum. Then bleed the brake system.

### 9    Rear brake backplate - removal and refitting

1    The brake backplate retaining bolts also retain the axle-shaft bearing and the axle-shaft itself in position. Fortunately it is rarely necessary to remove the backplate.
2    Begin by removing the appropriate roadwheel, brake drum and brake shoes as directed in Section 7, of this Chapter. Then remove the slave cylinder as directed in Section 8.

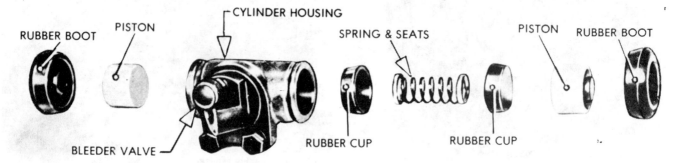

Fig. 9.11. Rear brake slave cylinder components (Sec. 8)

3   Using a socket spanner with an extension unbolt the backplate and
axle bearing retaining plate from the rear axle tube.
4   Withdraw the axle-shaft and then lift the backplate from the axle.
Be prepared to renew the oil seal on the end of the axle tube.
5   Refitting follows the reversal of the removal procedure. Ensure
that all the bolts are tightened to the torques specified at the beginning
of this Chapter.

### 10 Handbrake - adjustment and cable renewal

1   The handbrake system comprises a lever fitted with a pawl and rack,
a relay rod attached to the cable, and a cable which fastens to an actuating lever in each rear brake assembly and passes through a tensioning
saddle retained on the rear end of the relay rod (photo).
2   The action of the brake begins when the hand lever is raised and the
relay rod is pulled forward. This movement creates equal tension in the
cable connected to the actuating levers in the brakes. Inside the brake
assembly the tension in the cable forces the rearward shoe against the
drum, and the forward shoe against the drum via the forked strip
between that shoe and the actuating lever (Fig. 9.14).
3   The handbrake system is reckoned to be correctly adjusted when the
brakes begin to be applied at the third notch on the lever rack.

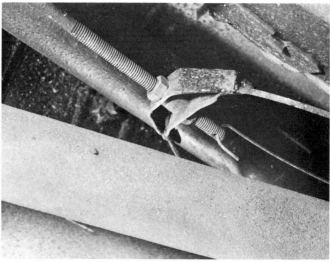

10.1 Handbrake relay rod

#### Adjustment
4   Before adjusting the handbrake ensure that the rear brake shoe
positions have been correctly adjusted as described in Section 7, of
this Chapter.
5   Usually the handbrake mechanism requires adjustment to accommodate wear and stretch in the rod and cable system. It follows that if it
becomes necessary to adjust the handbrake linkage regularly, monthly,
then the cable is suspect and should be renewed.
6   To adjust the system, drive the rear of the car up onto a pair of
ramps and chock the front wheels; put the car in gear and release the
handbrake.
7   From underneath the car loosen the nuts retaining the cable saddle
in position on the rear end of the relay rod, and turn them so as to
move the saddle forward on the rod. Re-apply the handbrake and
count the notches passed by the hand lever. The hand lever should
begin to apply the brakes after the third notch and be fully applied
at the fourth or fifth. When the cable saddle has been moved to the
correct position, tighten the retaining nuts (Fig. 9.12).

#### Handbrake cable renewal
8   Jack-up the rear of the car and support on firmly based axle stands,
chock the front wheels, put the car in gear and release the handbrake.
Remove the rear wheels and both brake drums.
9   From underneath the car, loosen the nuts retaining the cable
saddle on the rear end of the relay rod. Remove the nuts and the
saddle from the relay rod. Extract the cable from the saddle.
10  Next, unhook the ends of the cable from the actuating levers in
the rear brake assemblies, and finally, take the slotted bushing,
through which the cable passes, out of the backplate (Fig. 9.13).
11  The cable and sleeving can now be removed from the backing
plates and taken from the car.
12  If the cable assembly has been removed because the cable has
jammed or rusted solid in the sleeve, then, once rust solvent has been
applied and the cable freed, grease may be applied to prevent further
rusting and subsequent seizure again.
13  Replacement of the cable assembly follows the reversal of the
removal procedure. Remember to adjust the mechanism as directed
in paragraphs 4 to 7, of this Section. Apply grease liberally to the saddle
groove.

#### Handbrake lever assembly - removal and refitting
14  The handbrake lever assembly is a simple mechanism and is retained
in the transmission tunnel by two bolts. Jack-up the rear of the car and
support on firmly based axle stands. Chock the front wheels, put the
car in gear and release the handbrake.
15  From inside the car, remove the centre console (Fig. 9.15 and
Section 11 in Chapter 13) and pull the carpet back from around the
lever. Remove the two bolts in the side of the transmission tunnel
that retain the lever assembly in position.
16  From underneath the car loosen and remove the nuts securing the

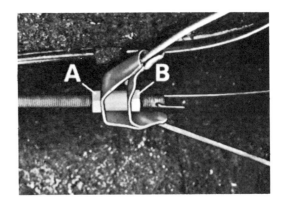

**Fig. 9.12. Handbrake cable adjuster (Sec. 10)**

A   Front adjuster nut                         B   Rear adjuster nut

**Fig. 9.13. Brake cable locking clip on backplate (Sec. 10)**

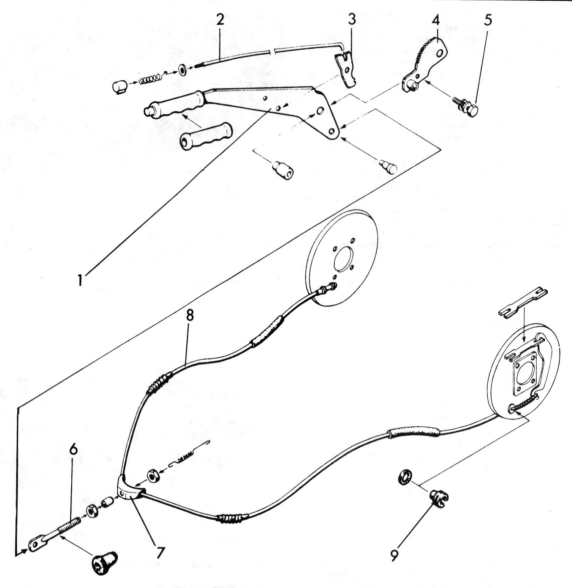

**Fig. 9.14. Handbrake system components (Sec. 10)**

1  *Handbrake lever*
2  *Button pushrod acting
   on pawl*
3  *Rack pawl*

4  *Lever rack*
5  *Lever assembly attachment
   bolt*

6  *Relay rod*
7  *Cable saddle*
8  *Cable assembly*

9  *Split bush retaining
   cable sleeve in the
   backplate*

cable saddle to the rear end of the relay rod and remove the saddle.
Disconnect the wire from the brake switch (Fig. 9.16).
17  The lever assembly can now be extracted from the transmission
tunnel inside the car.
18  The lever assembly is a riveted construction and can be easily
dismantled with a small drift and file.
19  On refitting the handbrake assembly to the car coat the relay rod
grommet with molybdenum disulphide grease, and smear medium
grease to the pawl and rack in the hand lever assembly.

## 11  Hydraulic pipes and hoses - inspection, removal and refitting

1  Periodically, and certainly well in advance of the MOT Test, all
brakes pipes, connections and unions should be completely and
carefully examined. Fig. 9.17 shows the composition of such pipes
and unions in the systems.
2  Examine first all the unions for signs of leaks. Then look at the
flexible hoses for signs of fraying and chafing (as well as for leaks).
This is only a preliminary inspection of the flexible hoses, as exterior
condition does not necessarily indicate interior condition which

will be considered later (photo).
3  The steel pipes must be examined equally carefully. They must be
thoroughly cleaned and examined for signs of dents or other percussive
damage, rust and corrosion. Rust and corrosion should be scraped off,
and, if the depth of pitting in the pipes is significant, they will require
renewal. This is most likely in those areas underneath the chassis and
along the rear suspension arms where the pipes are exposed to the full
force of road and weather conditions (photo).
4  If any section of pipe is to be removed, first take off the fluid
reservoir cap, line it with a piece of polythene film to make it airtight
and screw it back on. This will minimise the amount of fluid dripping
out of the system when the pipes are removed.
5  Rigid pipe removal is usually quite straightforward. The unions at
each end are undone and the pipe drawn out of the connection. The
clips which may hold it to the car body are bent back and it is then
removed. Underneath the car the exposed union can be particularly
stubborn, defying the efforts of an open ended spanner. As few people
will have the special split ring spanner required, a self-grip wrench
(mole) is the only answer. If the pipe is being renewed, new unions
will be provided. If not, then one will have to put up with the possibility of burring over the flats on the unions and of using a self-grip

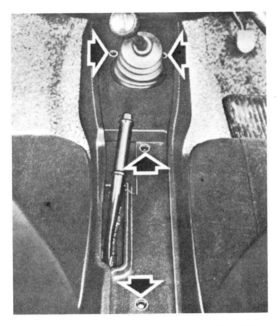

Fig. 9.15. Centre console retaining screws (Sec. 10)

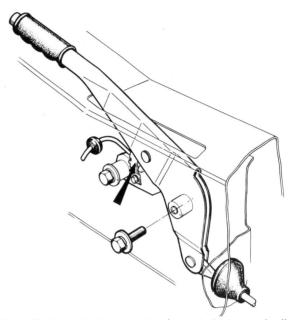

Fig. 9.16. Handbrake lever assembly (arrow indicates warning light switch). (Sec. 10)

11.2 Front brake hose union

11.3 Location of brake pipe union on rear axle

wrench for replacement also.

6  Flexible hoses are always fitted to a rigid support bracket where they join a rigid pipe, the bracket being fixed to the chassis or rear suspension arm. The rigid pipe unions must first be removed from the flexible union. Then the locknut securing the flexible pipe to the bracket must be unscrewed, releasing the end of the pipe from the bracket. As these connections are usually exposed they are, more often than not, rusted up and a penetrating fluid is virtually essential to aid removal. When undoing them, both halves must be supported as the bracket is not strong enough to support the torque required to undo the nut and can be snapped off easily.

7  Once the flexible hose is removed, examine the internal bore. If clear of fluid it should be possible to see through it. Any specks of rubber which come out, or signs of restriction in the bore, mean that the inner lining is breaking up and the hose must be renewed.

0  Rigid pipes which need renewing can usually be purchased at your local garage where they have the pipe, unions and special tools to make them up. All that they need to know is the pipe length required and the type of flare used at the ends of the pipe. These

may be different at each end of the same pipe. If possible, it is a good idea to take the old pipe along as a pattern.

9  Installation of pipes is a straightforward reversal of the removal procedure. It is best to get all the sets (bends) made prior to installation. Also, any acute bends should be put in by the garage on a bending machine otherwise there is the possibility of kinking them, and restricting the bore area and thus, fluid flow.

10 With the pipes replaced, remove the polythene from the reservoir cap and bleed the system as described in Section 2.

## 12 Master cylinder - removal and replacement

1  Apply the handbrake and chock the front wheels. Drain the fluid from the master cylinder reservoir and master cylinder by attaching a plastic bleed tube to one of the front brake bleed valves. Undo the valve one turn and then pump the fluid out into a clean glass container by means of the brake pedal. Hold the brake pedal against the floor at the end of each stroke and tighten the bleed valve. When the pedal

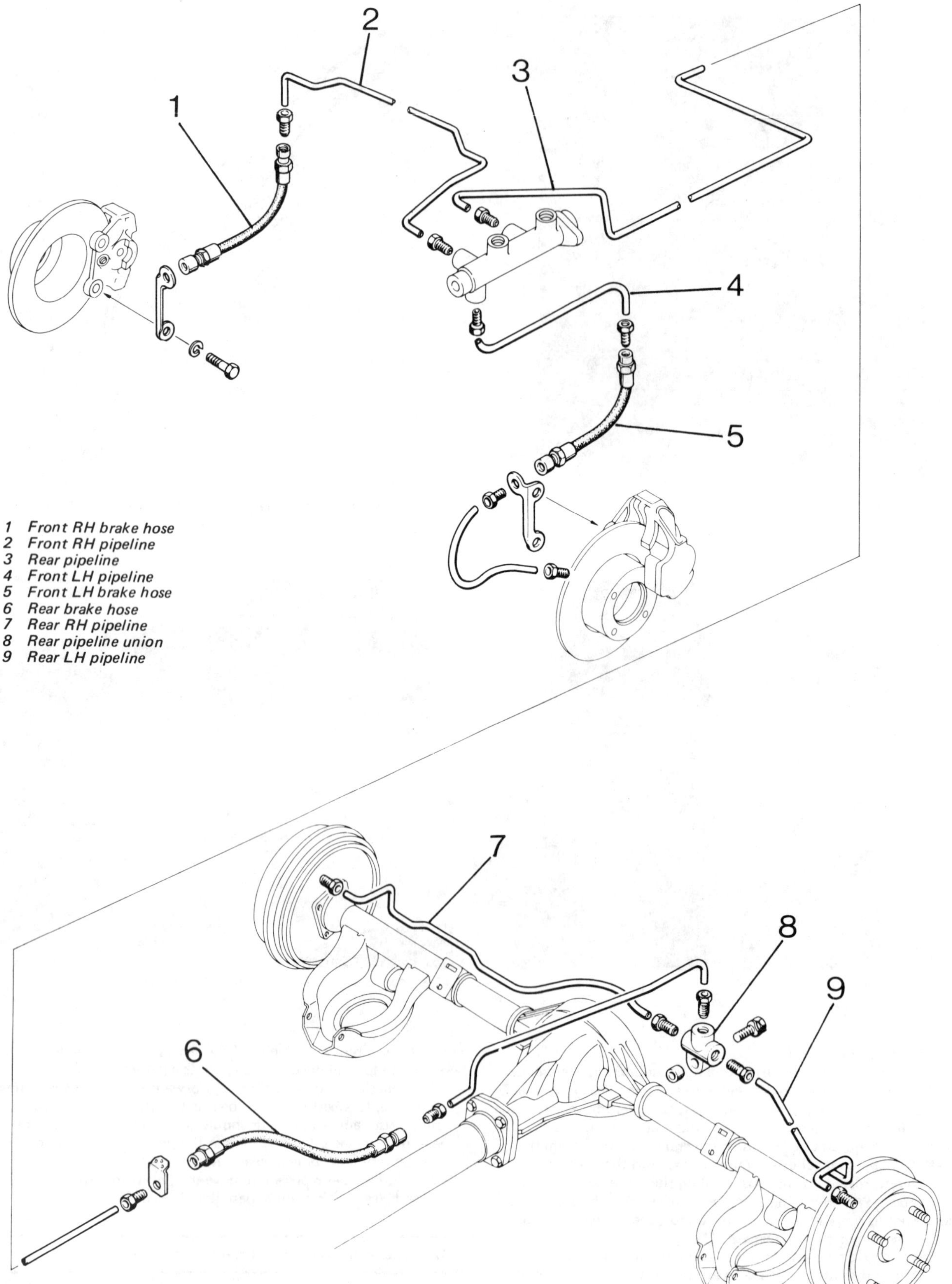

1 Front RH brake hose
2 Front RH pipeline
3 Rear pipeline
4 Front LH pipeline
5 Front LH brake hose
6 Rear brake hose
7 Rear RH pipeline
8 Rear pipeline union
9 Rear LH pipeline

Fig. 9.17. Brake hoses and pipelines (Sec. 11)

has returned to its normal position, loosen the bleed valve and repeat the process until the master cylinder reservoir is empty.

2   Wipe the area around the hydraulic pipe unions on the master cylinder. Undo the union nuts and lift out the hydraulic pipes.

3   Undo and remove the two nuts and spring washers that secure the master cylinder to the servo unit, and remove the clutch cable clip (Fig. 9.18).

4   Lift away the master cylinder taking care not to allow any hydraulic fluid to drip onto the paintwork.

5   Refitting the master cylinder follows the reversal of the removal procedure. Use a new 'O' ring between the tandem brake cylinder and servo unit.

6   Tighten the securing nuts to the specified torque; refit brake pipes and bleed the brake system.

## 13 Master cylinder - renovation

1   Remove the master cylinder without the brake servo as described in Section 12, of this Chapter.

2   Work on a clean bench and with clean tools. Any dirt introduced into the system can ruin many hours work.

3   Begin by removing the plastic reservoir from the master cylinder. The reservoirs are retained by two pipe unions.

4   Now remove the piston stop screw which is fitted in the top of the cylinder between the two reservoir ports (Fig. 9.19).

5   Mount the master cylinder in a vice and then push the primary piston downwards into the cylinder and retain by inserting a smooth rod into the reservoir port nearest the mounting flange. Once the primary piston is held down, the snap-ring near the mouth of the master cylinder can be removed. Extract the rod holding the primary piston (Fig. 9.20).

6   The primary and secondary pistons with their seals and spacing springs can now be removed from the cylinder.

7   Finally, remove the check valve by unscrewing the valve connector and extract the valve and spring (Fig. 9.21).

8   Lift the seals from the two pistons, and then proceed to clean all the component parts in new, clean brake fluid or methylated spirits. **No other solvent should be used.**

9   Inspect the cylinder bores and piston surfaces for scores, nicks, scratches and other defects. A new cylinder assembly should be fitted if any defects are found in the existing one, and in any event whenever the cylinder assembly is dismantled a new repair kit of seals and clips should be used on reassembly.

Fig. 9.18. Master cylinder pipeline connections (Sec. 12)

1   Rear brakes outlet
2   Front LH brake outlet
3   Front RH brake outlet

Fig. 9.20. Retaining the primary piston forwards using a piece of wire (Sec. 13)

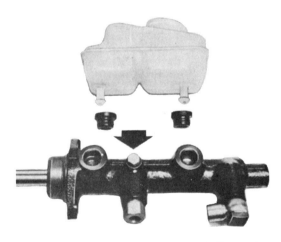

Fig. 9.19. Master cylinder and reservoir - arrow indicates piston stop screw (Sec. 13)

Fig. 9.21. The check valve removed from master cylinder body (Sec. 13)

10 On reassembly of the master cylinder coat all the components with clean hydraulic fluid. Refit the seals to the pistons, making sure that the seal lip is facing the correct way. The secondary piston centre and forward seal lips should face forwards. The rear seal on the secondary piston should face rearwards. Both seals on the primary piston should face forwards.

11 Insert the piston assembly carefully into the cylinder making sure that the seal lips are not damaged in any way. Push the primary piston down into the cylinder again whilst a **new** snap-ring is fitted to retain the pistons in the cylinder.

12 Install the check valve spring, valve and connector and tighten the connector.

13 Next, refit the piston stop screw.

14 The reservoirs should be fitted next. Lubricate the seals with new fluid before mounting the reservoirs on the master cylinder. Retain them in position with the special cylindrical clips. Do not use any force when refitting the reservoirs.

15 Finally, refit the reservoir covers. The master cylinder is now ready to be refitted to the car.

## 14 Brake servo unit - description and maintenance

### Description

1 A vacuum servo unit is fitted into the brake hydraulic circuit in

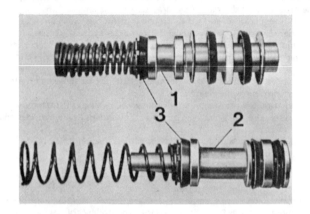

Fig. 9.22. Master cylinder pistons and springs (Sec. 13)

1 Primary piston
2 Secondary piston
3 Front seals

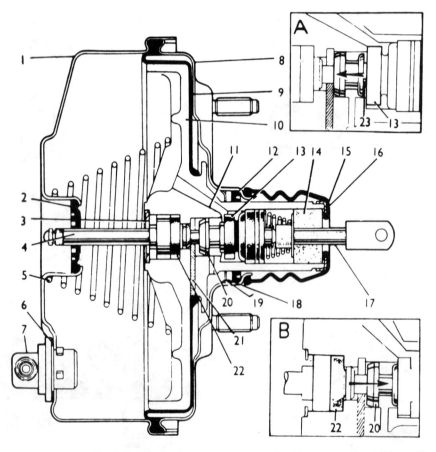

Fig. 9.23. Sectional view of Servo unit (Sec. 14)

| | | | | | |
|---|---|---|---|---|---|
| 1 | Front shell | 8 | Rear shell | 16 | End cap |
| 2 | Seal and plate assembly | 9 | Diaphragm | 17 | Valve operating rod assembly |
| 3 | Retainer (Sprag washer) | 10 | Diaphragm plate | 18 | Bearing |
| 4 | Pushrod (hydraulic) | 11 | Vacuum port | 19 | Retainer |
| 5 | Diaphragm return spring | 12 | Seal | 20 | Control piston |
| 6 | 'O' ring | 13 | Control valve | 21 | Valve retaining plate |
| 7 | Non-return valve | 14 | Filter | 22 | Reaction disc |
| | | 15 | Dust cover | 23 | Atmospheric port |

Insets:   A   Control valve closed, control piston moved forward - atmospheric port open
          B   Pressure from diaphragm plate causes reaction disc to extrude, presses back control piston and closes atmospheric port

series with the master cylinder, to provide power assistance to the driver when the brake pedal is depressed.

The unit operates by vacuum obtained from the induction manifold and comprises, basically, a booster diaphragm and a non-return valve.

The servo unit and hydraulic master cylinder are connected together so that the servo unit piston rod acts as the master cylinder pushrod. The driver's braking effort is transmitted through another pushrod to the servo unit piston and its built-in control system. The servo unit piston does not fit tightly into the cylinder, but has a strong diaphragm to keep its edges in constant contact with the cylinder wall so assuring an air tight seal between the two parts. The forward chamber is held under vacuum conditions created in the inlet manifold of the engine and, during periods when the brake pedal is not in use, the controls open a passage to the rear chamber so placing it under vacuum. When the brake pedal is depressed, the vacuum passage to the rear chamber is cut off and the chamber opened to atmospheric pressure. The consequent rush of air pushes the servo piston forward in the vacuum chamber and operates the main pushrod to the master cylinder. The controls are designed so that assistance is given under all conditions and, when the brakes are not required, vacuum in the rear chamber is established when the brake pedal is released. Air from the atmosphere entering the rear chamber is passed through a small air filter.

*Maintenance and adjustments*

2   The brake servo unit operation can be checked easily without any special tools. Proceed as follows:

3   Stop the engine and clear the servo of any vacuum by depressing the brake pedal several times.

4   Once the servo is cleared, keep the brake pedal depressed and start the engine. If the servo unit is in proper working order, the brake pedal should move further downwards, under even foot pressure, due to the effect of the inlet manifold vacuum on the servo diaphragms.

5   If the brake pedal does not move further downwards the servo system is not operating properly, and the vacuum hoses from the inlet manifold to the servo should be inspected. The vacuum control valve should also be checked. This valve is in the vacuum hose to prevent air flowing into the vacuum side of the servo from the inlet manifold when the engine stops. It is in effect a one way valve.

6   If the brake servo operates properly in the test, but still gives less effective service on the road, the air filter through which air flows into the servo should be inspected. A dirty filter will limit the formation of a difference in pressure across the servo diaphragm.

7   The servo unit itself cannot be repaired and therefore a complete replacement is necessary if the measures described are not effective.

8   *Air filter replacement:* From inside the car, detach the brake pedal from the servo pushrod, then remove the rubber boot over the pushrod housing and air filter (Fig. 9.24).

9   Once the boot has been removed, extract the filter, silencer and retainer from the servo housing bore.

10  Refitting follows the reversal of the removal procedure. The retainer can be driven into position with a light soft-faced hammer. The slots in the filter and silencer should be spaced by 180 degrees.

11  *Vacuum control valve:* The valve is located in the vacuum hose to prevent air flowing into the servo when the engine stops. It is not repairable and therefore when defective must be renewed.

12  The valve should be located near to the inlet manifold union and the arrows on the valve casing should point towards the inlet manifold. Make sure that all the hose clips are properly located and tightened: The system must be air tight (Fig. 9.25).

### 15 Brake servo unit - removal and refitting

1   Remove the master cylinder as directed in Section 12, of this Chapter.

2   Disconnect the vacuum hose from the vacuum servo unit.

3   Detach the brake pedal from the servo pushrod and then undo and remove the four nuts and washers attaching the servo to the bulkhead support.

4   Lift the servo unit from the car.

5   Refitting follows the reversal of the removal procedure. The nuts securing the servo unit to the bulkhead support should be tightened to the specified torque.

**Fig. 9.24. Servo unit air filter (Sec. 14)**

A   Inlet air filter
B   Air flow silencer
C   Silencer and filter retaining ring

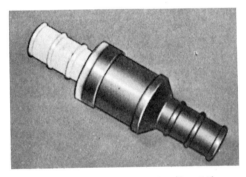

**Fig. 9.25. Vacuum control valve (Sec. 14)**

### 16 Stop light switch - removal and refitting

1   The braking 'stop' light switch is mounted on the brake pedal support.

2   Removal is straightforward, needing only the detachment of the electrical leads from the switch and then unscrewing the switch from the support.

3   The switch acts to close the electrical contacts when the plunger is released.

### 17 Brake and clutch pedals - removal and refitting

1   The best method of removing the clutch and brake pedals is to remove the complete mounting bracket assembly from inside the car.

2   First remove the clevis pin securing the brake pushrod to the brake pedal and then unhook the clutch cable from the clutch pedal.

3   Disconnect the wires from the brake light switch.

4   Remove the two bolts and one nut securing the pedal mounting bracket to the dash panel and left-hand support plate (see Fig. 9.27).

5   Unhook the clutch pedal return spring from the support plate, (Fig. 9.28), and lift out the pedals complete with mounting bracket and shaft.

6   Refer to Fig. 9.26 and slide the clutch pedal and shims off the shaft.

7   Remove the two spacing clips and shims from the shaft and slide off the brake pedal.

8   Check the pedal bushes for wear and renew if necessary. It is unlikely that the pedal shaft is worn, but if it is, it should be replaced with a new one.

9   Refit the bracket and pedals using the reverse procedure to dismantling. Ensure the pedal return springs are fitted correctly

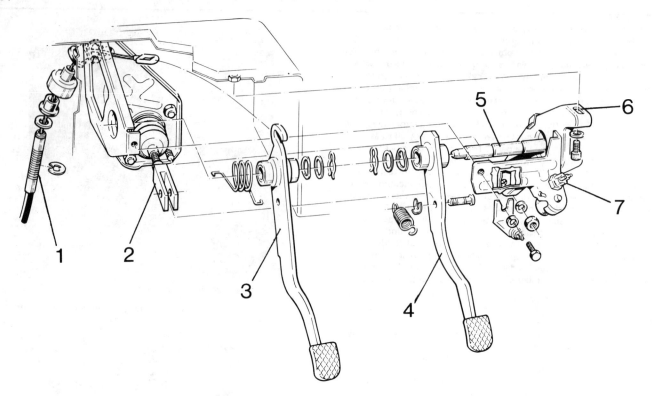

**Fig. 9.26. Brake and clutch pedal assembly (Sec. 17)**

1  Clutch cable
2  Brake pushrod
3  Clutch pedal
4  Brake pedal
5  Pedal support shaft
6  Support bracket
7  Stoplight switch

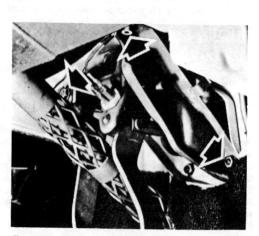

**Fig. 9.27. Support bracket mounting bolts (Sec. 17)**

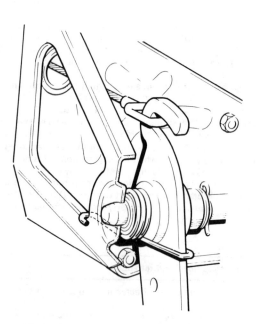

**Fig. 9.28. Clutch pedal return spring (Sec. 17)**

and check the brake pedal adjustment as described in the following Section.

## 18 Brake pedal play - adjustment

1  Before checking the pedal play, stop the engine and depress the pedal several times to clear the servo of any vacuum.
2  When the servo has been cleared, there should be a noticeable play of 0.24 to 0.35 inches at the pedal pad before the pedal and pushrod engages the servo piston.
3  The free play can be adjusted by disconnecting the pushrod, slackening the locknut and screwing the forkend in or out to obtain the correct free-travel. Do not forget to tighten the locknut after the correct adjustment has been obtained.

## 19 Brake pressure control valve

1  A brake pressure sensing valve is located in the engine compartment on the lower left-hand side (see Fig. 9.29).
2  The valve is connected into the hydraulic pipeline to the rear brakes and is basically a reducing valve. Under heavy braking conditions the fluid pressure to the front brakes is maintained at the normal rate, while the valve reduces the pressure to the rear brakes, thus minimising the possibility of the rear wheels locking.
3  The valve can be removed by undoing the two hydraulic lines and the bolt retaining it to the bracket. The valve cannot be dismantled and

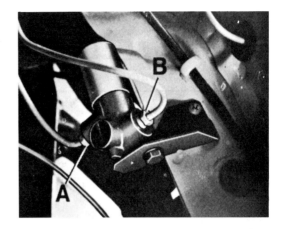

Fig. 9.29. Brake pressure control valve (Sec. 19)

A   Inlet pipe                                             B   Outlet pipe

if faulty should be replaced with a new one.
4  After refitting the valve it will be necessary to bleed the brakes as described in Section 2.

## 20 Fault diagnosis - braking system

*Before diagnosing faults from the following chart, check that any braking irregularities are not caused by:*

1  *Uneven and incorrect tyre pressures.*
2  *Incorrect 'mix' of radial and crossply tyres.*
3  *Wear in the steering mechanism.*
4  *Defects in the suspension and dampers.*
5  *Misalignment of the bodyframe.*

| Symptom | Reason/s |
| --- | --- |
| Pedal travels a long way before the brakes operate | Brake shoes set too far from the drums. |
| Stopping ability poor, even though pedal pressure is firm | Linings, discs or drums badly worn or scored.<br>One or more wheel hydraulic cylinders seized, resulting in some brake shoes not pressing against the drums (or pads against discs).<br>Brake linings contaminated with oil.<br>Wrong type of linings fitted (too hard).<br>Brake shoes wrongly assembled. Servo unit not functioning. |
| Car veers to one side when the brakes are applied | Brake pads or linings on one side are contaminated with oil.<br>Hydraulic wheel cylinder(s) on one side partially or fully seized.<br>A mixture of lining materials fitted between sides.<br>Brake discs not matched.<br>Unequal wear between sides caused by partially seized wheel cylinders. |
| Pedal feels spongy when the brakes are applied | Air is present in the hydraulic system. |
| Pedal feels springy when the brakes are applied | Brake linings not bedded into the drums (after fitting new ones).<br>Master cylinder or brake backplate mounting bolts loose.<br>Severe wear in brake drums causing distortion when brakes are applied. Discs out of true. |
| Pedal travels right down with little or no resistance and brakes are virtually non-operative | Leak in hydraulic system resulting in lack of pressure for operating wheel cylinders.<br>If no signs of leakage are apparent the master cylinder internal seals are failing to sustain pressure. |
| Binding, juddering, overheating | One or a combination of reasons given in the foregoing Sections. |

# Chapter 10 Electrical system

*For modifications, and information applicable to later models, see Supplement at end of manual*

**Contents**

**Specifications**

| | |
|---|---|
| **Battery** ... ... ... ... ... ... ... ... ... | 12 volt, 44 amp. hour at 20 hour rate |

**Alternator (Bosch type)**

| | |
|---|---|
| Voltage ... ... ... ... ... ... ... ... ... | 12 |
| Output ... ... ... ... ... ... ... ... ... | 45 amp |
| Rotor resistance (± 5%) ... ... ... ... ... ... | 4.2 ohms |
| Stator resistance (± 5%) ... ... ... ... ... ... | 0.19 ohms |
| Brush length ... ... ... ... ... ... ... | 0.2 in (5 mm) minimum protrusion |
| Slip rings: | |
| Permissible eccentricity ... ... ... ... ... ... | 0.001 in (0.03 mm) maximum |
| Minimum diameter ... ... ... ... ... ... ... | 1.24 in (31.5 mm) |
| Regulator: | |
| Type ... ... ... ... ... ... ... ... | ADN 1/4V |
| Voltage setting ... ... ... ... ... ... ... | 13.9 - 14.8 volts |

**Alternator (Delco-Remy type)**

| | |
|---|---|
| Voltage ... ... ... ... ... ... ... ... ... | 12 |
| Output ... ... ... ... ... ... ... ... ... | 45 amp |
| Rotor resistance (± 5%) ... ... ... ... ... ... | 2.8 ohms |
| Stator resistance (± 5%) ... ... ... ... ... ... | 0.24 ohms |
| Brush length ... ... ... ... ... ... ... | 0.4 in (10 mm) minimum |
| Brush spring pressure ... ... ... ... ... ... | 8 - 13 oz f (2.2 - 3.6 N) |
| Slip rings: | |
| Permissible eccentricity ... ... ... ... ... ... | 0.003 in (0.07 mm) maximum |
| Minimum diameter ... ... ... ... ... ... ... | 0.864 in (21.95 mm) |

**Starter motor (Bosch type)**

| | |
|---|---|
| Brush length ... ... ... ... ... ... ... | 0.51 in (13 mm) minimum |
| Brush spring pressure ... ... ... ... ... ... | 40 - 47 oz f (11.12 - 13.10 N) |
| Commutator: | |
| Diameter after skimming ... ... ... ... ... ... | 1.29 in (32.8 mm) minimum |
| Permissible eccentricity ... ... ... ... ... ... | 0.001 in (0.03 mm) maximum |
| Armature endfloat ... ... ... ... ... ... ... | 0.0004 - 0.012 in (0.01 - 0.30 mm) |

Solenoid pull-in voltage ... ... ... ... ... ... ... 7.5 minimum
Starter test data:
    Free-running current ... ... ... ... ... ... ... 35 - 55 amp at 6,000 - 8,000 rev/min at 11.5 volts
    Lock torque ... ... ... ... ... ... ... ... ... 9 lb f ft (12.3 N m) at 320 - 410 amp

## Starter motor (Delco-Remy)
Brush length ... ... ... ... ... ... ... ... ... 0.38 in (9.5 mm) minimum
Brush spring pressure at 0.25 in (6 mm) ... ... ... ... ... 38 - 64 oz f (10.6 - 17.8 N)
Commutator:
    Diameter after skimming ... ... ... ... ... ... ... 1.46 in (37 mm) minimum
    Permissible eccentricity ... ... ... ... ... ... ... 0.002 in (0.05 mm) maximum
Thickness of shift-lever pegs ... ... ... ... ... ... ... 0.20 in (5 mm) minimum
Solenoid test data:
    Pull-in resistance ... ... ... ... ... ... ... ... 0.21 - 0.27 ohm
    Hold-in resistance ... ... ... ... ... ... ... ... 0.85 - 1.12 ohm
    Pull-in voltage ... ... ... ... ... ... ... ... 7.7 maximum
Starter test data:
    Free-running current ... ... ... ... ... ... ... 43 - 51 amp at 7,400 - 9,000 rev/min at 10.6 volts
    Lock torque ... ... ... ... ... ... ... ... ... 8 lb f ft (11.2 N m) at 325 amp

## Lamp bulb data

| Lamp | Watts | Type |
|---|---|---|
| Head ... ... ... ... ... ... ... ... | 45/40 ... ... ... ... | Unified European cap |
| Side ... ... ... ... ... ... ... ... | 4 ... ... ... ... | Miniature centre contact |
| Tail/stop ... ... ... ... ... ... ... ... | 5/21 ... ... ... ... | Small bayonet cap (offset pins) |
| Turn signal ... ... ... ... ... ... ... ... | 21 ... ... ... ... | Small centre contact |
| Side repeater ... ... ... ... ... ... ... ... | 5 ... ... ... ... | Miniature bayonet cap |
| Number plate ... ... ... ... ... ... ... ... | 5 ... ... ... ... | Wedge-base capless |
| Reverse ... ... ... ... ... ... ... ... | 21 ... ... ... ... | Small centre contact |
| Fog ... ... ... ... ... ... ... ... | 55 ... ... ... ... | Quartz halogen H3 |
| Fog rear guard ... ... ... ... ... ... ... ... | 21 ... ... ... ... | Small centre contact |
| Interior ... ... ... ... ... ... ... ... | 10 ... ... ... ... | Festoon |
| Engine compartment and luggage trunk ... ... ... | 5 ... ... ... ... | Festoon |
| Instrument illumination<br>Turn signal indicator<br>Oil pressure warning<br>Main beam warning<br>Hazard warning indicator<br>Parking brake and clutch wear indicator<br>Cigar lighter/clock/glove compartment<br>Automatic transmission selector<br>Rear window demist and heater motor switches | 1.2 ... ... ... ... | Miniature wedge-base capless |
| Alternator warning ... ... ... ... ... ... | 3 ... ... ... ... | Wedge-base capless |

## Fuses

| Fuse | Amps | Circuit |
|---|---|---|
| No. 1 | 5 amp | Right-hand side and tail lamps. |
| No. 2 | 5 amp | Left-hand side and tail lamps, number plate lamp, instrument lamps, illumination for ventilator fan motor and rear window demist switches. Where applicable, fog rear guard lamps, cigar lighter/clock/glove compartment bulb, automatic transmission selector lamp, fog lamp switch illumination and engine compartment lamp. |
| No. 3 | 8 amp | Interior lamp, headlamp flasher, hazard warning system and where applicable luggage trunk lamp, radio and clock. |
| No. 4 | 8 amp | Windscreen wipers and wash and carburettor automatic choke. |
| No. 5 | 8 amp | Ventilator fan motor, reverse lamps and where applicable starter inhibitor switch (automatic transmission). |
| No. 6 | 8 amp | Stop lamps and turn signal lamps. |
| No. 7 | 16 amp | Rear window demist. |
| No. 8 | 8 amp | Horn and where applicable cigar lighter element and fog lamp switch. |
| No. 9 | 8 amp | Spare. |
| No. 10 | 8 amp | Where applicable, fog lamp relay. |

## Torque wrench settings

| | lb f in | kg f cm |
|---|---|---|
| Alternator through bolts: | | |
|     Bosch ... ... ... ... ... ... ... ... ... ... | 48 | 55 |
|     Delco-Remy ... ... ... ... ... ... ... ... ... | 62 | 70 |

| | lb f ft | kg f m |
|---|---|---|
| Alternator pulley nut: | | |
|     Bosch ... ... ... ... ... ... ... ... ... ... | 30 | 4.1 |
|     Delco-Remy ... ... ... ... ... ... ... ... ... | 50 | 6.8 |
| Starter through bolts ... ... ... ... ... ... ... | 49 | 6.6 |

## 1  General description

The major components of the 12 volt negative earth system comprise a 12 volt battery, an alternator (driven from the crankshaft pulley), and a starter motor.

The battery supplies a steady amount of current for the ignition, lighting and other electrical circuits and provides a reserve of power when the current consumed by the electrical equipment exceeds that being produced by the alternator.

The alternator has its own regulator which ensures a high output if the battery is in a low state of charge and the demand from the electrical equipment is high, and a low output if the battery is fully charged and there is little demand for the electrical equipment.

When fitting electrical accessories to cars with a negative earth system it is important, if they contain silicone diodes or transistors, that they are connected correctly; otherwise serious damage may result to the components concerned. Items such as radios, tape players, electronic ignition systems, electronic tachometer, automatic dipping etc, should all be checked for correct polarity.

It is important that the battery positive lead is always disconnected if the battery is to be boost charged, also if body repairs are to be carried out using electric welding equipment - the alternator must be disconnected otherwise serious damage can be caused. Whenever the battery has to be disconnected it must always be reconnected with the negative terminal earthed.

## 2  Battery - maintenance and inspection

1  Check the battery electrolyte level weekly, by lifting off the cover or removing the individual cell plugs. The tops of the plates should be just covered by the electrolyte. If not, add distilled water so that they are just covered. Do not add extra water with the idea of reducing the intervals of topping-up. This will merely dilute the electrolyte and reduce charging and current retention efficiency. On batteries fitted with patent covers, troughs, glass balls and so on, follow the instructions marked on the cover of the battery to ensure correct addition of water.
2  Keep the battery clean and dry all over by wiping it with a dry cloth. A damp top surface could cause tracking between the two terminal posts with consequent draining of power.
3  Every three months remove the battery and check the support tray clamp and battery terminal connections for signs of corrosion - usually indicated by a whitish green crystalline deposit. Wash this off with clean water to which a little ammonia or washing soda has been added. Then treat the terminals with petroleum jelly (vaseline) and the battery mounting with suitable protective paint to prevent the metal being eaten away. Clean the battery thoroughly and repair any cracks with a proprietary sealer. If there has been any excessive leakage the appropriate cell may need an addition of electrolyte rather than just distilled water.
4  If the electrolyte level needs an excessive amount of replenishment but no leaks are apparent, it could be due to over-charging as a result of the battery having been run down and then left to recharge from the vehicle rather than an outside source. If the battery has been heavily discharged for one reason or another it is best to have it continuously charged at a low amperage for a period of many hours. If it is charged from the car's system under such conditions the charging will be intermittent and greatly varied in intensity. This does not do the battery any good at all. If the battery needs topping-up frequently, even when it is known to be in good condition and not too old, then the voltage regulator should be checked to ensure that the charging output is being correctly controlled. An elderly battery, however, may need topping-up more than a new one because it needs to take in more charging current. Do not worry about this provided it gives satisfactory service.
5  When checking a battery's condition a hydrometer should be used. On some batteries where the terminals of each of the six cells are exposed, a discharge tester can be used to check the condition of any one cell also. On modern batteries the use of a discharge tester is no longer regarded as useful as the replacement or repair of cells is not an economic proposition. The tables in the following Section give the hydrometer readings for various states of charge. A further check can be made when the battery is undergoing a charge. If, towards the end of the charge, when the cells are meant to be 'gassing' (bubbling), one cell appears not to be, then it indicates that the cell or cells in question are probably breaking down and the life of the battery is limited.

## 3  Battery - charging and electrolyte replenishment

1  It is possible that in winter when the load on the battery cannot be recuperated during normal driving time external charging is desirable. This is best done over night at a 'trickle' rate of 1 - 1.5 amps. Alternatively a 3 - 4 amp rate can be used over a period of four hours or so. Check the specific gravity in the latter case and stop the charge when the reading is correct. Most modern charging sets reduce the rate automatically when the fully charged state is neared. Rapid boost charges of 30 - 60 amps or more may get you out of trouble or can be used on a battery that has seen better days anyhow. They are not advisable for a good battery that may have run flat for some reason. It is recommended that the battery leads are disconnected before connecting any mains charger, to avoid damaging the alternator.
2  Electrolyte replenishment should not normally be necessary unless an accident or some other cause such as contamination arises. If it is necessary then it is best first to charge the battery completely and then tip out all the remaining liquid from all cells. Then acquire a quantity of mixed electrolyte from a battery shop or garage according to the specifications in the table given next. The quantity required will depend on the type of battery but 3 - 4 pints should be more than enough for most. When the electrolyte has been put into the battery a slow charge - not exceeding one amp - should be given for as long as is necessary to fully charge the battery. This could be up to 36 hours.

Specific gravities for hydrometer readings (check each cell) - 12 volt batteries:

|  | Climate below 80°F (26.7°C) | Climate above 80°F (26.7°C) |
|---|---|---|
| Fully charged | 1.270 - 1.290 | 1.210 - 1.230 |
| Half-charged | 1.190 - 1.210 | 1.120 - 1.150 |
| Discharged completely | 1.110 - 1.130 | 1.050 - 1.070 |

**Note:** If the electrolyte temperature is significantly different from 60°F (15.6°C) then the specific gravity reading will be affected. For every 5° F (2.8°C) it will increase or decrease with the temperature by 0.002.

When the vehicle is being used in cold climates it is essential to maintain the battery fully charged because the charge affects the freezing point of the electrolyte. The densities below have been corrected to suit measurement at 80°F (26.7°C):

| | | |
|---|---|---|
| Specific gravity | 1.200 freezes | −35°F |
| Specific gravity | 1.160 freezes | 0°F |

## 4  Battery - long term storage

If the battery is to be stored for a long time (either in or out of the vehicle) it must be fully charged and the electrolyte level checked every 30 days. The battery will self discharge and therefore it will be necessary to charge at a 5 amp rate periodically to maintain full charge.

Self discharging will proceed faster in warm conditions and therefore wet batteries should be stored in a cool place.

## 5  Battery - removal and refitting

1  Remove the negative earth connector first (to prevent accidental shorting) and then the positive lead and connector.
2  Remove the battery hold down bracket and carefully lift out the battery. It will weigh in the order of 45 lbs (20.4 kg) and it should be handled carefully to prevent spillage of electrolyte. Electrolyte is highly corrosive (sulphuric acid) and if any gets onto your skin or clothes you should rinse with copious amounts of water.
3  Refitting follows the exact reversal of the removal procedure - replacing the positive lead first.

## 6  Alternator - general description, removal and refitting

1  Either a Bosch or Delco-Remy alternator may be fitted. Both types are similar in construction, comprising, basically, an aluminium casing housing a three-phase star-connected stator. A rotor carrying the field windings rotates within the stator and is belt-driven from the crankshaft pulley.
2  In the case of the Bosch alternator, the voltage regulator is a separate unit located on the wheelhouse panel in the engine compartment.

The Delco-Remy alternator is fitted with an integral voltage regulator located within the end casing.

3    The main advantage of the alternator over its predecessor, the dynamo, lies in its ability to provide a high charge at low revolutions. Driving slowly in heavy traffic with a dynamo invariably means no charge is reaching the battery. In similar conditions even with the wiper, heater, lights and perhaps radio switched on the alternator will ensure a charge reaches the battery.

4    To remove the alternator, first disconnect the negative (earth) battery terminal.

5    Unplug and unscrew all the wiring connectors from the rear of the alternator.

6    Undo and remove the fan belt tension adjustment bolt from the alternator and retrieve the lock washer, plain washer and nut.

7    Next loosen the pivot bolt beneath the alternator and push the unit towards the engine to permit the fan belt to be removed from the alternator pulley.

8    Now swing the alternator down to expose the pivot bolt which can then be removed to release the unit from the engine. **Note:** An earthing wire may be connected from the alternator through bolt to the rear mounting bracket retaining bolt, in which case the bolt will have to be removed and the wire disconnected.

9    Refit the alternator using the reverse procedure to removal. Set the tension of the drivebelt so that there is 0.32in (8mm) deflection midway between the alternator and water pump pulleys. If a new belt is fitted, the deflection should be 0.20in (5mm).

---

### 7    Alternator - fault diagnosis

Due to the specialist knowledge and equipment required to test or service an alternator it is recommended that if the performance is suspect the car be taken to an automobile electrician who will have the facilities for such work. Because of this recommendation, information is limited to the inspection and renewal of the brushes. Should the alternator not charge or the system be suspect the following points may be checked before seeking further assistance:

1    Check the fan belt tension, as described in Section 6.
2    Check the battery, as described in Section 2.
3    Check all electrical cable connections for cleanliness and security.

---

### 8    Alternator brushes (Delco-Remy) - inspection, removal and refitting

1    Remove the alternator from the engine, as described in Section 6.
2    Scribe a line across the stator casing and front end cover to ensure correct location when reassembling.
3    Remove the three through-bolts (Fig. 10.1) and prise the front cover and rotor away from the rear end casing and stator.
4    Remove the three nuts and washers securing the stator leads to the

Fig. 10.1 Delco-Remy alternator through-bolts (Sec. 8)

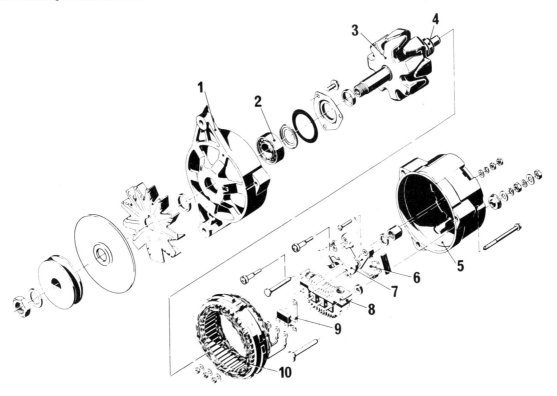

Fig. 10.2. Exploded view of Delco-Remy alternator (Sec. 8)

| | | | |
|---|---|---|---|
| 1  Drive end bracket | 4  Slip rings | 6  Regulator | 8  Rectifier |
| 2  Drive end bearing | 5  Slip-ring end bracket | 7  Brush holder | 9  Auxiliary diodes (Diode Trio) |
| 3  Rotor | | | 10  Stator |

Fig. 10.3. Stator and diode terminal nuts, (Delco-Remy). (Sec. 8)

Fig. 10.4. Brush holder retaining screws (Delco-Remy). (Sec. 8)

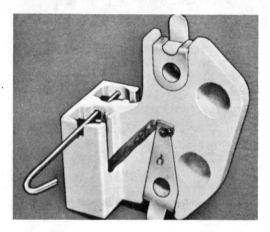

Fig. 10.5. Retracting the brushes (Delco-Remy). (Sec. 8)

Fig. 10.6. Brush retracting wire insert through alternator end casing (Delco-Remy). (Sec. 8)

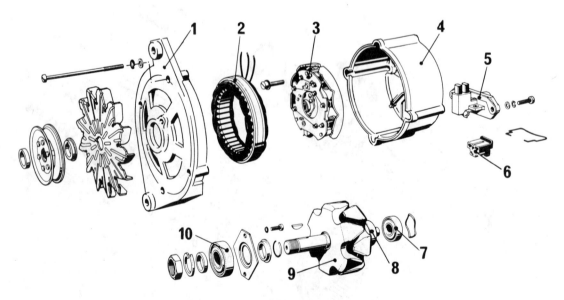

Fig. 10.7. Exploded view of Bosch alternator (Sec. 9)

| | |
|---|---|
| 1 Drive end bracket | 6 Connector plug |
| 2 Stator | 7 Slip ring end bearing |
| 3 Heat sink plate | 8 Slip rings |
| 4 Slip ring end bracket | 9 Rotor |
| 5 Brush holder | 10 Drive end bearing |

rectifier and lift away the stator assembly, remove the terminal screw and lift out the diode bracket (see Fig. 10.3).

5  Undo the two screws retaining the brushholder and voltage regulator to the end casing and remove the brushholder assembly (Fig. 10.4). Note that the inner screw is insulated.

6  Check that the brushes move freely in the guides and that the length is within the limit given in the Specifications. If any doubt exists regarding the condition of the brushes the best policy is to renew them.

7  To fit new brushes, unsolder the old brush leads from the brushholder and solder on the new leads in exactly the same place.

8  Check that the new brushes move freely in the guides.

9  Before refitting the brushholder assembly retain the brushes in the retracted position using a piece of insulated wire as shown in Fig. 10.5.

10  Refit the brushholder so that the wire protrudes through the slot in the end casing as shown in Fig. 10.6.

11  Refit the diode bracket and stator to the casing making sure the stator leads are in their correct positions.

12  Assemble the front casing and rotor to the stator casing ensuring that the scribe marks are aligned. Insert the three through bolts and tighten.

13  Now carefully pull the piece of wire out of the end casing slot so that the brushes drop onto the rotor slip ring.

14  The alternator can now be refitted to the car and tested.

### 9  Alternator brushes (Bosch) - inspection, removal and refitting

1  Undo and remove the two screws, spring and plain washers that secure the brush box to the rear of the brush end housing. Lift away the brush box (Fig. 10.8).

2  Check that the carbon brushes are able to slide smoothly in their guides without any sign of binding.

3  Measure the length of brushes and if they have worn below the specified limit, they must be renewed.

4  Hold the brush wire with a pair of engineer's pliers and unsolder

it from the brush box. Lift away the two brushes.

5  Insert the new brushes and check to make sure that they are free to move in their guides. If they bind, lightly polish with a very fine file.

6  Solder the brush wire ends to the brush box taking care that solder is not allowed to pass to the stranded wire.

7  Whenever new brushes are fitted new springs should also be fitted.

8  Refitting the brush box is the reverse sequence to removal.

### 10  Starter motor - general description

1  G.M. have fitted Delco-Remy and Bosch starters during the production of this range of cars. They are both of the pre-engaging type and comprise a DC series wound motor switched by a solenoid

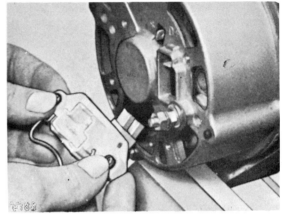

Fig. 10.8. Removing the brushholder (Bosch). (Sec. 9)

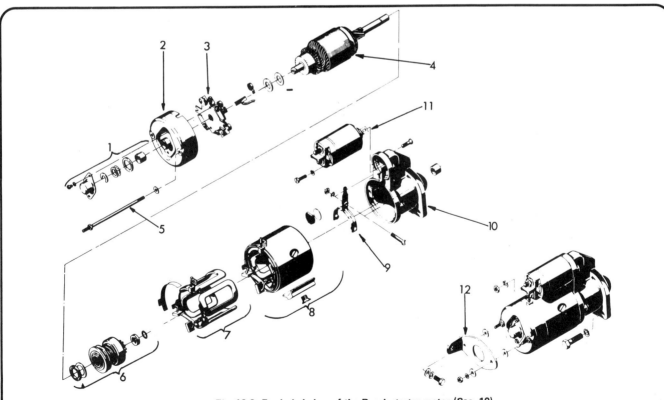

Fig. 10.9. Exploded view of the Bosch starter motor (Sec. 10)

| | | | | | |
|---|---|---|---|---|---|
| 1 | Armature forward end cap and bearing assembly | 3 | Brush holding frame | 6 | Pinion carriage |
| 2 | Motor forward end fitting | 4 | Armature | 7 | Field windings |
| | | 5 | Through-bolts | 8 | Motor casing |
| | | | | 9 | Pinion carriage actuation lever |

| | |
|---|---|
| 10 | Starter motor end housing |
| 11 | Solenoid |
| 12 | Forward support bracket |

**Fig. 10.10. Exploded view of the Delco-Remy starter motor (Sec. 10)**

1 Forward end plate and bearing
2 Through bolt
3 Negative brushes and holder
4 Solenoid
5 Pinion carriage shift lever
6 Through bolt sleeve
7 Armature
8 Positive brushes and field winding
9 Pinion carriage
10 Pinion carriage locating rings
11 Motor end casing

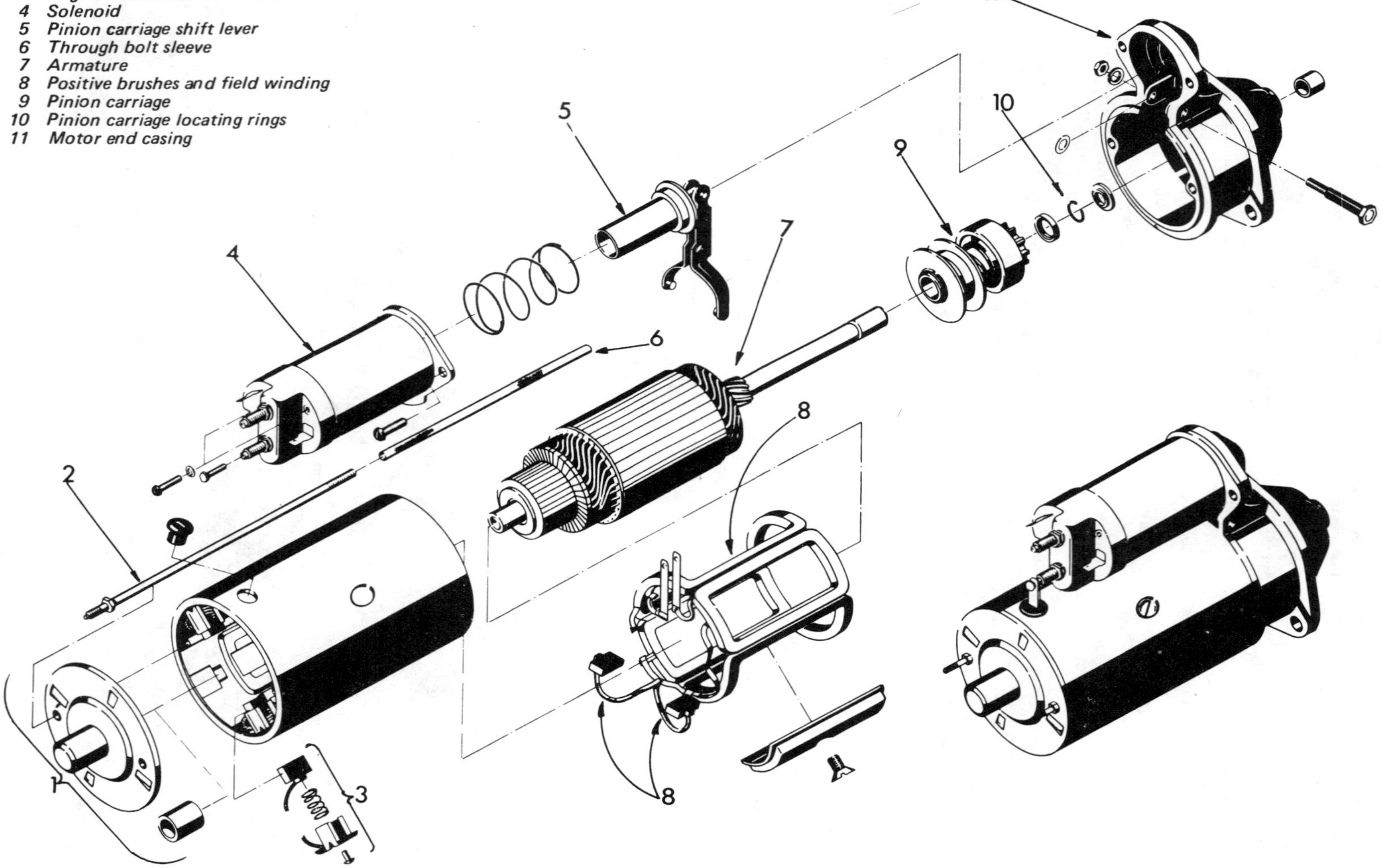

mounted on the top of the motor. The solenoid also serves to move the motor pinion into engagement with the ring gear on the flywheel periphery, before the switch contacts are closed to supply electrical power to the starter motor. The motor pinion is mounted on a carriage which engages a spiral spline on the motor shaft. The carriage incorporates an overspeed clutch which allows the pinion gear to be driven at a speed greater than starter motor speed when the engine starts. Once the engine has started and the starter switch is released, the solenoid cuts off the power from the motor and moves the pinion and carriage back from engagement with the flywheel ring gear.

2   The construction of the two makes of starter motor is quite similar and the removal, refitting, dismantling, inspection and reassembly procedures detailed here will serve for both motors. Significant differences will be noted.

## 11 Starter motor - in-situ testing

1   If the starter motor fails to turn the engine when the switch is operated there are four possible reasons why:

  a) *The battery is faulty.*
  b) *The electrical connections between the switch, solenoid, battery and starter motor are somewhere failing to pass the necessary current from the battery through the starter to earth.*
  c) *The solenoid switch is faulty.*
  d) *The starter motor is either jammed or electrically defective.*

2   To check the battery, switch on the headlights. If they dim after a few seconds the battery is in a discharged state. If the lights glow brightly, operate the starter switch and see what happens to the lights. If they dim then you know that power is reaching the starter motor but failing to turn it. Therefore check that it is not jammed by placing the car in gear (manual transmission only) and rocking it to-and-fro. Should the motor not be jammed, it will have to be removed for proper inspection. If the starter turns slowly when switched on proceed to the next check.

3   If, when the starter switch is operated the lights stay bright, then insufficient power is reaching the motor. Remove the battery connections, starter/solenoid power connections and the engine earth strap and thoroughly clean them and refit them.

Smear petroleum vaseline around the battery connections to prevent corrosion. Corroded connections are the most frequent cause of electric system malfunctions.

4   When the above checks and cleaning tasks have been carried out, but without success, you will have possibly heard a clicking noise each time the starter switch is operated. This is the solenoid switch operating, but it does not necessarily follow that the main contacts are closing properly (if no clicking has been heard from the solenoid, it is certainly defective). The solenoid contact can be checked by putting a voltmeter or bulb across the main cable connection on the starter side of the solenoid and earth. When the switch is operated, there should be a reading or lighted bulb. **Do not put a bulb across the two solenoid power connections.** If there is no reading or lighted bulb, the solenoid unit is faulty and should be replaced.

5   Finally, if it is established that the solenoid is not faulty and 12 volts are getting to the starter, then the motor is faulty and should be removed for inspection.

## 12 Starter motor - removal and refitting

1   With the engine in the car, the starter is quite accessible at the lower right-hand side of the engine. It is secured to the clutch bellhousing and engine cylinder block by two bolts and a terminal stud on the front end of the starter motor.

2   Remove the earth (negative) lead from the battery and then proceed to disconnect the solenoid and motor electrical connections. Identify the leads as necessary to ensure correct refitment.

3   Then remove the bolts which secure the solenoid - motor assembly to the engine. The motor can be lifted clear.

4   Refitting the starter motor assembly is the exact reversal of the removal procedure.

## 13 Starter motor - renovation

1   Such is the inherent reliability and strength of the starter motors fitted, that it is very unlikely that a motor will need dismantling until it is totally worn out and in need of replacement as a whole.

2   If, however, the motor is only a couple of years old or so and a pinion carriage, solenoid system or brush fault is suspected then remove the motor from the engine and dismantle as described in the following Sections.

## 14 Starter solenoid - removal and refitting

1   The solenoid is retained by two bolts to the pinion carriage operating mechanism casing. Remove the two bolts, retrieve the lock-washers and remove the electrical power connection to the motor. Extract the solenoid from the end casing.

2   **Note:** The Bosch starter/solenoid assembly differs from the Delco-Remy described above - the solenoid is retained by two screws to the end casing and is extracted after unhooking the solenoid switch shaft from the pinion carriage actuating arm mounted in the end casing.

3   Replacement of the solenoid follows the reversal of removal.

## 15 Starter motor brushes - inspection and replacement

### Bosch

1   With the starter removed from the engine and on a clean bench, begin by removing the armature end cap which is secured by two small screws on the front end of the motor. Remove the armature retaining clip, washers and the rubber sealing ring which were exposed. Undo and remove the two long bolts which hold the motor assembly together. The front end cover can now be removed to reveal the brushes and mounting plate.

2   Take the brushes from the holder and slip the holder off the armature shaft. Retrieve the spacer washers between the brush plate and the armature block (Fig. 10.11).

3   Inspect the brushes; if they are worn down to less than the minimum length given in the Specifications, they should be replaced. Where field brushes are obtained without lead wires attached, wash the old brushes and clean the existing wires, then locate the new brushes on the wires and splay the wire ends into the countersunk area. When soldering in place new brushes, hold the connecting wire in a pair of pliers to prevent molten solder running into the wire strands and destroying its flexibility. A 12 to 15 watt 'pencil' soldering iron is quite sufficient for this task.

4   Wipe the starter motor armature and commutator clean with a non-fluffy rag wetted with carbon tetrachloride.

5   Reassemble the brushes into the holder, refit the holder over the armature shaft remembering to fit the two washers between the holder and armature.

6   Refit the motor end cover and secure with two long bolts.

Fig. 10.11. Removing the brushholder from the Bosch starter motor (Note the spacers). (Sec. 15)

7 Refit the armature shaft end cap after fitting the rubber sealing ring, washer and shaft clip.

*Delco-Remy*

8 Again with the motor removed from the engine and ready on a clean bench, begin by undoing and removing the two long bolts which hold the motor assembly together.

9 The front end plate can then be removed from the motor to reveal the brushes, holders and armature of the motor (Fig. 10.12).

10 The brush holders are secured to the motor casing by rivets.

11 The 'positive' brushes are connected to the static field windings; the negative brushes are connected to the motor casing.

12 If the brushes are worn to less than the minimum length given in the Specifications, they should be replaced; always replace all four.

13 When soldering new positive brushes, hold the connecting wires in a pair of pliers to prevent the solder from running into the wire strands - reducing its flexibility. Use a 12 to 15 watt pencil soldering iron.

14 The negative brushes are replaced complete with the holder. Drill out the rivet holding the worn brush and mounting in place, remove and discard the worn brush unit. Offer up the new brush and mounting, insert the rivet from the inside of the casing and with a light hammer and punch close the rivet to secure the new brush mounting.

15 Clean the motor armature and commutator with a non-fluffy rag, wet with carbon tetrachloride.

16 Refit the armature into the motor and slip the brushes into position on the commutator.

17 Refit the motor end plate and screw in the long bolts which hold the motor assembly together. Check that the motor shaft turns freely, without any hint of an obstruction.

### 16 Starter motor - pinion carriage mechanism

1 With the starter motor removed from the engine and placed on a clean bench - remove the solenoid unit as detailed in Section 14, of this Chapter.

2 Then remove the motor casing end plate as directed in Section 15, when it is needed to be removed in order to gain access to the brushes.

3 *Bosch:* Remove the brushes from the brushholder, and slip holder off the armature shaft - retrieving the two spacing washers.

4 Pull the motor casing complete with static field windings off the armature, which is still held in the motor assembly rear end casing.

5 Undo the nut and remove the bolt which is the pivot for the pinion carriage actuating lever, mounted in the rear end casing (Fig. 10.13).

6 The end casing can now be separated from the armature and pin assembly.

7 Lift the forked lever from the pinion carriage.

8 Next remove the compensating washer from the rear end of the armature shaft and tap the snap-ring retaining ring back toward the pinion carriage to reveal the snap-ring.

9 With a small screwdriver prise the snap-ring open and slip it off the motor shaft. Clean burrs off the edge of the ring groove.

10 Slide the pinion carriage off the motor shaft. The pinion carriage cannot be dismantled and if deemed faulty should be replaced. The spiral spline on which the pinion runs should be thoroughly cleaned and then lightly lubricated with grease.

11 Reassembly follows the exact reversal of the dismantling procedure.

12 Make sure during reassembly of Delco-Remy motors that the long bolts which hold the assembly together, pass through the insulating sleeves which protect the static field windings.

### 17 Starter motor - checking armature and static field windings

1 Follow the instructions given in Section 16, of this Chapter and dismantle the motor to gain access to the armature and the motor casing with the static field windings attached.

2 The armature windings may be checked for a short onto the motor shaft/armature core, and for an open circuit in the windings.

3 Using a test circuit comprising two probes, a bulb and 12V battery, touch the commutator bars with one probe whilst holding the other against the armature metal (see Fig. 10.14). The test bulb should not light up.

4 To check the armature windings for open circuit, replace the bulb with an ammeter (0 to 10 amp). Touch commutator bars (90° spaced)

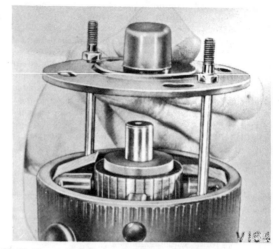

**Fig. 10.12. Removing the endplate from the Delco-Remy starter motor (Sec. 15)**

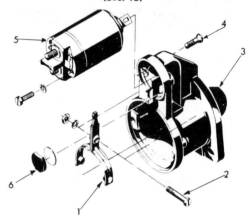

**Fig. 10.13. Exploded view of the starter motor rear end casing (Sec. 16)**

1   Pinion carriage shift lever      4   Solenoid securing screw
2   Shift lever pivot bolt           5   Solenoid
3   Main casing                  6   Rubber buffer

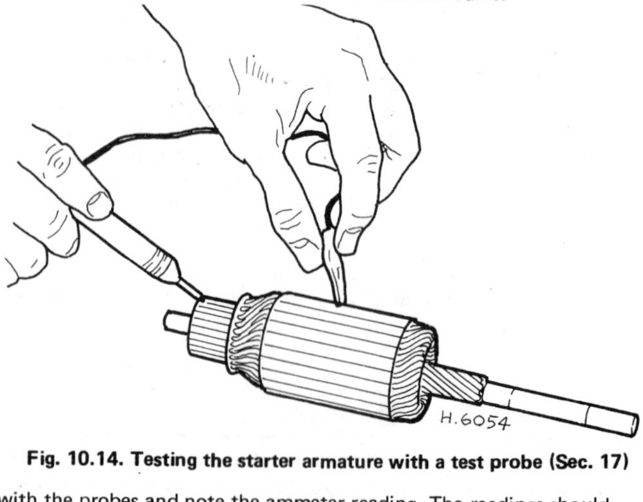

**Fig. 10.14. Testing the starter armature with a test probe (Sec. 17)**

with the probes and note the ammeter reading. The readings should all be the same; considerable deviation (25%) indicates open circuits or windings insulation breakdown.

5 The battery and bulb circuit is used to check the static field windings. Touch one probe onto each winding termination and hold the other against the metal of the motor casing. The test bulb must not light up. Remember to touch the positive brushes to check for short circuits properly.

6 Faulty armatures or field windings should be replaced - though

individual new spares may be difficult to obtain and it will possibly be necessary to purchase an exchange motor unit.

### 18 Windscreen wiper mechanism - fault diagnosis and rectification

1   Should the windscreen wipers fail, or work very slowly, then check the terminals on the motor for loose connections, and make sure the insulation of all the wiring is not cracked or broken thus causing a short circuit. If this is in order then check the current the motor is taking by connecting an ammeter in the circuit and turning on the wiper switch. Consumption should be between 2.3 and 3.1 amps.
2   If no current is passing through the motor, check that the switch is operating correctly.

### 19 Windscreen wiper components - removal and refitting

*Wiper blades*
1   To remove the wiper blades, depress the retaining catch on the

wiper arm and slide the blade off the pivot pin (see Fig. 10.15).
2   Refit the blades using the reverse procedure to removal.

*Wiper arms*
3   First prise off the plastic cap or lift the hinged cover from the base of the wiper arm (photo).
4   The arm can now be prised off the spindle using a wide-bladed screwdriver, after removing the nut.
5   With the wiper spindles in the 'parked' position, refit the blades in the positions shown in Fig. 10.17.

*Windscreen wiper motor and linkage*
6   Open the bonnet and disconnect the negative battery terminal.
7   Make a note of the positions of the wiring connections on the wiper motor and disconnect them.
8   Remove the wiper arms and remove the spindle retaining nuts and

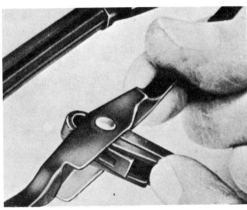

Fig. 10.15. Removing a windscreen wiper blade (Sec. 19)

19.3 Removing the wiper arm cap (early models)

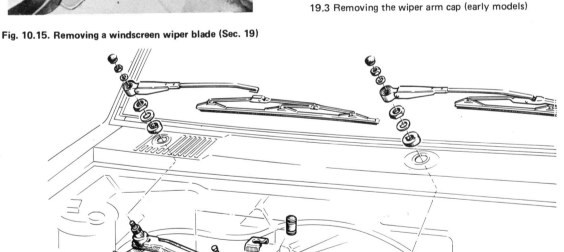

Fig. 10.16. View of windscreen wiper components (Sec. 19)

rubber spacers.

9   To enable the spindles to clear the shroud panel, it is necessary to remove the crank arm from the motor (Fig. 10.18).

10 Prise out the rubber grommet from the mounting bracket and lift out the complete wiper motor and linkage assembly from under the shroud panel.

11 The motor can be detached from the mounting bracket by removing the three retaining screws.

12 The linkage assembly cannot be serviced, so if the bushes are worn, a new assembly should be obtained.

13 Refit the motor and linkage assembly using the reverse procedure to removal. Before refitting the crank arm, ensure the motor is in the parked position and fit the arm onto the motor spindle so that it is in a horizontal position between the two arrows on the left of the mounting bracket.

## 20 Windscreen wiper motor - renovation

1   Release the two spring clips and pull the casing off the armature and gear housing (Fig. 10.20).

2   Remove the four screws and lift off the gear housing cover. The main gear and driveshaft can now be withdrawn from the housing, do not lose the thrust washer on the driveshaft.

3   Slacken the bearing retaining nut, as shown in Fig. 10.21, and withdraw the armature and bearing assembly, taking care not to contaminate the brushes with grease.

4   The brush plate assembly can be removed from the gear housing by undoing the three retaining screws.

5   Check the bushes and bearing for wear and replace if necessary. The brushes should be renewed as a matter of course.

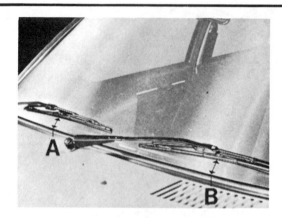

**Fig. 10.17. Correct position of wiper blades**

*A = 1.8 inches (45 mm)*          *B = 2 inches (50 mm)*

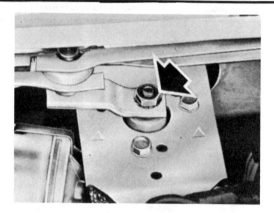

**Fig. 10.18. Wiper motor crank arm securing nut**

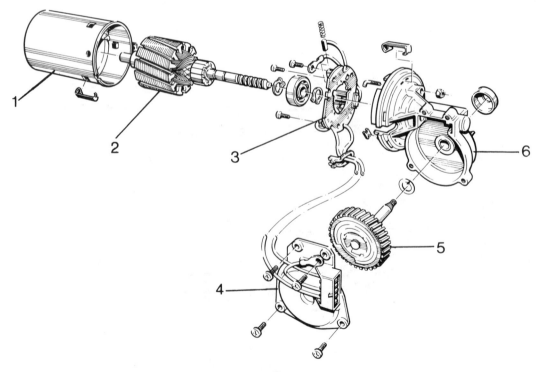

**Fig. 10.19. Exploded view of wiper motor**

| | | |
|---|---|---|
| 1   Outer casing | 3   Brushholder plate | 5   Drive gear and shaft |
| 2   Armature | 4   Contact cover | 6   Gear housing |

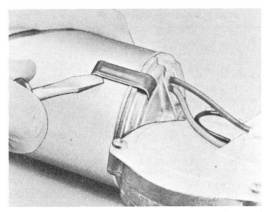

Fig. 10.20. Removing the casing retaining clips (Sec. 20)

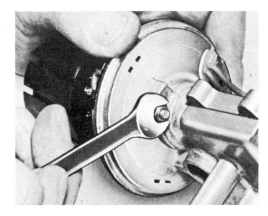

Fig. 10.21. Undoing the bearing retainer nut (Sec. 20)

Fig. 10.22. Location of horn (Sec. 21)

22.1 Lifting out the horn button

6   Clean the contacts on the gear housing cover using very fine emery paper.
7   Clean the commutator with a piece of clean cloth soaked in solvent and check that the insulation between the segments is free from metallic dust.
8   If nothing obviously wrong can be found with the motor, take the armature to an electrical specialist and have it checked for insulation failure.
9   Wash out the gear housing in petrol and repack with grease.
10 To refit the armature and bearing, retract the brushes out of the way, and carefully insert the armature shaft and bearing into the gear housing.
11 Before tightening the bearing retaining nut make sure the 'L' shaped retainer is hooked over the outer race of the bearing.
12 Continue to reassemble the motor using the reverse procedure to dismantling.
13 Finally refit the motor to the car, as described in Section 19.

## 21 Horn - testing, removal and replacement

1   On models with a radiator grille, a single horn is located behind the grille, which needs removing in order to allow access. On models without a grille, the horn is located on the front panel adjacent to the radiator (Fig. 10.22), access being gained through the radiator air intake.
2   If the horn fails to operate, disconnect the two wires from the horn.
3   Connect a test-lamp across the two wires and get someone to press the horn button. If the lamp illuminates the horn is at fault and should be renewed .
4   If the lamp does not light up, the horn switch may be at fault and should be checked as described in Section 22.

5   To remove the horn, disconnect the two wires from the rear of the horn, remove the retaining bolt and lift the horn away from the car.

## 22 Horn button switch - removal, inspection and refitting

1   Disconnect the battery, and then carefully prise out the horn button from the centre of the steering wheel (photo). On two-spoked steering wheels the button is disconnected from the horn wire connector by depressing the locking tag. On four-spoked wheels, the two wire connectors are similarly disconnected.
2   Bend back the locking tabs from the steering wheel nut. Undo and remove the nut together with the locking tab washer.
3   Mark the shaft and wheel boss to ensure correct alignment on reassembly.
4   Remove the wheel as described in Chapter 11.
5   The slip track on the fixed column switch assembly is now exposed, as well as the horn contact in the steering wheel boss.
6   Inspect and clean contacts. It is not possible to dismantle the two-spoke wheel further and if the switch incorporated in the wheel is faulty, renewal is the only course of action. The four-spoke wheel has additional contacts under the flexible area of the spokes. Access to these is gained by removal of the cover on the underside of the wheel. This is secured by claws which engage in the steering wheel hub. Prise out each claw in turn, at the same time carefully levering the cover free of the spokes.
7   Refitting follows the reversal of removal except that the return pins and cams associated with the direction indicator cancel mechanism should be lightly greased before the wheel is refitted.
8   Tighten the wheel retaining nut and remember to lock the nut by bending up another tab.

## 23 Flasher unit - removal and refitting

1   The direction indicator lights and hazard warning lights are operated by the same flasher unit. The unit is plugged into the fusebox located on the right-hand side of the steering column below the instrument panel (Fig. 10.23). To unplug the unit, simply pull it out in a downward direction. When refitting a new unit, align the terminals with those in the fusebox and push it home.

Fig. 10.23. Location of flasher unit (Sec. 23)

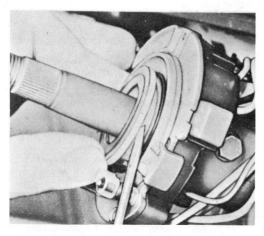

Fig. 10.24. Removing the horn contact ring (Sec. 24)

Fig. 10.26. Location of indent ball and spring in switch yoke (Sec. 24)

## 24 Steering column combination switch - removal and refitting

1   The steering column combination switch is a complex unit that provides the following facilities:

*Turn signal.*
*Headlamp dip and flasher.*
*Windscreen wiper and washer.*
*Hazard warning.*

2   The combination switch is not repairable and, with the exception of the wiper/washer switch, failure of one of the switch facilities means that the complete assembly must be renewed.
3   First remove the steering wheel and steering column cowls, as described in Chapter 11.
4   Prise out the horn contact ring from the centre of the switch yoke (Fig. 10.24).
5   Using a small diameter punch, tap out the pin securing the control arm to the yoke (Fig. 10.25).
6   Remove the large C-clip from the switch housing. Hold the indicator switch cams out of the way and lift the yoke off the steering column. Take care not to lose the ball and spring from the yoke indent (see Fig. 10.26).
7   Disconnect the wiring harness plugs and remove the three bolts securing the combination switch to the steering column.
8   The switch can now be lifted off the column.
9   To remove the wiper switch from the operating arm, lift up the retaining clip, as shown in Fig. 10.27, and pull the switch off the arm.

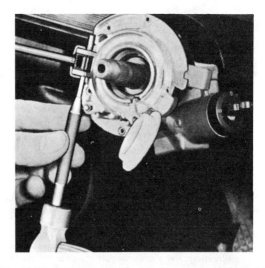

Fig. 10.25. Driving out the turn indicator arm pin (Sec. 24)

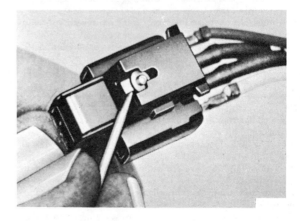

Fig. 10.27. Removing wiper switch from control arm (Sec. 24)

10 The switch assembly is refitted using the reverse procedure to removal. Care should be taken not to overtighten the three securing bolts. When installing the yoke, do not forget to refit the indent ball and spring.

## 25 Ignition switch and steering lock - removal and replacement

1 First remove the lower steering column shroud by undoing the two retaining screws.
2 Turn the ignition key to the '1' position and remove the lock cylinder by pressing in the retainer button using a piece of wire inserted in the hole shown in Fig. 10.28.
3 The ignition and starter switch can be withdrawn after removing the two screws from the switch housing (see Fig. 10.29).
4 Refit the ignition switch and lock using the reverse procedure to removal.

## 26 Headlights - alignment and adjustment

1 Alignment is achieved by adjustment with two nylon special bolts to be found on the headlight retaining frame. They are accessible from the inside of the engine compartment (photo).
2 To avoid dazzling oncoming traffic due to incorrect setting, and contravening the lighting laws, it is strongly recommended that the headlights are aligned by a garage equipped with the proper optical type beam setter.

## 27 Headlight bulbs - removal and replacement

1 Open the bonnet and remove the large plastic cap from the rear of

the headlight assembly by rotating it anticlockwise (photo).
2 Pull off the electrical plug connector (photo).
3 Remove the bulb retaining plate by pushing it inwards and turning it anticlockwise. The sidelight bulb can now be removed if required (photo).
4 Lift the headlamp bulb out of the reflector assembly (photo).
5 Refit the bulb using the reverse procedure to removal. Note that the metal rim on the bulb has a projection which must engage in the slot on the reflector.

## 28 Headlights - removal and refitting

1 Open the bonnet and remove the bulb retaining plate, as described in the previous Section.
2 Remove the wires from the bulb retaining plate, prise out the wiring grommet and pull the harness out of the headlight shell.
3 Remove the indicator bulb and holder if it is the type that fits in the headlight shell.
4 Undo the four retaining nuts and lift out the complete headlight assembly from the front of the car.
5 Refitting follows the reverse procedure to removal.

## 29 Headlight on/off switch - removal and refitting

1 Push in the two spring clips on each side of the switch body and pull the switch from the instrument panel (Fig. 10.30).
2 Disconnect the electrical plug from the rear of the switch, but make sure that the plug does not fall back through the switch aperture in the instrument panel.
3 Refit the switch using the reverse procedure to removal.

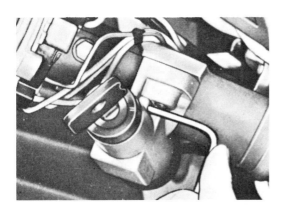

Fig. 10.28. Pressing in the lock cylinder retaining pin (Sec. 25)

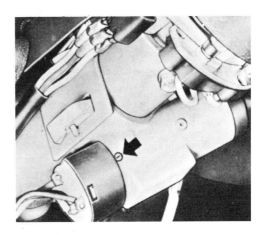

Fig. 10.29. Location of ignition switch retaining screw (Sec. 25)

26.1 The inside headlight adjusting screw

27.1 Removing the plastic cover from the rear of the headlight unit

27.2 Disconnecting the headlight electrical plug

27.3 Headlight bulb retaining plate, note side light bulb

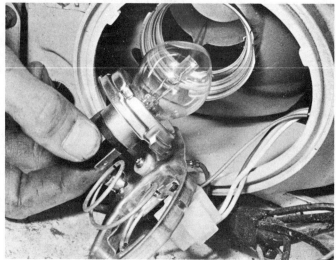

27.4 Withdrawing headlight bulb

2   On some models the turn indicator light is plugged into the head-light shell. To remove it, open the bonnet and simply pull the light assembly from the aperture.
3   Refit the lights using the reverse procedure to removal .

## 31  Rear light cluster - removal and replacement

1   Access to the rear light cluster bulbs is gained from inside the luggage compartment.
2   On saloon models, remove the bulbholders by turning them anti-clockwise (photo).
3   On Coupe models, the bulbholder is removed by pressing in the two plastic clips on the bulbholder and pulling it out.
4   To remove the complete light cluster assembly, first unplug the electrical connector by lifting up the locking tab (photo).
5   Undo the four retaining bolts (five on Coupe models), and lift away the complete light cluster assembly from the rear of the car.
6   Refitting is the reversal of the removal procedure.

Fig. 10.30. Removing the headlight switch (Sec. 29)

## 32  Interior and luggage compartment lights - removal and replacement

1   To remove the interior light lens, carefully ease it out of the roof aperture using a thin-bladed screwdriver (photo).
2   The festoon-type bulb can then be replaced or, if necessary the wires disconnected and the lens assembly removed.
3   The luggage compartment light is removed in a similar manner to the interior light.
4   Refitting is the reverse procedure to removal.

## 30  Front turn indicator lights - removal and replacement

1   On cars equipped with turn signal lights located below the front bumper, remove the two lens securing screws to gain access to the bulb. To remove the complete light assembly, undo the two retaining screws and disconnect the electrical wires.

31.2 Removing a rear light bulb - typical

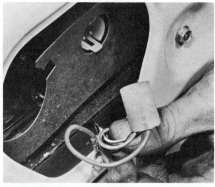

31.4 Removing the electrical plug from the rear light cluster

32.1 Interior light assembly removed

## 33 Rear window demist and ventilation fan switches - removal and replacement

1  Both the rear window and ventilation fan switches and their associated indicator lights are removed in an identical manner.
2  Make a hook out of a piece of thick wire and pull the switch assembly from the panel by engaging the hook in the indicator light recess as shown in Fig. 10.31..
3  To remove the switch assembly from the car, disconnect the electrical plug and bulbholder.
4  If a new bulb is fitted its operation should be checked before pushing the switch light assembly back into place.

## 34 Instrument housing - removal and refitting

**Note:** *For information on the upper and lower instrument panels, refer to Chapter 13, Section 16.*

1  Before commencing any electrical work on the vehicle and any repairs on the instrument assembly, disconnect the negative battery cable first.
2  Remove the steering wheel and steering column cowls, as described in Chapter 11.
3  Remove the rear window demist and ventilation fan switches, as described in the previous Section.
4  Undo the two switch panel retaining screws, one in each switch

aperture, and carefully pull the switch panel away.
5  To remove the instrument panel cowl, undo the two screws underneath the top of the cowl and the screw at each bottom corner (Fig. 10.32).
6  Pull the cowl away from the top first to disengage the two clips.
7  Remove the two heater control knobs by pulling them off the levers.
8  Undo the two screws (one on each side), retaining the instrument frame and lens and disconnect the lighting switch and instrument lamp plugs at the side of the frame.
9  The instrument frame and lens can now be lifted away.
10  Remove the retaining screws and withdraw the instrument facia.
11  The fuel and water temperature gauges, speedometer and warning lamp bulbs are now accessible (Fig. 10. 33).

## 35 Fuel and temperature gauges - removal and refitting

1  Both the gauges are sealed units and if faulty, must be renewed. If both gauges fail simultaneously, the voltage stabilizer on the rear of the printed circuit board should be checked (see Section 37).
2  To gain access to the gauges, it is necessary to remove the instrument facia as described in the previous Section.
3  The gauges are removed by undoing the two retaining screws and pulling them out of the sockets in the printed circuit board.

Fig. 10.31. Removing the ventilation fan switch using a wire hook (Sec. 33)

Fig. 10.32. Position of instrument panel cowl retaining screws (Sec. 34)

A  Upper screws (2)          B  Lower screws (2)

Fig. 10.33. Instruments and warning lights exposed after removal of facia panel (Sec. 34)

1  *Alternator warning bulb*          3  *Turn signal*          5  *Hazard warning*
2  *Brake and clutch warning*          4  *Main beam*          6  *Oil pressure warning*

## 36 Speedometer - removal and refitting

1  First remove the instrument facia panel as described in Section 34.
2  Undo the two retaining screws and lift away the speedometer, leaving the cable attached to the instrument panel casing.
3  To remove the cable from the rear of the casing, simply press down the spring clip and withdraw the cable.
4  Refitting is a reversal of the removal procedure. Make sure that the speedometer driveshaft has correctly engaged the cable before tightening the retaining screws.

## 37 Printed circuit board - removal and refitting

1  Remove the instrument facia panel and instruments, as described in the previous Sections.
2  Remove the four screws retaining the instrument housing to the panel.
3  Detach the speedometer cable and multipin socket from the rear of the instrument housing.
4  Remove the single retaining screw shown in Fig. 10.34, and move the board as far as possible to the right before carefully lifting it out of the instrument housing.
5  The voltage stabiliser, which plugs into the back of the printed circuit board can now be removed if required.
6  Refitting is a reversal of the removal procedure.

Fig. 10.34. Location of printed circuit board retaining screw (Sec. 37)

## 38 Fuel tank sender unit - testing

1  To check the fuel tank sender unit for correct operation, obtain a 40 ohm resistor from a radio dealer and connect it between the sender unit wire and earth (see Fig. 10. 35).
2  With the resistor in position, switch on the ignition and check that the gauge pointer moves slowly to the 'FULL' position.
3  If the gauge operates when earthed via the resistor, but not when connected to the tank sender unit terminal, then the sender unit is faulty and should be renewed (refer to Chapter 3).
4  The water temperature gauge and sender unit can be checked in an identical manner.

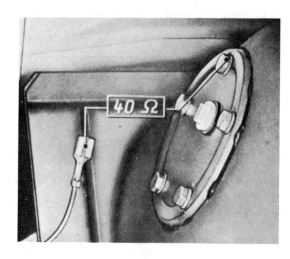

Fig. 10.35. Method of testing fuel sender unit using a 40 Ohm resistor (Sec. 38)

## 39 Electric clock - removal and replacement

1  The clock is a push fit in the lower section of the instrument panel.
2  To remove it, open the glovebox, insert a finger through the access hole and push the clock out of the panel.
3  The bulb can be renewed by pulling the bulbholder from the rear of the clock.
4  Replace the clock by pushing firmly back into the panel aperture.

## 40 Fuses - general

1  Fuse failure may be diagnosed by the simultaneous failure of several electrical systems. The blown fuse may be identified by the electrical systems which are inoperative.
2  For information on the fuse numbers and the services they protect, refer to the Specifications at the beginning of this Chapter.
3  The fuses are located behind a removable panel below the instrument panel on the right of the steering column (photo).
4  If a fuse blows it must be replaced with a fuse of the same amps rating. If the new fuse immediately blows when the particular electrical service is operated there is a fault in the system and the circuit must be carefully inspected to find the cause of the trouble.

## 41 Switches and relays - general

### *Interior lamp door switches*

1  The plunger type interior lamp switches are fitted to each front door pillar.
2  To check the operation of the switch undo the single screw and withdraw the switch. Disconnect the terminal and earth it against the

40.3 Location of fuse panel

door pillar and check that the interior lamp illuminates.

### Stoplamp switch

3   The stoplamp switch is located on the brake pedal support bracket.
4   To remove it, disconnect the two wiring terminals and unscrew the switch from the bracket.
5   If the brake lights have failed, the switch can be checked by bridging the circuit between the two wires. If the brake lights now work, the switch is faulty and should be renewed.

### Parking brake lever switch

6   To remove the parking brake warning switch, remove the centre console, as described in Chapter 9.
7   Undo the single retaining screw, disconnect the wiring terminal and remove the switch.
8   If the switch is suspect, it can be bypassed by earthing the wire and checking that the brake warning lamp illuminates.

### Reversing light switch

9   The reversing light switch is screwed into the rear of the gearbox and is operated from inside the gearbox by the reverse gear striking fork.
10  The switch can be removed by disconnecting the wiring terminals and unscrewing it from the gearbox.
11  When refitting the switch make sure the sealing ring is in position.

### Oil pressure switch

12  This switch is located behind the exhaust manifold near the rear of the engine (photo). Detach the lead and unscrew the switch from the engine block if thought to be faulty.
13  If the pressure warning light fails to glow when it should, the switch may be checked by disconnecting its lead and touching it onto the block.
14  The warning light should glow when its lead is touched to the engine block. If the light does not glow; check the warning bulb.

### Windscreen wiper relay

15  The wiper relay ensures that the wipers continue to operate for approximately four cycles after the wiper/washer button is released to clear the screen of water.
16  The relay is secured to the front wheelhouse panel by a single screw (Fig. 10.36). The unit cannot be repaired and if faulty must be renewed.

### Rear window demist relay

17  This relay ensures that the circuit to the rear window demister element is not closed unless the alternator is on line. This prevents excessive discharging of the battery.
18  The relay is plugged directly into the fuseblock next to the turn indicator flasher unit.

---

### 42 Cigar lighter - removal and replacement

1   The cigar lighter is retained in the lower instrument panel by means of a slotted plate (Fig. 10.37).
2   To remove the lighter, first pull out the element and then, holding the mounting plate, rotate the lighter body 90° using a pair of thin-nosed pliers. Withdraw the lighter body and disconnect the electrical terminals.
3   Refit the lighter using the reverse procedure to removal.

---

### 43 Radios and tape players - fitting (general)

   A radio or tape player is an expensive item to buy and will only give its best performance if fitted properly. It is useless to expect concert hall performance from a unit that is suspended from the dash panel on string with its speaker resting on the back seat or parcel shelf! If you do not wish to do the installation yourself there are many in-car entertainment specialists' who can do the fitting for you.
   Make sure the unit purchased is of the same polarity as the car, and ensure that units with adjustable polarity are correctly set before commencing installation.
   It is difficult to give specific information with regard to fitting, as final positioning of the radio/tape player, speakers and aerial is entirely a matter of personal preference, However, the following paragraphs give

41.12 Oil pressure switch

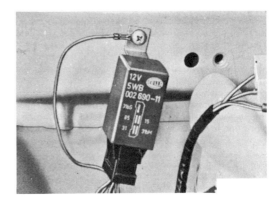

Fig. 10.36. Windscreen wiper relay — typical (Sec. 41)

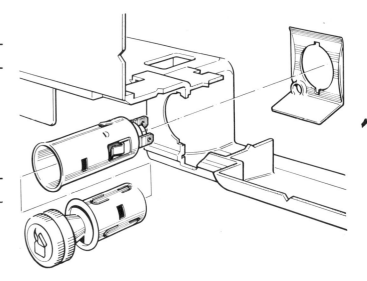

Fig. 10.37. Component parts of cigar lighter (Sec. 42)

guidelines to follow, which are relevant to all installations.

### Radios

Most radios are a standardised size of 7 inches wide, by 2 inches deep - this ensures that they will fit into the radio aperture provided in most cars. If your car does not have such an aperture, then the radio must be fitted in a suitable position either in, or beneath, the dashpanel. Alternatively, a special console can be purchased which will fit between the dashpanel and the floor, or on the transmission tunnel. These consoles can also be used for additional switches and instrumentation if required. Where no radio aperture is provided, the following points should be borne in mind before deciding exactly where to fit the unit:

a) *The unit must be within easy reach of the driver wearing a seat belt.*

b) *The unit must not be mounted in close proximity to an electronic tachometer, the ignition switch and its wiring, or the flasher unit and associated wiring.*

c) *The unit must be mounted within reach of the aerial lead, and in such a place that the aerial lead will not have to be routed near the components detailed in the preceding paragraph 'b'.*

d) *The unit should not be positioned in a place where it might cause injury to the car occupants in an accident; for instance, under the dashpanel above the driver's or passengers' legs.*

e) *The unit must be fitted really securely.*

Some radios will have mounting brackets provided together with instructions: others will need to be fitted using drilled and slotted metal strips, bent to form mounting brackets - these strips are available from most accessory shops. The unit must be properly earthed, by fitting a separate earthing lead between the casing of the radio and the vehicle frame.

Use the radio manufacturers' instructions when wiring the radio into the vehicle's electrical system. If no instructions are available refer to the relevant wiring diagram to find the location of the radio 'feed' connection in the vehicle's wiring circuit. A 1-2 amp 'in-line' fuse must be fitted in the radio's feed wire - a choke may also be necessary (see next Section).

The type of aerial used, and its fitted position is a matter of personal preference. In general the taller the aerial, the better the reception. It is best to fit a fully retractable aerial - especially, if a mechanical car-wash is used or if you live in an area where cars tend to be vandalised. In this respect electric aerials which are raised and lowered automatically when switching the radio on or off are convenient, but are more likely to give trouble than the manual type.

When choosing a site for the aerial the following points should be considered:

a) *The aerial lead should be as short as possible - this means that the aerial should be mounted at the front of the car.*

b) *The aerial must be mounted as far away from the distributor and HT leads as possible.*

c) *The part of the aerial which protrudes beneath the mounting point must not foul the roadwheels, or anything else.*

d) *If possible the aerial should be positioned so that the coaxial lead does not have to be routed through the engine compartment.*

e) *The plane of the panel on which the aerial is mounted should not be so steeply angled that the aerial cannot be mounted vertically (in relation to the 'end-on' aspect of the car). Most aerials have a small amount of adjustment available.*

Having decided on a mounting position, a relatively large hole will have to be made in the panel. The exact size of the hole will depend upon the specific aerial being fitted, although, generally, the hole required is of ¾ inch (19 mm) diameter. On metal bodied cars, a 'tank-cutter' of the relevant diameter is the best tool to use for making the hole. This tool needs a small diameter pilot hole drilled through the panel, through which, the tool clamping bolt is inserted. On GRP bodied cars a 'hole-saw' is the best tool to use. Again, this tool will require the drilling of a small pilot hole. When the hole has been made the raw edges should be de-burred with a file and then painted, to prevent corrosion.

Fit the aerial according to the manufacturer's instructions. If the aerial is very tall, or if it protrudes beneath the mounting panel for a considerable distance, it is a good idea to fit a stay between the aerial

and the vehicle frame. This stay can be manufactured from the slotted and drilled metal strips previously mentioned. The stay should be securely screwed or bolted in place. For best reception it is advisable to fit an earth lead between the aerial and the vehicle frame - this is essential for GRP bodied cars.

It will probably be necessary to drill one or two holes through body-work panels in order to feed the aerial lead into the interior of the car. Where this is the case ensure that the holes are fitted with rubber grommets to protect the cable, and to stop possible entry of water.

Positioning and fitting of the speaker depends mainly on its type. Generally, the speaker is designed to fit directly into the aperture already provided in the car (usually in the shelf behind the rear seats, or in the top of the dashpanel). Where this is the case, fitting the speaker is just a matter of removing the protective grille from the aperture and screwing or bolting the speaker in place. Take great care not to damage the speaker diaphragm whilst doing this. It is a good idea to fit a 'gasket' between the speaker frame and the mounting panel, in order to prevent vibration - some speakers will already have such a gasket fitted.

If a 'pod' type speaker was supplied with the radio, the best acoustic results will normally be obtained by mounting it on the shelf behind the rear seat. The pod can be secured to the mounting panel with self-tapping screws.

When connecting a rear mounted speaker to the radio, the wires should be routed through the vehicle beneath the carpets or floor mats - preferably the middle, or along the side of the floorpan, where they will not be trodden on by passengers. Make the relevant connections as directed by the radio manufacturer.

By now you will have several yards of additional wiring in the car, use PVC tape to secure this wiring out of harm's way. Do not leave electrical leads dangling. Ensure that all new electrical connections are properly made (wires twisted together will not do) and completely secure.

The radio should now be working, but before you pack away your tools it will be necessary to 'trim' the radio to the aerial. If specific instructions are not provided by the radio manufacturer, proceed as follows. Find a station with a low signal strength on the medium-wave band, slowly, turn the trim screw of the radio in, or out, until the loudest reception of the selected station is obtained - the set is then trimmed to the aerial.

### Tape players

Fitting instructions for both cartridge and cassette stereo type players are the same and in general the same rules apply as when fitting a radio. Tape players are not usually prone to electrical interference like radio - although it can occur - so positioning is not so critical. If possible the player should be mounted on an 'even-keel.' Also, it must be possible for a driver wearing a seat belt to reach the unit in order to change or turn over tapes.

For the best results from speakers designed to be recessed into a panel, mount them so that the back of the speaker protrudes into an enclosed chamber within the car (eg. door interiors or the boot cavity).

To fit recessed type speakers in the front doors, first check that there is sufficient room to mount the speakers in each door without it fouling the latch or window winding mechanism. Hold the speaker against the skin of the door, and draw a line around the periphery of the speaker. With the speaker removed draw a second 'cutting' line, within the first, to allow enough room for the entry of the speaker back, but at the same time, providing a broad seat for the speaker flange. When you are sure that the 'cutting-line' is correct, drill a series of holes around its periphery. Pass a hacksaw blade through one of the holes and then cut through the metal between the holes until the centre section of the panel falls out.

De-burr the edges of the hole and then paint the raw metal to prevent corrosion. Cut a corresponding hole in the door trim panel - ensuring that it will be completely covered by the speaker grille. Now drill a hole in the door edge and a corresponding hole in the door surround. These holes are to feed the speaker leads through - so fit grommets. Pass the speaker leads through the door trim, door skin and out through the holes in the side of the door and door surround. Refit the door trim panel and then secure the speaker to the door using self-tapping screws. Note: If the speaker is fitted with a shield to prevent water dripping on it, ensure that this shield is at the top.

Pod type speakers can be fastened to the shelf behind the rear seat, or anywhere else offering a corresponding mounting point on each side of the car. If the pod speakers are mounted on each side of the shelf behind the rear seat, it is a good idea to drill several large diameter holes

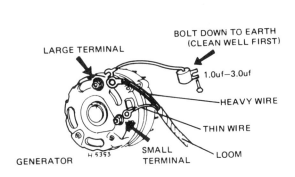

Fig. 10.38. Connecting a capacitor to the alternator (Sec. 44)

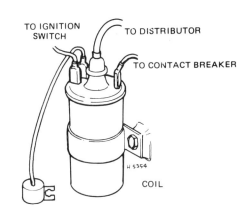

Fig. 10.39. Connecting a capacitor to the HT coil (Sec. 44)

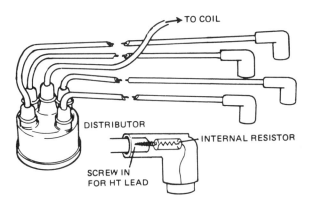

Resistive spark plug caps

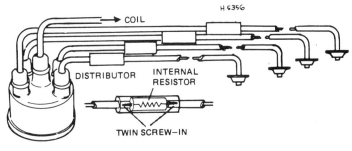

'In-line' suppressors

Fig. 10.40. Ignition HT lead suppporessors (Sec. 44)

through to the boot cavity beneath each speaker - this will improve the sound reproduction. Pod speakers sometimes offer a better reproduction quality if they face the rear window - which then acts as a reflector - so it is worthwhile to do a little experimenting before finally fixing the speaker.

## 44 Radios and tape players - suppression of interference (general)

To eliminate buzzes and other unwanted noises, costs very little and is not as difficult as sometimes thought. With a modicum of common sense and patience and following the instructions in the following paragraphs, interference can be virtually eliminated.

The first cause for concern is the generator. The noise this makes over the radio is like an electric mixer and the noise speeds up when you rev up (if you wish to prove the point, you can remove the drivebelt and try it). The remedy for this is simple; connect a 1.0 uf - 3.0 uf capacitor between earth, probably the bolt that holds down the generator base, and the *large* terminal on the dynamo or alternator. This is most important for if you connect it to the small terminal, you will probably damage the generator permanently (see Fig. 10.38).

A second common cause of electrical interference is the ignition system. Here a 1.0 ohm capacitor must be connected between earth and the 'SW' or '+' terminal on the coil (see Fig. 10.39). This may stop the tick-tick-tick sound that comes over the speaker. Next comes the spark itself.

There are several ways of curing interference from the ignition HT system. One is to use carbon film HT leads but these have a tendency to 'snap' inside and you don't know then, why you are firing on only half your cylinders. So the second, and more successful method is to use resistive spark plug caps (see Fig. 10.40) of about 10,000 ohm to 15,000 ohm resistance. If, due to lack of room, these cannot be used, an alternative is to use 'in-line' suppressors (Fig. 10.40) - if the interference is not too bad, you may get away with only one suppressor in the coil to distributor line. If the interference does continue (a 'clacking'

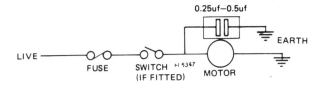

Fig. 10.41. Correct method of suppressing an electric motor (Sec. 44)

noise) then doctor all HT leads.

At this stage, it is advisable to check that the radio is well earthed, also the aerial, and to see that the aerial plug is pushed well into the set and that the radio is properly trimmed (see preceding Section). In addition, check that the wire which supplies the power to the set is as short as possible and does not wander all over the car. At this stage, it is a good idea to check that the fuse is of the correct rating. For most sets this will be about 1 to 2 amps.

At this point, the more usual causes of interference have been suppressed. If the problem still exists, a look at the causes of interference may help to pinpoint the component generating the stray electrical discharges.

The radio picks up electromagnetic waves in the air; now some are made by radio stations and other broadcasters and some, not wanted, are made by the car. The home made signals are produced by stray electrical discharges floating around the car. Common producers of these signals are electric motors; ie, the windshield wipers, electric screen washers, electric window winders, heater fan or an electric aerial if fitted. Other sources of interference are electric fuel pumps, flashing turn signals, and instruments. The remedy for these cases is shown in Fig. 10.41 for an electronic motor whose interference is not too bad and Fig. 10. 42 for instrument suppression. Turn signals are not normally supressed. In recent years, radio manufacturer's have included in the line (live) of the radio, in addition to the fuse, an 'in-line' choke. If

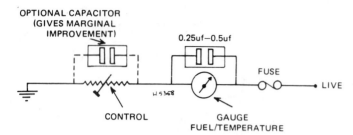

**Fig. 10.42. Method of suppressing instruments (Sec. 44)**

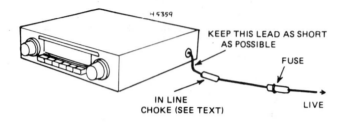

**Fig. 10.43. Fitting an in-line choke (Sec. 44)**

your installation lacks one of these, put one in as shown in Fig. 10.43. All the foregoing components are available from radio shops or accessory shops. For a transistor radio, a 2A choke should be adequate. If you have an electric clock fitted this should be suppressed by connecting a 0.5 uf capacitor directly across it as shown for a motor in Fig. 10.41.

If after all this, you are still experiencing radio interference, first assess how bad it is, for the human ear can filter out unobtrusive unwanted noises quite easily. But if you are still adamant about eradicating the noise, then continue.

As a first step, a few 'experts' seem to favour a screen between the radio and the engine. This is O.K. as far as it goes, literally! - for the whole set is screened and if interference can get past that then a small piece of aluminium is not going to stop it.

A more sensible way of screening is to discover if interference is coming down the wires. First, take the live lead; interference can get between the set and the choke (hence the reason for keeping the wires short). One remedy here is to screen the wire and this is done by buying screened wire and fitting that. The loudspeaker lead could be screened also to prevent 'pick-up' getting back to the radio - although this is unlikely.

Without doubt, the worst source of radio interference comes from the ignition HT leads, even if they have been suppressed. The ideal way of suppressing these is to slide screening tubes over the leads themselves.

As this is impractical, we can place an aluminium shield over the majority of the lead areas. In a vee - or twin-cam engine, this is relatively easy but for a straight engine the results are not particularly good.

Now for the really impossible cases, here are a few tips to try out Where metal comes into contact with metal, an electrical disturbance is caused which is why good clean connections are essential. To remove interference due to overlapping or butting panels you must bridge the join with a wide braided earth strap (like that from the frame to the engine/transmission). The most common moving parts that could create noise and should be strapped are, in order of importance.

a) Silencer to frame.
b) Exhaust pipe to engine block and frame.
c) Air cleaner to frame.
d) Front and rear bumpers to frame.
e) Steering column to frame.
f) Hood and trunk lids to frame.
g) Hood frame to frame on soft tops.

These faults are most pronounced when (1) the engine is idling, (2) labouring under load. Although the moving parts are already connected with nuts, bolts, etc, these do tent to rust and corrode, thus creating a high resistance interference source.

If you have a 'ragged' sounding pulse when mobile, this could be wheel or tyre static. This can be cured by buying some anti-static powder and sprinkling it liberally inside the tyres.

If the interference takes the shape of a high pitched screeching noise that changes its note when the car is in motion and only comes now and then, this could be related to the aerial, especially if it is of the telescopic or whip type. This source can be cured quite simply by pushing a small rubber ball on top of the aerial (yes, really!) as this breaks the electric field before it can form; but it would be much better to buy yourself a new aerial of a reputable brand. If, on the other hand, you are getting a loud rushing sound every time you brake, then this is brake static. This effect is most prominent on hot dry days and is cured only by fitting a special kit, which is quite expensive.

In conclusion, it is pointed out that it is relatively easy, and therefore cheap to eliminate 95 per cent of all noises, but to eliminate the final 5 per cent is time and money consuming. It is up to the individual to decide if it is worth it. Please remember also, that you will not get concert hall performance from a cheap radio.

Finally, at the beginning of this Section are mentioned tape players; these are not usually affected by interference but in a very bad case, the best remedies are the first three suggestions plus using a 3 - 5 amp choke in the 'live' line and in incurable cases screen the live and speaker wires.

**Note:** If your car is fitted with electronic ignition, then it is not recommended that either the spark plug resistors or the ignition coil capacitor be fitted as these may damage the system. Most electronic ignition unit have built-in suppression and should, therefore, not cause interference.

**45 Fault diagnosis - electrical system**

| Symptom | Reason/s |
| --- | --- |
| No voltage at starter motor | Battery discharged.<br>Battery defective internally.<br>Battery terminal leads loose or earth lead not securely attached to body.<br>Loose or broken connections in starter motor circuit.<br>Starter motor switch or solenoid faulty. |
| Voltage at starter motor: faulty motor | Starter motor pinion jammed in mesh with flywheel gear ring.<br>Starter brushes badly worn, sticking, or brush wires loose.<br>Commutator dirty, worn or burnt.<br>Starter motor armature faulty.<br>Field coils earthed. |
| Electrical defects | Battery in discharged condition.<br>Starter brushes badly worn, sticking, or brush wires loose.<br>Loose wires in starter motor circuit. |
| Dirt or oil on drive gear | Starter motor pinion sticking on the screwed sleeve. |
| Mechanical damage | Pinion or flywheel gear teeth broken or worn. |
| Lack of attention or mechanical damage | Pinion or flywheel gear teeth broken or worn.<br>Starter drive main spring broken.<br>Starter motor retaining bolts loose. |
| Wear or damage | Battery defective internally.<br>Electrolyte level too low or electrolyte too weak due to leakage.<br>Plate separators no longer fully effective.<br>Battery plates severely sulphated. |
| Insufficient current flow to keep battery charged | Fan belt slipping.<br>Battery terminal connections loose or corroded.<br>Alternator not charging properly.<br>Short in lighting circuit causing continual battery drain.<br>Regulator unit not working correctly. |
| Alternator not charging* | Fan belt loose and slipping, or broken.<br>Brushes worn, sticking, broken or dirty.<br>Brush springs weak or broken. |

*If all appears to be well but the alternator is still not charging, take the car to an automobile electrician for checking of the alternator and regulator.*

| | |
| --- | --- |
| Battery will not hold charge for more than a few days | Battery defective internally.<br>Electrolyte level too low or electrolyte too weak due to leakage.<br>Plate separators no longer fully effective.<br>Battery plates severely sulphated.<br>Fan/alternator belt slipping.<br>Battery terminal connections loose or corroded.<br>Alternator not charging properly.<br>Short in lighting circuit causing continual battery drain.<br>Regulator unit not working correctly. |
| Ignition light fails to go out, battery runs flat in a few days | Fan belt loose and slipping or broken.<br>Alternator faulty. |

**Failure of individual electrical equipment to function correctly is dealt with alphabetically, below.**

| | |
| --- | --- |
| Fuel gauge gives no reading | Fuel tank empty!<br>Electric cable between tank sender unit and gauge earthed or loose.<br>Fuel gauge case not earthed.<br>Fuel gauge supply cable interrupted.<br>Fuel gauge unit broken. |
| Fuel gauge registers full all the time | Electric cable between tank unit and gauge broken or disconnected. |
| Horn operates all the time | Horn push either earthed or stuck down.<br>Horn cable to horn push earthed. |

| Symptom | Reason/s |
| --- | --- |
| Horn fails to operate | Blown fuse.<br>Cable or cable connection loose, broken or disconnected.<br>Horn has an internal fault. |
| Horn emits intermittent or unsatisfactory noise | Cable connections loose.<br>Horn incorrectly adjusted (where applicable). |
| Lights do not come on | If engine not running, battery discharged.<br>Light bulb filament burnt out or bulbs broken.<br>Wire connections loose, disconnected or broken.<br>Light switch shorting or otherwise faulty. |
| Lights come on but fade out | If engine not running battery discharged. |
| Lights give very poor illumination | Lamp glasses dirty.<br>Reflector tarnished or dirty.<br>Lamps badly out of adjustment.<br>Incorrect bulb with too low wattage fitted.<br>Existing bulbs old and badly discoloured.<br>Electrical wiring too thin not allowing full current to pass. |
| Lights work erratically - flashing on and off, especially over bumps | Battery terminals or earth connections loose.<br>Lights not earthing properly.<br>Contacts in light switch faulty. |
| Wiper motor fails to work | Blown fuse.<br>Wire connections loose, disconnected or broken.<br>Brushes badly worn.<br>Armature worn or faulty.<br>Field coils faulty. |
| Wiper motor works very slowly and takes excessive current | Commutator dirty, greasy or burnt.<br>Drive to spindles bent or unlubricated.<br>Drive spindle binding or damaged.<br>Armature bearings dry or unaligned.<br>Armature badly worn or faulty. |
| Wiper motor works slowly and takes little current | Brushes badly worn.<br>Commutator dirty, greasy or burnt.<br>Armature badly worn or faulty. |
| Wiper motor works but wiper blades remain static | Linkage disengaged or faulty.<br>Drive spindle damaged or worn.<br>Wiper motor gearbox parts badly worn. |

**Key to Fig. 10.44 Wiring diagram (see pages 160 & 161)**

1  Right-hand front turn signal lamp
2  Right-hand headlamp
   a) Headlamp bulb
   b) Sidelamp bulb
3  Fog lamps
4  Horn
5  Left-hand headlamp
   a) Headlamp bulb
   b) Sidelamp bulb
6  Left-hand sidelamp
7  Windscreen washer pump
8  Ignition coil
9  Distributor
10  Delco-Remy alternator
11  Bosch alternator
12  Bosch voltage regulator
13  Starter
14  Engine compartment lamp
15  Temperature gauge engine unit
16  Oil pressure switch
17  Flasher unit
18  Rear window demist relay
19  Fog lamp relay
20  Connector for driving lamp relay
21  Windshield washer relay
22  Battery
23  Carburettor automatic choke
24  Interior lamp
25  Windscreen wiper motor
26  Right-hand door switch
27  Instrument lamp bulbs
28  Ventilator fan motor
29  Ignition key-start switch
30  Fusebox
31  Left-hand door switch
32  Main and interior lighting switch

33  Steering column combination switch
34  Instruments
   a) Voltage stabilizer
   b) Parking brake and clutch wear indicator
   c) Main beam warning
   d) Oil pressure warning
   e) Alternator warning
   f) Turn signal indicator
   g) Hazard warning indicator
   h) Fuel gauge
   i) Temperature gauge
35  Cigar lighter
36  Clock
37  Cigar light/clock/glove compartment lamp
38  Clutch wear indicator switch
39  Parking brake switch
40  Radio
41  Fuel gauge tank unit
42  Ventilator fan motor switch
43  Fog lamp switch
44  Starter inhibitor switch (automatic transmission)
45  Selector lever lamp (automatic transmission)
46  Reverse lamp switch
47  Stop lamp switch
48  Fog rear guard lamp switch
49  Rear window demist switch
50  Rear window demist element
51  Luggage trunk lamp
52  Luggage trunk lamp switch
53  Rear lamps
   a) Turn signal bulb
   b) Tail lamp bulb
   c) Stop lamp bulb
   d) Reverse lamp bulb
54  Fog rear guard lamp
55  Number plate lamp

**Colour code**

| | | | | | | | | |
|---|---|---|---|---|---|---|---|---|
| BL | = | blue | GR | = | grey | WS | = | white |
| BR | = | brown | GN | = | green | SW | = | black |
| GE | = | yellow | RT | = | red | LI | = | purple |

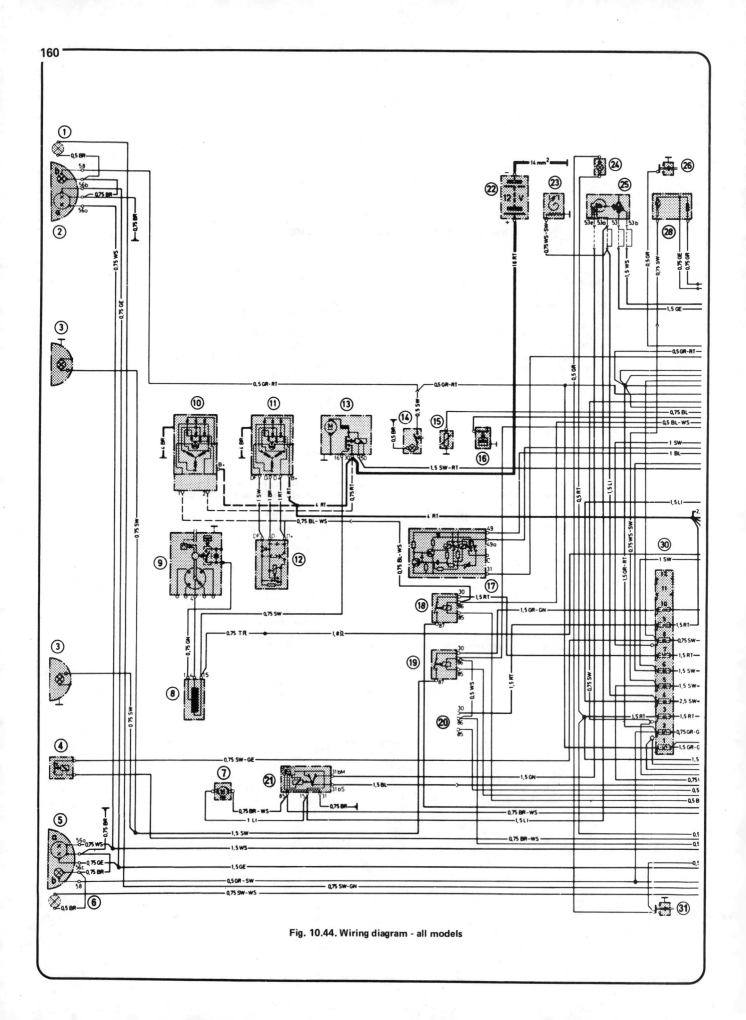

Fig. 10.44. Wiring diagram - all models

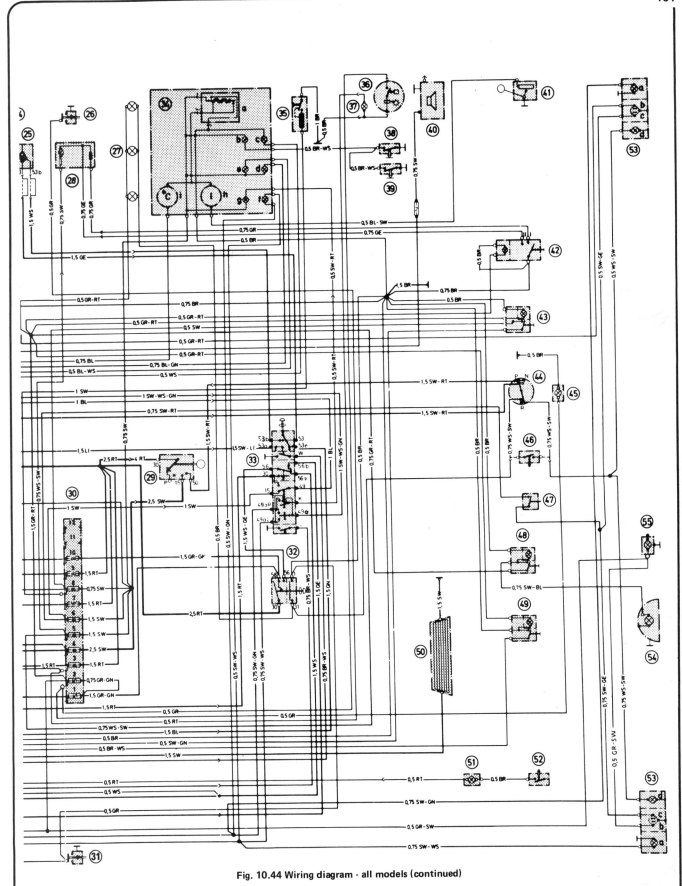

**Fig. 10.44 Wiring diagram - all models (continued)**

# Chapter 11 Suspension and steering

*For modifications, and information applicable to later models, see Supplement at end of manual*

## Contents

## Specifications

### Front suspension

| | |
|---|---|
| Type ... ... ... ... ... ... ... ... ... ... | Upper and lower wishbone, coil spring telescopic shock absorbers, stabiliser bar |
| Hub bearing endfloat ... ... ... ... ... ... ... | 0.001 to 0.004 in (0.02 to 0.10 mm) |
| Camber ... .... ... ... ... ... ... ... | 0° 20' positive to 1° 10' negative |
| Castor ... ... ... ... ... .:. ... ... | 3° positive to 5° 30' negative |
| Toe-in ... ... ... ... ... ... ... ... | 0.11 - 0.19 in (2.8 - 4.8 mm) |
| Toe-out on turns ... ... ... ... ... ... | Outside wheel 18° 25' to 19° 55' from straight ahead with inside wheel at 20° |

### Rear suspension

| | |
|---|---|
| Type ... ... ... ... ... ... ... ... ... | Trailing arm, coil spring, Panhard rod and stabiliser bar. Telescopic shock absorbers |

### Steering

| | |
|---|---|
| Type ... ... ... ... ... ... ... ... | Rack and pinion with collapsible column and flexible coupling |
| Turning circle (between kerbs) ... ... ... ... ... | 30.2 ft (9.2 m) |
| Number of turns (lock-to-lock) ... ... ... ... ... | 3.5 |
| Steering wheel diameter ... ... ... ... ... ... | 14¾ in (374.7 mm) |

### Wheel bearing grease type/specification

... ... ... ... Multi-purpose lithium based grease (Duckhams LB 10)

### Wheels and tyres

*Wheel and tyre sizes vary depending on the model specification. For information on individual cars refer to the Owners Handbook*

| Tyre pressures: | Front | Rear |
|---|---|---|
| Up to 3 occupants: | | |
|   165SR tyres .. ... ... ... ... ... ... ... ... | 24 psi | 24 psi |
|   185/70 SR tyres: | | |
|     Except Coupe 2000, Hatchback 2000 ... ... ... ... | 23 psi | 23 psi |
|     Coupe 2000, Hatchback 2000 ... ... ... ... | 26 psi | 26 psi |
| At maximum load: | | |
|   165SR tyres .. ... ... ... ... ... ... ... | 29 psi | 29 psi |
|   185/70SR tyres: | | |
|     Except Coupe 2000, Hatchback 2000 ... ... ... ... | 26 psi | 26 psi |
|     Coupe 2000, Hatchback 2000 ... ... ... ... | 29 psi | 29 psi |

### Torque wrench settings

| | lb f ft | kg f m |
|---|---|---|
| *Front suspension:* | | |
|   Upper arm pivot bolts ... ... ... ... ... ... ... | 47 | 6.4 |
|   Lower arm pivot bolts ... ... ... ... ... ... ... | 49 | 6.7 |
|   Crossmember brace bolts ... ... ... ... ... ... | 59 | 8.1 |
|   Crossmember upper bolts ... ... ... ... ... ... | 55 | 7.6 |
|   Upper swivel balljoint flange nuts ... ... ... ... | 30 | 4.1 |
|   Upper swivel balljoint to stub axle nut ... ... ... ... | 44 | 6.0 |
|   Lower swivel balljoint to stub axle nut ... ... ... ... | 58 | 8.0 |
|   Stabiliser bar clamp bolts ... ... ... ... ... | 15 | 2.1 |
|   Shock absorber lower mounting bolts ... ... ... ... | 30 | 4.1 |

| Torque wrench settings | | | | | | | | | lb f ft | kg f m |
|---|---|---|---|---|---|---|---|---|---|---|
| *Rear suspension:* | | | | | | | | | | |
| Panhard rod to body | ... | ... | ... | ... | ... | ... | ... | ... | 72 | 9.8 |
| Panhard rod to axle casing | ... | ... | ... | ... | ... | ... | ... | ... | 81 | 11 |
| Suspension arm pivot bolts | ... | ... | ... | ... | ... | ... | ... | ... | 50 | 6.9 |
| Pinion extension to crossmember | ... | ... | ... | ... | ... | ... | ... | ... | 15 | 2.1 |
| Shock absorber lower mountings | ... | ... | ... | ... | ... | ... | ... | ... | 32 | 4.4 |
| *Steering:* | | | | | | | | | | |
| Steering wheel nut | ... | ... | ... | ... | ... | ... | ... | ... | 11 | 1.4 |
| Column upper bracket nuts | ... | ... | ... | ... | ... | ... | ... | ... | 10 | 1.3 |
| Column lower shear bolt (initially) | ... | ... | ... | ... | ... | ... | ... | ... | 15 | 2.1 |
| Flexible coupling pinch bolt | ... | ... | ... | ... | ... | ... | ... | ... | 13 | 1.7 |
| Pinion shaft retaining nut | ... | ... | ... | ... | ... | ... | ... | ... | 11 | 1.4 |
| Rack preload adjuster screw locknut | ... | ... | ... | ... | ... | ... | ... | ... | 50 | 6.9 |
| Trackrod inner balljoint to rack | ... | ... | ... | ... | ... | ... | ... | ... | 66 | 9.1 |
| Trackrod-end taper pin nuts | ... | ... | ... | ... | ... | ... | ... | ... | 35 | 4.8 |
| Trackrod-end locknuts | ... | ... | ... | ... | ... | ... | ... | ... | 30 | 4.1 |
| Steering gear mounting bolts | ... | ... | ... | ... | ... | ... | ... | ... | 33 | 4.5 |
| *Wheels:* | | | | | | | | | | |
| Roadwheel nuts | ... | ... | ... | ... | ... | ... | ... | ... | 68 | 9.4 |

## 1 General description

1   The front suspension is of the independent upper and lower wishbone type-incorporating coil springs and double acting shock absorbers. The suspension arms are mounted to a crossmember at their inner ends and balljoints at their outer ends carry the stub axle. A stabiliser bar is mounted on the underbody and linked to the lower suspension arms.

2   The rear suspension is of the coil spring type and the rear axle is located by two suspension arms attached to the axle tubes and short crossmember supporting the front of the pinion extension housing. A Panhard rod controls side movement of the axle and a stabiliser bar and double acting shock absorbers are incorporated in the suspension system.

3   The steering gear is of rack and pinion type, mounted on the front suspension crossmember. The steering column is of energy absorbing type and incorporates a flexible coupling at its point of attachment to the steering pinion.

## 2 Maintenance and inspection

1   At regular intervals, inspect the condition of all flexible gaiters,

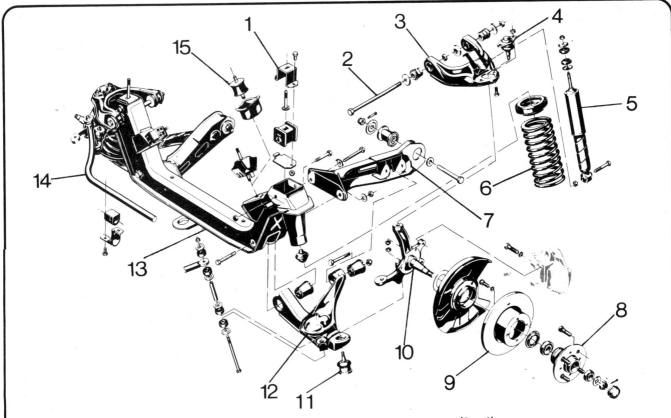

Fig. 11.1. Exploded view of front suspension components (Sec. 1)

| | | | | | | |
|---|---|---|---|---|---|---|
| 1 | Crossmember mounting bracket | 5 | Shock absorber | 9 | Front brake disc | 13 Main crossmember |
| 2 | Upper arm pivot bolt | 6 | Road spring | 10 | Front stub axle | 14 Stabiliser bar |
| 3 | Upper arm | 7 | Crossmember brace | 11 | Lower arm balljoint | 15 Engine mounting (two types) |
| 4 | Upper arm balljoint | 8 | Front hub | 12 | Lower arm | |

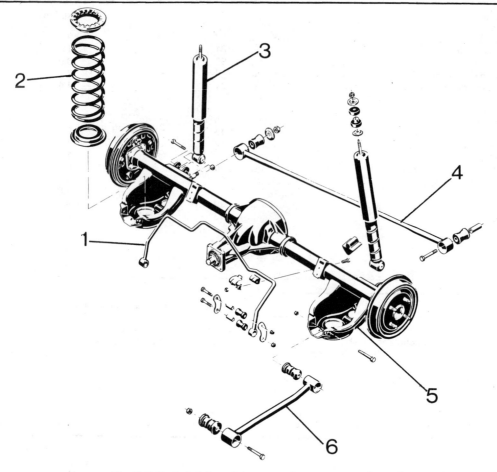

**Fig. 11.2. Exploded view of rear suspension components (Sec. 1)**

1   *Stabiliser bar*                3   *Shock absorber*                5   *Rear axle assembly*
2   *Road spring*                   4   *Panhard rod (track rod)*        6   *Suspension arm*

balljoint dust excluders and rubber suspension bushes. Renew any that have split or deteriorated, as described in the appropriate Section of this Chapter.

2   At the same time, check the torque of all nuts and bolts on suspension components and steering assemblies in accordance with those listed in the Specifications.

3   At the intervals specified in Routine Maintenance, adjust or lubricate the front hubs and check the front wheel alignment.

## 3   Front shock absorbers - removal, testing and installation

1   Do not remove a front shock absorber if the front roadwheels are hanging free with the front end jacked up under the crossmember. Either remove a shock absorber when the roadwheels are on the ground, or if the front end is jacked-up, place a supporting jack under the suspension lower arm.

2   Unscrew and remove the pivot bolt from the shock absorber lower mounting eye (photo).

3   Working within the engine compartment, unscrew and remove the shock absorber upper mounting nut (photo).

4   To test the shock absorber for serviceability, grip the lower mounting eye in the jaws of a vice so that the shock absorber is held vertically and then fully extend and retract the unit ten or twelve times. There should be a considerable resistance in both directions during every movement. Any jerkiness or lack of resistance will indicate the need for renewal.

5   The rubber mounting bushes can be renewed simply by detaching them.

6   Installation is a reversal of removal, tighten the lower pivot bolt to the specified torque and the upper mounting nut, so that the threaded spindle is exposed by the amount shown in the diagram (Fig. 11.3).

## 4   Front hub - adjustment and lubrication

1   Jack-up the front roadwheel and remove the hub cap and the roadwheel.

2   Prise off the dust cap and withdraw the split pin.

3   Withdraw the caliper disc pads as described in Chapter 9.

4   Spin the roadwheel in the forward direction of rotation, at the same time, tightening the hub nut to a torque of 20 lb f ft (2.7 kg f m).

5   Unscrew the hub nut until a feeler blade (0.001 to 0.004 in - 0.002 to 0.10 mm) can be inserted between the rear face of the nut and the thrust washer.

6   Insert a new split pin, bending its ends well over and refit the dust cap.

7   Refit the disc pads, roadwheel and hub cap and lower the car to the ground.

8   If the bearings are to be repacked with grease, carry out the operations described in paragraphs 1 and 2 and then remove the disc caliper, as described in Chapter 9, and tie it up out of the way with a piece of wire to avoid straining the brake flexible hose. There is no need to disconnect the hydraulic line.

9   Unscrew and remove the hub nut and extract the thrust washer.

10 Pull the hub/disc assembly slightly towards you. This will eject the outer bearing race which can be removed. Now pull the hub/disc from the stub axle.

11 All old grease should now be wiped carefully from the bearings and hub recesses and fresh grease worked into the rollers. Take care not to damage the oil seal and do not pack any grease into the recess in the hub interior between the bearings.

12 Installation is a reversal of removal, but offer the hub squarely to the stub axle so as not to damage the lips of the seal.

13 Adjust the bearings as previously described.

3.2 Front shock absorber lower mounting

3.3 Front shock absorber upper mounting

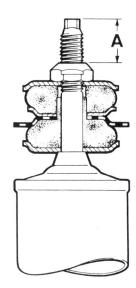

**Fig. 11.3. Front shock absorber installation (Sec. 3)**
**(Dimension A = 0.8 in/20 mm)**

**5   Front hub bearings and seal - renewal**

1   Remove the hub/disc, as described in the preceding Section.
2   Lever out the oil seal from the inner hub recess.
3   Withdraw the inner roller race.
4   The bearing tracks may now be drifted from the hub using a suitable rod.
5   Do not mix bearing components as they are supplied as matched sets. Install the tracks by reversing the removal process and always install a new oil seal.
6   Pack grease into the bearings, install the hub/disc and adjust as described in the preceding Section.

**6   Front stabiliser bar - removal and installation**

1   Disconnect the links which secure the ends of the stabiliser bar to the suspension lower arms.
2   Unscrew and remove the bolts which secure the clamps to the body-frame and withdraw the stabiliser bar from the car.
3   Installation is a reversal of removal, but make sure that the clamp insulating rubbers have their split facing the front of the car.

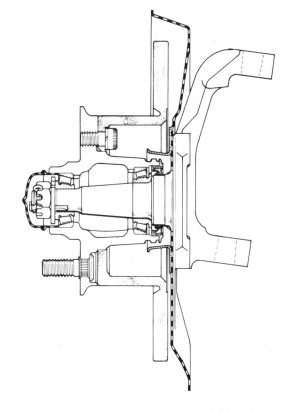

**Fig. 11.4. Cross-section of front hub (Sec. 4)**

4   Assemble the end link rubber bushes as shown in the diagram and tighten the link nuts so that the overall dimension of the mounting bush components is also as specified in the diagram (Fig. 11.5).

**7   Front road springs - removal and installation**

1   Jack-up the front of the car and support it securely under the front crossmember.
2   Slacken the suspension lower arm inner pivot bolts and disconnect the stabiliser bar end link bolts from the suspension arms.
3   Using a suitable compressor, compress the coil spring onto the suspension lower arm (Fig. 11.6).
4   Disconnect the suspension lower arm balljoint from the stub axle.
5   Remove the pivot bolts from the inner ends of the suspension arm

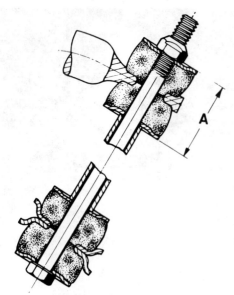

Fig. 11.5. Stabiliser bar end mounting (Sec. 6)
(Dimension A = 1.5 in/38 mm)

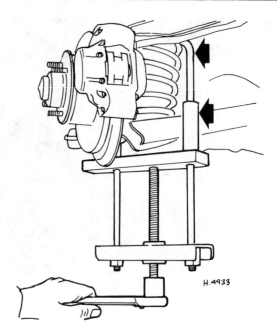

Fig. 11.6. Compressing a front spring (Sec. 7)

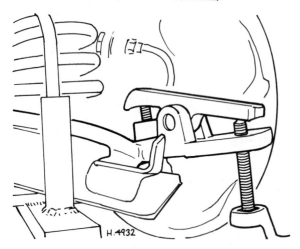

Fig. 11.7. Disconnecting a front suspension lower balljoint (Sec. 8)

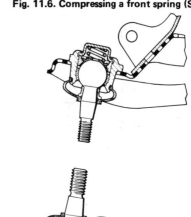

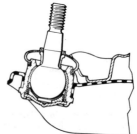

Fig. 11.8. Cross-section of upper and lower balljoints (Sec. 8)

and withdraw the arm complete with coil spring still in its compressed state.

6   The compressor can be carefully released and the spring separated from the suspension arm.

7   Reassembly is a reversal of removal, but make sure that the end of the coil spring, which is straight, locates correctly in the suspension lower arm recess.

8   Fit the rubber insulator to the top end of the spring before installing it.

9   Tighten all suspension nuts and bolts to the specified torque settings given in the Specifications Section at the beginning of this Chapter.

---

**8   Front suspension arm balljoints - checking for wear and renewal**

---

1   Raise the front of the car and support its weight under the suspension lower arms.

2   Hold each of the balljoints in turn and rock the roadwheel in the vertical plane. Any slackness must not be confused with incorrect hub endfloat.

3   Where wear is detected, renew the joint according to type, as described in the following paragraphs.

4   Remove the roadwheel and partially compress the roadspring as described in the preceding Section.

*Upper balljoint*

5   Scribe round the balljoint mounting plate to mark its position in relation to the suspension upper arm. Failure to do this will mean that the new joint will not take up the setting of the original and the camber will be altered (see Section 25).

6   Disconnect the balljoint taper pin from the stub axle using a suitable separator.

7   Unscrew and remove the nuts which secure the balljoint to the upper arm.

8   Installation is a reversal of removal, but tighten the retaining nuts to the specified torque. Check the front wheel alignment and steering angles at the first opportunity

*Lower balljoint*

9   Remove the suspension lower arm, as described in Section 7.

10  The lower balljoint is splined externally and is pressed with considerable force into the suspension lower arm. Unless suitable pressing facilities are available it is best to take the arm to your dealer to have the old balljoint removed and the new one installed.

11  After installation, check the front wheel alignment and steering angles at the first opportunity.

## 9  Front suspension upper arm - removal, servicing and installation

1   Raise the front of the car and support it under the suspension lower arm. Remove the roadwheel.
2   Partially compress the roadspring as described in Section 7.
3   Disconnect the upper balljoint from the stub axle.
4   Disconnect the shock absorber lower mounting.
5   Support the front hub on a block to avoid straining the flexible brake hose.
6   Unscrew and remove the suspension arm inner pivot bolt and withdraw the arm, taking great care to observe the positions of the castor spacers (see Section 25).
7   Renewal of the suspension arm bushes can be carried out using a press or a bolt and nut with suitable tubular distance pieces. When installing the new bushes note their correct location in relation to the front of the car (Fig. 11.10).
8   Installation is a reversal of removal, but refit the castor spacers in their original positions and have the front wheel alignment and steering angles checked at the first opportunity.
9   Tighten the suspension arm pivot bolt to the specified torque only when the weight of the car is on the roadwheels.

## 10  Front suspension lower arm - removal, servicing and installation

1   Removal of the arm complete with spring is described in Section 7. Gently release the compressor and remove the roadspring from the arm.
2   If the bushes are worn, a press will be required or a bolt and nut and suitable distance pieces.
3   The new bushes should be installed so that the flanges are towards the rear of the car and with the cut-outs uppermost. Make sure that the flanges of the bushes are in contact with the arm.
4   Installation is a reversal of removal, but tighten the pivot bolts to the specified torque when the weight of the car is on the roadwheels.

## 11  Crossmember braces - removal and replacement

1   The crossmember braces are bolted to the front crossmember with the rear ends attached to the chassis sidemember via rubber bushes (photo).
2   First remove the nut attaching the lower suspension arm to the brace bolt, and then the brace rear mounting bolt, (see Fig. 11.12).
3   **Bend** back the tab washers and remove the steering gear securing bolt and the lower suspension arm pivot bolt that retains the front end of the brace to the crossmember.
4   If the bush needs renewing it will have to be forced out of the brace using a press or a bolt and nut and suitable distance pieces.
5   When installing a new bush, ensure that the larger boss faces outwards from the car and the lug on the bush points downwards.
6   Install the braces using the reverse procedure to removal. Before tightening the bolts to the specified torque, ensure the weight of the car is on the roadwheels.

## 12  Front crossmember - removal and installation

1   Unscrew the pinch bolt from the steering column flexible coupling

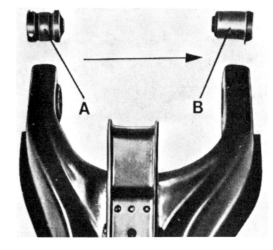

**Fig. 11.10. Correct installation of upper suspension arm bushes (Sec. 9)**

*A   Rear bush*                    *B   Front bush*

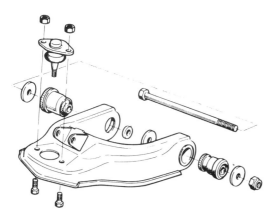

**Fig. 11.9. Upper suspension arm components (Sec. 9)**

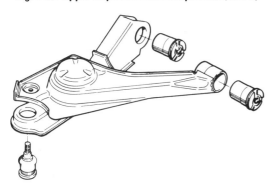

**Fig. 11.11. Lower suspension arm components (Sec. 10)**

11.1. Front crossmember brace

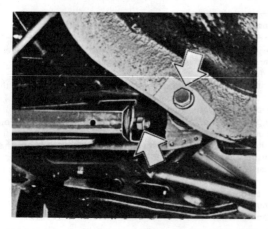

**Fig. 11.12. Rear crossmember brace attachment points (Sec. 11)**

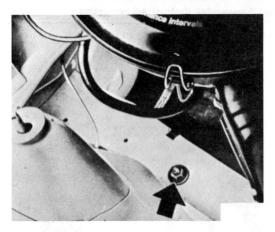

**Fig. 11.13. Crossmember attachment nut (Sec. 12)**

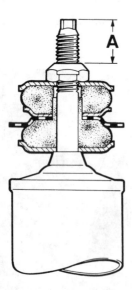

**Fig. 11.14. Rear shock absorber installation (Sec. 13)**
**(Dimension A = 0.44 in/11 mm)**

and separate the steering shaft from the pinion, after withdrawing the bolts which hold the rack and pinion assembly to the crossmember and pulling the assembly downwards.

2  With the weight of the car on the roadwheels, disconnect the shock absorber lower mountings and detach the stabiliser bar clamps from the bodyframe.

3  Disconnect both front flexible hoses from the rigid brake lines and extract the clips from the support brackets. Plug the hoses.

4  Support the weight of the engine (either by attaching a hoist or placing a jack with insulating wooden block under the sump) and disconnect the engine front mountings.

5  Remove the crossmember braces as described in Section 11.

6  From inside the engine compartment, remove the two crossmember retaining nuts (see Fig. 11.13).

7  The complete crossmember and front suspension assembly can now be removed from the car.

8  Refit the crossmember assembly using the reverse procedure to removal. Ensure all mounting bolts and nuts are tightened to the specified torque settings.

### 13 Rear shock absorber - removal, testing and installation

1  Jack-up and support the weight of the car under the rear axle.

2  Disconnect the lower mounting by removing the pivot nut.

3  From inside the luggage compartment remove the fuel tank trim panel as described in Chapter 3.

4  Prise off the plastic cap, covering the top of the shock absorber mounting, and remove the securing nut.

5  The shock absorber can now be withdrawn from beneath the car and tested as described in Section 3 of this Chapter.

6  When installing a shock absorber, ensure that the upper mounting rubbers and washers are in the correct order and the securing nut is tightened down to the dimension shown in Fig. 11.14.

### 14 Rear stabiliser bar - removal and installation

1  Refer to Fig. 11.15 and unbolt the rubber insulator clamps securing the stabiliser bar to the rear axle casing.

2  Remove the nuts and bolts securing the end links to the underbody of the car (photo).

3  Installation is the reverse procedure to removal.

### 15 Panhard rod - removal, servicing and installation

1  The Panhard rod is located between a bodyframe anchorage and a bracket on the left-hand axle tube (photo).

2  Removal is simply a matter of unscrewing and removing the securing nuts.

3  If the flexible bushes are worn, press the old ones out or draw them out using a nut and bolt and a tubular distance piece. To facilitate insertion of the new ones, dip them in soapy water.

4  Installation is a reversal of removal, but tighten the two nuts to the specified torque with the weight of the car on the roadwheels.

### 16 Rear suspension arm - removal and installation

1  Release the handbrake control lever and prise the handbrake cable from the small clip which is located on the underside of the suspension arm. If there is not enough slack in the cable, release the equaliser on the relay rod (Chapter 9).

2  Unscrew and remove the two suspension arm pivot bolts and remove the arm from its anchorage (photo).

3  If the flexible bushes are worn or have deteriorated press them out or draw them out using a bolt, nut and tubular distance piece. Installation of the new bushes will be faciliated if they are dipped in soapy water.

4  Installation is a reversal of removal, but remember to pull the handbrake cable beneath the arm before inserting the pivot bolts.

5  Before tightening the pivot bolts to the specified torque, ensure the weight of the car is being supported by the rear axle.

14.2 Rear stabiliser bar-to-body linkage

15.1 Panhard rod-to-body attachment point

16.2 Forward end of suspension arm

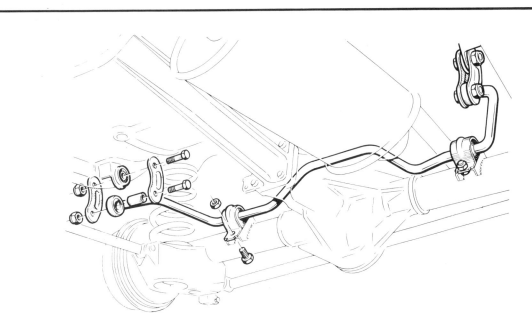

Fig. 11.15. Installation of rear stabiliser bar (Sec. 14)

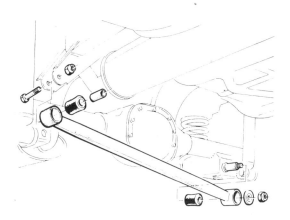

Fig. 11.16. Location of Panhard rod (Sec. 15)

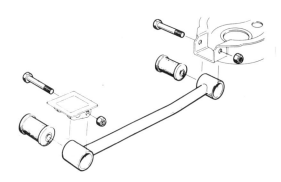

Fig. 11.17. Suspension arm and components (Sec. 16)

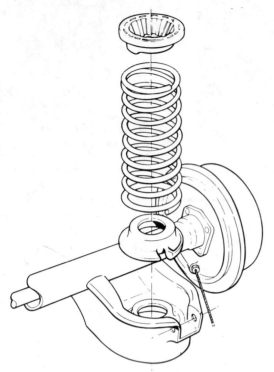

Fig. 11.18. Installation of rear spring (Sec. 17)

## 17 Rear road spring - removal and installation

1   Jack-up the rear of the car and support the bodyframe side members on stands. Place a jack under the rear axle differential unit.
2   Disconnect the stabiliser bar 'U' shaped clamps from the under-body.
3   Slacken the suspension arm pivot bolts.
4   Disconnect the shock absorber lower mounting on the side from which the spring is being removed. If both springs are being removed, disconnect one shock absorber at a time.
5   Now lower the axle gently, avoiding any strain on the flexible brake hose. Pull downwards on the spring and extract it together with flexible seats.
6   When installing a spring make sure that the straightened end of the spring locates in the axle tube seat, also, that the step in the upper seat is in contact with the end of the spring coil.
7   Make sure the weight of the car is on the rear axle before tightening the suspension arm pivot bolts to the specified torque.

## 18 Steering wheel - removal and installation

1   Set the front roadwheels in the straight-ahead position.
2   Prise out the medallion located in the centre of the steering wheel.
3   Unscrew and remove the now exposed steering wheel retaining nut.
4   Mark the relative position of the wheel to the steering shaft by dot punching the end faces.
5   Maintaining pressure with the thumbs on the end of the shaft, pull the steering wheel off its splines. On no account attempt to jar it off, as this may damage the inbuilt column collapsible plastic retainers. If the wheel is excessively tight, use a suitable puller.
6   When installing the steering wheel, mate the alignment marks before pressing it fully home on the splines.
7   Ensure that the projections and slots of the striker bush, cancelling sleeve and lugs are correctly engaged before tightening the steering wheel retaining nut to the specified torque.

## 19 Steering column shrouds - removal and refitting

1   Remove the two securing screws and remove the bottom shroud.
2   To remove the top shroud, it is necessary to undo the two screws

Fig. 11.19. RH side lower instrument panel securing screws (Sec. 19)

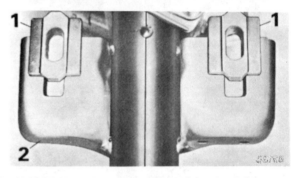

Fig. 11.20 Steering column upper bracket (2) and pads (1) in sheared position. (Sec. 20)

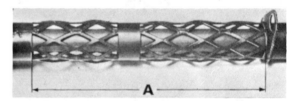

Fig. 11.21. Collapsible section of steering column (Sec. 20)

securing the lower, right-hand side of the instrument panel, (Fig. 11.19). and remove the upper column mounting nuts.
3   Lower the steering column just enough to remove the top shroud.
4   Refit the shrouds using the reverse sequence to removal.

## 20 Steering column - inspection for damage

1   In the event of a front end collision, however slight, the collapsible type steering column should be examined for damage.
2   Check for gaps between the column upper mounting pads and bracket. If gaps similar to those shown in Fig. 11.20 are to be seen, then the column has partially collapsed due to the plastic retainers having sheared.
3   If the overall length of the lattice section of the column is less than 10.37 in (263.5 mm) then again the column has suffered partial collapse (see Fig. 11.21).
4   Where damage to the steering column has been proved, then the column must be renewed.
5   Checking the steering shaft can only be carried out after its removal from the column, as described in Section 21.

## 21 Steering column - removal, servicing and installation

1   Remove the flexible coupling pinch bolt.
2   Remove the column lower mounting bolt by drilling a hole in its

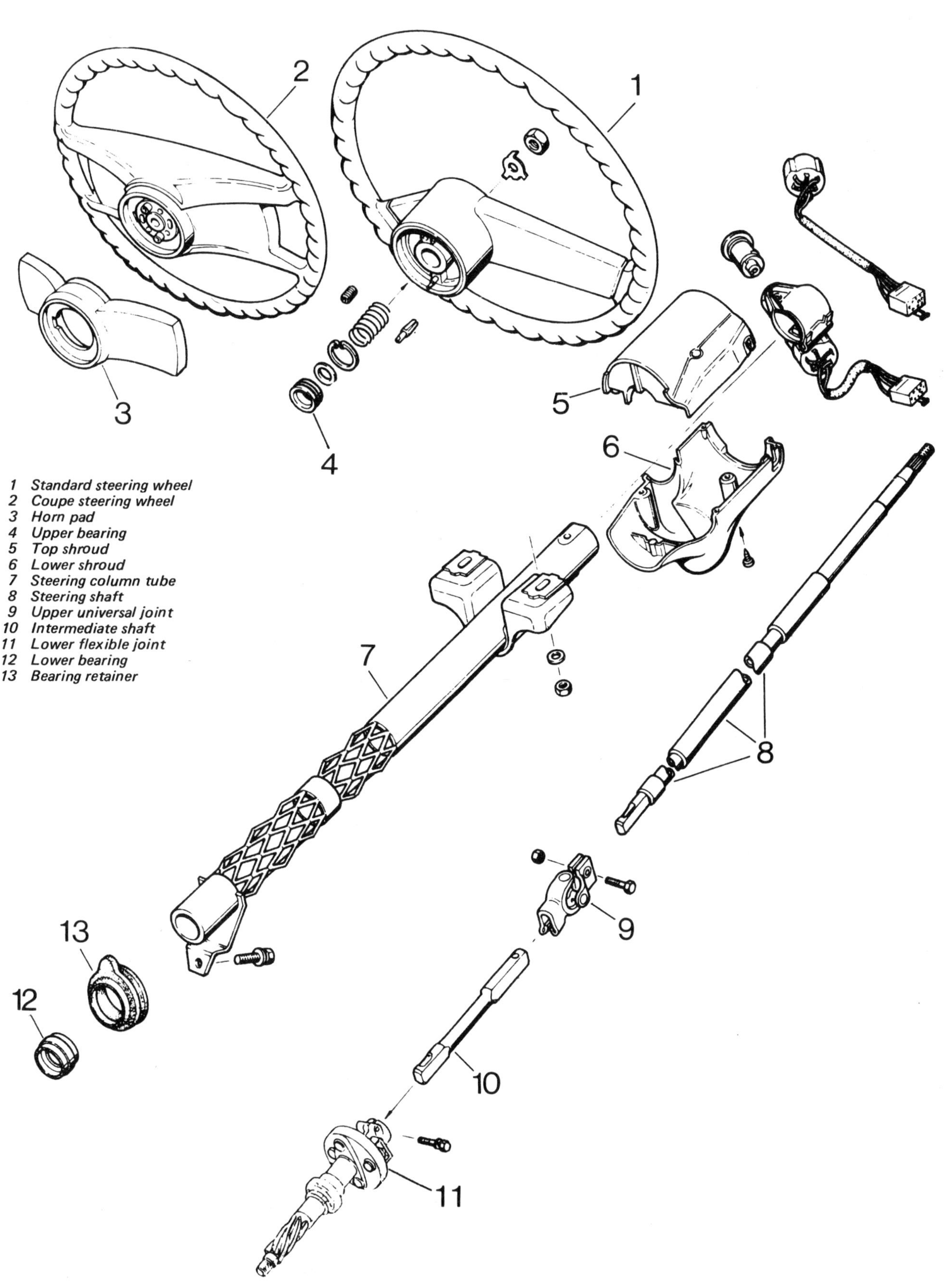

1  Standard steering wheel
2  Coupe steering wheel
3  Horn pad
4  Upper bearing
5  Top shroud
6  Lower shroud
7  Steering column tube
8  Steering shaft
9  Upper universal joint
10  Intermediate shaft
11  Lower flexible joint
12  Lower bearing
13  Bearing retainer

Fig. 11.22. Exploded view of steering column (Sec. 21)

centre (1/8 in - 3.0 mm twist drill) and unscrewing it with a screw extractor. Access to this bolt can only be gained after removal of the clutch and brake pedal assemblies as described in Chapter 9.

3  Remove the steering column upper shrouds.

4  Disconnect the lead from the battery negative terminal and then disconnect the plugs to the column switches.

5  Remove the column upper bracket bolts and withdraw the column assembly into the car interior. If the flexible coupling will not disengage easily, do not attempt to tap it off but turn the steering wheel from side-to-side fractionally and also insert a thick bladed screwdriver in the coupling clamp slot.

6  Remove the steering wheel (Section 18).

7  Withdraw the combination switch (Chapter 10).

8  Unlock the steering column lock by turning the ignition key to position 'I'.

9  Extract the upper bearing inner circlip and gently tap the upper end of the shaft to partially eject it from the column.

10  The lower ball bearing assembly can be prised out of the plastic retainer in the steering column. Ensure that the inner and outer bearing tracks are removed together (See Fig. 11.24). The shaft can now be withdrawn.

11  The column upper bearing and rubber sleeve can be extracted after removing the circlip and washer.

12  Renew any worn components and check that the shaft has not partially collapsed due to impact or collision. To do this, measure the overall length which must not be more, or less, than 31.59 in (802 mm).

13  Commence reassembly, by packing the upper bearing with grease

and placing the rubber sleeve over it before pressing them into the column. Fit the shaft into the column and push the lower bearing back into the nylon retainer on the lower end of the column. **Note:** Pack the bearing with grease before installation.

14  Press the shaft fully into the column using hand pressure only, pulling on the upper end of the shaft. Do not be tempted to tap the shaft into the column as this will cause the plastic inserts of the collapsible mechanism to shear.

15  Check that the steering column gaiter is in good condition and fitted securely to the aperture in the toe board.

16  Lower the column into position, making sure that the cut-out in the shaft is towards the pinch bolt side of the flexible coupling clamp. The different designs of the couplings and direction of entry of the clamp pinch bolt between LHD and RHD cars should be noted.

17  Install the mounting bracket bolts and the pinch bolt finger-tight and then install a new lower mounting bolt to a torque of 15 lb f ft (1.9 kg f m) only.

18  Tighten the upper mounting bracket bolts and the coupling pinch bolt to the specified torque and then return to the lower mounting bolt and tighten it until its head shears off.

19  Install the steering column combination switch, the steering wheel and the column shrouds.

20  Reconnect the electrical harness plugs and battery.

21  Reassemble the clutch and brake pedals.

## 22 Steering column lock - removal and installation

1  Remove the steering column, as described in the preceding Section.

2  Drill the centre of the bolt which secures the lock clamp to the column with a 1/8 in (3 mm) twist drill. Remove the bolt with a screw extractor.

3  When installing the lock use a new shear bolt, but only tighten it enough to hold the lock securely to the column and then check the operation of the lock by inserting the ignition key and ensuring that the tongue of the lock engages smoothly and positively in the shaft cut-out. Adjust the position of the lock if necessary, and then finally tighten the bolt fully until the head shears off.

## 23 Steering gear - removal, overhaul and installation

1  Jack up the front of the car and support it on axle stands. Apply the handbrake. Disconnect the track rod ends from the steering arms using a suitable separator tool.

2  Unscrew and remove the pinch bolt from the steering shaft flexible coupling.

3  Unscrew and remove the bolts which hold the steering gear to the crossmember and lift the gear away. If the flexible coupling is difficult to disengage, do not tap it from the steering shaft but turn the steering wheel from side to side and also insert a thick bladed screwdriver in the coupling clamp slot to expand it slightly.

4  Release the trackrod end locknuts and unscrew and remove the trackrod ends and the locknuts.

5  Release the clamps and withdraw the dust excluding bellows.

6  Using two open-ended spanners, hold the rack quite still and unscrew the inner balljoint assemblies.

7  Release the locknut and withdraw the adjusting screw, spring, washer and thrust bearing.

8  Withdraw the dust cover, hold the pinion shaft quite still and unscrew the pinion retaining nut.

9  Extract the pinion shaft.

10  Extract the rack from the pinion end of the steering gear housing to avoid damaging the housing bushes.

11  Extract the circlip and drive out the lower pinion shaft bearing. (Fig. 11.27).

12  Examine all components for wear and renew as necessary. If the upper pinion shaft needle bearing must be renewed, press it out using a suitable tubular drift or spacer and install the new one in a similar way.

13  Commence reassembly by installing the pinion shaft lower bearing and securing with a new circlip.

14  Fill the rack housing between the bushes with 2 oz (50 g) of recommended grease.

15  Install the rack from the pinion end of the housing and then centralise it so that it protrudes an equal amount at each end of the housing.

16  Apply grease to the pinion shaft and housing and install the shaft so

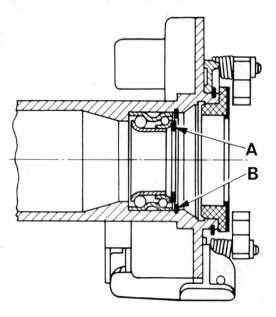

**Fig. 11.23. Sectional view of upper steering column bearing (Sec. 21)**

*A  Thrust ring*                    *B  Retaining snap-ring*

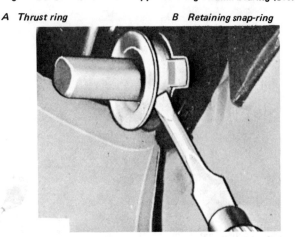

**Fig. 11.24. Prising out the lower steering column bearing (Sec. 21)**

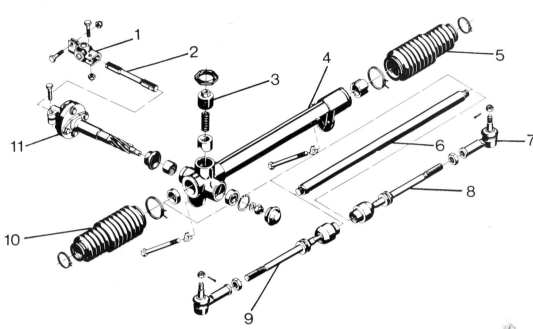

**Fig. 11.25. Exploded view of steering gear (Sec. 23)**

| 1 | Upper universal joint | 4 | Gear housing | 7 | Balljoint | 10 | Rubber bellows (RH) |
| 2 | Intermediate shaft | 5 | Rubber bellows (LH) | 8 | Inner rod and balljoint (LH) | 11 | Pinion shaft |
| 3 | Adjusting screw | 6 | Rack gear | 9 | Inner rod and balljoint (RH) | | |

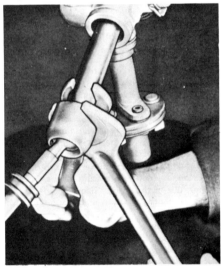

**Fig. 11.26. Removing inner balljoint (Sec. 23)**

that the slot in the coupling is aligned with the rack thrust bearing adjusting screw. Install the thrust washer to the pinion shaft and tighten the retaining nut to a torque of 11 lb f ft (1.5 kg f m) only.

17 Install the rack thrust bearing, spring and adjusting screw and with the rack still centralised, tighten the adjusting screw until a slight resistance is felt and then back off the screw between 30 and 60°. Tighten the locknut to a torque of 50 lb f ft (6.8 kg f m) and check that the pinion will move the rack over its full length of travel without binding.

18 Fit the inner balljoint assemblies and tighten to the specified torque and stake securely.

19 Install the flexible bellows but do not tighten the clamps at this stage.

20 Spin on the trackrod end locknuts and then screw on the trackrod ends an equal amount.

21 Centre the rack and offer up the steering gear so that the flat on the steering shaft is in alignment with the pinion coupling flange.

22 Tighten the steering gear mounting bolts to the specified torque.

23 Install the flexible coupling pinch bolt and tighten to the specified torque.

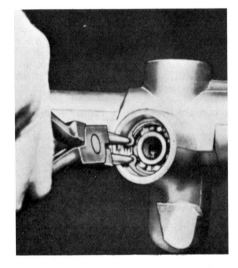

**Fig. 11.27. Lower pinion bearing circlip (Sec. 23)**

24 Connect the trackrod end balljoints to the steering arms and then adjust the front wheel toe-in, as described in Section 25 after lowering the car to the ground.

## 24 Trackrod end balljoints - testing and renewal

1 Periodically inspect the condition of the trackrod end balljoint dust excluding boots. If they are split, the complete joint will have to be renewed as the boots are not supplied separately.

2 The balljoints are spring loaded with nylon seats and require no lubrication.

3 If any free movement in a vertical direction can be felt when the trackrod is gripped and moved up and down, then the balljoint is worn and must be renewed.

4 Release the trackrod end locknut one quarter turn only.

5 Disconnect the trackrod end from the steering arm using a suitable separator.

6 Unscrew and remove the trackrod end, at the same time, holding the trackrod quite still so that the rack bellows are not twisted.

7 Screw on the new trackrod end to the same relative position as the

**Fig. 11.28. Trackrod end showing spanner flats (Sec. 24)**

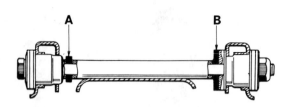

**Fig. 11.29. Front suspension upper arm spacers which control the castor angle (Sec. 25)**

old one, so that the locknut will require one quarter turn only to lock it. Hold the trackrod end in its correct attitude using the flats provided.
8    Make sure that the balljoint taper pin is clean and unlubricated and connect it to the steering arm.
9    Check the front wheel alignment, as described in Section 25.

### 25 Steering angles and front wheel alignment

1    Accurate front wheel alignment is essential for good steering and slow tyre wear. Before considering the steering angle, check that the tyres are correctly inflated, that the front wheels are not buckled, the hub bearings are not worn or incorrectly adjusted and that the steering linkage is in good order, without slackness or wear at the joints.
2    Wheel alignment consists of four factors:
**Camber** *is the angle at which the front wheels are set from the vertical when viewed from the front of the car. Positive camber is the amount (in degrees) that the wheels are tilted outwards at the top from the vertical.*
*Adjustment of the camber angle is carried out by rotating the suspension upper swivel joint flange through 180°. This movement will alter the camber angle by 0° 50'.*
3    **Castor** *is the angle between the steering axis and a vertical line when viewed from each side of the car. Positive castor is when the steering axis is inclined rearward.*
*Adjustment of the castor angle is carried out by varying the thickness of the spacers located between the suspension upper arm and crossmember. Due to the need for special gauges, it is not recommended that either the camber or castor angles are altered by the home mechanic.*
4    **Steering axis** *inclination is the angle, when viewed from the front of the car, between the vertical and an imaginary line drawn between the upper and lower suspension pivots.*
5    **Toe-in** *is the amount by which the distance between the front inside edges of the roadwheels (measured at the hub height) is less than the diametrically opposite distance measured between the rear inside edges of the front roadwheels.*
6    Front wheel tracking (toe-in) checks are best carried out with modern setting equipment, but a reasonably accurate alternative and adjustment procedure may be carried out as follows:
7    Place the car on level ground with the wheels in the straight-ahead position.
8    Obtain or make a toe-in gauge. One may be easily made from tubing, cranked to clear the sump and bellhousing, having an adjustable nut and setscrew at one end.
9    Using the gauge, measure the distance between the two inner wheel rims at hub height at the rear of the wheels.
10  Rotate the wheels (by pushing the car forwards) through 180° (half a turn) and again using the gauge, measure the distance at hub height between the two inner wheel rims at the front of the wheels. This measurement should be between 0.11 - 0.19 in (2.8 to 4.8 ,mm), less than that previously taken at the rear of the wheel and represents the correct toe-in.
11  Where the toe-in is found to be incorrect, slacken the trackrod end locknuts and the rack bellows outer clips.
12  Rotate each of the trackrods **an equal amount** and then recheck the toe-in. When adjustment is correct, tighten the locknuts, holding the trackrod ends in the centres of their arcs of travel.

### 26 Wheels and tyres -- general care and maintenance

Wheels and tyres should give no real problems in use provided that a close eye is kept on them with regard to excessive wear or damage. To this end, the following points should be noted.
Ensure that tyre pressures are checked regularly and maintained correctly. Checking should be carried out with the tyres cold and not immediately after the vehicle has been in use. If the pressures are checked with the tyres hot, an apparently high reading will be obtained owing to heat expansion. Under no circumstances should an attempt be made to reduce the pressures to the quoted cold reading in this instance, or effective underinflation will result.
Underinflation will cause overheating of the tyre owing to excessive flexing of the casing, and the tread will not sit correctly on the road surface. This will cause a consequent loss of adhesion and excessive wear, not to mention the danger of sudden tyre failure due to heat build-up.
Overinflation will cause rapid wear of the centre part of the tyre tread coupled with reduced adhesion, harsher ride, and the danger of shock damage occurring in the tyre casing.
Regularly check the tyres for damage in the form of cuts or bulges, especially in the sidewalls. Remove any nails or stones embedded in the tread before they penetrate the tyre to cause deflation. If removal of a nail *does* reveal that the tyre has been punctured, refit the nail so that its point of penetration is marked. Then immediately change the wheel and have the tyre repaired by a tyre dealer. Do *not* drive on a tyre in such a condition. In many cases a puncture can be simply repaired by the use of an inner tube of the correct size and type. If in any doubt as to the possible consequences of any damage found, consult your local tyre dealer for advice.
Periodically remove the wheels and clean any dirt or mud from the inside and outside surfaces. Examine the wheel rims for signs of rusting, corrosion or other damage. Light alloy wheels are easily damaged by 'kerbing' whilst parking, and similarly steel wheels may become dented or buckled. Renewal of the wheel is very often the only course of remedial action possible.
The balance of each wheel and tyre assembly should be maintained to avoid excessive wear, not only to the tyres but also to the steering and suspension components. Wheel imbalance is normally signified by vibration through the vehicle's bodyshell, although in many cases it is particularly noticeable through the steering wheel. Conversely, it should be noted that wear or damage in suspension or steering components may cause excessive tyre wear. Out-of-round or out-of-true tyres, damaged wheels and wheel bearing wear/maladjustment also fall into this category. Balancing will not usually cure vibration caused by such wear.
Wheel balancing may be carried out with the wheel either on or off the vehicle. If balanced on the vehicle, ensure that the wheel-to-hub relationship is marked in some way prior to subsequent wheel removal so that it may be refitted in its original position.
General tyre wear is influenced to a large degree by driving style — harsh braking and acceleration or fast cornering will all produce more rapid tyre wear. Interchanging of tyres may result in more even wear, but this should only be carried out where there is no mix of tyre types on the vehicle. However, it is worth bearing in mind that if this is completely effective, the added expense of replacing a complete set of

tyres simultaneously is incurred, which may prove financially restrictive for many owners.

Front tyres may wear unevenly as a result of wheel misalignment. The front wheels should always be correctly aligned according to the settings specified by the vehicle manufacturer.

Legal restrictions apply to the mixing of tyre types on a vehicle. Basically this means that a vehicle must not have tyres of differing construction on the same axle. Although it is not recommended to mix tyre types between front axle and rear axle, the only legally permissible combination is crossply at the front and radial at the rear. When mixing radial ply tyres, textile braced radials must always go on the front axle, with steel braced radials at the rear. An obvious disadvantage of such mixing is the necessity to carry two spare tyres to avoid contravening the law in the event of a puncture.

In the UK, the Motor Vehicles Construction and Use Regulations apply to many aspects of tyre fitting and usage. It is suggested that a copy of these regulations is obtained from your local police if in doubt as to the current legal requirements with regard to tyre condition, minimum tread depth, etc.

## 27 Fault diagnosis – suspension and steering

| Symptoms | Reasons |
| --- | --- |
| Lost motion at steering wheel | Wear in rack and pinion. Wear in trackrod end balljoints. |
| Steering wander | Wear in gear or linkage. Incorrect front wheel alignment. Incorrectly adjusted or worn front hub bearings. Worn suspension swivel balljoints. |
| Heavy or stiff steering | Incorrect front wheel alignment. Seized balljoint. Dry rack assembly. Distorted shaft/column. |
| Wheel wobble and vibration | Roadwheels out of balance. Roadwheel buckled. Incorrect front wheel alignment. Faulty shock absorber. Weak coil spring. |
| Excessive pitching or rolling on corners or during braking | Faulty shock absorber. Weak or broken coil spring. |

# Chapter 12 Bodywork and fittings

*For modifications, and information applicable to later models, see Supplement at end of manual*

## Contents

## 1 General description

The vehicle body structure is a welded fabrication of many individual shaped panels to form a 'monocoque' bodyshell. Certain areas are strengthened locally to provide for suspension system, steering system, engine support anchorages and transmission. The resultant structure is very strong and rigid.

It is as well to remember that monocoque structures have no discreet load paths and all metal is stressed to an extent. It is essential therefore to maintain the whole bodyshell both top and underside, inside and outside, clean and corrosion free. Every effort should be made to keep the underside of the car as clear of mud and dirt accumulations as possible. If you were fortunate enough to acquire a new car then it is advisable to have it rust proofed and undersealed at one of the specialist workshops who guarantee their work.

## 2 Maintenance - exterior

1 The general condition of a car's bodywork is the one thing that significantly affects its value. Maintenance is easy but needs to be regular and particular. Neglect - particularly after minor damage - can quickly lead to further deterioration and costly repair bills. It is important to keep watch on those parts of the bodywork not immediately visible, for example the underside, inside all the wheel arches and the lower part of the engine compartment.
2 The basic maintenance routine for the bodywork is washing, preferably with a lot of water from a hose. This will remove all the loose solids which may have stuck to the car. It is important to flush these off in such a way as to prevent grit from scratching the finish. The wheel arches and underbody need washing in the same way to remove any accumulated mud which will retain moisture and tend to encourage rust. Paradoxically enough, the best time to clean the underbody and wheel arches is in the wet weather when the mud is thoroughly wet and soft. In very wet weather the underbody is usually cleaned of large accumulations automatically and this is a good time for inspection.
3 Periodically it is a good idea to have the whole of the underside of the car steam cleaned, engine compartment included, for removal of accumulation of oily grime which sometimes collects thickly in areas

near the engine and gearbox, so that a thorough inspection can be carried out to see what minor repairs and renovations are necessary.

If steam facilities are not available there are one or two excellent grease solvents available which can be brush applied. The dirt can then be simply hosed off. Any signs of rust on the underside panels and chassis members must be attended to immediately. Thorough wire brushing followed by treatment with an anti-rust compound, primer and underbody sealer will prevent continued deterioration. If not dealt with the car could eventually become structurally unsound, and therefore, unsafe.
4 After washing the paintwork wipe it off with a chamois leather to give a clear unspotted finish. A coat of clear wax polish will give added protection against chemical pollutants in the air and will survive several subsequent washings. If the paintwork sheen has dulled or oxidised use a cleaner/polisher combination to restore the brilliance of the shine. This requires a little more effort but it usually is because regular washing has been neglected. Always check that door and drain holes and pipes are completely clear so that water can drain out. Brightwork should be treated the same way as paintwork. Windscreens and windows can be kept clear of smeary film which often appears, if a little ammonia is added to the water. If glass work is scratched, a good rub with a proprietary metal polish will often clean it. Never use any form of wax or other paint/chromium polish on glass.

## 3 Maintenance - interior

The flooring cover, usually carpet, should be brushed or vacuum cleaned regularly to keep it free from grit. If badly stained, remove it from the car for scrubbing and sponging and make quite sure that it is dry before replacement. Seat and interior trim panels can be kept clean with a wipe over with a damp cloth. If they do become stained (which can be more apparent on light coloured upholstery) use a little liquid detergent and a soft nailbrush to scour the grime out of the grain of the material. Do not forget to keep the headlining clean in the same way as the upholstery. When using liquid cleaners inside the car do not over-wet the surfaces being cleaned. Excessive damp could get into the upholstery seams and padded interior, causing stains, offensive odours or even rot. If the inside of the car gets wet accidentally it is worthwhile taking some trouble to dry it out properly. **Do not** use oil or electric heaters inside the car for this purpose. If, when removing mats for cleaning, there are signs of damp underneath, all the interior of the car floor should be uncovered and the point of water entry found. It may be only a missing grommet, but it could be a rusted through floor panel and this demands immediate attention as described in the previous Section. More often than not both sides of the panel will require treatment.

## 4  Minor body damage - repair

*The photographic sequences on pages 182 and 183 illustrate the operations detailed in the following sub-sections.*
**Note:** *For more detailed information about bodywork repair, the Haynes Publishing Group publish a book by Lindsay Porter called The Car Bodywork Repair Manual. This incorporates information on such aspects as rust treatment, painting and glass fibre repairs, as well as details on more ambitious repairs involving welding and panel beating.*

### Repair of minor scratches in bodywork

If the scratch is very superficial, and does not penetrate to the metal of the bodywork, repair is very simple. Lightly rub the area of the scratch with a paintwork renovator, or a very fine cutting paste, to remove loose paint from the scratch and to clear the surrounding bodywork of wax polish. Rinse the area with clean water.

Apply touch-up paint to the scratch using a fine paint brush, continue to apply fine layers of paint until the surface of the paint in the scratch is level with the surrounding paintwork. Allow the new paint at least two weeks to harden: then blend it into the surrounding paintwork by rubbing the scratch area with a paintwork renovator or a very fine cutting paste. Finally, apply wax polish.

Where the scratch has penetrated right through to the metal of the bodywork, causing the metal to rust, a different repair technique is required. Remove any loose rust from the bottom of the scratch with a penknife, then apply rust inhibiting paint to prevent the formation of rust in the future. Using a rubber or nylon applicator fill the scratch with bodystopper paste. If required, this paste can be mixed with cellulose thinners to provide a very thin paste which is ideal for filling narrow scratches. Before the stopper-paste in the scratch hardens, wrap a piece of smooth cotton rag around the top of a finger. Dip the finger in cellulose thinners and then quickly sweep it across the surface of the stopper-paste in the scratch; this will ensure that the surface of the stopper-paste is slightly hollowed. The scratch can now be painted over as described earlier in this Section.

### Repair of dents in bodywork

When deep denting of the vehicle's bodywork has taken place, the first task is to pull the dent out, until the affected bodywork almost attains its original shape. There is little point in trying to restore the original shape completely, as the metal in the damaged area will have stretched on impact and cannot be reshaped fully to its original contour. It is better to bring the level of the dent up to a point which is about 1/8 in (3 mm) below the level of the surrounding bodywork. In cases where the dent is very shallow anyway, it is not worth trying to pull it out at all. If the underside of the dent is accessible, it can be hammered out gently from behind, using a mallet with a wooden or plastic head. Whilst doing this, hold a suitable block of wood firmly against the outside of the panel to absorb the impact from the hammer blows and thus prevent a large area of the bodywork from being 'belled-out'.

Should the dent be in a section of the bodywork which has a double skin or some other factor making it inaccessible from behind, a different technique is called for. Drill several small holes through the metal inside the area — particularly in the deeper section. Then screw long self-tapping screws into the holes just sufficiently for them to gain a good purchase in the metal. Now the dent can be pulled out by pulling on the protruding heads of the screws with a pair of pliers.

The next stage of the repair is the removal of the paint from the damaged area, and from an inch or so of the surrounding 'sound' bodywork. This is accomplished most easily by using a wire brush or abrasive pad on a power drill, although it can be done just as effectively by hand using sheets of abrasive paper. To complete the preparation for filling, score the surface of the bare metal with a screwdriver or the tang of a file, or alternatively, drill small holes in the affected area. This will provide a really good 'key' for the filler paste.

To complete the repair see the Section on filling and re-spraying.

### Repair of rust holes or gashes in bodywork

Remove all paint from the affected area and from an inch or so of the surrounding 'sound' bodywork, using an abrasive pad or a wire brush on a power drill. If these are not available a few sheets of abrasive paper will do the job just as effectively. With the paint removed you will be able to gauge the severity of the corrosion and therefore decide whether to renew the whole panel (if this is possible) or to repair the affected area. New body panels are not as expensive as most people think and it is often quicker and more satisfactory to fit a new panel than to attempt to repair large areas of corrosion.

Remove all fittings from the affected area except those which will act as a guide to the original shape of the damaged bodywork (eg headlamp shells etc). Then, using tin snips or a hacksaw blade, remove all loose metal and any other metal badly affected by corrosion. Hammer the edges of the hole inwards in order to create a slight depression for the filler paste.

Wire brush the affected area to remove the powdery rust from the surface of the remaining metal. Paint the affected area with rust inhibiting paint; if the back of the rusted area is accessible treat this also.

Before filling can take place it will be necessary to block the hole in some way. This can be achieved by the use of aluminium or plastic mesh, or aluminium tape.

Aluminium or plastic mesh is probably the best material to use for a large hole. Cut a piece to the approximate size and shape of the hole to be filled, then position it in the hole so that its edges are below the level of the surrounding bodywork. It can be retained in position by several blobs of filler paste around its periphery.

Aluminium tape should be used for small or very narrow holes. Pull a piece off the roll and trim it to the approximate size and shape required, then pull off the backing paper (if used) and stick the tape over the hole; it can be overlapped if the thickness of one piece is insufficient. Burnish down the edges of the tape with the handle of a screwdriver or similar, to ensure that the tape is securely attached to the metal underneath.

### Bodywork repairs — filling and re-spraying

Before using this Section, see the Sections on dent, deep scratch, rust holes and gash repairs.

Many types of bodyfiller are available, but generally speaking those proprietary kits which contain a tin of filler paste and a tube of resin hardener are best for this type of repair. A wide, flexible plastic or nylon applicator will be found invaluable for imparting a smooth and well contoured finish to the surface of the filler.

Mix up a little filler on a clean piece of card or board — measure the hardener carefully (follow the maker's instructions on the pack) otherwise the filler will set too rapidly or too slowly. Using the applicator across the surface of the filler to achieve the correct contour and to level the filler surface. As soon as a contour that approximates to the correct one is achieved, stop working the paste — if you carry on too long the paste will become sticky and begin to 'pick up' on the applicator. Continue to add thin layers of filler paste at twenty-minute intervals until the level of the filler is just proud of the surrounding bodywork.

Once the filler has hardened, excess can be removed using a metal plane or file. From then on, progressively finer grades of abrasive paper should be used, starting with a 40 grade production paper and finishing with 400 grade wet-and-dry paper. Always wrap the abrasive paper around a flat rubber, cork or wooden block — otherwise the surface of the filler will not be completely flat. During the smoothing of the filler surface the wet-and-dry paper should be periodically rinsed in water. This will ensure that a very smooth finish is imparted to the filler at the final stage.

At this stage the 'dent' should be surrounded by a ring of bare metal, which in turn should be encircled by the finely 'feathered' edge of the good paintwork. Rinse the repair area with clean water, until all of the dust produced by the rubbing-down operation has gone.

Spray the whole repair area with a light coat of primer — this will show up any imperfections in the surface of the filler. Repair these imperfections with fresh filler paste or bodystopper, and once more smooth the surface with abrasive paper. If bodystopper is used, it can be mixed with cellulose thinners to form a really thin paste which is ideal for filling small holes. Repeat this spray and repair procedure until you are satisfied that the surface of the filler, and the feathered edge of the paintwork are perfect. Clean the repair area with clean water and allow to dry fully.

The repair area is now ready for final spraying. Paint spraying must be carried out in a warm, dry, windless and dust free atmosphere. This condition can be created artificially if you have access to a large indoor working area, but if you are forced to work in the open, you will have to pick your day very carefully. If you are working indoors, dousing the floor in the work area with water will help to settle the dust which would otherwise be in the atmosphere. If the repair area is confined to one body panel, mask off the surrounding panels; this will help to minimise the effects of a slight mis-match in paint colours. Bodywork fittings (eg chrome strips, door handles etc) will also need to be masked off. Use genuine masking tape and several thicknesses of newspaper for the masking operations.

Before commencing to spray, agitate the aerosol can thoroughly, then spray a test area (an old tin, or similar) until the technique is mastered. Cover the repair area with a thick coat of primer; the thickness should be built up using several thin layers of paint rather than one thick one. Using 400 grade wet-and-dry paper, rub down the surface of the primer until it is really smooth. While doing this, the work area should be thoroughly doused with water, and the wet-and-dry paper periodically rinsed in water. Allow to dry before spraying on more paint.

Spray on the top coat, again building up the thickness by using several thin layers of paint. Start spraying in the centre of the repair area and then, using a circular motion, work outwards until the whole repair area and about 2 inches of the surrounding original paintwork is covered. Remove all masking material 10 to 15 minutes after spraying on the final coat of paint.

Allow the new paint at least two weeks to harden, then, using a paintwork renovator or a very fine cutting paste, blend the edges of the paint into the existing paintwork. Finally, apply wax polish.

## 5  Major body damage - repair

1  Because the body is built on the monocoque principle, major damage must be repaired by a competent body repairer with the necessary jigs and equipment.
2  In the event of a crash that resulted in buckling of body panels, or damage to the roadwheels the car must be taken to a G.M. dealer or body repairer where the bodyshell and suspension alignment may be checked.
3  Bodyshell and/or suspension mis-alignment will cause excessive wear of the tyres, steering system and possibly transmission. The handling of the car will also be affected adversely.

## 6  Hinges, door catches and locks - maintenance

1  Oil the hinges of the bonnet, boot and doors with a drop, or two, of light oil, periodically. A good time is after the car has been washed.
2  Oil the bonnet release catch pivot pin and the safety catch pivot pin, periodically.
3  Do not over-lubricate door latches and strikers. Normally a little oil on the end of the rotary pinion spindle and a thin smear of high melting point grease on the striker pinion teeth and shoe spring plunger are adequate. Make sure that before lubrication they are wiped thoroughly clean and correctly adjusted.

## 7  Doors - tracing of rattles and rectification

1  Check first that the door is not loose at the hinges and that the latch is holding it firmly in position. Check also that the door lines up with the aperture in the body.
2  If the hinges are loose or the door is out of alignment it will be necessary to detach it from the hinges as described in Section 8.
3  If the latch is holding the door correctly it should be possible to press the door inwards fractionally against the rubber weatherstrip. If not, adjust the striker plate as described in Section 9.
4  Other rattles from the door would be caused by wear or looseness in the window winder, the glass channels and sill strips, or the door handles and remote control arm; all of which are described in following Sections.

## 8  Door hinges - pin removal and setting

1  The two halves of the door hinges are welded to the door and frame respectively.
2  To detach the doors, first drill or grind out the pivot rivet from the door check link.
3  Remove the sealing plugs from the hinge roll pins and drive the pins out using a suitably sized punch. If difficulty is experienced, a special cable-type extracting tool No. VR 2105 is available from your G.M. dealer. Get someone to support the weight of the door while the pins are being withdrawn.
4  When installing the hinge pins, tap them in as shown in Fig. 12.2 before hanging the door.
5  As the door hinge plates are welded to both the door pillar and the door frame, no adjustment for incorrect door alignment can be carried out other than by prising the pillar hinge plates using an adjustable wrench. This should be done very carefully and only a fraction at a time before rechecking the alignment.
6  Wear in the hinge pin holes will cause a door to drop and if the condition cannot be remedied by drilling and fitting oversize pins, then new hinge plates will have to be installed - very definitely a job for your G.M. dealer.

## 9  Door latch striker - adjustment

1  When the door is shut the panel should be flush with the bodywork and firm pressure on the door should move it inwards a fractional amount. If the door is difficult to latch or is loose when closed, the striker can be adjusted by slackening it using the correct sized Allen key and moving the striker in the required direction. Forward or rearward

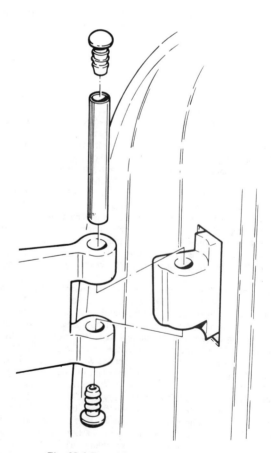

Fig. 12.1 Door hinge components (Sec. 8)

Fig. 12.2. Position of hinge pins prior to installation of door (Sec. 8)

movement of the striker can be achieved by the use of packing washers. (Fig. 12.3).

2　To ascertain the point of contact between the door lock fork and the striker, place some plasticine around the striker shaft and close the door several times. The contact mark in the plasticine should be approximately in the centre of the striker shaft.

## 10 Door interior handles and trim panel - removal and replacement

1　The doors are the usual pressed steel panel construction specially strengthened to resist sideways impact into the car. The door is retained on the bodyshell by two hinges which are welded to the door and the front door pillar. The exterior fittings are secured from the door interior: the interior handles clip onto the spindles which project through the trim from the respective mechanisms bolted to the door interior structure.

2　In order to gain access to any component attached to the door it will be necessary to begin by removing the interior facing fittings and trim.

3　Make a note of the position of the window regulator handle on the interior face, so that it can be refitted in its original position.

4　Depress the bezel around the handle spindle and with a piece of piano wire fashioned into a small hook, pull the wire clip retaining the handle on the splined end of the spindle, out of its slots (Fig. 12.4) (photos).

5　The handle and bezel can now be removed from the spindle and then the door lock button unscrewed.

6　The door handle/armrest is secured by a couple of screws and once these are undone and removed this handle may be lifted from the door (photo).

7　On Coupe models the combined armrest and door pull can be removed by pulling back the capping from the top of the door pull section and rotating the armrest upwards.

8　The door latch escutcheon should be carefully prised off on Saloon models. In the case of Coupe models the escutcheon plate is integral with the door trim panel and need not be removed.

9　To remove the ashtray, press down the stubber (Fig. 12.5), and lift it out. Undo the screw retaining the ashtray housing and prise the housing off the mounting bracket.

10　Having removed all the handles the trim may be prised from the door structure. Use a wide bladed screwdriver or similar and insert it between the door panel and the trim panel. Lever the trim panel very carefully away from the door. This action will release the trim panel retaining clips.

11　Refitting follows the reversal of the removal procedure. When refitting the window regulator handle, push the spring clip fully home, hold the handle onto the splined shaft and strike the handle with the palm of the hand. Make sure that the water deflection sheet is properly stuck to the inner door panel and the window regulator spring is in place (photo), before the trim panel is refitted (Fig. 12.6).

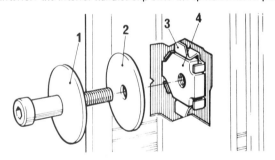

Fig. 12.3. Door latch striker (Sec. 9)

1　Striker shaft
2　Spacer
3　Anchor
4　Anchor nut

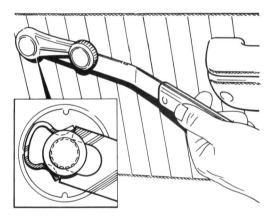

Fig. 12.4. Removing window regulator handle (Sec. 10)

10.4a Removing the window regulator handle

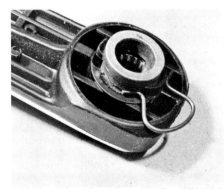

10.4b Close-up of the window regulator handle retaining clip (withdrawn)

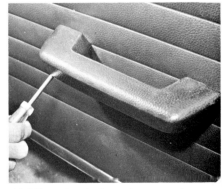

10.6 Removing the front door armrest

Fig. 12.5. Lifting out the ashtray from door trim panel (Sec. 10)

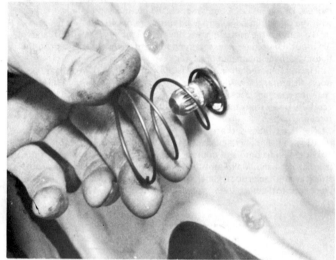

10.11 Replacing the window regulator shaft spring

Fig. 12.6. Sticking the water deflection sheet back onto the inner door panel (Sec. 10)

## 11 Door exterior fittings - removal and replacement

1  All the exterior fittings are secured in position by screws which pass through from the inside of the door.
2  Remove the interior handles and trim panel, as detailed in Section 10, to gain access to the screw retaining the exterior fittings.
3  The nuts and bolts which retain the exterior handle, door lock and latch are now fully exposed and can be undone to enable the appropriate component to be removed.

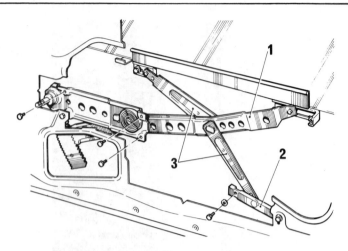

Fig. 12.7. Window regulator components (Coupe models). (Sec. 12)

1  Main arm
2  Support channel
3  Balance arms

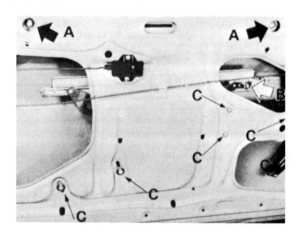

Fig. 12.8. Window regulator securing bolts (Coupe models). (Sec. 12)

A  Upper stop bolts
B  Balance arm bolt
C  Regulator securing bolts

4  Replacement of those components follows the reversal of the removal procedure.

## 12 Door window glass and regulator (Coupe models) - removal and replacement

1  Remove the door trim panel, as described in Section 10.
2  Undo the two bolts securing the window upper stops and the single bolt retaining the upper balance arm to glass support channel.
3  Refer to Fig. 12.8, and remove the six bolts securing the regulator assembly and lower balance arm support channel to door inner panel.
4  The regulator assembly can now be withdrawn through the large aperture in the door inner panel.
5  To withdraw the window glass, disengage the lower run channels and lift out the glass, rear end first from the top of the door.
6  Refit the window glass and regulator using the reverse procedure to removal. The glass should be adjusted for alignment as follows. The height adjustment is carried out using the upper stop bolts so that the top of the glass sits just below the lip of the weatherstrip. In order to ensure  that the glass does not tilt when lowering, adjust the support channel at the two securing bolts in the slotted holes with the window fully raised. Sideways movement is adjusted at the balance arm bolt.

### 13 Front door window glass and regulator (Saloon models) - removal and replacement

1  Remove the door interior trim panel, as described in Section 10.
2  Temporarily refit the window regulator handle and wind down the glass until the cable to glass support clamps come into view in the door apertures.
3  Unscrew the clamp bolts to release the glass support channel (photo).
4  Remove the door waist inner and outer weatherstrips.
5  Unscrew and remove the two lower bolts from the glass front channel guide and slacken the upper one (Fig. 12.10).
6  Lift the glass, turn it slightly and withdraw it towards the inner side of the door frame.
7  If a new glass is being installed, fit the support channel to its lower edge in accordance with the diagram (Fig. 12.9).
8  Turn the window regulator handle until it can be rotated no further

13.3 Glass support cable clamp

(anticlockwise on right-hand door, clockwise on left-hand door). Now turn the handle in the opposite direction until the notch on the cable drum appears in the door aperture. Continue turning until it appears for the second time. Do not move the regulator from this position.
9  Install the glass squarely so that it engages in the rear guide channel and then bolt the support channel to cable clamps into position by inserting a socket wrench through the door apertures.
10  Install the glass front guide channel bolts.
11  Any adjustment to the glass can be carried out by moving the cable clamps slightly or by moving the position of the front guide channel. The rear guide channel is secured at its lower end by a bolt and at its upper end by a clip.
12  To withdraw the window regulator, first remove the window glass as described previously.
13  Slacken the bolt which secures the cable tension roller.
14  Unscrew and remove the three screws which secure the regulator assembly to the door inner panel. Withdraw the assembly from the door cavity, complete with the continuous cable, having lifted the cable from the rollers.
15  The regulator assemblies are not interchangeable and are marked 'L' or 'R' on the inside face of the drum.
16  Commence installation by fitting the regulator to the door panel, making sure that the rubber sealing ring is located between the panel and the regulator spindle.
17  Position the regulator drum so that the inner cable attachment is pointing towards the rear lower roller. Wrap the cable around that roller.
18  Keeping tension in the cable, rotate the regulator drum (anticlockwise on RH door, clockwise on LH door) until 4 grooves on the drum are full, and the outer cable attachment is vertical (Fig. 12.11). Ensure the outer cable doesn't wind onto the drum.
19  Wrap the cable around the other rollers (Fig. 12.12) ensuring the cable does not become kinked. When the cable is correctly installed, apply hand pressure to the adjustable roller (2) and tighten the roller locking nut/bolt.

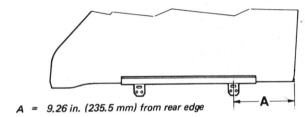

A  =  9.26 in. (235.5 mm) from rear edge

**Fig. 12.9. Correct location of door glass in support channel (Saloon models). (Sec. 13)**

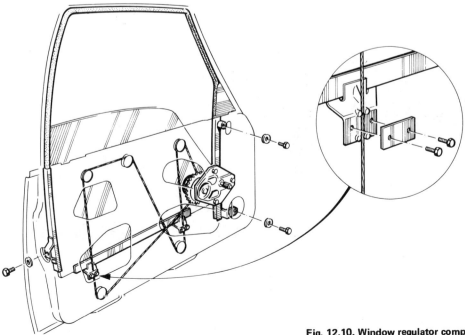

**Fig. 12.10. Window regulator components (Front door, Saloon models). (Sec. 13)**

This sequence of photographs deals with the repair of the dent and paintwork damage shown in this photo. The procedure will be similar for the repair of a hole. It should be noted that the procedures given here are simplified — more explicit instructions will be found in the text

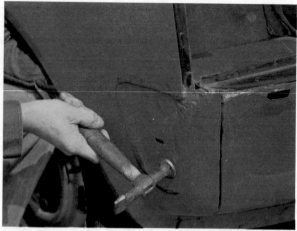

In the case of a dent the first job — after removing surrounding trim — is to hammer out the dent where access is possible. This will minimise filling. Here, the large dent having been hammered out, the damaged area is being made slightly concave

Now all paint must be removed from the damaged area, by rubbing with coarse abrasive paper. Alternatively, a wire brush or abrasive pad can be used in a power drill. Where the repair area meets good paintwork, the edge of the paintwork should be 'feathered', using a finer grade of abrasive paper

In the case of a hole caused by rusting, all damaged sheet-metal should be cut away before proceeding to this stage. Here, the damaged area is being treated with rust remover and inhibitor before being filled

Mix the body filler according to its manufacturer's instructions. In the case of corrosion damage, it will be necessary to block off any large holes before filling — this can be done with aluminium or plastic mesh, or aluminium tape. Make sure the area is absolutely clean before ...

... applying the filler. Filler should be applied with a flexible applicator, as shown, for best results; the wooden spatula being used for confined areas. Apply thin layers of filler at 20-minute intervals, until the surface of the filler is slightly proud of the surrounding bodywork

Initial shaping can be done with a Surform plane or Dreadnought file. Then, using progressively finer grades of wet-and-dry paper, wrapped around a sanding block, and copious amounts of clean water, rub down the filler until really smooth and flat. Again, feather the edges of adjoining paintwork

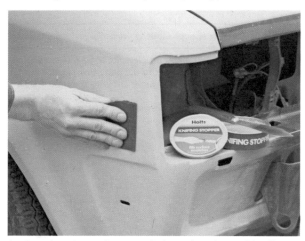

Again, using plenty of water, rub down the primer with a fine grade wet-and-dry paper (400 grade is probably best) until it is really smooth and well blended into the surrounding paintwork. Any remaining imperfections can now be filled by carefully applied knifing stopper paste

The top coat can now be applied. When working out of doors, pick a dry, warm and wind-free day. Ensure surrounding areas are protected from over-spray. Agitate the aerosol thoroughly, then spray the centre of the repair area, working outwards with a circular motion. Apply the paint as several thin coats

The whole repair area can now be sprayed or brush-painted with primer. If spraying, ensure adjoining areas are protected from over-spray. Note that at least one inch of the surrounding sound paintwork should be coated with primer. Primer has a 'thick' consistency, so will find small imperfections

When the stopper has hardened, rub down the repair area again before applying the final coat of primer. Before rubbing down this last coat of primer, ensure the repair area is blemish-free — use more stopper if necessary. To ensure that the surface of the primer is really smooth use some finishing compound

After a period of about two weeks, which the paint needs to harden fully, the surface of the repaired area can be 'cut' with a mild cutting compound prior to wax polishing. When carrying out bodywork repairs, remember that the quality of the finished job is proportional to the time and effort expended

Fig. 12.11. Attachment of cable to window regulator drum (Saloon models). (Sec. 13)

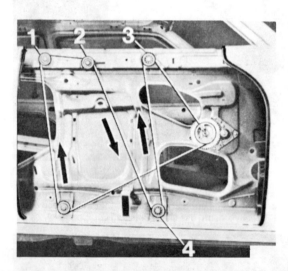

Fig. 12.12. Correct layout of window winding cable (viewed from the inside of the door). (Sec. 13)

Fig. 12.13. Rear door window regulator retaining bolts (Sec. 14)

20 Carry out the operations described in paragraphs 8 and 9 of this Section.
21 Check for smooth operation and apply oil to the cable rollers and grease to the cable itself. Refit the door interior trim panel.

## 14 Rear door window glass and regulator (Saloon models) - removal and replacement

1 First remove the door trim panel following the basic procedure given in Section 10.
2 Remove the three securing screws shown in Fig. 12.13 and lift out the regulator assembly through the aperture in the inner door panel.
3 To remove the window glass, remove the rear window channel by undoing the two screws on the upper window channel and the bolt on the inner door panel (see Fig. 12.14).
4 The glass can be lifted out through the door upper frame on the inside of the door (see Fig. 12.15).
5 If it is required to remove the rear door fixed quarter glass at this stage, it can be withdrawn by simply pulling it forwards (see Fig. 12.16).
6 Replace the window glass and regulator using the reverse procedure to removal.

## 15 Rear quarter light (Coupe models) - removal and installation

1 To remove the quarterlight, unscrew the three self-tapping screws which hold the link type fastener to the body side panel.
2 Pull the glass hinges out of engagement with the rubber grommets located in the door lock pillar.
3 If a new body flange weatherstrip is being fitted, make sure that the

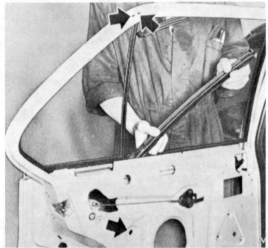

Fig. 12.14. Removing the rear window glass channel (Sec. 14)

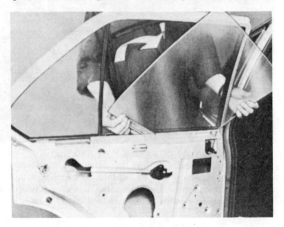

Fig. 12.15. Removing the rear door window (Sec. 14)

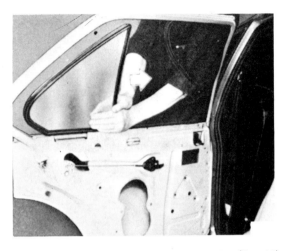

Fig. 12.16. Lifting out the rear door quarter glass (Sec. 14)

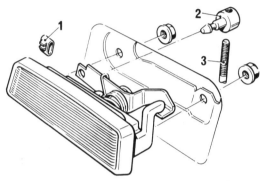

Fig. 12.18. Door handle components (Sec. 16)

1   Retaining clip          3   Release rod
2   Adjusting nut

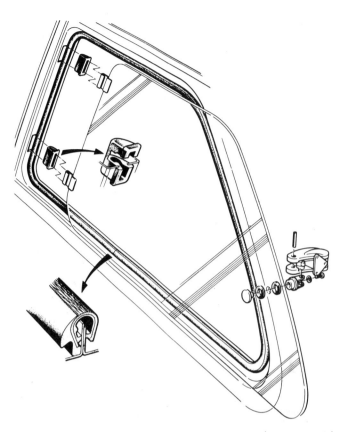

Fig. 12.17. Exploded view of rear opening quarter light (Coupe models)
(Sec. 15)

lip is to the outside and that the ends of the strip butt together at the
centre of the bottom run.
4   If new rubber hinge grommets are being installed, make sure that
their flat sides are outwards and when inserting the hinges, take care
not to push the grommets into the pillar cavity.

## 16 Door locks - removal and replacement

1   Remove the interior door handles and trim panel, as described in
Section 10.
2   On Saloon car models, unscrew the door locking button.
3   The remote control handle can be removed after extracting the two
screws.
4   Temporarily replace the window regulator handle and wind the glass
fully up.
5   Unscrew and remove the two nuts which secure the outside door
handle. Prise the adjusting nut '2' (Fig. 12.18) from its retaining clip '1'
and withdraw the handle assembly.
6   To remove the lock cylinder, extract the sliding clip '1' (Fig.12. 19)
and disconnect the rod '3'. The lock assembly can now be withdrawn
from within the door.
7   Installation is a reversal of removal but carry out the following
adjustments.
8   When fitting the outside handle, adjust the nut on the release rod so
that all free movement is eliminated. Apply a little grease to rubbing
surfaces.
9   Before tightening remote control handle mounting plate screws,
press the mounting forward with the finger to eliminate any free-
movement. The holes in the mounting plate are elongated for this
purpose.
10 On four-door saloon models the rear door lock is similar to the front

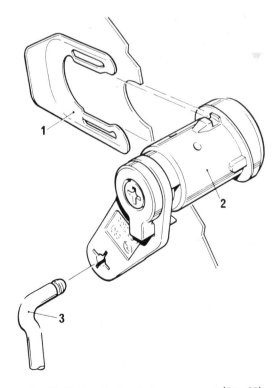

Fig. 12.19. Door lock cylinder components (Sec. 16)

1   Sliding clip
2   Cylinder
3   Connecting rod

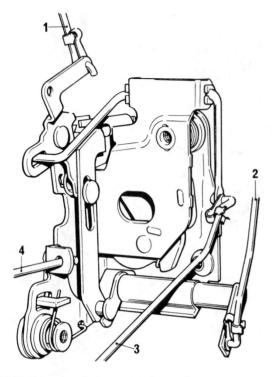

**Fig. 12.20. Front door lock assembly (Sec. 16)**

1  Internal lock plunger          3  Cylinder lock connecting rod
   connecting rod                 4  Remote control rod
2  Exterior handle connecting rod

**Fig. 12.22. Removing the luggage compartment lock barrel (Sec. 17)**

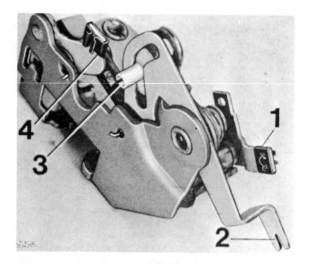

**Fig. 12.21. Rear door lock assembly (Sec. 16)**

1  Outside handle lever
2  Child safety catch
3  Remote control lever
4  Lock button lever

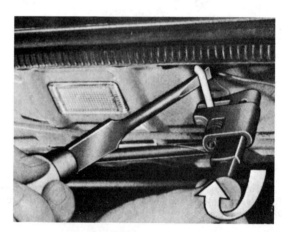

**Fig. 12.23. Releasing the luggage compartment hinge torsion rod (Sec. 18)**

but is operated by three rods and incorporates a child-safety catch (see Fig. 12.21).
11  All three control rods must be removed before the lock can be withdrawn through the inner door panel aperture.
12  The rear door handle is also similar to the front, but the lock assembly must first be removed to gain access to the handle securing nuts.

**17 Luggage compartment lock and lock cylinder - removal and replacement**

1  The lock is secured to the luggage compartment lid frame by two screws, and the key cylinder is retained on the lid shell by a spring clip.
2  Undo the two screws fastening the lock assembly to the lid and lift off the lock.
3  The lock cylinder can now be removed by prising off the spring clip, as shown in Fig. 12.22.
4  The lock barrel can be removed from the cylinder by prising off the retaining ring and inserting the key to align the lock wards.
5  When refitting the lock cylinder a length of tubing can be used to push the spring retaining clip over the cylinder. Ensure that the tag on

the spring clip is pointing towards the hinged end of the boot lid.

**18 Luggage compartment lid - removal and replacement**

1  The luggage compartment lid incorporates torque rods to support it in the open position.
2  To remove the torque rods, unhook the anchored end from the centre of the underside of the parcel shelf by twisting the rod upward using an adjustable wrench and prising the hooked end out of the hole with a screwdriver (Fig. 12.23).
3  The other end of the rod can be withdrawn from the hinge and removed from the car.
4  Mark the position of the hinges on the luggage compartment lid, and with someone supporting the weight of the lid, remove the retaining bolts and lift the lid away from the car.
5  If the position of the lid requires adjustment, the lid should be refitted and repositioned using the movement available through the slotted holes in the hinges (Fig. 12.24).
6  The striker hook on the luggage compartment sill can also be adjusted up or down by slackening the securing bolt.

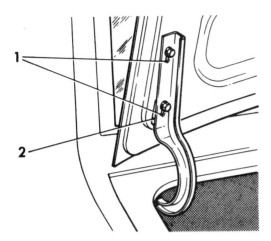

**Fig. 12.24. Luggage compartment lid hinge (Sec. 18)**

*1 Adjustment slots*          *2 Lid*

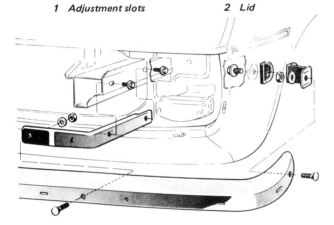

**Fig. 12.25. Front bumper attachment points (Sec. 21)**

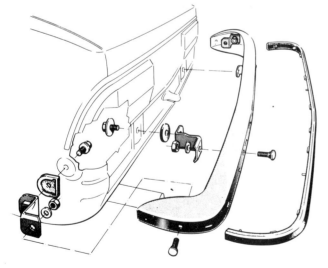

**Fig. 12.26. Rear bumper attachment points (Sec. 21)**

## 19 Engine compartment bonnet and catch assembly - removal and replacement

1   The bonnet is held to the hinges by two bolts on each side.
2   To remove the bonnet first mark the position of the hinges with a pencil. Remove one bolt from each side and then, with the help of someone, remove the other two, and lift the bonnet clear. Be careful when resting the bonnet against a wall, that the paint is not chipped,

particularly at the back corners. Pad the edges resting against rough surfaces with some paper or rag.
3   Replacement is a straightforward reversal of the removal procedure, once again requiring assistance. Line-up the hinges to the marks, nip the bolts up just enough to hold and close the bonnet. Check that it is central in the body opening and then tighten the bolts.
4   The bonnet lock assembly can be removed from the front end panel by removing the two retaining bolts, lifting off the lock and unhooking the release cable.
5   If it is found that the bonnet is hard to close or will not close fully, the lock securing bolts should be slackened and the lock assembly moved within the adjustment slots until the correct position is obtained.

## 20 Windscreens (front and rear) - removal and replacement

1   Where a windscreen is to be replaced then, if it is due to shattering, the facia air vents should be covered before attempting removal. Adhesive sheeting is useful to stick to the outside of the glass to enable large areas of crystallised glass to be removed.
2   Where the screen is to be removed intact or is of laminated type, then an assistant will be required. First release the rubber surround from the bodywork by running a blunt, small screwdriver around and under the rubber weatherstrip both inside and outside the car. This operation will break the adhesive of the sealer originally used. Take care not to damage the paintwork or catch the rubber surround with the screwdriver. Remove the windscreen wiper arms and interior mirror and place a protective cover on the bonnet.
3   Have your assistant push the inner lip of the rubber surround off the flange of the windscreen body aperture. Once the rubber surround starts to peel off the flange, the screen may be forced gently outwards by careful hand pressure. The second person should support and remove the screen complete with rubber surround and metal beading as it comes out.
4   Remove the bright moulding from the rubber surround.
5   Before fitting a windscreen, ensure that the rubber surround is completely free from old sealant and glass fragments, and has not hardened or cracked. Fit the rubber surround to the glass and apply a bead of suitable sealant between the glass outer edge and sealing strip.
6   Clean old sealant from the bodyflange.
7   Cut a piece of strong cord greater in length than the periphery of the glass and insert it into the body flange locating channel of the rubber surround.
8   Apply a thin bead of sealant to the face of the rubber channel which will eventually mate with the body.
9   Offer the windscreen to the body aperture and pass the ends of the cord, previously fitted and located at bottom centre into the vehicle interior.
10 Press the windscreen into place, at the same time have an assistant pull the cords to engage the lip of the rubber channel over the body flange.
11 Remove any excess sealant with a paraffin soaked rag.
12 Refit the bright moulding to the rubber surround. A special tool will facilitate this operation but take care not to tear the lips of the rubber.

## 21 Bumpers and other exterior bright trim - removal and replacement

1   All bumpers and overriders are bolt on assemblies. Removal is straightforward, but the nuts and bolt threads will probably require penetrating oil because they are invariably rusted.
2   The protective rubber strips on the front and rear bumpers are retained in place by spring clips and studs (Fig. 12.27). The bumper must be removed from the car before the strips can be removed.
3   The body trim both internally and externally is of very simple construction. Its removal is obvious in each case. If a screw is not visible then it is either a push-on, or slide-on fit. Check each part - and never force anything.

## 22 Heater control cables - removal and replacement

1   Refer to Chapter 10, and remove the instrument panel assembly to gain access to the heater control levers and cables.
2   To remove the cables from the control levers, release the outer cables from the clips and rotate the inner cable or lever until the clevis

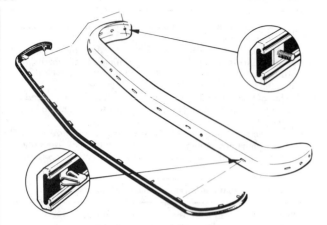

Fig. 12.27. Installation of bumper rubber strip (Sec. 21)

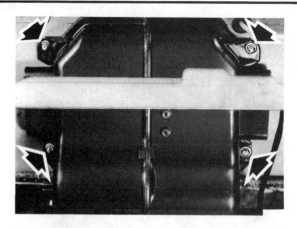

Fig. 12.28. Heater lower casing attachments (arrowed) (Sec. 23)

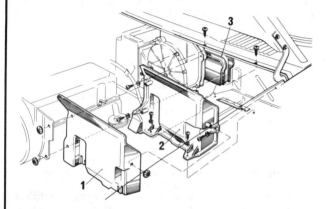

Fig. 12.29. Heater installation (Sec. 23)

| | | | |
|---|---|---|---|
| 1 | Moulded noise insulator | 3 | Scuttle panel deflector |
| 2 | Ventilator intake closing panel | | |

Fig. 12.30. Heater upper casing attachments (arrowed) (Sec. 23)

Fig. 12.31. Heater radiator securing cover (Sec. 23)

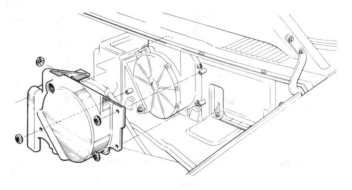

Fig. 12.32. Installation of ventilation fan cover (Sec. 24)

Fig. 12.33. Ventilation fan retaining screw (Sec. 24)

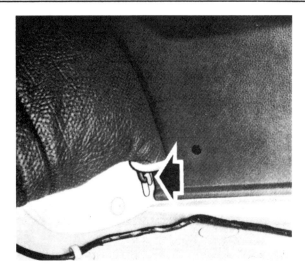

Fig. 12.34. Rear seat backrest lower securing hook (Sec. 25)

gain access to the heater control levers and cables.

2   To remove the cables from the control levers, release the outer cables from the clips and rotate the inner cable or lever until the clevis pin can be released.

3   Release the lower ends of the cables from the heater control valves and withdraw them from the car.

4   When refitting the cables, ensure that the temperature and distribution control valve levers are in the fully rearward position and the control levers are in the upward position.

### 23  Heater radiator assembly - removal and refitting

1   Drain the cooling system, as described in Chapter 2.

2   Disconnect the two heater hoses from the heater core inlet and outlet pipes.

3   Remove the switch panel and the right- and left-hand lower instrument panels as described in Chapter 10, Section 34.

4   Remove the three nuts and the self-tapping bolt securing the heater lower casing (Fig. 12.28) and remove the casing.

5   Prise out the three spring clips from the moulded noise insulator (Fig. 12.29) to gain access to the screws securing the ventilator intake closing panel.

6   Remove the seven screws from the ventilator intake closing panel and remove the panel.

7   Remove the three screws from the heater upper casing (Fig. 12.30) and remove the casing.

8   Remove the two screws from the heater core (Fig. 12.31) and detach the throttle linkage from the intake manifold to provide the necessary clearance for withdrawal of the radiator.

9   Refit the core by reversing the removal operations. On reassembly, apply sealer to the heater upper and lower casing joints to ensure a good seal between the heater casing and body panels.

10  Check the operation of the controls and then adjust if necessary. Adjustment of cables should be made with the control levers in the upward position and the distribution and temperature control flap levers in the fully rearward position. When installing the retaining clips, ensure that the outer cables do not restrict flap lever movement.

11  Refill the cooling system.

### 24  Ventilator fan - removal and replacement

1   The two-speed ventilator fan is located in the engine compartment on the rear bulkhead. The motor is not repairable, and if faulty must be replaced with a new unit.

2   To gain access to the fan assembly, release the four spring clips and lift off the moulded fan cover (Fig. 12.29).

3   Release the clips from around the edge of the fan inner cover and remove the cover.

4   Remove the single retaining screw (Fig. 12.33), and pull the fan and motor assembly from the two retaining lugs. Disconnect the electrical leads and remove the assembly from the car.

5   Refit the fan and motor assembly using the reverse procedure to removal. Apply some sealing compound between the inner fan cover joint faces before installation.

6   For information on removal of the fan switch and indicator light, refer to Chapter 10.

### 25  Front and rear seats - removal and replacement

1   The front bucket seats can be removed by detaching the two clamps retaining the front seat bar to the floor and releasing the rear safety catch.

2   When installing a front seat, ensure the guide tongue is located beneath the inner seat stop retaining rail.

3   The rear seat cushion can be removed by pulling the front of the seat upwards to release it from the two floor mounted spring clips.

4   Install the cushion by pushing it rearwards as far as possible, and then pushing down on the front edge.

5   To remove the rear seat backrest, first remove the seat cushion as described previously and unhook the wire loops at the base of the seat (see Fig. 12.34).

6   Lift the seatback upwards to release it from the top brackets and remove it from the car.

7   Refit the seatback using the reverse procedure to removal.

# Chapter 13 Supplement:
# Revisions and information on later models

## Contents

## 1 Introduction

This Supplement covers information and procedures for later models. In particular it covers the 1.8 overhead camshaft and 2.0 cam-in-head engines, fuel injection equipment, five-speed manual gearbox, and bodywork differences for Hatchback models.

The Sections in the Supplement follows the same order as the Chapters to which they relate, and the Specifications are all grouped together for convenience.

It is recommended that before any particular operation is undertaken, reference be made to the appropriate Section(s) of the Supplement. In this way, any changes to procedure or components can be noted before referring to the main Chapters.

## 2 Specifications

*The Specifications below are supplementary to, or revisions of, those at the beginning of the preceding Chapters.*

### Engine 2.0 cih
#### General
As 19S except for the following:

| | |
|---|---|
| Engine code number ................................................................. | 20S (carburettor), 20E (fuel injection) |
| Capacity ................................................................................... | 1979 cc (121 cu in) |
| Compression ratio ................................................................... | 9.0:1 |
| Compression pressure (hot) ................................................... | 140 lbf/in² (9.7 bar) |
| Valve clearances (hot) – hydraulic tappet ............................. | 1 revolution preload |
| Inlet valve maximum opening ................................................ | 110° ATDC |
| Camshaft lift, peak to base ................................................... | 1.576 in (40.10 mm) |
| Cylinder bore ......................................................................... | 3.740 in (95.00 mm) |
| Piston ring gap: | |
|    Top and centre ring ......................................................... | 0.016 to 0.026 in (0.40 to 0.65 mm) |
|    Scraper ring ..................................................................... | 0.010 to 0.016 in (0.25 to 0.40 mm) |

### Engine 1.8 ohc
#### General

| | |
|---|---|
| Type ........................................................................................ | Four cylinder in-line, overhead camshaft |
| Engine code number ............................................................... | 18S |
| Bore ........................................................................................ | 84.8 mm (3.34 in) |
| Stroke ..................................................................................... | 79.5 mm (3.13 in) |
| Displacement .......................................................................... | 1796 cc (109.5 cu in) |

| | |
|---|---|
| Max bhp | 90 at 5400 rpm |
| Max torque | 143 Nm (105.5 lbf ft) at 3000 to 3400 rpm |
| Compression ratio | 9.2 : 1 |
| Firing order | 1-3-4-2 |
| No 1 cylinder location | Timing belt cover end |

## Lubrication system

| | |
|---|---|
| Oil capacity: | |
|     With filter change | 3.75 litre (6.6 Imp pint) |
|     Without filter change | 3.5 litre (6.2 Imp pint) |
| Dipstick MIN to MAX quantity | 1.0 litre (1.8 Imp pint) |
| Oil pressure at idle with engine at operating temperature | 1.5 bar (22 lbf/in²) |

## Cylinder block (crankcase)

| | |
|---|---|
| Material | Cast-iron |
| Maximum cylinder bore out-of-round | 0.013 mm |
| Maximum permissible taper | 0.013 mm |
| Maximum rebore oversize | 0.5 mm |

## Crankshaft

| | |
|---|---|
| Number of main bearings | 5 |
| Main bearing journal diameter | 57.982 to 57.995 mm |
| Crankpin diameter | 48.971 to 48.987 mm |
| Undersizes | 0.25 and 0.50 mm |
| Crankshaft endfloat | 0.07 to 0.3 mm |
| Main bearing running clearance | 0.015 to 0.04 mm |
| Big-end running clearance | 0.019 to 0.063 mm |
| Big-end side-play | 0.07 to 0.24 mm |

## Camshaft

| | |
|---|---|
| Identification code | C |
| Endfloat | 0.09 to 0.21 mm |
| Cam lift | 6.12 mm |
| Camshaft journal diameters: | |
|     No 1 | 42.455 to 42.470 mm |
|     No 2 | 42.705 to 42.720 mm |
|     No 3 | 42.955 to 42.970 mm |
|     No 4 | 43.205 to 43.220 mm |
|     No 5 | 43.455 to 43.370 mm |
| Camshaft bearing (direct in housing) diameters: | |
|     No 1 | 42.500 to 42.525 mm |
|     No 2 | 42.750 to 42.775 mm |
|     No 3 | 43.000 to 43.025 mm |
|     No 4 | 43.250 to 43.275 mm |
|     No 5 | 43.500 to 43.525 mm |

## Pistons and rings

| | |
|---|---|
| Type | Alloy, recessed head |
| Piston-to-bore clearance | 0.02 mm |
| Number of piston rings | 2 compression, 1 oil control |
| Ring end gap: | |
|     Compression | 0.3 to 0.5 mm |
|     Oil control (rail) | 0.40 to 1.40 mm |
| Ring gap offset | 180° |
| Gudgeon pin: | |
|     Length | 70.0 mm |
|     Diameter | 23.0 mm |
|     Fit | Interference in connecting rod |
|     Clearance in piston | 0.011 to 0.014 mm |

## Cylinder head

| | |
|---|---|
| Material | Light alloy |
| Maximum permissible distortion of sealing face | 0.025 mm |
| Overall height of cylinder head | 95.75 to 96.25 mm |
| Valve seat width: | |
|     Inlet | 1.3 to 1.4 mm |
|     Exhaust | 1.7 to 1.8 mm |

## Valves

| | |
|---|---|
| Valve clearance | Automatic by hydraulic valve lifters (cam followers) |
| Valve stem-to-guide clearance: | |
|     Inlet | 0.015 to 0.042 mm |
|     Exhaust | 0.03 to 0.06 mm |

| | |
|---|---|
| Valve seat angle | 44° |
| Valve guide installed height | 80.95 to 81.85 mm |
| Valve stem diameter: | |
|     Inlet | 7.795 to 7.985 mm |
|     Exhaust | 7.957 to 7.970 mm |
| Oversizes | 0.075, 0.150, 0.250 mm |
| Valve guide bore (standard) | 8.000 to 8.017 mm |

## Flywheel

| | |
|---|---|
| Maximum thickness reduction at driven plate and pressure plate cover contact surfaces | 0.3 mm |

## Oil pump

| | |
|---|---|
| Tooth play (gear to gear) | 0.1 to 0.2 mm |
| Clearance (outer gear to housing) | 0.03 to 0.1 mm |

## Torque wrench settings

| | Nm | lbf ft |
|---|---|---|
| Flywheel (or driveplate) to crankshaft | 60 | 44 |
| Main bearing cap bolts | 80 | 59 |
| Oil pump mounting bolts | 6 | 4 |
| Oil pump relief valve cap | 30 | 22 |
| Alternator bracket bolts | 40 | 29 |
| Big-end cap bolts | 50 | 37 |
| Sump pan bolts | 5 | 4 |
| Cylinder head bolts: | | |
|     Stage 1 | 25 | 18 |
|     Stage 2 | Turn bolt through 60° | |
|     Stage 3 | Turn bolt through 60° | |
|     Stage 4 | Turn bolt through 60° | |
|     Stage 5 | Tighten a further 30° to 50° after warm-up | |
| Camshaft sprocket bolt | 45 | 33 |
| Torsional damper bolt | 60 | 44 |
| Starter motor bolts | 45 | 33 |
| Manifold bolts and nuts | 22 | 16 |
| Engine mounting bracket to crankcase | 50 | 37 |
| Engine mounting bracket to transmission | 30 | 22 |
| Engine mountings to bodyframe | 40 | 30 |
| Oil pressure switch | 30 | 22 |
| Oil drain plug | 45 | 33 |

## *Cooling system*
## Cooling system capacity (including heater)

| | |
|---|---|
| 18S/20E (manual gearbox) | 6.8 litres (12.0 pints) |
| 18S/20E (automatic transmission) | 6.7 litres (11.8 pints) |
| 20S (manual gearbox) | 6.2 litres (10.9 pints) |
| 20S (automatic transmission) | 6.1 litres (10.7 pints) |

## *Fuel system*
## Carburettor

| | |
|---|---|
| Type | GM Varajet II |
| Auxiliary system | Additional idling mixture |
| Throttle flap diameter | 35 mm (primary), 46 mm (secondary) |
| Venturi | 28 mm |
| Main jet | 92 |
| Partial load needle | 12 |
| Idling speed | 800 to 850 rpm (except five-speed) |
| | 900 to 950 rpm (five-speed) |
| Ignition control vacuum | 0.1 to 0.6 in Hg (1 to 15 mm Hg) or |
| | 0.8 to 8.0 in $H_2O$ (20 to 200 mm $H_2O$) |
| Exhaust gas emission (idling) | 1 to 2% CO |
| Fast idling speed (hot) | 2000 to 2100 rpm |
| Choke flap gap: | |
|     20S | 4.5 mm |
|     18S | A  3.7 to 4.3 mm |
| | B  2.7 to 3.3 mm |
| | C  9.5 to 10.5 mm |
| Pump piston setting | 7.8 to 8.2 mm |
| Clearance – baffle plate lever to pull rod | 0.1 to 0.3 mm |

## *Fuel injection system*

| | |
|---|---|
| Regulated pressure | 42 ± 3 lbf/in² (3 ± 0.2 bar) |
| Electric fuel pump output | 1.5 to 2.0 litres/min |
| Idle speed | 850 to 900 rpm |
| Exhaust gas emission (idling) | 0.5% CO maximum |

| Torque wrench settings | Nm | lbf ft |
|---|---|---|
| Fuel pump (ohc) .................................................. | 18 | 13 |
| Fuel injectors .................................................. | 32 | 23 |

## *Ignition system*
### General
| | |
|---|---|
| System type (later models) ................................ | Electronic (breakerless), Bosch or AC Delco |
| Firing order ....................................................... | 1-3-4-2 |

### Distributor
| | |
|---|---|
| Direction of rotation (viewed from top of cap): | |
| 1.8 ohc ....................................................... | Anti-clockwise |
| 2.0 cih ....................................................... | Clockwise |
| Dwell angle .................................................... | Electronically controlled |
| Rotor resistance ............................................. | 1000 ohms approx |

### Ignition timing
| | |
|---|---|
| Static ............................................................ | See text |
| At idle speed ................................................. | Timing marks in alignment |
| Location of marks: | |
| 1.8 ohc ....................................................... | Pulley and pointer |
| 2.0 cih ....................................................... | Flywheel and pointer |

### Ignition coil
| | |
|---|---|
| Type ............................................................. | Bosch KW12V or equivalent |
| Primary resistance ......................................... | 0.6 to 0.9 ohms |

### Spark plugs
| | |
|---|---|
| Make and type: | |
| 1.8 models .................................................. | Champion RN7YC, CR 42 CXLS, or equivalent |
| 1.6/1.9/2.0 models ...................................... | Champion RL82YC, CR 42 CFS, or equivalent |
| Electrode gap ................................................ | 0.7 to 0.8 mm (0.028 to 0.032 in) |

| Torque wrench settings | Nm | lbf ft |
|---|---|---|
| Spark plugs (1.8 ohc) ...................................... | 20 | 15 |
| Distributor clamp nuts ..................................... | 22 | 16 |

## *Clutch*
### Friction plate facings (1984 on models) ............
Asbestos-free

## *Manual gearbox (5-speed)*
### Gearbox type ...................................................
240

### Gear ratios
| | |
|---|---|
| First .............................................................. | 3.717 : 1 |
| Second .......................................................... | 2.019 : 1 |
| Third ............................................................. | 1.316 : 1 |
| Fourth ........................................................... | 1.000 : 1 |
| Fifth .............................................................. | 0.804 : 1 |
| Reverse ......................................................... | 3.445 : 1 |

### Lubricant capacity ..........................................
1.4 litres (2.5 pints)

### Reverse idler gear pinion-to-plate clearance ....
0.1 mm (0.004 in)

### Fifth gear pinion-to-retaining nut clearance .......
0.05 to 0.10 mm (0.002 to 0.004 in)

### Mainshaft bearing spacer thicknesses ..............
0.3, 0.4 and 0.5 mm (0.012, 0.016 and 0.020 in)

### Input shaft bearing spacer thicknesses ..............
2.3, 2.4, 2.5 and 2.6 mm (0.091, 0.094, 0.098 and 0.102 in)

### Clutch release bearing guide
| | |
|---|---|
| Spacer thicknesses ........................................ | 1.3, 1.4 and 1.5 mm (0.052, 0.055 and 0.059 in) |
| Maximum axial play ........................................ | 0.05 mm (0.002 in) |

### Selector fork end minimum thickness ...............
4.90 to 4.96 mm (0.19 to 0.20 in)

### Synchroniser ring-to-pinion teeth clearance
| | |
|---|---|
| Used ring ...................................................... | 1.0 mm (0.04 in) minimum |
| New ring ....................................................... | 1.0 to 1.5 mm (0.04 to 0.06 in) |

| Torque wrench settings | Nm | lbf ft |
|---|---|---|
| Support plate mounting bolt .............................. | 25 | 18 |
| Selector rail end support bolt ............................ | 25 | 18 |

Underbonnet view of a 1.8 ohc engine

1  Brake servo non-return valve
2  Heater housing
3  Battery
4  Front suspension upper
   mounting

5  Brake pressure control valve
6  Distributor
7  Ignition coil
8  Distributor

9  Engine oil filler cap
10  Top hose
11  Radiator
12  Radiator cap

13  Alternator
14  Fuel pump
15  Throttle cable
16  Brake master cylinder

17  Carburettor
18  Brake fluid reservoir
19  Washer reservoir
20  Oil level dipstick

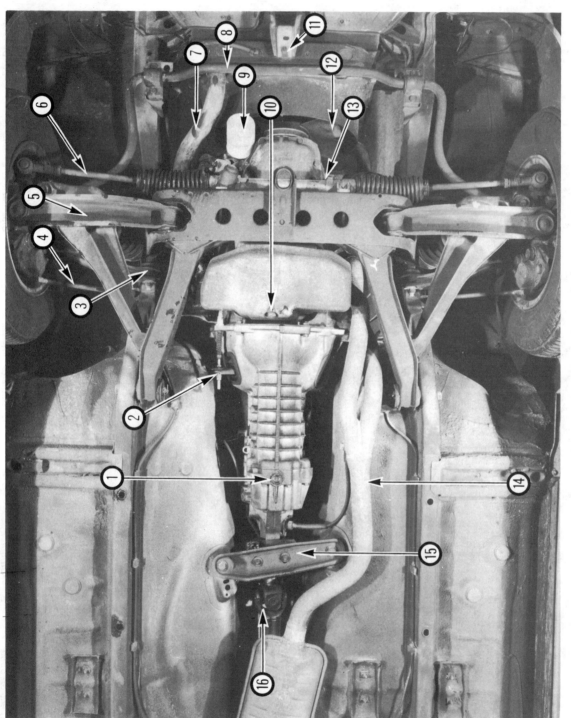

**View of front underbody**

1  Five-speed gearbox drain plug
2  Clutch release lever and cable
3  Front suspension upper arm inner pivot
4  Flexible brake hydraulic hose
5  Front suspension lower arm
6  Steering track rod
7  Bottom hose
8  Front stabiliser bar
9  Oil filter
10  Engine oil drain plug
11  Radiator bottom mounting
12  Fan blades
13  Steering gear
14  Front exhaust pipe
15  Gearbox mounting crossmember
16  Propeller shaft

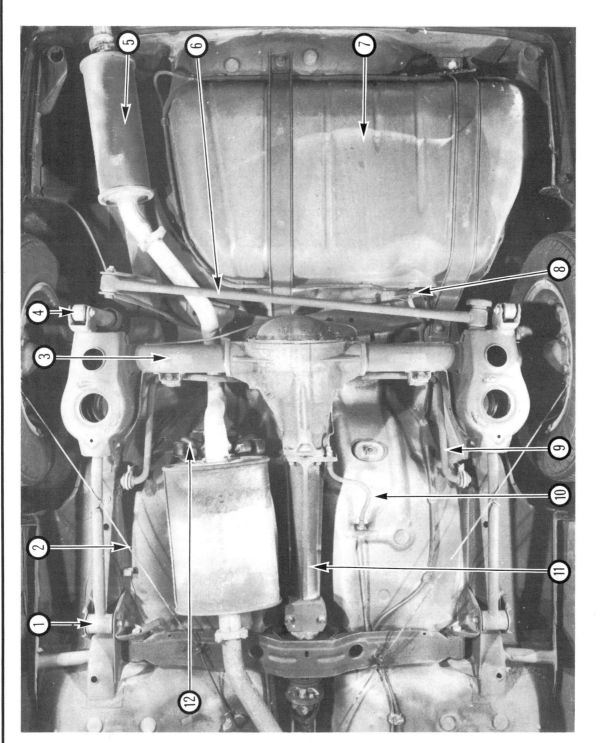

**View of rear under-body**

1  Rear suspension arm front
    mounting
2  Handbrake cable

3  Rear axle assembly
4  Rear shock absorber lower
    mounting

5  Rear exhaust system
6  Panhard rod
7  Fuel tank

8  Fuel gauge sender unit
9  Rear stabiliser bar
10 Flexible brake hudraulic hose

11 Rear axle extension
12 Exhaust system mounting

| | Nm | lbf ft |
|---|---|---|
| Fifth gear detent plug | 60 | 43 |
| Reverse idler shaft bolts | 25 | 18 |
| Reverse idler gear plate bolt | 25 | 18 |
| Casing bolts | 25 | 18 |
| Clutch release guide bolts | 10 | 7 |

*Rear axle*
## Axle ratios
| | |
|---|---|
| 1.8S engine | 3.67:1 |
| 2.0S/2.0E engines | 3.44:1 |

## Oil capacity (1.8S, 2.0S and 2.0E) ....... 1.2 litre (2.1 pint)

*Braking system*
## Brake pedal free-travel ....... 0.24 to 0.35 in (6 to 9 mm)

## Disc brakes (Manta-B)
| | |
|---|---|
| Disc diameter | 9.69 in (246 mm) |
| Permissible run-out | 0.004 in (0.1 mm) |

## Drum brakes (Manta-B)
| | |
|---|---|
| Drum diameter | 9.06 in (230 mm) |

## Torque wrench settings
| | lbf ft | kgf m |
|---|---|---|
| Disc to hub | 40 | 5.5 |
| Master cylinder | 13 | 1.8 |
| Brake caliper to steering knuckle | 69 | 9.5 |

*Electrical system*
## Battery rating ....... 36, 44, 55 or 66 amp hour at 20 hour rate

## Alternator (Delco-Remy)
| | |
|---|---|
| Voltage regulator setting | 14.45 ± 0.25 volt |

*Suspension and steering*
## Front suspension
| | |
|---|---|
| Camber (see text) | 0° to 1°30′ negative |
| Castor: | |
|    Manta-CC | 3°45′ positive to 6°15′ positive |
|    Manta, Manta GT/E and CC | 4° positive to 6°30′ positive |
| Toe-in (Manta) | 1.0 to 3.0 mm (0.04 to 0.12 in) laden, or 1.0 to 4.0 mm (0.04 to 0.16 in) unladen |

## Wheels and tyres
| | Front | Rear |
|---|---|---|
| Tyre pressures (195/60 HR 14): | | |
|    Up to 3 occupants | 26 psi | 26 psi |
|    At maximum load | 28.5 psi | 31 psi |

## 3  Routine maintenance

1  In common with other manufacturers GM have reduced the frequency of maintenance on all their models. As from 1983 models maintenance need only be carried out on a 9000 mile (15 000 km) or 12 months basis although some owners may still prefer to use the frequency given in the Routine Maintenance section at the beginning of the manual.
2  Disc pads should be checked at 9000 miles (15 000 km) or 12 months and rear drum brakes at 18 000 miles (30 000 km) or 24 months.
3  The brake fluid should be renewed every 12 months regardless of the mileage accumulated.
4  The engine oil and oil filter should be renewed on a 9000 mile (15 000 km) or 6 months basis.

## 4  Engine (cih)

*General description (2.0 litre engine)*
1  Apart from an increase in bore size to achieve the increased capacity, the only difference between the 19S and 2.0 litre engines is that the 2.0 litre engines are fitted with hydraulic tappets, which are self-adjusting. Note that two versions of the 2.0 litre engine are available – the 20S, with a carburettor, and the 20E, with fuel injection.

*Hydraulic tappets – principle of operation*
2  The hydraulic tappet consists of a hollow body, into which fits a bucket-shaped plunger which has a ball valve in its lower face. The top end of the plunger is fitted with a cap which bears against the valve cam.
3  The tappet body and the plunger have drillings through which oil passes to the inside of the plunger and from thence, through the ball valve, to the chamber at the bottom of the body.
4  A spring in the cavity below the plunger forces the plunger upwards to keep the plunger cap in contact with the cam, but as the cam rotates to open the valve, the pressure on the plunger causes the ball valve in its base to close. This traps the oil in the cavity beneath the plunger and prevents the plunger being pushed down into the tappet body.
5  While the engine is running, oil is fed to the tappets continuously, from drillings in the cylinder head. Any excess oil drains back to the sump and is recirculated.

*Hydraulic tappets – initial adjustment after overhaul*
6  Rotate the crankshaft until one of the pistons is at TDC and both the valves for that cylinder are closed.
7  Slacken the adjusting nut on the rockers of those valves until there is a slight clearance between the rocker and the tip of the valve stem.

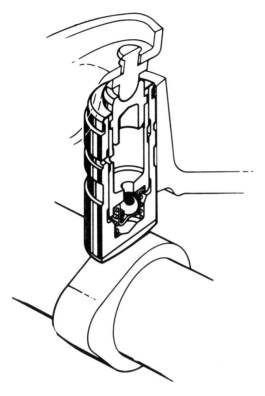

**Fig. 13.1 Hydraulic tappet – sectional view (Sec 4)**

8   Tighten the rocker adjusting nut until the clearance is eliminated and the spring inside the hydraulic tappet can be felt to be starting to compress. Repeat the operation for the valves of each cylinder.

### Hydraulic tappets – final adjustment after overhaul

9   Make up a temporary chain guard and oil baffle from 18 or 20 swg mild steel sheet (Fig. 13.3).
10  Run the engine until it achieves normal operating temperature and then switch it off, remove the rocker cover and fit the temporary chain guard.
11  Start the engine, and when it is again at normal operating

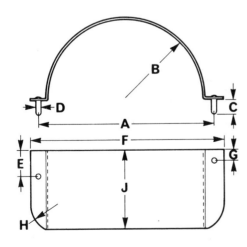

**Fig. 13.3 Temporary chain guard (Sec 4)**

| | | | | |
|---|---|---|---|---|
| A | = | 6.61 in (168 mm) | F = | 7.09 in (180 mm) |
| R | = | 2.95 in (75 mm) | G = | 0.40 in (10 mm) |
| C | = | 0.47 in (12 mm) | H = | 0.98 in (25 mm) |
| D | = | 0.19 in (4.8 mm) | J = | 2.76 in (70 mm) |
| E | = | 0.91 in (23 mm) | | |

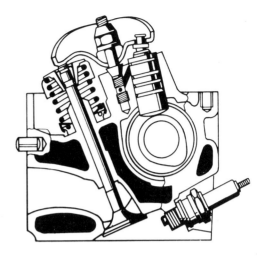

**Fig. 13.2 Hydraulic tappet lubrication system (Sec 4)**

temperature and running at idling speed, slacken one of the rocker adjusting nuts until the rocker arm starts rattling.
12  Tighten the rocker nut slowly until the rocker arm stops rattling. Tighten the nut by a further quarter turn and then wait ten seconds for the engine to run smoothly again. Tighten the nut a further quarter turn and again wait for ten seconds, then repeat the sequence another twice so that the nut has been advanced by a quarter turn four times.
13  It is important that this procedure is followed exactly, because this method of adjustment preloads the plunger slowly and allows the tappet to adjust itself to the changed preload. By so doing, the risk of plunger damage or of the engine running unevenly through compression loss is eliminated.
14  The adjusting sequence must be carried out on each rocker arm in turn. Finally, stop the engine, remove the temporary chain guard and refit the rocker cover.

### Hydraulic tappets – dismantling and reassembly

15  Remove the rocker cover, loosen the rocker adjusting nuts until the rocker arms can be swung off the valves and tappets, and extract the tappets, taking care to note the position from which each tappet is removed.
16  Push the plunger into the tappet against the pressure of the internal spring and prise the retaining cap off the end of the tappet.
17  Remove the rocker seat, the plunger and the spring from the tappet body and keep the parts of each tappet together so that there is no possibility of getting them mixed up with the parts of any other tappet.
18  Clean all components in solvent to remove all traces of dirt and varnish and leave the parts to dry.
19  Check that the plunger moves freely in the tappet bore and that with the compensating spring removed, the plunger will drop under its own weight to the bottom of the tappet bore. If any part is defective, renew the whole assembly.

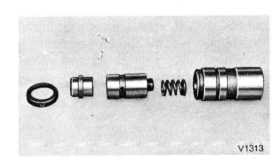

**Fig. 13.4 Hydraulic tappet components (Sec 4)**

20 Insert the spring, insert the plunger and retaining cap and press the retaining cap on to the end of the tappet body.
21 Immerse each tappet in clean engine oil and work the plunger up and down until the tappet is primed.
22 Refitting is a reversal of the removal procedure. Once fitted, it will be necessary to adjust the tappets as detailed earlier in this Section.

## Hydraulic tappets – fault diagnosis

| Symptom | Reason(s) |
| --- | --- |
| Hard knocking noise | Tappet plunger jammed tight in housing |
| Moderate knocking noise | Incorrect tappet adjustment Leaking check ball valve Worn plunger and/or body bore |
| Intermittent clicking | Dirt particle on ball valve seat Ball valve ball not spherical |
| Restricted engine speed | Incorrect tappet adjustment Leaking check ball valve Scuffing of plunger wall, or body bore |
| General noise | Incorrect tappet adjustment Insufficient oil supply |

## Valve clearances (non-hydraulic) – adjustment

23 GM specify adjustment of the valve clearances with the engine running as described in Chapter 1 Section 48, however the following procedure is given to enable owners to adjust the clearances with the engine stationary.
24 With the rocker cover removed turn the engine until valve number 8 is fully open. Valve number 1 can now be checked and if necessary adjusted.
25 Insert the correct feeler blade between the rocker arm and the end of the valve stem. If it is not a firm sliding fit use a ring spanner to turn the rocker nut as required.
26 Check and adjust the remaining clearances in the same manner using the following order:

| Valve fully open | Valve to adjust |
| --- | --- |
| 8 | 1 |
| 6 | 3 |
| 4 | 5 |
| 7 | 2 |
| 1 | 8 |
| 3 | 6 |
| 5 | 4 |
| 2 | 7 |

27 On completion refit the rocker cover.

## Oil pump cover to oil pump housing seal – 20E engine

28 From December 1984 on, a liquid sealant is used between the oil pump cover and the oil pump housing on the 2.0 litre fuel injection engine.
29 When refitting the pump cover, the mating surfaces of the cover and the pump housing should be thoroughly cleaned, and a thin layer of proprietary sealing compound applied.
30 On no account should a paper gasket be used, as this may upset gear tolerances and cause low oil pressure at idle.

---

## 5  Engine – 1.8 ohc

### General description

1   The engine is of four-cylinder, overhead camshaft type. The cylinder head is of light alloy construction while the cylinder block is of cast-iron. The cylinder head is of crossflow design. The crankshaft runs in five main bearings. The camshaft is supported in non-renewable bearings and is driven by a toothed belt from a sprocket on the crankshaft.
2   Valve adjustment is not required as the valve lifters (cam followers) are of the hydraulic self-adjusting type. A torsional damper is fitted to the crankshaft front end.

### Main operations possible with engine in car

3   The following operations may be carried out without having to remove the engine from the vehicle:

   *(a) Removal and refitting of oil pressure regulator valve*
   *(b) Renewal of camshaft drivebelt*
   *(c) Removal and refitting of cylinder head*
   *(d) Removal and refitting of camshaft housing*
   *(e) Removal and refitting of camshaft*
   *(f) Removal and refitting of sump*
   *(g) Removal and refitting of oil pump*
   *(h) Removal and refitting of pistons/connecting rods*
   *(i) Removal and refitting of flywheel (transmission detached)*
   *(j) Renewal of crankshaft front oil seal*
   *(k) Renewal of crankshaft rear oil seal (transmission detached)*
   *(l) Renewal of engine/transmission mountings*
   *(m) Removal and refitting of ancillary components (coolant pump, fuel pump, manifolds, distributor etc)*

### Oil pressure regulator valve – removal and refitting

4   From just to the rear of the crankshaft pulley, unscrew the pressure regulator valve plug and extract the spring and plunger.
5   Renew the spring if it is distorted or weak (compare it with a new one if possible).
6   If the plunger is scored, renew it.
7   Clean out the plunger hole and reassemble.

### Camshaft drivebelt – renewal

8   Unscrew and remove the drivebelt cover, removing cooling system components as necessary.
9   Using a socket spanner on the crankshaft pulley bolt, turn the crankshaft until No 1 piston is rising on its compression stroke. The notch in the rim of the crankshaft pulley should be aligned with the timing pointer and represents ignition timing at the specified degrees BTDC, **not** TDC which is not marked on these engines. The camshaft sprocket mark will be in alignment with the mark on the belt cover backplate (photo).

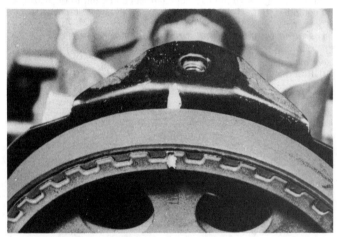

5.9 Camshaft sprocket timing marks

10 Remove the alternator drivebelt, the crankshaft torsional damper and the distributor (see Section 9). Remove the distributor drivebelt.
11 Drain the cooling system.
12 Release the coolant pump mounting bolts just enough to be able to swivel the pump and to release the tension of the drivebelt.
13 If the drivebelt is to be used again, note its running direction before removing it.
14 Take the belt off the sprockets and fit the new one without moving the set position of the camshaft or crankshaft.
15 Engage the new belt over the sprockets and apply some tension by moving the coolant pump.
16 Refit the torsional damper and then check that the pulley notch is still in alignment with the timing pointer and that the camshaft sprocket mark is aligned with the groove in the plate behind it. If not, release the belt tension and readjust the position of the sprockets as necessary.

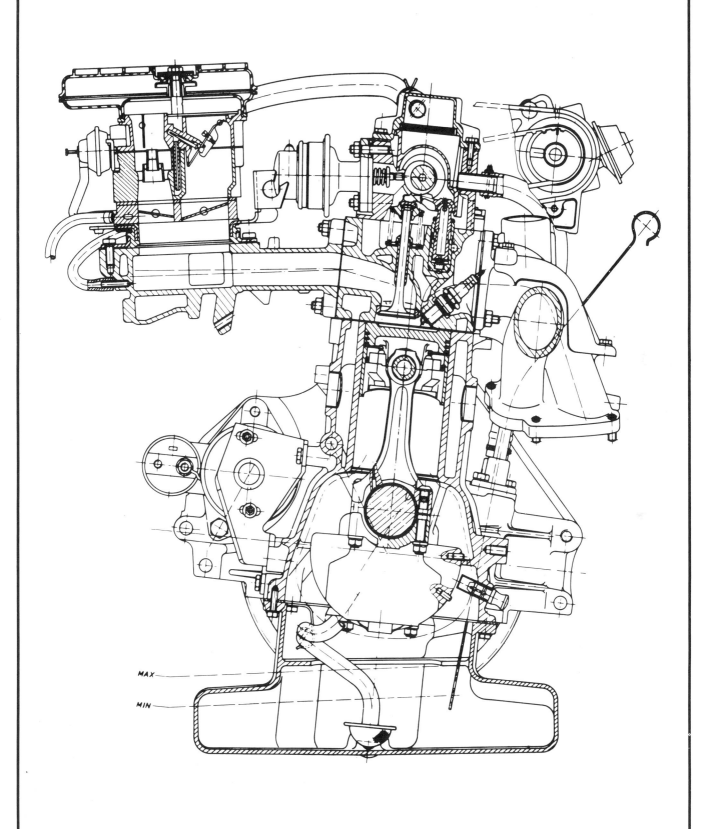

MAX

MIN

Fig. 13.5 Sectional view of 18S ohc engine (Sec 5)

17 The belt tension should now be adjusted in the following way. Partially tighten the clamping screws on the coolant pump and using the thumb and forefinger, twist the belt through 90°. If with moderate effort, the belt twists too easily or will not reach the full 90°, increase or decrease the tension as necessary by moving the coolant pump; a hexagon is moulded into the pump to turn it with a spanner. If the belt is overtightened, it will usually be heard to hum when the engine is running. Fully tighten the coolant pump bolts (photos).

18 Refit the remaining components in the reverse order to removal. Refill the cooling system and reset the ignition timing on completion.

*Cylinder head – removal and refitting*
19 The cylinder head should only be removed from a cold engine.
20 Disconnect the battery.
21 Refer to Chapter 2 and drain the coolant. Ignore the reference to cylinder block draining.
22 Remove the air cleaner, see Section 8 of this Chapter.
23 Disconnect the fuel hoses from the fuel pump and plug their open ends.
24 Disconnect the control cables and electrical leads from the carburettor.

25 Disconnect the heater hose and the vacuum pipe from the intake manifold.
26 Disconnect the lead from the temperature sensor on the intake manifold.
27 Remove the alternator drivebelt.
28 Remove the cover from the camshaft drivebelt and then set No 1 piston on the firing stroke.
29 Remove the distributor (see Section 9 of this Chapter).
30 Remove the camshaft cover.
31 Check that the mark on the camshaft sprocket is in alignment with the one on the camshaft housing.
32 Disconnect the exhaust downpipe from the manifold (photo).
33 Disconnect the spark plug cables and the coil-to-distributor cap HT lead.
34 Release the coolant pump bolts, move the pump to relieve the tension on the toothed belt and slip the belt from the sprockets.
35 Unscrew the cylinder head bolts and remove them. Work from the outside to inside in a spiral pattern, unscrewing them first by a quarter turn and then by half a turn.
36 Lift off the camshaft housing. This is located on dowels. Lift straight upwards.
37 Lift off the cylinder head. If it is stuck, tap it gently with a plastic-faced hammer.

5.17A Checking camshaft drivebelt tension

5.17B Adjusting camshaft drivebelt tension

5.17C Tightening the coolant pump bolts after tensioning the drivebelt

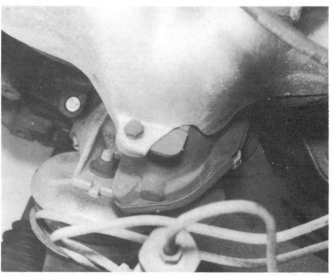

5.32 Exhaust downpipe connection to manifold

38 Peel away the cylinder head gasket and discard it.

39 Remove the rocker arms and thrust pads from the cylinder head. Withdraw the hydraulic valve lifters and immerse them in a container of clean engine oil to avoid any possibility of them draining. Keep all components in their original order if they are to be refitted.

40 Clean the cylinder block and the cylinder head free from carbon and old pieces of gasket by careful scraping. Take care not to damage the cylinder head, which is made of light alloy and is easily scored. Cover the coolant passages and other openings with masking tape or rag to prevent dirt and carbon falling in. Mop out oil from the bolt holes; hydraulic pressure could crack the block when the bolts are screwed in if oil is left in the holes.

41 When all is clean, locate a new gasket on the block so that the word 'OBEN' can be read from above.

42 Refit the hydraulic lifters, thrust pads and rocker arms to the cylinder head in their original order. If new hydraulic lifters are being used, initially immerse each one in a container of clean engine oil and compress it (by hand) several times to charge it.

43 With the mating surfaces scrupulously clean, locate the cylinder head on the block so that the positioning dowels engage in their holes.

44 Apply jointing compound to the mating flanges of the cylinder head and the camshaft housing and refit the camshaft housing to the cylinder head (camshaft sprocket marks in alignment).

45 The cylinder head bolts on ohc engines are tightened down by an angular method, as opposed to a conventional torque wrench method. This involves turning each bolt an equal number of degrees, resulting in a more even 'holding down' effect of the cylinder head, as each bolt travels the same depth into the block. However, a torque wrench must be used in the initial stage when settling the head down against valve spring pressure. The tightening must be carried out in five stages as given in the Specifications. Tighten the bolts progressively from the centre working outwards in a spiral pattern.

46 Fit and tension the camshaft drivebelt, then, refit the belt cover.

47 Fit the camshaft cover using a new gasket.

48 Fit and tension the alternator drivebelt.

49 Reconnect the vacuum pipe and heater hose.

50 Refit the distributor (see Section 9 of this Chapter).

51 Fit the coolant pipe clamp to the intake manifold and connect the control cables and electrical leads to the carburettor.

52 Reconnect the fuel pipes to the pump.

53 Connect the exhaust pipe to the manifold.

54 Connect the lead to the temperature sensor on the intake manifold.

55 Fill the cooling system and bleed it as described in Chapter 2.

56 Reconnect the battery.

57 Fit the air cleaner.

*Camshaft housing and camshaft – dismantling and reassembly*

*Refer also to Section 6*

58 With the camshaft housing removed from the cylinder head as previously described, make sure that the fuel pump is withdrawn where applicable.

59 Fit an open-ended spanner to the flats on the camshaft. Hold the camshaft and unscrew the camshaft sprocket retaining bolt. Pull off the sprocket.

60 At the opposite end of the camshaft housing unbolt the plate and remove the gasket, then use an Allen key to unscrew the two screws which retain the camshaft retaining plate.

61 Withdraw the retaining plate.

62 Remove the camshaft carefully out of the rear end of the camshaft housing taking care not to damage the camshaft bearing surfaces. Remove the front oil seal.

63 Before refitting the camshaft, oil the bearings.

64 Fit the camshaft retaining plate with fixing screws and then check the camshaft endfloat. If it exceeds the specified limit, renew the retaining plate.

65 Refit the rear plate with a new gasket.

66 Drive in a new front oil seal having smeared the sealing lip with oil, then refit the camshaft sprocket. Hold the camshaft steady and tighten the sprocket retaining bolt to the specified torque.

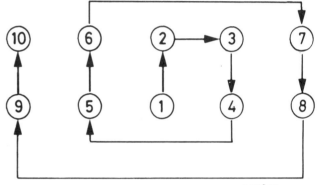

*H 12303*

Fig. 13.6 Cylinder head bolt tightening sequence (Sec 5)

*Sump – removal and refitting*

67 It is necessary to lift the front of the engine slightly to effect sump removal, and also to lower the front axle crossmember. Remove the air cleaner then unbolt the radiator cowl and locate the cowl over the fan blades.

68 Unscrew the top nuts from both front engine mountings.

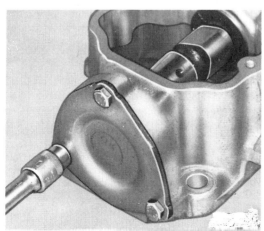

Fig. 13.7 Removing the plate from the rear of the camshaft housing (Sec 5)

Fig. 13.8 Camshaft retaining plate screws (arrowed) (Sec 5)

69 Jack up the front of the car and support on axle stands. Drain the engine oil (photo). Connect a hoist to the front of the engine and lift it slightly.
70 Unbolt the bellhousing cover plate, then unbolt the front axle crossmember arms from the underbody. Use a block of wood to wedge the arms down.
71 Remove the securing bolts and lower the sump. Remove the gasket and clean both mating surfaces.
72 To refit the sump, apply jointing compound to the mating surface corners. Smear each side of the new gasket with grease and press it onto the cylinder block. Coat the threads of each bolt with locking compound, position the sump and fit and tighten the bolts.
73 Refit the remaining items in reverse order then refill the engine with oil.

*Oil pump – removal and refitting*
74 Remove the camshaft drivebelt as previously described. Remove the belt cover backplate. For better access the radiator can be removed.
75 Using two screwdrivers as levers, prise off the belt sprocket from the front end of the crankshaft. Remove the Woodruff key.
76 Remove the sump as previously described.
77 Remove the oil pump pick-up pipe and strainer.
78 Unbolt the oil pump from the cylinder block and remove it.
79 Refer to paragraphs 132 to 137 for details of oil pump overhaul.
80 Before refitting the oil pump, steps must be taken to protect the seal lips from damage or turning back on the shoulder at the front end of the crankshaft. To do this, grease the seal lips and then bind tape around the crankshaft to form a gentle taper. Locate a new gasket.
81 Refit the oil pump and unwind and remove the tape.
82 Tighten the bolts to the specified torque and fit the Woodruff key and belt sprocket.
83 Refit the pick-up pipe and strainer, the sump, the drivebelt and its cover as previously described.
84 Refit the crankshaft pulley and the drivebelt and fill the engine with oil. Refit the radiator if removed.

*Pistons and connecting rods – removal and refitting*
85 Remove the cylinder head and sump.
86 Remove the oil pump pick-up pipe and strainer.
87 Remove the pistons and connecting rods with reference to Chapter 1, Sections 16 and 18. Make alignment marks for use when refitting.
88 Refit the pistons and connecting rods with reference to Chapter 1, Section 40; note that the piston orientation marks are not on the crown but on the underside (photo).
89 Refit the big-end bearing caps with reference to Chapter 1, Section 41 referring to the Specifications at the beginning of this Chapter for the torque wrench setting.
90 Refit the oil pump pick-up pipe and strainer, the cylinder head and the sump.

*Flywheel – removal and refitting*
91 Refer to Chapter 5 and remove the clutch assembly.
92 Although the flywheel bolt holes are offset so that it can only be fitted in one position, it will make fitting easier if the flywheel-to-crankshaft flange alignment is marked before removal.
93 Jam the flywheel starter ring gear and using a ring spanner or socket, unscrew the bolts from the flywheel. As the heads of these bolts are very shallow, if a chamfered type of socket is being used, it is best to grind it to ensure more positive engagement.
94 Remove the flywheel.
95 Refit by reversing the removal operations, but apply thread locking compound to the bolts and tighten them to the correct torque.

*Crankshaft front oil seal – renewal*
96 Disconnect the battery earth lead. Remove the radiator and its cowl.
97 Remove the camshaft drivebelt as previously described. If it is oil-soaked it must be renewed.
98 Using two screwdrivers as levers, prise the sprocket from the crankshaft. Remove the Woodruff key.
99 Punch or drill a small hole in the metal face of the oil seal and

5.69 Removing the engine sump drain plug

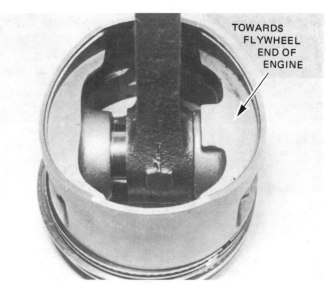
5.88 Identifying contour on underside of piston

screw in a self-tapping screw. Use the head of the screw to lever out the seal.
100 Fill the lips of the new seal with grease and tape the step on the crankshaft as previously described.
101 Using a piece of tubing, tap the oil seal into position. Refit the Woodruff key.
102 Refit the remaining components in the reverse order to removal.

*Crankshaft rear oil seal – renewal*
103 Remove the flywheel.
104 Punch or drill a small hole in the metal face of the oil seal and screw in a self-tapping screw. Grasp the screw head with pliers and pull the seal out, having first noted its fitted position.
105 Lightly grease the lips and outer periphery of the new seal. Press the seal carefully into its location as far as it will go, using finger pressure and keeping it square to the housing. Place a piece of flat wood across the seal and tap it fully home to its previously noted position.
106 Refit the flywheel.

*Engine/transmission mountings – renewal*
107 Take the weight of the engine/transmission on a hoist, or jack and a wooden block used as an insulator.
108 Unbolt the mounting brackets from the crankcase or

5.108A Lower view of left-hand engine mounting

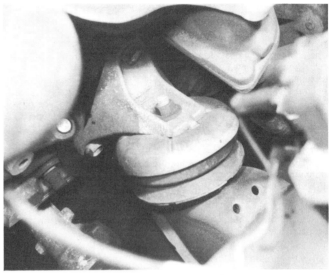

5.108B Upper view of left-hand engine mounting

5.108C Lower view of right-hand engine mounting

transmission casing and the body frame member and separate the brackets from the flexible member (photos).

109 Refit the mountings with the new flexible components, but have the bolts only 'nipped up' initially.

110 Once the hoist or jack has been removed, tighten all bolts to the specified torque with the weight of the engine/transmission on the mountings.

### Engine – methods of removal

111 Refer to Section 4 of Chapter 1.

### Engine – removal

112 The procedure for removing the 1.8 ohc engine (with or without transmission) is similar to that given in Chapter 1.

113 During removal, exercise a degree of common sense. If slight discrepancies in design between the car being worked on and that shown exist, then take care to label or note the position of mating components; do not rely on memory. Double check before lifting the engine out to ensure that all necessary components have been disconnected.

### Engine dismantling – general

114 Before attempting to dismantle the engine, read Section 7 of Chapter 1, ignoring paragraph 10.

### Engine ancillary components – removal

115 The following ancillary components should be removed before engine dismantling begins. Refer to the appropriate sub-Sections of this Chapter and to the main Chapters of the manual for the necessary procedures.

    (a)   Alternator
    (b)   Fuel pump
    (c)   Thermostat
    (d)   Inlet manifold
    (e)   Carburettor
    (f)   Distributor
    (g)   Coolant pump
    (h)   Exhaust manifold

### Engine – complete dismantling

116 With the engine removed from the vehicle and suitably positioned on a solid working surface, remove the following:

    (a)   Camshaft drivebelt
    (b)   Cylinder head
    (c)   Sump
    (d)   Oil pump and oil pick-up pipe
    (e)   Pistons/connecting rods
    (f)   Clutch and flywheel

117 Invert the engine so that it is standing on the top surface of the cylinder block.

118 The main bearing caps are numbered 1 to 4 from the drivebelt end of the engine. The rear cap is not marked. To ensure that the caps are refitted the correct way round, note that the numbers are read from the coolant pump side when the crankcase is inverted.

119 Unscrew and remove the main bearing cap bolts and tap off the caps. If the bearing shells are to be used again, keep them with their respective caps. The original shells are colour coded and if used again must be returned to their original locations.

120 Note that the centre bearing shell incorporates thrust flanges to control crankshaft endfloat.

121 Lift the crankshaft from the crankcase. Extract the upper half shells and again identify their position in the crankcase if they are to be used again.

122 Unbolt and remove the drivebelt cover backing plate if still in position.

123 The rubber plug located adjacent to the bellhousing flange on the crankcase covers the aperture for installation of a TDC sensor. This sensor when connected to a suitable monitoring unit, indicates TDC from the position of the contact pins set in the crankshaft counterbalance weight.

## Lubrication and crankcase ventilation systems – description and maintenance

124 Oil pressure for all moving components is provided by a gear type oil pump which is driven from the front end of the crankshaft. The crankshaft has flats for this purpose.

125 The pump draws oil from the sump through a pick-up pipe and strainer and pumps it through the oil filter and oil galleries to the engine friction surfaces.

126 A pressure regulator valve is screwed into the body of the oil pump. A relief valve, located in the oil filter mounting base, opens, should the filter block due to clogging caused by neglected servicing. An oil pressure switch is screwed into the pump casing.

127 The cylinder bores are lubricated by oil splash from the sump.

128 The hydraulic valve lifters are pressurised with oil to maintain optimum valve clearance at all times.

129 The crankcase ventilation system is designed to draw oil fumes and blow-by gas (combustion gas which has passed the piston rings) from the crankcase into the air cleaner, whence they are drawn into the engine and burnt during the normal combustion cycle.

130 The oil separator can be unbolted from the crankcase, washed out with paraffin and shaken dry. Clean out the connecting pipes at the same time (photo).

131 Periodically check the pipes for security and condition.

5.130 Crankcase ventilation system oil separator

## Oil pump – overhaul

132 With the oil pump removed from the vehicle, withdraw the rear cover. The cross-head fixing screws are very tight and an impact driver will be required to remove them (photo).

133 Check the clearance between the inner and outer gear teeth and the outer gear and the pump body (photos).

134 Using a straight-edge across the pump cover flange, measure the gear endfloat (photo).

135 If any of the clearances are outside the specified tolerance, renew the components as necessary. Note that the outer gear face is marked for position (photo).

136 The pressure regulator valve can be unscrewed from the oil pump housing and the components cleaned and examined (photo).

137 Renew the oil seal as a matter of course. Carefully lever it from position with the flat of a screwdriver. Use a socket of the appropriate diameter to tap the new seal into position.

## Cylinder head – dismantling, examination, renovation and decarbonising

138 With the cylinder head removed, clean away external dirt.

139 Remove the rocker arms and thrust pads from the cylinder head. Withdraw the hydraulic valve lifters and immerse them in a container of clean engine oil to avoid any possibility of them draining. Keep all components in their original order if they are to be refitted.

5.132 Removing the oil pump rear cover screws

5.133A Checking oil pump gear tooth clearance

5.133B Checking oil pump gear-to-body clearance

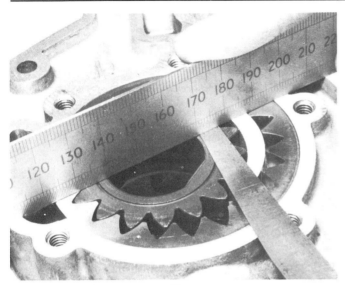

5.134 Checking oil pump gear endfloat

5.135 Oil pump gear positioning mark (arrowed)

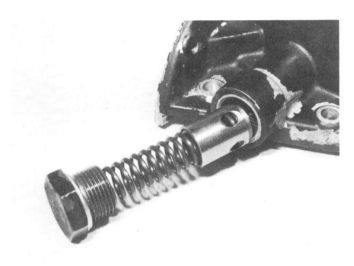

5.136 Oil pump pressure regulator valve components

140 Using a method similar to that given in Section 13 of Chapter 1, remove the valves.

141 If worn valve guides are evident, have them renewed professionally.

142 Refer to Section 33 of Chapter 1 and decarbonise the cylinder head and piston crowns. Bear in mind that the cylinder head is of light alloy construction and can be easily damaged.

143 Refer to Section 31 of Chapter 1 and examine the valves and valve seats.

144 Check that all valve springs are intact. If any one is broken, all should be renewed. Check the free height of the springs against new ones. Springs suffer from fatigue and it is a good idea to renew them even if they look serviceable.

145 The cylinder head can be checked for warping either by placing it on a piece of plate glass or using a straight-edge and feeler blades. If there is any doubt or if its block face is corroded, have it re-faced by your dealer or motor engineering works.

*Engine – examination and renovation, general*
146 Refer to Section 23 of Chapter 1

*Crankshaft – examination and renovation*
147 Refer to Section 24 of Chapter 1 and to the Specifications at

the beginning of this Chapter. Also check the spigot bearing in the end of the crankshaft for wear as described later.

*Big-end and main bearing shells – examination and renovation*
148 Refer to Section 25 of Chapter 1.

*Cylinder bore – examination and renovation*
149 Refer to Section 26 of Chapter 1 and to the Specifications given at the beginning of this Chapter.

*Pistons and piston rings – examination and renovation*
150 Refer to Section 27 of Chapter 1 and to the Specifications in this Chapter.

151 When removing the rings, keep them in order so that they may be refitted in their original location. The second ring has its upper surface marked TOP.

152 Before checking for piston ring groove wear, check each groove using a section of old piston ring ground to a suitable width as a scraper. Take care to remove only the carbon deposits and not to remove metal or score the piston lands. Protect your fingers – piston rings are sharp!

153 If new rings (or pistons and rings) are to be fitted to an existing bore the top ring must be stepped to clear the wear ridge at the top of the bore, or the bore must be de-ridged.

154 Check the clearance and end gap of any new rings as previously described. If a ring is slightly tight in its groove it may be rubbed down using an oilstone or a sheet of carborundum paper laid on a sheet of glass. If the end gap is inadequate, the ring can be carefully ground until the specified clearance is achieved.

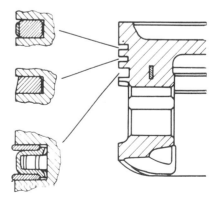

Fig. 13.9 Piston ring details (Sec 5)

155 If new pistons are to be installed they will be selected from the grades available after measuring the bores. Normally the appropriate oversize pistons are supplied by the repairer when the block is rebored. Whenever new piston rings are being installed, the glaze on original cylinder bores should be 'broken' using either abrasive paper or a glaze removing tool in an electric drill. If abrasive paper is used, use strokes at 60° to the bore centre line to create a cross-hatching effect.

### Connecting rods – examination and renovation
156 Refer to Section 28 of Chapter 1.
157 The gudgeon pins are an interference (shrink) fit in the connecting rod small end. Removal and refitting of pistons to rods is a job for your dealer, as would be any remedial action required if the gudgeon pin is no longer an interference fit in the rod.

### Flywheel – examination and renovation
158 Details of flywheel ring gear examination and renewal are given in Section 35 of Chapter 1.
159 Inspect the machined face of the flywheel as described in Chapter 5, Section 7.

### Driveplate (automatic transmission) – examination and renovation
160 Should the starter ring gear on the driveplate require renewal, renew the driveplate complete.

### Crankshaft spigot bearing – renewal
161 If the needle bearing in the centre of the crankshaft flange is worn, fill it with grease and tap in a close-fitting rod. Hydraulic pressure will remove it. Alternatively, a very small extractor having a claw type leg may be used. When tapping the new bearing into position, make sure that the chamfered side of the bearing enters first.
162 A spigot bearing may not be fitted to later engines.

### Camshaft – examination and renovation
163 With the camshaft removed, examine the bearings for signs of obvious wear and pitting. If evident, a new camshaft housing will probably be required.
164 The camshaft itself should show no marks or scoring on the journal or cam lobe surfaces. If evident, renew the camshaft.
165 The camshaft retaining plate should appear unworn and without grooves. In any event, check the camshaft endfloat and fit a new plate where necessary.
166 The housing front oil seal should always be renewed at major overhaul. A filter is incorporated in the camshaft housing cover. Remove it and wash thoroughly in petrol and allow to dry.

### Camshaft drivebelt – examination and renovation
167 Closely inspect the belt for cracking, fraying, oil contamination or tooth deformation. Where evident, renew the belt.
168 If the belt has been in use for 30 000 miles (48 000 km) or more, it is recommended that it is renewed even if it appears in good condition.
169 Whenever the original belt is to be removed but is going to be used again, always note its running direction before removing it. It is even worthwhile marking the tooth engagement points on each sprocket. As the belt will have worn in a set position, refitting it in exactly the same way will prevent any increase in noise which might otherwise occur when the engine is running.

### Valve lifters, rockers and thrust pads – examination and renovation
170 Any signs of wear in a hydraulic lifter can only be rectified by renewal, the unit cannot be dismantled.
171 Inspect the rockers and thrust pads for wear or grooving. Again, renew if evident.

### Engine reassembly – general
172 Refer to Section 36 of Chapter 1.
173 It is recommended that all self-locking nuts are renewed.
174 The order of assembly given in Chapter 1 differs from that described in the following paragraphs and references to the timing chain and case should be ignored.

### Crankshaft and main bearings – reassembly
175 Read paragraphs 1 to 3 of Section 37, Chapter 1.
176 The central bearing shell takes up the crankshaft endfloat. Note that the half-shells fitted to the cylinder block all have oil duct holes, while only the centre main bearing cap half-shell has an oil duct hole (photos).
177 When the shells are fully located in the crankcase and bearing caps, lubricate them with clean engine oil.
178 Fill the lips of a new crankshaft oil seal with grease and fit it to the end of the crankshaft (photo).
179 Carefully install the crankshaft into position in the crankcase.
180 Lubricate the crankshaft main bearing journals and then refit the centre and intermediate main bearing caps. Tighten the retaining bolts to the specified torque.
181 Clean the grooves of the rear main bearing cap free from old sealant and thinly coat its mating surfaces with sealing compound. Fit the cap and tighten the bolts to the specified torque (photos). Now fill the grooves in the bearing cap with RTV type gasket compound. Inject straight from the tube until the material is seen to exude from the cap joints to prove that any trapped air has been expelled.
182 Fit the front main bearing cap but before fitting the retaining bolts, smear them with sealant, and then tighten to the specified torque wrench setting. Check that the bearing cap is exactly flush with the end face of the crankcase as it is tightened.
183 Now rotate the crankshaft and check that it turns freely, and shows no signs of binding or tight spots. Check that the crankshaft endfloat is within the limits specified. Alternative centre bearing shells are available if necessary to adjust the endfloat. The endfloat can be checked using a dial gauge or with feeler blades inserted between the flange of the centre bearing shell and the machined surface of the crankshaft. Before measuring, make sure that the crankshaft has been forced fully towards one end of the crankcase to give the widest gap at the measuring location (photo).

### Piston rings – reassembly
184 Read paragraphs 1 and 2 of Section 39, Chapter 1.
185 Follow the manufacturer's instructions carefully when fitting rings to ensure that they are correctly fitted. Several variations of compression and oil control rings are available and it is of the utmost importance that they be located correctly in their grooves.
186 When the rings are in position check that the compression rings are free to expand and contract in their grooves. Certain types of multi-segment oil control rings are a light interference fit in their grooves and this may not therefore apply to them. When all rings are in position on the pistons move them around to bring each ring gap to be some 180° away from the gap on the adjacent ring. With the original type of oil control ring, ensure that the gap of the upper rail is offset by 25 to 50 mm (1 to 2 in) to the left of the spacer gap. Offset the gap of the lower rail the same distance to the right.

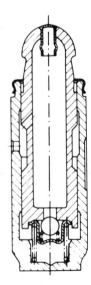

**Fig. 13.10 Sectional view of a hydraulic valve lifter (Sec 5)**

5.176A Centre main bearing shell showing thrust flanges

5.176B Centre main bearing shell showing locating notch

5.178 Crankshaft rear oil seal

5.181A Fitting the rear main bearing cap

5.181B Injecting sealant into rear main bearing cap grooves

5.183 Checking crankshaft endfloat

### Pistons and connecting rods – refitting

187 Refer to Sections 40 and 41 of Chapter 1, ignoring the instructions on rod and bearing alignment. Check that the rod markings are towards the side of the engine as noted before dismantling. This is very important as the piston crowns do not have front directional marks.

### Oil pump and sump – refitting

188 Refit the oil pump as described in paragraphs 80 to 82 (photos).

5.188A Crankshaft step taped

5.188B Fitting the oil pump

189 Refit the oil pick-up pipe and strainer.
190 Refit the sump, using a new gasket.
191 Stand the engine on the sump and fit the Woodruff key to the crankshaft.

### Flywheel – refitting

192 Offer the flywheel to the crankshaft rear mounting flange.
193 Apply thread locking compound to the bolt threads and screw in the bolts.
194 Jam the starter ring gear teeth and tighten the bolts to the specified torque.

### Cylinder head and camshaft housing – reassembly and refitting

195 Ensure that all valves and springs are clean and free from carbon deposits and that the ports and valve guides in the cylinder head have no carbon dust or valve grinding paste left in them.
196 Starting at one end of the cylinder head, fit new valve stem oil seals to the ends of the valve guides (photo). Refer also to Section 6.
197 Oil the stem of the first valve and insert it into its guide. The valves must be installed into the seats into which they have been ground, which in the case of the original valves will mean that their original sequence of fitting is retained.
198 With inlet valves, fit the spring seat making sure it is the correct way up. With exhaust valves fit the valve rotator. Fit the valve spring (photos).
199 Place the cap over the spring with the recessed part inside the coil of the spring (photo).
200 Using a method similar to that given in Section 45, Chapter 1, fit the valve stem cotters.
201 Lubricate the hydraulic valve lifters and insert them into their bores in the cylinder head (photo). If new hydraulic valve lifters are being used, initially immerse each one in a container of clean engine oil and compress it (by hand) several times to charge it.
202 Fit the rockers and the thrust pads, also new spark plugs of the specified type (photos).
203 Fit the thermostat into its seat, use a new sealing ring and fit the thermostat housing cover. Tighten the bolts to the specified torque.
204 Refit the camshaft to its housing as described in paragraphs 63 to 66 (photos).
205 Set the engine with Nos 1 and 4 pistons at TDC.
206 Refit and secure the cylinder head as described in paragraphs 41 to 45.
207 Fit the coolant pump (Section 7), but leave the bolts loose pending drivebelt adjustment.
208 Fit the camshaft drivebelt backplate.
209 Fit the drivebelt sprocket to the crankshaft nose.
210 Fit and tension the camshaft drivebelt as described in paragraphs 15 to 17.
211 Fit the camshaft housing cover using a new gasket.
212 Fit the distributor and the camshaft drivebelt front cover.
213 Fit the inlet and exhaust manifolds, using new gaskets.
214 Refit all ancillary components.

### Engine – refitting

215 The procedure is similar to that described in Chapter 1, Section 51.
216 Do not rush engine refitting but take time to ensure every component is properly reconnected and that connections are made in a logical order. Recheck connections for security before attempting to start the engine.

### Engine – initial start-up after overhaul

217 Refer to Section 52 of Chapter 1. If a new camshaft has been fitted, refer to the running-in procedure given in Section 6 of this Chapter. Expect some initial noise from the hydraulic valve lifters until they are properly pressurized with oil.

## 6 Engine (1.8 ohc) modifications

### Valve stem oil seals

1 From late 1983 GM have fitted improved valve stem oil seals. Fig. 13.11 shows the difference between the old and modified seals.
2 When fitting a modified seal, slide it carefully over the valve stem, taking care not to damage the seal lip. Using gentle thumb pressure, push the seal over the valve guide until the seal bead locates in the guide groove. Do not push the seal bead beyond the groove, otherwise the seal is ineffective.

### TIG camshaft – running-in

3 GM recommend a strict running-in procedure for the TIG camshaft introduced from the start of 18S engine production.
4 Coat all bearing surfaces of the camshaft with MoS$_2$

5.196 Fitting a valve stem oil seal

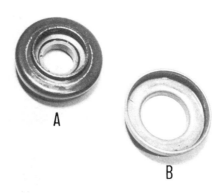

5.198A Exhaust valve rotator (A) and inlet valve spring seat (B)

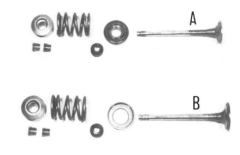

5.198B Valve components – exhaust (A) and inlet (B)

5.199 Fitting a valve spring and cap

5.201 Fitting a hydraulic valve lifter to the cylinder head

5.202A Fitting a thrust pad

5.202B Fitting a rocker

5.204A Camshaft retaining plate

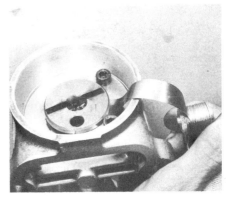

5.204B Checking camshaft endfloat

Fig. 13.11 Valve stem oil seals – old type (A) and new type (B) (Sec 6)

at idling speed but run it for 4 minutes at the following engine speeds:

  *1 minute at 2000 rpm*
  *1 minute at 1500 rpm*
  *1 minute at 3000 rpm*
  *1 minute at 2000 rpm*

6   The engine oil (but not the filter) must be renewed at the first 600 mile (1000 km) interval after camshaft renewal.

*Valve lifters and rockers – removal and refitting (using special tool)*

7   GM have now introduced a tool which allows removal of the

valve lifters and rockers without the need for prior removal of the camshaft. The tool No is KM565.

8   If it is possible to borrow or hire the tool from a GM dealer, then fit it as follows.

9   Position the appropriate piston at BDC. Locate the tool with the valve spring cap and tighten down on the tool until the rocker, thrust pad and valve lifter can be removed.

10  Refit all components by reversing the removal operation.

### 7   Cooling system

*Thermostat – operating temperature*

1   On some models, a different thermostat has been fitted and the opening temperature is 198°F (92°C) instead of 189°F (87°C).

2   Before testing a thermostat for correct opening temperature, check whether it is the later type, which can be identified by the opening temperature of 92°C stamped on the upper side of the thermostat flange (Fig. 13.13).

*Thermostat housing (cih engines) – modification*

3   As from 1981 a modified thermostat housing may be fitted to cih engines. The new housing does not incorporate a cover as the thermostat is located directly in the housing outlet being retained by a spring clip.

4   Although the housings are interchangeable for fitment to the cylinder head, the radiator top hoses are different due to the direction of the outlets.

*Thermostat (1.8 ohc engine) – removal, testing and refitting*

5   Drain the cooling system as described in Chapter 2.

6   Detach the hose from the thermostat housing on the left-hand side of the cylinder head just below the distributor.

7   Unbolt the housing and withdraw the thermostat.

8   The procedure for testing the thermostat is given in Chapter 2.

9   Renew the thermostat seal and the housing gasket. Ensure all mating surfaces are clean, locate the thermostat and its housing and tighten the securing bolts evenly to prevent distortion. Secure the hose and replenish the cooling system.

*Water pump gasket (cih engines) – modification*

10  As from 1983 the water pump gasket on cih engines incorporates a silicone bead for improved sealing. The earlier gasket quite often was the cause of leakage which could easily be mistaken for a faulty water pump flange.

*Water pump (1.8 ohc engine) – removal and refitting*

11  Disconnect the battery negative lead.

12  Remove the radiator as described in Chapter 2.

13  Remove the fanbelt (Chapter 2) then unbolt and remove the timing cover halves (photos).

14  Turn the engine to align the timing marks on the camshaft sprocket and crankshaft pulley as described in Section 5 of this Chapter.

15  Remove the cooling fan assembly with reference to paragraphs 27 and 28.

16  Loosen the water pump retaining bolts then rotate its body anti-clockwise to release the tension of the camshaft drivebelt. The drivebelt can then be released from the water pump.

17  Unbolt and remove the camshaft drivebelt rear cover.

18  Remove the bolts and withdraw the water pump from the cylinder block (photo).

19  Although the pump can be dismantled and reassembled, a press and several special tools are necessary and it is considered that the work is outside the scope of the home mechanic. For this reason a defective pump should be renewed.

20  Before fitting the pump, clean its mounting in the engine block and fit a new O-ring seal to the pump body (photo). Apply a light coating of silicone type grease to the O-ring and pump-to-block contact surfaces in order to reduce corrosion, which would prevent movement of the pump when tensioning the timing belt. Suitable grease is supplied under Part No 90167353 by your GM dealer. Install the pump in the block and fit the three retaining bolts and washers, but only hand tighten them at this stage (photo). The

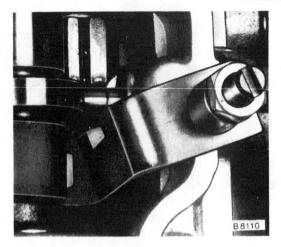

Fig. 13.12 Special tool No KM 565 in use (Sec 6)

Fig. 13.13 Later thermostat with 92°C stamped on flange (Sec 7)

Fig. 13.14 Thermostat housing on the 1.8 ohc engine (Sec 7)

cut-out in the pump flange must be positioned as shown to act as the adjustment limit stop when the pump is rotated to tension the camshaft drivebelt. Refit the belt rear cover.

21  Refit and tension the camshaft drivebelt with reference to Section 5. It will be found easier to engage the belt on the water pump first then on the camshaft sprocket.

22  Refit the cooling fan assembly followed by the timing cover halves.

23  Refit and tension the fanbelt, refit the radiator, and refill the cooling system with reference to Chapter 2.

24  Re-connect the battery negative lead.

*Temperature-controlled visco fan – operation, removal and refitting*

25  Later models are fitted with a temperature-controlled viscous coupled cooling fan (photo). The viscous coupling slips at low

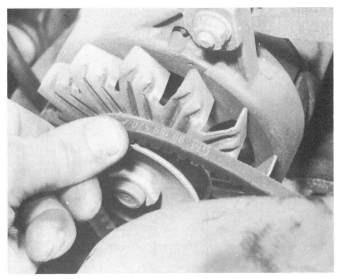

7.13A Removing the fanbelt

7.13B The timing cover halves

7.18 Removing the water pump

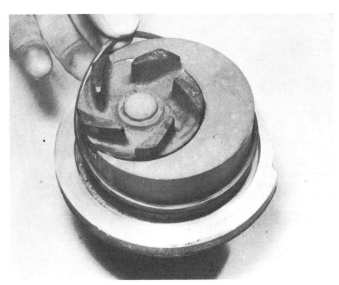

7.20A Water pump O-ring seal

7.20B Water pump correctly fitted – adjustment limit stops arrowed

7.25 Temperature-controlled viscous coupled cooling fan

temperatures, so reducing power loss and noise. At high temperatures the coupling slip is reduced and the fan speed rises.

26  The fan and coupling cannot be repaired and if defective or leaking must be renewed.

27  Before attempting removal of the visco fan, obtain an open-ended spanner which will fit closely over the flats of the fan carrier whilst clearing the fan holding nut. A spanner which is too thick can be modified by grinding a chamfer of the necessary width on one side of both of its flats.

28  Gain access to the fan by removing the cowling and radiator. **Note:** *The fan holding nut has a left-hand thread.* Whilst holding the fan carrier steady, remove the holding nut and withdraw the fan assembly. Avoid placing the fan on its face as this can damage the moving pin.

### Fanbelt – renewal

29  Where a new fanbelt has been fitted, start the engine and allow it to idle. Over a five minute period, accelerate the engine several times before allowing it to return to idle.

30  After five minutes, the new belt will have adapted to the pulley profiles and stretched slightly. Stop the engine and recheck the belt tension.

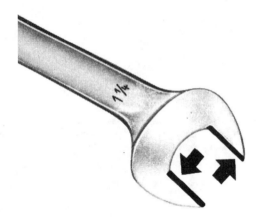

Fig. 13.16 Chamfer the jaws of a $1^1/4$ inch open-ended spanner for removing the visco fan (Sec 7)

## 8  Carburation, fuel injection, fuel and exhaust systems

### GM Varajet II carburettor – general

1  The 20S and 18S carburettor engines are fitted with a GM Varajet II carburettor of twin barrel downdraught type. The two barrels operate successively, the primary barrel being opened by a lever connected, via a cable, to the accelerator pedal. The secondary throttle barrel is opened by a mechanical link between the throttles. An automatic choke is fitted, the choke flap spindle rotation being controlled by the tension of a bi-metal spring. When the ignition is switched on, a heating element near the bi-metal spring is energised. As the temperature of the spring rises, its tension decreases and the throttle flap opens.

### GM Varajet II carburettor – dismantling, inspection and reassembly

2  Remove the fuel union nut and withdraw the fuel filter. Remove the three fixing screws and lift the cover off the automatic choke (photo).

3  Remove the accelerator pump lever pivot bolt and withdraw the lever.

4  Prise off the clips retaining the choke flap linkage and the fast idle cam assembly and pull the linkages off their pivots.

5  Remove the screws from the float chamber cover and prise off the cover, taking care to ensure that the gasket is not broken. Where applicable remove the screen from the float chamber aperture. The immersion tubes are permanently secured to the carburettor cover.

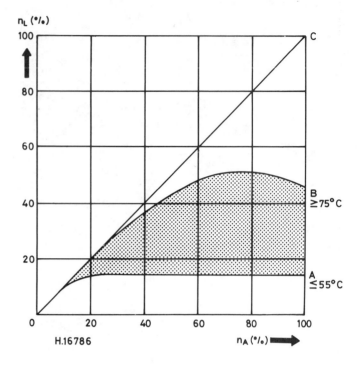

Fig. 13.15 Temperature-controlled visco fan operational graph (Sec 7)

A  Fully disengaged        nA Driving speed
B  Fully engaged           nL Fan speed
C  Directly driven fan

Take care not to damage the tubes, otherwise a new cover will be necessary (photos).

6  Remove the piston of the accelerator pump and lift the spring out of the pump bore (photos).

7  Lift off the joint gasket. The gasket is cut so that it can be removed leaving the partial load needle valve assembly in position.

8  Lift out the float chamber filler piece and remove the float and the needle valve (photos).

9  Unscrew the slotted retainer (if fitted) and lift out the partial load needle valve piston assembly, taking care not to damage the needle. Withdraw the piston return spring and place it in a container with the piston assembly.

10  Grip the pump suction valve spring retainer with a pair of pointed pliers and pull the retainer out of its bore in the float chamber.

11  Use a well fitting screwdriver to screw out the main jet and the float needle seat, and then invert the float chamber over a container to catch the balls from the accelerator pump bore and the suction valve spring drilling.

12  Remove the four screws securing the throttle flap body to the float chamber body. Separate the throttle flap body from the float chamber, taking care not to damage the gasket. Clean and inspect all the components.

13  Ensure that the end of the primary barrel flap return spring engages on the connecting link as shown in Fig. 13.29, and check that the throttle flap and linkage operate freely.

14  Reassembly is the reverse of dismantling, but the following points need to be noted carefully.

15  Insert the smaller ball (4 mm) into the accelerator pump bore and the larger ball (4.8 mm) into the drilling for the suction valve spring. Ensure that the pump ball locates in the seating recess as shown in Fig. 13.31.

16  Fit the spring on top of the suction valve ball. Carefully fit the piston and the needle into their respective drillings then screw in the piston retainer or press in the plastic plug flush.

17  Install the float needle by first hooking the valve spring over the

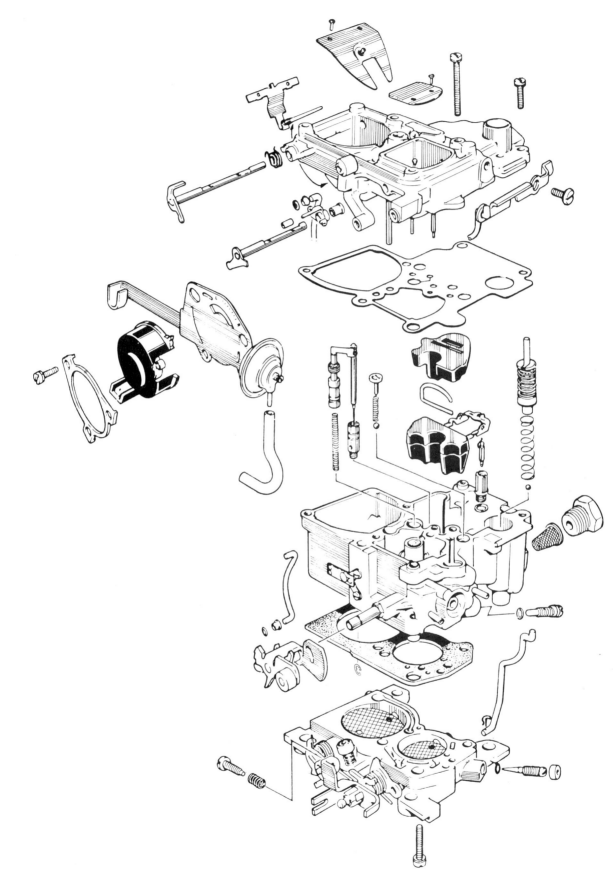

Fig. 13.17 GM Varajet II carburettor – exploded view (Sec 8)

Fig. 13.18 Fuel filter (Sec 8)

Fig. 13.19 Automatic choke cover screws (Sec 8)

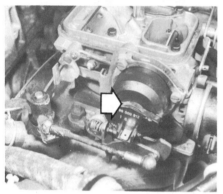

8.2 Automatic choke unit

8.5A Top view of carburettor showing cover screws

8.5B Removing the cover

8.5C Underside of carburettor cover

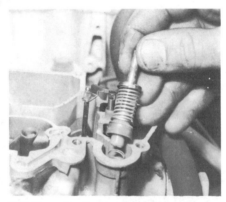

8.6A Removing the accelerator pump piston ...

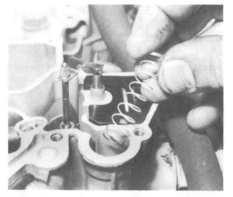

8.6B ... and spring

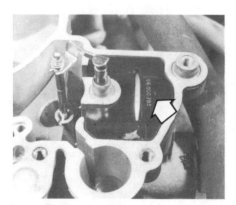

8.8A Remove the filler piece ...

8.8B ... and float assembly

8.8C View of carburettor with float removed

Fig. 13.20 Accelerator pump lever pivot screw (Sec 8)

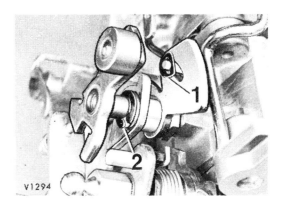

Fig. 13.21 Linkage retaining clips (Sec 8)

1    Choke flap clip                2    Fast idle cam clip

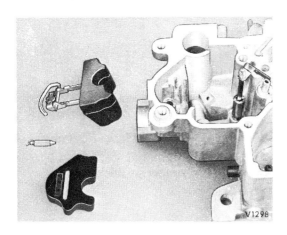

Fig. 13.22 Float needle, float and filler piece (Sec 8)

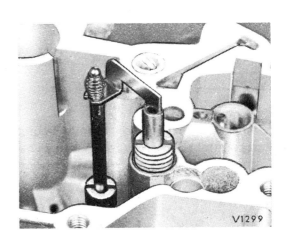

Fig. 13.23 Removing the partial load piston retainer (Sec 8)

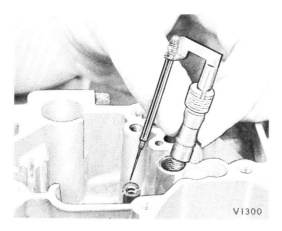

Fig. 12.24 Lifting out the needle and piston (Sec 8)

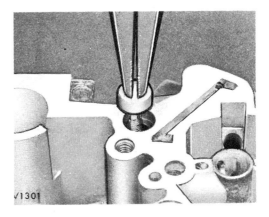

Fig. 13.25 Removing the pump suction valve spring retainer (Sec 8)

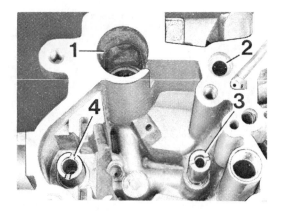

Fig. 13.26 Parts to be removed from the float chamber (Sec 8)

1  Accelerator pump check ball     3  Main jet
2  Suction valve check ball        4  Float needle valve seat

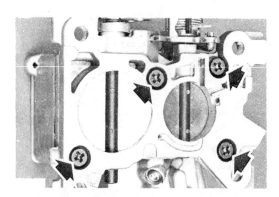

Fig. 13.27 Throttle flap body fixing screws (Sec 8)

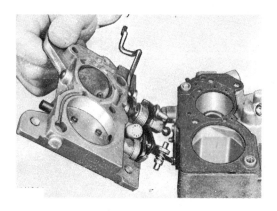

Fig. 13.28 Removing the throttle flap body, leaving gasket (Sec 8)

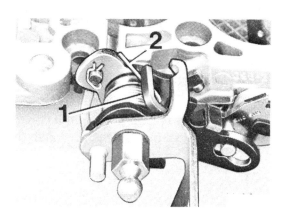

Fig. 13.29 Primary barrel flap linkage (Sec 8)
*End of spring (2) engages connecting link (1) as shown*

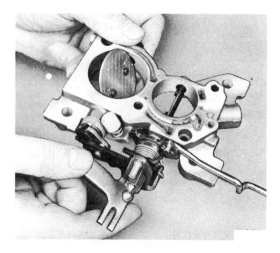

Fig. 13.30 Checking throttle flaps for free movement (Sec 8)

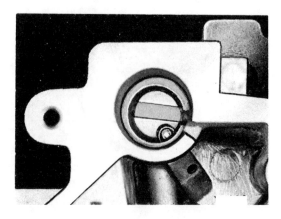

Fig. 13.31 Location of accelerator pump check ball (Sec 8)

platform as shown in Fig. 13.32. Lower the valve into its seat and guide the float pivot clip into the vertical slots in the float chamber. The clip may be installed either way round, but its endplay must be between 0.1 and 0.3 mm (0.004 and 0.012 in). Bend it if necessary.

18 Fit the filler piece into the float chamber so that the slot in the filler piece locates over the float pivot clip.

19 When fitting the carburettor cover on to the float chamber, ensure that the accelerator pump piston moves freely in its bore.

20 Engage the end of the bi-metal coil on the tang of the choke flap (Fig. 13.35) and position the choke cover so that the pointer coincides with the marks shown in Figs. 13.36 and 13.37.

### GM Varajet II carburettor – settings and adjustments
**Idling adjustment**

21 When the engine idling speed is adjusted during manufacture, the stop screw setting of the primary barrel throttle flap is adjusted relative to the vacuum valve at the carburettor ignition vacuum advance connection. The screw is then sealed with a plastic cap and should not be disturbed, because incorrect positioning of the throttle flap at idling speed can affect the ignition vacuum advance timing and the carburettor progression system.

22 Idling speed may be varied by adjusting the additional idling mixture screw (Fig. 13.38) without this having any appreciable

Fig. 13.32 Correct position of float needle spring (arrowed) (Sec 8)

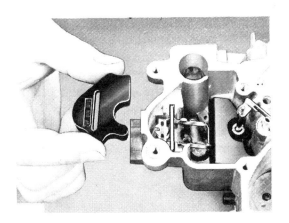

Fig. 13.33 Filler piece, showing slot to locate pivot clip (Sec 8)

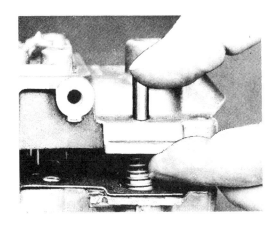

Fig. 13.34 Checking accelerator pump free movement when installing carburettor cover (Sec 8)

Fig. 13.35 Installing automatic choke cover (Sec 8)

| 1 | Bi-metal coil end | 2 | Choke flap tang |
|---|---|---|---|

Fig. 13.36 Choke cover position on cih engines (Sec 8)

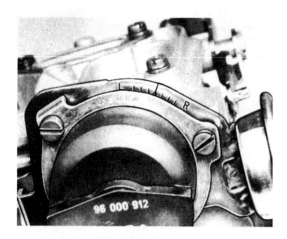

Fig. 13.37 Choke cover position on ohc engines (Sec 8)

Fig. 13.38 Carburettor idling adjustment (Sec 8)

1  Vacuum advance connection     3  Mixture control screw
2  Additional idling mixture screw

effect on the idling air/fuel mixture. The smaller screw is the mixture control screw and should not be tampered with unless a CO meter is available. Adjustment of this screw is only necessary when the carbon monoxide (CO) content is outside the specified limits (photos).
23 Idling speed should not be adjusted unless the engine is at operating temperature, the air cleaner is installed and the temperature compensator air bleed is closed. Additionally, on cars with automatic transmission, the selector lever should be in the 'P' position.

**Fast idling adjustment**
24 Check that the normal idling adjustment is satisfactory and that the engine is at normal operating temperature.
25 Remove the air cleaner and seal the vacuum connection on the carburettor which operates the temperature control system on the air cleaner (Fig. 3.2 in Chapter 3).
26 Open the throttle flap slightly and position the fast idle cam so that when the throttle flap is released, the regulating screw locates on the centre step of the cam (3-step cam – Fig. 13.39) or the 4th (second highest) step (5-step cam).
27 Start the engine without depressing the accelerator pedal and the engine should run at 2000 rpm. If necessary, adjust the regulating screw.

Fig. 13.39 Regulating screw on centre step of cam (Sec 8)

8.22A Adjusting the additional idling mixture screw

8.22B Adjusting the mixture control screw

## Automatic choke setting

28  The setting of the automatic choke should be as shown in Figs. 13.36 and 13.37, with the pointer on the choke cover coinciding with the relevant mark.

29  At this setting the choke flap should open fully in two to three minutes from starting the engine from cold. If the time taken is outside these limits, do not attempt to alter it by changing the choke setting, but fit a new choke cover.

## Pump piston setting

30  With the choke flap fully open and the primary throttle flap in the idling position, depress the pump rod with a screwdriver and measure the distance between the top of the rod and the pump lever (A' in Fig. 13.40). The dimension should be 0.307 to 0.323 in (7.8 to 8.2 mm)

31  To adjust the setting, bend the pump lever at point 'B'.

## Automatic transmission throttle damper

32  On cars with automatic transmission, a throttle damper is fitted to the carburettor to cushion the last part of throttle movement to the closed position and so prevent the engine from stalling. It should not be necessary to alter the original setting, but if adjustment is required, proceed as follows. Run the engine to achieve normal operating temperature and then check that the idling speed is correct, adjust if necessary.

33  For 20S engines stop the engine and hold the throttle partially open so that the damper·plunger moves out the full extent of its travel, and measure the distance from the tip of the plunger to the damper housing (dimension 'A' in Fig. 13.41). Allow the throttle to close to its idling position and measure the plunger projection in this position. The difference between the two dimensions should be 0.14 in (3.5 mm).

34  If necessary, adjust the position of the damper by releasing the locknut and turning the threaded rod to obtain correct plunger travel. Tighten the locknut when the adjustment is satisfactory.

35  For 18S engines stop the engine and check that the damper pin is depressed by 3.0 mm (0.12 in). If adjustment is necessary unscrew the damper until the pin is just touching the lever then screw it in three or four turns.

## Choke flap gap (engine running) – 20S engine

36  With the engine running at normal operating temperature and with the air cleaner removed, position the fast idle cam so that the regulating screw locates on the centre step of the cam (3-step cam) or the 4th (second highest) step (5-step cam).

37  Rotate the choke flap to its limit in the closing direction and measure the gap between the edge of the flap and the barrel bore (dimension 'A' in Fig. 13.42). If the gap is not within the limits 0.169 to 0.185 in (4.3 to 4.7 mm), adjust it as follows.

38  Rotate the stop screw on the vacuum unit (Fig. 13.43) to alter the choke gap, but if the gap is found be to too small, bend the end of the choke linkage backwards to increase the clearance between

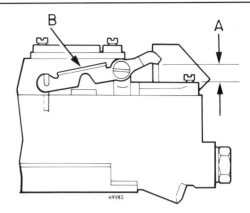

Fig.13.40 Accelerator pump piston setting (Sec 8)

A  Setting dimension          B  Lever adjustment point

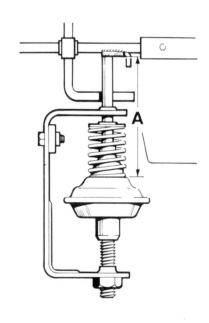

Fig. 13.41 Throttle damper adjustment – 20S engines (Sec 8)

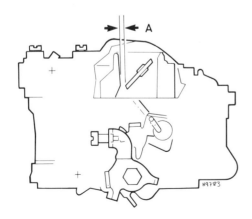

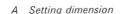

Fig. 13.42 Choke flap setting – 20S engine (Sec 8)

A  Setting dimension

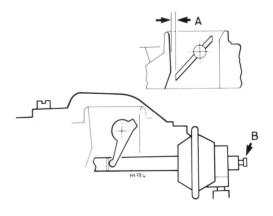

Fig. 13.43 Choke flap adjustment – 20S engine (Sec 8)

A  Choke flap gap          B  Stop screw

the stop and the baffle plate lever, before adjusting the stop screw.
39 After adjusting the choke flap setting, check the clearance between the baffle plate lever and the pull rod when the rod is fully extended (dimension 'A' in Fig. 13.44). The clearance should be 0.004 to 0.012 in (0.1 to 0.3 mm) and can be adjusted by bending the end of the pull rod.

### Choke flap gap (engine staionary) – 20S engine

40 Position the automatic choke linkage so that the choke flap is closed and the fast idle regulating screw is on the centre step of the cam (3-step cam) or the 4th (second highest) step (5-step cam).
41 Apply suction to the vacuum unit to overcome the tension of the bi-metal spring in the choke cover and move the baffle plate lever to its contact stop.
42 The gap between the edge of the choke plate and the barrel bore should be the same as for the engine running condition (paragraph 37) and adjustment is made in the same way as the engine running condition.

### Choke flap gap – 18S engine

43 With the air cleaner removed position the fast idle screw on the top step of the cam. If the choke flap is not completely shut (ie because the engine is warm) use a rubber band to keep it shut.
44 Apply vacuum to the choke vacuum unit then using a drill check that the gap (A) between the choke flap and wall is as given in the Specifications. If necessary turn the adjusting screw on the vacuum unit. If the gap is too small bend the linkage to provide clearance between the stop and vacuum unit cover.
45 Reposition the fast idle screw on the second highest cam step. Open and release the choke flap by hand and allow it to take up its position; a drill of diameter 'B' (see Specifications) should fit snugly between the flap and the carburettor wall.
46 If adjustment of gap 'B' is required, remove the carburettor and the choke cover. Bend the rod which connects the cam disc to the choke flap lever until the gap is correct. Refit the carburettor and recheck gap 'A' (paragraph 44).
47 Using the rubber band to apply closing force to the choke flap, open the throttle wide and check that the choke flap opens to gap 'C' (see Specifications). Adjust if necessary by bending the tag on the fast idle cam disc (Fig. 13.45).

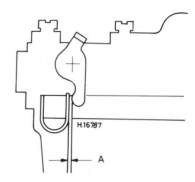

Fig. 13.44 Baffle plate lever to pull rod clearance (A) – 20S engine (Sec 8)

### Part load regulator screw adjustment – 18S engine

48 Problems such as jerking or hesitation at light throttle openings, or excessive fuel consumption despite moderate driving habits, may be due to incorrect adjustment of the part load regulator screw.
49 It is emphasised that this adjustment should not be attempted until all other possible causes of the problems mentioned have been investigated.
50 Remove the carburettor from the vehicle.
51 Prise out the metal plug covering the part load regulator screw (adjacent to the fuel inlet union).
52 If stalling or hesitation is the reason for adjustment – ie the mixture is too weak – turn the screw one-quarter turn anti-clockwise.
53 If excessive fuel consumption is the problem – ie the mixture is too rich – turn the screw one-quarter turn clockwise.
54 Refit the carburettor and test drive the vehicle to see if any improvement has occurred. If necessary a further adjustment can be made, but **do not** deviate from the original setting by more than half a turn of the screw.
55 Fit a new metal plug on completion, where this is required by law.

Fig. 13.45 Bend tag (G) to adjust wide throttle choke gap – 18S engine (Sec 8)

Fig. 13.46 Part load regulator adjusting screw – 18S engine (Sec 8)

**Float level check**

56 Remove the carburettor cover and the float chamber filler piece.
57 Depress the float shaft and arm at the same time (Fig. 13.47) then use a depth micrometer or vernier to check that the distance from the upper carburettor face to the float is 35.0 mm (1.38 in). If not, bend the float arm as necessary.
58 Refit the filler piece and the cover.

*Solex 32/32 DIDTA carburettor – adjustments*
**Idling adjustments**

59 When the engine idling speed is adjusted during manufacture, the stop screw setting of the primary barrel throttle flap is adjusted relative to the vacuum value at the carburettor ignition vacuum advance connection. The screw is then sealed with a plastic cap and should not be disturbed, because incorrect positioning of the throttle flap at idling speed can affect the ignition vacuum advance timing and the carburettor progression system.
60 Minor adjustments to idling speed can be carried out by turning the air volume screw and the mixture control screw (Fig. 13.49). Anti-clockwise rotation of the air volume screw weakens the

mixture and anti-clockwise rotation of the mixture control screw enriches the mixture.
61 Idling speed should only be adjusted when the engine is at normal operating temperature, with the air cleaner fitted and the temperature compensator air bleed closed. On cars with automatic transmission, idling adjustment should be made with the selector in the 'N' position.
62 At the correct idling speed of 800 to 850 rpm, the carbon monoxide (CO) content of the exhaust should be between 1.5 and 2.5% and the idling cannot be considered to be correct unless the CO level has been checked.
63 If the correct idling speed and exhaust emission conditions cannot be obtained, it is likely that the primary, or secondary, throttle flap is set incorrectly and this should be rectified by an Opel or Solex agent.

**Fast idle cam setting**

64 When adjusting fast idling, the fast idle lever should be on the top step of the fast idle cam (Fig. 13.50) and the top edge of the lever should align with the centre of the cam step as shown.
65 To adjust the cam position, attach an elastic band to the choke

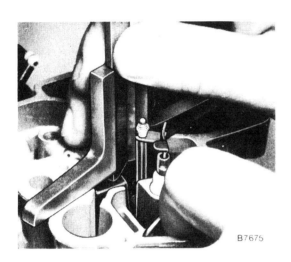

Fig. 13.47 Checking the float level dimension (Sec 8)

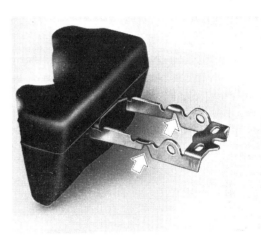

Fig. 13.48 Float arm adjustment points (Sec 8)

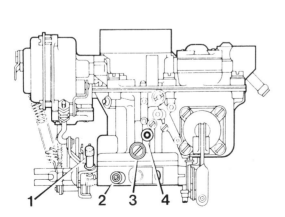

Fig. 13.49 Carburettor idling adjustment
(Solex 32/32 DIDTA) (Sec 8)

1  Throttle flap stop screw
2  Mixture control screw
3  Air volume screw
4  Ignition vacuum advance connection

Fig. 13.50 Fast idle cam (Solex 32/32 DIDTA) (Sec 8)

1  Fast idle cam
2  Fast idle lever

lever plate to hold the choke flap closed. Referring to Fig. 13.51, bend the lever to move the cam plate in the required direction until it is correctly positioned on the fast idle lever.

66 Check that there is a gap of 0.098 to 0.118 in (2.5 to 3.0 mm) between the edge of the choke flap and the barrel bore when the vacuum controlled override unit is fully depressed. If it is necessary to adjust the gap, bend the choke lever pin.

**Automatic transmission throttle damper**

67 The throttle damper fitted to the Solex 32/32 DIDTA carburettor is similar to that on the GM Varajet II carburettor and its adjustment is identical to that described in paragraphs 32 to 35.

*Solex 35 PDSI carburettor – adjustments*
**Idling adjustment**

68 Idling adjustment is similar to that of the Solex 32/32 DIDTA carburettor except that idling speed may be varied by adjustment of the additional idling mixture screw (Fig. 13.52), without appreciably altering the idling air/fuel mixture.

69 Adjustment of the air/fuel mixture is achieved by the additional idling mixture screw in conjunction with the mixture control screw, subject to the same exhaust gas requirements as described in paragraphs 62 and 63.

**Fast idling**

70 The fast idling speed is determined by the choke connecting linkage and no adjustment is necessary except to ensure that the fast idle adjusting screw just touches the throttle spindle lever when the throttle flap is closed.

**Automatic transmission throttle damper**

71 The throttle damper fitted to the Solex 35 PDSI carburettor is similar to that on the GM Varajet II carburettor and its adjustment is identical with that described in paragraphs 32 to 35.

*Zenith 35/40 INAT carburettor – adjustments*
**Idling adjustment**

72 The procedure is identical with that detailed for the GM Varajet II carburettor in paragraphs 21 to 23 except that the limits of carbon monoxide in the exhaust are 1.5% to 2.5%. Reference should be made to Fig. 13.53 for the position of the additional idling mixture screw and the mixture control screw.

**Fast idling**

73 Ensure that the engine is at normal operating temperature and that the idling speed is correct.

74 Open the throttle and close the choke flap to place the fast idle screw on the highest step of the cam (Fig. 13.54). The choke flap may be closed by raising the choke connecting rod to its fullest extent.

75 Start the engine without depressing the accelerator pedal and the engine should run at 2700 rpm.

76 To adjust the fast idling speed, stop the engine and open the throttle fully to expose the stop screw through a hole in the automatic choke housing. Turn the screw a small amount in a clockwise direction and again check the fast idling speed. If the alteration is in the wrong direction, stop the engine and turn the screw anti-clockwise a small amount before re-checking. Continue making small changes to the stop screw position until the engine runs at 2700 rpm.

**Automatic choke**

77 The setting of the automatic choke cover, which controls the time which the choke takes to open, is described in Chapter 3, Section 7.

78 To check the travel stop setting of the vacuum controlled override unit, close the choke flap and attach a rubber band to the choke intermediate lever to hold the flap closed (Fig. 13.56). Lift the vacuum diaphragm to the full extent of its travel and check that a gap of 0.106 to 0.114 in (2.7 to 2.9 mm) exists between the edge of the choke flap and the barrel bore.

79 To check the choke flap rod linkage setting, hold the choke flap closed and check that the distance between the intermediate lever and the vacuum diaphragm pull rod boss (dimension 'A' in Fig. 13.57) is 0.008 to 0.040 in (0.2 to 1.0 mm).

80 To adjust the setting, remove the plastic cap from the carburettor

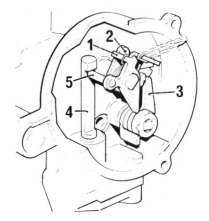

**Fig. 13.51 Fast idle cam adjustment (Solex 32/32 DIDTA) (Sec 8)**

| | |
|---|---|
| 1   Adjustment lever | 4   Vacuum controlled override |
| 2   Cam plate |      unit |
| 3   Fast idle lever | 5   Adjustment pin |

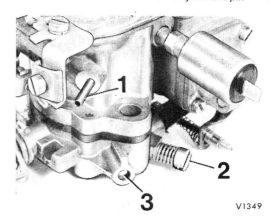

**Fig. 13.52 Carburettor idling adjustment (Solex 35 PDSI) (Sec 8)**

| | |
|---|---|
| 1   Vacuum advance connection | 3   Mixture control screw |
| 2   Additional idling mixture | |
|      screw | |

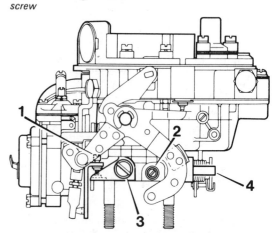

**Fig. 13.53 Carburettor idling adjustment (Zenith 35/40 INAT) (Sec 8)**

| | |
|---|---|
| 1   Throttle stop screw | 4   Ignition vacuum control |
| 2   Mixture control screw |      inlet |
| 3   Additional idling mixture screw | |

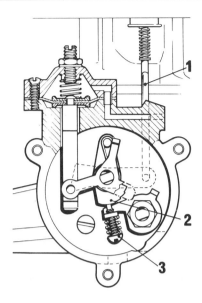

Fig. 13.54 Fast idle cam (Zenith 35/40 INAT) (Sec 8)

1   Choke connecting rod        3   Fast idle screw
2   Cam

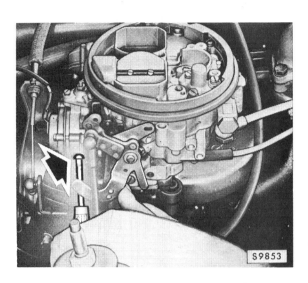

Fig. 13.55 Fast idle speed adjustment screw (Sec 8)

Fig. 13.56 Vacuum travel stop screw (Sec 8)

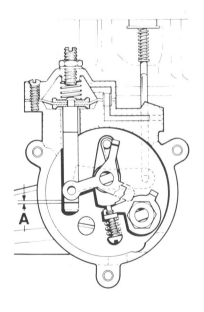

Fig. 13.57 Choke flap linkage setting (A) (Sec 8)

cover, slacken the choke rod clamp screw, adjust the rod to give the correct setting and then tighten the clamp (Fig. 13.58).

### Secondary barrel throttle flap setting
81  To prevent the secondary barrel throttle flap (Fig. 13.59) from jamming in the closed position, the throttle flap stop screw should be adjusted to give a gap of 0.002 in (0.05 mm) between the edge of the flap and the barrel bore. This clearance is about a quarter of a turn of the stop screw from the flap closed position.
82  The foregoing adjustment is important, because an excessive clearance of the secondary throttle flap can make it impossible to obtain correct engine idling speed.

### Throttle flap link roller
83  To ensure correct roller contact on the primary barrel throttle flap lever, the link lever screw (Fig. 13.60) should be adjusted to give a gap of 0.004 to 0.008 in (0.1 to 0.2 mm) between the end of the screw and the secondary barrel throttle flap lever with the primary barrel throttle flap closed.

### Float chamber vent valve setting
84  The float chamber vent valve setting (Fig. 13.61) is correct when there is a gap of 0.06 to 0.07 in (1.5 to 1.8 mm) between the throttle stop screw and its abutment when the air vent lever is just touching the base of the air vent valve.

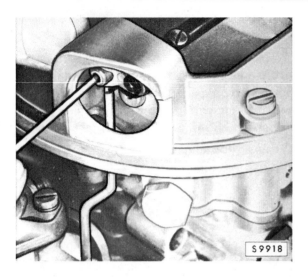

Fig. 13.58 Choke flap linkage adjustment (Sec 8)

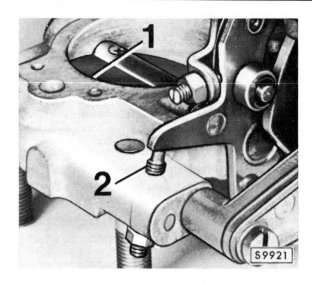

Fig. 13.59 Secondary barrel throttle flap setting (Sec 8)

1   *Throttle flap*                    2   *Stop screw*

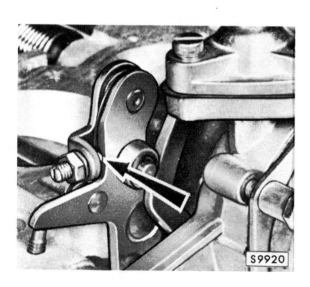

Fig. 13.60 Throttle flap link roller setting – adjust gap
(arrowed) (Sec 8)

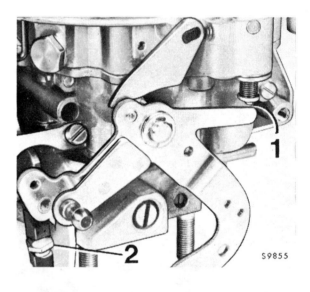

Fig. 13.61 Float chamber vent valve setting (Sec 8)

1   *Gap between vent valve and lever*
2   *Intermediate link adjustment*

85  To alter the setting, adjust the length of the intermediate link. Do not alter the setting of the throttle stop screw, because this will alter the ignition vacuum advance and also disturb the carburettor primary barrel progression system.

**Automatic transmission throttle damper**

86  The throttle damper fitted to the Zenith 35/40 INAT carburettor is similar to that on the GM Varajet II carburettor and its adjustment is identical to that described in paragraphs 32 to 35.

*Fuel tank (Hatchback) – removal and refitting*

87  The fuel tank is strapped to the underbody.

88  Removal and refitting of the tank is similar to that of the saloon models described in Chapter 3, Section 12, except that the tank is released by removing the nuts and bolts securing the tank straps (photos).

*Fuel pump (ohc engine) – removal and refitting*

89  The pump is mounted on the camshaft housing and actuated by a pushrod from an eccentric cam on the camshaft. The pump is of the semi-sealed type; no repairs are possible.

90  Refer to Section 10 of Chapter 3, paragraph 6 onwards, for details of pump servicing.

91  Pump removal is simply a matter of disconnecting the fuel pipes, plugging the pipe ends. unscrewing the two securing nuts and carefully withdrawing the pump from the camshaft housing.

92  Before refitting the pump, check that both mating surfaces are clean and then renew the base gasket. Push the pump into position and prevent it from tilting when the securing nuts are tightened. Reconnect the fuel pipes and after starting the engine, check for leaks.

*Fuel gauge sender unit (Hatchback) – removal and refitting*
93 Raise and support the rear of the car.
94 Syphon the fuel from the tank.
95 Disconnect the hoses and wiring then turn the retaining ring anti-clockwise and withdraw the unit (photo).
96 Refitting is a reversal of removal, but make sure that the wiring terminal is horizontal otherwise incorrect readings will be given.

*Air filter element (ohc engine) – removal and refitting*
97 Release the clips around the air cleaner body and pull the cover section forwards (photos).
98 Extract the filter element (photo).
99 To remove the complete air cleaner disconnect the vacuum and crankcase ventilation hoses, and unscrew the nut securing the air

cleaner to the carburettor (photos). Also disconnect the cold and warm air ducts.
100 Refitting is a reversal of removal (photo).

*L-Jetronic fuel injection system – general*
101 The principal components and general layout of the system are shown in Fig. 13.62. The circuit diagram of the system is appended to Section 14 of this Chapter. Idle speed and mixture adjustment are similar to the operations described for the LE-Jetronic system.
**Fuel metering**
102 Fuel metering is affected by the air intake sensor (Fig. 13.63) which senses the flow rate by a stator flap in an air intake chamber. As the flap swivels with increased airflow, a potentiometer, to which it is coupled, varies the voltage of a control signal to the control unit. The stator flap is balanced by a balance flap and associated balance chamber.

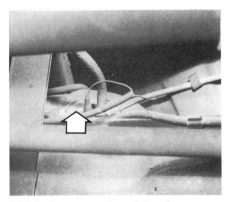

8.95 Fuel gauge sender unit location

8.97A Release the clips ...

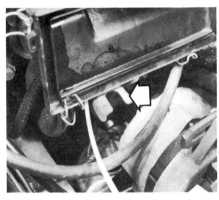

8.97B ... and pull the air cleaner cover from the support

8.98 Removing the air filter element

8.99A Disconnect the temperature control flap vacuum hose ...

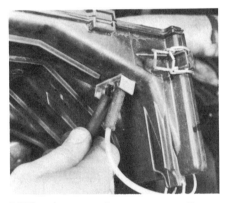

8.99B ... the temperature sensor vacuum hose ...

8.99C ... the crankcase ventilation hose ...

8.99D ... and unscrew the retaining nut

8.100 Showing the air cleaner assembly refitted

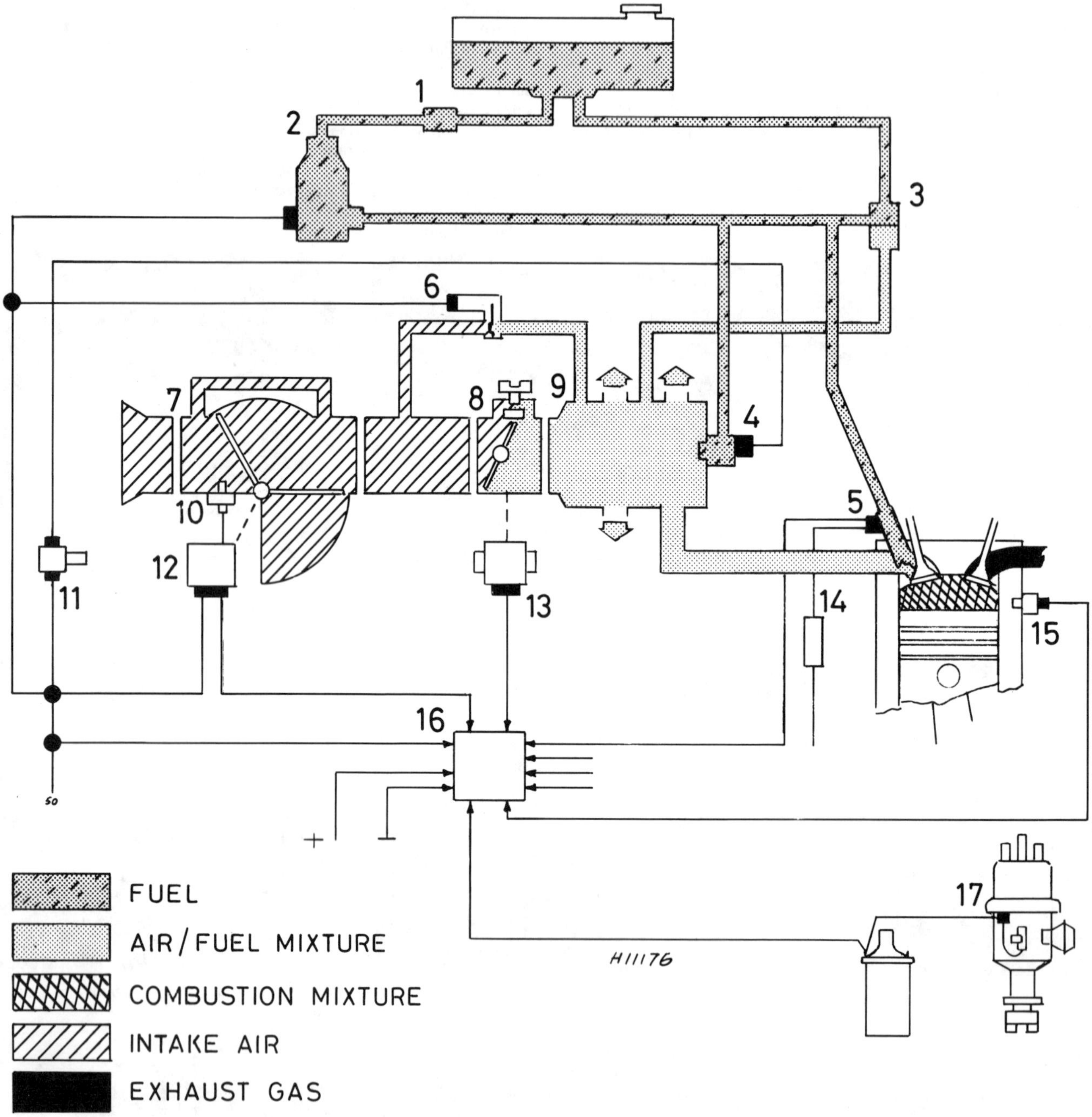

1
2
3
4
5
6
7
8
9
10
11
12
13
14
15
16
17
50
+
FUEL
AIR/FUEL MIXTURE
COMBUSTION MIXTURE
INTAKE AIR
EXHAUST GAS
H11176


**Fig. 13.62 L-Jetronic system schematic diagram (Sec 8)**

*1 Fuel filter*
*2 Fuel pump*
*3 Pressure regulator*
*4 Cold start valve*
*5 Injector*
*6 Auxiliary air regulator*
*7 Intake air sensor*
*8 Throttle valve housing*
*9 Intake air distributor*
*10 Temperature sensor I*
*11 Thermo-time switch*
*12 Potentiometer with fuel pump switch*
*13 Throttle valve switch*
*14 Resistor*
*15 Temperature sensor II*
*16 Control unit*
*17 Ignition contact breaker points*

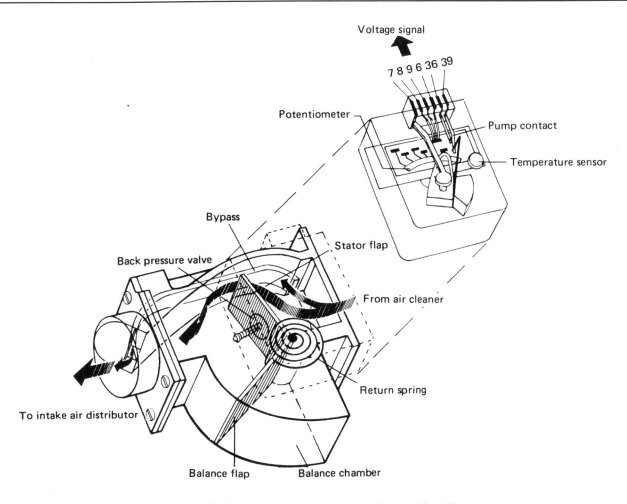

Fig. 13.63 Air intake sensor schematic diagram (Sec 8)

103 A contact on the potentiometer operates the fuel pump, to prevent fuel being pumped into the system if the engine is stationary.

104 A temperature sensor (I) in the air intake provides a control signal so that the quantity of fuel supplied is dependent upon the temperature of the air intake, and a contact on the throttle switch provides for full load enrichment.

### Injection timing

105 The injection timing is controlled by the ignition contact breaker points and the rate of operation of the contact breaker points is used as a measure of engine speed.

106 On alternate openings of the contact breaker points (ie every revolution of the crankshaft), the control unit triggers all four injectors and delivers half the required quantity of fuel. There are thus two injections of fuel, each of half the quantity required every complete engine cycle of two revolutions of the crankshaft.

### Temperature sensor II

107 This sensor is fitted in the coolant flow of the cylinder head and provides the control signal for enrichment during engine starting and warm up.

### Control unit

108 The control unit is a 'computer' which is fed with information on air intake, engine speed, air intake temperature, engine temperature and throttle pedal position. From these signals it determines the quantity of fuel to be injected.

### Pressure regulator

109 The pressure regulator maintains a constant difference between the fuel pressure and the pressure of the intake air.

### Auxiliary regulators

110 The auxiliary regulator is an electrically heated bi-metal gate valve in the auxiliary air line. It provides additional air when the cold start valve is in operation so that the optimum ratio of fuel to air is maintained.

### Barometric compensator

111 This is an optional unit which may be fitted. Its purpose is to prevent excessively rich mixtures when the car is operating at high altitudes where the air is less dense, and it is operative at above 3280 ft (1000 m).

### Electronically controlled fuel injection system precautions

112 The following precautions are necessary to prevent damage to the semiconductor components used in the system.

113 Never attempt to start the engine unless the battery is connected and its polarity is correct.

114 Do not use a boost charger to start the engine.

115 Never disconnect the battery while the engine is running.

116 Before testing the L-Jetronic system, check that the ignition timing and dwell angle are correct and that spark plugs of the correct specification and gap are fitted.

117 Remove the control unit if the car is being heated to above 176°F (80°C), eg for paint drying.

118 Ensure that all plug connections are free from corrosion and that the plug connections of the wiring harness are properly mated.

119 Never connect, or disconnect the wiring harness plugs to the control unit while the ignition is switched on.

120 When spinning the engine to test compression, disconnect the *red* power supply cable to the relay combination by disconnecting the plug near the battery.

## L-Jetronic components – removal and refitting

### Control unit
121 Press the spring clip of the left-hand end of the wiring harness plug and lift off the plug (Fig. 13.64).
122 Remove the three screws securing the control unit to the side panel (Fig. 13.65) and remove the unit.
123 It is necessary to remove the side panel trim from the front footwell to gain access to the unit.
124 Refitting is the reversal of removal.

### Air filter element
125 Release the four toggle fasteners and fold the air meter and top part of the air filter towards the engine.
126 Remove the filter from the bottom part of the casing.
127 Refitting is the reverse of removal, but fit a new filter if the one which was removed is heavily contaminated.

### Air meter
128 Release the four toggle fasteners of the air filter and unscrew the clip securing the rubber gaiter.
129 Disconnect the six-pole plug connection to the wiring harness.
130 Remove the air meter together with the top part of the air filter and then separate the parts by unscrewing the air meter.
131 Before refitting the air meter in the reverse order of removal, clean the back-up flap with a clean lint-free cloth.
132 Push the back-up flap to its stop by hand and ensure that it moves freely over the full range of travel.

### Relay combination
133 Disconnect wiring harness plug 'A' and fuel injection system plug 'B' (Fig. 13.68).
134 Remove the single fixing screw and remove the relay.
135 When connecting the plugs to the relay unit on refitting, ensure that all the terminals are properly seated in the plug and that the conductors are secure.
136 When testing fuel pressure, or pump delivery, connect the red/black cable of starter terminal '50' in plug 'A' to the red cable of terminal '30'. This prevents the starter from operating and injecting fuel into the inlet manifold.

### Compensating resistance
137 The compensating resistors are protected by a cover secured with two screws (Fig. 13.69).
138 The circuit from the resistors via the relay combination to the fuel pump is protected by its own fuse, which is in the fusebox in the passenger compartment (Chapter 10, Section 40).

### Wiring harness earth connection
139 The wiring harness earth connection is shown in Fig. 13.70.
140 Whenever removing or refitting any part of the system check that this connection is clean and secure, because a poor earth connection has an adverse effect on the operation of the entire system.

### Throttle valve switch
141 Disconnect the three-pin plug.
142 Remove the two fixing screws and pull the switch off the throttle valve spindle.
143 Refitting is the reverse of removal; there is no provision for adjusting the switch.

### Temperature sensor II
144 Partially drain the cooling system (Chapter 2), collecting the coolant for re-use.
145 Disconnect the white two-pin plug from the switch and unscrew the switch, using a 19 mm socket wrench.
146 Clean the threads of the switch and apply sealant to them before installing the switch.
147 After refitting the switch, top up the cooling system.

### Thermal timing switch
148 Partially drain the cooling system (Chapter 2), collecting the coolant for re-use.
149 Disconnect the brown two-pin plug from the switch, using a 24 mm socket wrench.
150 Clean the threads of the switch and apply sealant to them before fitting the switch.
151 After fitting the switch, top up the cooling system.

### Cold start valve
152 Disconnect the blue plug from the valve.
153 Unscrew the clip on the fuel pipe and carefully pull off the fuel pipe.
154 Remove the two screws from the valve flange and remove the valve and gasket from the inlet manifold.
155 When refitting the valve, ensure that the gasket is in good condition and that the fuel pipe is fitted properly and its clip tightened.

### Auxiliary air valve
156 Disconnect the black two-pin plug from the valve.
157 Loosen the clips on the two hoses and carefully pull the hoses off.
158 Remove the two fixing screws and remove the valve.
159 Before refitting the valve, check that when cold the valve port is open.
160 After refitting the valve, connect the hoses, ensuring that they fit properly, and then tighten the hose clips.

### Injectors
161 Injectors can only be removed in pairs.
162 Release the clips of the two hoses to a pair of injectors and disconnect the hose from the pipe stub.
163 Remove the bolt securing the injector support and pull out the injector assembly, taking care not to damage the injector needles.
164 When refitting the injectors, it is again necessary to avoid damaging the injector needles. Ensure that the rubber sealing rings are in good condition and that the injector hoses are properly fitted to the stub pipes, with the hose clips tight.

### Fuel pressure regulator
165 Release the clips on the fuel pressure and fuel return pipes and disconnect the pipes.
166 Pull the regulator off the end of the vacuum hose.
167 The fuel pressure regulator cannot be adjusted and if the fuel pressure is incorrect, a new regulator must be fitted.
168 When fitting a new regulator, ensure that the hoses are in good condition and that the clips on the pipes are tight.

### Fuel supply system
169 The fuel system has an electric fuel pump with suction and return pipes to the fuel tank, the general arrangement of components being as Fig. 13.77.
170 The pump and filters are an assembly and it is removed as follows.
171 Fit a clamp to the fuel suction and pressure pipes to stop fuel escaping – a self-gripping wrench is very effective for this.
172 Release the clips on the suction pipe to the pre-filter and on the pressure pipe from the filter, and detach the pipes, being careful to note which pipe is which.
173 Pull the electrical connections off the fuel pump and remove the three nuts securing the assembly to the underbody.
174 Refit the pump and filter assembly by reversing the removal operations, taking care that the hoses are connected correctly and that their clips are tight.
175 Reconnect the electrical leads to the pump, ensuring that the blue cable is connected to the positive terminal and the brown cable to the negative terminal.

## L-Jetronic components – testing
176 The following checks will enable the malfunctioning of a component in the system to be identified, but a comprehensive check of the system's operation is best entrusted to an Opel dealer with the necessary specialised equipment.

### Air meter
177 With the ignition switched off and the wiring harness disconnected, the following readings should be obtained if the unit is satisfactory:

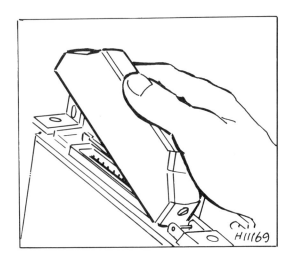

Fig. 13.64 Removing the control unit plug (Sec 8)

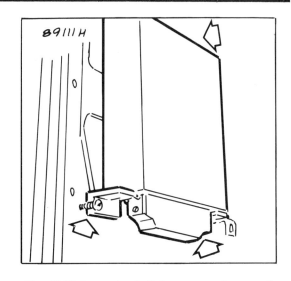

Fig. 13.65 Control unit fixing screws (arrowed) (Sec 8)

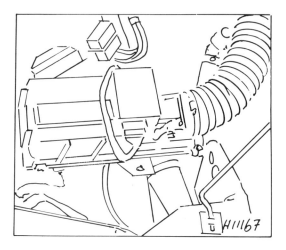

Fig. 13.66 Air filter assembly (Sec 8)

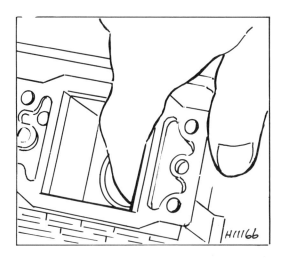

Fig. 13.67 Testing back-up flap movement (Sec 8)

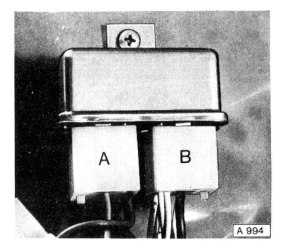

Fig. 13.68 Relay combination (Sec 8)

A   Harness plug          B   Fuel injection system plug

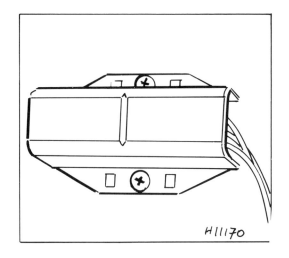

Fig. 13.69 Compensating resistors (Sec 8)

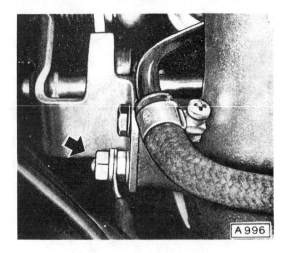

Fig. 13.70 Wiring harness earth connection (Sec 8)

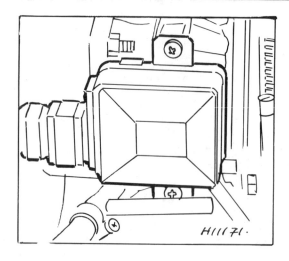

Fig. 13.71 Throttle valve switch (Sec 8)

Fig. 13.72 Temperature sensor II (arrowed) (Sec 8)

Fig. 13.73 Cold start valve (Sec 8)

Fig. 13.74 Auxiliary air valve (Sec 8)

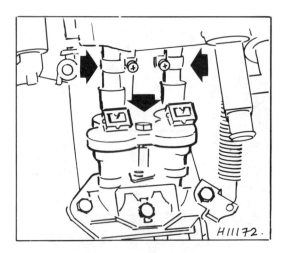

Fig. 13.75 Removing the fuel injectors (Sec 8)

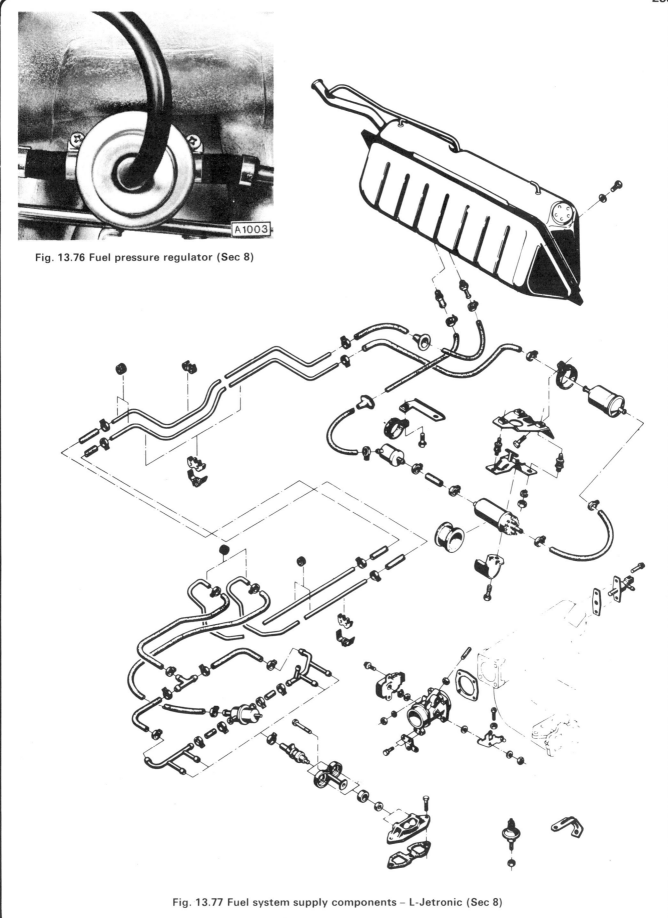

Fig. 13.76 Fuel pressure regulator (Sec 8)

A1003

Fig. 13.77 Fuel system supply components – L-Jetronic (Sec 8)

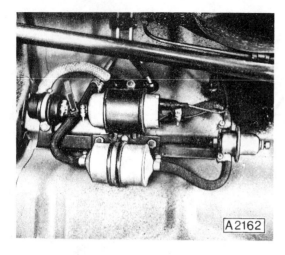

Fig. 13.78 Fuel pump and filter installation (Sec 8)

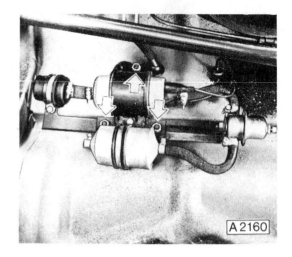

Fig. 13.79 Pump and filter assembly fixings (arrowed)
(Sec 8)

Fig. 13.80 Pump and filter assembly fuel flow (Sec 8)

*Ohmmeter connected to terminals 6 and 7; reading of about 50 ohms*
*Ohmmeter connected to terminals 6 and 8; reading of about 180 ohms*
*Ohmmeter connected to terminals 8 and 9; reading of about 100 ohms*

### Compensating resistance
178 Disconnect the compensating resistance from the circuit and measure the resistance value of the resistance. This should be between 5.5 and 6.5 ohms.
179 The resistance between the terminals of the injector valve, with the valve disconnected from the harness is between 2 and 3 ohms.

### Throttle valve switch
180 Disconnect the plug from the switch and connect an ohmmeter between terminal 3 and terminal 18. With the throttle closed, the switch should be open, giving a meter reading of infinity.
181 Depress the throttle pedal fully and the switch should close and give an ohmmeter reading of zero.

### Temperature sensor II
182 With the wiring harness plug disconnected from the temperature sensor, connect an ohmmeter between contacts 13 and

49 on the sensor. The reading obtained will depend upon the temperature of the engine as follows:

*At + 80°C, reading of 0.15 to 0.35 K ohms*
*At + 60°C, reading of 0.3 to 0.5 K ohms*
*At + 40°C, reading of 0.55 to 0.95 K ohms*
*At + 20°C, reading of 1.3 to 8.5 K ohms*

### Thermal timing switch
183 With the wiring harness plug disconnected from the switch, connect an ohmmeter between switch terminals 45 and 46. The following meter readings should be obtained:

*At a temperature above +35°C, a reading of 50 to 75 ohms*
*At a temperature below +35°C, a reading of 3 to 5 ohms*

### Cold start valve
184 Check that the valve is receiving an electrical signal by disconnecting the plug from the valve and connecting a test lamp between terminals 45 and 46 of the plug. Operate the starter switch and the test lamp should light.
185 If the lamp lights, test the valve by reconnecting the plug and removing the valve from the inlet manifold. Operate the starter briefly and check that the valve injects fuel, taking great care to ensure that the fuel emerging from the valve cannot be ignited.

### Auxiliary air valve
186 Disconnect the hoses from the valve and check visually that when the valve is cold, the ports are open.
187 Check the resistance between the valve terminals with an ohmmeter; a reading of about 30 ohms should be obtained. If this is satisfactory, connect a 12 volt battery between the valve terminals and check that when the valve has had time to heat up, the ports are closed.

### Fuel pressure regulator
188 Connect a pressure gauge with a range of up to 50 lbf/in², or 4 bar, into the hose to the cold start valve. Disconnect the hose from the pressure regulator to the intake pipe and blank off the opening in the intake pipe.
189 Start the engine and if the regulator is satisfactory, the indicated pressure will be in excess of 40 lbf/in² (3 bar).

### *LE Jetronic fuel injection system – general*
190 The LE Jetronic system is similar to the L Jetronic system previously described except for the following differences.
191 A cold start booster eliminates the need for a separate cold start valve and thermal timing switch.
192 A control relay incorporating a timing element and switch relay cuts off the fuel supply immediately after the engine stops.

## LE Jetronic fuel injection system – adjustments
### Idle speed and mixture adjustment
193 With the engine at normal operating temperature, connect a tachometer to it if one is not already fitted as standard equipment.
194 Check the idle speed against that given in the Specifications. If necessary, correct it by turning the regulating screw on the throttle connecting piece (photo).
195 To check the mixture (CO level), connect an exhaust gas analyser in accordance with its maker's instructions. Again the engine must be at normal operating temperature, and the ignition system must be correctly adjusted.
196 If the CO content deviates from that specified, remove the cap from the bypass screw on the airflow sensor (photo). Turn the screw in a clockwise direction to enrich the mixture or anti-clockwise to weaken it.
197 On completion of the adjustment, fit a new cap to the bypass screw.
198 Failure to bring the CO content within the specified tolerance will indicate a fault in the system, or a well worn engine.

### Throttle valve adjustment
199 Make sure that the throttle valve plate is closed. Refer to Fig. 13.81 or 13.82 as appropriate.
200 Unscrew both the throttle valve stop screw and locknut until they are clear of their cam, then screw the screw in again until it just contacts the cam. Now give it a further quarter of a turn and tighten its locknut.
201 On manual transmission models, release the locknuts on the connecting rod and adjust its length by rotating it so that dimension X is as shown in Fig. 13.81.

### Throttle valve switch adjustment
202 Release the switch mounting screws (photo) and rotate the switch in an anti-clockwise direction until resistance is felt. Tighten the screws.
203 Have an assistant open the throttle valve slightly by depressing the accelerator pedal. A click should be heard from the switch. A click should also be heard when the pedal is released.

## LE Jetronic components – removal and refitting
204 It is not possible to repair the main components of the fuel injection system. In the event of a fault occurring, it is best to have the fault isolated by your GM dealer or a fuel system specialist as special equipment will be necessary. However, once the problem has been diagnosed, there is no reason why the defective component cannot be renewed by carrying out the following instructions.

### Throttle valve housing
205 Release the securing clips and disconnect the flexible ducting which connects the throttle valve housing with the airflow sensor.
206 Disconnect the coolant hoses from the throttle control housing. If the ends of the hoses are retained in their highest position there will be no loss of coolant. If the engine is still warm when this work is being carried out then the system pressure must be released before disconnecting the hoses. Do this by gently unscrewing the expansion bottle cap.
207 Pull the distributor vacuum hose from the throttle valve housing.
208 Disconnect the brake servo vacuum hose and the crankcase ventilation system hose from the throttle valve housing.
209 Disconnect and plug the fuel hoses from the distribution tube pipe stubs. Note that the hose with the white band is located nearer the alternator. Do not connect these hoses incorrectly.

8.194 Idle speed adjusting screw and locknut (LE-Jetronic)

8.196 Adjusting the idle mixture with an Allen key (LE-Jetronic)

8.202 Throttle valve switch

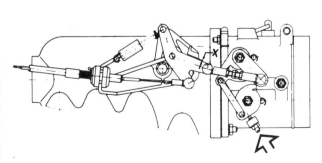

**Fig. 13.81 Throttle linkage (manual transmission) – LE-Jetronic (Sec 8)**

*Stop screw is arrowed*        X = 0.5 mm (0.020 in)

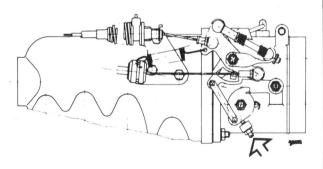

**Fig. 13.82 Throttle linkage (automatic transmission) – LE-Jetronic (Sec 8)**

*Stop screw is arrowed*

210 Release the wiring harness by disconnecting all the plugs and the earth connections. These include:

    *(a) Airflow sensor plug*
    *(b) Coolant temperature sensor*
    *(c) Fuel injectors*
    *(d) Throttle valve switch*
    *(e) Auxiliary air valve*
    *(f) Cam cover earth screw*

211 Disconnect the throttle cable from the throttle valve housing. Where the cable has a ball end, release it by removing the wire clip (photo). The end fitting of the cable outer can be released from its bracket by removing the E-clip. Where the cable has a cylindrical end and passes over a pulley arrangement, put slack in the cable inner by rotating the pulley against spring pressure and detach the cable end. Release the cable outer from its retaining bracket (photo).
212 Unscrew the throttle valve housing fixing nuts. The lower ones are difficult to reach, but present no problem to remove if a small socket or ring spanner is used.
213 Lift the throttle housing away (photo).
214 Peel off the flange gasket; renew it on reassembly.
215 Refitting is a reversal of removal, but note the wiring harness connections. Number 4 fuel injector is nearest the flywheel housing (photo).

### Throttle valve switch
216 Disconnect the three-pin wiring plug.
217 Unscrew the two mounting screws and pull the switch from the throttle valve spindle.
218 Refitting is a reversal of removal, but adjust the switch as described previously.

### Fuel pump
219 Refer to paragraphs 169 to 175 of this Section.

### Fuel filter
220 The fuel filter is adjacent to the fuel pump.
221 Clamp the fuel hoses to prevent loss of fuel when they are disconnected. Self-locking grips are useful for this. Disconnect the hoses and remove the filter.
222 Refitting is a reversal of removal. Observe the AUS (out) marking on the filter showing the direction of fuel flow (photo).

### Fuel injectors
223 Ensure that the engine is cool to eliminate the danger of fuel igniting. Do not smoke, and guard against external sources of ignition.
224 Release the hose clamps and pull the fuel distribution pipe from the hoses of the injectors. Catch as much fuel as possible.
225 Disconnect the wiring plug.
226 Unscrew the retaining bolts and withdraw the injector from its holder, taking care not to damage the needle valve.
227 Refitting is a reversal of removal, but renew the sealing rings if there is any doubt about their condition.

### Airflow sensor
228 The airflow sensor is attached to the inboard side of the air cleaner housing.
229 Pull the wiring harness plug from the airflow sensor. Release the securing band and remove the rubber trunking.
230 Release the toggle locks and remove the airflow sensor with the upper part of the air cleaner housing.
231 Unbolt the airflow sensor from the air cleaner housing.
232 Check the airflow sensor flap valve for free movement, without any jerkiness.

### Control unit
233 The control unit is attached to the side of the front footwell (right-hand side for UK models) behind the trim (photo).
234 With the trim detached, pull the plug from the unit top after

8.211A Throttle cable (ball end fittings)

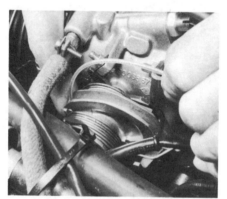

8.211B Throttle cable (cylindrical end fitting)

8.213 Throttle valve housing removed

8.222 Fuel filter

8.233 Fuel injection control unit

8.237 Coolant temperature sensor (LE-Jetronic)

8.240 Auxiliary air valve

8.245 Fuel injection control relay

8.248 Fuel pressure regulator

pressing aside its retaining spring. Remove the retaining screws and remove the unit.

235 Refitting is a reversal of removal. Check that the plug terminals are free from moisture before reconnecting.

### Coolant temperature sensor

236 Partially drain the cooling system, about 3 litres (5 pints) should be sufficient.

237 Disconnect the electrical lead and unscrew the sensor (photo).

238 Refitting is a reversal of removal.

239 Top up and bleed the cooling system as described in Chapter 2.

### Auxiliary air valve

240 This valve is located on the side of the camshaft housing/cylinder head (photo).

241 Pull the connecting plug from the valve.

242 Disconnect the hoses. Unscrew the two mounting bolts and remove the valve.

243 A check can be made on the serviceability of the valve by observing the regulator disc. With the valve cold, the disc should be open; with the valve hot (by connection to a 12V battery) the disc should be closed.

244 Refitting is a reversal of removal.

### Control relay

245 This relay may be located on the front suspension strut turret or the engine bay rear bulkhead (photo).

246 Pull the wiring plug and unclip the relay from its mounting.

247 Refitting is a reversal of removal.

### Fuel pressure regulator

248 The fuel pressure regulator is located between injectors 3 and 4 (photo).

249 Clamp the fuel hoses to prevent loss of fuel. Self-locking grips are useful for this.

250 Disconnect the fuel hoses and the vacuum hose from the pressure regulator.

251 Refitting is a reversal of removal.

### *Unleaded high octane petrol*

252 All models with 1.8 or 2.0 litre engines produced after 1980 may be successfully run on unleaded high octane (95 RON) petrol, noting the following guidelines:

*18S engine models: Unleaded fuel can be used at all times – retard the ignition timing by up to 5° if 'pinking' occurs*

*20S engine models, 1981 on: Use one tankful of leaded fuel after every five of unleaded – retard the ignition by 5° if 'pinking' occurs*

*20E engine models, up to February 1985: Use one tankful of leaded fuel after every five of unleaded – the ignition timing* **must** *be retarded 5°*

*20E engine models, March 1985 on: Unleaded fuel can be used at all times – the ignition timing* **must** *be retarded 5°*

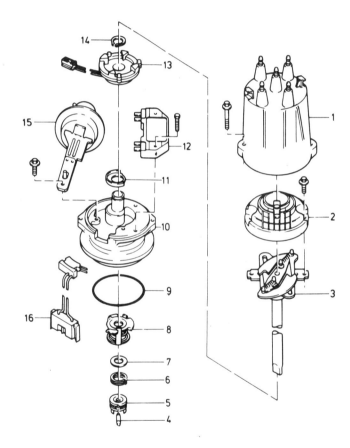

Fig. 13.83 Exploded view of AC Delco breakerless distributor (Sec 9)

| | | | |
|---|---|---|---|
| 1 | Distributor cap | 9 | O-ring |
| 2 | Rotor | 10 | Body |
| 3 | Shaft | 11 | Seal |
| 4 | Pin | 12 | Module |
| 5 | Drive dog | 13 | Induction sensor |
| 6 | Spring | 14 | Circlip |
| 7 | Washer | 15 | Vacuum unit |
| 8 | Spring | 16 | Plug |

## 9  Ignition system

### Electronic ignition system (all models)
#### Description
1   The electronic (breakerless) ignition system fitted to later models will be one of two types, either AC Delco or Bosch. Both systems are similar in that they require virtually no maintenance or adjustment.
2   The main components are a control unit, an ignition coil and a distributor.
3   Instead of the reluctor and pick-up on the AC Delco induction system, the Bosch system incorporates a permanent magnet, a detector/amplifier, and four vanes. When a vane is masking the detector/amplifier no voltage is induced in the detector, and under these conditions the control unit passes through the low tension windings of the coil.
4   Rotation of the distributor will uncover the detector and cause it to be influenced by the magnetic field of the permanent magnet. The Hall effect induces a small voltage in the detector plate which is then amplified and triggers the control unit to interrupt the low tension current in the coil.
5   The control unit in the Bosch system incorporates a circuit which switches off the low tension circuit if the time between consecutive signals exceeds 1.5 seconds. The coil and internal circuits are therefore protected if the ignition is left switched on inadvertently.
6   It is not recommended that this type of distributor is dismantled beyond the limits of the operations described in this Section.

#### Precautions
7   In view of the high voltage used in this system, care must be used when handling wiring or components with the ignition switched on. This is particularly important to anyone equipped with a cardiac pacemaker.
8   When cranking the engine with the HT leads disconnected – for example, when making a compression test – either disconnect the plug from the ignition control unit, or securely earth the coil HT terminal. If the coil is energised with the HT leads 'floating' there is a risk of insulation damage.
9   If it is wished to connect an independent tachometer to the breakerless ignition system, an adaptor cable may be needed in order to make contact with the ignition coil negative terminal (terminal 1, green lead). This is necessary if a completely insulated multiple plug is used to connect the coil into the ignition system.
10  When using such an adaptor cable, remember that dangerous voltages may be present at terminal 1. Always switch the ignition off before connecting or disconnecting equipment.

#### Ignition timing
11  Stroboscopic timing should be carried out as described in Chapter 4 (2.0 cih) or later in this Section (1.8 ohc).
12  Static timing as described in Chapter 4 is not possible with breakerless ignition. The position of the rotor arm stud when No 1 piston is firing is denoted by a mark on the rim of the distributor body.
13  Checking and adjusting the dwell angle is not required with breakerless distributors. The ignition timing itself should rarely need adjusting, except after overhaul or renewal of the distributor or related engine components.

#### Distributor removal and refitting
14  This procedure is as described in Chapter 4 (2.0 cih) or later in this Section (1.8 ohc).

#### Distributor dismantling and reassembly
15  Depending on the type of distributor, it will be obvious to what extent and by which method the distributor can be dismantled.
16  Detach the distributor cap, either by releasing its securing clips or by removing the Allen-headed screws.

17  Remove the rotor, after having removed its retaining screws or circlip.
18  Detach the wiring from the module.
19  Detach the vacuum unit by releasing its retaining screws. Remove the module.
20  Renew any defective components.
21  If a new module is being fitted, apply the silicone grease supplied with it between the module mounting base and the distributor body. Reassemble the distributor in conditions of utmost cleanliness.

#### Fault diagnosis
22  Total ignition failure or misfiring may be due to loose or disconnected wires or plugs, or to component malfunction. Misfiring may also be due to the same faults on the HT side as those described in Chapter 4, Section 12.
23  **Do not** remove plug caps whilst the engine is running in an attempt to locate a misfire. Personal electric shock and/or damage to the coil insulation may result.
24  Testing of the ignition system units should be left to a GM dealer or automobile electrician. Beware of haphazard testing by substitution – a fault in one component may damage other units.
25  If sealing compound is observed to have spilled from the coil cap, displacing the sealing plug, both the coil and the control unit should be renewed.
26  It is possible for the ignition system to malfunction when in close proximity to certain types of VHF radio transmitters. Consult your GM dealer if this is a problem.

### Electronic idle speed control (ISC) system (2.0 cih)
#### Description
27  From late 1982, GM have incorporated an ISC system in the electronic ignition system of vehicles fitted with the 2.0 cih engine. The ISC allows the engine to operate at its most efficient minimum idle speed whilst keeping the speed stable as electrical components are switched on.
28  Fig. 13.85 shows the layout of the ISC system. It operates as follows.
29  The signal emitted by the distributor is evaluated by the ISC which if necessary alters ignition timing to control engine speed. When engine load is increased, causing engine speed to drop, the ISC returns the engine speed to its previous setting.
30  It is possible to isolate the ISC from the ignition system so that in the event of component malfunction, the ISC can be prevented from adversely affecting ignition performance. To do this, simply unplug the two wiring connectors from the ISC unit and join them together.
31  On vehicles fitted with manual transmission and air conditioning, a vacuum switch in the ignition vacuum line isolates the ISC if the ignition vacuum rises beyond a certain level.

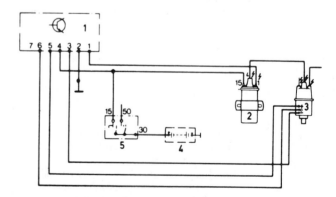

**Fig. 13.84 Schematic diagram of electronic ignition system. Lightning symbols denote high voltage (Sec 9)**

| | |
|---|---|
| 1   Control unit | 4   Battery |
| 2   Ignition coil | 5   Ignition switch |
| 3   Distributor | |

**Idle speed adjustment**

32 Before commencing adjustment, ensure that the ignition timing is correctly set and then run the engine until it reaches normal operating temperature.

33 On vehicles equipped with manual transmission, disconnect both wiring connectors from the ISC unit with the engine turned off. Join the connectors together and restart the engine. Adjust the idle speed to 700 to 750 rpm. Turn off the engine, reconnect both wiring connectors to the ISC and restart the engine. The ISC will automatically reset the idle speed to the correct value.

34 On vehicles equipped with automatic transmission, do not disconnect the ISC. Simply adjust the idle speed to the specified value.

**ISC unit test**

35 Obtain a timing light equipped with a timing indicator and connect it to the vehicle in accordance with the manufacturer's instructions.

36 Where the vehicle is equipped with manual transmission, check the ignition timing at idle speed. The timing must be seen to advance as electrical components such as the heated rear screen and headlights are switched on. If no timing change is apparent, fit a new ISC unit and retest.

37 Where the vehicle has automatic transmission, chock the wheels and apply the parking brake. Start the engine, allowing it to run at idle speed. Place the selector lever in 'D' and check the ignition timing, which must be more advanced than 5° BTDC. Select 'N' and check that the ignition timing has returned to 5° BTDC. If the test results do not correspond with those stated, renew the ISC unit and retest.

**Vacuum switch test**

38 In order to carry out this test, it is necessary to obtain a vacuum hand pump. If possible, hire or borrow this tool (no KM-J-23994-01) from your local GM dealer.

39 Disconnect the vacuum hose from the distributor and connect it to the vacuum pump. This hose must be in good condition and firmly connected to the carburettor stub. If in doubt, renew the hose before testing.

40 Fit a timing light equipped with a timing indicator. Start the engine and allow it to reach normal operating temperature. With the engine at idle, check the ignition timing which should be more advanced than 5° BTDC.

41 Operate the vacuum pump and apply approximately 150 mbar to the vacuum switch. The ignition timing should now return to 5° BTDC. If the test results do not indicate correct switch operation, substitute a new vacuum switch and retest.

*Temperature-controlled vacuum advance cut-out (2.0 cih)*

42 From mid 1983, GM have introduced a temperature-controlled vacuum advance cut-out system to vehicles fitted with the 2.0 cih engine and automatic transmission. This system reduces the nitrogen oxides (NOx) in the exhaust gases by inhibiting vacuum advance while the engine is cold. It does not function at ambient temperatures below 17°C (63°F).

43 The air temperature switch is located by the left-hand wing and the oil temperature switch on the oil pump.

*Distributor – removal and refitting (1.8 ohc)*

44 The distributor is mounted on the left-hand side of the cylinder head and is belt-driven from the front of the camshaft.

45 Gain access to the timing belt cover securing bolts by removing the appropriate cooling system components (fan belt, etc). Remove the covers. Mark the distributor body-to-engine alignment (photos).

46 Turn the engine so that the timing marks on the camshaft sprocket and distributor drivegear are aligned with the corresponding marks on the housing. The notch in the crankshaft pulley must also be aligned with the timing pointer on the oil pump housing (photos). These marks must remain aligned during the removal and refitting procedure.

47 Detach the distributor cap, and disconnect the distributor wiring (photos).

48 Unbolt the distributor body steady strut from the cylinder head. Disconnect the feed pipe from the vacuum advance unit (photo).

49 Remove the two distributor securing nuts and the steady strut.

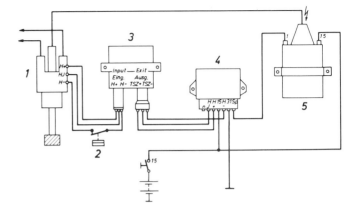

**Fig. 13.85 Idle speed control (ISC) system (Sec 9)**

| | |
|---|---|
| 1 Distributor | 4 Ignition control unit |
| 2 Vacuum switch | 5 Ignition coil |
| 3 ISC unit | |

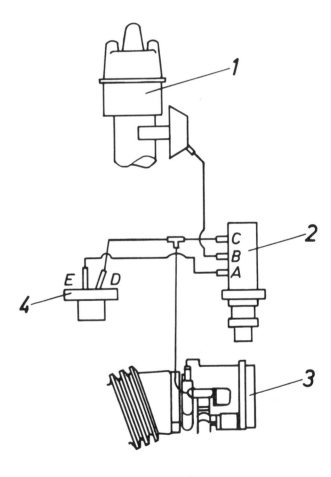

**Fig. 13.86 Hose routing – temperature controlled vacuum advance system (Sec 9)**

| | |
|---|---|
| 1 Distributor | 3 Carburettor/throttle valve |
| 2 Air temperature switch | (vacuum source) |
| | 4 Oil temperature switch |

9.45A Upper timing belt cover bolts

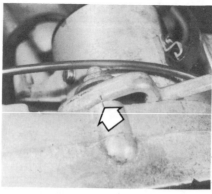

9.45B Mark the distributor body in relation to the housing

9.46A Camshaft sprocket and distributor drivegear alignment marks

9.46B Crankshaft pulley timing notch and pointer

9.47A Removing the distributor cap

9.47B Disconnecting the distributor wiring

9.48A Distributor body steady strut

9.48B Disconnecting the vacuum pipe

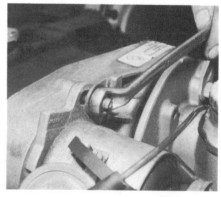

9.49A Unscrew the mounting nuts ...

9.49B ... release the toothed belt ...

9.49C ... and withdraw the distributor

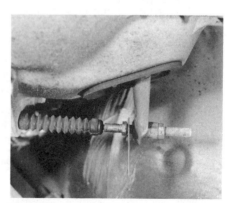

10.1 Clutch cable and fork on an 18S engine model

Pull the distributor carefully away from its mounting so that its drivegear slips free of the toothed belt. Remove the distributor (photos).
50 Refitting the distributor is a reversal of the removal procedure. Ensure that the distributor gear and camshaft sprocket are correctly aligned and that the distributor body is placed in its previously noted position before nipping tight the two securing nuts and fully tightening the steady strut-to-cylinder head bolt.
51 On completion of refitting, check the ignition timing as follows.

*Ignition timing – adjustment (1.8 ohc)*
52 Obtain a strobe light and connect it into the No 1 cylinder HT circuit, following the manufacturer's instructions. Dab a spot of white paint on the notch in the crankshaft pulley and on the corresponding pointer.
53 Run the engine at idling speed and point the strobe light at the timing marks. At idling speed the white paint marks should appear to be immediately opposite each other; open the throttle slightly and check that as the engine revolutions rise the spot on the crankshaft will move away from the pointer. This indicates the centrifugal advance mechanism is operating correctly.
54 If the timing marks do not line up under the strobe light, slightly slacken the distributor clamp nuts and carefully turn the distributor in its location to bring the marks into line. Retighten the clamp nuts.

*Retarding the ignition timing (for unleaded fuel)*
55 When using unleaded high octane fuel, the ignition timing may be retarded in the following way.
56 Turn the engine by means of the crankshaft pulley bolt, or by engaging top gear and pulling the car forward, until No 1 piston is at TDC on the firing stroke. This can be felt by removing No 1 spark plug and feeling for compression with your fingers as the engine is turned.
57 Make a mark on the crankshaft pulley in alignment with the timing mark, or pointer, on the engine.
58 On all engines except the 18S and 20E, this mark indicates 5° ignition retardation, and using this, adjust the ignition timing as described in Chapter 4, Section 8, retarding up to 5° as required.
59 On the 18S and 20E engines, the original pulley mark indicates 10° BTDC, and the new mark TDC; 5° ignition retardation, therefore, is central between the two.
60 Make a new timing mark on the crankshaft pulley, and adjust the ignition timing as described earlier in this Section (18S), or in Chapter 4, Section 8, using a stroboscopic timing method (20E).

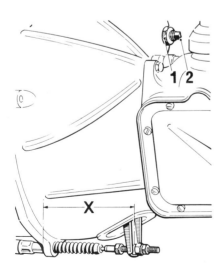

**Fig. 13.87 Clutch adjustment showing later cable with adjusting nuts for pedal height setting (Sec 10)**

| | |
|---|---|
| *1  Locknut* | *X  =  4.29 in (109 mm)* |
| *2  Pivot bolt* | |

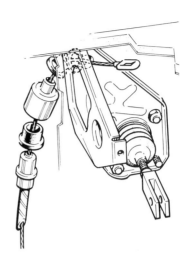

**Fig. 13.88 Clutch cable (pedal end) on later type (Sec 10)**

---

## 10  Clutch

*Clutch adjustment (later models)*
1  A revised clutch fork and cable were introduced on the 16S (1584 cc) models at engine No 492233 and in the 19S (1897 cc) models at engine No 1536240. All 20S (1979 cc) and 18S (1796 cc) models have the revised clutch assembly (photo).
2  The new clutch fork and cable can be installed on earlier vehicles, but it is necessary to use both parts together.
3  The adjustment of the clutch fork is identical to that described in Chapter 5, Section 2, and dimension 'X' (Fig. 13.87) is as given in Chapter 5, Fig. 5.2. However it is emphasised that this dimension must be achieved only by adjusting the ballstud bolt. Do not attempt to obtain dimension 'X' by using the adjuster nut at the clutch fork end of the cable.

*Clutch cable – renewal and adjustment (later models)*
4  The later type of clutch cable has an upper end which is non-adjustable (Fig. 13.88) and pedal adjustment is obtained by means of a screwed adjuster at the clutch fork end.
5  The method of renewing the cable is similar to that described in Chapter 3. First unhook the eye of the cable from the pedal end. Provided that the clutch pedal height is not too great, the pedal can be raised sufficiently to unhook the cable.
6  Remove the cable in similar manner to that for the non-adjustable cable.
7  Install a new cable as for the non-adjustable type and then adjust pedal height as follows.

**Pedal travel adjustment**
8  To ensure correct pedal travel, measure from the centre of the clutch pedal pad to the outer edge of the steering wheel (Fig. 13.89) and note this dimension 'B'.
9  Depress the clutch pedal fully, and while holding it depressed, again measure the distance from the centre of the pedal pad to the outside edge of the steering wheel. This dimension should be B + 5.9 in (B + 150 mm) and is the minimum distance which will ensure sufficient travel of the clutch fork to disengage the clutch fully.
10  The dimensions in paragraphs 8 and 9 can also be made using the front edge of the driver's seat as a datum.
11  If necessary turn the adjuster at the release lever end of the cable to achieve the correct dimension. Note that the released position of the clutch pedal is higher than that of the brake pedal. Also when correctly adjusted the distance between the clutch pedal and the pedal travel warning switch should be between 25.0 and 35.0 mm (0.98 and 1.38 in).

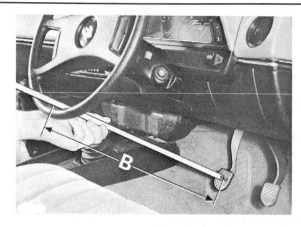

**Fig. 13.89 Checking clutch pedal travel adjustment (Sec 10)**

*Measure dimension B*

## Clutch assembly – modification
12  From mid-1983, GM have fitted a plastic thrust ring to the centre of the clutch spring. This prevents whirring noises emitting from the thrust bearing during clutch operation.
13  Fitting of the thrust ring will also reduce wear on the spring lugs, so it is a good idea to include its fitting as part of the clutch overhaul on pre-1983 vehicles.
14  When fitting a thrust ring, refer to Figs. 13.90 and 13.91 and fit the ring from the outside of the spring as shown, making sure that its retaining ring is correctly seated beneath the hooks.

## Clutch pressure plate (February 1987 on) – 1.8 ohc models
15  All Manta models with the 18S engine produced after February 1987 are equipped with a different clutch pressure plate, which requires the use of special tool KM-632 for removal and refitting. If this tool is not used, removal/refitting will result in damage to the internal spring tongues of the pressure plate. This tool bolts to the engine block, and depresses the clutch pressure plate during removal and refitting. It should be used in conjunction with clamps KM-526-A.

## 11  Manual gearbox (five speed)

### Removal and refitting
1    The procedure is similar to that described in Chapter 6, Section 2, however an outline of the work involved is given in the following paragraphs.
2    Raise the front of the car and support on axle stands. Apply the handbrake.
3    Remove the centre console (Section 16).
4    With neutral selected prise the gear lever boot from the flange and push it through the aperture.
5    Remove the propeller shaft (Chapter 7).
6    Disconnect the exhaust downpipe and the engine earth strap.
7    Unbolt the clutch cover plate.
8    Unbolt the underbody splash shield.
9    Disconnect the clutch cable, speedometer cable and reverse light switch wiring.
10  Support the gearbox with a trolley jack then unbolt the mounting crossmember from the underbody (photo).
11  Prise a block of wood between the engine sump and the steering gear then lower the gearbox.
12  Unscrew the nuts securing the gearchange rod to the bracket then remove the bolt securing the bracket to the gearbox.
13  Push back the spring sleeve and drive out the roll pin from the gearchange joint. The gearchange rod and bracket can now be removed.
14  Remove the gearbox-to-engine bolts and withdraw the gearbox.
15  Refitting is a reversal of removal with reference also to Chapter 6.

### Dismantling
16  Clean and dry the exterior of the gearbox. Position the unit on a firm, clean work surface, and drain the oil (photo).
17  Examine the rubber mounting bushes for deterioration. Renew any damaged bush. Should a bush seize in its housing, do not attempt to hammer the bush from position, but leave it to soak in releasing fluid for a time and then pull it from position with a tool made from a bolt, sleeve and washers as shown in Fig. 13.96.
18  Before fitting new mounting bushes, clean and lightly grease their housings to aid insertion. Pull them into position with the same tool as used for removal.
19  Remove the speedometer drive assembly retaining plate and nut. Using the flat of a screwdriver, carefully lever the drive assembly out of its location.
20  Unbolt the mounting bracket from the upper rear section of the transmission casing. It may prove difficult to release the bracket retaining bolts because of the locking compound applied to their threads during assembly.
21  Remove the spring sleeve from the end of the selector rod, followed by the retaining pin and joint.
22  Refer to Chapter 5 and remove the clutch release bearing and fork from the bellhousing. Renew the bellhousing gaiters if split or perished.

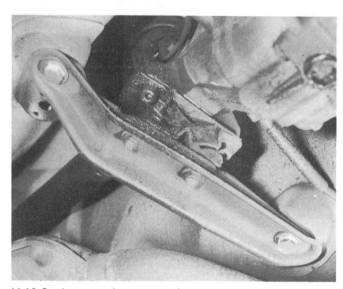

11.10 Gearbox mounting crossmember

11.16 Using a key and spanner to remove the gearbox drain plug

Fig. 13.90 Plastic thrust ring being fitted to clutch diaphragm spring – arrows show hooks (Sec 10)

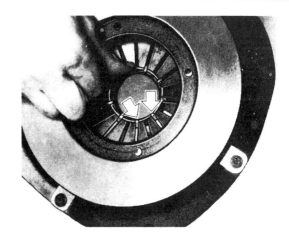

Fig. 13.91 The retaining ring engages the hooks (arrowed) (Sec 10)

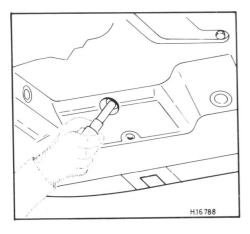

Fig. 13.92 Removing the underbody splash shield (Sec 11)

Fig. 13.93 Gearchange bracket bolt locations (Sec 11)

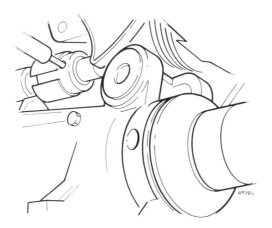

Fig. 13.94 Removing the roll pin from the gearchange joint (Sec 11)

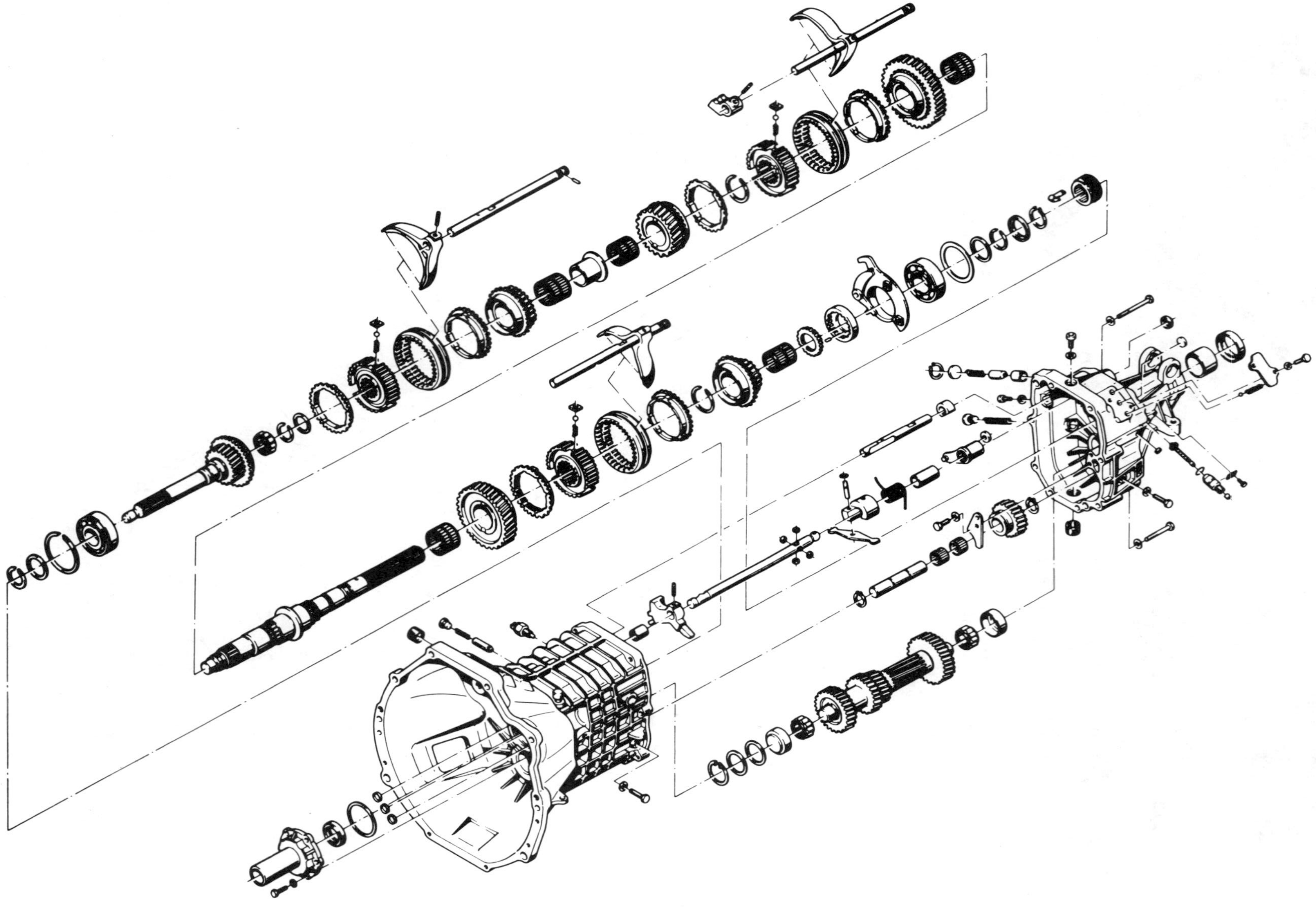

Fig. 13.95 Exploded view of five-speed gearbox (Sec 11)

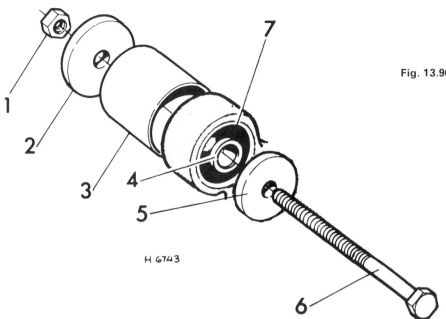

**Fig. 13.96 Mounting bush removal (Sec 11)**

1 Nut
2 Washer
3 Tube or socket
4 Brush inner
5 Washer
6 Bolt
7 Bush outer

H 6743

23 Remove the reverse light switch from the front section of the gearbox casing.

24 Pull the detent plug from the gearbox casing with a pair of pincers as shown in Fig. 13.97. Hook the detent spring and pin from their location.

25 Unbolt the clutch release bearing guide sleeve from the centre of the bellhousing and pull it off the input shaft. Retain the spacer ring(s).

26 Using a pair of circlip pliers, remove the retaining ring from the input shaft, followed by the spacer ring.

27 Release the two halves of the gearbox casing by removing the securing bolts. Note the fitted position of these bolts, making up a cardboard template if necessary. Drive the dowel pins slightly back into the casing front half.

28 Before attempting to separate the casing halves, remove the mounting bolts for the reverse idler gear shaft. With the casing rear half held in position, use a soft-faced hammer to separate the front half from it. Strike only on reinforced areas of the casing.

29 Upon separation, all gearbox internals should remain within the casing rear half. Support this casing half on the work surface.

30 Remove the three support plate mounting bolts shown in Fig. 13.98. Note that the bolts are of different lengths and must be refitted in their original locations.

31 Unbolt the reverse idler gear retaining plate. Support the shaft and remove the retaining plate. Remove the reverse idler gear and shaft, noting its fitted position.

32 Support the casing so that the shafts are vertical (open side uppermost). Remove the 5th gear detent retaining screw and the detent spring.

33 Remove the circlip which retains the reverse gear detent plug in position. Push the plug away from the circlip during removal. Spring pressure behind the plug will cause it to be ejected unless care is taken. Remove the plug, spring and detent pin.

34 Withdraw the transfer lever retaining pin. Note the fitted position of the lever and remove it.

35 Pull the selector rail from its end support in the casing. Unscrew the support retaining bolt and remove the support.

36 Support the adjacent selector rod (5th/reverse) with a block of

**Fig. 13.97 Removing the detent plug with a pair of pincers (Sec 11)**

B 7507

**Fig. 13.98 Support plate mounting bolts – arrowed bolt is 65 mm long (Sec 11)**

hardwood as shown in Fig. 13.99. Using a parallel pin punch, drive the retaining pin from the selector fork. Check that the fork moves independently of the rod. Detach the rod end support from the casing by removing its retaining bolt. Ease the rod assembly clear of the gearbox, taking care to retain the bearing rollers on the rod end.
37 Carefully release the selector rocker spring tension and withdraw the rocker assembly from the casing.
38 Unbolt the detent retaining plate from the casing. This plate will most likely be stuck in position with sealing compound, in which case it should be carefully levered free. The compound may also prevent the detent springs from popping free of the casing, in which case any dried compound must be removed before the springs are hooked free.
39 Place the end of a parallel pin punch against the edge of the 3rd/4th selector rod end cap. Strike the punch so that the cap is tilted through 90°. Remove the cap (photo).
40 Support the free end of the 3rd/4th selector rod and drive the selector fork retaining pin from position. Check the fork is free of the rod.
41 Using a soft metal drift, carefully drive the selector rod forward 20 mm (0.80 in). Doing this will release the detent balls which must be retained.
42 Support the casing so that the shafts are horizontal and the shaft ends readily accessible. GM now recommend that the casing around the mainshaft end be heated to approximately 80° C (176° F) to free the bearing. Place the casing in an oven or immerse it in boiling water. Do not use a naked flame or localised and excessive heat because of the risk of warping the casing.
43 With the casing heated and well supported, use a large soft metal drift and hammer to drive the mainshaft free. Remove the gearbox internals as an assembly and place them on a clean work surface. Retain any detent balls that fall from the casing, also the bearing spacer.

### Component examination

44 The principles for component examination are given in Section 4 of Chapter 6. Ignore any specific references to the 4-speed gearbox and note the following points.
45 The methods of measuring selector fork end wear and synchromesh ring wear are shown in the accompanying photographs. Wear limits are given in the Specifications.
46 If the reverse idler gear is not to be removed from the casing, then its clearance with the retaining plate must be checked before the casing halves are rejoined. See paragraph 101.
47 Should it prove necessary to renew bearings or spacers in either casing half, unless the job is obviously straightforward, entrust the task to your GM dealer who will have any special tools and replacement parts needed.

### Input shaft – dismantling and reassembly

48 It is not possible to dismantle the input shaft other than to remove the caged roller bearing from its end; this bearing should slip from position quite easily. If any one bearing surface is worn or damaged, renew the shaft complete (photo).

### Layshaft – renewal

49 The layshaft is machined as one solid assembly. If damage or excessive wear is apparent then the shaft must be renewed as a whole.

### Mainshaft – dismantling and reassembly

50 Using the flat of a small screwdriver, displace the speedometer drivegear retaining clip. Pull the gear off the shaft.
51 With the shaft vertical, place its splined end between the protected jaws of a vice and clamp it in position. Remove the 3rd/4th gear synchromesh bodies retaining circlip.
52 Remove the spacer. Remove the 3rd/4th gear synchromesh bodies, if necessary levering them from position with two screwdrivers positioned opposite to each other. Take care to keep the bodies together during removal, otherwise the springs and balls will be released.
53 Remove the synchromesh ring, the 3rd speed gear and the needle roller bearing assembly.
54 Pull the 2nd gear pinion and centre bush off the shaft (photo).
55 Remove the needle roller bearing followed by the synchromesh

**Fig. 13.99 Support the rod with a piece of wood and drive the pin out of the fork (Sec 11)**

ring. Do not allow any of the synchromesh rings to become interchanged.
56 Remove the 1st/2nd gear synchromesh bodies retaining circlip and remove the bodies, synchromesh ring, pinion and needle roller bearing.
57 Invert the mainshaft in the vice. Using circlip pliers, remove the first of the two circlips.
58 Remove the lockwasher by carefully levering it from position with the flat of a screwdriver. Remove the second circlip and the spacer.
59 Pull the bearing from the shaft end.
60 Using the flat of a large screwdriver, lever the torsion ring from position, taking care to retain the locating pin.
61 Remove the shaft support plate. Unscrew the thrust nut. Remove the 5th gear pinion/synchromesh ring and the needle roller bearing. Note that this bearing can be separated on one side to allow removal (photo).
62 Remove the 5th/reverse gear synchromesh bodies retaining circlip and carefully lever the bodies from position.
63 Remove the synchromesh ring, the reverse gear pinion and the needle roller bearing.
64 If dismantling the synchromesh bodies, keep each one separate to avoid mixing the component parts. To dismantle each body, carefully slide the outer sleeve off the hub, taking care to retain the springs, balls and slides.
65 Fatigued or broken springs will necessitate renewal. All springs must be of equal length. Renew worn slides or balls as a set (photo).
66 When reassembling a synchromesh body, take care fitting the slides; check that each one moves freely in its location and has its concave (or stepped) side facing outwards. Fit the springs and use one hand to hold all three in position.
67 Align the outer sleeve with the hub so that the recesses between the sleeve splines coincide with those of the hub (photo). Push the sleeve over the hub so that the slides and springs are retained in position. Place the assembly on the work surface and ease the sleeve back just enough for each ball to be fitted. With the balls fitted, fully align the sleeve and hub, checking that each slide is free to move.
68 Reassemble the mainshaft in conditions of absolute cleanliness. Lightly lubricate each bearing surface with the recommended gearbox oil.
69 With the shaft vertical, clamp its splined end between the protected jaws of a vice. Fit the needle roller bearing, 1st gear pinion and synchromesh ring (photos).
70 Fit the 1st/2nd gear synchromesh bodies so that the sleeve flange is uppermost. Fit the retaining circlip so that it is properly located in its groove. If necessary, tap the synchromesh bodies fully home using a length of metal tube of the appropriate diameter (photo).
71 Fit the synchromesh ring and the needle roller bearing. Using a method described earlier, heat the 2nd gear pinion and centre bush. Fit the pinion and bush over the shaft, tapping each component into position with a length of metal tube. The bush flange must face the pinion (photos).

11.39 Selector rod end cap

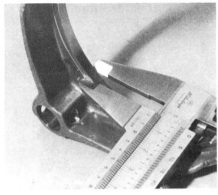

11.45A Measuring selector fork thickness

11.45B Measuring synchro ring-to-teeth clearance

11.48 Input shaft roller bearing

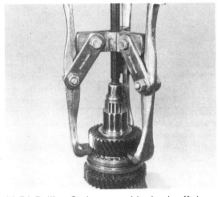

11.54 Pulling 2nd gear and its bush off the shaft

11.61 5th gear needle roller bearing

11.65 Synchro unit spring, ball and slide

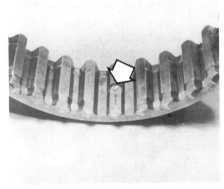

11.67 Synchro sleeve spine recess (arrowed)

11.69A 1st gear needle roller bearing ...

11.69B ... 1st gear pinion ...

11.69C ... and synchromesh ring

11.70 Using a piece of tube to fit 1st/2nd synchro body

11.71A Fitting 2nd gear synchro ring ...

11.71B ... 2nd gear bearing ...

11.71C ... 2nd gear pinion and bush

72 Fit the needle roller bearing, the 3rd gear pinion and the synchromesh ring. Push the 3rd/4th gear synchromesh bodies onto the shaft with the smaller central flange uppermost. Fit the spacer and retaining circlip. Check that the circlip is properly located in its groove (photos).

73 Invert the mainshaft in the vice. Fit the needle roller bearing, the reverse gear pinion and the synchromesh ring (photos).

74 Fit the 5th/reverse gear synchromesh bodies, taking care to align it correctly with the ring. Use a length of metal tube to tap the bodies home. Fit the retaining circlip (photos).

75 Fit the split needle roller bearing. Fit the synchromesh ring and the 5th gear pinion (photos). Screw the thrust nut onto the shaft finger tight, with the punch mark uppermost.

76 Select a 0.05 to 0.10 mm (0.002 to 0.004 in) feeler gauge and insert it between the underside of the nut and the 5th gear pinion.

Using finger pressure only, tighten the nut onto the gauge until the gauge can just be slid clear (photo).

77 Taking care not to move the nut, fit the torsion ring and retain it in position with the locating pin. Slight movement of the nut to allow ring alignment is permitted (photo).

78 Fit the shaft support plate with its centre flange uppermost. Position the bearing on the shaft end with its closed side uppermost. Keeping the bearing square to the shaft, use a length of metal tube of the same diameter as the bearing inner race to tap it into position (photo).

79 Fit the spacer, circlip, lockwasher and second circlip. Slide the speedometer drivegear retaining clip into the shaft groove and push the gear over it (photos). Reassembly of the mainshaft is now complete.

11.72A 3rd gear bearing ...

11.72B ... 3rd gear pinion ...

11.72C ... 3rd gear synchro ring ...

11.72D ... 3rd/4th synchro body ...

11.72E ... spacer and circlip

11.73A Reverse gear bearing ...

11.73B ... reverse gear pinion and synchro ring

11.74A Fitting 5th/reverse synchro body

11.74B 5th/reverse synchro secured with its circlip

11.75A 5th gear split bearing

11.75B 5th gear synchro ring and pinion

11.76 Tighten the nut onto the feeler blade

11.77 Nut secured with torsion ring and pin

11.78 Fitting the mainshaft bearing

11.79A Fit the spacer, circlip and lockwasher ...

11.79B ... and the second circlip

11.79C Speedometer drivegear clip

11.79D Speedometer drivegear

## Reassembly

80  Prior to reassembly, measure the total thickness of the mainshaft support plate and bearing. Note the measurement for future reference (photo).

81  Obtain two equal lengths of threaded rod. Each rod must screw securely into the holes provided in the support plate and should be of sufficient length to reach the mainshaft end (photo). GM provide these rods (known as guide pins) as tool No KM-442.

82  Fit the rods to the mainshaft support plate and then assemble the selector mechanisms to the mainshaft as shown in Fig. 13.100. Place the assembly on a clean piece of rag or paper to avoid contamination. Fit the input shaft to the mainshaft, making sure that the synchro ring and roller bearing are fitted (photo).

83  It is now necessary to determine the amount of mainshaft axial play. Measure the depth of the mainshaft bearing housing in the casing rear half (photo). With this measurement noted, subtract the thickness of support plate and bearing, noted earlier, from it. The resulting measurement will equal the thickness of the bearing spacer required. Spacers are available in thicknesses of 0.3 mm (0.012 in), 0.4 mm (0.016 in) and 0.5 mm (0.020 in).

84  Prepare the rear casing half by removing the selector rod seal (if not already done) with the flat of a screwdriver.

85  The housing for the five detent balls must be checked for cleanliness. Remove any hardened sealing compound. Ensure that

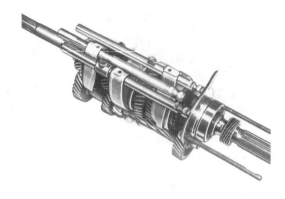

Fig. 13.100 Geartrains and selector components ready for refitting (Sec 11)

11.80 Measuring the thickness of the mainshaft support plate and bearing

11.81 Threaded rods screwed into the support plate

11.82 Synchro ring and bearing must be in position before input shaft is fitted to mainshaft

11.83 Measuring the depth of the mainshaft bearing housing

each ball can be pressed into position from the outside of the casing. If the holes appear too small, deburr their ends with a large drill (twisting by hand) until the balls enter freely.

86 Heat the casing as previously described around the mainshaft bearing housing. Fit the bearing spacer (photo). Support the casing upright in a vice.

87 Clasping the input shaft/mainshaft/selector mechanism/layshaft assembly in two hands, guide the support plate rods through the casing holes provided. Push the assembly into the casing, checking that the rods remain parallel (photo).

88 Keep a constant check on component alignment when fitting the gearbox internals. If it proves impossible to push the mainshaft bearing home by hand, fit nuts and plain washers to the rod ends and tighten each nut evenly, a little at a time, to pull the bearing into its housing. Ensure the mainshaft remains vertical and do not place excessive force on the nuts. Check for free rotation of both shafts during fitting.

89 With the mainshaft correctly fitted, remove one of the guide rods and replace it with the correct support plate mounting bolt. The bolt threads must be coated with locking compound. Remove the second guide rod and fit the remaining two bolts. Tighten each bolt to the specified torque.

90 Refer to Fig. 13.101 and fit the five detent balls as shown, smearing each one with grease so that it remains in position (photo). Use a small screwdriver to insert the middle two balls.

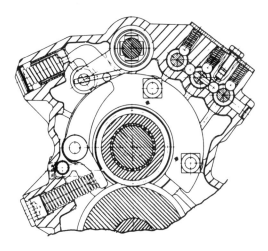

**Fig. 13.101 Sectional view of detent balls and springs (Sec 11)**

11.86 Fitting the mainshaft bearing spacer

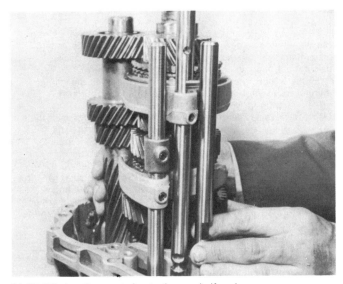

11.87 Offering the geartrains to the rear half casing

11.90A Fitting a detent ball

11.90B Pin in central selector rod

Manoeuvre the selector rods as necessary and remember to fit the pin into the centre rod (photo).

91 With all detent balls fitted and selector rods in position, insert the three springs. Coat the mating face of the retaining plate with sealing compound and bolt it in position (photo).

92 Refit the selector rocker assembly into the casing and using a pair of self-locking or flat-nosed pliers, tension the spring so that its end locks into the casing (photos). Push the spring end fully home with a screwdriver.

93 Fit the selector rod end support over the rocker assembly and fit its retaining bolt (photo). Coat the ball threads and shank with sealing compound.

94 Fit the selector rod through its end support and fork from the rear of the casing, ensuring that the end bearing rollers are all in position (photo). With the rod pushed fully home, secure the fork to it with the retaining pin, after having checked that the cut-outs in the shaft end are facing away from the group of three selector rods. The retaining pin must be fitted flush to the fork (photo).

95 Check that the other three selector forks are all secured to their rods; again, each retaining pin must be fitted flush to the fork.

96 Fit the selector rail end support into the casing (photo). The support retaining bolt must have its threads and shank coated with sealing compound before fitting. Tighten the bolt to the specified torque.

97 Push the selector rail into its end support, at the same time easing the transfer lever into position with its marked end toward the rail. Fit the lever retaining pin (photo).

98 Fit the reverse gear detent pin, spring and plug. Using a bar to hold the plug down against spring pressure, fit the circlip and ensure that it is fully home in its groove by placing the socket against it and tapping lightly with a hammer (photos).

99 Fit the 5th gear detent spring. Coat the threads of the spring retaining plug with sealing compound before fitting (photo). Tighten the plug to the specified torque.

100 Fit the reverse idler gear, tilting it slightly to clear the mainshaft pinion. Fit the shaft, complete with needle roller bearings and circlips, into the gear. If fitting the original shaft, place it in its originally noted position (photo). Coat the threads of the shaft-to-casing securing bolt with sealing compound. Align the shaft, fit the bolt and tighten it to the specified torque (photo).

101 Bolt the reverse idler gear retaining plate in position, finger tight. Obtain a narrow feeler gauge of 0.1 mm (0.004 in) thickness and insert it between the plate and pinion groove (photo). With the gauge a good sliding fit, tighten the plate retaining bolt to the specified torque. Recheck the clearance.

102 Fit the caged roller bearing, flanged end uppermost, to the layshaft end (photo).

103 Check the mating surface of each casing half for cleanliness and coat the surface of the assembled half with sealing compound. Make a final check to ensure the gearbox internals are correctly fitted and (where applicable) free to move. Lightly lubricate each bearing surface.

104 Align the casing front half over the shaft ends and push it down onto the rear half until the mating surfaces touch. Do not attempt to force the casing halves together or draw them together with the bolts. If unsuccessful, realign the front half and try again. Fit the casing bolts in their previously noted positions; the topmost right-hand bolt is the longest. Tighten the bolts a little at a time, working diagonally to avoid possible distortion, to the specified torque. Resite the dowel pins so that they are correctly positioned.

105 Fit the second of the reverse idler gear shaft securing bolts, coating its threads with sealing compound and tightening it to the specified torque.

106 If removed, refit the selector rod end covers so that they are flush with the casing (photo). These three covers are within the bellhousing.

107 It is now necessary to fit the spacer and retaining ring to the input shaft so that when fitted, the spacer prevents the ring from rotating. To do this, pull the shaft forward against its bearing, insert the outer edge of the ring into its groove and insert the spacer between it and the bearing inner race. Spacers are available in thicknesses of 2.3 mm (0.091 in), 2.4 mm (0.094 in), 2.5 mm (0.098 in) and 2.6 mm (0.102 in). Select a spacer which is a good firm fit and slide it over the shaft. Fit the retaining ring into its groove and check that it cannot be rotated (photo).

108 Before fitting the clutch release bearing guide sleeve over the

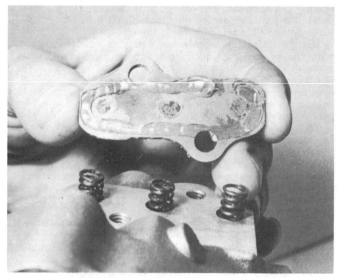
11.91 Fitting the detent spring retaining plate

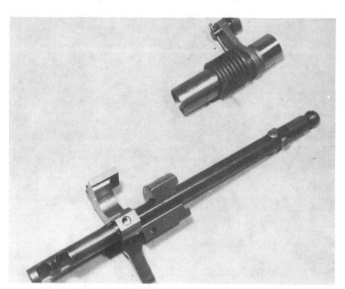
11.92A Selector rocker assembly

11.92B Selector rocker spring in casing

11.93 Tightening the selector rod end support retaining lock

11.94A Fitting the selector rod

11.94B Secure the fork to the rod with the pin

11.96 Selector rail end support (arrowed)

11.97 Selector rail and transfer lever fitted

11.98A Reverse detent components

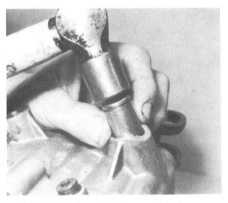

11.98B Settle the circlip by tapping the socket

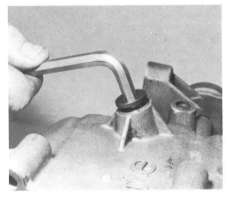

11.99 5th gear detent plug

11.100A Reverse idler shaft components

11.100B Fitting the reverse idler shaft

11.101 Feeler blade inserted between plate and groove

11.102 Layshaft bearing in position

11.106 Selector rod end covers

11.107 Input shaft spacer and retaining ring fitted

input shaft, determine the spacer ring thickness required. Do this by first measuring the distance between the bearing outer race and the casing-to-sleeve mating face (photo) (value W). Now measure the distance between the bearing surface of the sleeve flange and its lip edge (photo) (value X). Finally, measure the distance between the flange lip and its mating surface with the casing (photo) (value Y). Subtract Y from X and add W to the result to determine the total spacer thickness.

109 Spacer rings are available in thicknesses of 1.3 mm (0.052 in), 1.4 mm (0.055 in) and 1.5 mm (0.059 in). The maximum permissible axial play is 0.05 mm (0.002 in). Before fitting the selected ring(s), coat each one with grease.

110 Push the spacer rings(s) into the sleeve flange (photo). Coat the flange-to-casing mating surface with sealing compound, also the threads of the retaining bolts. Align the recess in the flange lip with the oilway in the casing and fit the guide sleeve. Tighten the retaining bolts evenly to the specified torque.

111 Fit the detent pin into the casing front half. The end roller of the pin must be parallel to the top surface of the gearbox. Fit the

11.108A Measuring the distance from the bearing outer race to the sleeve mating face

11.108B Measuring the distance from the sleeve bearing surface to the lip edge

11.108C Measuring the distance from the sleeve mating surface to the lip edge

11.110 Guide sleeve and spacer ring

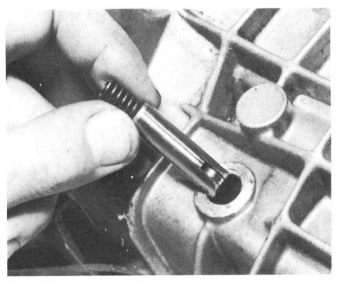

11.111A Fitting the detent pin ...

11.111B ... and its plug

11.112 Fitting the reverse light switch

spring and tap the plug home with a soft-faced hammer (photos).
112 Screw the reverse light switch into the casing front half, smearing a little sealing compound around its mating surface with the casing (photo).
113 Move to the rear of the gearbox and fit a new selector rod seal. Lightly grease the seal lip and outer edge before fitting and use a length of metal tube of the appropriate diameter to tap it home (photo).
114 Refit the joint, retaining pin and spring sleeve to the selector rod end (photo).
115 Refit the 3rd/4th selector rod end cap so that it is flush with the casing.
116 Bolt the mounting bracket to the upper rear section of gearbox casing. Coat the bolt threads with locking compound before fitting.
117 Renew the O-ring on the speedometer drive housing and smear it lightly with grease. Push the drive assembly into the casing and retain it with the plate and nut.
118 Refit the clutch release bearing and fork, with serviceable gaiters. Smear the bearing guide sleeve and input shaft splines with a molybdenum disulphide based grease.
119 Replenish the gearbox with the specified oil (photo). Reassembly of the gearbox is now complete.

11.113 Fitting the selector rod oil seal

11.114 The selector rod joint

11.119 Using the special key to unscrew the gearbox filler plug

## 12 Propeller shaft

*Forward section propeller shaft – removal and refitting*
1   On some models the forward section propeller shaft is attached to the pinion flange by two U-bolts instead of four conventional bolts. In this case the pinion flange is in the form of a split yoke for location of the two spider trunnions.
2   Removal and refitting of the propeller shaft is similar to that described in Chapter 7. Use a screwdriver to lever out the U-bolts, and when refitting them bend them as necessary so that they enter the split yoke holes freely. It is recommended that the locking tab plates are renewed whenever the propeller shaft is removed.

## 13 Braking system

*Front brake pads (floating caliper) – renewal*
1   Apply the handbrake, chock the rear wheels and jack up the

front of the car. Support the car securely on axle stands, then mark the relative position of the roadwheel to the hub; remove the roadwheel.
2   Drive out the brake pad retaining pins. **Note:** *Drive the retaining pins from the inside to the outside, and take care not to lose the spreader springs.*
3   Remove the outer brake pad followed by the inner one (which may require more effort that the outer pad) (photos). A special puller is available from the manufacturers, but this can be substituted by a piece of wire hooked through the holes for the brake pad retaining pins and pulled with a pair of pliers.
4   To fit replacement pads, insert a thin metal bar and carefully wedge open a gap sufficiently wide to insert a pad. Remove the cap from the brake master cylinder first however, as the brake fluid level will rise in the reservoir when the piston is moved back. It may be necessary to draw off some of the brake fluid to prevent it overflowing into the engine compartment.
5   The remainder of the procedure is the reverse of that adopted when removing the pads, however after completion depress the

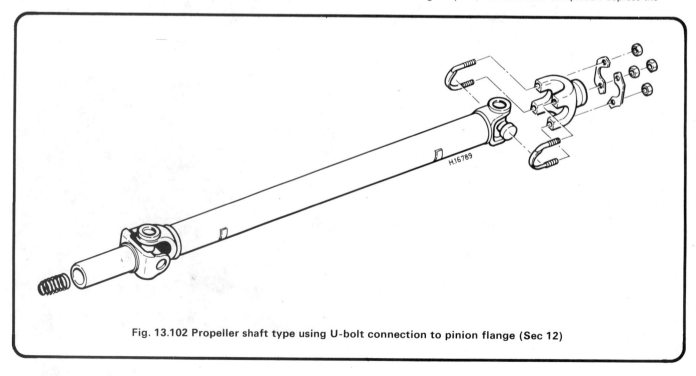

Fig. 13.102 Propeller shaft type using U-bolt connection to pinion flange (Sec 12)

13.3A Removing the outer brake pad

13.3B Removing the inner brake pad

13.5A Fitting the lower retaining pin ...

13.5B ... and upper retaining pin together with spreader springs

13.5C Front brake pads correctly fitted

13.9 Front brake caliper showing hose and union bolt

footbrake pedal several times to set the pads in their normal position (photos).

### Front brake caliper (floating type) – removal and refitting

6  Apply the handbrake, chock the rear wheels and jack up the front of the car. Support the car securely on axle stands, then mark the relative position of the roadwheel to the hub; remove the roadwheel.
7  Wipe the top of the brake fluid reservoir, unscrew the cap and place a thin sheet of polythene over the top. Refit the cap. This precaution should prevent leakage of fluid from the system when subsequently dismantled.
8  Remove the front brake pads as previously described.
9  Disconnect the hydraulic fluid hose by unscrewing the hollow union bolt (photo). Recover the sealing washers.
10  Extract the metal rings from the caps covering the two caliper mounting bolts using a small chisel if necessary.
11  Prise off the caps using a screwdriver.
12  Next, unscrew the caliper mounting bolts from the steering knuckle using an Allen key. The brake caliper can now be removed.
13  Refitting is a reversal of the above procedure (photo). Use new washers for the brake hose connection, and tighten the union bolt in the position shown in Fig. 13.106. Tighten the mounting bolts to the specified torque and after completion bleed the hydraulic system as described in Chapter 9.

### Front brake caliper (GMF floating type) – overhaul

14  With the caliper removed clean the external surfaces.
15  Using a chisel, release the sliding sleeve inner dust caps from the caliper housing.
16  Prise off the piston dust excluder.
17  Apply pressure to the outboard ends of the sliding sleeves until their dust caps can be disengaged from the sleeve grooves and removed.

18  Press the sliding sleeves from the caliper housing.
19  Place a thin piece of wood or hardboard on the end of the piston and apply air pressure to the fluid pipe connection on the caliper body. Only low air pressure will be required to eject the piston, such as is generated by a tyre foot pump.
20  Once the piston has been removed, pick out the seal from its groove in the cylinder, using a plastic or wooden instrument.
21  Inspect the surfaces of the piston and cylinder bore for scoring or evidence of metal-to-metal rubbing. If evident, renew the caliper

13.13 Fitted position of front brake caliper

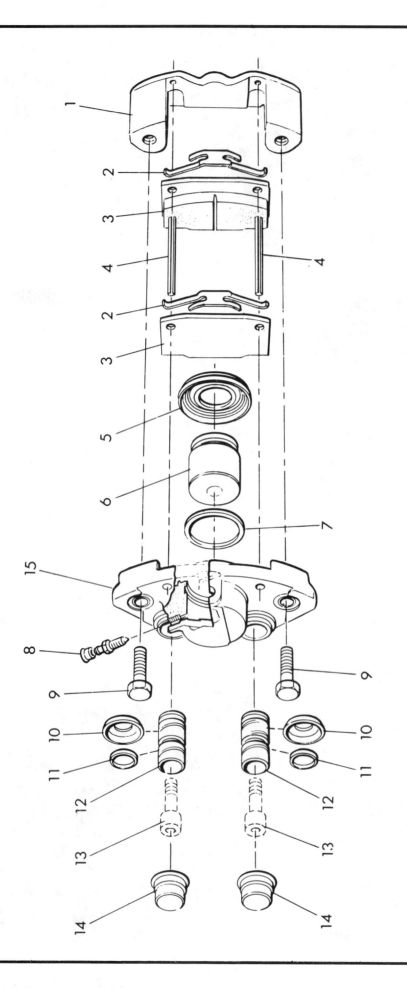

Fig. 13.103 Exploded view of GMF type floating front brake caliper and brake pads (Sec 13)

1  Caliper yoke
2  Spreader spring
3  Brake pad
4  Retaining pin
5  Piston boot

6  Piston
7  Piston seal
8  Bleed screw and cap
9  Bolt
10  Boot

11  Seal
12  Mounting sleeve
13  Allen bolt
14  Dust cap
15  Caliper housing

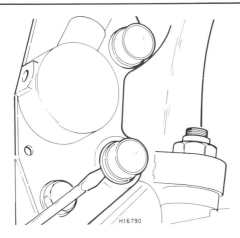

Fig. 13.104 Prising the caps from the front brake caliper mounting bolts (Sec 13)

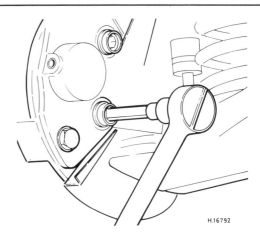

Fig. 13.105 Removing the front brake caliper mounting bolts (Sec 13)

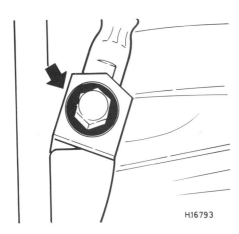

Fig. 13.106 Showing the correct fitted position of the caliper brake hose (Sec 13)

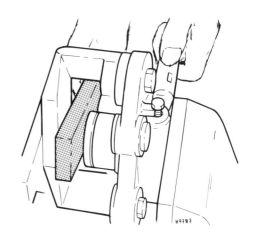

Fig. 13.107 Using air pressure to remove the piston from the caliper – GMF type shown (Sec 13)

complete. If these components are in good condition, discard the rubber seal and dust excluder and obtain a repair kit which will contain all the necessary replaceable items.

22 Clean the piston and cylinder bore with brake hydraulic fluid or methylated spirit – nothing else! When dry coat the sliding surfaces with brake cylinder paste or hydraulic fluid.

23 Commence reassembly by fitting the seal into the cylinder groove.

24 When the piston has been partially inserted, engage the new dust excluder with the groove in the piston.

25 Renew the sealing rings on the sliding sleeves, applying the special grease supplied in the repair kit to the sealing ring grooves. Make sure that the sealing ring is located in the centre groove.

26 Install the sliding sleeves so that the dust cap groove is towards the caliper bracket. Do not push the sleeves fully in at this stage. Install the new dust caps for the sliding sleeves onto their caliper housing collars. Use a piece of tubing to drive them fully home.

27 Depress the piston fully and secure the dust excluder to the housing, driving it fully home with a piece of suitable tubing.

*Front brake caliper (ATE floating type) – overhaul*
28 The procedure is similar to that described in paragraphs 14 to 27

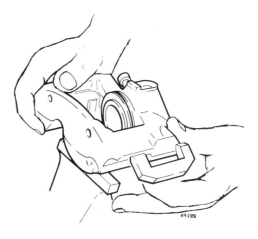

Fig. 13.108 Separating ATE caliper body from bracket (Sec 13)

except for the details given in the following paragraphs.

29 Mount the bracket in a vice then slide the caliper from the bracket. There are no sliding sleeves on the ATE caliper.

30 Use a screwdriver to extract the circlip from the piston dust excluder.

31 When refitting the caliper to the bracket check that the guide springs are correctly located, then insert the caliper (piston end first) pressing down as necessary against the springs. The piston end of the caliper should be flush with the inner face of the bracket.

32 The piston incorporates a recessed section which must be positioned as shown in Fig. 13.112, that is facing the bottom of the caliper at an angle of 45°. A card template may be made to ensure accurate positioning.

### Front brake disc (floating caliper models) – removal and refitting

33 Refer to Chapter 9, Section 5, however it is only necessary to remove the brake pads. The caliper can remain in position, the disc and hub being tilted as shown in Fig. 13.113.

### Rear brake drums – inspection

34 A certain amount of scoring of the brake drum surface is permissible. Drum removal is only necessary if the depth of scoring is more than 0.4 mm (0.015 in)

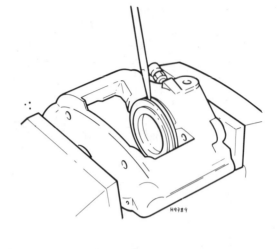

Fig. 13.109 Prising off the ATE caliper dust excluder circlip (Sec 13)

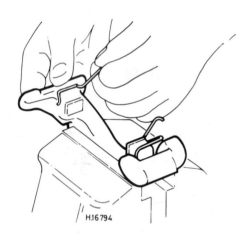

Fig. 13.110 Fitting ATE caliper bracket guide springs (Sec 13)

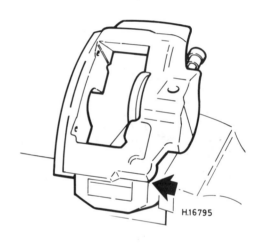

Fig. 13.111 Fit the ATE caliper on the bracket until the faces arrowed are flush (Sec 13)

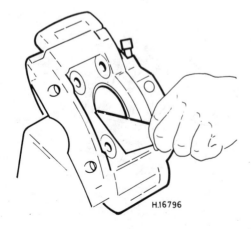

Fig. 13.112 Using a template to set the piston recess in the ATE caliper (Sec 13)

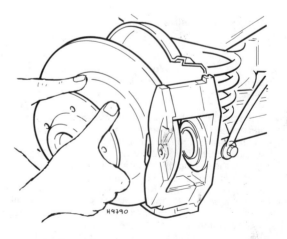

Fig. 13.113 Removing the front brake disc from the floating type caliper (Sec 13)

*Rear drum brakes (1984-on models) – general description*

35 The relay lever fitted to earlier drum brakes is now replaced by an automatic adjuster mechanism which comprises a threaded rod, pushrod sleeve, adjuster pinion and thermoclip. Upon operation of the brake, the lateral movement at the brake shoe arm is converted into rotary movement by the lever on the adjuster pinion, thereby compensating for shoe wear. The thermoclip is designed to expand at a preset temperature, thereby compensating for any increase in drum size due to increased temperature. If this were not so, the brakes might lock on when the drum cooled again.

*Rear brake shoes and drums (1984-on models) – removal and refitting*

36 During this operation, take care to keep the component parts of each brake assembly separate. The adjuster pinion, lever and return spring bracket will all be colour coded black (left-hand assembly) or silver (right-hand assembly). The threaded rods have left or right-hand threads and are identified by the letter L or R respectively.

37 The procedure for shoe removal and refitting is similar to that given in Section 7 of Chapter 9, but with the following differences (photos).

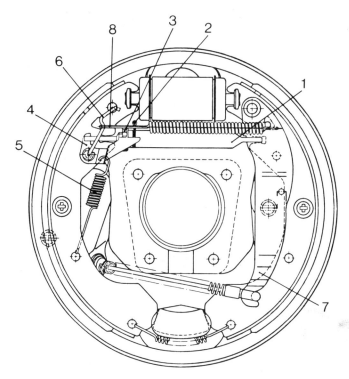

Fig. 13.114 Self-adjusting rear brake components for 1984-on models (Sec 13)

1  Strut
2  Thermoclip
3  Adjuster pinion
4  Adjuster lever
5  Adjuster lever return spring
6  Return spring bracket
7  Handbrake lever
8  Upper return spring

13.37A Self-adjusting rear brake

13.37B Upper return spring and self-adjusting strut

13.37C Lower anchor spring and handbrake cable connection

13.37D Adjuster lever return spring and steady spring

Fig. 13.115 Using a screwdriver to release the handbrake lever for difficult rear drum removal (Sec 13)

38 To facilitate drum removal, remove the plug from the backplate and, using the flat of a screwdriver, push the handbrake shoe lever until the stop pin slides down the side of the shoe web. This will cause the shoes to retract further and enable the drum to be removed.

39 After removal of the brake shoe return spring from its bracket, use the flat of a screwdriver to lever the bracket out of its location in the brake shoe.

40 Detach the adjuster lever from the brake shoe and disconnect its return spring.

41 In terms of removal, the automatic adjuster mechanism is the same as the relay lever fitted to earlier models.

42 When lubricating the areas of the backplate with which the shoes make contact, use 'Plastilube' or equivalent instead of the grease recommended in Chapter 9.

43 Refitting the shoes is the reverse sequence to removal, noting the following points.

44 Smear the threaded rod of the adjuster with a thin coat of silicone-based grease. Rotate the adjuster pinion back to its stop. Refit the adjuster mechanism, adjuster lever and return spring. Check that the spring washer fitted over the adjuster lever retaining pin of the brake shoe is not flattened; if so, renew it. Ensure that the thermoclip is fitted correctly, that is facing upwards.

45 Before refitting the brake drum ensure that the handbrake lever stop pin rests on the edge and not side of the shoe web. If the drum is fitted with the stop pin on the side of the web, and the footbrake then operated, the automatic adjuster will operate and when the handbrake is eventually applied the stop pin will position itself on the edge of the web causing the brakes to lock or overheat.

46 With the rear wheels refitted and the car on the ground, depress the brake pedal repeatedly (at least ten times) until it is no longer possible to hear the adjuster lever jumping across to the adjuster pinion. Once the lever ceases operation, adjustment is complete.

### Handbrake (1984-on models) – adjustment

47 Chock the front wheels then jack up the rear of the car and support on axle stands.

48 Apply the footbrake several times to ensure the rear shoes are correctly adjusted.

49 With the handbrake fully released check that both rear wheels turn freely.

50 Working under the car turn the adjustment nut(s) on the cable equalizer (on the handbrake lever threaded rod) until the rear wheels are partially locked, then back off the nut until the rear wheels are just free (photo).

51 Check that with the handbrake lever applied by two notches there is a slight drag on the rear wheels. The wheels should be firmly locked with the handbrake lever applied by five or six notches.

Fig. 13.116 Stop pin location on the handbrake lever (Sec 13)

Fig. 13.117 Levering out the return spring bracket (Sec 13)

### Master cylinder – general

52 The master cylinder described in Chapter 9 is of ATE manufacture. Later models may be fitted with a master cylinder of GMF manufacture and although most procedures are as described in Chapter 9, the following information should be noted.

53 The primary piston spring must be compressed in order to remove the circlip and gain access to the piston seal. GM use a special threaded tool to compress the spring. However, this can be substituted by a suitable G-clamp or valve spring compressor.

**Fig. 13.118 Correct fitting of adjuster strut end (arrowed) (Sec 13)**

*Brake pressure control valve – general*

54  On left-hand drive models the brake pressure control valve is located on a bracket beneath the master cylinder.

55  On early models the valve has only one inlet and one outlet and it operates as a limiter regardless of any additional pressure in the front brake circuit. However on later models the valve varies the pressure limit in the rear brake circuit according to the pressure in the front circuit. The latter type has four brake pipes connected to it and it is important that these pipes are located correctly (photo).

*Hydraulic system – additional bleeding methods*

56  One of the following alternative methods may be used to bleed the brake hydraulic system, in addition to the procedure described in Chapter 9, Section 2.

57  If the master cylinder or the pressure regulating valve have been disconnected and reconnected, then the complete system (both circuits) must be bled.

58  If a component of one circuit has been disturbed then only that particular circuit need be bled.

59  Unless the pressure bleeding method is being used, do not forget to keep the fluid level in the master cylinder reservoir topped up, to prevent air from being drawn into the system, which would make any work done worthless.

60  Before commencing operations, check that all system hoses and pipes are in good condition, with all unions tight and free from leaks.

13.50 Handbrake cable equalizer and adjustment nuts

61  Take great care not to allow hydraulic fluid to come into contact with the vehicle paintwork, as it is an effective paint stripper. Wash off any spilled fluid immediately with cold water.

62  As the system incorporates a vacuum servo, destroy the vacuum by giving several applications of the brake pedal in quick succession.

63  The car should be loaded with enough weight to actuate the pressure regulating valve before bleeding commences.

**Bleeding – using one-way valve kit**

64  There are a number of one-man, one-way brake bleeding kits available from motor accessory shops. It is recommended that one of these kits is used wherever possible as it will greatly simplify the bleeding operation, and also reduce the risk of air or fluid being drawn back into the system, quite apart from enabling the work to be done without the help of an assistant.

65  To use the kit, connect the tube to the bleed screw and open the screw one half a turn.

66  Depress the brake pedal fully and slowly release it. The one-way valve in the kit will prevent expelled air from returning at the end of each pedal downstroke. Repeat this operation several times to be sure of ejecting all air from the system. Some kits include a translucent container, which can be positioned so that the air bubbles can actually be seen being ejected from the system.

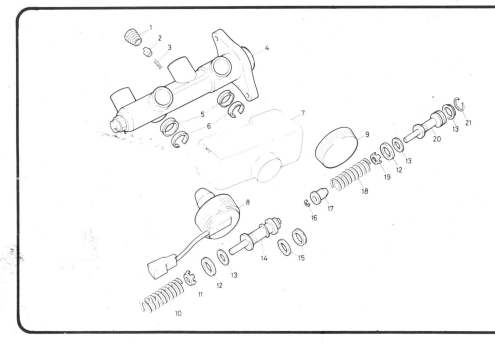

**Fig. 13.119 Exploded view of the GMF master cylinder (Sec 13)**

1   Check valve housing
2   Check valve
3   Return spring
4   Main body
5   Reservoir seals
6   Circlips
7   Reservoir
8   Cap with warning switch
9   Cap without warning switch
10  Secondary spring
11  Retainer
12  Cups
13  Washers
14  Secondary piston
15  Secondary seals
16  Circlip
17  Spring sleeve
18  Primary spring
19  Retainer
20  Primary piston
21  Circlip

67 Tighten the bleed screw, remove the tube and repeat the operations on the remaining brakes.
68 On completion, depress the brake pedal. If it still feels spongy, repeat the bleeding operations as air must still be trapped in the system.

**Bleeding – using a pressure bleeding kit**
69 These kits too are available from motor accessory shops, and are usually operated by air pressure from the spare tyre.
70 By connecting a pressurized container to the master cylinder fluid reservoir, bleeding is then carried out by simply opening each bleed screw in turn and allowing the fluid to run out, rather like turning on a tap, until no air is visible in the expelled fluid.
71 By using this method, the large reserve of hydraulic fluid provides a safeguard against air being drawn into the master

cylinder during bleeding, which often occurs if the fluid level in the reservoir is not maintained.
72 Pressure bleeding is particularly effective when bleeding 'difficult' systems, or when bleeding the complete system at time of routine fluid renewal.

**All methods**
73 When bleeding is completed, check and top up the fluid level in the master cylinder reservoir.
74 Check the feel of the brake pedal. If it feels at all spongy, air must still be present in the system and further bleeding is indicated. Failure to bleed satisfactorily after a reasonable period of the bleeding operation may be due to worn master cylinder seals.
75 Discard brake fluid which has been expelled. It is almost certain to be contaminated with moisture, air and dirt making it unsuitable for further use. Clean fluid should always be stored in an airtight container as it absorbs moisture readily (hygroscopic) which lowers its boiling point and could affect braking performance under severe conditions.

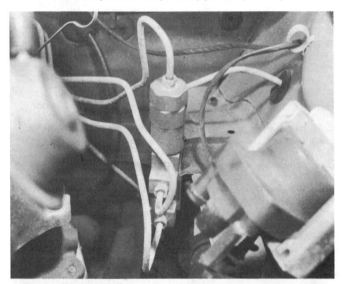

**Fig. 13.120 Using the special spring compressor to remove the circlip from the primary piston (Sec 13)**

13.55 Brake pressure control valve fitted to latter models

14.1 Maintenance-free battery

## 14 Electrical system

*Maintenance-free battery – general*
1 Later models are equipped with a maintenance-free battery which does not require regular topping-up of the electrolyte level (photo).
2 The state of charge of the battery can be determined from the built-in hydrometer with reference to Fig. 13.121. The hydrometer consists of a clear or light yellow plastic rod at the end of which is a green ball in a cage. With the battery at or above 65% state of charge the green ball floats and will appear as a green dot when viewed through the rod. Below 65% state of charge the green ball will sink from direct view causing a dark spot. If the electrolyte level drops below the hydrometer a clear or light yellow spot will be visible.
3 The battery may be charged using the method described in Chapter 10. When the green dot appears in the hydrometer the battery is sufficiently charged for normal use.

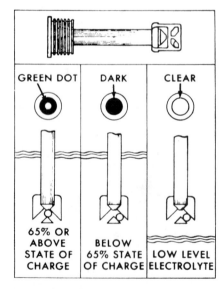

**Fig. 13.121 Built-in hydrometer fitted to the maintenance-free battery (Sec 14)**

*Battery cable – general*
4 On some 1982 and 1983 models fitted with the cih engine, it is important that the battery positive cable on the starter solenoid is positioned vertically otherwise it may touch surrounding components. It is also recommended that the cable is secured with straps as shown in Fig. 13.122.

*Tailgate wiper arm and motor – removal and refitting*
5 Disconnect the battery negative lead.

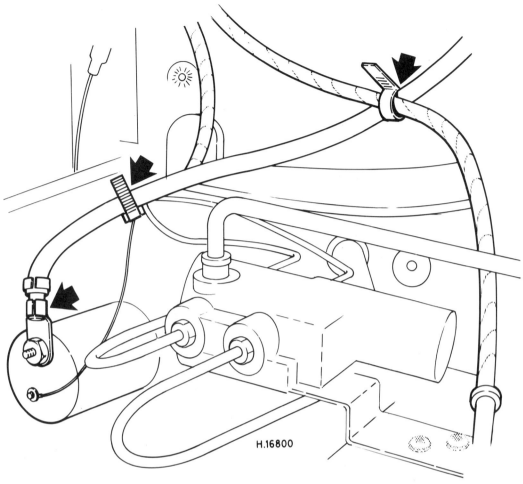

H.16800

**Fig. 13.122 Correct fitting of the battery cable on 1982/1983
cih engine models (Sec 14)**

6  Note the parked position of the wiper arm then lift the hinged
cap, unscrew the nut and withdraw the arm from the motor spindle
(photo).
7  Remove the rubber cap and unscrew the nut beneath it. Recover
the metal and rubber washers (photos).
8  Carefully prise the trim panel from the inside of the tailgate.
9  Separate the wiring at the connectors noting the relevant
positions of each wire (photo).
10 Unscrew the mounting bolts noting the location of the earth
cable where fitted, and withdraw the wiper motor from the tailgate
(photo).
11 Refitting is a reversal of removal.

*Tailgate washer pump – removal and refitting*
12 Disconnect the battery negative lead.
13 Open the tailgate and remove the floor cover. Remove the spare
wheel if necessary (photo).
14 Disconnect the wiring from the pump on the side of the washer
reservoir (photo).
15 Lift out the reservoir and empty its contents into a suitable
container.
16 Separate the pump from the reservoir by moving it sideways
under the shoulder then pulling it from the rubber gasket.
Disconnect the tubing.
17 Refitting is a reversal of removal. The washer jet should be
adjusted to direct the spray at the point shown in Fig. 13.123.

14.6 Tailgate wiper arm securing nut

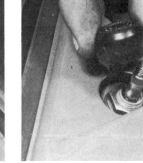

14.7A Remove the rubber cap ...

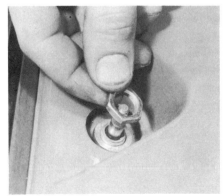

14.7B ... nut ...

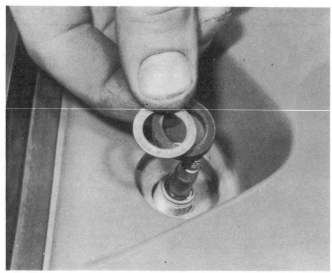

14.7C ... then the metal and rubber washers

14.9 Tailgate wiper motor wiring

14.10 Removing the tailgate wiper motor

14.13 View of spare wheel and tailgate washer reservoir

14.14 Tailgate washer reservoir showing wiring and tubing

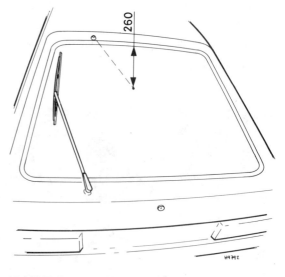

**Fig. 13.123 Tailgate washer jet adjustment point (Sec 14)**

*Dimension = 260.0 mm (10.24 in)*

*Tailgate wash/wipe switch – removal and refitting*

18 Disconnect the battery negative lead.
19 Remove the fusebox cover and the lower facia panel.
20 Using a small screwdriver press in the tab and pull off the switch knob.
21 Using circlip pliers unscrew the ring nut, then withdraw the switch from under the instrument panel and disconnect the wiring.
22 Refitting is a reversal of removal, but note that the location flat on the switch must be uppermost.

*Wiper motor – fault diagnosis*

23 On models with a wash/wipe delay facility, it is not unknown for the wiper motor to start spontaneously. This is caused by a voltage peak accidentally triggering the wiper motor control relay.
24 Various items of electrical equipment may produce these peaks including the following:

  *(a) Coil secondary (HT) winding defective (open-circuit)*
  *(b) Alternator voltage regulator defective*
  *(c) Washer pump wires too close to HT leads*
  *(d) Idle speed increase solenoid valve switching*
  *(e) Idle cut-off solenoid valve loose or defective*

25 The coil secondary winding may be checked with an ohmmeter. A small break in the wiring will show up as infinite resistance, even though the ignition system may function normally as the HT voltage can jump the break.
26 The alternator output can be checked with a voltmeter, and temporarily disconnecting the idle speed increase solenoid valve will show up a fault due to this component.

*Headlamp wash/wipe system – general*

27 Where this system is fitted, a combined windscreen and headlamp washer fluid reservoir will be found in the engine bay.
28 To remove a wiper arm, flip up the protective cap at the arm pivot and remove the arm retaining nut. Ease the arm off its splined spindle, having noted its fitted position (photos). If necessary, use the flat of a screwdriver to lever the arm free.
29 Refit the arm in its previously noted position, using a reversal of the removal sequence.
30 The washer jets are located in the front bumper and should be adjusted with a pin to direct the spray near the start of the wiper stroke.
31 To remove the wiper motor disconnect the battery negative lead, then remove the small panel in front of the radiator and separate the appropriate wiring connector. Release the wiring from the clips.
32 For better access the complete front bumper may be removed although this is not essential.
33 On Manta models remove the headlamp and direction indicator lamp.
34 Unscrew the mounting nuts/bolts and withdraw the wiper motor (photo). On Manta models one nut is accessible from beneath the front wheel arch.

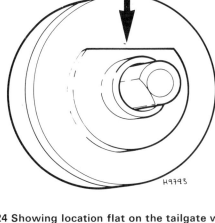

Fig. 13.124 Showing location flat on the tailgate wash/wipe switch (Sec 14)

14.28A Unscrew the nut ...

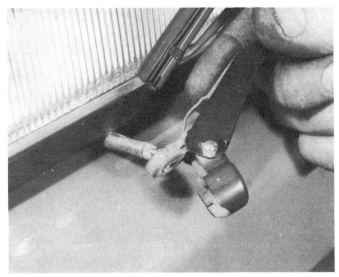

14.28B ... and remove the headlamp wiper arm

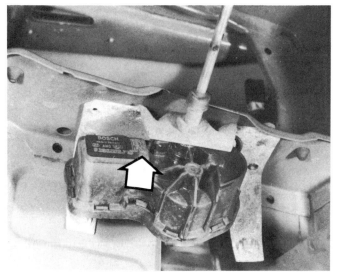

14.34 Headlamp wiper motor showing side reference R

35 Refitting is a reversal of removal. The wiper motors are handed and marked accordingly (L for left-hand, R for right-hand).

### Washer pump – removal and refitting

36 The pump for the windscreen and headlamp washers is attached to the combined reservoir. To remove it first remove and empty the reservoir. Disconnect the wiring and tubing and unscrew the pump from the reservoir. Note that the one pump supplies both the windscreen and headlamp washers, but the headlamp circuit incorporates a solenoid valve which operates in conjunction with the headlamp wipers (photo).
37 Refitting is a reversal of removal.

### Horn (Manta models) – removal and refitting

38 Access is gained either by removing the small panel in front of the radiator in the engine compartment or by removing the front bumper and spoiler.
39 Disconnect the battery negative lead then unscrew the mounting nut, disconnect the wiring and withdraw the horn (photo).
40 Refitting is a reversal of removal.

### Headlight bulb (later models) – renewal

41 Unscrew the large plastic cap from the rear of the headlight (photo).
42 Pull off the wiring connector (photo).

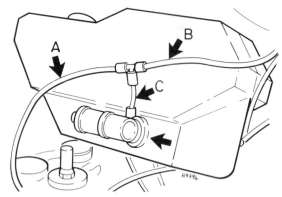

**Fig. 13.125 Washer pump location on the fluid reservoir (Sec 14)**

A   Tube to headlamp washer solenoid
B   Tube to windscreen washers
C   Pump outlet
    Additional arrow indicates pump retaining cap

43 Unhook the wire clip and remove the bulb (photos).
44 Fit the new bulb in reverse order, but do not touch the glass bulb. If necessary clean the bulb with methylated spirit.

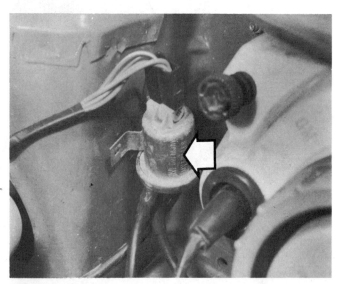

14.36 Headlamp washer solenoid valve

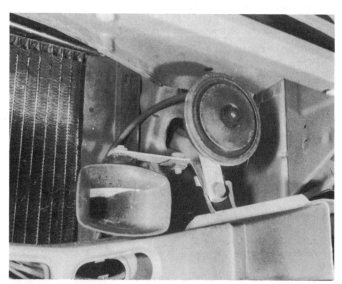

14.39 Horn location

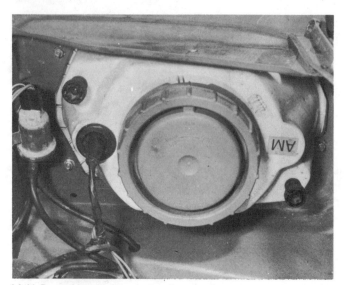

14.41 Rear of headlight unit showing plastic cap

14.42 Pull off the wiring connector

## Headlight unit (Manta models) – removal and refitting

45 Unscrew the large plastic cap from the rear of the headlight and disconnect the wiring from the headlight and sidelight bulbs.

46 Prise out the grommet and withdraw the wiring from the headlight unit (photo).

47 On models with a front spoiler remove the complete front bumper and spoiler.

48 Loosen the screws and slide out the trim strip from under both headlight units. Slots are provided in the strip so it is only necessary to loosen the screws (photos).

49 Unscrew the four mounting nuts and withdraw the headlight unit from the front of the car (photo).

50 Refitting is a reversal of removal, but finally adjust the headlight beam.

**Note:** *The limited edition Manta 'Exclusive' model is fitted with a four-headlamp system, but no details were available at the time of writing.*

## Sidelight bulb (Manta models) – renewal

51 Unscrew the large plastic cap from the rear of the headlight.

52 Pull out the sidelight bulbholder, then depress and twist the bulb to remove it (photo).

53 Fit the new bulb in reverse order.

## Front foglamp bulb – renewal

54 Unscrew the bottom crosshead screw and unhook the lens and reflector.

55 Release the wire clips and withdraw the bulb. Disconnect the wiring.

56 Fit the new bulb in reverse order making sure that the lugs on the bulbholder locate in the socket recesses.

## Front direction indicator bulb and light unit (Manta model) – removal and refitting

57 To remove the bulb unscrew the two screws and lift off the lens then depress and twist the bulb to remove it (photo).

14.43A Unhook the wire clip ...

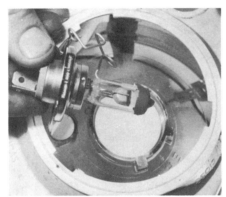

14.43B ... and remove the headlight bulb

14.46 Wiring grommet hole in rear of headlight unit

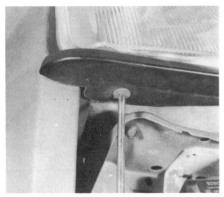

14.48A Loosen the screws ...

14.48B ... and remove the trim strip

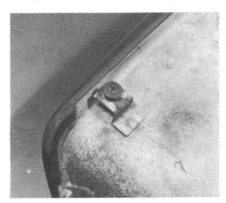

14.48C Trim strip mounting screw on the headlight (removed)

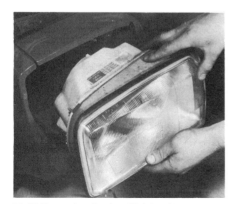

14.49 Removing the headlight unit

14.52 Removing the sidelight bulbholder

14.57 Removing the front direction indicator lens

58 To remove the light unit disconnect the wiring from the rear of the unit then unbolt the unit from the spoiler (photos).
59 Refitting is a reversal of removal.

*Rear light cluster bulbs and assembly (Manta models) – removal and refitting*
60 To remove a bulb first open the tailgate and remove the trim from the rear of the luggage compartment. Twist the appropriate bulbholder from the light unit then depress and twist the bulb to remove it (photos).
61 Unbolt the earth cable(s) from the rear panel then unbolt the assembly and withdraw it rearwards (photos).
62 Prise up the tabs and pull out the wiring multi-plug (photo). The assembly can now be removed.
63 Refitting is a reversal of removal.

*Number plate lamp bulb (early models) – renewal*
64 The rear number plate is illuminated by a single light behind the rear bumper.
65 To renew the bulb, remove the two screws securing the lens and ease the pointed end of the lens out of the lamp body. Remove the lens and the gasket (photo) to expose the bulb.
66 The bulbholder is retained by a clip and the bulbholder must be pulled out (photo) to remove the bulb.
67 Fit a new bulb and push the bulbholder back into the clip.
68 Refit the lens and gasket, taking care to ensure that the pointed end of the lens engages in its slot in the lamp body. If this is not done, there is a danger of cracking the lens when the lens screws are tightened.
69 Insert and tighten the lens screws.

14.58A Wiring to the rear of the front direction indicator light unit

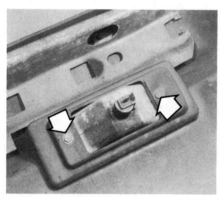

14.58B Mounting bolts for the front direction indicator light unit

14.60A View of rear light cluster with trim panel removed

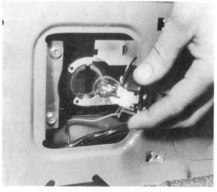

14.60B Removing a bulbholder

14.61A Earth cables for rear light cluster

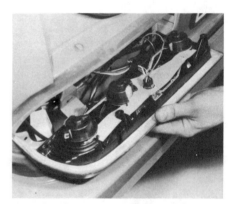

14.61B Removing the rear light cluster

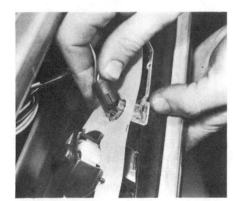

14.62 Disconnecting the multi-plug from the rear light cluster

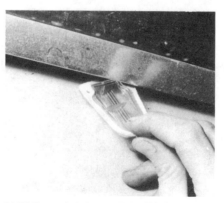

14.65 Removing the number plate lamp lens (early models)

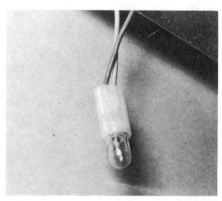

14.66 Number plate lamp bulb (early models)

*Number plate lamp bulb (later models) – renewal*
70 Prise the lamp from the rear bumper; it is retained by two plastic hooks.
71 Remove the bulbholder from the lens and cover then depress and twist the bulb to remove it (photos).
72 Fit the new bulb in reverse order.

*Rear foglamp bulb – renewal*
73 Undo the screws and remove the lens.
74 Depress and twist the bulb to remove it (photo).
75 Fit the new bulb in reverse order.

*Engine compartment light bulb – renewal*
76 Prise the lens from the bonnet and extract the festoon-type bulb from the spring teminals (photo).
77 Fit the new bulb in reverse order.

*Instrument housing – removal and refitting*
78 Disconnect the battery negative lead.
79 Remove the switches from the strip below the instrument housing.
80 Undo the screws and remove the switch strip (photo).

14.71A Remove the bulbholder from the lens and cover ...

14.71B ... then remove the bulb

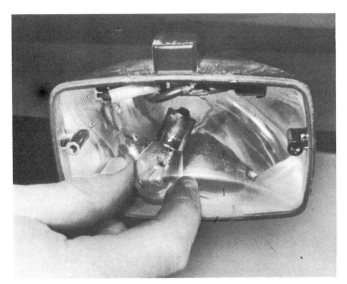

14.74 Removing the rear foglamp bulb

14.76 Engine compartment light unit and bulb

14.80 Removing the switch strip screws

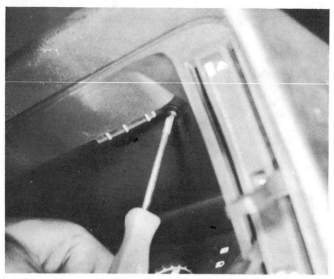

81 Undo the upper and lower screws and lift off the cowling (photos). It is retained by spring clips at the rear and on some models incorporates illumination lamp wiring.
82 Undo the instrument housing mounting screws (photo).
83 Note the position of the heater control cables then pull out the levers and unhook the cables and controls (photo).
84 Disconnect the wiring plugs and the speedometer cable, and release the heater cables from the rear of the housing. Withdraw the housing from the facia (photos).
85 If necessary the illumination and warning lamp bulbs may be removed by twisting them through 90° (photos).
86 Refitting is a reversal of removal.

*Luggage compartment light switch – removal and refitting*
87 The switch is located on the rear of the roof and is accessible with the tailgate open.
88 Remove the screw then pull out the switch and disconnect the wire (photo).
89 Refitting is a reversal of removal.

14.81A Instrument housing cowling upper screws ...

14.81B ... and lower screws

14.82 Instrument housing mounting screws

14.83 Heater controls and cables

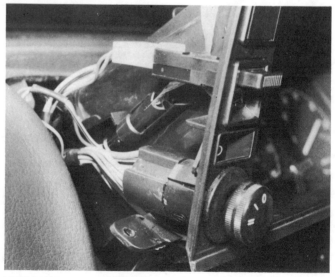

14.84A Wiring to left-hand side of instrument housing

14.84B Disconnect the wiring plugs ...

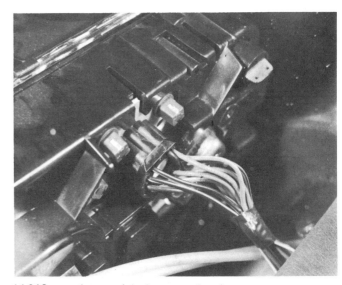

14.84C ... on the rear of the instrument housing

14.84D Showing the speedometer cable fitting

14.84E The heater control cables are secured with a Belleville washer

14.84F View of instrument housing wiring

14.84G Front and rear views of the instrument housing

14.85A The instrument housing incorporates round ...

14.85B ... and square bulbholders

14.88 Luggage compartment light switch removal

*Handbrake warning lamp switch – removal and refitting*
90  Raise the rear of the car and support on axle stands.
91  Unscrew the adjustment nut(s) and release the handbrake cable equalizer from the threaded rod.
92  Remove the passenger's seat, inner rail, and transmission tunnel cover.
93  Remove the centre console panel on manual gearbox models.
94  Lift the carpet and unbolt the handbrake lever from the floor.
95  Remove the switch and wiring.
96  Refitting is a reversal of removal but adjust the handbrake on completion.

*Rear loudspeakers (Hatchback) – installation*
97  Provision is made for the installation of rear speakers in the luggage compartment.
98  The fretted panel on each side is released by removing a screw and releasing two plastic clips (photo). Installation of the speakers should then be carried out according to the manufacturer's instructions.

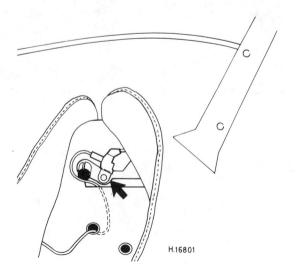

Fig. 13.126 Handbrake warning lamp switch location
(Sec 14)

14.98 Rear loudspeaker panel

## Radio interference – VHF/FM broadcasts

99 Reception of VHF/FM in an automobile is more prone to problems than the medium and long wavebands. Medium/long wave transmitters are capable of covering considerable distances, but VHF transmitters are restricted to line of sight, meaning ranges of 10 to 50 miles, depending upon the terrain, the effects of buildings and the transmitter power.

100 Because of the limited range it is necessary to retune on a long journey, and it may be better for those habitually travelling long distances or living in areas of poor provision of transmitters to use an AM radio working on medium/long wavebands.

101 When conditions are poor, interference can arise, and some of the suppression devices described previously fall off in performance at very high frequencies unless specifically designed for the VHF band. Available suppression devices include reactive HT cable, resistive distributor caps, screened plug caps, screened leads and resistive spark plugs.

102 For VHF/FM receiver installation the following points should be particularly noted:

(a) Earthing of the receiver chassis and the aerial mounting is important. Use a separate earthing wire at the radio, and scrape paint away at the aerial mounting.

(b) If possible, use a good quality roof aerial to obtain maximum height and distance from interference generating devices on the vehicle.

(c) Use of a high quality aerial downlead is important, since losses in cheap cable can be significant.

(d) The polarisation of FM transmissions may be horizontal, vertical, circular or slanted. Because of this the optimum mounting angle is at 45° to the vehicle roof.

103 On some later models, a transformer is fitted to eliminate buzzing which occurs when the vehicle parking lamps are in operation. Initially the transformer was of Striebel make, subsequently superseded by a Lucas unit (Part No 36522D).

## Radio interference – CB installations

104 In the UK, CB transmitter/receivers work within the 27 MHz and 934 MHz bands, using the FM mode. At present interest is concentrated on 27 MHz where the design and manufacture of equipment is less difficult. Maximum transmitted power is 4 watts, and 40 channels spaced 10 kHz apart within the range 27.60125 to 27.99125 MHz are available.

105 Aerials are the key to effective transmission and reception. Regulations limit the aerial length to 1.65 metres including the loading coil and any associated circuitry, so tuning the aerial is necessary to obtain optimum results. The choice of a CB aerial is dependent on whether it is to be permanently installed or removable, and the perforance will hinge on correct tuning and the location point on the vehicle. Common practice is to clip the aerial can be rapidly unscrewed. An alternative is to use the boot rim to render the aerial theftproof, but a popular solution is to use the 'magmount' – a type of mounting having a strong magnetic base clamping to the vehicle at any point, usually the roof.

106 Aerial location determines the signal distribution for both transmission and reception, but it is wise to choose a point away from the engine compartment to minimise interference from vehicle electrical equipment.

107 The aerial is subject to considerable wind and acceleration forces. Cheaper units will whip backwards and forwards and in so doing will alter the relationship with the metal surface of the vehicle with which it forms a ground plane aerial system. The radiation pattern will change correspondingly, giving rise to break-up of both incoming and outgoing signals.

108 Interference problems on the vehicle carrying CB equipment fall into two categories:

(a) Interference to bearby TV and radio receivers when transmitting.

(b) Interference to CB set reception due to electrical equipment on the vehicle.

109 Problems of break-through to TV and radio are not frequent, but can be difficult to solve. Mostly trouble is not detected or reported because the vehicle is moving and the symptoms rapidly disappear at the TV/radio receiver, but when the CB set is used as a base station any trouble with nearby receivers will soon result in a complaint.

110 It must not be assumed by the CB operator that his equipment is faultless, for much depends upon the design. Harmonics (that is, multiples) of 27 MHz may be transmitted unknowingly and these can fall into other user's bands. Where trouble of this nature occurs, low pass filters in the aerial or supply leads can help, and should be fitted in base station aerials as a matter of course. In stubborn cases it may be necessary to call for assistance from the licensing authority, or, if possible, to have the equipment checked by the manufacturers.

111 Interference received on the CB set from the vehicle equipment is, fortunately, not usually a severe problem. The precautions outlined previously for radio/cassette units apply, but there are some extra points worth noting.

112 It is common practice to use a slide-mount on CB equipment enabling the set to be easily removed for use as a base station, for example. Care must be taken that the slide mount fittings are properly earthed and that first class connection occurs between the set and slide-mount.

113 Vehicle manufacturers in the UK are required to provide suppression of electrical equipment to cover 40 to 250 MHz to protect TV and VHF radio bands. Such suppression appears to be adequately effective at 27 MHz, but suppression of individual items such as alternators/dynamos, clocks, stabilisers, flashers, wiper motors, etc, may still be necessary. The suppression capacitors and chokes available from auto-electrical suppliers for entertainment receivers will usually give the required results with CB equipment.

## Radio/cassette unit (standard fitment) – removal

114 From late 1986, some radio/cassette units fitted as standard equipment incorporate theft-deterrent fitting details.

115 This takes the form of four Allen screws, which blank off the spring release apertures in the radio/cassette front panel.

116 Before the unit can be removed, these screws must be removed using a 2 mm Allen key. The necessary removal tools can then be inserted.

## Headlamp dim-dip system – general

117 As from October 1987, all models are fitted with a headlamp dim-dip system to comply with current regulations.

118 The system is designed to prevent the car being driven on parking lamps only, and the headlamps are switched on with reduced intensity automatically as soon as the engine is started.

119 An essential part of the system is a voltage reducer (transformer) – the wiring circuit is shown in Fig. 13.132.

## Alternator – GT/E Exclusive models

120 A 55A alternator is fitted to GT/E Exclusive models. For all practical purposes, operations described for smaller output alternators apply (see Chapter 10).

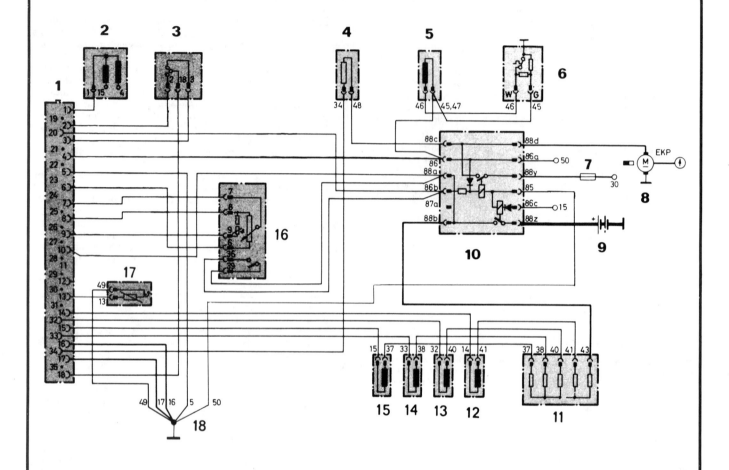

**Fig. 13.127 Wiring diagram – fuel injection system**

| | | | |
|---|---|---|---|
| 1 | Multiple connector | 10 | Relay combination |
| 2 | Ignition coil | 11 | Compensating resistor |
| 3 | Throttle valve switch | 12 | Injector, cyl 4 |
| 4 | Auxiliary air valve | 13 | Injector, cyl 3 |
| 5 | Cold start valve | 14 | Injector, cyl 2 |
| 6 | Thermal timing switch | 15 | Injector, cyl 1 |
| 7 | Fuse | 16 | Air meter |
| 8 | Fuel pump | 17 | Temperature sensor II |
| 9 | Battery | 18 | Earth terminal |

**Key to Fig. 13.128**

1 Turn signal lamp
2 Headlamps
  (a) High and low beams
  (b) Parking lamp
3 Fog light
4 Driving light
5 Horn
6 Windscreen washer pump
7 Windscreen washer relay
8 Ignition coil
9 Distributor
10 Alternator (Delco Remy)
11 Alternator (Bosch)
12 Voltage regulator (Bosch) installed at alternator
13 Starter
14 Engine compartment lamp
15 Remote thermometer sensor
16 Oil pressure sensor
17 Flasher
18 Rear window heater relay
19 Fog light relay
20 High beam relay
21 Marker light
22 Battery
23 Carburettor choke pre-heater
24 Passenger compartment lamp
25 Windscreen wiper motor
26 Door switch
27 Instrument lights
28 Blower
29 Ignition/starter switch
30 Fuse block
31 Marker light switch
32 Headlamp/passenger compartment lamp switch
33 Turn signal/windscreen wiper switch
34 Instruments
  (a) Voltage stabilizer
  (b) Parking brake and clutch monitor lamp
  (c) High beam indicator
  (d) Oil pressure lamp
  (e) Charging monitor lamp

  (f) Turn signal indicator lamp
  (g) Emergency flasher indicator lamp
  (h) Fuel gauge
35 Cigarette lighter
36 Clock
37 Clutch monitor switch
38 Parking brake monitor switch
39 Radio
40 Fuel level sender
41 Heater switch
42 Blower switch
43 Fog light switch
44 Gear selector lever switch
45 Gear selector lever light
46 Reversing light switch
47 Brake light switch
48 Rear fog light switch
49 Rear window heater grid switch
50 Rear window heater grid
51 Boot lamp
52 Boot lamp switch
53 Tail light group
  (a) Turn signal lamp
  (b) Tail lamp
  (c) Brake light
  (d) Reversing light
54 Rear fog light
55 Number plate lamp
56 Overpressure safety switch
57 Blower motor series resistors
58 Low-pressure switch
59 Blower relay
60 Air conditioning relay
61 Supplementary fan
62 Supplementary fan switch
63 Thermostat switch
64 Magnetic compressor clutch
65 Wiper motor (hatchback lid)
66 Wiper switch
67 Washer pump

**Colour Code**

| | | | | | |
|---|---|---|---|---|---|
| RT | = | red | GE | = | yellow |
| SW | = | black | LI | = | violet |
| WS | = | white | BL | = | blue |
| BR | = | brown | HBL | = | light blue |
| GR | = | grey | 1.8 | = | resistance wire |
| GN | = | green | | | |

Note: Wiring codes consist of a number, representing the cross-sectional area of the wire in mm², followed by the colour code as above

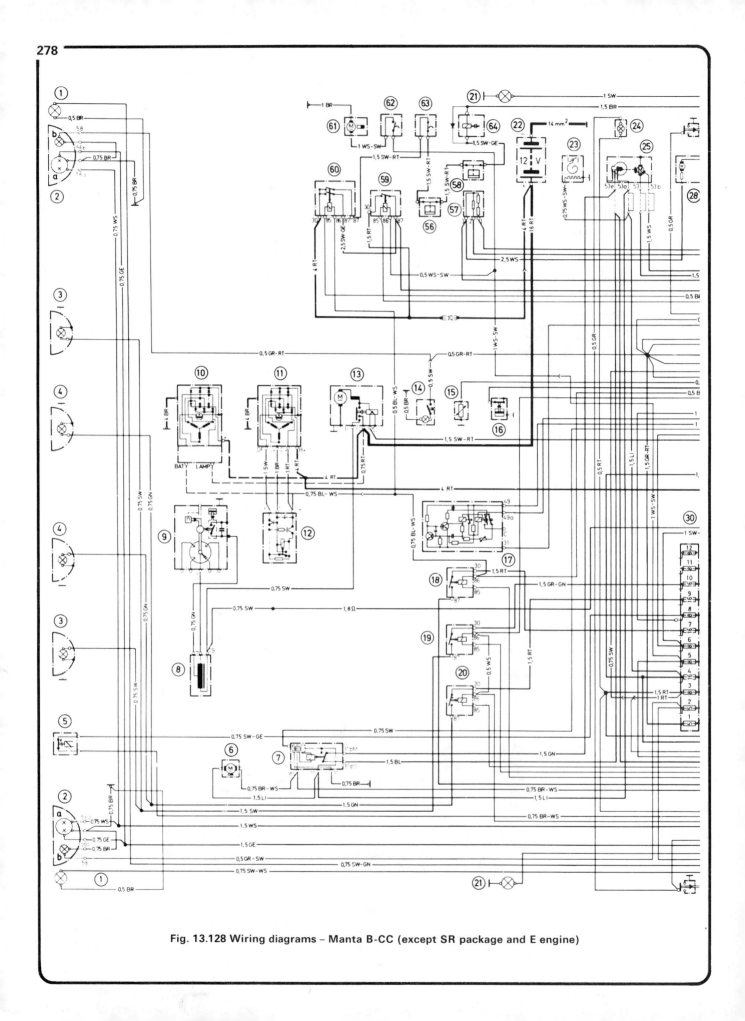

Fig. 13.128 Wiring diagrams – Manta B-CC (except SR package and E engine)

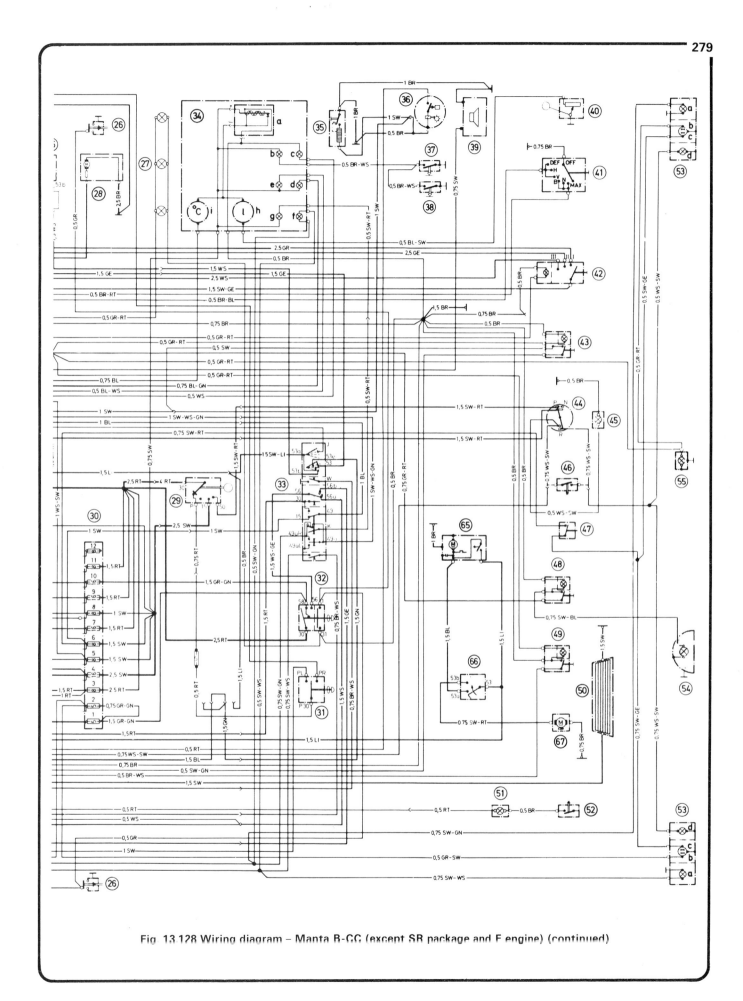

Fig. 13.128 Wiring diagram – Manta B-GC (except SR package and E engine) (continued)

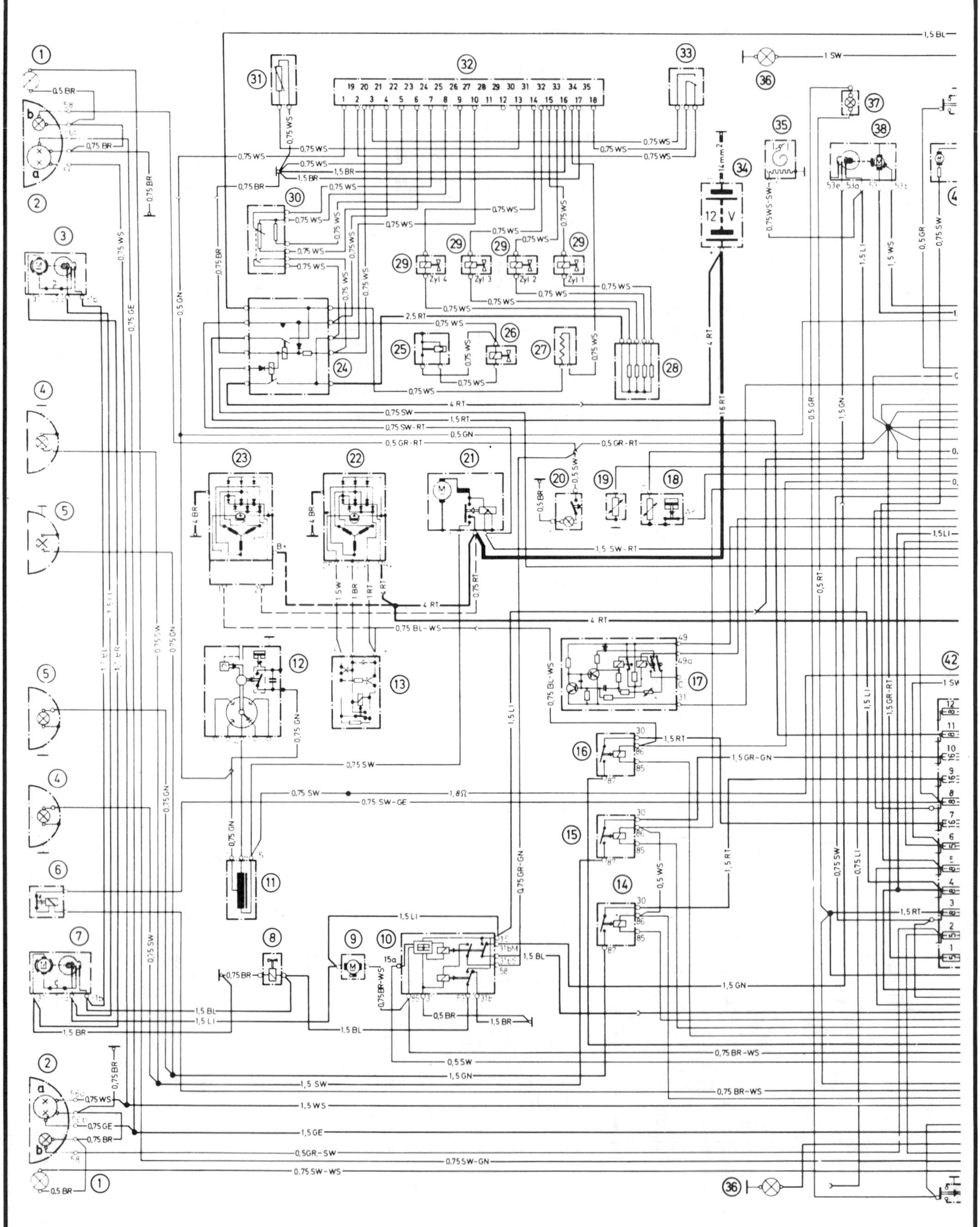

Fig. 13.129 Wiring diagram – Manta B-CC (SR package and E engine)

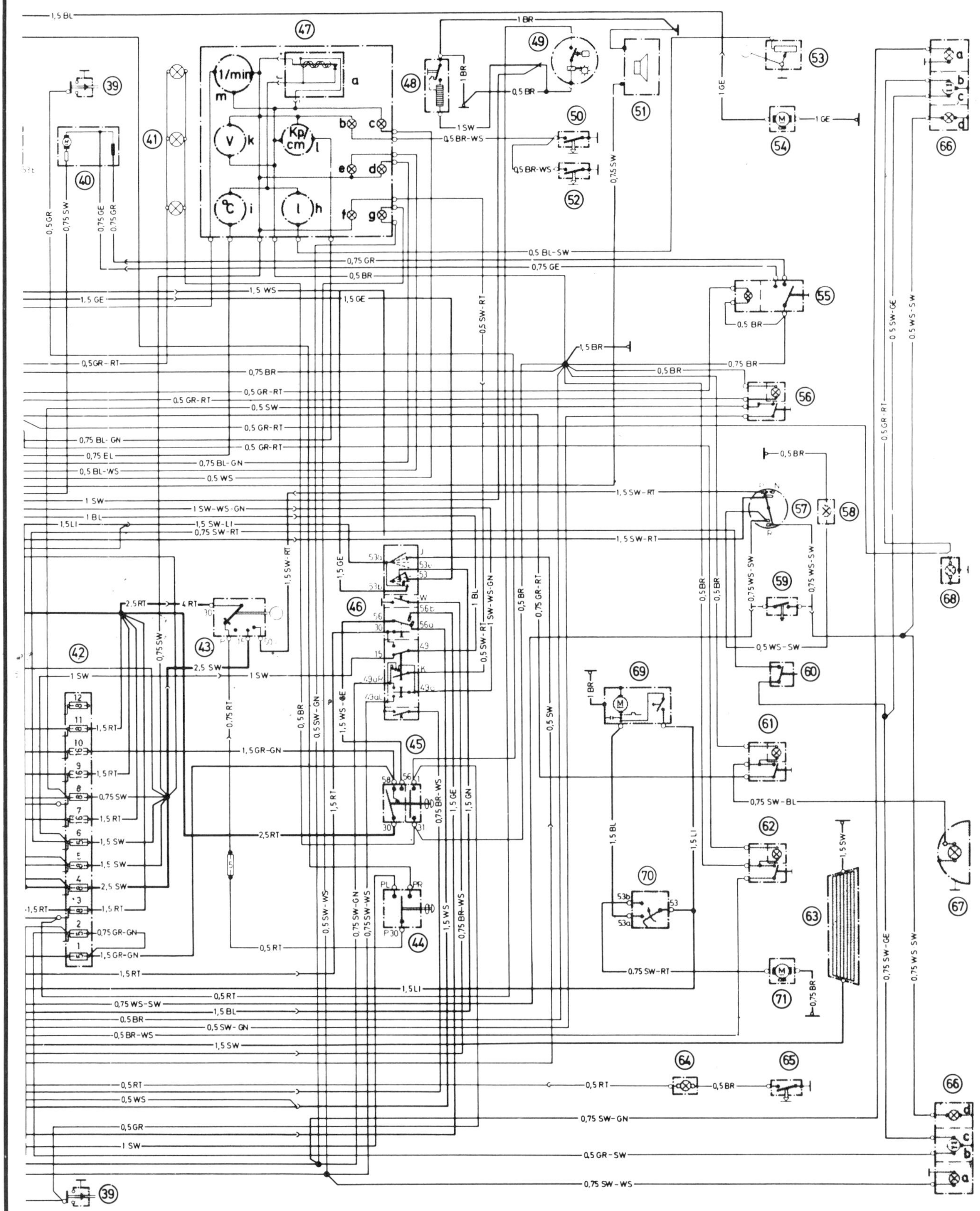

Fig. 13.129 Wiring diagram – Manta B-CC (SR package and E engine) (continued)

## Key to Fig. 13.129

| | |
|---|---|
| 1 | Turn signal |
| 2 | Headlamps |
| | (a) High and low beams |
| | (b) Parking lamp |
| 3 | Headlamp wiper motor, right |
| 4 | Foglight |
| 5 | Driving light |
| 6 | Horn |
| 7 | Headlamp wiper motor, left |
| 8 | Solenoid valve, headlamp washer system |
| 9 | Windscreen and headlamp washer pump |
| 10 | Windscreen and headlamp wipe/wash relay |
| 11 | Ignition coil |
| 12 | Distributor |
| 13 | Voltage regulator (Bosch), installed on alternator |
| 14 | High beam relay |
| 15 | Foglight relay |
| 16 | Rear window heater grid relay |
| 17 | Flasher |
| 18 | Oil pressure sensor |
| 19 | Remote thermometer sensor |
| 20 | Engine compartment lamp |
| 21 | Starter |
| 22 | Alternator (Bosch) |
| 23 | Alternator (Delco Remy) |
| 24 | Double relay for injection system (GT/E) |
| 25 | Thermo-time switch (GT/E) |
| 26 | Cold start valve (GT/E) |
| 27 | Auxiliary air valve (GT/E) |
| 28 | Series resistors (GT/E) |
| 29 | Solenoid valve (GT/E) |
| 30 | Air-flow sensor (GT/E) |
| 31 | Temperature sensor (GT/E) |
| 32 | Control unit (GT/E) |
| 33 | Throttle flap switch (GT/E) |
| 34 | Battery |
| 35 | Carburettor choke pre-heater |
| 36 | Marker light |
| 37 | Passenger compartment lamp |
| 38 | Windscreen wiper motor |
| 39 | Door switch |
| 40 | Blower |
| 41 | Instrument lights |
| 42 | Fuse block |
| 43 | Ignition/starter switch |
| 44 | Marker light switch |
| 45 | Headlamp/passenger compartment lamp switch |
| 46 | Turn signal/windscreen wiper switch |
| 47 | Instruments |
| | (a) Voltage stabilizer |
| | (b) Parking brake and clutch monitor lamp |
| | (c) High beam lamp |
| | (d) Oil pressure lamp |
| | (e) Charging monitor lamp |
| | (f) Emergency flasher lamp |
| | (g) Turn signal indicator |
| | (h) Fuel gauge |
| | (i) Remote thermometer |
| | (k) Voltmeter |
| | (l) Oil pressure gauge |
| | (m) Tachometer |
| 48 | Cigarette lighter |
| 49 | Clock |
| 50 | Clutch moniter switch |
| 51 | Radio |
| 52 | Parking brake monitor switch |
| 53 | Fuel level sender |
| 54 | Fuel pump (GT/E) |
| 55 | Blower switch |
| 56 | Fog light switch |
| 57 | Gear selector lever switch |
| 58 | Gear selector lever light |
| 59 | Reversing light switch |
| 60 | Brake light switch |
| 61 | Rear fog lght switch |
| 62 | Rear window heater switch |
| 63 | Rear window heater grid |
| 64 | Boot lamp |
| 65 | Boot lamp switch |
| 66 | Tail light group |
| | (a) Turn signal lamp |
| | (b) Tail lamp |
| | (c) Brake light |
| | (d) Reversing light |
| 67 | Rear fog light |
| 68 | Number plate light |
| 69 | Wiper motor (hatchback lid) |
| 70 | Windscreen wiper switch |
| 71 | Windscreen washer pump |

## Colour code

| | | | | | |
|---|---|---|---|---|---|
| RT | = | red | GE | = | yellow |
| SW | = | black | LI | = | violet |
| WS | = | white | BL | = | blue |
| BR | = | brown | HBL | = | light blue |
| GR | = | grey | 1.8 | = | resistance wire |
| GN | = | green | | | |

*Note: Wiring codes consist of a number, representing the cross-sectional area of the wire in mm², followed by the colour code as above*

## Key to Fig. 13.130

| Code | Description | Ref. |
|---|---|---|
| E1 | Parking lamp – right | 47 |
| E2 | Tail lamp – right | 48 |
| E3 | Number plate lamp | 50 |
| E4 | Parking lamp – left | 44 |
| E5 | Tail lamp – left | 45 |
| E6 | Engine compartment lamp | 51 |
| E7 | High beam – right | 60 |
| E8 | High beam – left | 59 |
| E9 | Low beam – right | 63 |
| E10 | Low beam – left | 62 |
| E11 | Instrument lights | 51 |
| E12 | Selector lever light | 109 |
| E13 | Boot lamp | 81 |
| E14 | Courtesy light | 92 |
| E17 | Reversing lamp – right | 106 |
| E18 | Reversing lamp – left | 107 |
| E19 | Heated rear window | 40 |
| E20 | Fog lamp – left | 158 |
| E21 | Fog lamp – right | 159 |
| E24 | Fog lamp – rear | 163 |
| E32 | Clock lamp | 98 |
| E35 | Parking lamp – left | 169 |
| E36 | Parking lamp – right | 171 |
| F1 to F12 | Fuses in fusebox | |
| F13 | Parking light fuse | 170 |
| F14 | Running light fuse | 202 |
| F19 | Trailer hitch fuse | 196 |
| F21 | Air conditioning fuse | 174 |
| F25 | Voltage stabilizer | 19 |
| G1 | Battery | 1 |
| G2 | Alternator | 14 |
| H1 | Receiver | 95 |
| H2 | Horn | 101 |
| H3 | Turn signal lamp telltale | 76 |
| H4 | Oil pressure telltale | 27 |
| H5 | Handbrake and hydraulic fluid telltale | 25 |
| H6 | Hazard warning telltale | 28 |
| H7 | Charging indicator light | 15 |
| H8 | High beam telltale | 61 |
| H9 | Stop-lamp – right | 68 |
| H10 | Stop-lamp – left | 64 |
| H11 | Front turn signal lamp – right | 76 |
| H12 | Rear turn signal lamp – right | 78 |
| H13 | Front turn signal lamp – left | 73 |
| H14 | Rear turn signal lamp – left | 75 |
| H17 | Trailer turn signal lamp telltale | 199 |
| H19 | Headlamps 'on' warning buzzer | 186, 187 |
| H20 | Choke 'on' telltale | 100 |
| K1 | Heated rear window relay | 39 |
| K2 | Flasher unit | 69 |
| K5 | Fog lamp relay | 156 to 159 |
| K6 | Air conditioning relay | 174 to 176 |
| K7 | Interval windscreen wiper relay | 178, 179 |
| K8 | Headlamp washer unit relay | 120 to 124 |
| K9 | Trailer flasher unit | 128 to 131 |
| K10 | Fuel injection unit timing control | 199, 201 |
| K15 | Ignition module | 213, 225 |
| K20 | Radiator fan relay | 8, 9, 29 to 33 |
| K24 | Running light relay | 241, 242 |
| K28 | Interval rear window wiper relay | 202, 203 |
| K30 | Fuel pump relay | 142 to 145 |
| K31 | Idling stabilizer control unit | 207, 209 |
| L2 | Ignition coil (transistorized system) | 32 to 35 |
| M1 | Starter | 9, 30 |
| M2 | Windscreen wiper motor | 7 |
| M3 | Heater blower motor | 118 to 122 |
| M4 | Radiator fan motor | 85 to 88 |
| M5 | Washer pump | 242 |
| M6 | Headlamp washer motor – left | 121 |
| M7 | Headlamp washer motor – right | 131 to 134 |
| M8 | Rear window wiper motor | 135 to 138 |
| M9 | Rear window washer pump | 139 to 142 |
| M10 | Air conditioning fan motor | 145 |
| M11 | Accessory fan motor | 183 |
| M21 | Electric fuel pump | 177 |
| P1 | Fuel gauge | 211 |
| P2 | Temperature gauge | 22 |
| P3 | Clock | 20 |
| P4 | Fuel sensor | 96, 97 |
| P5 | Temperature sensor | 22 |
| P7 | Tachometer | 20 |
| P8 | Oil pressure gauge | 113 |
| P9 | Voltmeter | 115 |
| P10 | Oil pressure sensor | 114 |
| P11 | Airflow meter | 115 |
| P12 | Temperature probe | 235 |
| R2 | Automatic excess-fuel starting device | 148 |
| R3 | Cigarette lighter | 99 |
| R6 | Air conditioning fan resistor | 178 |
| S1 | Starter switch | 7 |
| S2 | Light switch | 52 |
| S2.1 | Courtesy light switch | 90 |
| S2.3 | Parking light switch | 169 to 171 |
| S3 | Heater fan switch | 87 |
| S4 | Heater rear window switch | 39 |
| S5 | Turn signal switch assembly | 57 |
| S5.2 | High/flow beam switch | 70 to 76 |
| S5.3 | Turn signal/hazard warning switch | 101 |
| S5.5 | Horn switch | 119 |
| S5.6 | Interval windscreen wiper switch | 116 |
| S5.7 | Washer unit contact switch | 143 |
| S5.8 | Rear window washer contact switch | 107 |
| S7 | Reversing light switch | 65 |
| S8 | Stop-lamp switch | 7 |
| S10 | Automatic transmission switch | 25 |
| S11 | Brake fluid control switch | 24 |
| S12 | Clutch control switch | 26 |
| S13 | Handbrake 'on' telltale switch | 27 |
| S14 | Oil pressure switch | 81 |
| S15 | Boot light switch | 94 |
| S16 | Door contact switch – right | 92 |
| S17 | Door contact switch – left | 156 |
| S21 | Fog lamp switch | 163 |
| S22 | Rear foglamp switch | 182 |
| S24 | Air conditioning fan switch | 181 to 183 |
| S25 | Air conditioning switch | 174 |
| S26 | Inlet control evaporator switch | 174 |
| S27 | Compressor cut-off switch | 174 |
| S28 | Compressor cut-off switch | 174 |
| S29 | Accessory fan temperature switch | 174 |
| S44 | Throttle valve switch | 177, 241 |
| S47 | Door and headlamps 'on' contact warning switch | 235 |
| S50 | Choke valve cable switch | 187, 188 |
| S62 | Thermotime switch | 100 |
| S66 | Pressure switch | 235 |
| U1 | Voltage transformer | 35 |
| V2 | Headlamp washer diode | 203 to 207 |
| X1 | Trailer socket | 129 |
| X2 | Connector (auxiliary) | 191 to 197 |
| Y1 | Air conditioning compressor clutch | 95, 96, 98, 186, 196 |
| Y2 | Solenoid valve | 174 |
| Y4 | Headlamp washer solenoid valve | 172 |
| Y6 | Auxiliary air slide valve | 134 |
| Y7 | Solenoid valves | 235 |
| Y10 | Ignition distributor (transistorized system) | 235 |
| Y11 | Hall sensor | 11, 34 |
| Y15 | Cold start valve | 8, 9, 31, 32 |
| Y17 | Idle cut-off solenoid valve | 147 |

### Colour code

| | | | |
|---|---|---|---|
| BL | blue | GR | grey |
| BR | brown | GN | green |
| GE | yellow | HBL | light blue |
| LI | lilac | VI | violet |
| RT | red | WS | white |
| SW | black | | |

*Note: the wiring codes consist of the basic colour, the identification colour (in some instances), and the cross-sectioned area of the wire in mm$^2$*

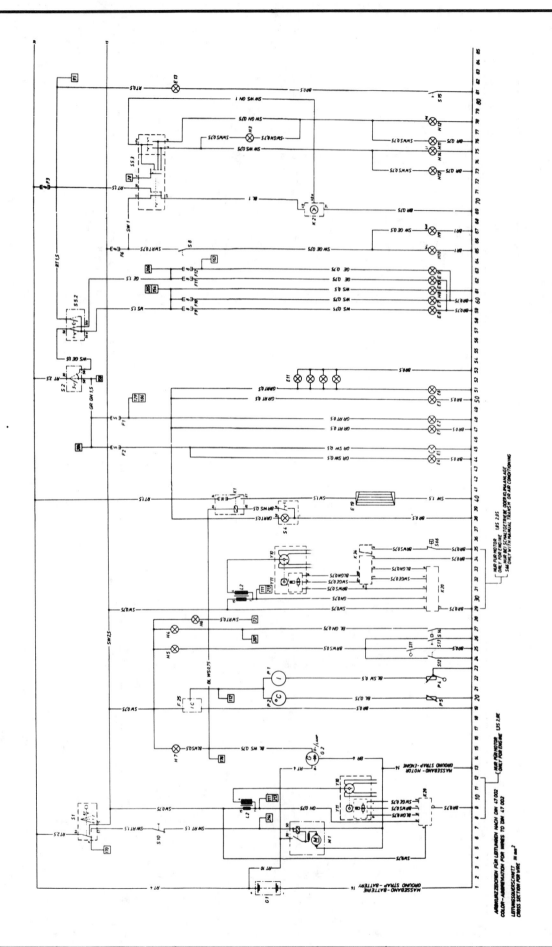

Fig. 13.130 Wiring diagram – Manta B and B-CC from May 1982

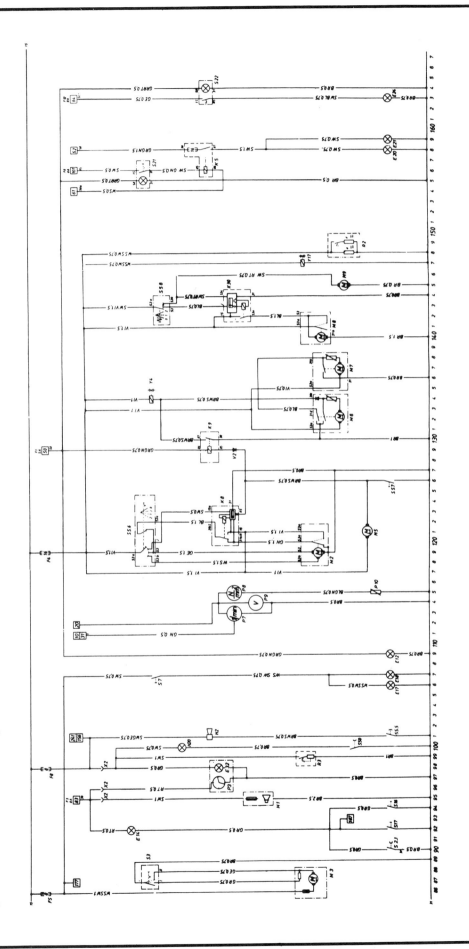

Fig. 13.130 Wiring diagram – Manta B and B-CC from May 1982 (continued)

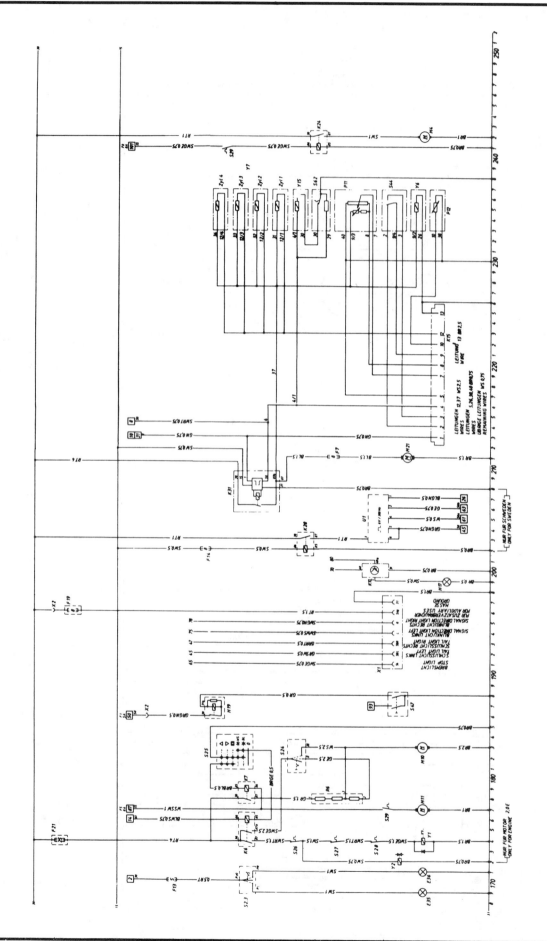

Fig. 13.130 Wiring diagram – Manta B and B-CC from May 1982 (continued)

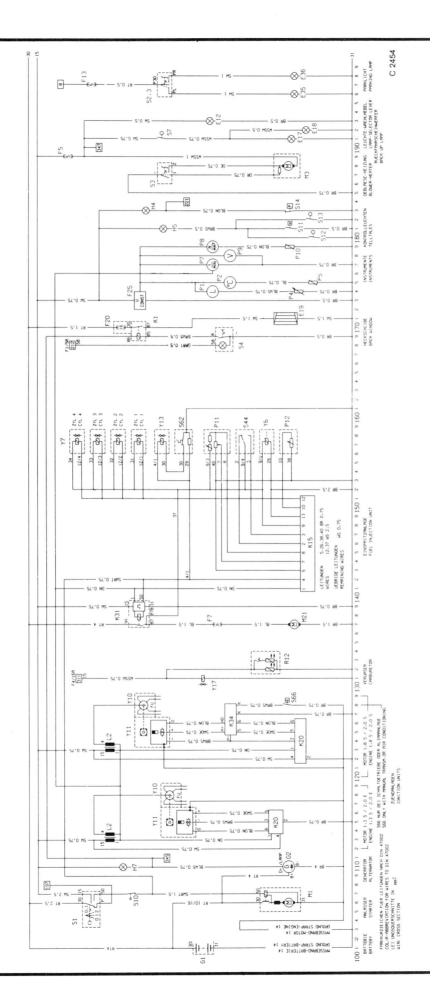

Fig. 13.131 Wiring diagram – Manta B from August 1985

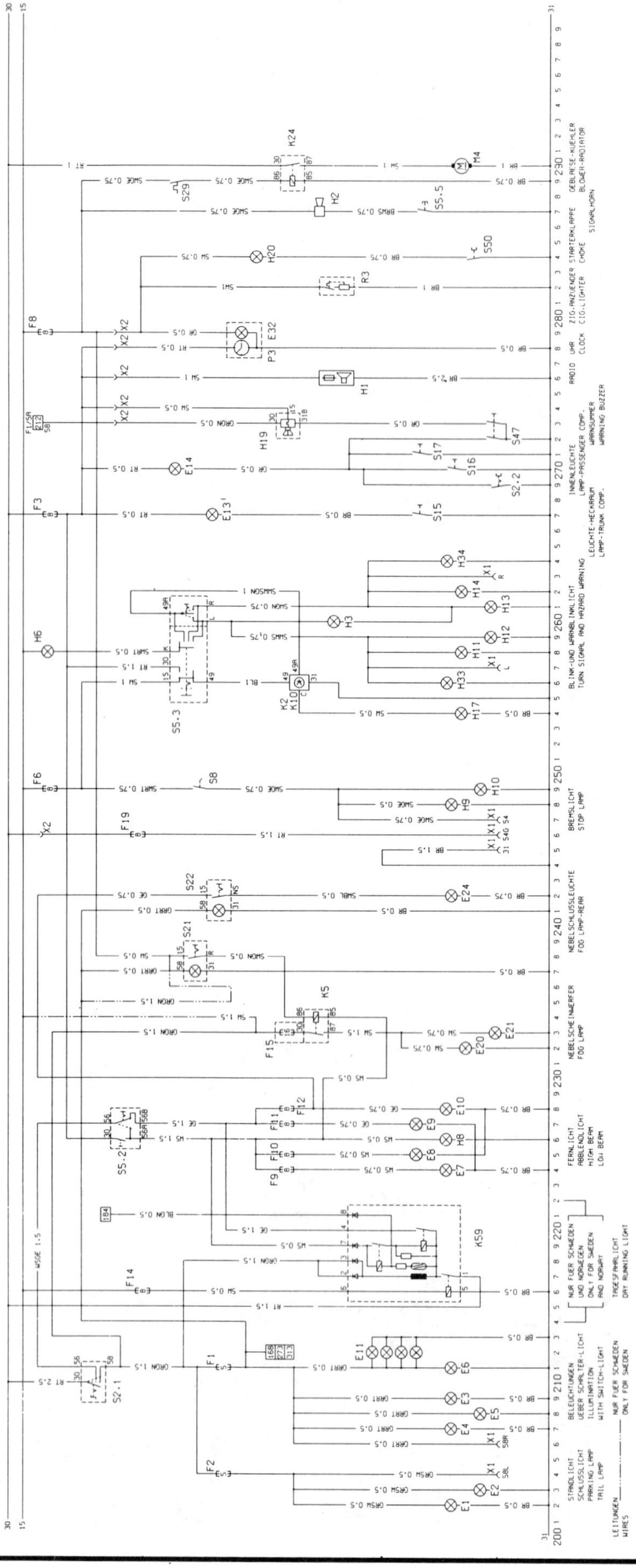

Fig. 13.131 Wiring diagram – Manta B from August 1985 (continued)

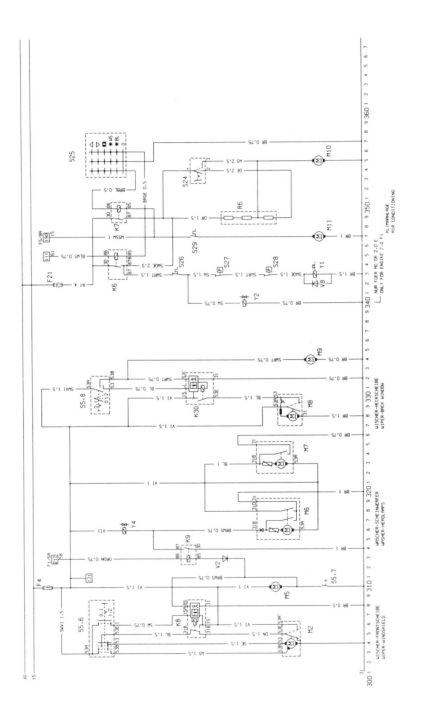

Fig. 13.131 Wiring diagram – Manta B from August 1985 (continued)

## Key to Fig. 13.131

| Code | Description | Track |
|---|---|---|
| E1 | Parking lamp – left | 202 |
| E2 | Tail lamp – left | 203 |
| E3 | Lamp – number plate | 109 |
| E4 | Parking lamp – right | 207 |
| E5 | Tail lamp – right | 208 |
| E6 | Lamp – engine compartment | 211 |
| E7 | High beam – left | 224 |
| E8 | High beam – right | 225 |
| E9 | Low beam – left | 227 |
| E10 | Low beam – right | 228 |
| E11 | Lights – instrument | 212 |
| E12 | Lamp – selector lever | 193 |
| E13 | Lamp – boot | 267 |
| E14 | Lamp – passenger compartment | 270 |
| E17 | Reversing lamp – left | 191 |
| E18 | Reversing lamp – right | 192 |
| E19 | Heated rear window | 171 |
| E20 | Fog lamp – left | 232 |
| E21 | Fog lamp – right | 233 |
| E24 | Fog lamp – rear | 242 |
| E32 | Lamp – clock | |
| E35 | Parking lamp – left | 196 |
| E36 | Parking lamp – right | 198 |
| F1 to F12 | Fuses in fuse box | |
| F13 | Fuse – reversing light | 195 |
| F14 | Fuse – day running light | 216 |
| F15 | Fuse – fog lamp | 233 |
| F19 | Fuse – trailer | 246 |
| F20 | Fuse – heated rear window | 170 |
| F21 | Fuse – air conditioning | 342 |
| F25 | Voltage stabilizer | 173 |
| G1 | Battery | 101 |
| G2 | Alternator | 110 |
| H1 | Receiver | 276 |
| H2 | Signal horn | 287 |
| H3 | Telltale – turn signal lamp | 260 |
| H4 | Telltale – oil pressure | 183 |
| H5 | Telltale – clutch, brake fluid & handbrake | 181 |
| H6 | Telltale – hazard warning system | 258 |
| H7 | Charging indicator light | 110 |
| H8 | Telltale – high beam | 226 |
| H9 | Stop-lamp – left | 248 |
| H10 | Stop-lamp – right | 249 |
| H11 | Turn signal lamp – front left | 258 |
| H12 | Turn signal lamp – rear, left | 259 |
| H13 | Turn signal lamp – front, right | 261 |
| H14 | Turn signal lamp – rear, right | 262 |
| H17 | Telltale – turn signal lamp, trailer | 254 |
| H19 | Buzzer – headlamps 'on' warning | 273,274 |
| H20 | Telltale – choke | 284 |
| H33 | Auxiliary turn signal lamp – left | 256 |
| H34 | Auxiliary turn signal lamp – right | 264 |
| K1 | Relay – heated rear window | 169,170 |
| K2 | Flasher unit | 255,256 |
| K5 | Relay – fog lamp | 233,234 |
| K6 | Relay – air conditioning | 343 to 345 |
| K7 | Relay – blower, air conditioning | 249,350 |
| K8 | Relay – interval, wiper, windshield | 305 to 308 |
| K9 | Relay – washer unit, headlamps | 313,314 |
| K10 | Flasher unit – trailer | 254 to 256 |
| K15 | Timing control – injection unit | 141 to 151 |
| K20 | Ignition module | 112 to 116, 122 to 126 |
| K24 | Relay – radiator fan | 289,290 |
| K30 | Relay – interval wiper, rear window | 330 to 332 |
| K31 | Relay – pump, fuel | 137 to 139 |
| K34 | Control unit – idle stabilization | 125 to 128 |
| K59 | Relay – running light | 215 to 221 |
| L2 | Ignition coil | 113,114,123,124 |
| M1 | Starter | 106,107 |
| M2 | Motor – windscreen wiper | 303 to 307 |
| M3 | Motor – radiator fan | 187 to 189 |
| M4 | Motor – radiator fan | 290 |
| M5 | Pump – washer, windshield | 310 |
| M6 | Motor – washer, headlamp left | 316 to 319 |
| M7 | Motor – wiper, headlamp right | 323 to 325 |
| M8 | Motor – wiper, back window | 328 to 330 |
| M9 | Pump – washer, back window | 334 |
| M10 | Motor – blower, air conditioning | 355 |
| M11 | Motor – blower, auxiliary | 347 |
| M21 | Fuel pump | 137 |
| P1 | Fuel indicator | 174 |
| P2 | Temperature indicator – engine | 175 |
| P3 | Clock | 278 |
| P4 | Sensor – fuel | 174 |
| P5 | Sensor – temperature, engine | 175 |
| P7 | Tachometer | 177 |
| P8 | Gauge – oil pressure | 179 |
| P9 | Voltmeter | 178 |
| P10 | Sensor – oil pressure | 179 |
| P11 | Air flow meter | 157 |
| P12 | Sensor – temperature, F1 | 157 |
| R3 | Cigarette lighter | 282 |
| R6 | Resistor – air conditioning fan | 349 |
| R12 | Automatic choke | 132 |
| S1 | Ignition switch | |
| S2 | Light switch assembly | 106 to 108 |
| S2.1 | Switch – light | 210,211 |
| S2.2 | Switch – passenger compartment light | 269 |
| S2.3 | Switch – parking lamp | 196 to 198 |
| S3 | Switch – blower, heater | 187,188 |
| S4 | Switch – back window, heated | 168,169 |
| S5 | Turn signal switch | |
| S5.2 | Switch – low beam | 226,227 |
| S5.3 | Switch – turn signal/hazard warning | 256 to 262 |
| S5.5 | Switch – horn | 287 |
| S5.6 | Switch – wiper windshield, interval | 303 to 305 |
| S5.7 | Contact switch – washer unit | 310 |
| S5.8 | Rear window washer contact switch | 331,332 |
| S7 | Switch – reversing lamp | 191 |
| S8 | Switch – stop-lamp | 249 |
| S10 | Switch – automatic transmission | 107 |
| S11 | Control switch – brake fluid | 181 |
| S12 | Control switch – clutch | 180 |
| S13 | Switch – parking brake | 182 |
| S14 | Switch – oil pressure | 183 |
| S15 | Switch – boot lamp | 267 |
| S16 | Contact switch – door, front left | 270 |
| S17 | Contact switch – door, front right | 271 |
| S21 | Switch – fog lamp, front | 237,238 |
| S22 | Switch – fog lamp, rear | 241,242 |
| S24 | Switch – blower, air conditioning | 354,355 |
| S25 | Rotary switch – air conditioning | 354 to 356 |
| S26 | Inlet control – evaporator | 343 |
| S27 | Pressure switch – air conditioning | 343 |
| S28 | Cut off switch – compressor | 343 |
| S29 | Switch – temperature, radiator | 289,347 |
| S44 | Switch – throttle valve | 157 |
| S47 | Contact switch – door and headlamps 'on' warning | 272,273 |
| S50 | Switch – Bowden cable, choke | 284 |
| S62 | Thermotime switch | 157 |
| S66 | Switch – vacuum | 128 |
| V2 | Diode – headlamp washer | 313 |
| V8 | Diode – compressor | |
| X1 | Socket – trailer | 204,206,245,246,247,257,263 |
| X2 | Connector – auxiliary | 246,273,274,276,278,279 |
| Y1 | Clutch – air conditioning compressor | 343 |
| Y2 | Solenoid valve | 340 |
| Y4 | Solenoid valve – headlamp washer | 316 |
| Y6 | Slide valve – auxiliary air | 157 |
| Y7 | Solenoid valves | 157 |
| Y10 | Ignition distributor – Hei, Hall sensor system | |
| Y11 | Hall sensor | 118,128 |
| Y13 | Cold start valve | 114 to 116,124 to 126 |
| Y17 | Solenoid valve – idle cut-off | 131 |

### Colour code

| Code | Colour |
|---|---|
| BL | Blue |
| BR | Brown |
| GE | Yellow |
| GR | Grey |
| GN | Green |
| HBL | Light blue |
| LI | Lilac |
| RT | Red |
| SW | Black |
| VI | Violet |
| WS | White |

Note: the wiring codes consist of the basic colour, the identification colour (in some instances), and the cross-sectional area of the wire in mm²

Numbers in boxes refer to the current track elsewhere in the diagram

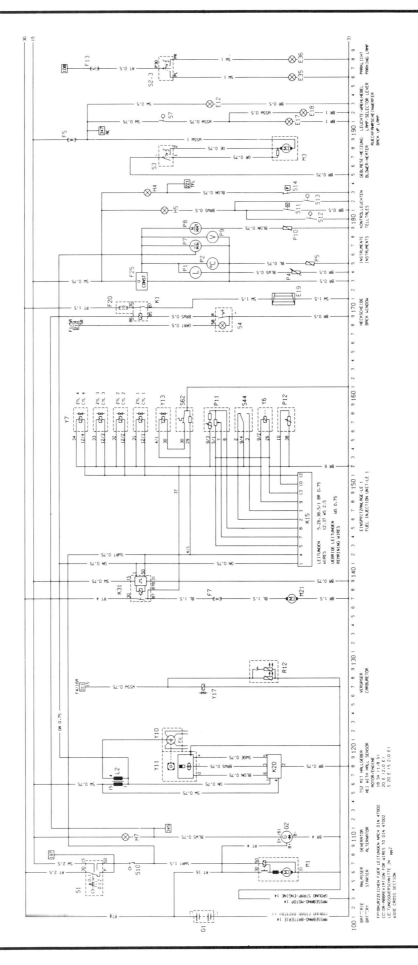

**Fig. 13.132 Wiring diagram – Manta B from August 1986**

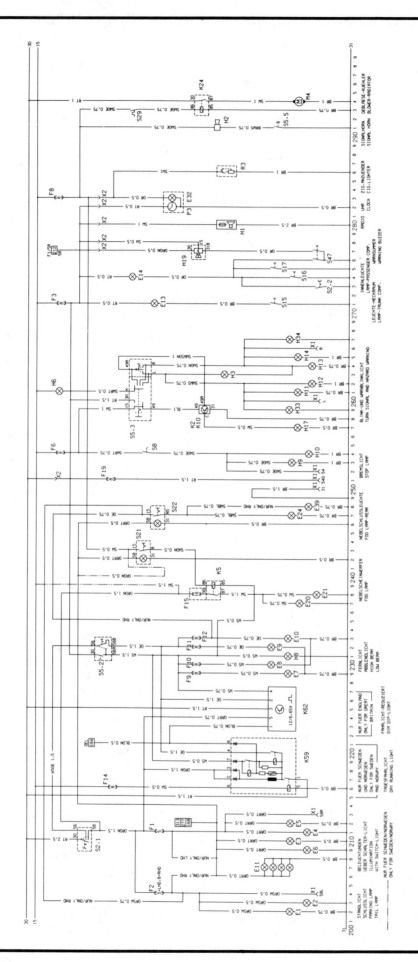

**Fig. 13.132 Wiring diagram – Manta B from August 1986 (continued)**

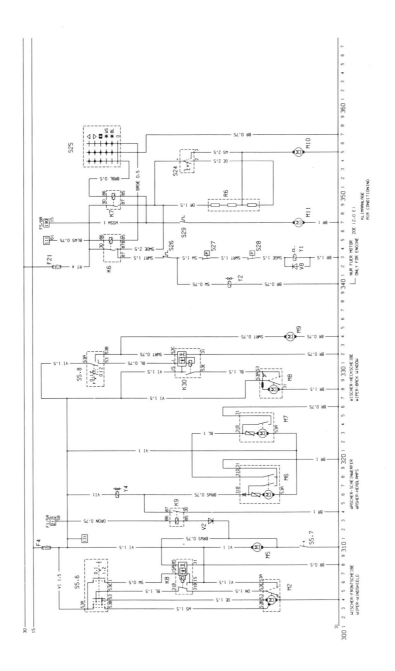

Fig. 13.132 Wiring diagram – Manta B from August 1986 (continued)

## Key to Fig. 13.132

| | | |
|---|---|---|
| E1 | Parking lamp – left | 202 |
| E2 | Tail lamp – left | 203 |
| E3 | Number plate lamp | 210 |
| E4 | Parking lamp – right | 211 |
| E5 | Tail lamp – right | 212 |
| E6 | Engine compartment lamp | 209 |
| E7 | Main beam – left | 229 |
| E8 | Main beam – right | 230 |
| E9 | Dipped beam – left | 232 |
| E10 | Dipped beam – right | 233 |
| E11 | Instrument lighting | 207 |
| E12 | Selector lever lamp | 193 |
| E13 | Luggage compartment lamp | 271 |
| E14 | Interior lamp | 274 |
| E17 | Reversing lamp – left | 191 |
| E18 | Reversing lamp – right | 192 |
| E19 | Heated rear window | 171 |
| E20 | Front foglamp – left | 237 |
| E21 | Front foglamp – right | 238 |
| E24 | Rear foglamp – left | 247 |
| E32 | Clock illumination | 283 |
| E35 | Parking lamp – left | 196 |
| E36 | Parking lamp – right | 198 |
| E39 | Rear foglamp – right | 248 |
| F1 to F12 | Fuses in fusebox | – |
| F13 | Fuse – parking light | 195 |
| F14 | Fuse – day running light | 216 |
| F15 | Fuse – foglamp | 238 |
| F19 | Fuse – trailer | 251 |
| F20 | Fuse – heated rear window | 170 |
| F21 | Fuse – air conditioning | 342 |
| F25 | Voltage stabiliser | 173 |
| G1 | Battery | 101 |
| G2 | Alternator | 110 |
| H1 | Receiver | 280 |
| H2 | Horn | 291 |
| H3 | Indicator telltale | 263 |
| H4 | Oil pressure telltale | 183 |
| H5 | Clutch, brake fluid, handbrake telltale | 181 |
| H6 | Hazard warning telltale | 261 |
| H7 | Charging indicator light | 110 |
| H8 | Main beam telltale | 231 |
| H9 | Stop-lamp – left | 253 |
| H10 | Stop-lamp – right | 254 |
| H11 | Indicator lamp – front left | 261 |
| H12 | Indicator lamp – rear left | 262 |
| H13 | Indicator lamp – front right | 264 |
| H14 | Indicator lamp – rear right | 265 |
| H17 | Indicator telltale – trailer | 257 |
| H19 | Headlamps-on buzzer | 277, 278 |
| H33 | Indicator repeater lamp – left | 259 |
| H34 | Indicator repeater lamp – right | 267 |
| K1 | Relay – heated rear window | 169, 170 |
| K2 | Flasher unit | 258, 259 |
| K5 | Relay – foglamp | 238, 239 |
| K6 | Relay – air conditioning | 343 to 345 |
| K7 | Relay – blower, air conditioning | 349, 350 |
| K8 | Relay – intermittent wipe | 305 to 308 |
| K9 | Relay – headlamp washer | 313, 314 |
| K10 | Flasher unit – trailer | 257 to 259 |
| K15 | Timing control – injection unit | 141 to 151 |
| K20 | Ignition module, HEI coil | 115 to 119 |
| K24 | Relay – radiator fan | 293, 294 |
| K30 | Relay – intermittent rear wipe | 330 to 332 |
| K31 | Relay – fuel pump | 137 to 139 |
| K59 | Relay – running light | 215 to 221 |
| K62 | Dim-dip lighting control unit | 223 to 227 |
| L2 | Ignition coil HEI, Hall sensor system | 116, 117 |
| M1 | Starter | 106, 107 |
| M2 | Windscreen wiper motor | 303 to 306 |
| M3 | Radiator fan motor | 187 to 189 |
| M4 | Radiator fan motor | 294 |
| M5 | Windscreen washer pump | 310 |
| M6 | Headlamp wiper motor – left | 316 to 319 |
| M7 | Headlamp wiper motor – right | 323 to 325 |
| M8 | Rear screen wiper motor | 328 to 330 |
| M9 | Rear screen washer pump | 334 |
| M10 | Air conditioning blower motor | 355 |
| M11 | Auxiliary blower motor | 347 |
| M21 | Fuel pump | 137 |
| P1 | Fuel gauge | 174 |
| P2 | Temperature gauge | 175 |
| P3 | Clock | 282 |
| P4 | Sensor – fuel | 174 |
| P5 | Sensor – engine temperature | 175 |
| P7 | Tachometer | 177 |
| P8 | Oil pressure gauge | 179 |
| P9 | Voltmeter | 178 |
| P10 | Sensor – oil pressure | 179 |
| P11 | Air flow meter | 157 |
| P12 | Temperature sensor, fuel injection | 157 |
| R3 | Cigarette lighter | 286 |
| R6 | Air conditioning blower resistor | 349 |
| R12 | Automatic choke | 128 |
| S1 | Ignition switch | 106 to 108 |
| S2 | Light switch assembly | – |
| S2.1 | Light switch | 210, 211 |
| S2.2 | Interior light switch | 273 |
| S2.3 | Parking light switch | 196 to 198 |
| S3 | Heater blower switch | 187, 188 |
| S4 | Heated rear window switch | 168, 169 |
| S5 | Indicator switch assembly | – |
| S5.2 | Dipped beam switch | 231, 232 |
| S5.3 | Indicator/hazard warning switch | 259 to 264 |
| S5.5 | Horn switch | 291 |
| S5.6 | Windscreen wiper interval switch | 303 to 305 |
| S5.7 | Windscreen washer switch | 310 |
| S5.8 | Rear screen washer switch | 331, 332 |
| S7 | Reversing lamp switch | 191 |
| S8 | Stop-lamp switch | 254 |
| S10 | Automatic transmission switch | 107 |
| S11 | Brake fluid control switch | 181 |
| S12 | Clutch control switch | 180 |
| S13 | Handbrake switch | 182 |
| S14 | Oil pressure switch | 183 |
| S15 | Luggage compartment light switch | 271 |
| S16 | Door switch – front left | 274 |
| S17 | Door switch – front right | 275 |
| S21 | Front foglamp switch | 242, 243 |
| S22 | Rear foglamp switch | 246, 247 |
| S24 | Air conditioning blower switch | 354, 355 |
| S25 | Air conditioning rotary switch | 354 to 356 |
| S26 | Evaporator inlet control | 343 |
| S27 | Air conditioning pressure switch | 343 |
| S28 | Compressor cut-off switch | 343 |
| S29 | Radiator temperature switch | 347 |
| S44 | Throttle valve switch | 157 |
| S47 | Door switch – headlamps on buzzer | 276, 277 |
| S62 | Thermotime switch | 157 |
| V2 | Headlamp washer diode | 313 |
| V8 | Compressor diode | 342 |
| X1 | Trailer socket | 204, 213, 250 to 252, 260, 266 |
| X2 | Connector, auxiliary users | 251, 277, 278, 280, 282, 283 |
| Y1 | Air conditioning compressor clutch | 343 |
| Y2 | Solenoid valve | 340 |
| Y4 | Headlamp washer solenoid valve | 316 |
| Y6 | Auxiliary air slide valve | 157 |
| Y7 | Solenoid valve | 157 |
| Y10 | Ignition distributor HEI – Hall sensor system | 121 |
| Y11 | Hall sensor | 117 to 119 |
| Y13 | Cold start valve | 157 |
| Y17 | Idle cut-off solenoid valve | 127 |

*For notes on use of diagrams, and colour code, see p.290. Not all items fitted to all models*

## 15 Suspension and steering

### Spare wheel and jack (Hatchback)

1   The spare wheel and jack are mounted beneath the floor of the luggage compartment.
2   Open the rear door and remove the floor covering of the luggage compartment.
3   Lift out the floor panel to expose the jack and the spare wheel (photo).

### Front shock absorber (Manta) – fitting

4   When fitting a front shock absorber to a Manta the upper mounting nut should be tightened so that the length of exposed spindle is $27.0 \pm 0.5$ mm ($1.1 \pm 0.2$ in). Refer to Chapter 11 Fig. 11.3.

### Front hub – adjustment

5   Jack up the front of the car and remove the roadwheel.
6   Remove the brake pads then prise off the hub grease cap and remove the split pin.
7   Loosen the nut to provide slight end play.
8   Using a torque wrench tighten the nut to 25 Nm (18 lbf ft) while turning the hub.
9   Unscrew the nut 90° ($^1/_4$ turn) and insert a new split pin. If the split pin holes are not aligned continue to unscrew the nut to the nearest hole. With the bearings correctly adjusted it should still be possible to move the thrust washer beneath the nut using a screwdriver.
10  Refit the cap and roadwheel, and lower the car to the ground.

### Front suspension upper balljoint

11  A revised balljoint and upper arm were fitted in 1977 in which the balljoint is 0.08 in (2.0 mm) nearer the centre of the car. The revised camber angle is 0° to 1° 30' negative.
12  The revised components can be identified by an indentation located on the upper arm on the inner side of the balljoint.

### Rear shock absorber (Manta) fitting

13  The rear shock absorber upper mounting on Manta-B GT/E models incorporates two locknuts and these should be tightened so that the length of exposed spindle is 6 mm (0.23 in). A single nut is fitted to other Manta models and the dimension should be 11 mm (0.44 in) for pre 1983 models as shown in Chapter 11 Fig. 11.14, or 9 mm (0.35 in) for 1983-on models (photo).

### Steering wheel (Manta) – removal and refitting

14  On some Manta models the horn push is located in the centre of the steering wheel. Access to the steering wheel nut is gained by removing the horn push and disconnecting the wire(s).

15.3 Jack and spare wheel (Hatchback)

15.13 Rear shock absorber upper mounting on a late Manta

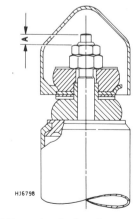

**Fig. 13.133 Rear shock absorber upper mounting tightening dimension for Manta B GT/E models (Sec 15)**

A = 6 mm (0.23 in)

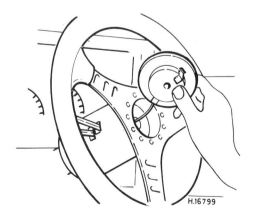

Fig. 13.134 Removing the horn push from the steering wheel (Sec 15)

## 16 Bodywork

### *Radiator grille – removal and refitting*

1  Prise the top of the grille from the fasteners then lift the grille out of the bottom mountings.
2  Refitting is a reversal of removal.

### *Door interior handles and trim panel (Manta) – removal and refitting*

3  Remove the screws from the arm rest/handle grip then swivel it upwards through 90° and release it from the trim panel (photos).
4  Prise the surround from the lock lever (photo).
5  Prise out the inner handle finger plate then remove the surround (photos).

6  Remove the window regulator handle and trim panel as described in Chapter 12.
7  Refitting is a reversal of removal.

### *Door exterior mirror (Manta) – removal and refitting*

8  Remove the trim panel as previously described.
9  Prise the centre disc from the mirror control knob.
10  The control knob must now be removed by levering out the four tags simultanously. Pull the knob from the control arm (photos).
11  Remove the mounting screws, lift off the inner plate, and withdraw the mirror from the door (photos).
12  Refitting is a reversal of removal, but make sure that the rubber gasket is located correctly before tightening the mounting screws (photo).

16.3A Arm rest in its normal position

16.3B Swivel the arm rest through 90° to remove it

16.4 Removing the lock lever surround

16.5A Remove the inner handle finger plate ...

16.5B ... and surround

16.10A Showing the four tags which retain the exterior mirror control knob

16.10B Removing the exterior mirror control knob

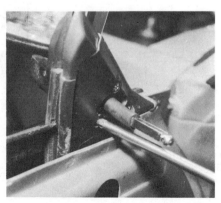

16.11A Remove the mounting screws and plate ...

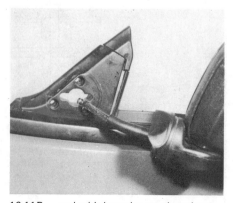

16.11B ... and withdraw the exterior mirror

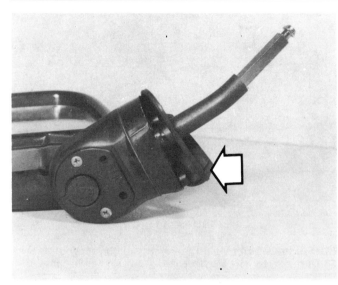

16.12 Showing the exterior mirror and rubber gasket

*Rear quarter window (Hatchback) – removal and refitting*
13 Using a piece of thin plastic, or a wooden wedge, carefully prise off the extractor grille between the door pillar and the quarter window (photo).
14 Remove the sealant covering the heads of the two hinge bolts (photo).
15 From inside the car, remove the three screws securing the quarter window catch.
16 While holding the quarter window in the open position, remove the two hinge screws and lift away the window with hinges and catch attached. Refitting is a reversal of the removal procedure.

*Door lock (Manta) – general*
17 On later models the inner locking knob is replaced by a slider control in the trim panel. The control is secured by two screws (photo).

*Hatchback lid – removal and refitting*
18 Open the rear door and disconnect the two cords from the tonneau.
19 Disconnect the electrical leads from the heated glass panel and free the cables from the cable clips (photo).
20 Using a small screwdriver, prise the plastic wedges from the upper ends of the lid stays and disconnect the stays from the door (photos).
21 Lower and close the door.
22 From inside the vehicle, prise out the cover plates from the headlining.
23 Remove the two bolts from the hinge on the left- and right-hand sides (photo).
24 Lift out the rear door with the hinges attached.
25 If the hinges are to be removed from the door, first mark round them with a pencil, so that they can be installed in exactly the same position (photo).
26 Refitting the rear door is the reverse of the removal sequence.

*Rear door lock (Hatchback) – removal and dismantling*
27 Prise out the plastic clips from the trim panel on the rear door and remove the panel.
28 Use a thin drift to release the mounting studs of the plastic plate and remove the plate (photo).
29 Disconnect the actuating rod from the latch.
30 With a tubular spanner, unscrew and remove the slotted nut from the lock cylinder and lift the lock cylinder out of the hatchback lid.
31 To remove the lock barrel, insert the ignition key into the lock. Prise off the circlip and remove the circlip and waved washer.
32 Withdraw the lock barrel from its housing.

16.13 Removing the rear extractor grille (Hatchback)

16.14 Rear quarter window hinge bolt (Hatchback)

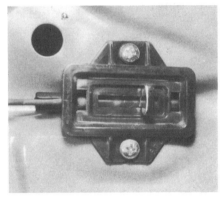

16.17 Door locking control (Manta)

16.19 Heated rear window connection (Hatchback)

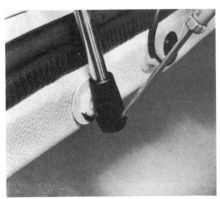

16.20A Prising out the lid stay wedge (Hatchback)

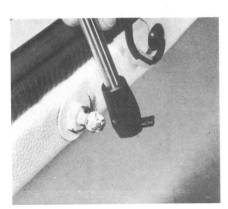

16.20B Disconnecting the lid stay (Hatchback)

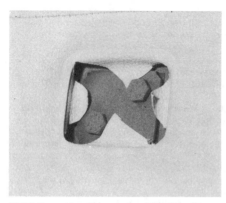

16.23 Rear door hinge bolts (Hatchback)

16.25 View of the hatchback lid hinge
(Hatchback)

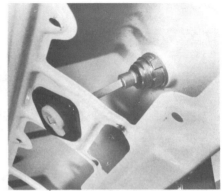

16.28 Rear door lock plastic plate
(Hatchback)

### Rear door latch (Hatchback) – removal and refitting
33 Prise out the plastic clips from the trim panel on the rear door
and remove the panel.
34 Remove the four screws securing the latch (photo).
35 Disconnect the actuating rod from the lock housing.
36 Refitting is the reverse of the removal operations, but before
connecting the actuating rod, check that the dimension from the
screwed end of the actuating rod to the centre of the stud is 0.55 in
(14 mm).

### Rear door glass (Hatchback) – removal and refitting
37 The removal and refitting of the rear door glass is similar to that
of the windscreen, described in Chapter 12, Section 20, with the
addition that it is necessary to disconnect the electrical cables to the
heating element before starting removal, and to reconnect them
when refitting has been completed.

### Rear tonneau (Hatchback) – removal and refitting
38 Open the rear door and disconnect the two cords from the
tonneau.
39 Pull the tonneau to the rear to disengage the securing hooks
(photo) and then lift the tonneau clear.
40 When refitting the tonneau, enter the hooks of the tonneau into
the slots and then push the tonneau forward to engage the hooks.
41 When the tonneau is in place, reconnect the two cords.

### Bonnet – removal and refitting
42 On later models the windscreen washer jets and engine
compartment light are fitted to the bonnet. Removal and refitting is
as described in Chapter 12, but additionally the washer tubing and
light wiring must be disconnected (photos).
43 The bonnet lock is located at the front of the engine
compartment and is secured by two bolts (photo).

16.34 Rear door latch fixing screws
(Hatchback)

16.39 Rear tonneau fixing hook
(Hatchback)

16.42A Washer tubing ...

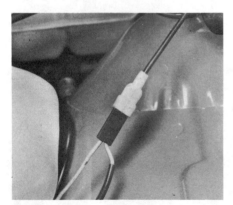

16.42B ... and light wiring on the bonnet

16.42C Showing bonnet hinge also tubing
and wiring entry point

16.43 Bonnet lock

*Bumpers (Manta) – removal and refitting*
44 To remove a front bumper raise the front of the car and support on axle stands. Unscrew all the mounting bolts and withdraw the bumper and brackets from the body box sections. Note that there are two bolts on each side of the bumper in addition to the bracket bolts. Disconnect the lighting wiring and the headlight washer tubing and withdraw the bumper. Refitting is a reversal of removal (photos).
45 To remove a rear bumper remove the luggage compartment floor panel and use a socket to remove the rear bolts. Unscrew the end mounting bolts from the outside. Disconnect the number plate light wiring and withdraw the bumper. Refitting is a reversal of removal (photos).

*Rear spoiler (Manta) – removal and refitting*
**Note:** *The limited edition Manta 'Exclusive' model has a*

*different rear spoiler to other Manta models. No removal/refitting details were available at the time of writing.*

46 Open the rear door (tailgate) then unscrew the mounting nuts and lift off the spoiler (photo).
47 Refitting is a reversal of removal.

*Centre console – removal and refitting*
48 Where fitted unclip and remove the cassette storage box (photo).
49 Prise out the plastic plugs then remove the screws and lift the console over the gear lever and handbrake lever (photos). On some automatic transmission models it may also be necessary to prise off the sealing strip cover and remove the flexible sealing strip from the base of the selector lever.
50 Refitting is a reversal of the above.

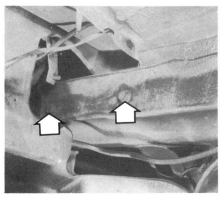
16.44A Remove the bracket bolts ...

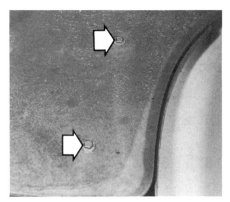
16.44B ... and side mounting bolts ...

16.44C ... and withdraw the front bumper

16.44D Showing box section location for front bumper brackets

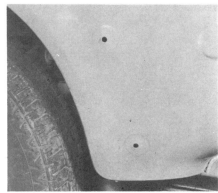
16.44E Showing front bumper side mounting holes

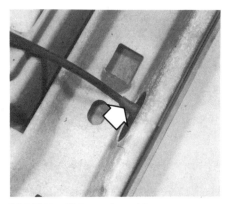
16.44F Headlight washer tubing connection to front bumper

16.44G Bracket fixings to front bumper

16.44H Front bumper side mounting nuts

16.45A Using a socket to unscrew the rear bumper rear bolts

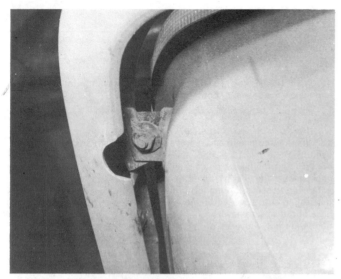

16.45B Rear bumper end mounting bolt

16.46 Rear spoiler mounting nut

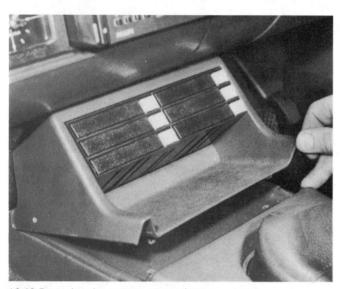

16.48 Removing the cassette storage box

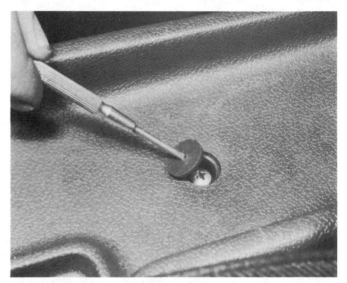

16.49A The rear screws are covered with plastic plugs

16.49B Front screw locations for the centre console

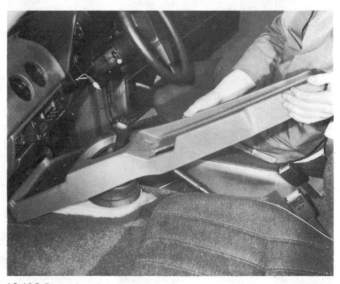

16.49C Removing the centre console

*Sun roof – removal and refitting*

51  Pull the handle down to position 'A' (Fig. 13.135), push the roof to the rear, unscrew the handle recess, and pivot the sun roof lining downwards at the retaining springs.

52  Pull the sun roof lining slightly inwards at the sides and unscrew the front and rear guide plates. Swivel the sun roof lining back up at the front tension springs.

53  Pull the sun roof forwards until the front edge of the slides ('B' in Fig. 13.137) is in line with the rounded part of the guide bead 'C'.

54  Angle the sun roof to one side and lift it out of the roof opening (Fig. 13.138).

55  Refitting is the reverse of removal, but before starting refitting, smear the sun roof runner rails with bearing grease and ensure that both supporting levers ('D' in Fig. 13.139) are pointing downwards and outwards.

56  When screwing on the sun roof front and rear retaining plates, make sure that the side control rod clips (1 and 2) are fitted as shown in Fig. 13.140.

*Sun roof lining – renewal*

57  Remove the sun roof, taking care not to scratch the roof paint-work.

58  Unhook the tensioning rail retaining springs at the front and then use a screwdriver to prise the retaining springs out of the tensioning rail (Fig. 13.141).

59  Use a screwdriver to bend back the retaining tongues of the rear tensioning rail and unhook the lining (Fig. 13.142).

60  Remove the clips from the pleats in the lining at the forward end of each side, and from the back edge, and pull out the front tensioning rail and the wire bow from the rear pockets of the lining.

61  Refitting is the reverse of removal, but note that the T-slots in the front rail point towards the front (Fig. 13.144) and the chamfered edge is as shown in Fig. 13.143.

*Sun roof control mechanism – removal and refitting*

62  Remove the sun roof and then its lining as described previously.

63  Unhook the retaining springs on the control rod hinge pins, tap the pins out and remove the control rods.

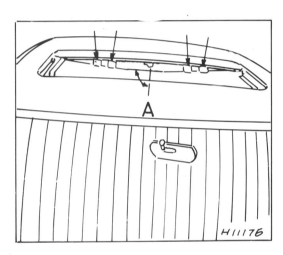

Fig. 13.135 Sun roof handle position (A) to remove sun roof (retaining springs arrowed) (Sec 16)

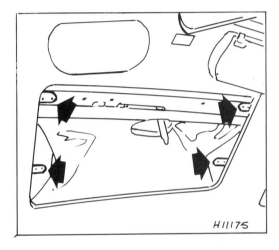

Fig. 13.136 Sun roof guide plates (arrowed) (Sec 16)

Fig. 13.137 Sun roof removal – front edge of slides (B) on same level as round part of guide bead (C) (Sec 16)

Fig. 13.138 Lifting out the sun roof (Sec 16)

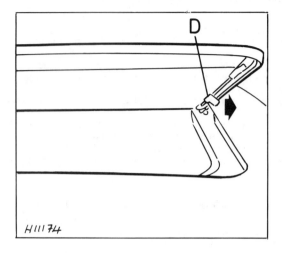

Fig. 13.139 Supporting lever D in position for installing sun roof (Sec 16)

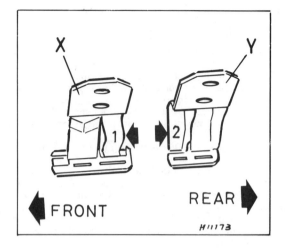

Fig. 13.140 Retaining plate positions (Sec 16)

X          Front                    Y          Rear

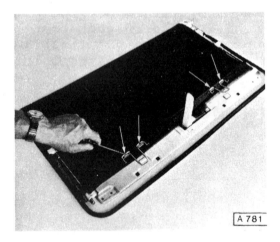

Fig. 13.141 Removing the retaining springs (Sec 16)

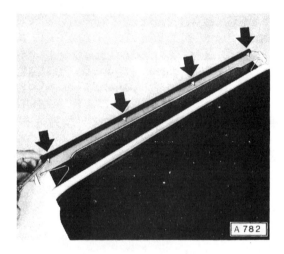

Fig. 13.142 Bending back the retaining tongues (Sec 16)

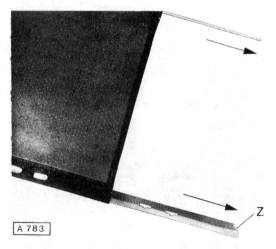

Fig. 13.143 Removing the tensioning rail and bow – note side slopes at 'Z' (Sec 16)

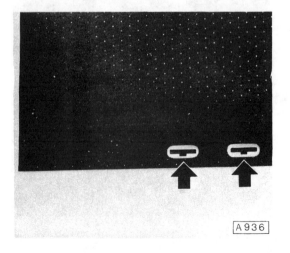

Fig. 13.144 Position of T-slots (Sec 16)

64 Use a pin punch to drive out the pivot pin of the handle and then unhook the end of the compensating spring from its hole in the handle.
65 Remove the handle with one stay attached to it and then remove the other stay.
66 Refitting is the reverse of removal.

*Instrument panel – removal and refitting*
67 The instrument panel is split into an upper and a lower half. The lower half may be removed and refitted independently of the upper, but the upper half can only be removed in sequence after the lower half.

**Lower instrument panel**
68 This panel is split into two unequal sections. The longer, left-hand section, incorporating glovebox, ashtray and apertures for cigar lighter, radio and clock, is secured to the panel support by eight screws and washers, three of them located inside the glovebox. The shorter, right-hand section, incorporating a detachable access cover for the fuse block, is secured to the panel support by two screws and washers.
69 To remove the panel, first remove the shorter, right-hand section. The screw at the right-hand end of the left-hand section will now

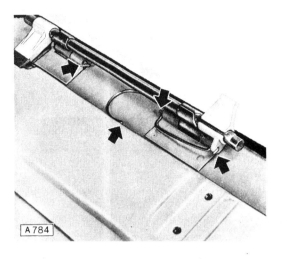

Fig. 13.145 Hinge pin retaining springs (Sec 16)

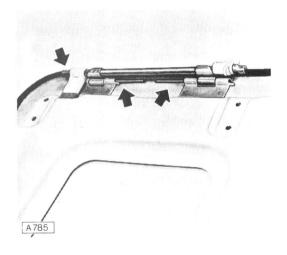

Fig 13.146 Removing the hinge pin (Sec 16)

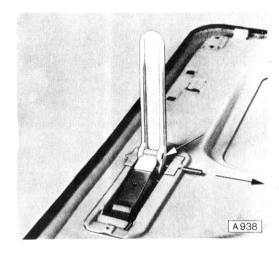

Fig. 13.147 Removing the pivot pin (Sec 16)

Fig. 13.148 Unhooking the compensating spring (Sec 16)

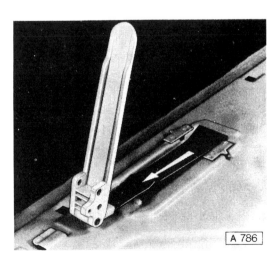

Fig. 13.149 Removing the handle and stay (Sec 16)

be accessible and this section may be removed by undoing the eight retaining screws. Refer to Fig. 13.150.

70 Refitting is a reversal of the above, remembering the longer, left-hand section must be refitted first. When refitting, ensure the panel is located on top of the support bracket, as shown in Fig. 13.151.

**Upper panel cover**

71 The instrument panel cover can only be removed once the lower panel has been removed (see above) and the instrument housing assembly also removed (see Chapter 10, Section 34).

72 The panel is secured by the three studs and washers below the windscreen, and in addition has three clips which engage with the panel support common to both upper and lower panel sections. Two screws securing the instrument cowl pass through the metal frame of the panel cover.

73 To remove, undo the three nuts and washers below the windscreen. Then carefully pull the panel away from the windscreen, disengaging it from the panel support. Detach the demist vents from their ducts and lift the panel away completely.

74 Refitting is a reversal of the above procedure.

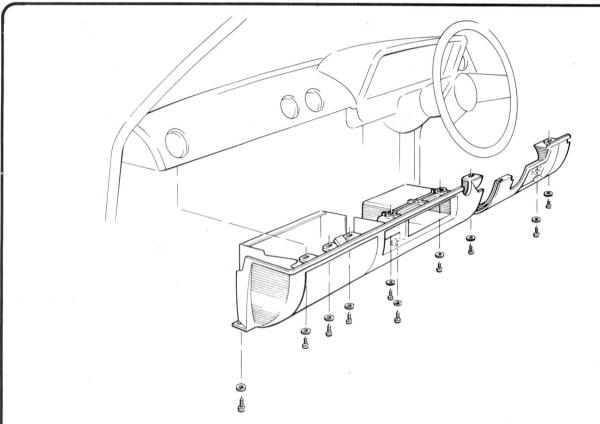

Fig. 13.150 Lower instrument panel retaining screws (Sec 16)

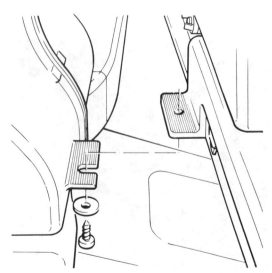

Fig. 13.151 Lower instrument panel location to support (Sec 16)

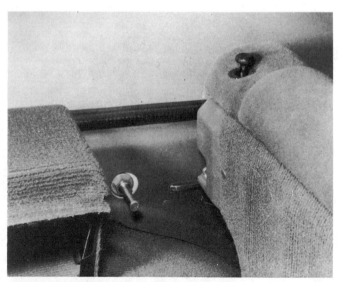

16.76 Rear seat locking knob and escutcheon (Hatchback)

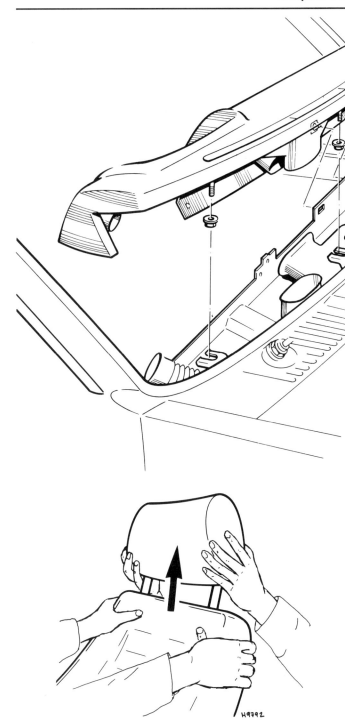

Fig. 13.152 Instrument panel cover retaining screws (Sec 16)

### Front seat head restraints (Manta) – removal and refitting

81 Have an assistant press the head restraint downwards, then depress the retaining springs with the thumbs as shown in Fig. 13.153. The assistant can now withdraw the head restraint sharply upwards.

82 Refitting is a reversal of removal.

### Plastic components

With the use of more and more plastic body components by the vehicle manufacturers (eg bumpers, spoilers, and in some cases major body panels), rectification of more serious damage to such items has become a matter of either entrusting repair work to a specialist in this field, or renewing complete components. Repair of such damage by the DIY owner is not really feasible owing to the cost of the equipment and materials required for effecting such repairs. The basic technique involves making a groove along the line of the crack in the plastic using a rotary burr in a power drill. The damaged part is then welded back together by using a hot air gun to heat up and fuse a plastic filler rod into the groove. Any excess plastic is then removed and the area rubbed down to a smooth finish. It is important that a filler rod of the correct plastic is used, as body components can be made of a variety of different types (eg polycarbonate, ABS, polypropylene).

Damage of a less serious nature (abrasions, minor cracks etc) can be repaired by the DIY owner using a two-part epoxy filler repair material. Once mixed in equal proportions, this is used in similar fashion to the bodywork filler used on metal panels. The filler is usually cured in twenty to thirty minutes, ready for sanding and painting.

If the owner is renewing a complete component himself, or if he has repaired it with epoxy filler, he will be left with the problem of finding a suitable paint for finishing which is compatible with the type of plastic used. At one time the use of a universal paint was not possible owing to the complex range of plastics encountered in body component applications. Standard paints, generally speaking, will not bond to plastic or rubber satisfactorily. However, it is now possible to obtain a plastic body parts finishing kit which consists of a pre-primer treatment, a primer and coloured top coat. Full instructions are normally supplied with a kit, but basically the method of use is to first apply the pre-primer to the component concerned and allow it to dry for up to 30 minutes. Then the primer is applied and left to dry for about an hour before finally applying the special coloured top coat. The result is a correctly coloured component where the paint will flex with the plastic or rubber, a property that standard paint does not normally possess.

Fig. 13.153 Removing the front seat head restraint (Sec 16)

### Rear seat (Hatchback) – removal and refitting

75 Release the rear seat from the floor bracket by pressing down the front edge of the seat and pushing the seat to the rear at the same time, and then lift the seat out.

76 Screw off the locking knob and remove the escutcheon from each side of the rear seat back (photo).

77 Press down along the entire width of the reinforcement strip of the rear seat back upholstery to disengage it from its retainer track.

78 Disengage the form wire of the rear seat from the three upper holders.

79 Fold the rear seat cushion downwards and disconnect the rear seat back form wire from the lower retainers.

80 Refitting is the reverse of the operations necessary for removal.

# Fault diagnosis

## Introduction

The vehicle owner who does his or her own maintenance according to the recommended schedules should not have to use this section of the manual very often. Modern component reliability is such that, provided those items subject to wear or deterioration are inspected or renewed at the specified intervals, sudden failure is comparatively rare. Faults do not usually just happen as a result of sudden failure, but develop over a period of time. Major mechanical failures in particular are usually preceded by characteristic symptoms over hundreds or even thousands of miles. Those components which do occasionally fail without warning are often small and easily carried in the vehicle.

With any fault finding, the first step is to decide where to begin investigations. Sometimes this is obvious, but on other occasions a little detective work will be necessary. The owner who makes half a dozen haphazard adjustments or replacements may be successful in curing a fault (or its symptoms), but he will be none the wiser if the fault recurs and he may well have spent more time and money than was necessary. A calm and logical approach will be found to be more satisfactory in the long run. Always take into account any warning signs or abnormalities that may have been noticed in the period preceding the fault — power loss, high or low gauge readings, unusual noises or smells, etc — and remember that failure of components such as fuses or spark plugs may only be pointers to some underlying fault.

The pages which follow here are intended to help in cases of failure to start or breakdown on the road. There is also a Fault Diagnosis Section at the end of each Chapter which should be consulted if the preliminary checks prove unfruitful. Whatever the fault, certain basic principles apply. These are as follows:

**Verify the fault.** This is simply a matter of being sure that you know what the symptoms are before starting work. This is particularly important if you are investigating a fault for someone else who may not have described it very accurately.

**Don't overlook the obvious.** For example, if the vehicle won't start, is there petrol in the tank? (Don't take anyone else's word on this particular point, and don't trust the fuel gauge either!) If an electrical fault is indicated, look for loose or broken wires before digging out the test gear.

**Cure the disease, not the symptom.** Substituting a flat battery with a fully charged one will get you off the hard shoulder, but if the underlying cause is not attended to, the new battery will go the same way. Similarly, changing oil-fouled spark plugs for a new set will get you moving again, but remember that the reason for the fouling (if it wasn't simply an incorrect grade of plug) will have to be established and corrected.

**Don't take anything for granted.** Particularly, don't forget that a 'new' component may itself be defective (especially if it's been rattling round in the boot for months), and don't leave components out of a fault diagnosis sequence just because they are new or recently fitted. When you do finally diagnose a difficult fault, you'll probably realise that all the evidence was there from the start.

## Electrical faults

Electrical faults can be more puzzling than straightforward mechanical failures, but they are no less susceptible to logical analysis if the basic principles of operation are understood. Vehicle electrical wiring exists in extremely unfavourable conditions — heat, vibration and chemical attack — and the first things to look for are loose or corroded connections and broken or chafed wires, especially where the wires pass through holes in the bodywork or are subject to vibration.

All metal-bodied vehicles in current production have one pole of the battery 'earthed', ie connected to the vehicle bodywork, and in nearly all modern vehicles it is the negative (−) terminal. The various electrical components — motors, bulb holders etc — are also connected to earth, either by means of a lead or directly by their mountings. Electric current flows through the component and then back to the battery via the bodywork. If the component mounting is loose or corroded, or if a good path back to the battery is not available, the circuit will be incomplete and malfunction will result. The engine and/or gearbox are also earthed by means of flexible metal straps to the body or subframe; if these straps are loose or missing, starter motor, generator and ignition trouble may result.

Assuming the earth return to be satisfactory, electrical faults will be due either to component malfunction or to defects in the current supply. Individual components are dealt with in Chapter 10. If supply wires are broken or cracked internally this results in an open-circuit, and the easiest way to check for this is to bypass the suspect wire temporarily with a length of wire having a crocodile clip or suitable connector at each end. Alternatively, a 12V test lamp can be used to verify the presence of supply voltage at various points along the wire and the break can be thus isolated.

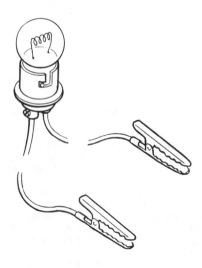

**A simple test lamp is useful for tracing electrical faults**

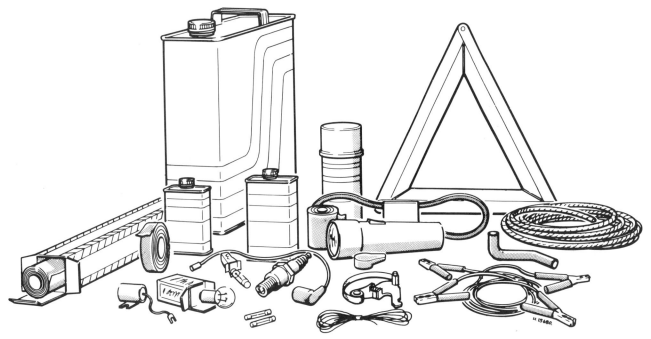

**Carrying a few spares can save you a long walk!**

If a bare portion of a live wire touches the bodywork or other earthed metal part, the electricity will take the low-resistance path thus formed back to the battery: this is known as a short-circuit. Hopefully a short-circuit will blow a fuse, but otherwise it may cause burning of the insulation (and possibly further short-circuits) or even a fire. This is why it is inadvisable to bypass persistently blowing fuses with silver foil or wire.

### Spares and tool kit

Most vehicles are supplied only with sufficient tools for wheel changing; the *Maintenance and minor repair* tool kit detailed in *Tools and working facilities,* with the addition of a hammer, is probably sufficient for those repairs that most motorists would consider attempting at the roadside. In addition a few items which can be fitted without too much trouble in the event of a breakdown should be carried. Experience and available space will modify the list below, but the following may save having to call on professional assistance:

> *Spark plugs, clean and correctly gapped*
> *HT lead and plug cap — long enough to reach the plug furthest from the distributor*
> *Distributor rotor, condenser and contact breaker points*
> *Drivebelt(s) — emergency type may suffice*
> *Spare fuses*
> *Set of principal light bulbs*
> *Tin of radiator sealer and hose bandage*
> *Exhaust bandage*
> *Roll of insulating tape*
> *Length of soft iron wire*
> *Length of electrical flex*
> *Torch or inspection lamp (can double as test lamp)*
> *Battery jump leads*
> *Tow-rope*
> *Ignition waterproofing aerosol*
> *Litre of engine oil*
> *Sealed can of hydraulic fluid*
> *Emergency windscreen*
> *Worm drive clips*
> *Tube of filler paste*

If spare fuel is carried, a can designed for the purpose should be used to minimise risks of leakage and collision damage. A first aid kit and a warning triangle, whilst not at present compulsory in the UK, are obviously sensible items to carry in addition to the above.

When touring abroad it may be advisable to carry additional spares which, even if you cannot fit them yourself, could save having to wait while parts are obtained. The items below may be worth considering:

> *Clutch and throttle cables*
> *Cylinder head gasket*
> *Alternator brushes*
> *Fuel pump repair kit*
> *Tyre valve core*

One of the motoring organisations will be able to advise on availability of fuel etc in foreign countries.

---

**Engine will not start**

---

### Engine fails to turn when starter operated

Flat battery (recharge, use jump leads, or push start)
Battery terminals loose or corroded
Battery earth to body defective
Engine earth strap loose or broken
Starter motor (or solenoid) wiring loose or broken
Automatic transmission selector in wrong position, or inhibitor switch faulty

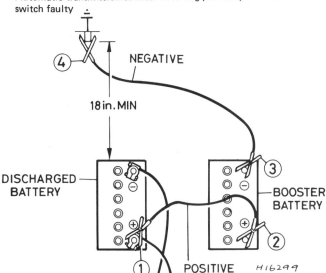

**Jump start lead connections for negative earth — connect leads in order shown**

Ignition/starter switch faulty
Major mechanical failure (seizure)
Starter or solenoid internal fault (see Chapter 10)

### Starter motor turns engine slowly

Partially discharged battery (recharge, use jump leads, or push start)
Battery terminals loose or corroded
Battery earth to body defective
Engine earth strap loose
Starter motor (or solenoid) wiring loose
Starter motor internal fault (see Chapter 10)

### Starter motor spins without turning engine

Flywheel gear teeth damaged or worn
Starter motor mounting bolts loose

### Engine turns normally but fails to start

Damp or dirty HT leads and distributor cap (crank engine and check for spark)
**Dirty** or incorrectly gapped distributor points (if applicable)
**No** fuel in tank (check for delivery at carburettor)
Excessive choke (hot engine) or insufficient choke (cold engine)
Fouled or incorrectly gapped spark plugs (remove, clean and regap)
Other ignition system fault (see Chapter 4)
Other fuel system fault (see Chapter 3)
Poor compression (see Chapter 1)
Major mechanical failure (eg camshaft drive)

### Engine fires but will not run

Insufficient choke (cold engine)
Air leaks at carburettor or inlet manifold
Fuel starvation (see Chapter 3)
Ballast resistor defective, or other ignition fault (see Chapter 4)

---

**Engine cuts out and will not restart**

### Engine cuts out suddenly — ignition fault

Loose or disconnected LT wires
Wet HT leads or distributor cap (after traversing water splash)
Coil or condenser failure (check for spark)
Other ignition fault (see Chapter 4)

### Engine misfires before cutting out — fuel fault

Fuel tank empty
Fuel pump defective or filter blocked (check for delivery)
Fuel tank filler vent blocked (suction will be evident on releasing cap)
Carburettor needle valve sticking
Carburettor jets blocked (fuel contaminated)
Other fuel system fault (see Chapter 3)

### Engine cuts out — other causes

Serious overheating
Major mechanical failure (eg camshaft drive)

---

**Engine overheats**

### Ignition (no-charge) warning light illuminated

Slack or broken drivebelt — retension or renew (Chapter 2)

### Ignition warning light not illuminated

Coolant loss due to internal or external leakage (see Chapter 2)
Thermostat defective
Low oil level
Brakes binding
Radiator clogged externally or internally
Engine waterways clogged
Ignition timing incorrect or automatic advance malfunctioning
Mixture too weak

**Note:** *Do not add cold water to an overheated engine or damage may result*

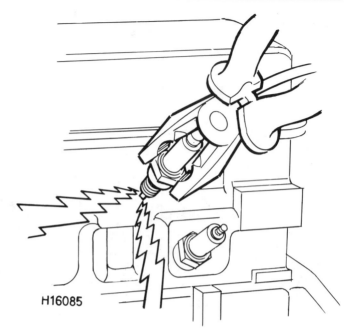

H16085

Crank engine and check for spark. Note use of insulated tool

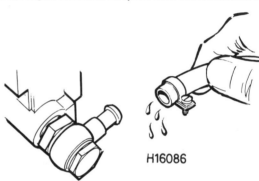

H16086

Remove fuel pipe from carburettor and check for fuel delivery. Disable ignition before cranking engine

**Slacken bolts to adjust fanbelt tension**
1 *Lower mounting bolt*
2 *Top mounting bolt*
3 *Adjusting bolt*

**Low engine oil pressure**

*Gauge reads low or warning light illuminated with engine running*
Oil level low or incorrect grade
Defective gauge or sender unit
Wire to sender unit earthed
Engine overheating
Oil filter clogged or bypass valve defective
Oil pressure relief valve defective
Oil pick-up strainer clogged
Oil pump worn or mountings loose
Worn main or big-end bearings

**Note:** *Low oil pressure in a high-mileage engine at tickover is not necessarily a cause for concern. Sudden pressure loss at speed is far more significant. In any event, check the gauge or warning light sender before condemning the engine.*

**Engine noises**

*Pre-ignition (pinking) on acceleration*
Incorrect grade of fuel
Ignition timing incorrect
Distributor faulty or worn
Worn or maladjusted carburettor
Excessive carbon build-up in engine

*Whistling or wheezing noises*
Leaking vacuum hose
Leaking carburettor or manifold gasket
Blowing head gasket

*Tapping or rattling*
Incorrect valve clearances
Worn valve gear
Worn timing chain
Broken piston ring (ticking noise)

*Knocking or thumping*
Unintentional mechanical contact (eg fan blades)
Worn fanbelt
Peripheral component fault (generator, water pump etc)
Worn big-end bearings (regular heavy knocking, perhaps less under load)
Worn main bearings (rumbling and knocking, perhaps worsening under load)
Piston slap (most noticeable when cold)

# General repair procedures

Whenever servicing, repair or overhaul work is carried out on the car or its components, it is necessary to observe the following procedures and instructions. This will assist in carrying out the operation efficiently and to a professional standard of workmanship.

## Joint mating faces and gaskets

Where a gasket is used between the mating faces of two components, ensure that it is renewed on reassembly, and fit it dry unless otherwise stated in the repair procedure. Make sure that the mating faces are clean and dry with all traces of old gasket removed. When cleaning a joint face, use a tool which is not likely to score or damage the face, and remove any burrs or nicks with an oilstone or fine file.

Make sure that tapped holes are cleaned with a pipe cleaner, and keep them free of jointing compound if this is being used unless specifically instructed otherwise.

Ensure that all orifices, channels or pipes are clear and blow through them, preferably using compressed air.

## Oil seals

Whenever an oil seal is removed from its working location, either individually or as part of an assembly, it should be renewed.

The very fine sealing lip of the seal is easily damaged and will not seal if the surface it contacts is not completely clean and free from scratches, nicks or grooves. If the original sealing surface of the component cannot be restored, the component should be renewed.

Protect the lips of the seal from any surface which may damage them in the course of fitting. Use tape or a conical sleeve where possible. Lubricate the seal lips with oil before fitting and, on dual lipped seals, fill the space between the lips with grease.

Unless otherwise stated, oil seals must be fitted with their sealing lips toward the lubricant to be sealed.

Use a tubular drift or block of wood of the appropriate size to install the seal and, if the seal housing is shouldered, drive the seal down to the shoulder. If the seal housing is unshouldered, the seal should be fitted with its face flush with the housing top face.

## Screw threads and fastenings

Always ensure that a blind tapped hole is completely free from oil, grease, water or other fluid before installing the bolt or stud. Failure to do this could cause the housing to crack due to the hydraulic action of the bolt or stud as it is screwed in.

When tightening a castellated nut to accept a split pin, tighten the nut to the specified torque, where applicable, and then tighten further to the next split pin hole. Never slacken the nut to align a split pin hole unless stated in the repair procedure.

When checking or retightening a nut or bolt to a specified torque setting, slacken the nut or bolt by a quarter of a turn, and then retighten to the specified setting.

## Locknuts, locktabs and washers

Any fastening which will rotate against a component or housing in the course of tightening should always have a washer between it and the relevant component or housing.

Spring or split washers should always be renewed when they are used to lock a critical component such as a big-end bearing retaining nut or bolt.

Locktabs which are folded over to retain a nut or bolt should always be renewed.

Self-locking nuts can be reused in non-critical areas, providing resistance can be felt when the locking portion passes over the bolt or stud thread.

Split pins must always be replaced with new ones of the correct size for the hole.

## Special tools

Some repair procedures in this manual entail the use of special tools such as a press, two or three-legged pullers, spring compressors etc. Wherever possible, suitable readily available alternatives to the manufacturer's special tools are described, and are shown in use. In some instances, where no alternative is possible, it has been necessary to resort to the use of a manufacturer's tool and this has been done for reasons of safety as well as the efficient completion of the repair operation. Unless you are highly skilled and have a thorough understanding of the procedure described, never attempt to bypass the use of any special tool when the procedure described specifies its use. Not only is there a very great risk of personal injury, but expensive damage could be caused to the components involved.

# Conversion factors

**Length (distance)**

| | | | | | |
|---|---|---|---|---|---|
| Inches (in) | X | 25.4 | = Millimetres (mm) | X 0.0394 | = Inches (in) |
| Feet (ft) | X | 0.305 | = Metres (m) | X 3.281 | = Feet (ft) |
| Miles | X | 1.609 | = Kilometres (km) | X 0.621 | = Miles |

**Volume (capacity)**

| | | | | | |
|---|---|---|---|---|---|
| Cubic inches (cu in; in³) | X | 16.387 | = Cubic centimetres (cc; cm³) | X 0.061 | = Cubic inches (cu in; in³) |
| Imperial pints (Imp pt) | X | 0.568 | = Litres (l) | X 1.76 | = Imperial pints (Imp pt) |
| Imperial quarts (Imp qt) | X | 1.137 | = Litres (l) | X 0.88 | = Imperial quarts (Imp qt) |
| Imperial quarts (Imp qt) | X | 1.201 | = US quarts (US qt) | X 0.833 | = Imperial quarts (Imp qt) |
| US quarts (US qt) | X | 0.946 | = Litres (l) | X 1.057 | = US quarts (US qt) |
| Imperial gallons (Imp gal) | X | 4.546 | = Litres (l) | X 0.22 | = Imperial gallons (Imp gal) |
| Imperial gallons (Imp gal) | X | 1.201 | = US gallons (US gal) | X 0.833 | = Imperial gallons (Imp gal) |
| US gallons (US gal) | X | 3.785 | = Litres (l) | X 0.264 | = US gallons (US gal) |

**Mass (weight)**

| | | | | | |
|---|---|---|---|---|---|
| Ounces (oz) | X | 28.35 | = Grams (g) | X 0.035 | = Ounces (oz) |
| Pounds (lb) | X | 0.454 | = Kilograms (kg) | X 2.205 | = Pounds (lb) |

**Force**

| | | | | | |
|---|---|---|---|---|---|
| Ounces-force (ozf; oz) | X | 0.278 | = Newtons (N) | X 3.6 | = Ounces-force (ozf; oz) |
| Pounds-force (lbf; lb) | X | 4.448 | = Newtons (N) | X 0.225 | = Pounds-force (lbf; lb) |
| Newtons (N) | X | 0.1 | = Kilograms-force (kgf; kg) | X 9.81 | = Newtons (N) |

**Pressure**

| | | | | | |
|---|---|---|---|---|---|
| Pounds-force per square inch (psi; lbf/in²; lb/in²) | X | 0.070 | = Kilograms-force per square centimetre (kgf/cm²; kg/cm²) | X 14.223 | = Pounds-force per square inch (psi; lbf/in²; lb/in²) |
| Pounds-force per square inch (psi; lbf/in²; lb/in²) | X | 0.068 | = Atmospheres (atm) | X 14.696 | = Pounds-force per square inch (psi; lbf/in²; lb/in²) |
| Pounds-force per square inch (psi; lbf/in²; lb/in²) | X | 0.069 | = Bars | X 14.5 | = Pounds-force per square inch (psi; lbf/in²; lb/in²) |
| Pounds-force per square inch (psi; lbf/in²; lb/in²) | X | 6.895 | = Kilopascals (kPa) | X 0.145 | = Pounds-force per square inch (psi; lbf/in²; lb/in²) |
| Kilopascals (kPa) | X | 0.01 | = Kilograms-force per square centimetre (kgf/cm²; kg/cm²) | X 98.1 | = Kilopascals (kPa) |
| Millibar (mbar) | X | 100 | = Pascals (Pa) | X 0.01 | = Millibar (mbar) |
| Millibar (mbar) | X | 0.0145 | = Pounds-force per square inch (psi; lbf/in²; lb/in²) | X 68.947 | = Millibar (mbar) |
| Millibar (mbar) | X | 0.75 | = Millimetres of mercury (mmHg) | X 1.333 | = Millibar (mbar) |
| Millibar (mbar) | X | 0.401 | = Inches of water (inH₂O) | X 2.491 | = Millibar (mbar) |
| Millimetres of mercury (mmHg) | X | 0.535 | = Inches of water (inH₂O) | X 1.868 | = Millimetres of mercury (mmHg) |
| Inches of water (inH₂O) | X | 0.036 | = Pounds-force per square inch (psi; lbf/in²; lb/in²) | X 27.68 | = Inches of water (inH₂O) |

**Torque (moment of force)**

| | | | | | |
|---|---|---|---|---|---|
| Pounds-force inches (lbf in; lb in) | X | 1.152 | = Kilograms-force centimetre (kgf cm; kg cm) | X 0.868 | = Pounds-force inches (lbf in; lb in) |
| Pounds-force inches (lbf in; lb in) | X | 0.113 | = Newton metres (Nm) | X 8.85 | = Pounds-force inches (lbf in; lb in) |
| Pounds-force inches (lbf in; lb in) | X | 0.083 | = Pounds-force feet (lbf ft; lb ft) | X 12 | = Pounds-force inches (lbf in; lb in) |
| Pounds-force feet (lbf ft; lb ft) | X | 0.138 | = Kilograms-force metres (kgf m; kg m) | X 7.233 | = Pounds-force feet (lbf ft; lb ft) |
| Pounds-force feet (lbf ft; lb ft) | X | 1.356 | = Newton metres (Nm) | X 0.738 | = Pounds-force feet (lbf ft; lb ft) |
| Newton metres (Nm) | X | 0.102 | = Kilograms-force metres (kgf m; kg m) | X 9.804 | = Newton metres (Nm) |

**Power**

| | | | | | |
|---|---|---|---|---|---|
| Horsepower (hp) | X | 745.7 | = Watts (W) | X 0.0013 | = Horsepower (hp) |

**Velocity (speed)**

| | | | | | |
|---|---|---|---|---|---|
| Miles per hour (miles/hr; mph) | X | 1.609 | = Kilometres per hour (km/hr; kph) | X 0.621 | = Miles per hour (miles/hr; mph) |

**Fuel consumption***

| | | | | | |
|---|---|---|---|---|---|
| Miles per gallon, Imperial (mpg) | X | 0.354 | = Kilometres per litre (km/l) | X 2.825 | = Miles per gallon, Imperial (mpg) |
| Miles per gallon, US (mpg) | X | 0.425 | = Kilometres per litre (km/l) | X 2.352 | = Miles per gallon, US (mpg) |

**Temperature**

Degrees Fahrenheit = (°C x 1.8) + 32          Degrees Celsius (Degrees Centigrade; °C) = (°F - 32) x 0.56

*It is common practice to convert from miles per gallon (mpg) to litres/100 kilometres (l/100km),
where mpg (Imperial) x l/100 km = 282 and mpg (US) x l/100 km = 235

# Index

Printed by
**J H Haynes & Co Ltd**
Sparkford  Nr Yeovil
Somerset  BA22  7JJ  England